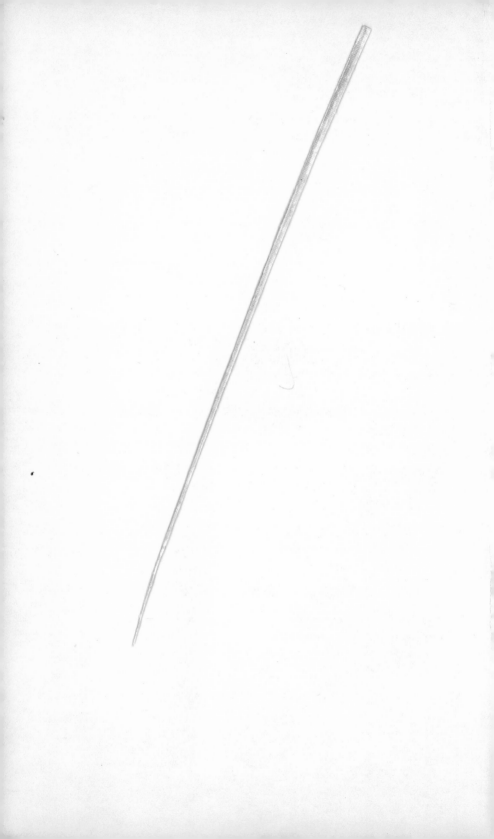

VOICE OF THE PEOPLE

Readings in
Public Opinion and Propaganda

McGRAW-HILL SERIES IN POLITICAL SCIENCE

Joseph P. Harris, *Consulting Editor*

* * *

Adrian · Governing Urban America: Structure, Politics, and Administration
Bone · American Politics and the Party System
Chase · The United Nations in Action
Christenson and McWilliams · Voice of the People: Readings in Public Opinion and Propaganda
Ebenstein · Political Thought in Perspective
Ferguson and McHenry · American Federal Government
Ferguson and McHenry · American System of Government
Ferguson and McHenry · Elements of American Government
Field · Governments in Modern Society
Frank · Cases on the Constitution
Gosnell, Lancaster, and Rankin · Fundamentals of American Government: National, State, and Local
Gosnell, Lancaster, and Rankin · Fundamentals of American National Government
Gross · The Legislative Struggle
Haas and Whiting · Dynamics of International Relations
Hartmann · Basic Documents of International Relations
Holloway · State and Local Government in the United States
Leonard · Elements of American Foreign Policy
Leonard · International Organization
Mangone · A Short History of International Organization
Millett · Government and Public Administration
Millett · Management in the Public Service
Neumann · European and Comparative Government
Pierson and Gil · Governments of Latin America
Pritchett · The American Constitution
Pritchett · American Constitutional Issues
Riemer · Problems of American Government
Roche and Stedman · The Dynamics of Democratic Government
Rodee, Anderson, and Christol · Introduction to Political Science
Strausz-Hupé and Possony · International Relations
Svarlien · An Introduction to the Law of Nations
Turner · Politics in the United States: Readings in Political Parties and Pressure Groups
Waldo · Ideas and Issues in Public Administration: A Book of Readings
Wilson · The American Political Mind
Wilson · Police Administration

VOICE OF THE PEOPLE

Readings in
Public Opinion and Propaganda

REO M. CHRISTENSON

Associate Professor of Government
Miami University
Oxford, Ohio

ROBERT O. McWILLIAMS

Professor of Political Science
Eastern Michigan University
Ypsilanti, Michigan

McGRAW-HILL BOOK COMPANY, INC.   1962

New York   San Francisco   Toronto   London

II

10780

Preface

There has long been a need—a widely felt and even a vociferously proclaimed need—for a nontechnical book of readings on public opinion and propaganda designed to contribute broadly to students' liberal education. While readings with a narrower goal (often preprofessional) and a different orientation serve a useful purpose, they do not adequately fulfill certain liberal arts objectives.

This anthology has been prepared to fill the void. To the best of our knowledge, it represents the first collection of readings in this field designed specifically for the nonspecialist, embracing selections with sufficient depth to supplement a textbook and sufficient breadth to stand alone. If such a collection can also be read with profit and pleasure by the general reader desiring to learn more about this area of human activity, so much the better. We sincerely believe that this is such a volume.

The materials chosen had to satisfy the following requirements: pertinence, percipience, and readability. We are firmly convinced that the typical undergraduate student will more readily absorb observations felicitously phrased than those of equal merit couched in "academese" or requiring methodological sophistication of the reader. This is not to say that we have sacrificed matter to manner. Nor is it to say that we have been uniformly successful in our search for the well-turned phrase. Nor, further, is there any intention to depreciate the carefully conceived and executed empirical studies of public opinion and propaganda, which contribute so much to the understanding of the expert—but, alas, also to the frustration of the uninitiated. But we do believe that those who are sensitive to matters of style as well as of content will find enjoyment in most of the excerpts. Certainly, if we may judge from the reactions of our own students who have been exposed to the type of material represented in this collection and who have found the experience intellectually exhilarating, this should be the case.

A word about sources: An examination of the Table of Contents will reveal an almost cavalier disregard of the convention that books of readings should consist largely of the efforts of academicians. They, to be sure, are generously represented, but so also are journalists, novelists, poets, philosophers, jurists—anyone, in fact, who has something to say which is relevant, lucid, and discerning and who, therefore, can illuminate significant aspects of the chosen area of inquiry.

And now about scope: We begin with a consideration of the nature of public opinion. A discussion of the dynamics of the public opinion process and of the role of public opinion in a democracy is followed by a consideration of the numerous factors which influence or determine opinion. The mass media of communication, both as molders and reflectors of public opinion and as instruments of propaganda, come in for close scrutiny. The principles, techniques, and effects of propaganda are considered, and several important types of propaganda (political propaganda, public relations, and advertising) are examined in some detail. The problems involved in the measurement of public opinion are discussed, and particular attention is given to that most hazardous of polling activities: election prediction. The reader will also find the presentation laced with liberal dollops of concern for various aspects of the problem of conformity to the dictates of public opinion: the myth or reality of the concept of the "mass mind," the tyranny of the majority, and censorship. And finally, the compilers invite a number of pundits to contest on the issue of the competence of public opinion adequately to discharge its awesome responsibilities in a free society.

We believe that such a collection of readings might find profitable employment in a variety of courses, whether offered as political science, sociology, social psychology, journalism, or communications. A course in public opinion and propaganda is a standard offering by several different disciplines, but courses in mass communications, political parties and pressure groups, political behavior, and even the introductory courses in the aforementioned disciplines might make good use of all or some of the selections provided. We have commented previously on the basically liberal arts approach of this collection, but eschewal of chi squares (actually, several quantitative studies *were* included as particularly relevant) does not detract from the value of the work even for the methodologically oriented student. After all, there is no one who will not profit from exposure to the Bryces, the Huxleys, and the Lippmanns.

Authors normally conclude their prefatory remarks by manfully shouldering responsibility for all errors discovered in their work. The position of the compiler is somewhat different in this regard: He is reproachable only for having chosen to reproduce the errors of *others*. We can only hope, then, to have assembled a group of contributors who are flawless as well as peerless.

Reo M. Christenson
Robert O. McWilliams

Contents

viii   Contents

Contents

CHAPTER I

The Nature of Public Opinion

What is public opinion? There is, of course, the oft-quoted observation of Montaigne that it is a "powerful, bold and unmeasurable party." The extent to which public opinion is unmeasurable and/or bold will be considered in the final two chapters of this volume, and Lord Bryce will speak to the issue of its potency in this chapter. We shall try, however, to go beyond evaluating Montaigne's sweeping generalization and to delineate the essential characteristics of this phenomenon.

Authorities are generally agreed that public opinion is an influential factor in human affairs, but they are obliged also to take note of its amorphous and fluid quality. Bryce, for example, has characterized it as "a real force, impalpable as the wind, yet a force, which all are trying to discover and nearly all obey." He denies that it is synonymous with "the aggregate of all that is thought and said on a subject" or that it is "merely the views of the majority." He would, however, have agreed with John Dewey who contended that public opinion requires "effective and organized inquiry."[1]

In the excerpt selected for this chapter from Bryce's *The American Commonwealth*, we are informed that public opinion is neither a recent nor a democratic invention but rather that it "has really been the chief and ultimate power in nearly all nations at nearly all times." Bryce traces the evolution of public opinion from its passive role in autocratic regimes to its active role in democracies. He then gives encouragement to the pollsters by suggesting that the final stage of this evolutionary process would be achieved if and when the popular will were continuously ascertainable.

To W. Phillips Davison falls the responsibility of discussing the nature of the public opinion process. And, as he points out, public opinion is not the sum of individual opinions but is that which emerges from the joint concern of a group of persons over the same issue and their consequent interaction as the result of that concern. The nature of this process from initial awareness through intragroup and intergroup communication and adjustment to the dissolution of public opinion is discussed in terms of a hypothetical mayoralty election campaign.

Thus, we have accepted a sociopsychological definition of public opinion. It is one which conceives of the process in terms of groups and issues: A group of people are faced by a common problem; they interact as a means of seeking a solution to that problem; and, on the basis of their discussion, they reach some sort of consensus. There are, then, as many publics as there are issues or controversies. Floyd Allport has elaborated this concept in the following systematic if somewhat turgid fashion: "The term public opinion is given its meaning with reference to a multi-individual situation

---

[1] John Dewey, *The Public and Its Problems,* Holt, Rinehart and Winston Company, New York, 1927, p. 177.

I

in which individuals are expressing themselves, or can be called upon to express themselves, as favoring or supporting (or else disfavoring or opposing) some definite condition, person, or proposal of widespread importance, in such a proportion of number, intensity, and constancy as to give rise to the probability of affecting action, directly or indirectly, toward the object concerned."[2]

Such a definition places its emphasis upon actual, functioning public opinion—upon concern, interaction, discussion, accommodation. It does not, however, deny that there are varying degrees of involvement in any given issue: from fanatical engrossment through moderate interest to substantial indifference. Those who are not presently involved may become so as discussion continues, and frequently, moreover, opinion leaders may try to manage the discussion so as not to disturb those slumbering on the periphery. In fact, there is even utility in the concept of "latent" public opinion, which involves no current controversy and discussion at all. Rather, this is public opinion which, given the basic beliefs, values, and motives of the people, would emerge if the occasion warranted. Thus, it is possible to state that there is latent public opinion with regard to an atheist becoming President of the United States. Much of what is *not* done in this world isn't done because of the influence of latent public opinion.[3]

President Lowell's contribution to this discussion of the nature of public opinion is to insist, in his words, "public opinion must be public," by which he means that, although public opinion involves controversy, it also requires minority acquiescence, i.e., a willingness on the part of minorities to accede to preponderant opinion. Without this willingness, there is neither "public" opinion nor democracy.

Pendleton Herring completes this introduction with some cogent remarks concerning the symbolic value of public opinion. Continual obeisance to the concept of rule by public opinion is regarded as having a positive value. However irrational or nebulous the concept, faith in it provides an important safeguard against irresponsible government.

I. THE UBIQUITY AND POWER OF PUBLIC OPINION
by James Bryce*

We talk of public opinion as a new force in the world, conspicuous only since governments began to be popular. Statesmen, even in the last genera-

[2] Floyd W. Allport, "Toward a Science of Public Opinion," *Public Opinion Quarterly*, vol. I, no. 1, p. 23, January, 1937.

[3] Cf. Leonard W. Doob, *Public Opinion and Propaganda*, Holt, Rinehart and Winston Company, New York, 1948, pp. 40-41.

* British lawyer, professor of law, member of Parliament, and diplomat. British Ambassador to the United States, 1907–1913. Author of *The Holy Roman Empire, The American Commonwealth, Modern Democracies*, and other works. The selection is from James Bryce, *The American Commonwealth*, Macmillan & Co., Ltd., London, 1889, vol. II, pp. 217-222.

tion, looked on it with some distrust or dislike. Sir Robert Peel, for instance, in a letter written in 1820, speaks with the air of a discoverer, of "that great compound of folly, weakness, prejudice, wrong feeling, right feeling, obstinacy, and newspaper paragraphs, which is called public opinion."

Yet opinion has really been the chief and ultimate power in nearly all nations at nearly all times. I do not mean merely the opinion of the class to which the rulers belong. Obviously the small oligarchy of Venice was influenced by the opinion of the Venetian nobility, as the absolute Czar is influenced now by the opinion of his court and his army. I mean the opinion, unspoken, unconscious, but not the less real and potent, of the masses of the people. Governments have always rested and, special cases apart, must rest, if not on the affection, then on the reverence or awe, if not on the active approval, then on the silent acquiescence of the numerical majority. It is only by rare exception that a monarch or an oligarchy has maintained authority against the will of the people. The despotisms of the East, although they usually began in conquest, did not stand by military force but by popular assent. So did the feudal kingdoms of mediaeval Europe. So do the despotisms of the Sultan (so far, at least, as regards his Mussulman subjects), of the Shah, and of the Chinese Emperor at this moment. The cases to the contrary are chiefly those of military tyrannies, such as existed in many of the Greek cities of antiquity, and in some of the Italian cities of the Renaissance, and such as exist now in the so-called republics of Central and South America. That even the Roman Empire, that eldest child of war and conquest, did not rest on force but on the consent and good-will of its subjects is shown by the smallness of its standing armies, nearly the whole of which were employed against frontier enemies, because there was rarely any internal revolt or disturbance to be feared. Belief in authority, and the love of established order, are among the strongest forces in human nature, and therefore in politics. The first supports governments *de jure*, the latter governments *de facto*. They combine to support a government which is *de jure* as well as *de facto*. Where the subjects are displeased, their discontent may appear perhaps in the epigrams which tempered the despotism of Louis XV in France, perhaps in the sympathy given to bandits like Robin Hood, perhaps in occasional insurrections like those of Constantinople under the Eastern Emperors. Of course, where there is no habit of combination to resist, discontent may remain for some time without this third means of expressing itself. But, even when the occupant of the throne is unpopular, the throne as an institution is in no danger so long as it can command the respect of the multitude and show itself equal to its duties.

In the earlier or simpler forms of political society public opinion is passive. It acquiesces in, rather than supports, the authority which exists, whatever its faults, because it knows of nothing better, because it sees no way to improvement, probably also because it is overawed by some kind of religious sanction. Human nature must have something to reverence, and the sovereign, because remote and potent and surrounded by pomp and splendour, seems to it mysterious and half divine. Worse administrations than those of Asiatic Turkey and Persia at this moment can hardly be imagined, yet the Mohammedan population show no signs of disaffection. The subjects of Darius and the subjects of Theebaw obeyed as a matter of course. They did not ask why they obeyed, for the habit of obedience was sufficient. They could, however, if disaffected, have at any moment overturned the throne, which had only, in both cases, an insignificant force of guards to protect it. During long ages the human mind did not ask itself—in many parts of the world does not even now ask itself—questions which seem to us the most obvious. Custom, as Pindar said, is king over all mortals and immortals, and custom prescribed obedience. When in any society opinion becomes self-conscious, when it begins to realize its force and question the rights of its rulers, that society is already progressing, and soon finds means of organizing resistance and compelling reform.

The difference therefore between despotically governed and free countries does not consist in the fact that the latter are ruled by opinion and the former by force, for both are generally ruled by opinion. It consists rather in this, that in the former the people instinctively obey a power which they do not know to be really of their own creation, and to stand by their own permission; whereas in the latter the people feel their supremacy, and consciously treat their rulers as their agents, while the rulers obey a power which they admit to have made and to be able to unmake them—the popular will. In both cases force is seldom necessary, or is needed only against small groups, because the habit of obedience replaces it. Conflicts and revolutions belong to the intermediate stage, when the people are awakening to the sense that they are truly the supreme power in the state, but when the rulers have not yet become aware that their authority is merely delegated. When superstition and the habit of submission have vanished from the whilome subjects, when the rulers, recognizing that they are no more than agents for the citizens, have in turn formed the habit of obedience, public opinion has become the active and controlling director of a business in which it was before the sleeping and generally forgotten partner. But even when this stage has been reached, as has now happened in most civilized States, there are differences in the degree and mode in and by which public opinion asserts itself. In some countries the habit of obeying rulers and officials is so strong that the people, once they have chosen the legislature or executive head by whom the officials are appointed, allow these officials almost as wide a range of authority as in the old days of despotism. Such people have a profound respect for government as government, and a reluctance, due either to theory or to mere laziness, perhaps to both, to interfere with its action. They say, "That is a matter for the Administration; we have nothing to do with it;" and stand as much aside or submit as humbly as if the government did not spring from their own will. Perhaps they practically leave themselves, like the Germans, in the hands of a venerated monarch and a forceful minister, giving these rulers a free hand so long as their policy moves in accord with the general sentiment of the nation, and maintains its glory. Perhaps while frequently changing their ministries, they nevertheless yield to each ministry, and to its executive subordinates all over the country, an authority great while it lasts, and largely controlling the action of the individual citizen. This seems to be still true of France. There are other countries in which, though the sphere of government is strictly limited by law, and the private citizen is little inclined to bow before an official, the habit has been to check the ministry chiefly through the legislature, and to review the conduct of both ministry and legislature only at long intervals, when an election of the legislature takes place. This was the case in England down till a recent period. Although the people ruled, they ruled not directly, but through the House of Commons, which they chose only once in five, six, or seven years, and which might at any given moment, represent rather the past than the present will of the nation.

I make these observations for the sake of indicating another form which the rule of the people may assume. We have distinguished three stages in the evolution of opinion from its unconscious and passive into its conscious and active condition. In the first it acquiesces in the will of the ruler whom it has been accustomed to obey. In the second conflicts arise between the ruling person or class, backed by those who are still disposed to obedience, on the one hand, and the more independent or progressive spirits on the other; and these conflicts are decided by arms. In the third stage the whilome ruler has submitted, and disputes are referred to the sovereign multitude, whose will is expressed at certain intervals upon slips of paper deposited in boxes, and is carried out by the minister or legislature to whom the popular mandate is entrusted. A fourth stage would be reached if the will of the majority of the citizens were to become ascertainable at all times, and without the need of its passing through a body of representatives, possibly even without the need of voting machinery at all. In such a state of things the sway of public opinion would have become more complete, because more continuous, than it is in those European countries which, like France, Italy, and England, look chiefly to parliaments as exponents of national sentiment. The authority would seem to remain all the while in the mass of the citizens. Popular government would have been pushed so far as almost to dispense with, or at any rate to anticipate, the legal modes in which the majority speaks its will at the polling booths; and this informal but direct control of the multitude would dwarf, if it did not supersede, the importance of those formal but occasional deliverances made at the elections of representatives. To such a condition of things the phrase, "Rule of public opinion," might be most properly applied, for public opinion would not only reign but govern.

The mechanical difficulties, as one may call them, of working such a method of government are obvious. How is the will of the majority to be ascertained except by counting votes? how, without the greatest inconvenience, can votes be frequently taken on all the chief questions that arise? No country has yet surmounted these inconveniences, though little Switzerland with its *Referendum* has faced and dealt with some of them. But what I desire to point out is that even where the machinery for weighing or measuring the popular will from week to week or month to month has not been, and is not likely to be, invented, there may nevertheless be a disposition on the part of the rulers, whether ministers or legislators, to act as if it existed; that is to say, to look incessantly for manifestations of current popular opinion, and to shape their course in accordance with their reading of those manifestations. Such a disposition will be accompanied by a constant oversight of public affairs by the mass of the citizens, and by a sense on their part that they are the true governors, and that their agents, executive and legislative, are rather servants than agents. Where this is the attitude of the people on the one hand and of the persons who do the actual work of governing on the other, it may fairly be said that there exists a kind of government materially, if not formally, different from the representative system as it presented itself to European thinkers and statesmen of the last generation. And it is to this kind of government that democratic nations seem to be tending. . . .

The excellence of popular government lies not so much in its wisdom— for it is as apt to err as other kinds of government—as in its strength. It has often been compared to a pyramid, the firmest based of all buildings.[1] Nobody can be blamed for obeying it. There is no appeal from its decisions. Once the principle that the will of the majority, honestly ascertained, must prevail, has soaked into the mind and formed the habits of a nation, that nation acquires not only stability, but immense effective force. It has no need to fear discussion and agitation. It can bend all its resources to the accomplishment of its collective ends. The friction that exists in countries where the laws or institutions handed down from former generations are incompatible with the feelings and wishes of the people has disappeared. A key has been found that will unlock every door. . . .

[1] This comparison is an old one: it is referred to by James Wilson in the Pennsylvania Convention of 1787.—Elliot's *Debates,* ii. 524.

2. THE PUBLIC OPINION PROCESS
by W. Phillips Davison *

Although the term "public opinion" was not used until the eighteenth century, the phenomenon itself has been noted and described by writers in ancient, medieval, and early modern times. Public opinion appears most often in urban societies and in those with relatively well-developed communication facilities, as for instance in the Greek city states, but it can also be observed, even if more rarely, in predominantly rural societies with rudimentary communications.[1] The existence of phenomena bearing strong resemblances to public opinion has been noted by anthropologists in primitive societies of widely varying characteristics.[2]

In ancient and medieval times writers who mention public opinion often

* Member of the social science staff of The RAND Corporation, and former editor of *The Public Opinion Quarterly.* The selection is from W. Phillips Davison, "The Public Opinion Process," *Public Opinion Quarterly,* vol. 22, issue 2, pp. 91-106, Summer, 1958. By permission of the author and publisher.

[1] Wilhelm Bauer, *Die Öffentliche Meinung in der Weltgeschichte,* Potsdam, 1930.

[2] Felix M. and Marie Keesing, *Elite Communication in Samoa: A Study of Leadership,* Stanford University Press, 1956; Margaret Mead, "Public Opinion Mechanisms Among Primitive Peoples," *Public Opinion Quarterly,* July, 1937.

refer to it as having mystical or divine properties. Early modern writers regard it as perceptible but indefinable. They usually agree on two of its aspects: that it is a consensus among a large number of people, and that this consensus somehow exercises force. The German poet Wieland has given us one of the first formal discussions of public opinion in his *Gespräch unter vier Augen* (1798):

> I, for my part, understand by it an opinion that gradually takes root among a whole people; especially among those who have the most influence when they work together as a group. In this way it wins the upper hand to such an extent that one meets it everywhere. It is an opinion that without being noticed takes possession of most heads, and even in situations where it does not dare to express itself out loud it can be recognized by a louder and louder muffled murmur. It then only requires some small opening that will allow it air, and it will break out with force. Then it can change whole nations in a brief time and give whole parts of the world a new configuration.

Wieland's description is similar to many others given in writings of approximately the same period.[3]

More recently, students have been able to agree substantially on a number of distinguishing marks of public opinion. A list of characteristics, which is still one of the best, was given by Floyd Allport more than twenty years ago.[4] He noted that public opinion involved verbalization and communication among many individuals, that some widely known issue was always involved, that public opinion represented action or a readiness for action by individuals who were aware that others were reacting to the same situation, and that it was ordinarily a transitory phenomenon. Other writers have pointed out that a majority is not necessarily involved, that public opinion must be distinguished from norms and customs, and that the effectiveness of public opinion in bringing about change depends on the political and societal context in which it operates. . . .

Our ability to measure the distribution of individual opinions in a population or the thematic content of communications is now far greater than our capacity to explain how the phenomenon that we call public opinion arises in the first place or why sustained propaganda will have very little effect in one situation while in another a series of whispers will produce a riot. . . .

Nevertheless, although the hazards are sufficiently apparent to discourage speculation in the realm of public opinion theory, and obviously have done so, the importance of the phenomenon suggested by its close relationship to major problems of political, social, and economic behavior is ample justification for renewed attempts. This article represents such an attempt.

A DEFINITION OF PUBLIC OPINION

The term "public opinion" will be used here in a sense suggested by Allport and will refer to action or readiness for action with regard to a given issue on the part of members of a public who are reacting in the

---

[3] *Cf.* Hans Speier, "Historical Development of Public Opinion," *Social Order and the Risks of War*, New York, Stewart, 1952.

[4] "Toward a Science of Public Opinion," *Public Opinion Quarterly*, January 1937.

expectation that others in the public are similarly oriented toward the same issue.

If we accept this definition as a tool for use in further inquiry, it raises a number of questions for investigation. How is the central issue in the public opinion process defined? What is a public? How are expectations as to the behavior of others formed? What effect do these expectations have on the attitudes and behavior of individual members of the public? What is the usual sequence of steps in the process by which public opinion is formed?

That the suggested definition is not completely adequate is indicated by the fact that a number of other questions are not immediately raised. The definition says nothing about communication, about opinion leadership, or about the role of primary groups. Yet we strongly suspect that these are somehow involved in the phenomenon under study. The part they play may be illuminated, however, if we examine the process by which public opinion is formed.

GENESIS OF AN ISSUE IN THE PRIMARY GROUP

A familiar allegory uses the analogy of seeds to illustrate the growth of ideas. The seeds are numbered in thousands, and are scattered over the landscape. Some fall on the rocks and fail to germinate. Others start to take root but soon die because they lack soil in sufficient depth or because they are smothered by faster-growing weeds. Only a few fall on earth where the conditions are right for continued growth and multiplication.

Similarly, there are many more issues that might provide the basis for mass movements than ever see the light of day. All men have grievances, inspirations, and ideas for improving society, but most of these die away in mutterings or casual conversations. An issue begins to take root only when it is communicated from one person to a second, who then carries it further in his own conversation. Most potential issues disappear from attention before this human chain grows to an appreciable length, but the few that survive form the basis for public opinions.

Let us take the hypothetical case of Center City. This is a town of some 30,000 persons, situated in a predominantly agricultural region. It serves as the market place for a wide area and has a relatively large population of small business men and white collar workers. It also has a few small factories and a junior college. Center City is governed by a mayor who was returned at the last election, in which the principal issue was a proposed sales tax. The mayor successfully opposed this tax, and the issue is now less controversial.

But one day a new factor is injected into the political life of the town. Mr. Jones, who runs a dry goods store on Main Street, receives a notice that the value of his residence has been reassessed. From now on he will have to pay almost half as much again in real estate tax as he has paid in previous years. He hurries down to the assessor's office to protest, but receives no satisfaction. He complains loud and long to his wife, his brother-in-law, his neighbors, and his friends on Main Street. The valuation of his property, he says, is way out of line with that placed on similar properties in the neighborhood.

As it happens, Mr. Jones is a popular man. He has many friends and is not known as one who constantly complains or makes hasty judgments. When he discusses his grievance against the city government with others, some of them remember grievances of their own: one has been treated inconsiderately by municipal employees, another has had difficulties with trash collection, a third dislikes the mayor personally because of a family squabble several years ago. In the minds of all those who interact in these discussions a generalized picture of maladministration is built up. Soon one cannot mention the city government in the circle frequented by Mr. Jones without eliciting the opinion that it is time for a change in city hall. A political issue has arisen.

Actually, we know very little about the formative stage of issues. This part of the public opinion process is usually buried in obscurity because it is unlikely to attract the attention of historians or journalists. Students of public opinion have ordinarily given attention to issues only after they have exploded into public view. Observation of small group behavior does, however, suggest the kind of process that is at work.[5]

The history of issues is complicated further by the fact that important ideas often appear independently at various times and places.[6] To which one of these points of origin should the idea that eventually emerges into public discussion be traced? Or is it the very fact that an idea has a number of apparently independent points of origin that is in part responsible for its subsequent growth?

But, however an issue germinates, we know that in order to survive and spread it must find one or more human groupings that are hospitable to it.[7] Otherwise, the originator will usually discard it or keep it to himself, since it interferes with the harmony of his social relationships. Those few who persist in expressing ideas that find no resonance among their daily associates are usually the lonely and embittered members of society.

EMERGENCE OF LEADERSHIP

Let us return to Mr. Jones and his friends in Center City. Their dissatisfaction with the local government soon comes to the attention of the Opposition Party. This party knows that several similarly disaffected groups exist in the city and, since an election is scheduled for the following year, decides it is time to fan the flames of dissatisfaction. Leaders of the Opposition Party are on good terms with the publisher of the *Center City Bugle* and arrange with him for a series of articles, based largely on leads sup-

---

[5] See especially the excellent summary of small group research in Elihu Katz and Paul F. Lazarsfeld, *Personal Influence,* The Free Press, 1955, pp. 31-116.

[6] The frequency of independent, but almost simultaneous, discoveries has been noted by historians of science. *Cf.* Robert K. Merton, "Priorities in Scientific Discovery," *American Sociological Review,* December 1957.

[7] Harold D. Lasswell has pointed to the significance of the small group as "a radiating nucleus for an idea." *Cf. Psychopathology and Politics,* University of Chicago Press, 1930, p. 187.

plied by the party, on inefficiency in the local government. These deal not only with tax valuations and trash collection, but also with police protection, street lighting, and other subjects about which there have been complaints. One result of these articles is that the mayor and city councilmen prepare to defend themselves. Another is that additional complaints and more information about alleged shortcomings of the city administration flow into the offices of the *Bugle* and the Opposition Party.

While the series of articles on local mismanagement is appearing, and as indignant responses can be heard from the mayor and his friends, the leader of the Opposition Party makes a series of speeches before trade and fraternal groups. His problem is that dissatisfaction with the government comes both from those who think tax valuations are too high and from those who favor extended city services, and who therefore are inferentially in favor of added taxes. To solve this problem, the opposition leader avoids mentioning the tax problem at all and concentrates on two slogans:

PUT CENTER CITY ON A BUSINESS BASIS

and

GIVE THE CITIZEN HIS MONEY'S WORTH

He states that the aims of both these slogans can be accomplished by returning the Opposition Party to office at the next election.

Thus, at this stage of the public opinion process, leadership transcending the original primary group or groups can be distinguished. Sometimes this leadership is provided by the original exponent of the issue in question, whose influence then begins to extend beyond the circle of those he knows personally. An example of such a situation is given in a recent study of a fluoridation controversy in Northampton, Massachusetts, where one of the original opponents of fluoridation succeeded in winning election as mayor and then continued his campaign from the mayor's office.[8] A similar situation is noted in an older study of a controversy over the location of a new school in a rural community. Here the men who had personal interests in the location of the new school, and who first expressed opinions about it, became community leaders as far as this issue was concerned.[9]

More often, however, ideas that are agitating small, face-to-face groups are taken up by men who are already concerned with mass manipulation and who have at their disposal the means of organization and publicity. Such ideas may be collected and exploited by leaders in one field or another with considerable self-consciousness. A speech writer for a prominent politician once asked the author prior to a presidential election whether he could suggest any lively foreign policy issue that had not recently been dealt with by some national figure. Political parties are increasingly ascertaining by public opinion polls what issues are most talked about throughout the population and then are tailoring their campaigns to fit these issues.

[8] Bernard and Judith Mausner, "A Study of the Anti-Scientific Attitude," *Scientific American*, February 1955.

[9] Richard L. Schank, "Test-Tube for Public Opinion: A Rural Community," *Public Opinion Quarterly*, January 1938.

When leadership takes over, simplification and generalization of the original ideas can usually be observed. The leader attempts to formulate the issues in such a manner that they will be understood by and be of interest to the largest possible number of people. A classic example of this adaptation process has been provided by Walter Lippmann in his analysis of a speech made by Charles Evans Hughes following his acceptance of the Republican presidential nomination in 1916.[10]

At this point it is possible to suggest a definition of leadership that may be useful in this discussion. A leader is one who, in the course of interacting with others, influences their attitudes and behavior more than they influence his. He can be distinguished from a spokesman, who merely registers the opinions of a group, and from a prestigeful follower, who lends authority to an existing pattern of attitudes and behavior. In practice, a leader often serves as spokesman and may seek to appear as a prestigeful follower, but if he actually is limited to one or the other of these roles he cannot be regarded as a leader. This definition is illustrated by the rapidly shifting patterns of leadership that can be observed in mob action. A mob leader falls from power and a new leader emerges when the behavior of the latter exerts more influence on the actions of the mob members than does the behavior of the former, who may then become a follower.[11]

INTER-GROUP COMMUNICATIONS

The most important characteristic of communications at this stage of the public opinion process is their ability to transmit facts and opinions about the issue concerned to members of many primary groups. Mass communications have the advantage of being able to reach large numbers of people simultaneously, but even when they are not available the same effect may be achieved, although more slowly and with infinitely more difficulty, through person-to-person communication systems. It is probably because of this fact that we are able to discern public opinion phenomena in societies where mass communications are poorly developed, or are under the rigid control of the state, even though we see these phenomena more rarely than in societies where mass communication systems are easily available to all currents of opinion.

Through inter-group communications the ideas that were originally developed as a result of interaction within face-to-face groups, and were then rationalized by opinion leaders, become available to large numbers of people who are not personally acquainted with each other. Some of those exposed pay no attention. Others find the new ideas incompatible with existing ideas on which they already base their behavior or with the norms of the groups to which they belong, and either consciously or unconsciously reject the new notions. If all, or nearly all, of the audience falls into one of these two categories, then the phenomenon we call public opinion never appears. If, on the other hand, a substantial number of individuals accept the new ideas there is a chance that public opinion may develop.

10 *Public Opinion*, Penguin Books, 1946, pp. 150-154; also p. 156.
11 Robert C. Myers, "Anti-Communist Mob Action: A Case Study," *Public Opinion Quarterly*, Spring 1948.

Those who agree or disagree with an issue propounded in inter-group communications are not scattered at random throughout the audience but are clustered in certain population categories. Those who agree may for example, be concentrated in the ranks of low income groups, younger people, Baptists, and Midwesterners; while those who disagree may be found more frequently among higher income groups, Episcopalians, and Easterners. Studies of public opinion have repeatedly found that the distribution of individual opinions on any given issue is correlated with the group composition of the audience in question.[12]

PERSONAL OPINIONS ON PUBLIC ISSUES

When a controversial idea is received by a significant number of persons in any segment of an audience, face-to-face discussions are likely to start again.[13] This process resembles the one that takes place in the original primary group where the issue is generated, except that this time group discussion proceeds in the awareness that many other people are thinking and talking about the same thing. Out of these discussions new formulations and leaders may emerge and these may modify the formulation presented in the first wave of inter-group communication or may merely reinforce it. A circular process is thus set up: an increasing volume of public communications stimulates more and more discussions, and the involvement of new groups and individuals leads to more public communication.

It is at this point that most of us enter the public opinion process. We rarely take part in the discussions that lead to the initial emergence of an issue, nor do we attempt to formulate or manipulate it. But we are constantly bombarded with ideas originating outside the realm of our personal acquaintanceship (although these may be relayed to us by relatives or friends) and we must disregard, reject, or consider each of these ideas. If we think about the issues involved and form attitudes about them, these attitudes are likely to be shaped not only by our existing attitudes but also by the attitudes prevalent among those with whom we have day to day relationships.[14]

Our attitudes and opinions about issues under public discussion are, however, also conditioned by our knowledge of the opinions and behavior of other groups. The statement attributed to Winston Churchill to the effect that if Hitler invaded Hell, he (Churchill) would say a favorable word for the Devil in the House of Commons is an extreme example of the way in which the actions or opinions of those outside our immediate group help to shape our attitudes on broader issues. "If they are fur it, then I'm agin' it." Studies of prestige suggestion have shown that our attitudes may be shaped by the views of those with whom we have few personal contacts as well as

[12] A familiar example is provided by Paul F. Lazarsfeld, Bernard Berelson, and Hazel Gaudet in *The People's Choice*, Columbia University Press, 1948, pp. 25-27.

[13] *Cf.* Elihu Katz, "The Two-Step Process of Communication: An Up-to-Date Report on an Hypothesis," *Public Opinion Quarterly*, Spring 1957.

[14] This process is illustrated by a great many studies. See especially the remarks on voting changes by social units in Bernard R. Berelson, Paul F. Lazarsfeld and William N. McPhee, *Voting*, University of Chicago Press, 1954, pp. 118-132.

by the attitudes of those with whom we live our daily lives. This is particularly true of people who would like to raise their social status and who therefore model their behavior on that of others with whom they may be acquainted only through press, radio, or television.

The process just described occurred in Center City. As a result of the agitation of the Opposition Party, informal discussions took place along Main Street, especially at lunch time, and in service clubs and fraternal organizations. Small businessmen tended to subscribe to the Opposition Party's slogans. Many white collar workers, who hoped some day to become store owners or managers, adjusted their opinions to those of the boss. In numerous cases their relatives and friends followed suit. Only among the mayor's immediate political following and in the ranks of labor was there strong sentiment in favor of the incumbent administration. A local union leader wrote the *Bugle* in support of the mayor, pointing out that the city government had successfully avoided a sales tax. But since the Opposition Party had said nothing about imposing such a tax most skilled and unskilled workers did not feel themselves threatened. As a matter of fact, only a minority joined in the lively discussions; most citizens were not greatly concerned with local politics. They remained silent during the discussions at which they were present, and at this point did not form any personal opinions at all.

EXPECTATIONS AS TO THE BEHAVIOR OF OTHERS

In the process of forming their own attitudes on public issues, people usually learn about the opinions of others beyond their own immediate circle of acquaintances. Indeed, they often attempt self-consciously to ascertain what these opinions are. They note views reported in the mass media and may even question taxi drivers or casual acquaintances they meet on the train as to the prevailing opinion on a given issue in one part of the country or another. More often, however, people learn about the opinion of others without realizing that they are seeking them.

This process might be called "personal sampling." It leads to a picture of the way members of other groups may be expected to react. From the few opinions that are accessible to us we generalize as to the opinions of large groups or whole populations. We decide, after three or four conversations, that "all the better people in town" feel in such and such a way about a given issue; or we may read a few Paris newspapers and conclude that Frenchmen are overwhelmingly in favor of halting atom bomb tests.

A study of reactions to a radio dramatization of H. G. Wells' *War of the Worlds* provides some excellent examples of the way the personal sampling process may be carried out, although in this case the sampling was in reference to a question of fact (whether or not there had really been an invasion from Mars) rather than to a question of opinion.[15] Walter Lippmann also notes this personal sampling process.[16]

The way in which expectations are formed, and the resulting nature of

[15] Hadley Cantril, *The Invasion From Mars*, Princeton University Press, 1947.
[16] *Op. cit.*, pp. 112-113.

these expectations, varies greatly from individual to individual and from case to case. Some people feel that they know how a given group will react even without sampling the opinions of any members of this group. ("Labor will never stand for that.") The less educated are likely to sample poorly or to project their own opinions onto the whole human race. ("Everybody knows that the earth is flat.") Or a very simple differentiation may be made between the probable difference in the views of good and bad people, or rich and poor. Those with more education are likely to make finer differentiations. But, however accurate or inaccurate these expectations are, they serve to provide an individual with a picture of the way people beyond the reach of his personal observation are likely to behave on any issue in which he is interested.

Practical propagandists are aware of the importance of the picture people form of the attitudes of others and seek to influence this, often by "rigging" the sample. During the Berlin blockade, for instance, East German communists sought to convince West Berliners that pro-communist opinion was strong in the city. They therefore started sending groups of three or four agitators, dressed in work clothes, into West Berlin. One of these would engage a passer-by in conversation on political questions and then, if another West Berliner joined in, the second communist would come up as if by chance, and so on.[17] Similarly, during the South Sea Bubble in 18th century London, the directors of the South Sea Company sent agents into Exchange Alley, where they attempted to create the impression that the stock of the company was in great demand.[18] It has been alleged that advertising agencies have resorted to analogous tactics by stationing operatives in rush-hour subways, with instructions to make loud-voiced comments to each other about the virtues of a given product or service. Such efforts to influence an individual's picture of public attitudes are more often unsuccessful than successful, since they usually are outweighed by other observations a person can easily make in the course of his everyday life.

As a result of prior information, observation, and personal sampling, people are able to locate their own position and the position of the groups to which they belong with regard to an issue. "We" are for it, "they" are against it, and the rest don't care.

The formation of expectations about the opinions and probable behavior of others could be seen in our hypothetical case of Center City. As a result of conversations, discussions, and reading of the *Bugle*, people who were interested in local politics decided that nearly all the business and professional men, and most of the better-paid white collar employees would vote for the Opposition Party at the next election. The politically conscious segment of labor clearly supported the mayor, but most factory workers showed little interest. White collar girls and housewives were also seen as indifferent. There were in fact very appreciable deviations from these patterns, but those who discussed politics in Center City ordinarily spoke as if the various population groups would vote as a unit.

[17] Berlin *Tagesspiegel*, July 1, 1948.
[18] Charles Mackay, *Extraordinary Popular Delusions and the Madness of Crowds*, L. C. Page and Company, 1932, p. 53.

ADJUSTMENT OF OPINIONS AND BEHAVIOR

Once expectations about the attitudes and behavior of others on a given issue have been formed, these expectations tend to influence the opinions and behavior, and even the attitudes, of the people who entertain them. They know that expressions in favor of an issue are likely to win respect or affection for them in one group and may provoke hostile reactions or indifference in other groups. Therefore, they are likely to speak or act in one way if they anticipate approbation and to remain silent or act in another way if they anticipate hostility or indifference. When emotions run high, people may even express support for a position they privately oppose.

This process can be observed most clearly in a crowd that is organized around a given issue. People who do not share the opinions as expressed by the crowd's leaders are likely to remain silent, fearing the disapproval of those around them. This very silence isolates others who may be opposed, since they conclude that, with the exception of themselves, all those present share the same attitudes. Even some who oppose the dominant opinion, or who do not care about it, may express approval by applauding, and thus adjust their behavior to the expected reactions of others present. Crowd members who gain cheers by riotous behavior will be encouraged to even greater excesses. A process is set up in which expectations produce behavioral adjustments, and these in turn reinforce expectations. When this has happened, public opinion has been formed.

It is at this last stage of the public opinion process that individuals who may be unconcerned with the issue at hand are drawn in. Although they may not have formed a personal attitude about the issue, and indeed may not be aware of its nature, they still cannot ignore the behavior of those about them who *do* feel strongly about it. They therefore adopt the opinions of these others. Most often they are involved through some primary group to which they belong, as when one politically concerned member of a family insists that the others vote, but they may also feel the impact of the opinions of those with whom they are not acquainted.[19] Jules Verne's imperturbable hero, Phineas Fogg, who arrived in San Francisco during an election rally in the course of girdling the world in eighty days, found that having no opinion about the local election left him in a highly exposed position. Women who have little interest in the latest trends of fashion still find themselves influenced by the dominant opinion among other women as to what is suitable attire for a given occasion. The fairy tale of the emperor's new clothes is also a case in point, in that all who were sensitive to the opinions of others maintained that they saw the clothes, while only the child, belonging to a population category that is often insensitive to grown-up opinions, announced that the emperor was naked.

In Center City, the process of behavioral adjustment on the basis of expectations was clearly observable. Speakers at business men's luncheons learned that jokes at the expense of the mayor were likely to provoke laughter. Even those who did not share the views of the Opposition Party usually joined politely in the merriment, although somewhat less heartily.

---

[19] *Cf.* Lazarsfeld, Berelson and Gaudet, *op. cit.,* p. 149.

Office seekers whose observations convinced them that the mayor would be
defeated made small contributions to the Opposition Party, or offered their
services as party workers. The minority along Main Street who favored the
mayor kept discreetly silent on the subject of local politics, except when
talking to personal friends.

When election day came, most of those who supported the Opposition
Party marched to the polls, taking with them their relatives of voting age
and their friends. A good turn-out was assured by the fact that these people
felt the eyes of their neighbors and associates upon them. The supporters of
the mayor, who did not feel an equal degree of pressure from the less-
interested members of their own group, showed a much lower incidence of
voting. The headline in the *Center City Bugle* on the following morning
ran:

PUBLIC OPINION SWEEPS MAYOR FROM OFFICE

Before leaving this final stage of the public opinion process, it may be
useful to attempt a definition of a public in the sense that it has been
referred to here. A public is a large collection of individuals (either assembled at one point or scattered throughout a wide area) who do not know
each other personally but who react to an issue with the expectation that
certain categories of others will display similar attitudes on the same issue.
It thus includes those whose behavior is influenced by the expected approval
or expected similar actions of others, even if they themselves have no
strongly held attitude about the issue in question. This definition does not,
however, include those who, even if they take the expected behavior of the
public into account in shaping their overt actions, feel no community of
interest with it. For example, social scientists studying a riot or a political
rally are not members of the rioting or rallying public when the term is
used in this sense.

As this last reservation suggests, the behavior of those who are not members of a given public may still be influenced by the public opinion that has
taken root there. Thus, the social scientists in question may be especially
discreet in their note-taking because they do not wish to arouse hostility
or suspicion on the part of the members of the public they are studying.
Similarly, military or political planners often take public opinion into
account as one datum, along with many others of both a social and a non-
social nature. They may be concerned with public opinions in a given area
along with the geographic location, raw materials, industrial plant, and
political leadership of this area.

It is clear, of course, that the expression "public" is also used frequently
in other ways: to refer to a population, to an audience, or to any collection
of persons distinguished by a single characteristic (e.g., the stockholders of
a company). In connection with discussions of public opinion, however, we
believe that a definition along the lines of the one we have offered is the
most useful. To use one of the other possible definitions leads to the anom-
aly that one can distinguish several public opinions among members of a
single public.

THE DISSOLUTION OF PUBLIC OPINION

One of the characteristics of public opinion that has been noted since early times is that it is a transitory phenomenon. It seems to arise spontaneously and to disappear imperceptibly. With the benefit of the scheme outlined above, we can offer some suggestions as to the various ways it disappears.

Since public opinion refers to attitudes and behavior polarized around an issue, it is clear that if the issue disappears the behavioral adjustment that characterizes public opinion will cease to have any purpose. A mob, for instance, will break up if the occasion for its gathering ceases to exist. Sometimes new goals are found as, for instance, when the mob turns its attention to destruction of property if the victim escapes, but this can be only a temporary stay. The mob members soon resume their normal patterns of life. A similar pattern of developments can be observed in the case of a political public after an election is over.

In other instances, public opinion on one issue is displaced by public opinion on another. At the same time that behavioral adjustment with regard to the first issue is at its height, a new wave of public opinion based on a different issue may be starting to form. This new issue attracts the attention of many members of the first public and a new public, possibly more powerful, is formed. Democratic statesmen who take actions that they know will be opposed by public opinion at the time often do so with the expectation that they will subsequently receive popular support when all the facts are known, or when the situation has been changed by new developments.

Public opinion may sometimes be broken up by superior physical force. The ringleaders may be arrested, all known adherents of a given viewpoint may be subjected to harsh penalties, or all communication among members of a public may be halted. If this repression is carried through relentlessly, individuals who initially composed the public may find their former behavioral adjustment incompatible with their personal safety or with the attainment of other values and adjust their behavior and even their attitudes to the new situation.

Public opinion may lead to the formation of customs or social norms before it is dissipated. The feminist movement managed to organize public opinion in such a manner that many of those who privately disagreed or who didn't care were led to adjust their behavior to conform to the pattern demanded by the militant minority. This pattern, subsequently buttressed by political and economic changes in many areas, then became established as a custom or norm. Feminism was no longer an issue, but people behaved in the manner demanded by the feminists because this was the way they had learned to behave. Their actions were no longer taken with reference to expected approval or hostility from others but either with no thought at all or else with reference to custom or social norms.

Finally, public opinion may also cease to exist when it has succeeded in having the issue around which it was organized embedded in formal laws or constitutions. The writers of *The Federalist* struggled hard to organize public opinion in favor of the constitution of the United States. After the constitution had been ratified, political behavior on many questions then became governed by reference to this formal instrument rather than by public opinion. It is only when a custom or law is seriously threatened that individual behavior may once again become polarized by reference to expectation of mass reactions.

A POSTSCRIPT ON TERMINOLOGY

Partially because of its long history and undefined character the term "public opinion" has been used to refer to a great many phenomena, in addition to phenomena of the type that have been described above. It may serve to clarify our discussion if we mention some of these usages and explain why they cannot be applied to the phenomenon we have attempted to describe.

A common usage is to refer to the findings of opinion polls as public opinion. If, for example, it is found that 80 per cent of eligible voters are in favor of increased federal grants for certain public works, it is sometimes said that public opinion supports legislation to this effect. But it may be that the issue has not been generally discussed. A majority of individual citizens may favor increased federal aid for highways, but their position is taken without reference to the expected behavior of others, because they have not been able to form an expectation about this behavior. They may not know that others share their opinions. In this case, the poll gives us the sum of individual opinions, but the process described in this article has not taken place, or has taken place among the members of only a relatively small public.

This, of course, is not to say that such survey findings are inaccurate or of no value. In some cases they enable us to predict (although not with very great accuracy) what majority and minority public opinion on an issue would be if it were to be formed. Furthermore, they may provide a useful guide for legislators, since in a democracy individual opinions may be as suitable a basis for legislative action as public opinion. The political leader who takes the sum of individual opinions as a guide, however, runs the risk that public opinion when formed later may be of a substantially different character.

An older usage treats public opinion as if it were represented by the dominant ideas expressed in public communications. This approach has been shaken by the observation that successful political candidates in hotly contested elections are often opposed by a heavy proportion of the mass media. It was dealt an even heavier blow when in 1956 the Hungarians rebelled against those who had enjoyed a near monopoly of the communication media for ten years. We are fairly certain that public communications do not necessarily reflect what people talk about in small groups, and even if the issues mentioned in headlines are discussed either approvingly or disapprovingly they may not serve as issues around which a public opinion process is centered.

A third usage refers to public opinion as an agent that enforces social norms, taboos, and so on. In a few cases this may be true, but ordinarily the process we have described does not appear to take place in such situations. A person who breaks a norm or violates a taboo is usually punished without reference to the expected attitudes or behavior of others in the group, and very little communication may take place. Those who administer the punishment play a role more like that of the traffic policeman who gives a ticket when he sees a law violated, while most group members who adhere to established norms or taboos do so not because of the expected behavior of those around them but because they feel that it is the right thing to do. That is, they will behave in the same manner even in private.

The most difficult distinction to maintain is the one between the public opinion process as we have described it here and the process that takes place in relatively small groups. In both cases we can see that similar individual predispositions and environmental influences may be involved, that communication and interaction take place, that expectations as to the attitudes and behavior of others are formed, and that the overt behavior of the self is adjusted to the expected behavior of others with respect to a given issue. At first sight it would appear that a distinction between the public opinion process and what we might call the group opinion process would be difficult to make.

Nevertheless, we believe that there are very important differences. Perhaps most important is the fact that a public is formed around a single issue, or a number of closely related issues, while the range of issues on which a small group may demand conformity from its members can be very great indeed.

A second difference is that the interaction process leading to the formation of group opinions takes place among people who are in frequent association, while the public opinion process involves people who may be united in a particular interaction process only once. Consequently, behavioral adjustment with regard to an issue on which there is consensus in a small group may actually be brought about more because of the past relations and expected future relations among members of the group than because of the dominant stand of the group members on this particular issue. Thus a faculty member may express agreement with a course of action suggested by his colleagues not because of the immediate appreciation he anticipates but because he feels he owes this support to his colleagues in view of their past indulgence to him, or perhaps because he is planning on submitting a proposal himself at a later meeting and does not want to prejudice its chances. Log-rolling in Congress is a similar case in point. A transitory public has no comparable past and future, but only a present.

A related distinction is that group members usually know each other, while members of a public may be total strangers. Adjustment in the group may therefore take place with reference to specific people ("these are my friends and I don't want to hurt their feelings"), while such a process is unlikely in a faceless public.

Indeed, the importance of the public in social processes seems to be related to the fact that, as distinct from the small group, it is a transitory, impersonal aggregate that is organized around a particular issue. These characteristics give it a great suppleness and versatility. The group opinion process is an extremely important component of the public opinion process, but the distinction between the two must be maintained if public opinion phenomena are to be explained adequately.

3. THE NEED FOR MINORITY ACQUIESCENCE IN A DEMOCRACY

by A. Lawrence Lowell *

Each of the two words that make up the expression "public opinion" is significant, and each of them may be examined by itself. To fulfil the requirement an opinion must be public, and it must be really an opinion. Let us begin with the first of these qualities.

OPINION OF A MAJORITY NOT ALWAYS PUBLIC

If two highwaymen meet a belated traveller on a dark road and propose to relieve him of his watch and wallet, it would clearly be an abuse of terms to say that in the assemblage on that lonely spot there was a public opinion in favor of a redistribution of property. Nor would it make any difference, for this purpose, whether there were two highwaymen and one traveller, or one robber and two victims. The absurdity in such a case of speaking about the duty of the minority to submit to the verdict of public opinion is self-evident; and it is not due to the fact that the three men on the road form part of a larger community, or that they are subject to the jurisdiction of a common government. The expression would be quite as inappropriate if no organized state existed; on a savage island, for example, where two cannibals were greedy to devour one shipwrecked mariner. In short the three men in each of the cases supposed do not form a community that is capable of a public opinion on the question involved. May this not be equally true under an organized government, among people that are for certain purposes a community?

To take an illustration nearer home. At the time of the Reconstruction that followed the American Civil War the question whether public opinion in a southern state was, or was not, in favor of extending the suffrage to the Negroes could not in any true sense be said to depend on which of the two races had a slight numerical majority. One opinion may have been public or general in regard to the whites, the other public or general in regard to the Negroes, but neither opinion was public or general in regard to the whole population. Examples of this kind could be multiplied indefinitely. They can be found in Ireland, in Austria-Hungary, in Turkey, in India, in any country where the cleavage of race, religion, or politics is

* Lawyer, professor of government, and president of Harvard University (1900–1933). Author of *Essays on Government, The Government of England, Public Opinion and Popular Government, Public Opinion in War and Peace,* and other works. The selection is from A. Lawrence Lowell, *Public Opinion and Popular Government,* rev. ed., Longmans, Green & Co., Inc., New York, 1921, pp. 4-14. By permission of the publisher.

sharp and deep enough to cut the community into fragments too far apart
for an accord on fundamental matters. When the Mohammedans spread
the faith of Islam by the sword, could the question whether public opinion
in a conquered country favored Christianity or Mohammedanism be said
to depend on a small preponderance in numbers of the Christians or the
followers of the Prophet; and were the minority under any obligation to
surrender their creed? The government was entirely in the hands of the
Mussulmans, but would it be rational to assert that if they numbered
ninety-nine thousand against one hundred thousand Christians public opinion in the country was against them, whereas if they were to massacre two
thousand of the Christians public opinion would then be on their side?
Likewise in Bohemia at the present day, where the Germans and the
Czechs are struggling for supremacy, would there not be an obvious fallacy
in claiming that whichever race could show a bare majority would have
the support of public opinion in requiring its own language to be taught
to all the children in the schools?

In all these instances an opinion cannot be public or general with respect to both elements in the state. For that purpose they are as distinct
as if they belonged to different commonwealths. You may count heads, you
may break heads, you may impose uniformity by force; but on the matters
at stake the two elements do not form a community capable of an opinion
that is in any rational sense public or general. As Mr. Bryce points out, a
great deal of confusion arises from using the term sometimes to mean
everybody's views, that is, the aggregate of all that is thought, and sometimes the views of the majority.[1] If we are to employ the term in a sense
that is significant for government, that imports any obligation moral or
political on the part of the minority, surely enough has been said to show
that the opinion of a mere majority does not by itself always suffice. Something more is clearly needed.

UNANIMITY NOT NECESSARY

But if the opinion of a majority does not of itself constitute a public
opinion, it is equally certain that unanimity is not required. To confine the
term to cases where there is no dissent would deprive it of all value and
would be equivalent to saying that it rarely, if ever, exists. Moreover,
unanimous opinion is of no importance for our purpose, because it is perfectly sure to be effective in any form of government, however despotic,
and it is, therefore, of no particular interest in the study of democracy.
Legislation by unanimity was actually tried in the kingdom of Poland,
where each member of the assembly had the right of *liberum veto* on any
measure, and it prevented progress, fostered violence, and spelled failure.
The Polish system has been lauded as the acme of liberty, but in fact it was
directly opposed to the fundamental principle of modern popular government; that is, the conduct of public affairs in accord with a public opinion
which is general, although not universal, and which implies under certain
conditions a duty on the part of the minority to submit.

[1] *American Commonwealth*, Ed. of 1910, vol. ii, p. 251.

ROUSSEAU'S COMMON WILL

If then unanimity is not necessary to public opinion and a majority is not enough, where shall we seek the essential elements of its existence? A suggestion much in point may be found in the speculations of the most ingenious political philosopher of the eighteenth century. In his *Contrat Social* Rousseau attempts to prove that in becoming a member of a state the natural man may remain perfectly free and continue to obey only his own will. He tells us that in forming a state men desire to enforce the common will of all the members; and he takes as the basis of all political action this common will, which is nearly akin to our idea of public opinion. Now, in order to reconcile the absolute freedom of every citizen to obey only his own volition, with the passing of laws in every civilized state against opposition, he says that when the assembled people are consulted on any measure, their votes express, not their personal wishes upon the subject, but their opinions in regard to the common will, and thus the defeated minority have not had their desires thwarted, but have simply been mistaken in their views about the common will. All men, he insists, want to give effect to this common will, which becomes, therefore, the universal will of everyone and is always carried out.

PUBLIC OPINION AND UNIVERSAL CONSENT

Though stated in a somewhat fanciful way, the theory contains a highly important truth, which may be clothed in a more modern dress. A body of men are politically capable of a public opinion only so far as they are agreed upon the ends and aims of government and upon the principles by which those ends shall be attained. They must be united, also, about the means whereby the action of the government is to be determined, in a conviction, for example, that the views of a majority—or it may be some other portion of their numbers—ought to prevail; and a political community as a whole is capable of public opinion only when this is true of the great bulk of the citizens. Such an assumption was implied, though usually not expressed in all theories of the Social Compact; and, indeed, it is involved in all theories that base rightful government upon the consent of the governed, for the consent required is not a universal approval by all the people of every measure enacted, but a consensus in regard to the legitimate character of the ruling authority and its right to decide the questions that arise.

The power of the courts in America to hold statutes unconstitutional furnishes an illustration of this doctrine. It rests upon a distinction between those things that may be done by ordinary legislative procedure and those that may not; the theory being that in the case of the former the people have consented to abide by the decision of the majority as expressed by their representatives, whereas in the case of matters not placed by the constitution within the competence of the legislature, the people as a whole have given no such consent. With regard to these they have agreed to abide only by a decree uttered in more solemn forms, or by the determination of something greater than a mere majority. The court, therefore, in holding a statute unconstitutional, is in effect deciding that it is not within the range of acts to which the whole people have given their consent; so that while the opinion in favor of the act may be an opinion of the majority of the voters, it is not a public opinion of the community, because it is not one where the people as a whole are united in a conviction that the views of the majority, at least as expressed through the ordinary channels, ought to prevail.

CONSENT AND FORCE

We have seen that in some countries the population has contained, and for that matter still contains, distinct elements which are sharply at odds upon the vital political questions of the day. In such a case the discordant forces may be violent enough to preclude a general consent that the opinion of the majority ought to prevail; but this is not always true. If they are not, the assumption which lies at the foundation of popular government remains unimpaired. If they are, the forms of democracy may still be in operation, although their meaning is essentially altered. It may be worth while to dwell on this contrast a moment because it makes clear the difference between true public opinion and the opinion of a majority.

Leaving out of account those doctrines whereby political authority is traced to a direct supernatural origin, government among men is commonly based in theory either on consent or on force, and in fact each of these factors plays a larger or smaller part in every civilized country. So far as the preponderating opinion is one which the minority does not share, but which it feels ought, as the opinion of the majority, to be carried out, the government is conducted by a true public opinion or by consent. So far as the preponderating opinion is one the execution of which the minority would resist by force if it could do so successfully, the government is based upon force. At times it may be necessary to give effect to an opinion of the majority against the violent resistance, or through the reluctant submission, of the minority. A violent resistance may involve the suppression of an armed insurrection or civil war. But even when there is no resort to actual force it remains true that in any case where the minority does not concede the right of the majority to decide, submission is yielded only to obviously superior strength; and obedience is the result of compulsion, not of public opinion. The power to carry out its will under such conditions must to some extent be inherent in every government. Habitual criminals are held in check by force everywhere. But in many nations at the present day there are great masses of well-intentioned citizens who do not admit the right of the majority to rule. These persons and the political parties in which they group themselves are termed irreconcilable, and when we speak of public opinion in that country we cannot include them. So far as they are concerned there can be no general or public opinion.

Let us be perfectly clear upon this point. The presence of irreconcilables does not mean that the government is illegitimate, or that it is not justified in enforcing its will upon the reluctant minority. That will depend upon other considerations. The use of force may be unavoidable if any settled government is to be upheld, if civic order is to be maintained. But it does mean that the fundamental assumption of popular government, the control of political affairs by an opinion which is truly public, is set aside. Florence may, or may not, have been justified in disfranchising her noble families, but Freeman was certainly right in his opinion that by so doing she lost her right to be called a democracy[2]—that is, a government by all the people—and it makes little difference for this purpose whether a part of the body politic is formally excluded from any share in public affairs or overawed by force into submission.

NUMBERS AND INTENSITY IN OPINION

One more remark must be made before quitting the subject of the relation of public opinion to the opinion of the majority. The late Gabriel Tarde, with his habitual keen insight, insisted on the importance of the intensity of belief as a factor in the spread of opinions.[3] There is a common impression that public opinion depends upon and is measured by the mere number of persons to be found on each side of a question; but this is far from accurate. If forty-nine per cent of a community feel very strongly on one side, and fifty-one per cent are lukewarmly on the other, the former opinion has the greater public force behind it and is certain to prevail ultimately if it does not at once. The ideas of people who possess the greatest knowledge of a subject are also of more weight than those of an equal number of ignorant persons. If, for example, all the physicians, backed by all other educated men, are confident that an impure water supply causes typhoid fever, while the rest of the people are mildly incredulous, it can hardly be said that public opinion is opposed to that notion. One man who holds his belief tenaciously counts for as much as several men who hold theirs weakly, because he is more aggressive, and thereby compels and overawes others into apparent agreement with him, or at least into silence and inaction. This is, perhaps, especially true of moral questions. It is not improbable that a large part of the accepted moral code is maintained by the earnestness of a minority, while more than half of the community is indifferent or unconvinced. In short, public opinion is not strictly the opinion of the numerical majority, and no form of its expression measures the mere majority, for individual views are always to some extent weighed as well as counted. Without attempting to consider how the weight attaching to intensity and intelligence can be accurately gauged, it is enough for our purpose to point out that when we speak of the opinion of a majority we mean, not the numerical, but the effective majority.

No doubt differences in the intensity of belief explain some sudden transformations in politics and in ethical standards, many people holding their views with so little conviction that they are ready to follow in the wake of any strong leader in thought or action. On the other hand they explain in part also cases where a law is enacted readily but enforced with difficulty; for the law may be carried through by a comparatively small body of very earnest men, who produce a disproportionate effect by the heat of their

[2] *Growth of the English Constitution*, chap. i, note 14.
[3] *Les Transformations du Pouvoir*, pp. 42 et seq.

conviction; while the bulk of the people are apathetic and unwilling to support the effort required to overcome a steady passive resistance to the enforcement of the law.

4. THE VALUE OF PUBLIC OPINION
AS A SOCIAL MYTH
by Pendleton Herring *

Like fog or smoke, public opinion is obvious in its larger manifestations, but intangible at closer view. Unlike our fatalistic acceptance of the weather, so much decried by Mark Twain, many try hard to do something about the climate of opinion when it proves unsatisfactory. Orators sometimes use hot air; propagandists set up smoke screens. Various methods of befogging the situation have been tried. Attempts at clarification are difficult. Nevertheless two aspects of public opinion are essential to the success of democratic politics.

Public opinion has vital importance as a symbol that need stand for no value other than directing human affairs through the consensus that emerges from discussion and persuasion. The validity of government by public opinion lies in the kind of social milieu it helps to establish and the attitude of mind that it encourages. Thus the concept, by referring to the "people" for the ultimate sanction of authority, retains flexibility and even uncertainty as to the focus of authority within our society. No ruling group can properly claim the sole right to speak for the people. Hitler apparently has mass support for his regime, but we must deny his right to claim the sanction of public opinion as we understand it under a democracy. Under our political creed power can never be crystallized in a final determinate human will. It rests rather upon an ever fresh interplay of forces.

There is the danger, to be sure, that under aggressive leadership and strong organization a large body of individuals will try to arrogate to themselves the sole right to act for the public. The result would be tyranny in the name of the mass. Men do not act as a mass without strong leadership, nor do they seek the fulfillment of a program without indoctrination; and these ends can be attained only through disciplined organization. Dissenters must be punished. Rule by public opinion implies no such continuity and agreement. It is protean by nature; and like Proteus it is mythical.

In a particular instance public opinion may be resolved into the control of institutions by individuals acting in concert. However, as an abstract belief, it does promote free discussion of ideas and adjustment of special interests—the essence of democracy. Belief in public opinion as a creed

* Former professor of government at Harvard University, former editor-in-chief of *Public Administration Review,* and president of the Social Science Research Council since 1948. Author of *Group Representation before Congress, Public Administration and the Public Interest, The Politics of Democracy, Presidential Leadership,* and other works. The selection is from pp. 305-307 and 309 of *The Politics of Democracy,* by Pendleton Herring. © Copyright 1940 by Pendleton Herring. Holt, Rinehart and Winston Company, New York. Reprinted by permission.

stimulates the interchange of thoughts and diffuses among individuals a sense of social responsibility.

The concept of public opinion embraces another characteristic of great importance. It sanctions the belief that even the opinions of people who are not direct participants in a process must not be ignored. In this sense public opinion is well described as "the views of those outside any given group which must be taken into account by those inside it, whether the group is an institution like the government, or a hospital board, or whether it is some unorganized elements such as spoilsmen of the countryside or slum landlords." In other words belief in public opinion imposes a decent respect for the opinions and standards of one's fellows even though their interests may not be immediately affected by one's actions.

This concept may be interpreted in many other ways. Numerous definitions of public opinion are available. Scholars cannot agree on a precise definition, and there is no authority to fix a formula. Yet the concept is nonetheless useful as a point of departure for varied inquiries. It brings into focus the attitudes, the sentiments, and the more or less articulate views of men taken not as individuals but in multiples. The fact that the term is general does not rob it of meaning; but it does indicate the limitations upon the concept as a tool of analysis. While public opinion, as such, eludes analysis, the fact of our belief in the concept is highly important.

Treated frankly as a social myth, public opinion holds implications highly significant for our political process. The concept of dictatorship of the proletariat is no less important for Soviet Russia than rule by public opinion is for us. Yet it is perhaps easier for us to see through this former phrase as an inadequate description of fact than to note the comparable limitations on our own theory of popular government. In neither case, however, does the significance of the concept lie in its accurate description of human behavior. It lives in the realm of ideology, whence it exerts its influence on the minds of men. As with all symbols, meaning is not to be found in the thing itself as a logical concept but rather in its effectiveness for evoking loyalties and sanctioning rule. A symbol may appear irrational, mystical, even fantastic, yet it may nonetheless give meaning and form to life for those who accept it. Belief in miracles has undoubtedly fostered the spirituality of religious-minded men. An anthropologist studying the history of religion would note its value for this purpose. He might regard similarly our deep faith in the will of the people. . . .

If we talk of what the "people" want, we reify an abstraction and accord it a moral conscience. Rightness or wrongness finds expression only through the individual. Whether a combination of individual judgments manifested as an expression of "public opinion" is right or wrong depends on the judgment of the individual. Political leaders may strive to strengthen their position by an ethical sanction of popular will. Such a sanction can be given only through a consensus of individual moral judgments.

To justify rule by the concept of public opinion does not require us to argue that public opinion is always ethically sound. We are not forced to argue that what the people want is right just because the people want it. This must remain a matter of subjective judgment.

Yet around the concept of public opinion an excrescence of unnecessary assumptions has gathered. Here we find shibboleths about the common will and the necessity that all good citizens participate in elections and hold opinions on public questions in order that this general-will concept be vindicated. The persistent failure of men to act in accordance with this picture merely stimulates the exhorters to greater efforts.

If the significance of public opinion were to be measured by such moral and rationalistic standards, the prospects for popular government would be discouraging. It is enough if we treat the concept of rule by public opinion as simply providing a milieu within which group opinions may compete. Belief in government by public opinion means belief in the validity of that process. It does not entail any assumptions as to the superior wisdom of mass opinion or the rationality of man. It is enough if we allow for the free interplay of opinion, the tolerance of opposition, and a widespread participation by interested citizens in the discussion of problems that touch them closely.

CHAPTER II

The Determinants of Public Opinion

Each of us experiences only a small portion of his environment, and our perception of that environment is encumbered in many ways. *How much* we see of what is going on around us and *how* we see it are determined in large part by the kind of perceptual equipment we possess, which in turn derives from what we begin with and what has happened to it along the way. In other words, our drives (innate and acquired), our emotional make-up, and our ongoing experiences may be viewed as lenses through which our perceptions and feelings are filtered, and all sorts of lenticular variations and aberrations are possible. That which is close at hand may be distinct, while that which is remote is blurred or imperceptible—or the reverse may be true. Or one may be permitted access to objects at varying distances but denied the opportunity of seeing them in an undistorted or anastigmatic manner. One's visual world may thus become a kind of amusement-park hall of mirrors. Or the lenses may be tinted in such a way as to prevent seeing things in their true colors. Or depth of field may be restricted to the degree of isolating objects from both foreground and background. Or one may be obliged to view his environment with too little perspective, causing all objects to appear equally important—or things may be seen with exaggerated perspective, whereby the proximate dwarfs the ultimate. Or angle of view may be narrowed (as though one were wearing blinders) to only that which is directly before one.

The foregoing remarks were not intended as a dissertation on optics but only as an analogical discussion of Man's limited access to reality. It serves, therefore, a similar purpose to Plato's famous "allegory of the cave," with which we begin this chapter, viz., to demonstrate, among other things, in admittedly oblique fashion that it is probably more valid to assert that "believing is seeing" than that "seeing is believing." We have attempted to elaborate upon this general theme with selections from a variety of sources. Taken as a whole, they represent a cataloguing of the more significant influences upon attitude formation; that is, they are in the nature of a search for causes or for those factors which are responsible for the way individuals perceive and react toward their environment.

In the first chapter, we provided an organic definition of public opinion, i.e., a definition which presupposes the interaction of concerned individuals seeking consensus; but opinions are held by individuals not groups. Not all opinions are "public" opinions in the sense in which we are using the term; many are purely private. But, public or private, they are the resultant of similar types of influences. Moreover, we are necessarily interested not only in how one *perceives* and *feels* but also in how one *behaves* as the result of those perceptions and feelings. Both attitude and behavior, therefore, are part of what we have in mind when we discuss "public opinion."[1] As a matter of fact, an attitude, as a "predisposition to experience, to be motivated by, and to act toward, a class of objects in a predictable manner,"[2] is not directly observable; we know of it only as it is verbalized as an opinion or manifested as behavior. Therefore, in this presentation we shall weave back and forth between "public" opinions and "private" opinions and between attitudes and behaviors as our *dependent* variables, recognizing that the dynamics of causation are similar in each instance.

There is no rigidly logical order in which the various influences upon attitude and behavior may be presented; but, after an initial brief discussion by Smith, Bruner, and White of the three major functions of holding an opinion (object appraisal, social adjustment, and externalization), we start with the more remote cultural and characterological determinants and move gradually inward until we are at last considering *intra*personal factors. Stuart Chase sets the pattern for this type of approach with his typically lucid discussion of five major cultural rings which surround George Adams, a hypothetical Connecticut filling station operator, and of what each contributes to molding his attitudes and behavior. The ways in which he is a product of civilization, of Western civilization, of Anglo-Saxon culture, of North American culture, and of New England culture are effectively illustrated. Gabriel Almond then presents, on the basis of a synthesis of the observations of various cultural anthropologists and other scholars, some psychocultural hypotheses about American character.

We turn next to the 1948 Elmira study of voting behavior for a number of perceptive observations by Berelson, Lazarsfeld, and McPhee on the relationship of political choice to group membership. The impact of certain demographic group memberships and identifications are examined first. This is followed by an investigation of primary group influences: family, friends, and coworkers. We continue the discussion of group determinants with an excerpt from an article by Arthur Kornhauser on public opinion and social class wherein are made some very discerning remarks about the difficulties involved in discovering *causes* instead of mere *correlates* of opinion. Finally, we return to a nineteenth-century classic, *An Essay on the Influence of Authority in Matters of Opinion*, for the last of the *inter*personal determinants: In the style of the Victorian scholar, Sir George Cornewall Lewis speaks of parents, teachers, and other authorities as influences upon opinion.

We begin the canvass of *intra*personal influences with Bertrand Russell's gloomy but articulate ruminations about the motives, aspirations, desires of modern man, especially those which have political importance. Scholars from many disciplines have, of course, wrestled with the problem of specifying man's basic needs or drives. Psychoanalyst Harry Stack Sullivan speaks of the pursuit of satisfaction (biological) and the pursuit of security

---

[1] *Cf.* Davison (p. 17), who states that "public opinion refers to attitude and behavior polarized around an issue."

[2] M. Brewster Smith, Jerome S. Bruner, and Robert W. White, *Opinions and Personality*, John Wiley & Sons, Inc., New York, 1956, p. 33.

(cultural);[3] psychologist A. H. Maslow of a needs hierarchy (physiological, safety, love, esteem, and self-actualization);[4] and political scientist Harold Lasswell in one of his earlier works of safety, income, and deference as representative values sought by man[5]—but philosopher Russell's observations will suffice for present purposes.

We might have resorted to clinical materials by way of illustration of personality determinants, for example, the case histories supplied by Lasswell in his *Psychopathology and Politics* and *Power and Personality* to demonstrate the validity of his formulation that the power-oriented individual displaces private motives on public objects and rationalizes such action in terms of public interest.[6] But out of consideration for the reader with limited psychological training, we shall resist this temptation and leave a more thorough exploration of psychodynamics to those interested in this approach. Instead, we have provided two exceptionally readable and nontechnical excerpts which deal with the relationship between certain motivational factors and the conversion to mass movements. The first consists of a number of aphoristic passages from Eric Hoffer's remarkable little work, *The True Believer,* and the second is Arthur Koestler's brief account of the factors impelling his conversion to communism.

One need not, of course, travel to either extreme of the politico-economic continuum in search of motivational determinants. We need examine neither the Koestlers nor the fascistoid personalities, who have received so much attention since the end of World War II. Consider, for example, the New Deal–Fair Deal–New Frontier Democrat whose liberal sentiments, however, they may be rationalized, represent primarily a strong identification with anyone who like himself is seen as having been "shortchanged" in life. Consider also his friend who arrived at identical sentiments from the differing route of hostility toward conservative parents and of resulting rejection of most things for which they stand. A great many political commitments—of either the Right or the Left—are explicable in just such terms as these.

The final category of determinants considered are events. These fit nowhere into the concept of concentric rings from civilization to psyche, but they are no less important and deserving of consideration. We need only refer back to the 1960 presidential election campaign and note the surprisingly good showing President Kennedy made in the first of the "Great Debates" on television, by which the issue of his "immaturity" was minimized. And we might also speculate about the possible impact on the campaign and the outcome of the election if the unfounded rumor of Khrushchev's fall from power had proved true. The Cantwell article provides a neat demonstration of the influence of events on public opinion in the con-

---

[3] Harry Stack Sullivan, *Conceptions of Modern Psychiatry,* The William Alanson White Psychiatric Foundation, Washington, D.C., 1947, Lecture I.

[4] A. H. Maslow, "A Theory of Human Motivations," *Psychological Review,* vol. 50, no. 4, pp. 370-396, July, 1943.

[5] Harold D. Lasswell, *World Politics and Personal Insecurity,* McGraw-Hill Book Company, Inc., New York, 1935, p. 3.

[6] Harold D. Lasswell, *Psychopathology and Politics,* University of Chicago Press, Chicago, 1930, pp. 75-77; and Harold D. Lasswell, *Power and Personality,* W. W. Norton & Company, Inc., New York, 1948, pp. 37-38.

text of the 1937 debate on President Roosevelt's proposal for reorganizing the Supreme Court.

The chapter ends on the theme with which it began—with a consideration of perceptual mechanisms which deprive us of the opportunity of knowing things as they really are. This is Walter Lippmann's excellent discussion of the nature and functioning of stereotypes.

We have by no means exhausted the infinite variety of external and internal influences upon opinion, but we have considered a number of the more important determinants. One should realize, of course, that any attempt to explain the status of opinion with regard to any particular issue in terms of *single* causative factors is naïve. Impressive and statistically significant correlations between two variables are easily obtained, but the more difficult task is demonstrating that the relationship is *causal* and that more satisfactory explanations are not possible on the basis of *other* factors. Readers and researchers alike are well advised to keep this caveat ever before them.

5. THE ALLEGORY OF THE CAVE

by Plato *

After this, I said, imagine the enlightenment or ignorance of our nature in a figure: Behold! human beings living in a sort of underground den, which has a mouth open towards the light and reaching all across the den; they have been here from their childhood, and have their legs and necks chained so that they cannot move, and can only see before them; for the chains are arranged in such a manner as to prevent them from turning round their heads. At a distance above and behind them the light of a fire is blazing, and between the fire and the prisoners there is a raised way; and you will see, if you look, a low wall built along the way, like the screen which marionette players have before them, over which they show the puppets.

I see, he said.

And do you see, I said, men passing along the wall carrying vessels, which appear over the wall; also figures of men and animals, made of wood and stone and various materials; and some of the passengers, as you would expect, are talking, and some of them are silent?

That is a strange image, he said, and they are strange prisoners.

Like ourselves, I replied; and they see only their own shadows, or the shadows of one another, which the fire throws on the opposite wall of the cave?

True, he said; how could they see anything but the shadows if they were never allowed to move their heads?

* Greek philosopher (427?–347 B.C.). Author of a number of dialogues including *Phaedrus, Symposium, Apology, Crito, Phaedo, The Republic, Timaeus,* and *Laws.* The selection is from Plato, *The Republic,* Book VII, pp. 341-344 of vol. II of *The Dialogues of Plato* (trans. B. Jowett), Charles Scribner's Sons, New York, 1887.

And of the objects which are being carried in like manner they would only see the shadows?

Yes, he said.

And if they were able to talk with one another, would they not suppose that they were naming what was actually before them?

Very true.

And suppose further that the prison had an echo which came from the other side, would they not be sure to fancy that the voice which they heard was that of a passing shadow?

No question, he replied.

There can be no question, I said, that the truth would be to them just nothing but the shadows of the images.

That is certain.

And now look again, and see how they are released and cured of their folly. At first, when any one of them is liberated and compelled suddenly to go up and turn his neck round and walk and look at the light, he will suffer sharp pains; the glare will distress him, and he will be unable to see the realities of which in his former state he had seen the shadows; and then imagine some one saying to him, that what he saw before was an illusion, but that now he is approaching real being and has a truer sight and vision of more real things,—what will be his reply? And you may further imagine that his instructor is pointing to the objects as they pass and requiring him to name them,—will he not be in a difficulty? Will he not fancy that the shadows which he formerly saw are truer than the objects which are now shown to him?

Far truer.

And if he is compelled to look at the light, will he not have a pain in his eyes which will make him turn away to take refuge in the object of vision which he can see, and which he will conceive to be clearer than the things which are now being shown to him?

True, he said.

And suppose once more, that he is reluctantly dragged up a steep and rugged ascent, and held fast and forced into the presence of the sun himself, do you not think that he will be pained and irritated, and when he approaches the light he will have his eyes dazzled, and will not be able to see any of the realities which are now affirmed to be the truth?

Not all in a moment, he said.

He will require to get accustomed to the sight of the upper world. And first he will see the shadows best, next the reflections of men and other objects in the water, and then the objects themselves; next he will gaze upon the light of the moon and the stars; and he will see the sky and the stars by night, better than the sun, or the light of the sun, by day?

Certainly.

And at last he will be able to see the sun, and not mere reflections of him in the water, but he will see him as he is in his own proper place, and not in another, and he will contemplate his nature.

Certainly.

And after this he will reason that the sun is he who gives the seasons and the years, and is the guardian of all that is in the visible world, and in a certain way the cause of all things which he and his fellows have been accustomed to behold?

Clearly, he said, he would come to the other first and to this afterwards.

And when he remembered his old habitation, and the wisdom of the den and his fellow-prisoners, do you not suppose that he would felicitate himself on the change, and pity them?

Certainly, he would.

And if they were in the habit of conferring honors on those who were quickest to observe and remember and foretell which of the shadows went before, and which followed after, and which were together, do you think that he would care for such honors and glories, or envy the possessors of them? Would he not say with Homer,—

"Better to be a poor man, and have a poor master,"

and endure anything, rather than to think and live after their manner?

Yes, he said, I think that he would rather suffer anything than live after their manner.

Imagine once more, I said, that such an one coming suddenly out of the sun were to be replaced in his old situation, is he not certain to have his eyes full of darkness?

Very true, he said.

And if there were a contest, and he had to compete in measuring the shadows with the prisoners who have never moved out of the den, during the time that his sight is weak, and before his eyes are steady (and the time which would be needed to acquire this new habit of sight might be very considerable), would he not be ridiculous? Men would say of him that up he went and down he comes without his eyes; and that there was no use in even thinking of ascending: and if any one tried to loose another and lead him up to the light, let them only catch the offender in the act, and they would put him to death.

No question, he said.

6. THE ADJUSTIVE FUNCTIONS OF OPINION

by M. Brewster Smith, Jerome S. Bruner, and Robert W. White *

What purpose is served by holding an opinion? Put more technically, the question becomes, "What adjustive functions of personality are served by the formation and maintenance of an opinion?"

* M. Brewster Smith, professor of psychology at University of California (Berkeley), former editor of *Journal of Social Issues* and *Journal of Abnormal and Social Psychology,* and coauthor of several works. Jerome S. Bruner, professor of psychology at Harvard University, former editor of *Public Opinion Quarterly,* and coauthor of several works. Robert W. White, professor of clinical psychology at Harvard University. Reprinted with permission from M. Brewster Smith, Jerome S. Bruner, and Robert W. White, *Opinions and Personality,* pp. 39-44, © copyright 1956, John Wiley & Sons, Inc., New York.

Let us say at the most general level that one's opinions or attitudes serve as mediators between the inner demands of the person and the outer environment—the material, social, and, most immediately, the informational environment of the person. Figures of speech may be misleading, yet we do well to think of a man's attitudes as his major equipment for dealing with reality. This equipment is not a product solely of basic needs and defenses nor is it fashioned directly according to the blueprint of the world in which the person finds himself. Nor is it simply borrowed ready-made from the groups to which he belongs or aspires. Something of all of these but not quite any one of them, it is, essentially, an apparatus for balancing the demands of inner functioning and the demands of the environment. One cannot predict a man's opinions by knowledge of his personality alone or of his environment alone. Both must enter into any predictive formula.

It is a mistake to restrict the concepts of attitude and opinion to those predispositions which have as their object the issues of contemporary social and political life. Such restriction overlooks the fact that these attitudes are embedded in larger systems of opinion which mediate between the most compelling pressures of the environment and the most imperious and pervasive needs. Perhaps someone will ask, "Why all this searching analysis of a man's half-baked attitudes toward Russia?"* The answer is this: look far enough into the origins of any opinion, and one will find not just an opinion but a sample of how the holder of that opinion copes with his world.

Rather than risk later misunderstanding we shall pause for a moment to examine the two meanings that can be attached to "having an opinion." Let us say first that one can *hold* an opinion and at the same time reserve option on when and how the opinion should be *expressed*. It is obvious that the two acts serve somewhat different functions. And while we may be inclined to say that the one is freer of constraints than the other—that a man may hold whatever view he likes so long as he is discreet in its expression—it is the better wisdom to attribute an equal lawfulness to each. Only in a most superficial sense is one "free" to hold whatever opinion he will. The illusion of free choice of opinion is scarcely borne out by closer analysis of the many inner and outer requirements that limit what a person will find acceptable. "I can't believe that," he will say; or, "What an irresponsible, almost despicable point of view that is!"

Once we have said that there is a lawful determination both in the opinions one holds and in the occasions and circumstances of their expression, we must then go on to say that the same laws do not hold for each. The two must be held separate, for separate but concurrent examination. It is true, of course, that the opinions permissible to express are, under some circumstances, the very opinions one wishes to hold. Or, quite the reverse, the rebel may find himself repelled by popular points of view whose expression savors to him of conformism. Such instances do not cancel the need for separate analysis.

* *Editors' Note:* This selection is taken from one of the introductory chapters of a detailed report on the findings and conclusions of an intensive study of ten men and their opinions about Russia by the Harvard Psychological Clinic.

In our discussion of the adjustive functions of opinion we shall make no special effort to incarcerate "holding" and "expressing" into separate and purified theoretical categories. They each present somewhat different problems for empirical analysis and we shall, where possible, analyze them separately. Our principal theoretical interest, as the reader must long ago have noted, is in the opinions *held* by the individual. It is a crucial but secondary theoretical problem how a man works out the strategy of their expression.[1]

There are three functions served by holding an opinion, and we shall call them *object appraisal, social adjustment,* and *externalization.* Let us note briefly the characteristics of each. . . .

Object Appraisal

We use this expression in the same sense in which psychoanalysts employ "reality testing." The holding of an attitude provides a ready aid in "sizing up" objects and events in the environment from the point of view of one's major interests and going concerns. Insofar as attitudes are predispositions to experience certain classes of objects, to be motivated by them, and to respond to them, it is evident that their existence permits the individual to check more quickly and efficiently the action-relevancy of the events in the environment around him. Presented with an object or event, he may categorize it in some class of objects and events for which a predisposition to action and experience exists. Once thus categorized, it becomes the focus of an already-established repertory of reactions and feelings, and the person is saved the energy-consuming and sometimes painful process of figuring out *de novo* how he shall relate himself to it. If the environmental fact either defies categorization or is categorized in such a way as to bring harmful consequences to the person, new attitudes may be developed or shifts in categorization may occur. In sum, then, attitudes aid us in classifying for action the objects of the environment, and they make appropriate response tendencies available for coping with these objects. This feature is a basis for holding attitudes in general as well as any particular array of attitudes. In it lies the function served by holding attitudes *per se*. Without them, we should be in the constant throes of determining the relevance of events, of fashioning decisions and of deciding upon actions—all *ab initio*. More specifically, object appraisal is the process whereby the person develops attitudes that are a creative solution to the problems posed by the existence of disparate internal demands and external or environmental demands.

Social Adjustment

Opinions can play another role: that of facilitating, disrupting, or simply maintaining an individual's relations with other individuals. It is in this

---

[1] If one should ask, "How do you know the opinion held by a person save by its expression?" we shall reply that we know it only in that way. Knowledge of a "held" opinion is based upon inference from observation of its expression under a variety of special situations—including those highly permissive diagnostic situations in which there is neither gain nor loss to be earned or incurred by expressing one's views.

realm particularly that one must take care to distinguish the functions served by holding an opinion and by expressing it, for the strategy of expression is of particular importance in maintaining or cementing one's relationship with what may be called "membership groups"—the individuals with whom one is in direct contact. Where there is a need to be accepted in the community, one will more readily and more forthrightly express acceptable attitudes while inhibiting or modulating the expression of less approved ones.

The function of social adjustment served by holding an opinion is at once more subtle and more complex. For it is by holding certain views that one identifies with, or, indeed, differentiates oneself from various "reference groups" within the population. By reference groups we mean here those groups in terms of whose standards the individual judges himself and with which he identifies or feels kinship. They may or may not correspond to the membership groups with which he has face-to-face commerce; moreover, certain reference groups may never be physically present to the individual for interaction. Representative of reference groups are such symbols as "intellectuals," "average middle-class Americans," "decent girls," and so on. The act of holding certain opinions, as Merton,[2] Centers,[3] Warner,[4] and various others have pointed out, is an act of affiliation with reference groups. It is a means of saying, "I am like them."

Reference groups may also play a negative role in opinion functioning. There are groups with which one seeks to reject kinship or identification. Thus, one of our subjects sought as hard to dissociate himself from the bourgeoisie as he sought to associate himself with the *avant-garde* left. When rebelliousness and rejection are prominent features in a man's adjustment, we may expect negative reference groups to play a prominent role in his opinion formation.

Two rather unique kinds of social adjustment can also be achieved by holding opinions of a certain kind. First, one may develop opinions as the expression of a need to be autonomous from others. Such declarations of autonomy—and we must distinguish the term from rebellion—are in a curious backhand way still another mode of identifying oneself with various reference groups. Thus one of our subjects showed a strong need for working out his opinions independently, unswayed by prevailing points of view. This procedure was for him a way of expressing his lack of dependence on others; but it was also a way of identifying with that nebulous category known as "independent and liberal thinkers." And second, it is sometimes convenient to indulge hostility toward others by holding opinions that are at odds with prevailing beliefs. If such an adjustment be neurotic in origin, it is nonetheless a form of negativism one occasionally encounters.

[2] R. K. Merton and A. S. Kitt, Contributions to the theory of reference-group behavior, In R. K. Merton and P. F. Lazarsfeld (eds.), *Continuities in social research,* Glencoe, Ill., Free Press, 1950.

[3] R. Centers, *The psychology of social classes,* Princeton, Princeton University Press, 1949.

[4] W. L. Warner and P. S. Lunt, *The social life of a modern community,* New Haven, Yale University Press, 1941.

The very act of holding an opinion, whatever its nature, may serve the social adjustment of the individual, as Riesman and Glazer have remarked.[5] Given identification with certain groups—let us take the reference group called "intellectuals"—the individual feels that he *must* have opinions on certain issues to maintain his sense of identification.

We must not, however, leave a false impression. The underlying motive gratified by holding and expressing opinions that aid our social adjustment is neither a conformity need nor its reverse, a need to rebel. A wide variety of psychological mechanisms is at work, motivating us to relate our destinies to those of the concrete membership groups around us and to those of the more remote reference groups to which we adhere. Requirements of ego defense, dependency needs, drives for autonomy, hostility, drives for status, and many other dynamisms may be involved.

Externalization

It would be all too easy to equate externalization of inner requirements with the classical conceptions of projection and displacement. These two mechanisms are two *examples* of what we mean by externalization. Externalization occurs when an individual, often responding unconsciously, senses an analogy between a perceived environmental event and some unresolved inner problem. He adopts an attitude toward the event in question which is a transformed version of his way of dealing with his inner difficulty. By doing so, he may succeed in reducing some of the anxiety which his own difficulty has been producing.

Perhaps an illustration will clarify the process. An adolescent develops a violent hatred for Fascism, the Nazis, and for Hitler, particularly during the 1930's. Although he is not accepted because of his age, he is aroused to the point of volunteering for the Abraham Lincoln Brigade during the Spanish Civil War. Upon entry of the United States into the War, he volunteers, is rejected, but flings himself into a lather of civilian war activity from which he derives a deep satisfaction.

Whence the tremendous intensity of this attitude? Leaving aside the realities of the situation, the grave threat with which Fascism *did* in fact confront the world and which our subject sensed, why was there such an extraordinarily intense compulsion to do something about his feelings? Analysis reveals in this man a strong and unresolved fear of rejection by powerful figures who can be reached neither through their sympathies nor through their intellect: the figure of an inchoate, powerful, cruel, but basically unreachable force. We need not examine the genesis of this deeply repressed fear. It suffices that it existed. The emergence of Hitler and the Nazis served for the adolescent as a concretization or "binding" for this fearsome and rejecting figure. Hitler in a unique way could serve as the apotheosis of that figure which could be reached neither by sympathy nor by reason. Energies previously directed at coping with the inner problem could now be liberated and focussed on an external object. If anxiety could thereby be reduced, so much the better.

[5] D. Riesman and N. Glazer, The meaning of opinion, *Public Opinion Quarterly*, 1948, **12**, 633-648.

We present this case not only to illustrate externalization but also to show how it differs from run-of-the-mill displacement. Certainly the case illustrates displacement, but that is not all: there are also externalization of affect and externalization of action. An external object is treated in terms relevant to an internal problem: where the internal rejecting figure could not be destroyed by direct assault, the externalized object could become a target for highly energized, creatively destructive planning and action. If the externalization proved an adaptive one, that is partly the good fortune of history and partly the result of adequate object appraisal. The fact that there were active membership groups and palpable reference groups with whom our young man could align himself also helped.

7. THE CONCENTRIC RINGS OF CULTURE
by Stuart Chase *

Another way to bring the culture concept home is to take a neighbor in one's community and try to find out the sources of the cultures which have molded him. Warner and Lunt in their excellent *Yankee City* series have done this in statistical and scholarly detail, but we will be content with a more impressionistic survey.

Here, for instance, is George Rutherford Adams, an imaginary character who runs a garage, filling station, and milk bar in Middleburg, Connecticut. On the Warner and Lunt six-class scale, he would be a member of the lower middle class which, when bracketed with the upper middle, contains the most energetic and dependable citizens in the community. He is thirty-one years old, five feet nine, weighs one hundred and fifty-eight pounds, and was a bombardier with the 16th Air Force in the war. He is a Legionnaire, an Elk, and an active member of the Middleburg Volunteer Fire Company; he goes to the Congregational Church half a dozen times a year. Junior is four, and the baby is eighteen months. His wife taught seventh grade in the Hill School before he married her.

George likes to listen to ball games over the radio as he works in his shop, and he loves to go trout fishing in the spring. He is a Republican in town politics, but twice he voted for Franklin Roosevelt. He is well regarded in Middleburg, for at one time or another his wrecker, a 1930 Pierce Arrow, has pulled nearly everyone in town out of a ditch.

What kind of being is George Rutherford Adams? What shaped him? How did he get to be what he is? We know that he is the product of a group and the culture which goes with it. What group and what culture? Here we encounter a hierarchy of attachments and loyalties. George is not the product of a single culture, as the Greenland Eskimo is (or was), but

* Professional writer on economic, political, and social problems. Author of *The Tragedy of Waste, The Economy of Abundance, Rich Land, Poor Land, The Tyranny of Words, Democracy under Pressure, Men at Work, The Proper Study of Mankind, Some Things Worth Knowing,* and numerous other works. The selection is from *The Proper Study of Mankind,* Harper & Brothers, New York, 1948, pp. 69-74. Copyright 1948 by Stuart Chase. Reprinted by permission of Harper & Brothers.

of a whole ring of cultures, one inside the next. His group, meanwhile, is now so large that it covers a continent—though we can also distinguish a number of subgroups to which George belongs.

He identifies himself loyally with Middleburg, with Connecticut, with New England, in a declining scale. His major loyalty, however, is to the USA, with its three million square miles and 145 million neighbors.* This has now become his community, his We-group, in the most binding sense of the term, as it is mine, and probably yours—unless you live in Texas, which is a special case. It is so by the test of a common culture as well as by national sovereignty. The concrete highway, even more than the railroad, has broken up the old local patterns, and is making "home" mean to Americans a place where you can get a good ice-cream soda, decent service at a filling station, beauty shops, ice-water, sports writers who make sense, and Bing Crosby. . . .

The nation has also become George's *economic* unit in these days of fresh vegetables from California, lumber from Oregon, and oil from Louisiana. In the times of Obadiah Adams, deacon of the Methodist Church, blacksmith of Middleburg, and George's great-great-grandfather, the town came first, Connecticut also claimed a fierce loyalty, but New York State was practically a foreign country separated by a tariff wall. America, reaching way out to the wilds of Ohio, was a pretty vague concept to Obadiah. He never went fifty miles from where he was born in all his life. His economic region lay within that radius; even the iron for his horseshoes came from the Connecticut hills. He knew the face and name of everyone in town, and many in the region.

George has heard much about rugged individualism. He may think he is on his own, above the crowd, responsible only to himself and to his God, but the facts do not bear out his assumptions. In Middleburg there are many, many things he might like to do, but cannot do, because the folkways forbid it. For instance, he may not whistle in church, or grow a beard, or strike a woman, or eat with his fingers, or take off his clothes in public on a hot day, or wear brown shoes with a tuxedo or bright colors at a funeral, or appear at the Elks' Hall with a patch on his coat. His freedoms are strictly relative. George can choose his necktie from the rack, but he must wear a necktie at the appropriate times. Certain foods highly prized among many peoples, such as eels, snails, certain kinds of grubs, he does not think fit to eat. Although his hunger is physical and common to all men, his recognition of how he will satisfy it is cultural.

Superstitions have declined somewhat since Obadiah's day, but George still avoids walking under ladders, would rather not sign a contract on Friday the thirteenth, and wants no black cats to cross the road. He is perfectly sure, too, that Ellery Sanford can find water every time with that willow wand.

Where did these codes and beliefs come from? They started coming to George at the moment the doctor slapped him on the back, and he let out his first yell. They came from parents, teachers, schoolmates, relatives,

* *Editors' Note:* The present population of the United States is, of course, considerably larger than this.

truck drivers, drill sergeants, ministers, policemen, store-keepers, the drug store gang, from nearly everyone who crossed George's path during his impressionable years. Think, for instance, of all the people who taught him to talk, including the voices on the radio.

Where did *they* get the codes? From the generation which inducted them. There was nothing floating in the air; codes always come from people. A few of the simpler habits, like drinking from a cup, or sitting on a chair rather than on the ground, may have been handed down unchanged for twenty generations. Altogether we can identify at least five major cultural rings from which most of George's behavior is derived.

1. To begin with the broadest, he is a product of *civilization.* For more than 6,000 years the group from which he descends has practiced a widespread division of labor and city living, based on the invention of a storable grain. This marks off his behavior from nature peoples who never developed cities, writing, architecture, or mathematics. At the same time it connects George with the peoples of India, China, Persia, and other areas where civilization as defined has been long in evidence. To him personally it means, among other things, living in a house, going to school, eating cereals, paying taxes, using money.

2. Next comes *Western civilization* as distinct from other civilizations. From this source George gets the Christian religion, many of his standards of right and wrong, Arabic numerals, nationalism and the sovereign state, modern science and technology, tinkering with machines, music in the diatonic scale, the free market—now, alas, much corrupted with monopolies and government controls—property rights, pecuniary emulation, and military conscription, to name a few.

3. The next smaller ring is *Anglo-Saxon culture*—that part of Western civilization in which English is spoken. Here George learns his language— *the most important single element in his entire cultural inheritance.* Without language the members of the group could not communicate, and would rapidly disintegrate. Man would cease to be a human being. Here, too, he learns to vote and believe in *habeas corpus,* the Bill of Rights, political democracy, the idea of progress, and romantic love as the only proper basis for marriage. He acquires a streak of Puritanism, a strong sense of superiority to foreigners, and the ability to cover up his emotions. He is taught to disapprove of people who shout and weep and wave their hands. For a grown man to cry in the presence of others is humiliating in the extreme. He stands nearer the Iroquois than the Latin peoples in this respect, but nearer the Latins in his public laughter.

4. Next comes *North American culture,* which George shares with English-speaking Canadians, but not with Mexicans. Here he picks up many words and place names and a few customs—like canoeing and corn roasts— which derive from the Indians. More than half the forty-eight states have Indian names, including his own Connecticut. He has been heavily influenced by the frontier pattern, for even New England was the frontier a few generations ago. This pattern helps to reinforce George's individualism and a certain social irresponsibility, especially toward public property and resources. Cut out, get out, move West, was the frontiersman's idea. The

Pacific has long since been reached, but the irresponsibility remains, a cultural lag. It is shown in the fabulous wastes of top soil, timber, grasslands, natural gas, wastes which mean nothing whatever to George, but which communities in Europe could not tolerate. It is shown in the political immaturity and awkwardness of most Americans when faced with international contacts. There is nothing in their culture to help them cope with such situations.

Here are other patterns that North America gives to George: the great motor car complex on which he makes his living, Hollywood, radio habits, the comics, mass production, bathrooms, a sublime belief in education, service clubs, baseball, the success story, a power of laughing at himself, juke boxes, jazz bands, and a propensity to spoil his children. Notice that we are mixing up material things with customs and attitudes, but so they are mixed in the cultural stream.

5. *New England* is the last ring. Though most of George's habits were learned there, its unique contributions to his way of life are few; far fewer than in Obadiah's case. George is more tolerant of Negroes, coming from an abolitionist area, than many Americans. New England has given him some favorite dishes, such as clam chowder with milk; a nasal twang in his speech, a disposition to be close-mouthed, to be thrifty and count his pennies, and to be suspicious of the neighbors; the moral virtue of early rising and hard work.

The Old Man of the Sea

We have given only the roughest indication of the items in each ring. To prepare a full account of the habits which George has learned, and largely follows without taking thought, would fill a library. Reflect a moment on the unthinking customs you yourself follow in a single day—from the time you get out of bed in the morning until you snap off the light at night. There must be thousands of them.

It is obvious that most of George's artifacts, habits, and systems of belief come from Western civilization, from the Anglo-Saxon culture, and from North America. The first has been in existence since Socrates, say for twenty-five hundred years; the second since Chaucer, say six hundred years; the third since Captain John Smith, say three hundred years, but Indian additions to the last reach back much further; Indian corn probably antedated Homer.

George Rutherford Adams is an amalgam of these far-flung influences. Wherever he goes he carries this great cultural load—like the Old Man of the Sea. Nobody can get at him, talk to him, tell him anything except in relation to this burden. When he met Chinese, Burmese, or Dutch during his overseas service, he judged them by these standards, built into his nervous system as the transmission is built into a car. If he should take a tourist cruise in the Caribbean, he will judge Haitians, Cubans, Mexicans in a similar way. Unless he is aware of his reaction, it is unlikely that he will judge them fairly. Because their culture rings are somewhat different, many things they do will vary from what he does in similar circumstances, and he will blame them for it. At times the blame may flare into anger.

If we compare George with such a person as Laughing Boy, the Navaho hero of Oliver LaFarge's novel by that name, we see a strange and significant contrast. George is caught in a whirl of cultural rings, and an interdependent society far beyond the face-to-face range, which make his way of life more complicated and uncertain than that of the Indian. George can never be so sure what is the right thing to do, as Laughing Boy learned to be. His loyalties do not run to a single tribe, a definite cosmology, a straight and narrow path in all of life's main turnings.

George does not belong to anything very hard since he left the Air Force. He is worried, despite the breezy way he comes out to fill up your car. He had to borrow so much money to start his business, and prices have been so high. He is not sure what is in store for him and the family. He does not see clearly where he is going, or the country, or the world. The bomb, now, and those Russians, and the next depression. . . .

Laughing Boy's world was steady as a rock; but George's sometimes seems to be breaking apart.

8. CHARACTEROLOGICAL DETERMINANTS
by Gabriel A. Almond *

In the systematic inventory which follows we have made an effort to include only those observations which have continually recurred and those which seem to have an inherent plausibility, recognizing that the criterion of "plausibility" is a purely subjective one.

1. General Value Orientation

The characteristic American value orientation would appear to consist of the following interrelated traits.

a. The degree of atomization in the United States is perhaps greater than in any other culture. The American is primarily concerned with "private" values, as distinguished from social-group, political, or religious-moral values. His concern with private, worldly success is his most absorbing aim. In this regard it may be suggested by way of hypothesis that in other cultures there is a greater stress on corporate loyalties and values and a greater personal involvement with political issues or with other-worldly religious values.

b. The "attachment" of the American to his private values is characterized by an extreme degree of competitiveness. He views himself and his family as in a state of competition with other individuals and families for success and achievement. American culture tends to be atomistic rather than corporate, and the pressure of movement "upward," toward achievement, is intense. Here again a hypothesis might be proposed that in other

---

* Professor of international affairs and of politics at Princeton University. Author of *The American People and Foreign Policy, The Appeals of Communism,* and several other works. The selection is from pp. 48-53 of *The American People and Foreign Policy* by Gabriel A. Almond, copyright, 1950, by Harcourt, Brace & World, Inc., New York. By permission.

cultures individual competition for success tends to be more localized within specific classes or regions, tends to be subordinated to, or assimilated in, political competition, and tends to be muted by religious conceptions of life.

c. The American views himself and his family as in a state of competition with other individuals and families for values which are largely "material" in character. What he appears to want are the material evidences of success—money, position, and the consumer-goods of the moment. While the stress is toward money, or what money can buy, the important thing is not the money itself, but the sense of accomplishment or fulfillment which it gives. This sense of accomplishment rests on matching and exceeding the material standard of community and social class; it requires external approval and conformity. Because of the stress in the American value system on having what others want, and because of the great emphasis on the elaboration of material culture, the American tends to be caught up in an endless race for constantly changing goals—the "newest" in housing, the "latest" in locomotion, the most "fashionable" in dress and appearance. This love of innovation, improvement, and change tends to be confined to the material culture. Attitudes toward human and social relations tend to be more conservative. By way of hypothetical comparison it may be said that in other cultures the criteria of accomplishment are more stable. Religious salvation and political resentment provide greater consolation for the poor and the failures. The material culture tends to be hemmed in by tradition. The criteria of achievement have a more stable subjective basis in the sense of craftsmanship, esthetic and intellectual subtlety, and the fulfillment of social and religious routines.

d. There are certain derivative elements of this general value orientation which call for comment. First, intense individualistic competitiveness, in which the primary aim is to get more of what other people want, produces diffuse hostile tension and general apprehension and anxiety, which pervades every aspect of the culture including the competing unit itself, the family. The fear of failure and the apprehension over the hostility which is involved in one's relations with other persons produce on the one hand an extraordinary need for affection and reassurance, and on the other, an extraordinary tendency to resort to physiological and spiritual narcosis. In other words, as a consequence of being impelled by cultural pressure toward relationships in which one is aggressively pitted against others, the resulting unease and apprehension is characteristically mitigated by demands for external response, attention, and warmth, or by resort to escapism. Thus an excessive concern with sexuality, an excessive resort to alcohol, and, what is a uniquely American form of narcosis of the soul—the widespread addiction to highly stimulating mass entertainment, the radio, movies, comics, and the like—provide culturally legitimate modes of discharging hostility and allaying anxiety.

Thus, by way of summary, the value orientation of the American tends to be atomistic rather than corporate, worldly rather than unworldly, highly mobile rather than traditional, compulsive rather than relaxed, and externally directed rather than autonomous. Needless to say, these are presented as hypothetical tendencies, which are supported only by an inadequate and quite heterogeneous body of evidence.

2. Value Expectations

The American is an optimist as to ends and an improviser as to means. The riches of his heritage and the mobility of his social order have produced a generally euphoric tendency, that is, the expectation that one can by effort and good will achieve or approximate one's goals. This overt optimism is so compulsive an element in the American culture that factors which threaten it, such as failure, old age, and death, are pressed from the focus of attention and handled in perfunctory ways. This belief that "things can be done" is coupled with a faith in common sense and "know-how" with regard to means. The American has a double approach to complex reasoning and theory. He has great respect for systematic thinking and planning in relation to technological and organizational problems. But even this type of intellectualism is brought down to earth by referring to it as "know-how." Know-how implies both the possession of formal technical knowledge and the capacity to improvise and overcome obstacles on the basis of a "feel" for the problem or the situation. In complicated questions of social and public policy there is a genuine distrust of complex and subtle reasoning and a preference for an earthy "common sense." Thus, in these important areas his compulsive optimism, his anti-intellectualism, and his simple rationalism leave the American vulnerable to deflation and pessimism when his expectations are thwarted and when threats and dangers are not effectively warded off by improvisations. This vulnerability is, to be sure, balanced by a certain flexibility and experimentalism, a willingness to try new approaches. If Americans typically avoid the rigidity of dogma in dealing with new problems, they also typically fail to reap the advantages of thoughtful policy-planning. What is involved here is not so much a net loss, but rather the failure to realize the net gain that would result from a greater intellectual discipline.

3. Attitudes toward Authority and Morality

The American tends to "cut authority down to his own size." He has a respect for achievement and a toleration of order-enforcing agencies, but a distrust of arbitrary or traditional authority. This attitude toward authority also carries over into the field of tradition and custom. Certainly the urban American, and many of the rural ones as well, are not seriously limited by traditional methods of doing things. They are iconoclasts with respect to earlier aspects of culture, and conformists in relation to the most recent value changes. They reject what was done in the past, and they conform to the new things that are being done *now*. But again this iconoclasm is especially noticeable in the sphere of material culture. A greater conservatism obtains in relation to social and political matters. This social and political conservatism is not unique to Americans. What seems to be unique is this combination of mobility of material values and fundamentalism with regard to social and political values.

Similar trends are observable in American attitudes toward moral norms.

The norms of Christianity still constitute an important theme in contemporary American culture. Since these moral standards are in obvious and continual rivalry with the competitive ethic, Americans tend to suffer from ambivalence and conflicts in determining what is "proper." Under normal circumstances this conflict does not appear to have a seriously laming effect. It tends to be disposed of by adding a moral coloration to actions which are really motivated by expediency, and an expediential coloration to actions which are motivated by moral and humanitarian values. These tendencies are related to a rather widespread naive belief in the compatibility of morality and expediency. While this ambivalence is a factor which generally affects American behavior, there is also a characteristic pendulum movement between the two ethics. Thus, if generous actions, motivated by moral and humanitarian considerations, are accepted without gratitude, are misinterpreted, or are unrequited, a "cynical" rejection of humanitarianism may follow, resulting from the humiliation at having been "played for a sucker." To yield to humanitarian impulses in the "market place" or to moderate one's own demands in the light of "Christian" considerations, to give without the expectation of receiving, to suffer injury without retaliation—these are impulses which have a partial validity; but it is dangerous to give way to them since they dull the edge of competitiveness, confuse and retard the forward course of action.

9. GROUP DETERMINANTS OF VOTING BEHAVIOR

by Bernard R. Berelson, Paul F. Lazarsfeld, and William N. McPhee *

The relation of group memberships and identifications to political choice is central to the problem of consensus and cleavage in a political democracy. If the "community interest" were in actuality the basis for political decision in our society, that would not necessarily mean that all men would have to agree: some could be right and others wrong, or some logical and others illogical, or some perceptive and others unperceptive. However, in that case, we could assume that political differences would distribute themselves at random throughout the society, that is, that they would not be correlated with basic social groupings. But they are.

In contemporary America, political events and social differentiation have combined to produce three major types of political cleavage: (1) occupa-

* Bernard R. Berelson, professor of library science and of social sciences at the University of Chicago, author of *The Library's Public* and *Content Analysis,* coauthor of *What Reading Does to People, The People's Choice,* and *Voting,* and coeditor of *Reader in Communication and Public Opinion.* Paul F. Lazarsfeld, professor of sociology and director of the Bureau of Applied Social Research at Columbia University, author and coauthor of numerous books, including *Radio and the Printed Page, Radio Listening in America, Continuities in Social Research, The People's Choice, Voting,* and *Personal Influence.* The selection is reprinted from pp. 54-75, 88-101, and 114-115 of *Voting: A Study of Opinion Formation in a Presidential Campaign* by Bernard R. Berelson, Paul F. Lazarsfeld, and William N. McPhee, by permission of The University of Chicago Press, Chicago. Copyright 1954 by The University of Chicago. All charts and tables and several footnotes are omitted from this selection by permission.

tional, income, and status cleavages; (2) religious, racial, and ethnic cleavages; and (3) regional and urban-rural cleavages.[1] For the large majority of the population political experience is organized around major social identifications, associations, and memberships. One's own private political convictions are not so private or so much one's own as they may seem—or as one might wish them to be. In political affairs of the mid-twentieth century the kinds of social experience most persistently underlying political choices are those centering on class, ethnic, and ecological differences. Such social bases of political traditions are the subject matter of the present chapter.

SOCIOECONOMIC STATUS

In our discussion of social differentiation in politics, the place to start is the "obvious" place: the effect of differing socioeconomic status upon political attitudes. If there is one social characteristic that is generally admitted to affect opinion on public affairs, at least since 1932, this is it. Although voting along socioeconomic lines is generally recognized as characteristic of this country since the depression of the 1930's, it is much older than that— as old, in fact, as the Republic itself.

Class Affiliation

Socioeconomic status—as measured here by an index composed of the breadwinner's occupation, education, and interviewer's rating—is directly related to the final vote decision. The higher the socioeconomic status (SES), the more Republican the vote; put crudely, richer people vote Republican more than poorer people.

Class Identification

Nor is this relationship by any means limited to the so-called objective measures of socioeconomic status. It also appears when socioeconomic status is measured in terms of the respondent's own class identification—his own feeling as to the class in which he belongs. With socioeconomic status controlled, class identification exerts an independent influence upon the vote, especially on the lower socioeconomic status level.

"Class-consciousness"

Since the norms of the general community are more favorable to middle-class and business groups, it is more likely that they will achieve political solidarity than the working class, especially in this small-town environment. Particularly in towns like Elmira, the development of a "class conscious" vote is inhibited by the status of the dominant community ideology centered in the middle class and its rural forebears. As a result the workers show less political solidarity and more political ambivalence. In 1948 Elmira the business, professional, and white-collar groups supported the

---

[1] By virtue of the design of this *community* study, this factor of place of residence was not included. However, occasional comparisons with other regions or the country as a whole are made, and the influence of the Republican predominance in Elmira is evident at many points.

Republicans fully 75 per cent; the workers split their vote almost fifty-fifty. There is a more cohesive business vote than labor vote. Were this not the case generally, the closeness of the Republican-Democratic vote in this country would not exist because of the strong numerical majority held by wage workers over salaried employees and independent entrepreneurs and professionals. The working class splits its vote more than does the business class.[2]

This fact can be explained in at least two ways. On the one hand, the workers could have a class-conscious ideology but be split on which party expresses it better. On the other hand, the workers could be themselves split on the matter of ideology itself, especially in a middle-class community like Elmira. The latter seems to be the case. There is little class-consciousness among workers in Elmira and hence no great tendency toward uniform political action.

Now this matter of ideology is not easy to gauge in a few survey questions. What would class-consciousness mean in a town like Elmira? Presumably it would be manifested by such elements as these: response to verbal symbols like "big business" (negative) and "labor" (positive); a conviction that existing institutions are managed in disregard of the workers' rights and interests; a feeling of solidarity with other workers that would express itself in a desire to associate with them in leisure-time and other private activities; and, finally, the desire for a political movement specifically dedicated to the interest of the working class. Accordingly a number of questions were devised to see whether workers consider themselves a special group in the population by such criteria. At least by this test there is little class-consciousness in Elmira. While there are some differences between the workers and other occupations on these items, they are slight (except in the case of attitudes toward labor unions). Workers do not particularly distrust social institutions, or feel unduly handicapped by their social position, or show interest in their own rather than other groups, or have deviant ambitions for their children, or advocate a political party for labor. At bottom, the working class is loyal to the dominant middle-class ideology symbolized by the "American way of life."

Yet the political history of the last twenty years in this country reveals a number of actual and potential clashes between economic interests of the different classes. What this seems to mean in Elmira is that the workers are in an ambivalent position in which their political values are derived from the dominant culture at the same time that their interest in social prestige and economic security is to some extent blocked by the interests of the dominant groups. American cultural values and actual life-experience are mutually reinforcing for upper and middle classes in the society, and

[2] An important circumstance making for greater political harmony within the business group is simply their greater rate of political activity within the community. They belong to more organizations than the labor group, they talk politics more, and they are looked to more for political advice. They not only reassure themselves through such activities; they also set a political "tone" for the entire community. And they were in positions to do so: about 80 per cent of the occupational elite of the community were Republicans and about 75 per cent of the officers of clubs and organizations.

accordingly they exhibit a high degree of political consensus. But cultural values and life-experience are often in contradiction for the workers, and accordingly they are more ambivalent and, as we shall see, more unstable in their political support. It takes a depression or a heated political campaign directly aimed at economic interest to bring out their "class vote" sharply against the norms of the "larger community."

Political Generations

The relationship between socioeconomic status (SES) and vote is partly a function of the political conditions under which each generation comes of age. The younger generation raised in the New Deal era showed a high tendency to vote along the socioeconomic class lines associated with the Roosevelt elections. Their elders, introduced to politics in the Republican 1920's, are not so far apart on class lines. Acceptance of the political norms current at the time of political initiation does not stop there; it tends to perpetuate itself through succeeding elections. Recognizing that young voters of the 1930's and later were more Democratic than their elders, many observers concluded that young "liberals" would grow up into old "conservatives." But a whole "political generation" may have been developing for whom the socioeconomic problems of their youth served as bases for permanent political norms—a semipermanent generation that would later bulge the ranks of the Democrats in certain age groups much as the crop of postwar babies is bulging different grades in school as they grow up. Presumably an age generation can be transformed by political events and social conditions into a political generation based on class considerations— a generation that retains its allegiances and norms while succeeding generations are moving in another direction. In addition, in a community like Elmira there is no difference by age at the higher socioeconomic status levels, but at the middle and lower levels there is a tendency for people to become more Republican as they grow older—as the political climate of the community "rubs off" on them.

MINORITY RELIGIOUS AND ETHNIC STATUS

Now let us turn to another basic differentiation within the electorate. The United States has been characterized by many political observers as a nation composed of blocs of minority voters. While the history of American politics attests to the general ineffectiveness of minority political parties, it also demonstrates the importance of the minority social vote— an electorate composed of so-called "hyphenated Americans." Racial, religious, and ethnic groups have demonstrated a unity in their voting allegiance that has led some observers to assign them a place of increasing importance in determining the outcome of elections. For example, Samuel Lubell, in *The Future of American Politics*, concludes that "for the immediate future the prospects point to an intensification of "League of Nations' politics. . . . Virtually none of the underdog groups has obtained the full recognition of its numbers" (p. 79). Politicians have always been concerned with organizing the "Negro vote" or the "Jewish vote" or the "Italian vote." Such minority voters are quite numerous, especially in crucial metropolitan areas; they offer a common characteristic to which the politician can appeal; and they possess the internal cohesion, and often organization, essential for delivering a solid bloc vote.

A basic difference in political support within the electorate exists between the white native-born Protestant voters, representing the "majority" group in American society, on the one hand, and a number of racial, ethnic, and religious minority groups, on the other.

Now it is generally recognized that such minority groups are tied to the Democratic machine in the big cities, where they constitute a large segment of the party's support. But Elmira is a small upstate town with little machine politics and not a great deal of organized minority activity. Even in this small, quiet community there is a sharp differential in vote between minority ethnic groups and "pure Americans." Even here the election can be clearly seen as a contest between the minority groups and the dominant majority—the former supporting the Democrats and the latter the Republicans. Let us analyze first the Catholic group and then review the situation for the other minority groups.

The Catholic Vote

The relation between votes and socioeconomic status is, after all, "reasonable" in view of the acknowledged relationship between politics and economic problems. In aiding or retarding unionism, in levying taxes upon incomes and profits, in distributing public aid, in financing social security—in these and countless other ways the government participates in what is called "class legislation." No wonder, then, that different classes vote differently.

But what of Catholicism? At first glance it seems to have no direct connection with American politics in 1948. The political issues indirectly involving Catholics were such matters as United States relations with Spain, the Vatican envoy, and the treatment of parochial schools under proposed federal aid to education. These were not salient in the 1948 campaign. Yet Catholics in the Republican community of Elmira voted Republican less than half as much as the Protestants.

To some extent, of course, this tendency reflects a historical identification. The Democratic party in New York State has been traditionally associated with the Catholics (Tammany Hall, Al Smith, Jim Farley, Ed Flynn, et al.), and national party leaders have been Catholics, particularly the chairmen of the Democratic National Committee over the last twenty-five years. In addition, there is a long-term connection between the party and the church stemming from the great immigration waves of the nineteenth century. But such considerations do not account for contemporary Catholic allegiance to the Democrats.

Independent of Other Factors

Now, in the first place, the Catholic vote is not simply a spurious reflection of other demographic factors. For example, Catholics are on a lower (average) income level than Protestants, and this condition is sometimes thought to be responsible for the apparent correlation between religion and political attitudes. However, the correlation in Elmira is genuine. No matter what demographic variable is controlled, the relationship between Catholic affiliation and party preference significantly remains. Not only that, but the religious affiliation (and the ethnic differences it represents) appears to be a stronger influence upon vote than any other single factor. For example, on each socioeconomic status level about half as many Catholics vote Republican as Protestants. Catholics of high status vote more Democratic than do Protestants of low status; thus Catholic affiliation is stronger than socioeconomic status in determining vote. In Elmira the Catholics have almost achieved the socioeconomic position of the Protestants, but this has not basically deflected their vote from the Democratic candidate.

Here, then, we find a condition not anticipated nor endorsed by classical political theorists: a nonpolitical, associative factor with strong influence upon the electoral decision. Regardless of other demographic characteristics —and despite democratic claims, protestations, or theories to the contrary— there is a strong "religious vote" in this country.

Independent of Attitudes

And, still more, ideological or attitudinal position on the issues is no more powerful an influence than religion. An index of "liberalism," based on socioeconomic issues of the time, illustrates the matter. Conservative Catholics—that is, those who agree in substance with the Republican position on big business, unions, and price control—are no more Republican than liberal Protestants. At each step of this liberalism-conservatism score Catholics are much more Democratic than Protestants. In this respect vote is as much conditioned by who one is as by what one believes.

Catholics and "Catholics"

The importance of religious affiliation in affecting political decision can be tested still further. To this point we have dealt simply with the report that one "belongs" to a religion; but there is belonging and belonging. If religious affiliation is operative, it should be even stronger among the more deeply religious or among those more intimately connected with the church. And that is so. The longer Catholics have lived in Elmira (i.e., the longer they have been associated with their co-religionists in this institution), the more Democratic do they vote. Similarly, the longer Protestants have lived in Elmira, the more Republican they become, probably in response to the predominantly Republican climate of opinion in the town. But Catholics become more Democratic despite the prevailing opinion climate, illustrating to some extent their group isolation, at least as far as politics is concerned. And the more intimately Catholic they feel, as indicated by their assertion that their religious group is among their "most important" identifications, the more Democratic they vote. (The fact that this is not so for the Protestants suggests the lack of a particular religious orientation to their vote.)

Thus, the more intensely religious status is felt or the more pervasive its influence, the more powerful its effect upon vote. (This effect, incidentally, derives from in-group association and mutual reinforcement—in ways we shall analyze later—rather than from direct suggestion or pressure. Close observation of political activity among formal Catholic organizations, including the local church, failed to reveal any attempt to "deliver" the Catholic vote. The result derived from informal social relations, not formal institutional pressure.)

Religion and Political Involvement

Actually the effect of religious affiliation depends also upon the voter's involvement in politics. The more deeply Catholics are involved, the less effect religion as such has upon their vote. It was the politically *uninterested* Catholics who followed religious affiliation most frequently in determining their vote. The more involved Catholics had certain political considerations on which to base their decision as to how to vote; the less involved simply followed the lead of the religious group.

Long-term Age Trend

With all this, 1948 marked a weakening of the Catholic vote in Elmira. In 1940 and again in 1944 about 85 per cent of Elmira Catholics claimed to have voted Democratic, and in 1948 this proportion had fallen to about 65 per cent. The likelihood of a trend away from the Democratic party on the part of Catholics is further suggested by the vote of different age groups. Political observers generally seem to believe that younger people— out of greater "liberalism"—have been more Democratic in recent years. But this is a complicated matter. The younger Protestants do vote more Democratic, but the younger Catholics vote more Republican. Thus the younger generation of Catholics voted less by religion than their elders, and in time this may diminish the difference between the two religious groups. The largest difference between Protestants and Catholics exists among the older people (70 percentage points); among the middle-aged this difference has fallen to about 40 percentage points and among the younger people to less than 30. The succession of generations seems to be softening the religious difference.

To recapitulate, here is a social characteristic that is not directly involved in political issues but nevertheless makes a big difference in vote. Catholics vote differently from Protestants, and this difference is not simply a function of differing demographic or ideological positions. Regardless of socioeconomic status level or age or even political attitude, Catholics vote more Democratic than do Protestants. And the more closely they are bound to their religion, the more Democratic they are.

Other Minorities

What about the other minority groups in Elmira? In most respects the story is the same. As we have noted, Italians, Negroes, and Jews voted heavily Democratic in Elmira in 1948—82 per cent of the Italian-Americans, 81 per cent of the Negroes, and 67 of the Jews. And, as in the case of the Catholics, the vote for Truman is not particularly affected by differences in socioeconomic status. Even among the highest-income Jewish voters the ratio of Truman to Dewey voters is about three to one. There is little variance by socioeconomic status level within the Negro group, and on each socioeconomic status level the Italians are more Democratic than the non-ethnic native-born.

Contrary to the tendency among Catholics, however, the younger Negroes and Jews supported the Democrats even more strongly than their elders. Thus the educated youth may serve as the standardbearers of these more newly active minorities, just as youth led the disintegration of older cleavages between Catholics and Protestants. In any case, the younger generation in these minority groups is more Democratic than the younger generation of Catholics.

But in the case of psychological identification and social interaction with the group, these minorities are the same as the Catholics—the more closely the members identified with their minority group, the stronger their Democratic vote. Regardless of the particular measure, those minority members who feel close to their own group (or who feel hostile to the out-group) are more likely to express the group's political preference (i.e., vote Democratic) than their fellows.

Minority voting patterns are closely linked to the social and psychological forces that determine intergroup relations in the United States today. In the political arena, as in other spheres of community life, the intergroup tension present in most American communities results in a difference of opinion between the members of minority and "majority" groups. This division of political support is expected behavior on the part of both groups. During an election campaign it becomes an overtly expressed and openly recognized political alignment, reinforced by the stereotyped expectations of both sides. Different voting patterns become one of the prevailing practices of the community—"the way we do things around here."

THE SOCIAL TRANSMISSION OF POLITICAL CHOICES

In Elmira, then, it is the socioeconomic classes, on the one hand, and the religious and ethnic groups, on the other, that serve as the social carriers of political traditions. In the country at large, to these two kinds of differentiation in the population is added the ecological division of region or size of community (e.g., the metropolitan area as against the small town). In contrast, there are only minor differences in voting between men and women or between young and old or, indeed, on any other characteristic.

Why do certain characteristics make a difference and not others? Why is there not a distinctive women's vote or a sharp cleavage along age lines or, for that matter, a more or less random dispersal of the votes of individuals? In part this is a matter of timing, that is, of the historical period in which our study happens to be made. But, if a number of such studies had been made over the entire span of the two-party system, it is likely that most of them would have found similar differences in voting by class, ethnic, and ecological blocs of the American population. Why are such bases of political cleavage so persistent?

Explanations of a political character are prominent; for example, the explanation that such people have group interests in common and represent convenient blocs for political appeal and mobilization. Thus, in simplified terms, Jews vote Democratic "because" of Roosevelt's interventionist stand against Hitler; Negroes, "because" of the relief and welfare program of the New Deal; and both "because" of civil rights legislation. Less understood, however, are the social conditions that contribute to the success of such political mobilization—and, more importantly, to its persistence. Voting blocs are often perpetuated so long after group needs and political alternatives have changed that it is unrealistic to speak of active, contemporary "interests" being involved in more than a few of the voting differences between groups that exist in the country at a given time. Why do the others persist with such force?

There appear to be three ways in which social relations contribute to the maintenance of political differences.

First, there is the necessary condition of an economic division of labor or a physical separation or a social differentiation in the population such that people of unlike characteristics are affected in different ways by a single political policy. In other words, it is necessary to have a social basis for a political interest. It would be difficult in contemporary America, for example, to maintain strong voting differences by sex, because there are few policy issues persisting over a period of time that affect men and women differently. *Differentiation* is a condition for disagreement.

Second, a necessary condition for the persistence of political differences is their *transmission* to succeeding generations. Parents and children sharing the same characteristics provide a condition of continuity in which political choices can be taught, however subtly and unconsciously, by the one to the other. Some such transmission is necessary so that voting traditions do not die out. This presumably is a reason why youth movements in politics are often less stable or persistent than other bases of voting traditions that can more easily be transmitted from generation to generation. Similarly, a political movement based on the special interests of old age (e.g., pensions) has difficulty in maintaining itself because of the necessary absence of a generational tie. *Transmission* is a condition for persistence.

Finally, given the origin of a voting difference in one generation and the transmittibility of it to the next, another condition is necessary for it to survive in the succeeding generation. Members of the social groups involved must be substantially more in contact with one another, socially and physically, than they are with opposing groups. Political traditions are maintained through marriage and through living and working with socially alike, and hence politically like-minded, people. *Contact* is a condition for consensus.

In sum, the conditions underlying persistent voting cleavages seem to be (1) initial social differentiation such that the consequences of political policy are materially or symbolically different for different groups; (2) conditions of transmittibility from generation to generation; and (3) conditions of physical and social proximity providing for continued in-group contact in succeeding generations. In contemporary America these conditions are best met in *class*, in *ethnic*, and in *ecological* divisions of the population. They continue to provide, then, the most durable social bases for political cleavage.

*   *   *

The social differences politically relevant in Elmira have been described. Now we inquire more closely into the ways they are transmitted and maintained through small groups—the political role of family, friends, and co-workers. We have dealt, so to speak, with the social *what;* now we deal with the *how* and *why.*

THE FAMILY AND VOTE

How does a vote start with each new generation of citizens? Where should we look for the roots of political belief?

The "Hereditary Vote"

We should look first where we find the roots of personality, of religious and ethical values, of general cultural tastes—within the parental family. The family's influence upon vote begins long before the individual reaches voting age. A "hereditary vote"—the influence of the political tradition of one generation upon the political conviction of the next—is suggested by the association between the respondents and their fathers. The association is particularly strong among the younger voters—four out of five with Republican fathers voted Republican in 1948, and two out of three with Democratic fathers voted Democratic even in this Republican town. In other words, about 75 per cent of the first voters in the community sided with their fathers in their political choice.[3] And a high proportion of the total group, regardless of age, continue the political partisanship of their fathers in later life. The parental family, and the constellation of social and psychological forces expressed through and around it, initiates a political disposition that with proper reinforcement carries through life.

This "inheritance" of political position is naturally maintained by the several characteristics held in common by family members; that is, it operates within the broad factors of socioeconomic status and religion that distinguish both parents and children. Where these associations or loyalties are in conflict, the father's traditional vote is modified, though a noticeable influence still persists. Where father's vote and social position are reinforcing, the children's vote is quite predictable.

The modification of parental loyalty by the child's social status is revealed in intergenerational mobility. The children who have "moved up" in the world are more likely to vote Republican than those who have remained roughly in their father's social strata. The comparative social status of the son or daughter is a qualifying factor to the father's political tradition.

[3] Some of the correlation, of course, must be a projection of present convictions into the memory of the father's past vote, but this ambiguity in recollection should be at a minimum among the youngest voters, most of whom are still living with or near their parents. Among them the correlation of own and father's vote is the highest of all.

Conversely, most of the deviants in class voting can be explained in terms of father's traditional vote. About two-thirds of upper socioeconomic-status Democrats and lower socioeconomic-status Republicans were voting in line with their fathers.

Bases of Generational Stability

How does this political continuity between parent and child come about? Two conditions stand out: the first is a quality of the young voters; the second, a quality of the families in which they are brought up.

Contributing to the young voter's conformity with the parental tradition is his lack of involvement in politics. There is a belief in this country that youth is politically radical; closer to the truth is the proposition that young people do not care much about politics. True, there are some indications that the young people carry the seeds of political deviation from traditional voting patterns; that is, they are more idealistic, more independent (or at least inconsistent), in their opinions. But in the end they do not carry through: they do not pay much attention to political materials, they tend not to vote, they are less likely to care if the opposition wins, and—this is the payoff—they fail to carry through deviant voting intentions. Thus the age group most expected to "revolt" from tradition is least likely to go through with it in practice. And, because of that, here is an important link in the transmission of part of the political heritage, from generation to generation—and an element of stability in the political system.

The second condition contributing to generational stability is this: about 90 per cent of those adult family members living together in the same house who had made up their minds agreed on their voting intentions in late October; all relationships within the immediate family had about the same level of agreement. Here is primary group solidarity of a high order. In the end many American families vote *as a unit*, making joint decisions in voting as in spending parts of the common family income. Indeed, it would not be inappropriate to consider the family as the primary unit of voting analysis, just as for some problems in economics the household or the spending unit is taken as the basis of study. There would be advantages to understanding voting decisions in this way—as the joint pooling of experience, information, and partisanship by several members of the primary and extended family into the crystallization or change of family voting traditions.

The young voter is brought up, then, in a one-sided political atmosphere. In addition, such homogeneity extends beyond the family to the whole circle of people with whom the youth associates as he comes to political age —his family's friends as well as his own. For example, because of social similarities, the youth is likely to marry within his political tradition. To the extent that parents bring up their children in a "one-party" climate of opinion like that provided by the primary-group homogeneity of middle-aged Elmirans, that environment provides strong pressures toward the perpetuation of political uniformities from one generation to the next. Just as young people learn from their elders, say, the religion and the table manners appropriate to their situation, so do they learn the appropriate political beliefs. His environment does not provide the young adult with clear political alternatives on a more or less random basis but rather a "natural selection" of the "correct way of life" as applied to politics. As he comes to voting age, the young voter's political consciousness is no *tabula rasa* on which various interests can contend; it is preshaped in particular political directions, as it is in other ways. And this process of socializing the ongoing generation in political matters, informal and nonpurposive as it is, provides an element of generational stability in the American political system.

PERSONAL ASSOCIATIONS AND VOTE

In addition to his family, the voter lives his day-to-day life largely in the company of his friends and his co-workers. This study collected information on the political preferences of three of the respondent's closest friends and three of his closest co-workers. With the family, they make up the primary social groups whose members mold each other's political opinions as well as other behavior.

In passing, we might remark that this view of friends and co-workers as "groups" within which the voter is a "member" is the customary but not entirely appropriate image. Actually, friends and co-workers serve less as closed cliques than as *contact points* through whom the individual is connected to whole networks of social relations that affect political behavior. The networks are organized in major socioeconomic and ethnic blocs, and at their center are the main institutions of the community and its ultimate leadership. Thus, one's personal associations are not distinct entities from class and ethnic strata but rather connect the individual to others in such strata. Data on the voter's friends and co-workers reveal how he is "hooked into" the larger community and hence partly indicate which social interests are more likely to influence him in his political choices.

Political Character of the Personal Environment

By and large, the voter is tied into a network of personal associations that is both homogeneous and congenial. Republican voters are more likely to have Republican friends and co-workers, and Democratic voters are more likely to have Democratic. The homogeneity is slightly greater for friends, since the voters can choose them more freely than co-workers, but for both groups the agreement within small clusters of personal associates is high—and higher for Republicans in this particular community. Only about one in five Republicans has a Democrat among his immediate associates, and about two in five Democrats have a Republican. For the community as a whole the proportion with associates from the *other* party is about 25 per cent. In a democracy the individual is expected to have available to him, not only in formal channels of communication but in informal channels of personal contact, a rich variety of experience, a diversity of information, a competition of ideas, and a maximum number of choices. Yet for this the individual is partly dependent on the accumulated information, aggregate experience, and collective judgment of his friends and co-workers (and that larger community to which he is connected through them). Most voters, and especially those of the majority party, carry on these personal associations in what approaches a political monopoly.[4]

Moreover, the political complexion of one's friends is related to one's own social position. Those predisposed toward a Democratic vote (e.g., working-class people and Catholics) are more likely to have Democratic friends; and conversely for those predisposed Republican. Here, again, the general complexion of the Republican community is apparent, but the differential between groups is too. Friends transmit the predispositional tendencies of class and religion; in a sense, such predispositions *are* mainly the accumulated influence of like-positioned and hence like-minded associates on each other.

The political homogeneity of personal associations increases as the voter grows older and settles more and more into his life-pattern. Only half of the young *first* voters are in agreement with all three of their close friends, and almost 30 per cent disagree with two or all three of them. The young people just coming to voting age are establishing new families and finding their way into new jobs, new neighborhoods, and new associations that provide opportunities for political inconsistencies and conflicts. Their elders— and this means those from age thirty-five on—come to fall into agreeable associations through the very process of living in jobs, communities, organizations. Thus political homogeneity of the primary environment, high to start with, becomes even higher with the passage of time.

Friends, Co-workers, and Voting

The data can be rearranged to show the harmony between one's own vote and the vote of his associates in a different sense—the respondent's vote as a *consequence* of the preferences of his associates. Again eliminating the "Don't know's" and the unknowns, we find an agreement in over 85 per cent of the extreme cases;* and, when the political complexion of friends and co-workers is divided, the distribution of the respondents' votes reflects the nature of the division.

More than that, friends and co-workers also affect the strength of conviction with which the vote preference is held. It is voters with homogeneous and agreeable associates who believe strongly in the rightness of their candidate and party. Those with friends in both camps are less sure of their vote. Thus, the political conviction of the individual is closely bound to the

[4] The effect of the politics of one's friends is also clear between elections. Those 1944 Republicans with a majority of Republican friends stayed Republican (98 per cent); those 1944 Democrats with a majority of Democratic friends stayed Democratic, even in Elmira (91 per cent). But those in conflict between their earlier allegiance and their current friendships divided, in effect, with the community (i.e., 63 per cent Republican). A campaign catches some individuals in a personal environment contradictory to their own voting tradition and produces a kind of political exchange of social captives.

* *Editors' Note:* By "extreme cases" is meant those in which all three of the respondent's closest friends identify with the same political party or in which all three of his closest co-workers have the same partisan preference.

political character of his personal relations—or at least his perception of their political complexion. A sense of security about one's judgment seems to be a function of the congeniality of the personal environment; here, as elsewhere in the realm of political attitudes and behavior, the private political conscience of the citizen rests upon a near-by group norm represented by the people around him. Without their full support it is not easy to hold strong political attitudes, and relatively few people do.

Friends, the Community, and Breakage in the Vote

Finally, what of the inevitable discords between the small cluster of personal associates with whom the individual voter lives and the larger community in which he lives? It is customary to say that what matters for the voter is the social environment *close* to him; and so it does. When the primary group of friends or co-workers is united in political opinion, then the respondent's vote is firm. When Democratic primary groups are "solid," the party vote is not significantly lower than for "solid" Republican groups (i.e., each side loses only about 12 or 15 per cent in deviations). The strong community majority for the Republicans has little effect because it has little access to persons within homogeneous Democratic groups.

But when the primary environment is internally *divided* the effect of the distant community can be seen. Then the Republicans get a higher proportion of the vote. If friends and co-workers are divided two-to-one Republican, the vote goes about three-fourths Republican; but, if they are two-to-one Democratic, the vote goes only about half Democratic. It is as though the average vote in *mixed* primary groups was moved some distance to the Republican side. The impact of the larger community is thus most evident among voters with discordant or disagreeing primary groups. When the voter's close associates do not provide him with a single, clear political direction—when instead they offer an alternative—then wider associations in the surrounding community reinforce one position over the other.

The same effect can be seen within each socioeconomic status and religious category. With supporting friends entirely of the "right" party (the traditional party of the stratum), each of the subgroups is 90 per cent "solid" in vote. But, in almost every intermediate case, the Republican-disposed category with a mixed group of friends retains a stronger vote for its party than its Democratic counterpart. Protestants with one Democratic friend (of three) "lose" only 15 per cent of their vote to the Democrats, but Catholics with one Republican friend "lose" 36 per cent of theirs.

In general, then, the Republicans get more than their random share of the adjustment to a conflicting environment, because of the pervasive Republican atmosphere of Elmira that thus tends to perpetuate itself. The surrounding majority gets the benefit of the operation of cross-pressures. One might call this the "breakage" effect, borrowing a term from horse-racing circles. In the parimutuel system people bet against and influence one another. But, when the result is settled in round sums, the odd pennies left over—the breakage—go to the track or to the state in the background. In our case the breakage in small-group adjustment goes to the Republican community. At any one moment the breakage may be trivial, as it is at the crack; but over a period of time it is considerable. For example, the heavier Republican vote of older people in Elmira may be the result of just such attrition from the give-and-take of primary groups. With advancing age, a steady toll is taken of former Democrats in the Republican community....

THE SOCIAL GROUP AND THE POLITICAL SYSTEM

Underlying the influence of the social group is the ambiguity of political stimuli. The individualistic tradition of thinking about politics, as typically expressed in democratic theory, implies that it is possible and reasonably convenient for the voter to see clear-cut alternatives: to judge the differences between candidates, weigh the relevance of the issues to his own needs, and then rightly or wrongly "decide" what to do. The scheme implied in this tradition of thinking about politics requires a reasonably clear political choice that can be responded to directly by the individual, but this is not always, or even usually, the case.

Suppose we think of two polar types of modern elections. An unusual type of election (e.g., 1936) presents a clear-cut and easily understood program that had major consequences for a large number of voters, that was highlighted by dramatic events, and that was symbolized by a magnetic candidate. At the opposite pole there is an election period (e.g., 1948) in which voters can find no clear programs, no simple picture of what is at stake, no visible consequences win or lose for the average citizen, no appealing and dramatic candidates—in short, a thoroughly ordinary period against the backdrop of reasonably stable times during which the citizen would prefer to be left undisturbed in the normal pursuit of job and family activities.

In situations of high ambiguity, according to the evidence of psychological experiments, two kinds of behavior occur that we have encountered in this political analysis. First, with no clear directives from stimuli outside themselves, people are likely to fall back on directive forces within themselves. This means that voters are likely to fall back on early allegiances, experiences, values, and norms—for example, those associated with being raised as a member of the working class or a minority group. Second, voters are likely to be especially vulnerable to less relevant influences than direct political stimuli. If voters cannot test the appropriateness of their decisions by reference to political consequences, then they are especially likely to be influenced by other, nonpolitical facts—for example, what trusted people around them are doing. As a result, old interests and traditions of class and minority blocs are brought to bear upon the determination of today's vote. In this process the principal agencies are not Machiavellian manipulators, as is commonly supposed when bloc votes are delivered at the polls, but the ordinary family, friends, co-workers, and fellow organization members with whom we are all surrounded. In short, the influences to which voters are most susceptible are opinions of trusted people expressed to one another.

10. PUBLIC OPINION AND SOCIAL CLASS

by Arthur Kornhauser [*]

In American society sharp differences of opinion on public questions are considered natural. But why should members of a common culture not see eye to eye on matters of public policy? Do social and political oppositions reflect divergent self-interest arising from economic relationships? Or are the differences traceable to variation in noneconomic goals associated with age, sex, education, race, religion, location and size of community, and family history? Or is it a matter of differences in exposure to the information and ideas on which the opinions are based? Or should major emphasis be placed on subtle subjective explanations associated with variables of individual personality? Or does a true understanding of public opinion determinants involve all these and additional factors interacting as parts of a continuous complex social process?

The most confident and vigorous answer to the problem over the past century has been that of the Marxists, in terms of economically determined class consciousness and class conflict. The momentous impact of Marxian views on the modern world, the heated controversy regarding the issue of class cleavages and class interests in American life, the conviction on the part of many scholarly social scientists that the class analysis of social behavior contains important elements of truth—all constitute ample reason for focusing attention on the problem of class position as a determinant of public opinion in our society.

Is class an important causal determinant or explanatory factor (along with other determinants, of course) of given opinions? Corresponding questions have to be asked regarding possible noneconomic determinants of opinion.

Since the inception of scientific research on public opinion, a large body of data has been amassed that demonstrates the linkage of opinions with personal and social facts about the people who hold the views. Prominent among these relationships is that between socioeconomic status and attitudes on a number of social and political issues. Before we embark on a critical analysis, it will be valuable to review a few examples of these research results and the conclusions drawn from them.

Examples of occupational and income class differences on single opinion questions are scattered through the reports of polls by Gallup, Roper, and other agencies. From recent *Public Opinion Quarterly* poll summaries one may take such comparisons as these:

> A Gallup question this spring asks whether the Taft-Hartley law is unfair and should be changed to give labor more strength. Among manual workers

[*] Professor of psychology at Wayne State University and consultant in industrial psychology. Author of *Detroit as the People See It*, coauthor of *Industrial Conflict* and *When Labor Votes*, and editor of *Problems of Power in American Democracy*. The selection is from Arthur Kornhauser, "Public Opinion and Social Class," *American Journal of Sociology*, vol. 55, issue no. 4, pp. 333-345, January, 1950. Reprinted by permission of the University of Chicago Press, Chicago.

49% agree while 34% disagree; business and professional people disagree 70% to 20%; white collar employees fall between. Thus the percentages agreeing run—business and professional 20%, white collar 32%, manual workers, 49%.[1]

A *Fortune* Survey question last winter inquired whether government regulation of business has gone too far, is in right amount, or "do you think we need even more?" In the business and professional sample, 51% think government regulation has gone too far, as against 32% of factory workers.[2]

A *Fortune* question asks whether the government should do more than it has done to improve the condition of poor people. By income classes, the persons saying government should do more are as follows: Prosperous 28%; Upper Middle 35%; Lower Middle 44%; Poor 57%.[3]

Substantially greater differences than these have been found in a number of studies specifically concerned with class relationships; for example, in the works of Cantril, Centers, Alfred Jones, Kornhauser, and others. A wealth of qualitative observations by Robert and Helen Lynd, W. Lloyd Warner and his associates, and in other community studies, offer similar findings.

There are also important studies of voting behavior in relation to the socioeconomic status and other characteristics of the voter. In recent decades, and especially in our northern cities, the election analyses reflect a pronounced association between class position and political alignment.

The opinion surveys and political and social studies as a whole indicate that class differences are greatest in regard to issues that obviously and directly affect the interests of people at upper, middle, and lower levels differently. Rather consistently the lower income groups are more in favor of government control of business and extending government welfare activities, sacrificing certain institutional property rights and unlimited opportunities for individual achievement in the interests of increasing security, overcoming the concentration of influence in the hands of the wealthy. There is also evidence that the poorer groups have more extreme nationalistic attitudes, greater religious traditionalism, and generally a more restricted outlook on the world, associated presumably with limited education.

It is tempting to catch up the main differences in a simple generalization that upper classes are more conservative, lower classes more radical; that the former rest content with things as they have been, while the have-nots desire reform. A number of studies explicitly marshal evidence to support this proposition. Dr. Centers, for example, employing a set of six questions on which he bases an index of radicalism-conservatism, discovers decided differences between the several social classes in percentages of radicals and conservatives. My own results in Chicago in 1937 pointed strongly in the same direction, but I emphasized the large amount of overlap between the classes and the variations depending on types of issues considered.

If one accepts a definition of radical and conservative opinion that is limited to question responses pertaining to distribution of income, regula-

[1] *Public Opinion Quarterly*, XIII (1949), 353.
[2] *Ibid.*, XII (1948–49), 759-60.
[3] *Ibid.*, p. 781.

tion of economic affairs in the interests of the common man, and similar economic-political reforms, there can be little doubt that pronounced differences are found in relation to socioeconomic status. Questions on other issues, however (religious doctrine, international questions, race relations, for example), fail to support the conception of a neat general pattern of radicalism-conservatism in which social classes manifest consistent contrasts. The differences, in general, are in directions to be expected if people's opinions coincide with their own self-interest as they perceive it and the means to advance it. Be it noted, however, that there are great numbers of exceptions—substantial minorities who do not go along with their fellows who are similarly situated. We are dealing with average tendencies, differences in distribution of opinion, and not with clear-cut cleavages between the classes.

Alongside the evidence on the relations of class to opinions stand even more extensive data describing opinion variations by other social and personality characteristics. The opinion research investigator almost automatically tabulates his response material by sex, age, and education of respondents; not infrequently also by size of community, section of the country, religion, race, national origins, and other factors. Depending principally on the issues under study, any or all of these variables may show substantial relationships to opinion. In respect to deep-lying questions of social, economic, and political change, the socioeconomic class differences are usually accompanied by—and entwined with—variations in these factors as well. Most of these personality characteristics are associated in some degree with class position and, to complicate the picture further, they likewise manifest intricate relationships among themselves.

In general, the noneconomic characteristics bear a less consistent and less marked correlation with the attitudes of the kind we are considering than do the income and occupational differences. Nevertheless, the relations are decidedly significant. They serve notice even on the superficial investigator—as well as on the naïve or overenthusiastic Marxist—that variations in public opinion cannot be ascribed to any single determinant. . . .

While economic position may thus prove more closely related to opinion than are the other objective characteristics, this finding is eclipsed in significance by the more important point that *many* factors are involved which *together* must be taken into account in understanding the uniformities and variations in public opinion. The figures bring us face to face with the intricate problem of multiple causation and the insistent question of the meaning of determinants of opinion. . . .

How does public opinion come to be what it is? It is assumed that our interest attaches to causal determinants; mere statistical correlations of the opinions under study, mere lists of concomitants, though sometimes labeled determinants, will not suffice. We seek dynamic delineations of the essential social-psychological processes by which public opinion takes its shape.

If one seriously sets out to discover causal determinants of public opinion, he is overwhelmed at once by the limitless possibilities. He cannot consider everything that has happened in the society and to the society that might make opinions different from what they otherwise would be. He is compelled to limit his undertaking in two basic respects, both of which are too often overlooked in the enthusiastic pursuit of results.

The first limitation is that the investigator must make explicit and specific what he is setting out to explain. To find determinants of public opinion in general is patently impossible. The scientific project is to account for certain differences in public opinion. Why are social-political views in one city or region different from those found elsewhere? Why are they different this year from last year or a generation ago and how are they changed by particular influences? At a given time and place, why do the opinions differ from one subdivision of the population to another? These three questions point to quite different research problems; each requires its own type of research attack. The last of the three is the only one of direct interest in the present discussion. In what degree do class position and related characteristics account for the distribution of opinion on public issues in our society?

This emphasis on explaining opinion differences in our society should not hide the complementary problem of understanding larger uniformities of opinion as well. We are simply by-passing these related questions of explaining how and why public opinion in American society differs from that in other nations or cultures and from various alternative possible states of opinion. Likewise, no attention is given here to explaining historical changes of opinion even in our own society. Determinants are necessarily related to a specified set of variations. Confusion is inevitable unless we keep clearly in mind the class of differences to be explained. Quite different studies and answers would be necessary to explain why corn crops are better in one region than another, why better in one year than another, and why better on Farm A than across the fence on Farm B. The comparison of Farm A with Farm B may lead to the conclusion that important determinants of crop size are the farmer's judgment, skill, and effort, the number of years the land has been worked, the amount of fertilizer used, etc. But the actual size of crops on both farms, compared, say, with other regions and years, may be due to the amount of rainfall, sunshine, soil type, and available seed corn. Differences between A and B may be insignificant in the larger frame of reference. Let us not be deceived by a parallel overemphasis on differences in opinion by class, age, religion, and the like; there are also highly important uniformities when compared with opinions in China or in medieval Europe.

The other basic limitation is the problem of knowing under what total set of conditions the causal relationships hold. How far can the determinants established on the basis of certain observations be expected to operate in like manner when somewhat different situations are involved? Is our knowledge of determinants of public opinion confined to particular situations as they have been, or can the conclusions be generalized and applied to future situations? Even when we confine ourselves to the American scene, serious difficulties cannot be escaped. We still have the question of how far the same relations obtain in different sections of the nation, among different population groups, and under different economic and political conditions occurring as a consequence of social-historical changes at home and over the world.

Determinants are such only within a specified system of variables. All sorts of factors outside that system must be assumed to remain uniform or to have no significant effects on the relationships studied. We safeguard ourselves with qualifying expressions such as "other things being equal," "under the same conditions," or "all else remaining constant." But it is transparently evident that we do not know whether the new situation is "essentially the same" or even what we mean by the phrase.

In a great deal of our research what is implied by determinants is a set of quantitative factors so interrelated in a closed system that each variable is predictable (within a specified margin of error) from the others. As applied to public opinion, this conception of determinants leads to a table of correlation coefficients or a set of regression equations and a readiness to stop there. In the closed system of these particular variables, taking all else as fixed, the opinions in question are "determined" with known degrees of probability by the set of correlated factors. But this tells nothing directly about causal relations, about the time sequences, and, above all, about the host of influential conditions outside the systems of measured variables. This last is a fatal weakness.

Consider a case in point. A number of studies show a correlation between socioeconomic level and nonvoting. People at low occupational levels including prominently unskilled and semiskilled industrial workers are found to lack political interest and to remain away from the polls in disproportionately large numbers. But in a subsequent election the labor-union leadership in certain industrial communities has become aroused over a Taft-Hartley law. Is working-class status now still a determinant of noninterest and nonvoting, or must we conclude that the determinant was such only under certain undefined conditions that previously existed? How valuable is a scientific generalization about political behavior that is true only until a new issue or new political incentives enter the picture?

In any such instance, knowledge can and should be extended by properly designed inquiry concerning surrounding variables believed to be relevant. Although the investigator can never include all possible conditioning variables, he can steadily increase the probability with which the determinants may be expected to operate by confirming that they do so operate in a wider and wider variety of contexts. At the same time it must be humbly acknowledged that we have no way to study the influence of new conjunctures of conditions until after they occur. Hence empirical demonstrations of causal factors are always subject to upset without notice when unforeseen changes intrude.

The key to salvation is less faith in data and correlations and greater devotion to underlying social and psychological theory. The difficulties grow out of the fact that determinants are determinative only as they function within concrete intricate social contexts. They are always parts of a whole and can be rewardingly investigated only when they are so conceived. The investigator can never lose sight of the larger social setting and the way in which public opinion emerges as a product of the sociopsychological interactions in society.

The opinions are formed in the interplay of complex personalities in the course of infinitely varied relations of each person to the groups, institutions, individuals, and conditions of life that surround him, interact with him, provide his gratifications, and impose upon him his deprivations. The opinions that comprise public opinion are formed as other components of personality are formed—as parts of the total social learning process. Studies of determinants accordingly need constantly to weave back and forth between empirical relationships of separate factors and systematic conceptual formulations of how these factors operate—what other conditions they depend on and what intervening variables mediate between the observed causes and observed effects.

Our original question—whether social class and personal characteristics are determinants of public opinion—must be construed to inquire not simply whether these factors are correlated with opinion differences but whether they fit into, and thus furnish support for, a coherent generalized account of the way public opinion comes to be what it is. Perhaps the "determinants" should better be called "indicators" of causal sequences. The sequences are arrived at by joining together many pieces of knowledge from all available sources to construct a social-psychological account of behavior, attitudes, and public opinion.

As a concrete example, consider again the simple relation of social-economic level to nonvoting and the precarious conclusion that low occupational status is a determinant of nonvoting behavior. Even a hurried consideration of why people vote or do not vote would lead one to interesting speculation regarding the different ways voting is perceived and evaluated and the dependence of these meanings on previous education and intellectual ability, on political influences in the respondents' circle, on views of their own roles, self-interest, and aspirations and the relation of these to the election, their beliefs about their own powers to change things, their appraisal of alternative means available to them for achieving their objectives, etc. The investigator would collect and analyze data bearing on these processes to the best of his ability. Further, however, in the inevitable absence of adequate information, he would so qualify his conclusions as to leave no doubt that these applied only to the time, place, and conditions studied and that such and such other conditions might well lead to drastic changes in the conclusions.

The empirical relationship discovered in the past would then serve merely as a point of departure in trying to gain true understanding of what would be likely to occur in the changed circumstances. New conditions would be weighed and predictions of probable changes in public opinion affecting nonvoting would be arrived at by inferring the motivations and behavior people would develop under the new conditions. Occupation would no longer be viewed as a fixed determinant of attitude toward voting; it is now seen as only one element in a shifting dynamic social process.

Class position is essentially a name for a network of social and psychological influence affecting persons. These influences are the determinants of opinion, as they enter into the development and functioning of personalities. Specific static determinants, statistically demonstrated, are useful indicators; they serve to suggest underlying determinative interpretations; they can never replace them.

An extensive literature is developing in recent years on the technical aspects of the problem of opinion determinants. The heart of the procedures is the "analytical breakdown" or simultaneous cross-tabulation of three or more variables. A simple example, from the well-known Erie County study [4] opinion data showed the Democratic vote intention was greater among Catholics than among Protestants. The question arises whether this is merely a reflection of occupational income differences between the religious groups, since the results also showed that Protestants tended to be higher on the socioeconomic scale. The answer is found by means of a cross-tabulation in which Catholics' and Protestants' vote intentions are compared separately at four economic levels. It turns out that the relation of religious affiliation to voting is independent of the socioeconomic factors. This leads the investigators to conclude that "on each socioeconomic status level religious affiliation plays an important role in determining political affiliation."

Clearly this type of information is of enormous value to the investigator. If the vote relations to religion had disappeared within the several economic groupings, it would have indicated that the socioeconomic factor was the explanation for the correlations of vote with religion, and no further interpretation of the religious influence as such would have been attempted. The procedure serves as an enlightening check on the analysts' speculations and hypotheses regarding possible explanatory factors; it also frequently suggests new lines of interpretation for further exploration. It contributes insight into relationships among the numerous class variables and other personal characteristics which is a necessary step toward further understanding of class influences on opinion.

Important and useful as the cross-tabulation and partial correlation procedures can be, we should not overlook their serious limitations and frequent abuses. One set of limitations arises from the indefinitely great number of variables involved in a complete analysis and the resulting inconclusiveness of the actual cross-tabulations. Consider, for example, an analysis of education, income, and vote. If the statistical relation between education and vote persists when economic status is ruled out, this does not demonstrate that schooling is a causal determinant. For, clearly, what one cross-tabulation has given, another cross-tabulation may take away. Until each factor is tried, there remains a possibility that one of them or a combination—say, ethnic group membership, religion, home environment, care in childhood, types of companions, etc.—may explain the original relationship between education and voting preference.

Conversely, the absence of a correlation in a given breakdown does not mean that the factor involved is to be discarded as a possible determinant. Its relation to the given opinion effect may have been hidden by the play

[4] P. F. Lazarsfeld, B. Berelson, and H. Gaudet, *The People's Choice* (New York: Duell, Sloan & Pearce, 1944).

of some other variable. Cantril reports a good case in point.[5] A simple tabulation of isolationist opinion in 1940 showed no association of opinion with age groups. When the same data were tabulated by age and by economic status together, a decided relation of age to isolationism was revealed. At the upper economic level young people were much more isolationist; at the lower economic level older people were significantly more isolationist. These relations canceled each other when the classes were combined.

The point is that there is no natural stopping place in the statistical analysis: there is no point at which the conclusion is final either that a particular variable is a determinant or that it is not. The analysis can proceed as long as the analyst can think of further promising variables. Moreover, it is, of course, possible that a simultaneous analysis of four or five or more variables would reveal relations not appearing with combinations of three. For practical reasons, however, these further breakdowns are ordinarily impossible.

This lack of finality does not condemn the cross-tabulation procedure. It does argue for extreme caution in drawing conclusions and for open-mindedness and comprehensive guiding theory in formulating further hypotheses.

A related set of perplexing questions is illustrated by a similar type of material. An analysis of economic status and education in relation to opinions on public issues is conducted to answer the question whether economic position or educational attainment has more weight in the determination of opinion. But to conclude that education is a determining influence is to assume that persons with different amounts of schooling at each economic level are alike in all other respects—that they are the same kinds of persons except for education. Obviously, if they also differ in other respects, no conclusion is justified about the effect of education. Is it reasonable to assume, however, that a person with grade-school education at a low economic level is the same kind of person as a college graduate at that lowest level? Surely college graduates in lowest occupations tend to be there in spite of their education and by reason of some personal or social characteristics that handicap them. Similarly it seems unreasonable to suppose that the grade-school graduate at the poorest economic level and his fellow grade-school graduate who has mounted to the top ranks are alike save for differences dependent upon their contrasting economic conditions. The selection that has taken place in terms of intellectual and personality traits cannot be ignored. Yet it is ignored by some of even the most technically skilled analysts.

To reiterate: the variables loosely incorporated in class position are so numerous and complexly interrelated that they defy neat conclusions that try to relate selected ones of these variables to public opinion. The fruitful alternative is rather to utilize knowledge provided by analysis of these variables as clues or indicators to a fuller, more rounded understanding of the processes of social interaction and personal development which actually determine opinion.

[5] Hadley Cantril, *Gauging Public Opinion* (Princeton: Princeton University Press, 1944), p. 178.

This discussion of research on determinants of opinion consists primarily of warnings. First are the two broad cautions: that the search for causal determinants is always directed at explaining specified differences in public opinion, not public opinion as a whole, and that the explanations are always limited to the particular conditions under which they hold true and that the defining of these conditions is indispensable. While careless interpretation of research on opinion determinants sometimes transgresses the first principle, much more common and serious lapses occur in respect to the second. Rarely, indeed, does one find any serious attempt to specify the conditions under which the research conclusions are true and to warn of important uncontrolled variables that may invalidate them.

Finally, the point has been stressed that inquiry into personal and class variables may contribute valuable clues to the dynamic interpretation of how public opinion is determined, but the analysis of these variables does not itself yield stable scientific conclusions. The empirical research dealing with these factors must be woven much more successfully than it has been into a structure of coherent social psychological theory and integrated with all the research knowledge that can be accumulated through other types of research on the problem.

11. ON THE EXTENT OF OPINIONS FOUNDED UPON AUTHORITY

by George Cornewall Lewis *

§ 1. The opinions of all children and young persons are necessarily derived from their parents and teachers, either without any knowledge, or with a very imperfect knowledge, of the grounds on which they rest, or the objections to which they may be liable. Even in cases where the reason is given with the opinion, the belief of a child is often determined rather by the authority of the teacher, than by the force of the argument. The subjects connected with the relations of physical objects, as well as with morals and religion, which are early presented to the mind of a child, often involve considerations so numerous, so complex, and so remote from his limited experience, that a full explanation of them would necessarily bewilder, rather than enlighten his understanding. Much instruction, too, is conveyed to a child in language, the full import of which he cannot comprehend. Words are often counters, not money, to children. They counterfeit processes of thought, rather than represent them. Much of the benefit of such early tuition consists in its familiarising the child with the names of ideas, which in its mind are still invested only with a vague and shadowy form,

* Nineteenth-century (1806–1863) English statesman and author. Member of Parliament, Chancellor of the Exchequer, Secretary for War, and other governmental positions. Author of *Enquiry into the Credibility of the Early Roman History, An Essay on the Influence of Authority in Matters of Opinion, Dialogue on the Best Form of Government,* and other works. The selection is from George Cornewall Lewis, *An Essay on the Influence of Authority in Matters of Opinion,* 2d ed., Longmans, Green & Co., Ltd., London, 1875, pp. 7-14.

and in habituating it to the use of the great instrument of thought and dis-course—language. Hence, in the education of children, a respect for the teacher as teacher, and for his precepts, independently of his reasons for them, is necessary: and it is important to inculcate principles and truths, even though the evidence of them is not, and cannot be, fully understood.

In this manner a person grows up, having imbibed, almost unconsciously, from his parents, teachers, and friends, the opinions and sentiments on religion, morality, government, history, and the relations of external nature, which are current in his country, at his time, among the persons under whose tuition he has been placed, and with whom he has associated.

This transmission of opinions from one generation to another, in a lump, (like the succession of property *per universitatem,* according to the expression of the Roman lawyers,) which results from family influences and the authority exercised by the parent and the senior upon the mind of the child and the junior, doubtless contains a considerable alloy of evil, inas-much as it perpetuates error in combination with truth, and affords no test for their discrimination. But it is mainly this process which, in each com-munity, connects the present with the past, and creates a unity and con-tinuity of national character and feeling. It is the insensible and incessant propagation of opinions from the old to the young within the circle of every family, and the uninquiring adoption by the growing generation of the moral and intellectual ideas of their immediate predecessors, which give to each nation its distinctive attributes—which enable it to maintain its char-acteristic peculiarities, and which prevent the general level of civilisation throughout the country from receding or becoming irregular. The traditions of civilisation, if we may use the expression, are, to a great extent, per-petuated by the implicit faith of children in the authority of their parents.

§ 2. To what extent a man, when his reason becomes mature, and he is emancipated from parental control, will modify the opinions with which he has been imbued during his childhood, depends upon the circumstances of his subsequent life.

If he belongs to the working-classes, he will probably, unless his circum-stances be peculiar, retain these opinions through life, with little verification or enlargement. His opportunities for observation will be principally con-fined to his relations with his employer, together with the manual opera-tions in which he is occupied. Owing to the cheapness of newspapers and tracts, he may occasionally obtain imperfect and partial glimpses into some of the political questions of the day; but he can rarely exercise any inde-pendent judgment, except upon the matters with which his labour makes him personally conversant. This description applies particularly to the agricultural labourers, who are not within the influence of the more stirring life of towns. "A great part of mankind" (says Locke) "are, by the natural and unalterable state of things in this world, and the constitution of human affairs, unavoidably given over to invincible ignorance of those proofs on which others build, and which are necessary to establish those opinions; the greatest part of men, having much to do to get the means of living, are not in a condition to look after those of learned and laborious inquiries."[1]

---

[1] *Essay on the Understanding,* B. IV. c. xx. § 2.

With the middle classes, there is more opportunity for the independent formation of opinions, by the acquirement of knowledge and observation of the world. Their time is, however, from an early age, engrossed with their industrial pursuits. Their daily business, combined with the care of their families, necessarily consumes the chief part of their attention, and leaves few opportunities for study and reflection. Such knowledge, however, and fitness for judgment as springs from special skill, and from a familiar acquaintance with the mechanical processes of certain arts, trades, and manufactures, will often be found in this class.

With regard to the wealthier classes,[2] comprising a large number of persons who have received a liberal education, and have leisure and means for study, observation, investigation, and reflection, the facilities for the independent formation of opinions are greater. But many of these, particularly the more energetic, are occupied with business and the affairs of active life, which either leave little time for reading and thought, or restrict it to one subject. Others consume a large portion of their time in amusements, or, at the most, in pursuits of mere curiosity; and still more acquiesce, without examination, in the opinions current amongst their friends and associates. Even persons of a speculative turn of mind, having leisure for speculation, confine their thoughts to a limited class of subjects, and entertain on all other subjects opinions mainly derived from authority. For example, a mathematician takes his historical and political opinions, a moral philosopher or an historian takes his physical opinions, on trust. The difficulty and labour of original thought and investigation are great; the number of subjects is enormous; every year adds to the stock of known facts, both in history and physics. The invention of printing and paper, by multiplying and perpetuating the records of facts and opinions, has rendered it impossible even for a professed student to explore more than certain portions of the field of knowledge. Hence, the use of reviews, manuals, compendia, encyclopaedias, and other books of reference, which serve as guides to the character of works, which contain results and opinions without the scaffolding by which they were constructed, and abridge intellectual labour.

§ 3. Men in general, with regard even to their opinions, are influenced by the prevailing fashion. They fear singularity more than error; they accept numbers as the index of truth; and they follow the crowd. The dislike of labour, the fear of unpopularity, the danger even of setting up individual opinion against established convictions and the voice of the multitude, contribute to strengthen this inclination. In the voting of political bodies, it is necessary to make the decision depend upon the numerical majority. But although everybody is aware that numbers are not a test of truth, yet many persons, while they recognise this maxim in theory, violate it in practice, and accept opinions simply because they are entertained by the people at large. It may be added, that a state of doubt, or suspense, as to opinions, particularly on important subjects, is painful to most minds, and men are impatient of the delay, or unwilling to make the exertion needful for the independent examination of the evidence and arguments on both sides of a

[2] See the remarks of Locke, ib. § 6.

disputed question. Hence, they are prone to cut the knot by accepting without verification, or with a very partial examination of its grounds, the opinion of some person whom, for any reason, they look to with respect, and whom they consider a competent judge in the matter. This feeling is naturally much strengthened by a conviction which the modesty and candour of most persons will suggest to them—viz., that if they do their best to form an independent judgment, they are not more likely to be right than other persons who have previously examined the subject, and whose opinions are known.

§ 4. There is a further motive which induces us to rely upon the judgment of persons whom we believe to have previously examined a subject with care and attention, and to be competent to form a sound opinion upon it. Even if we have, at some former time, gone through a process of study and examination, and have arrived at a given conclusion, the reasons for that conclusion do not always remain present to our mind. We may hold the opinion, rather upon the recollection of our having once ascertained it to be well grounded, than from a present perception of its grounds. "I confess (says Locke) in the opinions men have, and firmly stick to, in the world, their assent is not always from an actual view of the reasons that at first prevailed with them; it being in many cases almost impossible, and in most very hard, even for those who have very admirable memories, to retain all the proofs which, upon a due examination, made them embrace that side of the question. It suffices that they have once with care and fairness sifted the matter as far as they could, and that they have searched into all the particulars that they could imagine to give any light to the question, and with the best of their skill cast up the account upon the whole evidence; and thus, having once found on which side the probability appeared to them, after as full and exact an inquiry as they can make, they lay up the conclusion in their memories as a truth they have discovered; and for the future they remain satisfied with the testimony of their memories, that this is the opinion that, by the proofs they have once seen of it, deserves such a degree of their assent as they afford it. This is all that the greatest part of men are capable of doing in regulating their opinions and judgments; unless a man will exact of them either to retain distinctly in their memories all the proofs concerning any probable truths, and that, too, in the same order and regular deduction of consequences in which they have formerly placed or seen them, which sometimes is enough to fill a large volume on one single question; or else they must require a man, for every opinion that he embraces, every day to examine the proofs, both which are impossible. It is unavoidable, therefore, that the memory be relied on in the case, and that men be persuaded of several opinions, whereof the proofs are not actually in their thoughts—nay, which perhaps they are not able actually to recal. Without this, the greatest part of men must be either very sceptics, or change every moment, and yield themselves up to whoever, having lately studied the question, offers them arguments, which, for want of memory, they are not able presently to answer."[3]

[3] *On the Understanding*, B. IV. c. xvi. §§ 1 and 2.

As is very clearly explained in the preceding passage of Locke, our belief in a matter of opinion often rests upon our memory of an investigation which we have formerly made; we rely on a process of reasoning which we remember that we went through though we cannot now recollect its several steps, and only recal its final result: we know that we had once sufficient reasons for the opinion, though the reasons themselves are no longer in our thoughts; so that we believe, as it were, *upon our own authority;* we refer to a foregone process of inquiry, as a ground of present belief, in the faith that it was adequately performed, but without feeling the force of the reasons by which our mind was originally satisfied. If men did not thus fall back upon their own authority; if they did not for a time hold to an opinion in the confidence that their previous assent to it had been founded on adequate reasons, though these reasons may have faded from their memory, they would, as Locke truly remarks, be perpetually floating about in doubt, or they would be at the mercy of any person who had a readier and more retentive memory than themselves, or who happened from accidental circumstances to have mastered the arguments on one side of the question. There is one class of cases in particular, which may be referred to as illustrating our habit of entertaining opinions without any accurate memory of their grounds. This is, the estimates which we form of the characters of persons either in private or public life; our judgment of a man's character is derived from observing a number of successive acts, forming in the aggregate his general course of conduct. Now in proportion as our opportunities for observation are multiplied, our judgment is likely to be correct; but the facts from which our ultimate opinion is collected are so numerous, and often so trivial in themselves, that however sound the opinion may be, a large part of them necessarily soon vanish from the memory.

Being thus familiarised with the habit of entertaining an opinion without any present consciousness of its grounds, and from a mere remembrance of a process of investigation which we formerly went through, it is easy to transfer this origin of belief to *another* person, and to accept an opinion because that other person, (whom, moreover, we believe to be more competent to judge in the matter than ourselves) has gone through a similar process of investigation. Being accustomed to treat his former self as a sort of *alter ego,* and practically to divide his own identity, a man can easily apply the same mode of reference to another person. At all events, such a ground of belief is quite legitimate until we are able to examine the question for ourselves; and is far preferable to the alternative of a temporary suspension of belief (which in practical matters may tend to serious evils) or subjection to a sophistical advocate whose business it is to present one side of the case in a favourable point of view.

§ 5. In the preceding remarks, we have had chiefly in view those general opinions which are termed speculative; and which, although they in fact ultimately determine men's conduct, yet have not an immediate bearing upon practice. The extensive department of Practice, however, also involves a constant succession of questions which cause a man to hesitate as to the course to be pursued, which give rise to diversity of opinions, and require the interference of a competent judge for their solution. In many of the

affairs of private life, it is customary to follow the advice of professional
and other persons having had an appropriate training and peculiar experience in the subject matter. Thus a physician is consulted in questions of
health, a lawyer in legal questions, an architect or engineer in questions of building, a gardener in questions of horticulture, a sailor in questions
of navigation, and the like. There is likewise frequent occasion in the administration of justice, and the transaction of public business, for appealing to
the opinion of persons of professional and special knowledge. In practical
affairs, too, many opinions are formed upon the authority of the civil government, of public bodies and persons in conspicuous and responsible positions, of the heads of churches and religious bodies, of universities, acad-
emies, and places of learning, and of leaders of parties, and other voluntary
associations.

For the present, we merely indicate these sources of authority, as influencing the opinions of numerous persons: and we merely point out, in
general terms, the extent of the opinions accepted upon trust, and formed
without independent investigation, or a knowledge of the grounds on which
they rest.

12. THE SPRINGS OF HUMAN ACTION
by Bertrand Russell *

1

If politics is to become scientific, and if the event is not to be constantly
surprising, it is imperative that our political thinking should penetrate more
deeply into the springs of human action. All human activity is prompted by
desire. There is a wholly fallacious theory advanced by earnest moralists to
the effect that it is possible to resist desire in the interests of duty and moral
principle. I say this is fallacious, not because no man ever acts from a
sense of duty, but because duty has no hold on him unless he desires to be
dutiful. If you wish to know what men will do, you must know not only, or
principally, their material circumstances, but rather the whole system of
their desires with their relative strengths.

There are some desires which, though very powerful, have not, as a rule,
any great *political* importance. Most men at some period of their lives
desire to marry. But as a rule they can satisfy this desire without having
to take any political action. There are, of course, exceptions. The rape of
the Sabine women is a case in point. And the development of northern
Australia is seriously impeded by the fact that the vigorous young men
who ought to do the work dislike being wholly deprived of female society.
But such cases are unusual, and in general the interest that men and
women take in each other has little influence upon politics.

* Philosopher and author, recipient in 1950 of the Nobel Prize for literature. Coauthor of *Principia Mathematica* (with Dr. A. N. Whitehead) and author of *Power,
A History of Western Philosophy, Human Knowledge,* and numerous other works. The
selection is from Bertrand Russell, "The Springs of Human Action," *The Atlantic
Monthly*, vol. 189, pp. 27-31, March, 1952. By permission of the author.

The desires that are politically important may be divided into a primary and secondary group. In the primary group come the necessities of life: food and shelter and clothing. When these things become very scarce, there is no limit to the efforts that men will make, or to the violence that they will display, in the hope of securing them. It is said by students of the earliest history that, on four separate occasions, drought in Arabia caused the population of that country to overflow into surrounding regions, with immense effects, political, cultural, and religious. The last of these four occasions was the rise of Islam. The gradual spread of Germanic tribes from southern Russia to England, and thence to San Francisco, had similar motives. Undoubtedly the desire for food has been, and still is, one of the main causes of great political events.

But man differs from other animals in one very important respect, and that is that he has some desires which are, so to speak, infinite, which can never be fully gratified, and which would keep him restless even in Paradise. The boa constrictor, when he has had an adequate meal, goes to sleep, and does not wake until he needs another meal. Human beings, for the most part, are not like this. When the Arabs, who had been used to living sparingly on a few dates, acquired the riches of the Eastern Roman Empire, and dwelt in palaces of almost unbelievable luxury, they did not, on that account, become inactive. Hunger could no longer be a motive, for Greek slaves supplied them with exquisite viands at the slightest nod. But other desires kept them active: four in particular, which can be labeled *acquisitiveness, rivalry, vanity,* and *love of power.*

Acquisitiveness—the wish to possess as much as possible of goods, or the title to goods—is a motive which, I suppose, has its origin in a combination of fear and the desire for necessaries. I once befriended two little girls from Esthonia, who had narrowly escaped death from starvation in a famine. They lived in my family and of course had plenty to eat. But they spent all their leisure visiting neighboring farms and stealing potatoes, which they hoarded.

Rockefeller, who in his infancy had experienced great poverty, spent his adult life in a similar manner. Similarly, the Arab chieftains on their silken Byzantine divans could not forget the desert, and hoarded riches far beyond any possible physical needs. But whatever may be the psychoanalysis of acquisitiveness, no one can deny that it is one of the great motives—especially among the more powerful, for, as I have said before, it is one of the infinite motives. However much you may acquire, you will always wish to acquire more; satiety is a dream which will always elude you.

But acquisitiveness, although it is the mainspring of the capitalist system, is by no means the most powerful of the motives that survive the conquest of hunger. Rivalry is a much stronger motive. Over and over again in Mohammedan history, dynasties have come to grief because the sons of a sultan by different mothers could not agree, and in the resulting civil war universal ruin resulted. The same sort of thing happens in modern Europe. The world would be a happier place than it is if acquisitiveness were always stronger than rivalry. But, in fact, a great many men will cheerfully face impoverishment if they can thereby secure complete ruin for their rivals. Hence the present level of income tax.

Vanity is a motive of immense potency. Anyone who has much to do with children knows how they are constantly performing some antic, and saying "Look at me." "Look at me" is one of the most fundamental desires of the human heart. It can take innumerable forms, from buffoonery to the pursuit of posthumous fame. There was a Renaissance Italian princeling who was asked by the priest on his deathbed if he had anything to repent of. "Yes," he said. "There is one thing. On one occasion I had a visit from the Emperor and the Pope simultaneously. I took them to the top of my tower to see the view, and I neglected the opportunity to throw them both down, which would have given me immortal fame." History does not relate whether the priest gave him absolution.

One of the troubles about vanity is that it grows with what it feeds on. The more you are talked about, the more you will wish to be talked about.

The condemned murderer, I am told, who is allowed to see the account of his trial in the press is indignant if he finds a newspaper which has reported it inadequately. And the more he finds about himself in other papers, the more indignant he will be. Politicians and literary men are in the same case. And the more famous they become, the more difficult the press cutting agency finds it to satisfy them. It is scarcely possible to exaggerate the influence of vanity throughout the range of human life, from the child of three to the potentate at whose frown the world trembles. Mankind have even committed the impiety of attributing similar desires to the Deity, whom they imagine avid for continual praise.

2

But great as the influence of the motives we have been considering, there is one which outweighs them all. I mean the love of power. Love of power is closely akin to vanity, but is not by any means the same thing. What vanity needs for its satisfaction is glory, and it is easy to have glory without power. The people who enjoy the greatest glory in the United States are film stars; but they can be put in their place by the Committee on Un-American Activities, which enjoys no glory whatever. In England, the King has more glory than the Prime Minister, but the Prime Minister has more power than the King. Many people prefer glory to power, but on the whole these people have less effect upon the course of events than those who prefer power to glory. When Blücher, in 1814, saw Napoleon's palaces, he said: "Wasn't he a fool to have all this and to go running after Moscow." Napoleon, who certainly was not destitute of vanity, preferred power when he had to choose. To Blücher, this choice seemed foolish. Power, like vanity, is insatiable. Nothing short of omnipotence could satisfy it completely. And as it is especially the vice of energetic men, the casual efficacy of love of power is out of all proportion to its frequency. It is, indeed, by far the strongest motive in the lives of important men.

Love of power is greatly increased by the experience of power, and this applies to petty power as well as to that of potentates. In the happy days before 1914, when well-to-do ladies could acquire a host of servants, their pleasure in exercising power over the domestic steadily increased with age. Similarly, in any autocratic regime, the holders of power become increasingly tyrannical with experience of the delights that power can afford. Since power over human beings is shown in making them do what they would rather not do, the man who is actuated by love of power is more apt to inflict pain than to permit pleasure. If you ask your boss for leave of absence from the office on some legitimate occasion, his love of power will derive more satisfaction from a refusal than from a consent. If you require a building permit, the petty official concerned will obviously get more pleasure from saying "No" than from saying "Yes." It is this sort of thing which makes the love of power such a dangerous motive.

But it has other sides which are more desirable. The pursuit of knowledge is, I think, mainly actuated by love of power. And so are all advances in scientific technique. In politics, also, a reformer may have just as strong a love of power as a despot. It would be a complete mistake to decry love of power altogether as a motive. Whether you will be led by this motive to actions which are useful or to actions which are pernicious depends upon the social system and upon your capacities. If your capacities are theoretical or technical, you will contribute to knowledge or technique, and, as a rule, your activity will be useful. If you are a politician, you *may* be actuated by love of power, but as a rule this motive will join itself on to the desire to see some state of affairs realized which for some reason you prefer to the status quo. A great general may, like Alcibiades, be quite indifferent as to which side he fights on, but most generals have preferred to fight for their own country, and have, therefore, had other motives besides love of power.

Love of power as nearly pure as possible is to be seen in various types of men. The purest type is that of the *Éminence Grise*—the power behind the throne that never appears in public, and merely hugs itself with the secret thought: "How little these puppets know who is pulling the strings." Baron Holstein, who controlled the foreign policy of the German Empire from 1890 to 1906, illustrates this type to perfection. He lived in a slum; he never appeared in society; he avoided meeting the Emperor, except on one single occasion when the Emperor's importunity could not be resisted; he refused all invitations to court functions, on the ground that he possessed no court dress. He had acquired secrets which enabled him to blackmail the Chancellor and many of the Kaiser's intimates. He used the power of blackmail, not to acquire wealth, or any other obvious advantage, but merely to compel the adoption of the foreign policy that he preferred. In the East, similar characters are not very uncommon among eunuchs.

3

I come now to other motives, which, though in a sense less fundamental than those we have been considering, are still of considerable importance. The first of these is love of excitement. When white men first effect contact with some unspoiled race of savages, they offer them all kinds of benefits, from the light of the Gospel to pumpkin pie. These, however, much as we may regret it, most savages receive with indifference. What they really value among the gifts that we bring them is intoxicating liquor, which enables them, for the first time in their lives, to have the illusion, for a few brief moments, that it is better to be alive than dead. Red Indians, while they were still unaffected by white men, would smoke their pipes, not calmly as we do, but orgiastically, inhaling so deeply that they sank into a faint. And when excitement by means of nicotine failed, a patriotic orator would stir them up to attack a neighboring tribe, which would give them all the enjoyment that we (according to our temperament) derive from baseball or a general election.

The pleasure of gambling consists almost entirely in excitement. Monsieur Huc, the Jesuit missionary, describes Chinese traders at the Great Wall in winter, gambling until they lost all their cash, then proceeding to lose all their merchandise, and at last gambling away their clothes and going out naked to die of cold. With civilized men, as with primitive Red Indian tribes, it is, I think, chiefly love of excitement which makes the populace applaud when war breaks out; the emotion is exactly the same as at a football match, although the results are not comparable.

What is serious about excitement is that so many forms are destructive. It is destructive in those who cannot resist excess in alcohol or gambling. It is destructive when it takes the form of mob violence. And above all it is destructive when it leads to war. It is so deep a need that it will find harmful outlets of this kind unless innocent outlets are at hand. There are such innocent outlets at present in sport, and in politics so long as it is kept within constitutional bounds. But these are not sufficient, especially as the kind of politics that is most exciting is also the kind that does most harm. Civilized life has grown altogether too tame, and, if it is to be stable, it must provide harmless outlets for the impulses which our remote ancestors satisfied in hunting. In Australia, where people are few and rabbits are many, I watched a whole populace satisfying the primitive impulse in the primitive manner by the skillful slaughter of many thousands of rabbits. But in London or New York, where people are many and rabbits are few, some other means must be found to gratify primitive impulse.

I think every big town should contain artificial waterfalls that people could descend in very fragile canoes, and they should contain bathing pools full of mechanical sharks. Any persons found advocating preventive war should be condemned to two hours a day with these ingenious monsters. More seriously, pains should be taken to provide constructive outlets for the love of excitement. Nothing in the world is more exciting than a moment of sudden discovery or invention, and many more people are capable of experiencing such moments than is sometimes thought.

Interwoven with many other political motives are two closely relating passions to which human beings are regrettably prone: I mean fear and hate. It is normal to hate what we fear, and it happens frequently, though not always, that we fear what we hate. I think it may be taken as the rule among primitive men that they both fear and hate whatever is unfamiliar. They have their own herd, originally a very small one. And within one herd, all are friends, unless there is some special ground of enmity. Other herds are potential or actual enemies; a single member of one of them who strays by accident will be killed. An alien herd as a whole will be avoided or fought, according to circumstances.

It is this primitive mechanism which still controls our instinctive reaction to foreign nations. The completely untraveled person will view all foreigners as the savage regards a member of another herd. But the man who has traveled, or who has studied international politics, will have discovered that, if his herd is to prosper, it must, to some degree, become amalgamated with other herds. If someone says to you: "The French are your brothers," your first, instinctive feeling will be: "Nonsense. They shrug their shoulders and talk French. And I am even told that they eat frogs." If he explains to you that we may have to fight the Russians; that, if so, it will be desirable to defend the line of the Rhine; and that, if the line of the Rhine is to be defended, the help of the French is essential, you will begin to see what he means when he says that the French are your brothers. But if some fellow traveler were to go on to say that the Russians also are your brothers, he would be unable to persuade you, unless he could show that we are in danger from the Martians. We love those who hate our enemies, and if we had no enemies there would be very few people whom we should love, unless we could learn to have a more open and generous temperament than most people have at present.

All this, however, is only true so long as we are concerned solely with attitudes towards other human beings. You might regard the soil as your enemy because it yields reluctantly a niggardly subsistence. You might regard Mother Nature in general as your enemy, and envisage human life as a struggle to get the better of Mother Nature. If men viewed life in this way, coöperation of the whole human race would become easy. And men could easily be brought to view life in this way if schools, newspapers, and politicians devoted themselves to this end. But schools are out to teach patriotism; newspapers are out to stir up excitement; and politicians are out to get re-elected. None of the three, therefore, can do anything whatever toward saving the human race from reciprocal suicide.

There are two ways of coping with fear: one is to diminish the external danger, and the other is to cultivate Stoic endurance. The latter can be reinforced, except where immediate action is necessary, by turning our thoughts away from the cause of fear. The conquest of fear is of very great importance. Fear is in itself degrading; it easily becomes an obsession; it produces hate of that which is feared, and it leads headlong to excesses of cruelty. Nothing has so beneficent an effect on human beings as security. If an international system could be established which would remove the fear of war, the improvement in the everyday mentality of everyday people would be enormous and very rapid. Fear, at present, overshadows the world. The atom bomb and the bacterial bomb, wielded by the wicked communist or the wicked capitalist as the case may be, make Washington and the Kremlin tremble, and drive men further and further along the road towards the abyss. If matters are to improve, the first and essential step is to find a way of diminishing fear.

The world at present is obsessed by the conflict of rival ideologies, and one of the apparent causes of conflict is the desire for the victory of our ideology and the defeat of the other. I do not think that the fundamental motive here has much to do with ideologies. I think the ideologies are merely a way of grouping people, and that the passions involved are merely those which always arise between rival groups. There are, of course, various reasons for hating communists. First and foremost, we believe that they wish to take away our property. But so do burglars, and although we disapprove of burglars, our attitude toward them is very different indeed from our attitude towards communists—chiefly because they do not inspire the same degree of fear. Secondly, we hate the communists because they are irreligious. But the Chinese have been irreligious since the eleventh century, and we only began to hate them when they turned out Chiang Kaishek. Thirdly, we hate the communists because they do not believe in democracy, but we consider this no reason for hating Franco. Fourthly, we hate them because they do not allow liberty; this we feel so strongly that we have decided to imitate them.

It is obvious that none of these are the real grounds for our hatred. We hate them because we fear them and they threaten us. If the Russians still adhered to the Orthodox religion, if they had instituted parliamentary government, and if they had a completely free press which daily vituperated us, then—provided they had armed forces as powerful as now—we should still hate them if they gave us ground for thinking them hostile.

You may have been feeling that I have allowed only for bad motives, or, at best, such as are ethically neutral. I am afraid they are, as a rule, more powerful than more altruistic motives, but I do not deny that altruistic motives exist, and may on occasion be effective. The agitation against slavery in England in the early nineteenth century was indubitably altruistic, and was thoroughly effective. Its altruism was proved by the fact that in 1833 British taxpayers paid many millions in compensation to Jamaican landowners for the liberation of their slaves, and also by the fact that at the Congress of Vienna the British Government was prepared to make important concessions with a view to inducing other nations to abandon the slave trade. This is an instance from the past, but present-day America affords instances equally remarkable. I will not go into these, as I do not wish to become embarked in current controversies.

I do not think that it can be questioned that sympathy is a genuine motive, and that some people at some times are made somewhat uncomfortable by the sufferings of other people. It is sympathy that has produced the many humanitarian advances of the last hundred years. We are shocked when we hear stories of the ill-treatment of lunatics, and there are now quite a number of asylums in which they are not ill-treated. Prisoners in Western countries are not supposed to be tortured, and when they are, there is an outcry if the facts are discovered. We do not approve of treating orphans as they are treated in *Oliver Twist*. In all these ways sympathy has been politically effective. If the fear of war were removed, its effectiveness would become much greater. Perhaps the best hope for the future of mankind is that ways will be found of increasing the scope and intensity of sympathy.

The time has come to sum up this discussion. Politics is concerned with herds rather than with individuals, and the passions which are important in politics are, therefore, those in which the various members of a given herd can feel alike. The broad instinctive mechanism upon which political edifices have to be built is one of coöperation within the herd and hostility towards other herds. The coöperation within the herd is never perfect. There are members who do not conform; who are, in the etymological sense, "egregious"—that is to say, outside the flock. These members are those who have fallen below, or risen above, the ordinary level. They are: idiots, criminals, prophets, and discoverers. A wise herd will learn to tolerate the eccentricity of those who rise above the average, and to treat with a minimum of ferocity those who fall below it.

As regards relations to other herds, modern technique has produced a conflict between self-interest and instinct. In old days, when two tribes went to war, one of them exterminated the other and annexed its territory. From the point of view of the victor, the whole operation was thoroughly satisfactory. The killing was not at all expensive, and the excitement was agreeable. It is not to be wondered at that, in such circumstances, war persisted. Unfortunately we still have the emotions appropriate to such primitive warfare, while the actual operation of war has changed completely. Killing an enemy in modern war is a very expensive operation. If you consider how many Germans were killed in the last war, and how much the victors are paying in income tax, you can, by a sum in long division, discover the cost of a dead German, and you will find it considerable. In the East, it is true, the enemies of the Germans have secured the ancient advantages of turning out the defeated population and occupying their lands. The Western victors, however, have secured no such advantages. It is obvious that modern war is not good business from a financial point of view. Although we won both the world wars, we should now be much richer if they had not occurred.

If men were actuated by self-interest, which they are not—except in the case of a few saints—the whole human race would coöperate. There would be no more wars, no more armies, no more navies, no more atom bombs. There would not be armies of propagandists employed in poisoning the minds of Nation A against Nation B, and reciprocally Nation B against Nation A. There would not be armies of officials at frontiers to prevent the entry of foreign books and foreign ideas, however excellent in themselves. There would not be customs barriers to ensure the existence of small enterprises where one big enterprise would be more economic. All this would happen very quickly if men desired their own happiness as ardently as they desire the misery of their neighbors. But, you will tell me, what is the use of these Utopian dreams? Moralists will see to it that we do not become wholly selfish, and until we do become wholly selfish, the millennium will be impossible.

I do not wish to seem to end upon a note of cynicism. I do not deny that there are better things than selfishness, and that some people achieve these things. I maintain, however, on the one hand, that there are few occasions upon which large bodies of men, such as politics is concerned with, can rise above selfishness, while, on the other hand, there are a very great many circumstances in which populations will fall below selfishness, if selfishness is interpreted as enlightened self-interest.

And among these occasions on which people fall below self-interest are most of the occasions on which they are convinced that they are acting from idealistic motives. Much that passes as idealism is disguised hatred or disguised love of power. When you see large masses of men swayed by what appear to be noble motives, it is well to look below the surface and ask yourself what it is that makes these motives effective. It is partly because it is so easy to be taken in by a façade of nobility that a psychological query, such as I have been attempting, is worth making. I would say, in conclusion, that if what I have said is right, the main thing needed to make the world happy is intelligence. And this, after all, is an optimistic conclusion, because intelligence is a thing that can be fostered by known methods of education.

13. ON THE MOTIVATIONS OF CONVERTS TO MASS MOVEMENTS

by Eric Hoffer*

2

There is in us a tendency to locate the shaping forces of our existence outside ourselves. Success and failure are unavoidably related in our minds with the state of things around us. Hence it is that people with a sense of fulfillment think it a good world and would like to conserve it as it is, while the frustrated favor radical change. The tendency to look for all causes outside ourselves persists even when it is clear that our state of being is the product of personal qualities such as ability, character, appearance, health and so on. "If anything ail a man," says Thoreau, "so that he does not perform his functions, if he have a pain in his bowels even . . . he forthwith sets about reforming—the world."

It is understandable that those who fail should incline to blame the world for their failure. The remarkable thing is that the successful, too, however much they pride themselves on their foresight, fortitude, thrift and other "sterling qualities," are at bottom convinced that their success is the result of a fortuitous combination of circumstances. The self-confidence of even the consistently successful is never absolute. They are never sure that they know all the ingredients which go into the making of their success. The outside world seems to them a precariously balanced mechanism, and

* Self-educated aphorist, analyst of mass movements, and San Francisco longshoreman. Author of *The True Believer* and *The Passionate State of Mind*. The selection is from Eric Hoffer, *The True Believer*, Harper & Brothers, New York, 1951, pp. 6-8, 11, 14-16, 23-24, 39, and 46-47. Copyright 1951 by Eric Hoffer. Reprinted by permission of Harper & Brothers.

so long as it ticks in their favor they are afraid to tinker with it. Thus the resistance to change and the ardent desire for it spring from the same conviction, and the one can be as vehement as the other.

3

Discontent by itself does not invariably create a desire for change. Other factors have to be present before discontent turns into disaffection. One of these is a sense of power.

Those who are awed by their surroundings do not think of change, no matter how miserable their condition. When our mode of life is so precarious as to make it patent that we cannot control the circumstances of our existence, we tend to stick to the proven and the familiar. We counteract a deep feeling of insecurity by making of our existence a fixed routine. We hereby acquire the illusion that we have tamed the unpredictable. Fisherfolk, nomads and farmers who have to contend with the willful elements, the creative worker who depends on inspiration, the savage awed by his surroundings—they all fear change. They face the world as they would an all-powerful jury. The abjectly poor, too, stand in awe of the world around them and are not hospitable to change. It is a dangerous life we live when hunger and cold are at our heels. There is thus a conservatism of the destitute as profound as the conservatism of the privileged, and the former is as much a factor in the perpetuation of a social order as the latter.

The men who rush into undertakings of vast change usually feel they are in possession of some irresistible power. The generation that made the French Revolution had an extravagant conception of the omnipotence of man's reason and the boundless range of his intelligence. Never, says de Tocqueville, had humanity been prouder of itself nor had it ever so much faith in its own omnipotence. And joined with this exaggerated self-confidence was a universal thirst for change which came unbidden to every mind. Lenin and the Bolsheviks who plunged recklessly into the chaos of the creation of a new world had blind faith in the omnipotence of Marxist doctrine. The Nazis had nothing as potent as that doctrine, but they had faith in an infallible leader and also faith in a new technique. For it is doubtful whether National Socialism would have made such rapid progress if it had not been for the electrifying conviction that the new techniques of blitzkrieg and propaganda made Germany irresistible.

Even the sober desire for progress is sustained by faith—faith in the intrinsic goodness of human nature and in the omnipotence of science. It is a defiant and blasphemous faith, not unlike that held by the men who set out to build "a city and a tower, whose top may reach unto heaven" and who believed that "nothing will be restrained from them, which they have imagined to do."

6

For men to plunge headlong into an undertaking of vast change, they must be intensely discontented yet not destitute, and they must have the feeling that by the possession of some potent doctrine, infallible leader or some new technique they have access to a source of irresistible power. They must also have an extravagant conception of the prospects and potentialities of the future. Finally, they must be wholly ignorant of the difficulties involved in their vast undertaking. Experience is a handicap. The men who started the French Revolution were wholly without political experience. The same is true of the Bolsheviks, Nazis and the revolutionaries in Asia. The experienced man of affairs is a latecomer. He enters the movement when it is already a going concern. It is perhaps the Englishman's political experience that keeps him shy of mass movements.

8

Faith in a holy cause is to a considerable extent a substitute for the lost faith in ourselves.

9

The less justified a man is in claiming excellence for his own self, the more ready is he to claim all excellence for his nation, his religion, his race or his holy cause.

10

A man is likely to mind his own business when it is worth minding. When it is not, he takes his mind off his own meaningless affairs by minding other people's business.

This minding of other people's business expresses itself in gossip, snooping and meddling, and also in feverish interest in communal, national and racial affairs. In running away from ourselves we either fall on our neighbor's shoulder or fly at his throat.

11

The burning conviction that we have a holy duty toward others is often a way of attaching our drowning selves to a passing raft. What looks like giving a hand is often a holding on for dear life. Take away our holy duties and you leave our lives puny and meaningless. There is no doubt that in exchanging a self-centered for a selfless life we gain enormously in self-esteem. The vanity of the selfless, even those who practice utmost humility, is boundless.

12

One of the most potent attractions of a mass movement is its offering of a substitute for individual hope. This attraction is particularly effective in a society imbued with the idea of progress. For in the conception of progress, "tomorrow" looms large, and the frustration resulting from having nothing to look forward to is the more poignant. Hermann Rauschning says of pre-Hitlerian Germany that "The feeling of having come to the end of all things was one of the worst troubles we endured after that lost war." In a modern society people can live without hope only when kept dazed

and out of breath by incessant hustling. The despair brought by unemployment comes not only from the threat of destitution, but from the sudden
view of a vast nothingness ahead. The unemployed are more likely to follow the peddlers of hope than the handers-out of relief.

Mass movements are usually accused of doping their followers with
hope of the future while cheating them of the enjoyment of the present
Yet to the frustrated the present is irremediably spoiled. Comforts and
pleasures cannot make it whole. No real content or comfort can ever arise
in their minds but from hope.

13

When our individual interests and prospects do not seem worth living
for, we are in desperate need of something apart from us to live for. All
forms of dedication, devotion, loyalty and self-surrender are in essence a
desperate clinging to something which might give worth and meaning to our
futile, spoiled lives. Hence the embracing of a substitute will necessarily be
passionate and extreme. We can have qualified confidence in ourselves, but
the faith we have in our nation, religion, race or holy cause has to be
extravagant and uncompromising. A substitute embraced in moderation
cannot supplant and efface the self we want to forget. We cannot be sure
that we have something worth living for unless we are ready to die for it.
This readiness to die is evidence to ourselves and others that what we had
to take as a substitute for an irrevocably missed or spoiled first choice is
indeed the best there ever was.

18

There is a tendency to judge a race, a nation or any distinct group by
its least worthy members. Though manifestly unfair, this tendency has
some justification. For the character and destiny of a group are often
determined by its inferior elements.

The inert mass of a nation, for instance, is in its middle section. The
decent, average people who do the nation's work in cities and on the land
are worked upon and shaped by minorities at both ends—the best and the
worst.

The superior individual, whether in politics, literature, science, commerce
or industry, plays a large role in shaping a nation, but so do individuals
at the other extreme—the failures, misfits, outcasts, criminals, and all those
who have lost their footing, or never had one, in the ranks of respectable
humanity. The game of history is usually played by the best and the worst
over the heads of the majority in the middle.

The reason that the inferior elements of a nation can exert a marked
influence on its course is that they are wholly without reverence toward the
present. They see their lives and the present as spoiled beyond remedy and
they are ready to waste and wreck both: hence their recklessness and their
will to chaos and anarchy. They also crave to dissolve their spoiled, meaningless selves in some soul-stirring spectacular communal undertaking—

hence their proclivity for united action. Thus they are among the early recruits of revolutions, mass migrations and of religious, racial and chauvinist movements, and they imprint their mark upon these upheavals and movements which shape a nation's character and history.

The discarded and rejected are often the raw material of a nation's future. The stone the builders reject becomes the cornerstone of a new world. A nation without dregs and malcontents is orderly, decent, peaceful and pleasant, but perhaps without the seed of things to come. It was not the irony of history that the undesired in the countries of Europe should have crossed an ocean to build a new world on this continent. Only they could do it.

34

A rising mass movement attracts and holds a following not by its doctrine and promises but by the refuge it offers from the anxieties, barrenness and meaninglessness of an individual existence. It cures the poignantly frustrated not by conferring on them an absolute truth or by remedying the difficulties and abuses which made their lives miserable, but by freeing them from their ineffectual selves—and it does this by enfolding and absorbing them into a closely knit and exultant corporate whole. . . .

37

The permanent misfits are those who because of a lack of talent or some irreparable defect in body or mind cannot do the one thing for which their whole being craves. No achievement, however spectacular, in other fields can give them a sense of fulfillment. Whatever they undertake becomes a passionate pursuit; but they never arrive, never pause. They demonstrate the fact that we can never have enough of that which we really do not want, and that we run fastest and farthest when we run from ourselves.

The permanent misfits can find salvation only in a complete separation from the self; and they usually find it by losing themselves in the compact collectivity of a mass movement. By renouncing individual will, judgment and ambition, and dedicating all their powers to the service of an eternal cause, they are at last lifted off the endless treadmill which can never lead them to fulfillment.

The most incurably frustrated—and, therefore, the most vehement—among the permanent misfits are those with an unfulfilled craving for creative work. Both those who try to write, paint, compose, etcetera, and fail decisively, and those who after tasting the elation of creativeness feel a drying up of the creative flow within and know that never again will they produce aught worth while, are alike in the grip of a desperate passion. Neither fame nor power nor riches nor even monumental achievements in other fields can still their hunger. Even the wholehearted dedication to a holy cause does not always cure them. Their unappeased hunger persists, and they are likely to become the most violent extremists in the service of their holy cause.

14. A SELF-ANALYSIS OF A CONVERSION TO COMMUNISM
by Arthur Koestler *

A faith is not acquired by reasoning. One does not fall in love with a woman, or enter the womb of a church, as a result of logical persuasion. Reason may defend an act of faith—but only after the act has been committed, and the man committed to the act. Persuasion may play a part in a man's conversion; but only the part of bringing to its full and conscious climax a process which has been maturing in regions where no persuasion can penetrate. A faith is not acquired; it grows like a tree. Its crown points to the sky; its roots grow downward into the past and are nourished by the dark sap of the ancestral humus.

From the psychologist's point of view, there is little difference between a revolutionary and a traditionalist faith. All true faith is uncompromising, radical, purist; hence the true traditionalist is always a revolutionary zealot in conflict with pharisaian society, with the lukewarm corrupters of the creed. And vice versa: the revolutionary's Utopia, which in appearance represents a complete break with the past, is always modeled on some image of the lost Paradise, of a legendary Golden Age. The classless Communist society, according to Marx and Engels, was to be a revival, at the end of the dialectical spiral, of the primitive Communist society which stood at its beginning. Thus all true faith involves a revolt against the believer's social environment, and the projection into the future of an ideal derived from the remote past. All Utopias are fed from the sources of mythology; the social engineer's blueprints are merely revised editions of the ancient text.

Devotion to pure Utopia, and revolt against a polluted society, are thus the two poles which provide the tension of all militant creeds. To ask which of the two makes the current flow—attraction by the ideal or repulsion by the social environment—is to ask the old question about the hen and the egg. To the psychiatrist, both the craving for Utopia and the rebellion against the status quo are symptoms of social maladjustment. To the social reformer, both are symptoms of a healthy rational attitude. The psychiatrist is apt to forget that smooth adjustment to a deformed society creates deformed individuals. The reformer is equally apt to forget that hatred, even of the objectively hateful, does not produce that charity and justice on which a utopian society must be based.

Thus each of the two attitudes, the sociologist's and the psychologist's, reflects a half-truth. It is true that the case-history of most revolutionaries and reformers reveals a neurotic conflict with family or society. But this

* Author and former foreign correspondent for European newspapers. Author of *Darkness at Noon, The Yogi and the Commissar, The Age of Longing, The Sleepwalkers,* and other works. The selection is from Arthur Koestler, in Richard Crossman (ed.), *The God That Failed,* Harper & Brothers, New York, 1949, pp. 15-21. Copyright 1949 by Richard Crossman. Reprinted by permission of Harper & Brothers.

only proves, to paraphrase Marx, that a moribund society creates its own morbid gravediggers.

It is also true that in the face of revolting injustice the only honorable attitude is to revolt, and to leave introspection for better times. But if we survey history and compare the lofty aims, in the name of which revolutions were started, and the sorry end to which they came, we see again and again how a polluted civilization pollutes its own revolutionary offspring.

Fitting the two half-truths—the sociologist's and the psychologist's—together, we conclude that if on the one hand oversensitivity to social injustice and obsessional craving for Utopia are signs of neurotic maladjustment, society may, on the other hand, reach a state of decay where the neurotic rebel causes more joy in heaven than the sane executive who orders pigs to be drowned under the eyes of starving men. This in fact was the state of our civilization when, in December, 1931, at the age of twenty-six, I joined the Communist Party of Germany.

I became converted because I was ripe for it and lived in a disintegrating society thirsting for faith. But the day when I was given my Party card was merely the climax of a development which had started long before I had read about the drowned pigs or heard the names of Marx and Lenin. Its roots reach back into childhood; and though each of us, comrades of the Pink Decade, had individual roots with different twists in them, we are products of, by and large, the same generation and cultural climate. It is this unity underlying diversity which makes me hope that my story is worth telling.

I was born in 1905 in Budapest; we lived there till 1919, when we moved to Vienna. Until the First World War we were comfortably off, a typical Continental middle-middle-class family: my father was the Hungarian representative of some old-established British and German textile manufacturers. In September, 1914, this form of existence, like so many others, came to an abrupt end; my father never found his feet again. He embarked on a number of ventures which became the more fantastic the more he lost self-confidence in a changed world. He opened a factory for radioactive soap; he backed several crank-inventions (everlasting electric bulbs, self-heating bed bricks and the like); and finally lost the remains of his capital in the Austrian inflation of the early 'twenties. I left home at twenty-one, and from that day became the only financial support of my parents.

At the age of nine, when our middle-class idyl collapsed, I had suddenly become conscious of the economic Facts of Life. As an only child, I continued to be pampered by my parents; but, well aware of the family crisis, and torn by pity for my father, who was of a generous and somewhat childlike disposition, I suffered a pang of guilt whenever they bought me books or toys. This continued later on, when every suit I bought for myself meant so much less to send home. Simultaneously, I developed a strong dislike of the obviously rich; not because they could afford to buy things (envy plays a much smaller part in social conflict than is generally assumed) but because they were able to do so without a guilty conscience. Thus I projected a personal predicament onto the structure of society at large.

It was certainly a tortuous way of acquiring a social conscience. But precisely because of the intimate nature of the conflict, the faith which grew out of it became an equally intimate part of my self. It did not, for some years, crystallize into a political creed; at first it took the form of a mawkishly sentimental attitude. Every contact with people poorer than myself was unbearable—the boy at school who had no gloves and red chilblains on his fingers, the former traveling salesman of my father's reduced to cadging occasional meals—all of them were additions to the load of guilt on my back. The analyst would have no difficulty in showing that the roots of this guilt-complex go deeper than the crisis in our household budget; but if he were to dig even deeper, piercing through the individual layers of the case, he would strike the archetypal pattern which has produced millions of particular variations on the same theme—"Woe, for they chant to the sound of harps and anoint themselves, but are not grieved for the affliction of the people."

Thus sensitized by a personal conflict, I was ripe for the shock of learning that wheat was burned, fruit artificially spoiled and pigs were drowned in the depression years to keep prices up and enable fat capitalists to chant to the sound of harps, while Europe trembled under the torn boots of hunger-marchers and my father hid his frayed cuffs under the table. The frayed cuffs and drowned pigs blended into one emotional explosion, as the fuse of the archetype was touched off. We sang the "Internationale," but the words might as well have been the older ones: "Woe to the shepherds who feed themselves, but feed not their flocks."

In other respects, too, the story is more typical than it seems. A considerable proportion of the middle classes in central Europe was, like ourselves, ruined by the inflation of the 'twenties. It was the beginning of Europe's decline. This disintegration of the middle strata of society started the fatal process of polarization which continues to this day. The pauperized bourgeois became rebels of the Right or Left; Schickelgrüber and Djugashwili shared about equally the benefits of the social migration. Those who refused to admit that they had become déclassé, who clung to the empty shell of gentility, joined the Nazis and found comfort in blaming their fate on Versailles and the Jews. Many did not even have that consolation; they lived on pointlessly, like a great black swarm of tired winterflies crawling over the dim windows of Europe, members of a class displaced by history.

The other half turned Left, thus confirming the prophecy of the "Communist Manifesto":

> Entire sections of the ruling classes are . . . precipitated into the proletariat, or are at least threatened in their conditions of existence. They . . . supply the proletariat with fresh elements of enlightenment and progress.

That "fresh element of enlightenment," I discovered to my delight, was I. As long as I had been nearly starving, I had regarded myself as a temporarily displaced offspring of the bourgeoisie. In 1931, when at last I had achieved a comfortable income, I found that it was time to join the ranks of the proletariat. But the irony of this sequence only occurred to me in retrospect.

The bourgeois family will vanish as a matter of course with the vanishing of Capital. . . . The bourgeois claptrap about the family and education, about the haloed correlation of parent and child, becomes all the more disgusting the more, by the action of modern industry, all family ties among the proletarians are torn asunder. . . .

Thus the "Communist Manifesto." Every page of Marx, and even more of Engels, brought a new revelation, and an intellectual delight which I had only experienced once before, at my first contact with Freud. Torn from its context, the above passage sounds ridiculous; as part of a closed system which made social philosophy fall into a lucid and comprehensive pattern, the demonstration of the historical relativity of institutions and ideals—of family, class, patriotism, bourgeois morality, sexual taboos—had the intoxicating effect of a sudden liberation from the rusty chains with which a pre-1914 middleclass childhood had cluttered one's mind. Today, when Marxist philosophy has degenerated into Byzantine cult and virtually every single tenet of the Marxist program has become twisted round into its opposite, it is difficult to recapture that mood of emotional fervor and intellectual bliss.

I was ripe to be converted, as a result of my personal case-history; thousands of other members of the intelligentsia and the middle classes of my generation were ripe for it, by virtue of other personal case-histories; but, however much these differed from case to case, they had a common denominator: the rapid disintegration of moral values, of the pre-1914 pattern of life in postwar Europe, and the simultaneous lure of the new revelation which had come from the East.

I joined the Party (which to this day remains "the" Party for all of us who once belonged to it) in 1931, at the beginning of that short-lived period of optimism, of that abortive spiritual renaissance, later known as the Pink Decade. The stars of that treacherous dawn were Barbusse, Romain Rolland, Gide and Malraux in France; Piscator, Becher, Renn, Brecht, Eisler, Säghers in Germany; Auden, Isherwood, Spender in England; Dos Passos, Upton Sinclair, Steinbeck in the United States. (Of course, not all of them were members of the Communist Party.) The cultural atmosphere was saturated with Progressive Writers' congresses, experimental theaters, committees for peace and against Fascism, societies for cultural relations with the USSR, Russian films and avant-garde magazines. It looked indeed as if the Western world, convulsed by the aftermath of war, scourged by inflation, depression, unemployment and the absence of a faith to live for, was at last going to

> Clear from the head the masses of impressive rubbish;
> Rally the lost and trembling forces of the will,
> Gather them up and let them loose upon the earth,
> Till they construct at last a human justice.
>
> *Auden*

The new star of Bethlehem had risen in the East; and for a modest sum, Intourist was prepared to allow you a short and well-focused glimpse of the Promised Land.

15. THE INFLUENCE OF EVENTS
UPON PUBLIC OPINION
by Frank V. Cantwell *

The rôle played by public opinion in a democracy, particularly as it effects the legislative process, has long been a subject for speculation by political scientists. The advent of controlled quota sampling permits of the study of this important relationship in measurable terms. The object of the present discussion is to trace the interaction of public opinion and the executive and legislative branches of government as they have dealt with a single public question—reorganization of the Supreme Court, as presented to Congress for consideration by President Roosevelt on February 5, 1937. Enlargement of the Supreme Court from nine to fifteen members was the most controversial feature of the general reorganization of the federal judiciary proposed by the President, aimed at speeding up the process of clearing cases through the federal court system, and making the system more "representative" of the wishes of the people.

The debate on enlargement of the Supreme Court provides a useful and interesting case study for several reasons. The case as a public issue has a definite beginning and end, ranging from the proposal of the judiciary reform bill by the President on February 5 to the death of Senator Joseph T. Robinson on July 14, 1937. As it was debated by public and legislators, the issue was a relatively clear-cut one, uncomplicated by side issues or utterly foreign events that might have influenced the course of either legislators or the public. Finally, and of decided importance, the American Institute of Public Opinion made weekly measurements of opinion toward the proposal during the entire period that reorganization of the Court was a public question. This permits the correlation of reliable opinion samplings with events in the debate and the observation of their relationship.

From this observation it is hoped to throw light on several specific questions: (1) What is the general nature of the relationship between the public and its legislators? (2) What are the forces at work which determine the direction that public opinion will take in a debate of this type? (3) Is there a noticeable tendency on the part of legislators to follow the guidance of public opinion, and if so, to what extent do legislators take their lead from the public? (4) To what extent do legislators attempt to swing opinion to their way of thinking? (5) Are there any phases of the relationship between the public and legislators that might be improved so as to make it more effective in approaching the process of deciding public policy?

I. THE DEBATE ON THE COURT BILL

From accounts of the Court debate as carried in the *New York Times,*

* Public opinion analyst and legislative assistant to Congressmen. The selection is from Frank V. Cantwell, "Public Opinion and the Legislative Process," *American Political Science Review,* vol. 40, issue no. 5, 924-935, October, 1946. Reprinted by permission. Several charts and tables are omitted from this selection by permission.

the following short outline of leading developments in the debate has been prepared:

Chronological Listing of Events in the Court Debate

February 5—President Roosevelt sends message to Congress recommending reorganization of the federal judiciary, including increasing the membership of the Supreme Court from nine to fifteen members. President reported "calm and confident," reflecting his conviction that he has a huge popular mandate for what he is doing. Message creates shock throughout country.

March 1—The Supreme Court upholds Congressional resolution abrogating payments in gold. Decision is of aid to New Deal.

March 4—President Roosevelt, in Democratic Victory Dinner speech, calls for party loyalty on the Supreme Court issue.

March 8—The President, in a fireside chat, assures Americans that, in proposing reorganization of the Court, he is seeking to protect them from the Court's usurpations.

March 9—Homer Cummings, Attorney-General, opens Administration arguments before Senate Judiciary Committee, saying the bill will restore the governmental machinery to its proper balance.

March 22—Senator Burton K. Wheeler opens opposition arguments before Senate Judiciary Committee and reads a statement from Chief Justice Charles E. Hughes saying enlargement of the Court is "unnecessary." Statement is said to have the approval of Justices Brandeis and Van Devanter.

March 29—The Supreme Court reverses Adkins v. Children's Hospital decision and holds constitutional minimum wage law of the state of Washington. Adkins case specifically overruled by 5–4 decision. Decision opens way for federal minimum wage legislation.

April 12—In handing down decisions in four specific cases, the Supreme Court upholds the National Labor Relations Act (Wagner Act). Decision in chief case is 5–4.

April 28—Senators Hatch, McCarran, and O'Mahoney, members of the Senate Judiciary Committee previously uncommitted on Supreme Court Bill, announce opposition on basis of testimony offered before the Committee.

May 10—Washington reports say that Justices Brandeis and Van Devanter will retire from Court in June.

May 18—Justice Willis Van Devanter, 78, retires.

May 24—The Supreme Court upholds the Social Security Act in ruling on three cases, two by 5–4 decisions.

June 14—The Senate Judiciary Committee reports unfavorably to the Senate on the Court bill, terming the proposal "a needless, futile, and utterly dangerous abandonment of constitutional principle." Vote is 10–8 against proposal.

July 14—Senator Joseph T. Robinson, majority leader of the Senate, dies suddenly. Supreme Court Bill will be abandoned.

An analysis has been prepared from two questions asked weekly by the Gallup Poll during the debate. The first question was asked during the period from February 15 to April 5, and reads: "Are you in favor of President Roosevelt's proposal regarding the Supreme Court?" The second question covers the period from April 12 to June 7, and reads: "Should Congress pass the President's Supreme Court plan?" In both questions, the Supreme Court plan was stated to be "President Roosevelt's." Possibly the use of the President's name might have introduced a bias, although throughout the debate, in the newspapers, on the radio, and in the halls of Congress, the plan was also identified with the President. In view of this very common identification, the possibility of such a bias is minimized. In any event, any tendency toward bias would not affect the validity of the figures as used in this study, since a bias would be constant.

Phase One of the Debate. The initial period in the debate extends from the introduction of the President's proposal on February 5 until the week immediately preceding the two speeches made by the President. In this early period public attitudes toward the proposal divided equally, 45 per cent of the people expressing approval of the proposal, and 45 per cent expressing disapproval, with 10 per cent in the "no opinion" category. These figures are from the Gallup Poll taken during the week of February 15. At approximately the same time, the *New York Times* reported that an informal poll of senators made by *Times* reporters showed that 32 senators were on record as favoring the proposal, 28 as against the proposal, while 35 remained uncommitted. Thus, while 90 per cent of the public had put themselves on record as favoring or disapproving the proposal, only 63 per cent of the senators had taken a definite stand. One week later, on February 17 the *Times* news columns carried this statement from a Washington staff member: "Conservative Democrats . . . especially those in the Senate, gagged at the proposals. . . . Many of them maintained a prudent silence, waiting to see how the cat of public opinion would jump."

In this first stage of the debate, newspapers and radio commentators began to take definite stands on the proposals, and senators and other public figures began to make statements setting forth their positions. Senator Norris declared against the bill; former Governor Alf Landon, who had carried the Republican standard in the presidential election a few months earlier, came out against the proposal; Senator Champ Clark declared against the scheme; and Senators Glass and Wheeler denounced it. The only figure of magnitude to raise his voice in favor of the proposal was Senator La Follette. In the face of this cumulation of official opinion against the proposal, public opinion began to turn against the plan, and by March 1 the Gallup Poll reported that the anti-proposal vote had grown to 48 per cent, while the pro-proposal vote had slumped to 41 per cent—a difference of 7 percentage points. The President and his advisers became aware that public sentiment was turning away from the proposal.

As early as February 15, the *Times* reported that Attorney-General Cummings and Senator Sherman Minton were planning to make appeals for public support of the plan. The *Times* news columns said: "The frank object of all these appeals is to induce the backers of the President to send telegrams and letters to their senators and representatives to offset the thousands received at the Capitol in the last few days in opposition to his sweeping plan for remaking the Supreme Court with more liberal-minded men." On February 19, the *Times* said: "On the showing of informal polls that the Administration's judiciary reform bill may hang on the decision of less than a dozen senators, President Roosevelt and the forces identified with him, particularly organized labor, intensified their efforts to insure its passage as a prerequisite to further New Deal legislation. . . . The opposition strategists in the Senate . . . were . . . making preparations for one of the stiffest legislative battles of recent years. They were making no particular effort to dig into the dwindling reservoir of unpledged senators, leaving that to the weight of the letters and telegrams still coming in from all parts of the country." Phase One of the debate may be summarized by saying that the President introduced the proposal with the hope that public opinion, which had given him a handsome victory in November, would provide the pressure necessary to push the proposal through Congress. This public pressure was not forthcoming, and the public had become increasingly hostile. Opposition senators were biding their time as they watched public opinion swing behind them. So far as the Administration was concerned, a counter-attack was necessary to win back public favor to the proposal.

Phase Two. The second phase of the debate may be entitled the Administration drive for public support. The outstanding development during this phase was the entry of the President directly into the discussion. With opinion turning away from the proposal, it became obvious that use of the most powerful weapon in the New Deal arsenal was indicated—a personal appeal from the President. Consequently, the President made two speeches to the nation within five days, an address at the Democratic Victory Dinner on March 4 and a fireside chat on March 8. The *New York Times* reported the fireside chat in these words: "He had no intention of packing the Court with 'spineless puppets.' He simply proposed to return the Court to its 'rightful and historic place' and save the Constitution from 'hardening of the arteries'." On the morning following the fireside chat, Attorney-General Cummings opened the Administration case before the Senate Judiciary Committee, saying that the proposal would restore the governmental machinery to its proper balance. The Gallup Poll for the week of March 1 immediately registered the impact of the President's speeches. The anti-proposal vote fell to 47 per cent and in two weeks dropped precipitately to 41 per cent, the lowest point reached by the No vote at any stage of the debate. On the other hand, the pro-proposal vote began a climb that was to last until March 29, rising from 41 to 45 per cent during the month. Success had apparently crowned the effort of the Administration to win the favor of public opinion, for the Yes vote now held a slim margin over the No vote. However, as will be seen, this margin was to prove far from decisive.

Phase Three. On March 22, the opposition forces swung back into action as Senator Burton Wheeler, chief of the anti-court reorganization forces, opened the opposition arguments before the Senate Judiciary Committee. As the first opposition witness, Senator Wheeler read a statement from Chief Justice Charles E. Hughes saying enlargement of the Court was "unnecessary"; and the statement was said to have the approval of Justices Brandeis and Van Devanter. During that week the No vote turned again and began a steady climb upward which was to mount almost steadily until the proposal was finally killed. Evidently, opposition arguments before the Judiciary Committee were sufficiently convincing to solidify the

No vote, and the poll findings show the constant strength of the opposition-ists among the public from this date onward.

Phase Four. The turning point in the debate was reached on March 29. On that day, the Supreme Court handed down a decision reversing an earlier decision in the Adkins v. Children's Hospital case. The effect was to hold constitutional the minimum wage law of the state of Washington, thus paving the way for federal minimum wage legislation, one of the chief objectives of the New Deal. The effect on public opinion of the switch by the Supreme Court was nothing short of profound. The Yes vote, or those in favor of reorganization, began a sharp slump from which it never fully recovered. In terms of percentages, the Yes vote dropped from a high of 45 per cent in the week before the reversed decision in the Adkins case to a low of 31 per cent on May 17. It is safe to say that the Administration lost its case before the public on the day when the Supreme Court did its famous about-face. It is to be noted, however, that the Yes vote which became estranged from the proposal did not shift into the No group, but fell into indecision and became allied with the No Opinion group. The growth of the No Opinion group almost matched, point for point, the decline in the Yes group. This phenomenon will be enlarged upon below.

From the beginning of Phase Two onward, the Senate Judiciary Committee had been holding extensive hearings at which educators, farm and labor leaders, women's group leaders, and the representatives of almost every special interest group in the nation appeared and presented their case. To what extent the members of the Judiciary Committee were "hold-ing off" from presenting the bill for a formal test on the Senate floor is difficult to tell with exactness. During this period, opinion was in a state of flux, and the Judiciary Committee served a valuable function by permitting opinion to crystallize. Some evidence of political maneuvering to take advantage of a favorable climate of opinion is revealed in a charge made by Senators Wheeler and Van Nuys on April 3, five days after the Supreme Court handed down the decision in the Adkins case. The *New York Times* reported the two Senators as charging Attorney-General Cummings with a "gag" attempt, based on reports that Mr. Cummings had hinted that he would like to see the Judiciary Committee bring the hearings to a close. The *Times* reported the Senators as saying: "There is no doubt the Attorney-General would like to close public hearings on this issue. . . . Hundreds of American citizens, holding responsible positions at the bar, in universities, and in the molding of public opinion have asked to be heard . . . it is the duty of the Senate Judiciary Committee to continue these hearings until every cross-section of public opinion has been given an opportunity to present its views." Senator Wheeler was astute enough to realize that the tide of opinion was running against the proposal, and that time was playing into the hands of the opposition, just as Mr. Cummings knew that time was playing against the Administration. The two opposition Senators realized the impact of the Supreme Court decision of March 29 on the public and were willing to continue the hearings of the Judiciary Committee until such time as the increased opposition they expected from the public should have an opportunity to register itself through witnesses at the hearings and through senatorial channels of sounding opinion. The Judiciary Committee did continue its hearings, and reports continued to furnish the bulk of newspaper and radio accounts of the reorganization debate. The incident is illustrative of the dependence that both sides placed upon the pressure of public opinion to furnish the force needed to carry the day. Opponents and proponents alike realized that without the backing of public opinion they were lost, and were anxiously trying to win opinion to their side, while waiting for opinion to crystallize sufficiently so that a clear-cut case of public support would be forthcoming.

On April 12, with the No vote holding a six per cent margin over the Yes vote, the Supreme Court handed down a decision upholding the National Labor Relations Act in rulings on four specific cases. In the chief case, the decision was five to four in favor of the act. Strangely enough, the effect of this decision on public opinion was the reverse of that in the Adkins case. The No vote went down slightly while the Yes vote mounted slightly. This reversal of opinion can be traced to the fact that the Administration immediately made capital of the two successive favorable decisions of the Court, following a series of reverses for the New Deal—maintaining that the two decisions proved the point that the Court was actually composed of human beings who were subject to error and could see the error of their ways. The Administration raised its famous cry that Court decisions rested on whether a Justice came down heads or tails, which indicated the need for a larger Court membership. This argument, although it had an immediate effect, was not powerful enough to change the trend of opinion, and the following week (April 19) the No vote rose three percentage points, while the Yes vote sank two points.

Phase Five. The next development of note in the debate occurred on May 10, when reports from Washington circled the country to the effect that Justices Brandeis and Van Devanter intended to retire from the Court in June. The effect of this report was to increase public indecision, which had been mounting steadily from the introduction of the proposal, and after the report had gained credence the No Opinion group stood at a high of 25 per cent on May 17. It is worth pausing to note the state of opinion at this time.

The data reveal that the opposition group had held its own, despite sharp dips. The Yes group, proponents of reorganization, had lost a total of 14 percentage points; the No Opinion group had risen from 10 per cent to 25 per cent; those who lost faith in their position did not feel powerfully enough affected to jump into the opposite camp, but that their reaction was to fall into a state of indecision. The gain for the No Opinion group represents the total defection from both the Yes and No groups. In other words, the public was still not clear upon a course of action, although the number of Yes people who were growing increasingly doubtful of their position was very much larger than the respective No group. The importance of this observation lies in the assumption that members of the Senate were idling along, waiting for a popular reaction. This was not to be forthcoming, since

the people were becoming increasingly indecisive. But for the next event
unfolding on May 18, it is difficult to say how long this deadlock between
the people and their legislators, each waiting for the other to act, might
have lasted.

Phase Six. The deadlock was broken on the date mentioned with announcement of the retirement from the Supreme Court of Justice Willis
Van Devanter at the age of seventy-eight. This announcement immediately
cleared the atmosphere, and both opponents and proponents of the court
reorganization proposal were enabled to make up their minds definitely.
Opinion had at last crystallized. The retirement of Justice Van Devanter
meant that the President would be able to appoint to the Court a Justice
more in sympathy with New Deal objectives. In turn, this appointment,
together with the recent "liberalization" of the Court in the Adkins and
Wagner Act decisions, meant that for all practical purposes the Court had
been reorganized. De facto reorganization apparently was satisfactory to
the public, and the No vote rose quickly until on June 7 opponents of court
reorganization had 50 per cent of the public behind them, while only 35 per
cent favored reorganization. The No Opinion vote sank rapidly from 25
per cent on May 17 to 15 per cent on June 7.

After the retirement of Justice Van Devanter, opinion crystallized more
rapidly in the direction of opposition to the proposal than in favor of it.
A total defection of 10 per cent of those originally favoring reorganization
can be noted, five per cent of these people switching their vote into opposition, while five per cent were unable to come to a decision and moved into
the No Opinion group.

This evident satisfaction of the people with the changed court situation
came as a great relief to legislators, who were now able to deal with the
delicate problem of de jure court reorganization. On June 14, with the
battle of public opinion decided, and with opinion firmly behind it, the
Senate Judiciary Committee reported unfavorably (ten to eight) to the
Senate on the Judiciary Reorganization Bill, terming the measure "a needless, futile, and utterly dangerous abandonment of constitutional principle."
Reorganization of the Court was no longer a public issue; and whatever
lingering inclination there might have been on the part of the Administration to press for court reform in the face of public opposition was dissipated by the death on July 14 of Senator Joseph T. Robinson, majority
leader of the Senate, who had thrown all of his strength into the fray on
behalf of the proposal.

II. CONCLUSIONS

Having examined in some detail the interplay between public opinion
and events in the court debate, it is now possible to form conclusions as to
the general nature of the relationship between the public and its legislators
as they deal jointly with a public question. In many respects, the debate on
the Court is typical of the problems which present themselves for solution
in our democracy. For this reason, the conclusions which follow have been
cast in such a form that they may be applied to understanding the nature

of any similar debate on a public question. At the same time, it must be borne in mind that so many diverse factors operate while a question runs its public course that these conclusions have applicability only in so far as the phenomena at work in a given situation are taken into consideration. Further study of the type of relationship under consideration will permit the understanding with considerable exactness of how public opinion and the legislative process affect each other. This, in turn, will enable the public and legislators to operate together at full efficiency; for it is undeniable that national questions must be solved by the joint action of the people and their elected legislative representatives.

1. *Legislators display an inclination to "wait on" public opinion to shape itself before dealing formally with questions.* This does not mean that senators were content merely to follow the lead of public opinion, for many made an effort to mold opinion to their way of thinking through radio addresses and personal appearances. It does mean that the great majority of senators were keenly aware of the existence of public opinion and hesitant to take action so long as its final direction was not absolutely certain. Although many senators committed themselves publicly during the course of the debate, at no time did either side show determination to force a showdown on the floor of the Senate, such hesitation seeming to stem from the uncertain condition of public opinion, which never registered above 50 per cent either for or against the proposal.

The function of the Senate Judiciary Committee as a sounding board is interesting. As long as any doubt remained about public sentiment toward the bill, the committee remained in session, and only when it was perfectly plain that public support for the proposal would not be forthcoming did it make its unfavorable report. During the extended period of public hearings, an amazing array of witnesses appeared before the committee and every possible type of argument for and against the proposal was brought forth. Doubtless this varied array of witnesses gave to the senators valuable clues as to public feeling on the proposal, and it was on the basis of testimony offered before the committee that Senators Hatch, McCarran, and O'Mahoney announced their opposition to the bill. The most useful function of the committee seems to have been to hold in abeyance the necessity of making a formal decision while senators waited in the hope that public opinion would develop in a decisive direction and render unnecessary a decision on the Senate floor.

2. *Events played a more important rôle than Congress or the President in shaping the direction of public opinion.* The six leading determinants of opinion in the debate were: (1) the President's Victory Dinner speech and fireside chat on the fourth and eighth of March; (2) the opening of the Administration case before the Senate Judiciary Committee on March 9; (3) the opening of opposition arguments against the proposal before the committee on March 22; (4) the decision of the Supreme Court overruling an earlier decision in the Adkins v. Children's Hospital case on March 29, which paved the way for federal minimum wage legislation and broke the succession of anti-New Deal decisions handed down by the Court;

(5) Washington reports, beginning on May 10, that Justices Brandeis and Van Devanter were planning to retire; and (6) the retirement on May 18 of Justice Van Devanter.

Of these six steps in the downfall of the Court proposal, three were attempts by government officials (the President and senators) to mobilize opinion in a particular direction. The other three were events in the sense of being unanticipated happenings beyond the province of either proponents or opponents of the proposal. While the President's speeches and the arguments given before the Senate Judiciary Committee affected public opinion measurably, they were incapable of affecting it decisively. The major event in opinion-determination was the decision of the Court in the Adkins case. From the time of this decision, the public Yes vote dropped off steadily, while the No vote rose. The second most important step in opinion-determination was the retirement of Justice Van Devanter, with the effect of crystallizing opinion which had been drifting into indecision as the debate wore on. As Cantril has said, "opinion is generally determined more by events than by words—unless those words are themselves interpreted as an 'event.'"[1]

3. *Public opinion cannot propose a course of action, and a healthy public opinion requires leadership.* Throughout the course of the debate public opinion was responsive to political moves and events. At no time was there observable any great spontaneous movement of opinion in a direction which would have indicated to legislators the necessity for taking a particular course of action that would have broken the deadlock. It is characteristic of public opinion that it cannot generate a proposal or series of proposals serving to satisfy its needs. Public opinion can indicate very powerfully the general area of its needs, but it remains for an individual or group of individuals to come forward with specific proposals toward which opinion can display approval or disapproval. We have seen how, during the course of the debate, the public support that fell away from both the Yes and No sides of the discussion tended to gather in the No Opinion category, where it remained in a state of indecision awaiting some new determining factor that would move it once more into the realm of decision. Those legislators who waited in the hope that public opinion would show them the way were waiting in vain. Public opinion in a democracy responds to leadership, and needs the stimulus of leadership in order to crystallize one way or the other on specific proposals. Legislators are perfectly correct in sounding opinion so that they may determine whether or not they are moving in a direction calculated to meet popular needs. It is completely fallacious for legislators to wait on public opinion to tell them what to do, because public opinion waits on leadership to supply the grist of fact and suggestion so that it can fulfill its function, which is the acceptance or rejection of proposals. In a sentence, when faced with a specific problem, public opinion will respond to proposals, but cannot generate them; generation of proposals is the function of the legislators.

[1] Hadley Cantril, *Gauging Public Opinion* (Princeton, 1944), p. 226.

16. STEREOTYPES
by Walter Lippmann *

1

Each of us lives and works on a small part of the earth's surface, moves in a small circle, and of these acquaintances knows only a few intimately. Of any public event that has wide effects we see at best only a phase and an aspect. This is as true of the eminent insiders who draft treaties, make laws, and issue orders, as it is of those who have treaties framed for them, laws promulgated to them, orders given at them. Inevitably our opinions cover a bigger space, a longer reach of time, a greater number of things, than we can directly observe. They have, therefore, to be pieced together out of what others have reported and what we can imagine.

Yet even the eyewitness does not bring back a naïve picture of the scene.[1] For experience seems to show that he himself brings something to the scene which later he takes away from it, that oftener than not what he imagines to be the account of an event is really a transfiguration of it. Few facts in consciousness seem to be merely given. Most facts in consciousness seem to be partly made. A report is the joint product of the knower and known, in which the rôle of the observer is always selective and usually creative. The facts we see depend on where we are placed, and the habits of our eyes.

An unfamiliar scene is like the baby's world, "one great, blooming, buzzing confusion."[2] This is the way, says Mr. John Dewey,[3] that any new thing strikes an adult, so far as the thing is really new and strange. "Foreign languages that we do not understand always seem jibberings, babblings, in which it is impossible to fix a definite, clear-cut, individualized

---

* Author, newspaper columnist, and former editor. Author of *A Preface to Politics, Public Opinion, The Phantom Public, A Preface to Morals, The Public Philosophy,* and numerous other works. The selection is from pp. 79-96 of Walter Lippmann, *Public Opinion,* copyright 1922 by The Macmillan Company, New York, and is used with the publisher's permission.

[1] *E. g. cf. Edmond Locard, L'Enquête Criminelle et les Méthodes Scientifiques.* A great deal of interesting material has been gathered in late years on the credibility of the witness, which shows, as an able reviewer of Dr. Locard's book says in *The Times* (London) Literary Supplement (August 18, 1921), that credibility varies as to classes of witnesses and classes of events, and also as to type of perception. Thus, perceptions of touch, odor, and taste have low evidential value. Our hearing is defective and arbitrary when it judges the source and direction of sound, and in listening to the talk of other people "words which are not heard will be supplied by the witness in all good faith. He will have a theory of the purport of the conversation, and will arrange the sounds he heard to fit it." Even visual perceptions are liable to great error, as in identification, recognition, judgment of distance, estimates of numbers, for example, the size of a crowd. In the untrained observer, the sense of time is highly variable. All these original weaknesses are complicated by tricks of memory, and the incessant creative quality of the imagination. *Cf.* also Sherrington, *The Integrative Action of the Nervous System,* pp. 318-327.

The late Professor Hugo Münsterberg wrote a popular book on this subject called *On the Witness Stand.*

[2] Wm. James, *Principles of Psychology,* vol. 1, p. 488.

[3] John Dewey, *How We Think,* p. 121.

group of sounds. The countryman in the crowded street, the landlubber at sea, the ignoramus in sport at a contest between experts in a complicated game, are further instances. Put an inexperienced man in a factory, and at first the work seems to him a meaningless medley. All strangers of another race proverbially look alike to the visiting stranger. Only gross differences of size or color are perceived by an outsider in a flock of sheep, each of which is perfectly individualized to the shepherd. A diffusive blur and an indiscriminately shifting suction characterize what we do not understand. The problem of the acquisition of meaning by things, or (stated in another way) of forming habits of simple apprehension, is thus the problem of introducing (1) *definiteness* and *distinction* and (2) *consistency* or *stability* of meaning into what is otherwise vague and wavering."

But the kind of definiteness and consistency introduced depends upon who introduces them. In a later passage[4] Dewey gives an example of how differently an experienced layman and a chemist might define the word metal. "Smoothness, hardness, glossiness, and brilliancy, heavy weight for its size . . . the serviceable properties of capacity for being hammered and pulled without breaking, of being softened by heat and hardened by cold, of retaining the shape and form given, of resistance to pressure and decay, would probably be included" in the layman's definition. But the chemist would likely as not ignore these esthetic and utilitarian qualities, and define a metal as "any chemical element that enters into combination with oxygen so as to form a base."

For the most part we do not first see, and then define, we define first and then see. In the great blooming, buzzing confusion of the outer world we pick out what our culture has already defined for us, and we tend to perceive that which we have picked out in the form stereotyped for us by our culture. Of the great men who assembled at Paris to settle the affairs of mankind, how many were there who were able to see much of the Europe about them, rather than their commitments about Europe? Could anyone have penetrated the mind of M. Clemenceau, would he have found there images of the Europe of 1919, or a great sediment of stereotyped ideas accumulated and hardened in a long and pugnacious existence? Did he see the Germans of 1919, or the German type as he had learned to see it since 1871? He saw the type, and among the reports that came to him from Germany, he took to heart those reports, and, it seems, those only, which fitted the type that was in his mind. If a junker blustered, that was an authentic German; if a labor leader confessed the guilt of the empire, he was not an authentic German.

At a Congress of Psychology in Göttingen an interesting experiment was made with a crowd of presumably trained observers.[5]

Not far from the hall in which the Congress was sitting there was a public fête with a masked ball. Suddenly the door of the hall was thrown open and

---

[4] *Op. cit.,* p. 133.

[5] A. von Gennep, *La formation des légendes*, pp. 158-159. Cited F. van Langenhove, *The Growth of a Legend*, pp. 120-122.

a clown rushed in madly pursued by a negro, revolver in hand. They stopped in the middle of the room fighting; the clown fell, the negro leapt upon him, fired, and then both rushed out of the hall. The whole incident hardly lasted twenty seconds.

The President asked those present to write immediately a report since there was sure to be a judicial inquiry. Forty reports were sent in. Only one had less than 20% of mistakes in regard to the principal facts; fourteen had 20% to 40% of mistakes; twelve from 40% to 50%; thirteen more than 50%. Moreover in twenty-four accounts 10% of the details were pure inventions and this proportion was exceeded in ten accounts and diminished in six. Briefly a quarter of the accounts were false.

It goes without saying that the whole scene had been arranged and even photographed in advance. The ten false reports may then be relegated to the category of tales and legends; twenty-four accounts are half legendary, and six have a value approximating to exact evidence.

Thus out of forty trained observers writing a responsible account of a scene that had just happened before their eyes, more than a majority saw a scene that had not taken place. What then did they see? One would suppose it was easier to tell what had occurred, than to invent something which had not occurred. They saw their stereotype of such a brawl. All of them had in the course of their lives acquired a series of images of brawls, and these images flickered before their eyes. In one man these images displaced less than 20% of the actual scene, in thirteen men more than half. In thirty-four out of the forty observers the stereotypes preëmpted at least one-tenth of the scene.

A distinguished art critic has said[6] that "what with the almost numberless shapes assumed by an object. . . . What with our insensitiveness and inattention, things scarcely would have for us features and outlines so determined and clear that we could recall them at will, but for the stereotyped shapes art has lent them." The truth is even broader than that, for the stereotyped shapes lent to the world come not merely from art, in the sense of painting and sculpture and literature, but from our moral codes and our social philosophies and our political agitations as well. Substitute in the following passage of Mr. Berenson's the words "politics," "business," and "society," for the word "art" and the sentences will be no less true: ". . . unless years devoted to the study of all schools of art have taught us also to see with our own eyes, we soon fall into the habit of moulding whatever we look at into the forms borrowed from the one art with which we are acquainted. There is our standard of artistic reality. Let anyone give us shapes and colors which we cannot instantly match in our paltry stock of hackneyed forms and tints, and we shake our heads at his failure to reproduce things as we know they certainly are, or we accuse him of insincerity."

Mr. Berenson speaks of our displeasure when a painter "does not visualize objects exactly as we do," and of the difficulty of appreciating the art of the Middle Ages because since then "our manner of visualizing forms

[6] Bernard Berenson, *The Central Italian Painters of the Renaissance*, pp. 60 *et seq.*

has changed in a thousand ways."[7] He goes on to show how in regard to the human figure we have been taught to see what we do see.

> Created by Donatello and Masaccio, and sanctioned by the Humanists, the new canon of the human figure, the new cast of features . . . presented to the ruling classes of that time the type of human being most likely to win the day in the combat of human forces. . . . Who had the power to break through this new standard of vision and, out of the chaos of things, to select shapes more definitely expressive of reality than those fixed by men of genius? No one had such power. People had perforce to see things in that way and in no other, and to see only the shapes depicted, to love only the ideals presented. . . .[8]

2

If we cannot fully understand the acts of other people, until we know what they think they know, then in order to do justice we have to appraise not only the information which has been at their disposal, but the minds through which they have filtered it. For the accepted types, the current patterns, the standard versions, intercept information on its way to consciousness. Americanization, for example, is superficially at least the substitution of American for European stereotypes. Thus the peasant who might see his landlord as if he were the lord of the manor, his employer as he saw the local magnate, is taught by Americanization to see the landlord and employer according to American standards. This constitutes a change of mind, which is, in effect, when the inoculation succeeds, a change of vision. His eye sees differently. One kindly gentlewoman has confessed that the stereotypes are of such overweening importance, that when hers are not indulged, she at least in unable to accept the brotherhood of man and the fatherhood of God:

> We are strangely affected by the clothes we wear. Garments create a mental and social atmosphere. What can be hoped for the Americanism of a man who insists on employing a London tailor? One's very food affects his Americanism. What kind of American consciousness can grow in the atmosphere of sauerkraut and Limburger cheese? Or what can you expect of the Americanism of the man whose breath always reeks of garlic?[9]

This lady might well have been the patron of a pageant which a friend of mine once attended. It was called the Melting Pot, and it was given on the Fourth of July in an automobile town where many foreign-born workers are employed. In the center of the baseball park at second base stood

---

[7] *Cf.* also his comment on *Dante's Visual Images, and his Early Illustrators* in *The Study and Criticism of Italian Art* (First Series), p. 13. "*We* cannot help dressing Virgil as a Roman, and giving him a 'classical profile' and 'statuesque carriage,' but Dante's visual image of Virgil was probably no less mediaeval, no more based on a critical reconstruction of antiquity, than his entire conception of the Roman poet. Fourteenth Century illustrators make Virgil look like a mediaeval scholar, dressed in cap and gown, and there is no reason why Dante's visual image of him should have been other than this."

[8] *The Central Italian Painters*, pp. 66-67.

[9] Cited by Mr. Edward Hale Bierstadt, *New Republic*, June 1, 1921, p. 21.

a huge wooden and canvas pot. There were flights of steps up to the rim on two sides. After the audience had settled itself, and the band had played, a procession came through an opening at one side of the field. It was made up of men of all the foreign nationalities employed in the factories. They wore their native costumes, they were singing their national songs; they danced their folk dances, and carried the banners of all Europe. The master of ceremonies was the principal of the grade school dressed as Uncle Sam. He led them to the pot. He directed them up the steps to the rim, and inside. He called them out again on the other side. They came, dressed in derby hats, coats, pants, vest, stiff collar and polka-dot tie, undoubtedly, said my friend, each with an Eversharp pencil in his pocket, and all singing the Star-Spangled Banner.

To the promoters of this pageant, and probably to most of the actors, it seemed as if they had managed to express the most intimate difficulty to friendly association between the older peoples of America and the newer. The contradiction of their stereotypes interfered with the full recognition of their common humanity. The people who change their names know this. They mean to change themselves, and the attitude of strangers toward them.

There is, of course, some connection between the scene outside and the mind through which we watch it, just as there are some long-haired men and short-haired women in radical gatherings. But to the hurried observer a slight connection is enough. If there are two bobbed heads and four beards in the audience, it will be a bobbed and bearded audience to the reporter who knows beforehand that such gatherings are composed of people with these tastes in the management of their hair. There is a connection between our vision and the facts, but it is often a strange connection. A man has rarely looked at a landscape, let us say, except to examine its possibilities for division into building lots, but he has seen a number of landscapes hanging in the parlor. And from them he has learned to think of a landscape as a rosy sunset, or as a country road with a church steeple and a silver moon. One day he goes to the country, and for hours he does not see a single landscape. Then the sun goes down looking rosy. At once he recognizes a landscape and exclaims that it is beautiful. But two days later, when he tries to recall what he saw, the odds are that he will remember chiefly some landscape in a parlor.

Unless he has been drunk or dreaming or insane he did see a sunset, but he saw in it, and above all remembers from it, more of what the oil painting taught him to observe, than what an impressionist painter, for example, or a cultivated Japanese would have seen and taken away with him. And the Japanese and the painter in turn will have seen and remembered more of the form they had learned, unless they happen to be the very rare people who find fresh sight for mankind. In untrained observation we pick recognizable signs out of the environment. The signs stand for ideas, and these ideas we fill out with our stock of images. We do not so much see this man and that sunset; rather we notice that the thing is man or sunset, and then see chiefly what our mind is already full of on those subjects.

3

There is economy in this. For the attempt to see all things freshly and in detail, rather than as types and generalities, is exhausting, and among busy affairs practically out of the question. In a circle of friends, and in relation to close associates or competitors, there is no shortcut through, and no substitute for, an individualized understanding. Those whom we love and admire most are the men and women whose consciousness is peopled thickly with persons rather than with types, who know us rather than the classification into which we might fit. For even without phrasing it to ourselves, we feel intuitively that all classification is in relation to some purpose not necessarily our own; that between two human beings no association has final dignity in which each does not take the other as an end in himself. There is a taint on any contact between two people which does not affirm as an axiom the personal inviolability of both.

But modern life is hurried and multifarious, above all physical distance separates men who are often in vital contact with each other, such as employer and employee, official and voter. There is neither time nor opportunity for intimate acquaintance. Instead we notice a trait which marks a well known type, and fill in the rest of the picture by means of the stereotypes we carry about in our heads. He is an agitator. That much we notice, or are told. Well, an agitator is this sort of person, and so *he* is this sort of person. He is an intellectual. He is a plutocrat. He is a foreigner. He is a "South European." He is from Back Bay. He is a Harvard Man. How different from the statement: he is a Yale Man. He is a regular fellow. He is a West Pointer. He is an old army sergeant. He is a Greenwich Villager: what don't we know about him then, and about her? He is an international banker. He is from Main Street.

The subtlest and most pervasive of all influences are those which create and maintain the repertory of stereotypes. We are told about the world before we see it. We imagine most things before we experience them. And those preconceptions, unless education has made us acutely aware, govern deeply the whole process of perception. They mark out certain objects as familiar or strange, emphasizing the difference, so that the slightly familiar is seen as very familiar, and the somewhat strange as sharply alien. They are aroused by small signs, which may vary from a true index to a vague analogy. Aroused, they flood fresh vision with older images, and project into the world what has been resurrected in memory. Were there no practical uniformities in the environment, there would be no economy and only error in the human habit of accepting foresight for sight. But there are uniformities sufficiently accurate, and the need of economizing attention is so inevitable, that the abandonment of all stereotypes for a wholly innocent approach to experience would impoverish human life.

What matters is the character of the stereotypes, and the gullibility with which we employ them. And these in the end depend upon those inclusive patterns which constitute our philosophy of life. If in that philosophy we assume that the world is codified according to a code which we possess, we are likely to make our reports of what is going on describe a world run by our code. But if our philosophy tells us that each man is only a small part of the world, that his intelligence catches at best only phases and aspects in a coarse net of ideas, then, when we use our stereotypes, we tend to know that they are only stereotypes, to hold them lightly, to modify them gladly. We tend, also, to realize more and more clearly when our ideas started, where they started, how they came to us, why we accepted them. All useful history is antiseptic in this fashion. It enables us to know what fairy tale, what school book, what tradition, what novel, play, picture, phrase, planted one preconception in this mind, another in that mind.

4

Those who wish to censor art do not at least underestimate this influence. They generally misunderstand it, and almost always they are absurdly bent on preventing other people from discovering anything not sanctioned by them. But at any rate, like Plato in his argument about the poets, they feel vaguely that the types acquired through fiction tend to be imposed on reality. Thus there can be little doubt that the moving picture is steadily building up imagery which is then evoked by the words people read in their newspapers. In the whole experience of the race there has been no aid to visualization comparable to the cinema. If a Florentine wished to visualize the saints, he could go to the frescoes in his church, where he might see a vision of saints standardized for his time by Giotto. If an Athenian wished to visualize the gods he went to the temples. But the number of objects which were pictured was not great. And in the East, where the spirit of the second commandment was widely accepted, the portraiture of concrete things was even more meager, and for that reason perhaps the faculty of practical decision was by so much reduced. In the western world, however, during the last few centuries there has been an enormous increase in the volume and scope of secular description, the word picture, the narrative, the illustrated narrative, and finally the moving picture and, perhaps, the talking picture.

Photographs have the kind of authority over imagination to-day, which the printed word had yesterday, and the spoken word before that. They seem utterly real. They come, we imagine, directly to us without human meddling, and they are the most effortless food for the mind conceivable. Any description in words, or even any inert picture, requires an effort of memory before a picture exists in the mind. But on the screen the whole process of observing, describing, reporting, and then imagining, has been accomplished for you. Without more trouble than is needed to stay awake the result which your imagination is always aiming at is reeled off on the screen. The shadowy idea becomes vivid; your hazy notion, let us say, of the Ku Klux Klan, thanks to Mr. Griffiths, takes vivid shape when you see the Birth of a Nation. Historically it may be the wrong shape, morally it may be a pernicious shape, but it is a shape, and I doubt whether anyone who has seen the film and does not know more about the Ku Klux Klan than Mr. Griffiths, will ever hear the name again without seeing those white horsemen.

5

And so when we speak of the mind of a group of people, of the French mind, the militarist mind, the bolshevik mind, we are liable to serious confusion unless we agree to separate the instinctive equipment from the stereotypes, the patterns, and the formulae which play so decisive a part in building up the mental world to which the native character is adapted and responds. Failure to make this distinction accounts for oceans of loose talk about collective minds, national souls, and race psychology. To be sure a stereotype may be so consistently and authoritatively transmitted in each generation from parent to child that it seems almost like a biological fact. In some respects, we may indeed have become, as Mr. Wallas says,[10] biologically parasitic upon our social heritage. But certainly there is not the least scientific evidence which would enable anyone to argue that men are born with the political habits of the country in which they are born. In so far as political habits are alike in a nation, the first places to look for an explanation are the nursery, the school, the church, not in that limbo inhabited by Group Minds and National Souls. Until you have thoroughly failed to see tradition being handed on from parents, teachers, priests, and uncles, it is a solecism of the worst order to ascribe political differences to the germ plasm.

It is possible to generalize tentatively and with a decent humility about comparative differences within the same category of education and experience. Yet even this is a tricky enterprise. For almost no two experiences are exactly alike, not even of two children in the same household. The older son never does have the experience of being the younger. And therefore, until we are able to discount the difference in nurture, we must withhold judgment about differences of nature. As well judge the productivity of two soils by comparing their yield before you know which is in Labrador and which in Iowa, whether they have been cultivated and enriched, exhausted, or allowed to run wild.

6

There is another reason, besides economy of effort, why we so often hold to our stereotypes when we might pursue a more disinterested vision. The systems of stereotypes may be the core of our personal tradition, the defenses of our position in society.

They are an ordered, more or less consistent picture of the world, to which our habits, our tastes, our capacities, our comforts and our hopes have adjusted themselves. They may not be a complete picture of the world, but they are a picture of a possible world to which we are adapted. In that world people and things have their well-known places, and do certain expected things. We feel at home there. We fit in. We are members. We know the way around. There we find the charm of the familiar, the normal, the dependable; its grooves and shapes are where we are accustomed to find them. And though we have abandoned much that might have tempted

[10] Graham Wallas, *Our Social Heritage*, p. 17.

us before we creased ourselves into that mould, once we are firmly in, it fits as snugly as an old shoe.

No wonder, then, that any disturbance of the stereotypes seems like an attack upon the foundations of the universe. It is an attack upon the foundations of *our* universe, and, where big things are at stake, we do not readily admit that there is any distinction between our universe and the universe. A world which turns out to be one in which those we honor are unworthy, and those we despise are noble, is nerve-racking. There is anarchy if our order of precedence is not the only possible one. For if the meek should indeed inherit the earth, if the first should be last, if those who are without sin alone may cast a stone, if to Caesar you render only the things that are Caesar's, then the foundations of self-respect would be shaken for those who have arranged their lives as if these maxims were not true.

A pattern of stereotypes is not neutral. It is not merely a way of substituting order for the great blooming, buzzing confusion of reality. It is not merely a short cut. It is all these things and something more. It is the guarantee of our self-respect; it is the projection upon the world of our own sense of our own value, our own position and our own rights. The stereotypes are, therefore, highly charged with the feelings that are attached to them. They are the fortress of our tradition, and behind its defenses we can continue to feel ourselves safe in the position we occupy.

CHAPTER III

The Mass Media:
The Role of the Press

With 58 million newspapers entering American homes daily, the fourth estate remains perhaps the most important single informational instrument in the nation. Television is pressing it hard, as Marya Mannes points out, but even TV commentators get most of their day-by-day education from the press. It is hard to imagine a future in which newspapers did not play an impressive role in educating the public about the complex, frightening, and exhilarating world in which we live.

Whether newspaper performance equals the challenge of its time is another question. The press has never been without its staunch defenders, men like Thomas Jefferson, e.g., nor has it lacked bitter critics, men like Thomas Jefferson, e.g. In both past and present, defenders and critics have something valid to say in support of their position.

Certainly, the international news services have some exceedingly capable and responsible journalists on their staffs. Newspapers like the *New York Times*, the *New York Herald Tribune*, the *Milwaukee Journal*, the *Atlanta Constitution*, the *Baltimore Sun*, the *Christian Science Monitor*, the *Denver Post*, and the *Louisville Courier-Journal* set a very high standard indeed. Equally certain, to cite Miss Mannes again, the great majority of United States newspapers fall dismally below the standard set by the better papers.

Louis Seltzer, although an editor himself, deplores the lack of really vigorous newspaper probing into local conditions which might involve treading on sensitive toes. Other responsible critics have pointed out that the press frequently is mousy, unimaginative, obsessed with trivia, crime, and scandal, and—most grievous of journalistic crimes—indisposed to give its readers a sufficiently large amount of raw news on national and international events to enable them to form tolerably intelligent opinions.

The press revels in its opportunity (and obligation) to sit in judgment on men, policies, and institutions. But it reacts with surprising indignation when it is attacked by "outsiders." For example, the Commission on Freedom of the Press, composed of some of the most eminent figures in the academic world, made some forthright remarks about the conduct of the press in 1947. In 1955, the chairman of the commission, Robert Hutchins, observed to the American Society of Newspaper Editors that "You were furious. Your president issued a statement in six paragraphs, in three of which he stated that the members of the Commission were 'left-wing' and in all of which he stated his conviction that, since most of the members of the Commission were professors without experience in the newspaper business, nothing they said could be of any importance, although it might be dangerous. . . ." Mr. Hutchins further observed: "A kind of neurotic sensitivity is characteristic of the press throughout the English-speaking world. The British papers were outraged by the report of the Royal Commission on the Press, which was almost as mild as ours. I don't know what makes you feel this way."[1]

The press gets considerable criticism as a collective entity but precious little on a paper-by-paper basis by responsible students. In the absence of an independent agency "to appraise and report annually upon the performance of the press," as the Hutchins Commission recommended, Professor Christenson has suggested closer scrutiny of the political role of the American newspaper in local affairs. His study dealt with the *Toledo Blade*, whose publisher, Paul Block, Jr., makes a cogent defense of the monopoly newspaper in America.

Mr. Block's views correspond closely to those of a number of writers who find no correlation between the degree of newspaper competition in a city and the quality of journalism in that city. It is not uncommon for observers, in listing what are believed to be the better United States newspapers, to invite attention to the sizable number of these which operate in one-publisher cities.

Others look less tolerantly on the trend to a monopoly press, believing that whatever reduces the number of independent voices in the community tends to reduce the diversity and clash of opinion which is so vital to a democracy. While some have deplored the effects of the great international news-gathering agencies in standardizing much of the news from coast to coast, Louis Lyons focuses on the commanding role of the newspaper chains in seizing control of so many approaches to the public mind. Mr. Lyons is disturbed by the dimensions and implications of "chain-store journalism" and by the dimming prospects for good journalism in general.

Then there is the question of the "one-party press," as Adlai Stevenson reminded the newspaper editors in 1952. The press is overwhelmingly Republican, which would seem to place Democratic presidential aspirants under a perennially heavy handicap. But if the editorial page has as little influence on presidential elections as it sometimes appears, perhaps the Democrats can rest more easily. Jefferson, Jackson, Wilson, Franklin D. Roosevelt, Truman, and Kennedy marched into the White House through withering fire from most of the nation's newspaper editors.

Others have wondered, however, if their majorities (or pluralities) might not have been substantially greater had the press been more equally divided. And not a few have speculated that the unprecedented popularity of Mr. Eisenhower in 1960, considering the decline of presidential prestige which normally occurs over two terms, was achieved at least in part because of the remarkably kid-gloved treatment he had received at the hands of the press—including *Time* Magazine. Ben Bagdikian's carefully documented study of the editorial slants in Henry Luce's influential weekly

[1] Speech by Robert M. Hutchins before The American Society of Newspaper Editors, Washington, D.C., Apr. 21, 1955.

suggest that this medium may have contributed something to the Eisenhower phenomenon. Mr. Bagdikian's comments on *U.S. News & World Report* call attention to a different kind of bias—quantitative bias and bias based on concepts of newsworthiness.

Although the number of newspaper and competitive cities steadily declines in America, the press remains a vigorous and vital institution. Its vitality will probably persist if it can attract able young people into journalism (better pay would help!), if critics continue to evaluate its performance, and if publishers never forget that the First Amendment's guarantee of freedom of the press reflected the Founding Fathers' assumption that the press is a public trust—not just another commercial enterprise.

17. A FOUNDING FATHER'S VARIOUS VIEWS

by Thomas Jefferson

To Carrington, 1787

I am persuaded myself that the good sense of the people will always be found to be the best army. They may be led astray for a moment, but will soon correct themselves. The people are the only censors of their governors; and even their errors will tend to keep these to the true principles of their institution. To punish these errors too severely would be to suppress the only safeguard of the public liberty. The way to prevent these irregular interpositions of the people, is to give them full information of their affairs through the channel of the public papers, and to contrive that those papers should penetrate the whole mass of the people. The basis of our governments being the opinion of the people, the very first object should be to keep that right; and were it left to me to decide whether we should have a government without newspapers, or newspapers without a government, I should not hesitate a moment to prefer the latter. But I should mean that every man should receive those papers, and be capable of reading them. I am convinced that those societies (as the Indians) which live without government, enjoy in their general mass an infinitely greater degree of happiness than those who live under the European governments. Among the former, public opinion is in the place of law, and restrains morals as powerfully as laws ever did anywhere. Among the latter, under pretense of governing, they have divided their nations into two classes, wolves and sheep. I do not exaggerate. This is a true picture of Europe. Cherish, therefore, the spirit of our people, and keep alive their attention. Do not be too severe upon their errors, but reclaim them by enlightening them. If once they become inattentive to the public affairs, you and I, and Congress and Assemblies, Judges and Governors, shall all become wolves. It seems to be the law of our general nature, in spite of individual exceptions; and experience declares that man is the only animal which devours his own kind; for I can apply no milder term to the governments of Europe, and to the general prey of the rich on the poor.

To J. Norvell, 1807

It is a melancholy truth, that a suppression of the press could not more completely deprive the nation of its benefits, than is done by its abandoned prostitution to falsehood. Nothing can now be believed which is seen in a newspaper. Truth itself becomes suspicious by being put into that polluted vehicle. The real extent of this state of misinformation is known only to those who are in situations to confront facts within their knowledge with the lies of the day. I really look with commiseration over the great body of my fellow citizens, who, reading newspapers, live and die in the belief, that they have known something of what has been passing in the world in their time; whereas the accounts they have read in newspapers are just as true a history of any other period of the world as of the present, except that the real names of the day are affixed to their fables. General facts may indeed be collected from them, such as that Europe is now at war, that Bonaparte has been a successful warrior . . . , but no details can be relied on. I will add, that the man who never looks into a newspaper is better informed than he who reads them; inasmuch as he who knows nothing is nearer to truth than he whose mind is filled with falsehoods and errors. . . .

Perhaps an editor might begin a reformation in some such way as this. Divide his paper into four chapters, heading the 1st, Truths. 2d, Probabilities. 3d, Possibilities. 4th, Lies. The first chapter would be very short.

18.   WHAT THE PRESS SHOULD BE— AND WHAT THE PRESS IS

The Commission on Freedom of the Press *

. . . Today our society needs, first, a truthful, comprehensive, and intelligent account of the day's events in a context which gives them meaning; second, a forum for the exchange of comment and criticism; third, a means of projecting the opinions and attitudes of the groups in the society to one another; fourth, a method of presenting and clarifying the goals and values of the society; and, fifth, a way of reaching every member of the society by the currents of information, thought, and feeling which the press supplies.

The Commission has no idea that these five ideal demands can ever be completely met. All of them cannot be met by any one medium; some do not apply at all to a particular unit; nor do all apply with equal relevance to all parts of the communications industry. The Commission does not suppose that these standards will be new to the managers of the press; they are drawn largely from their professions and practices.

* Reprinted from *A Free and Responsible Press* by the Commission on Freedom of the Press, the University of Chicago Press, Chicago, 1947, pp. 20-29, 52-62, 65-68. By permission of the University of Chicago Press.

A TRUTHFUL, COMPREHENSIVE, AND INTELLIGENT ACCOUNT
OF THE DAY'S EVENTS IN A CONTEXT WHICH GIVES THEM MEANING

The first requirement is that the media should be accurate. They should not lie.

Here the first link in the chain of responsibility is the reporter at the source of the news. He must be careful and competent. He must estimate correctly which sources are most authoritative. He must prefer firsthand observation to hearsay. He must know what questions to ask, what things to observe, and which items to report. His employer has the duty of training him to do his work as it ought to be done.

Of equal importance with reportorial accuracy are the identification of fact as fact and opinion as opinion, and their separation, so far as possible. This is necessary all the way from the reporter's file, up through the copy and makeup desks and editorial offices, to the final, published product. The distinction cannot, of course, be made absolute. There is no fact without a context and no factual report which is uncolored by the opinions of the reporter. But modern conditions require greater effort than ever to make the distinction between fact and opinion. In a simpler order of society published accounts of events within the experience of the community could be compared with other sources of information. Today this is usually impossible. The account of an isolated fact, however accurate in itself, may be misleading and, in effect, untrue.

The greatest danger here is in the communication of information internationally. The press now bears a responsibility in all countries, and particularly in democratic countries, where foreign policies are responsive to popular majorities, to report international events in such a way that they can be understood. It is no longer enough to report *the fact* truthfully. It is now necessary to report *the truth about the fact*.

In this country a similar obligation rests upon the press in reporting domestic news. The country has many groups which are partially insulated from one another and which need to be interpreted to one another. Factually correct but substantially untrue accounts of the behavior of members of one of these social islands can intensify the antagonisms of others toward them. A single incident will be accepted as a sample of group action unless the press has given a flow of information and interpretation concerning the relations between two racial groups such as to enable the reader to set a single event in its proper perspective. If it is allowed to pass as a sample of such action, the requirement that the press present an accurate account of the day's events in a context which gives them meaning has not been met.

A FORUM FOR THE EXCHANGE OF COMMENT AND CRITICISM

The second requirement means that the great agencies of mass communication should regard themselves as common carriers of public discussion. The units of the press have in varying degrees assumed this function and should assume the responsibilities which go with it, more generally and more explicitly.

It is vital to a free society that an idea should not be stifled by the circumstances of its birth. The press cannot and should not be expected to print everybody's ideas. But the giant units can and should assume the duty of publishing significant ideas contrary to their own, as a matter of objective reporting, distinct from their proper function of advocacy. Their control over the various ways of reaching the ear of America is such that, if they do not publish ideas which differ from their own, those ideas will never reach the ear of America. If that happens, one of the chief reasons for the freedom which these giants claim disappears.

Access to a unit of the press acting as a common carrier is possible in a number of ways, all of which, however, involve selection on the part of the managers of the unit. The individual whose views are not represented on an editorial page may reach an audience through a public statement reported as news, through a letter to the editor, through a statement printed in advertising space, or through a magazine article. But some seekers for space are bound to be disappointed and must resort to pamphlets or such duplicating devices as will spread their ideas to such public as will attend to them.

But all the important viewpoints and interests in the society should be represented in its agencies of mass communication. Those who have these viewpoints and interests cannot count on explaining them to their fellow-citizens through newspapers or radio stations of their own. Even if they could make the necessary investment, they could have no assurance that their publications would be read or their programs heard by the public outside their own adherents. An ideal combination would include general media, inevitably solicitous to present their own views, but setting forth other views fairly. As checks on their fairness, and partial safeguards against ignoring important matters, more specialized media of advocacy have a vital place. In the absence of such a combination the partially insulated groups in society will continue to be insulated. The unchallenged assumptions of each group will continue to harden into prejudice. The mass medium reaches across all groups; through the mass medium they can come to understand one another.

Whether a unit of the press is an advocate or a common carrier, it ought to identify the sources of its facts, opinions, and arguments so that the reader or listener can judge them. Persons who are presented with facts, opinions, and arguments are properly influenced by the general reliability of those who offer them. If the veracity of statements is to be appraised, those who offer them must be known.

Identification of source is necessary to a free society. Democracy, in time of peace, at least, has a justifiable confidence that full and free discussion will strengthen rather than weaken it. But, if the discussion is to have the effect for which democracy hopes, if it is to be really full and free, the names and the characters of the participants must not be hidden from view.

THE PROJECTION OF A REPRESENTATIVE PICTURE
OF THE CONSTITUENT GROUPS IN THE SOCIETY

This requirement is closely related to the two preceding. People make decisions in large part in terms of favorable or unfavorable images. They relate fact and opinion to stereotypes. Today the motion picture, the radio, the book, the magazine, the newspaper, and the comic strip are principal agents in creating and perpetuating these conventional conceptions. When the images they portray fail to present the social group truly, they tend to pervert judgment.

Such failure may occur indirectly and incidentally. Even if nothing is said about the Chinese in the dialogue of a film, yet if the Chinese appear in a succession of pictures as sinister drug addicts and militarists, an image of China is built which needs to be balanced by another. If the Negro appears in the stories published in magazines of national circulation only as a servant, if children figure constantly in radio dramas as impertinent and ungovernable brats—the image of the Negro and the American child is distorted. The plugging of special color and "hate" words in radio and press dispatches, in advertising copy, in news stories—such words as "ruthless," "confused," "bureaucratic"—performs inevitably the same image-making function.

Responsible performance here simply means that the images repeated and emphasized be such as are in total representative of the social group as it is. The truth about any social group, though it should not exclude its weaknesses and vices, includes also recognition of its values, its aspirations, and its common humanity. The Commission holds to the faith that if people are exposed to the inner truth of the life of a particular group, they will gradually build up respect for and understanding of it.

THE PRESENTATION AND CLARIFICATION OF THE
GOALS AND VALUES OF THE SOCIETY

The press has a similar responsibility with regard to the values and goals of our society as a whole. The mass media, whether or not they wish to do so, blur or clarify these ideals as they report the failings and achievements of every day. The Commission does not call upon the press to sentimentalize, to manipulate the facts for the purpose of painting a rosy picture. The Commission believes in realistic reporting of the events and forces that militate against the attainment of social goals as well as those which work for them. We must recognize, however, that the agencies of mass communication are an educational instrument, perhaps the most powerful there is; and they must assume a responsibility like that of educators in stating and clarifying the ideals toward which the community should strive.

FULL ACCESS TO THE DAY'S INTELLIGENCE

It is obvious that the amount of current information required by the citizens in a modern industrial society is far greater than that required in any earlier day. We do not assume that all citizens at all times will actually use all the material they receive. By necessity or choice large numbers of people voluntarily delegate analysis and decision to leaders whom they trust. Such leadership in our society is freely chosen and constantly changing; it is informal, unofficial, and flexible. Any citizen may at any time assume the power of decision. In this way government is carried on by consent.

But such leadership does not alter the need for the wide distribution of news and opinion. The leaders are not identified; we can inform them only by making information available to everybody....

Private enterprise in the field of communications has great achievements to its credit. The American press probably reaches as high a percentage of the population as that of any other country. Its technical equipment is certainly the best in the world. It has taken the lead in the introduction of many new techniques which have enormously increased the speed and the variety of communications. Whatever its shortcomings, the American press is less venal and less subservient to political and economic pressure than that of many other countries. The leading organs of the American press have achieved a standard of excellence unsurpassed anywhere in the world. It is necessary to keep these general comments in mind in order to see the criticisms which follow in the proper perspective.

The economic logic of private enterprise forces most units of the mass communications industry to seek an ever larger audience. The result is an omnibus product which includes something for everybody.

The communications industry, in building this omnibus, has not introduced new material into communication. It has transferred to mass communication what had formerly passed from person to person as gossip, rumor, and oral discussion. The oldest mass medium of which we have record, the *Acta diurna,* an official bulletin board publishing the news in the Rome of the first Caesars, was an omnibus vehicle including sports, crime, and other sensational events as well as news regarding public affairs and official propaganda. So, too, in England, when newspapers were strictly limited to serious intelligence for a small reading public, there was a literature of handbills and pamphlets specializing in crime news.

The American newspaper is now as much a medium of entertainment, specialized information, and advertising as it is of news. A solid evening of radio adds up to something like the reading of a mass-circulation newspaper except that the percentage of reporting and discussion of public affairs is even lower. It goes as low as zero in the case of some local stations, as low as 2 per cent in many, and up to 10 per cent in some network affiliates. The magazines of largest circulation provide a mixed menu of print, pictures, stories, articles, and gossip, to entertain and inform persons of all ages and tastes, with advertising occupying half or more of each issue. The motion picture, as everybody knows, has developed mainly and avowedly as a medium of mass entertainment.

We see, then, that information and discussion regarding public affairs are only a part, and often a minor part, of the output of the communications industry. On the other hand, such information and discussion as are included reach a far larger audience because of the low price which advertising and mass circulation make possible.

Information and discussion regarding public affairs, carried as a rider on the omnibus of mass communication, take on the character of the other passengers and become subject to the same laws that governed their selection: such information and discussion must be shaped so that they will pay their own way by attracting the maximum audience.

SCOOPS AND SENSATIONS

Hence the word "news" has come to mean something different from important new information. When a journalist says that a certain event is news, he does not mean that it is important in itself. Often it is; but about as often it is not. The journalist means by news something that has happened within the last few hours which will attract the interest of the customers. The criteria of interest are recency or firstness, proximity, combat, human interest, and novelty. Such criteria limit accuracy and significance.

The eager pursuit of these qualities is undoubtedly captivating to the participants, but to the world at large it seems often to lead to unfortunate excesses. The unauthorized "scoops"—at the end of the war, with announcements prematurely made only to be awkwardly withdrawn by the press associations and radio networks—unsettled people's confidence in the dependability of these news sources and marred the generally good war record of the press in safeguarding important announcements.

To attract the maximum audience, the press emphasizes the exceptional rather than the representative, the sensational rather than the significant. Many activities of the utmost social consequence lie below the surface of what are conventionally regarded as reportable incidents: more power machinery; fewer men tending machines; more hours of leisure; more schooling per child; decrease of intolerance; successful negotiation of labor contracts; increase of participation in music through the schools; increase in the sale of books of biography and history.

In most news media such matters are crowded out by stories of night-club murders, race riots, strike violence, and quarrels among public officials. The Commission does not object to the reporting of these incidents but to the preoccupation of the press with them. The press is preoccupied with them to such an extent that the citizen is not supplied the information and discussion he needs to discharge his responsibilities to the community.

The effort to attract the maximum audience means that each news account must be written to catch headlines. The result is not a continued story of the life of a people, but a series of vignettes, made to seem more significant than they really are. The sum of such discontinuous parts does not equal the whole because the parts have not been represented in their actual size and color in relation to the whole.

This was illustrated at the San Francisco Conference. This gathering necessarily followed a course governed by protocol; it involved proposal and counterproposal, preparation of texts, amendments and revisions, and eventual agreement by compromise.

On many days during the weeks the Conference was in session there was nothing to report. But the reporters had to send in their stories. Somehow there had to be news. The result on the lower levels was a series of personal items modeled after the Hollywood fan magazine and on the higher levels a distorted account of what took place. Because drama and tension were demanded by the editorial desks back home, drama and tension were manufactured at San Francisco. Hence calm was turned into the calm-before-the-storm. Silence became the silence-of-impending-conflict.

The passage of time became a portentous period of delay. So completely was the task of manufacturing suspense performed that, when after some weeks an acceptable charter was signed, the effect on newspaper readers was one of incredulous surprise. . . .

The worst offenders in this direction are to be found among the newspaper columnists and radio commentators. The members of this craft have come to perform an indispensable function in American public discussion. But they must attract the maximum audience, too. Some of them have thought that the way to do this is to supply the public with keyhole gossip, rumor, character assassination, and lies.

THE PRESSURE OF THE AUDIENCE

People seldom want to read or hear what does not please them; they seldom want others to read or hear what disagrees with their convictions or what presents an unfavorable picture of groups they belong to. When such groups are organized, they let the press know their objections to remarks concerning them. The press is therefore caught between its desire to please and extend its audience and its desire to give a picture of events and people as they really are.

The motion picture industry offers the most elaborate example of accommodation to the pressure of the audience. . . . This accommodation may not have gone quite so far as the present Code executive says it would have to go to satisfy all protestors: it has not limited the villain of the screen to "a native-born, white, American citizen, without a job, and without any political, social, religious, or fraternal affiliation of any kind." But pressure groups, because they have or are thought to have influence on attendance, have shaped the motion picture to their desires. Hollywood's efforts to develop the documentary film may be thwarted by its habit of yielding to this kind of intimidation.

Every branch of the communications industry is subject to the same sort of pressure. Publishers who stick to their guns have suffered for it. The managing editor of one of the principal papers of the country testified before the Commission that in his opinion his publication took a drop of more than 50,000 in circulation because of a policy displeasing to a well-organized pressure group.

It would be a mistake to assume that pressure is always bad just because it is pressure. Testimony before the Commission reveals that pressure groups often correct unconscious bias or mistakes and bring into view neglected areas of discussion. But the power of these groups and the importance of the mass media raise a serious question, to which we shall later return: How can a medium of communication which almost by definition must strive to please everybody perform the function which it should perform today?

THE BIAS OF OWNERS

The agencies of mass communication are big business, and their owners are big businessmen. The American consumers just prior to the war paid the forty thousand mass communication establishments nearly two and a half billion dollars for their services, representing one dollar out of every twenty-seven spent that year for all goods and services. The press is a large employer of labor. With its total wage and salary bill in the same year nearly a billion dollars, it provided about 4 per cent of the country's total salary and wage expenditures. The newspapers alone have more than 150,000 employees. The press is connected with other big business through the advertising of these businesses, upon which it depends for the major part of its revenue. The owners of the press, like the owners of other big businesses, are bank directors, bank borrowers, and heavy taxpayers in the upper brackets.

As William Allen White put it: "Too often the publisher of an American newspaper has made his money in some other calling than journalism. He is a rich man seeking power and prestige. He has the country club complex. The business manager of this absentee owner quickly is afflicted with the country club point of view. Soon the managing editor's wife nags him into it. And they all get the unconscious arrogance of conscious wealth. Therefore it is hard to get a modern American newspaper to go the distance necessary to print all the news about many topics." In the last thirty years, in Mr. White's opinion, newspapers "have veered from their traditional position as leaders of public opinion to mere peddlers and purveyors of news. . . . The newspapers have become commercial enterprises and hence fall into the current which is merging commercial enterprises along mercantile lines."

The same point is made with equal force by another distinguished editor, Virginius Dabney of the *Richmond Times-Dispatch* writing in the *Saturday Review of Literature:* "Today newspapers are Big Business, and they are run in that tradition. The publisher, who often knows little about the editorial side of the operation, usually is one of the leading business men in his community, and his editorial page, under normal circumstances, strongly reflects that point of view. Sometimes he gives his editor a free hand but far oftener he does not. He looks upon the paper primarily as a 'property' rather than as an instrument for public service." The typical American publisher, Mr. Dabney continues, "considers the important part of the paper to be the business management, and is convinced that so long as high salaries and lavish expenditures are made available ·to that management, the editorial department can drag along under a schedule of too much work and too little pay. Of course, such a publisher sees that the editorials in his paper are 'sound,' which is to say that they conform to his own weird views of society, and are largely unreadable."

Neither indictment is of universal application nor was it intended by its author to be so. There are, as Mr. Dabney says, "brilliant and honorable exceptions." But another highly respected editor, Erwin D. Canham of the *Christian Science Monitor,* thinks upper-bracket ownership and its big-business character important enough to stand at the head of his list of the "short-comings of today's American newspapers."

The published charges of distortion in the press resulting from the bias of its owners fall into the categories that might be expected. In 1935 the American Newspaper Publishers Association condemned the proposed Child Labor Amendment. The A.N.P.A. action with regard to the child labor provision of N.R.A. was characterized by the *St. Louis Star-Times* as "a disgrace to the newspaper industry." Bias is claimed against consumer co-operatives, against food and drug regulation, against Federal Trade Commission orders designed to suppress fraudulent advertising, and against F.C.C. regulations affecting newspaper-owned broadcasting stations. Other claims involve affiliations with suppliers of raw paper stock and their affiliations with electric power companies. Still others arise from the ownership of outside businesses by the owners of the press. Many people believe that the press is biased in matters of national fiscal policy.

ADVERTISING AND SALES TALK

One of the criticisms repeatedly made is that the press is dominated by its advertisers. The evidence of dictation of policy by advertisers is not impressive. Such dictation seems to occur among the weaker units. As a newspaper becomes financially stable, it becomes more independent and tends to resist pressure from advertisers. . . .

MUTUAL CRITICISM

One of the most effective ways of improving the press is blocked by the press itself. By a kind of unwritten law the press ignores the errors and misrepresentations, the lies and scandals, of which its members are guilty. The retraction by John O'Donnell in the *Washington Times-Herald* and *New York Daily News* of his widely resented statement that the victim of General Patton's slapping incident was a Jewish soldier and that because of this the General's later removal from area control in Germany was urged by prominent American leaders, also Jews, was mentioned by only one other daily newspaper in New York. Mayor La Guardia, when he was in office, freely criticized the press and was as freely quoted in the New York papers. After he became a columnist and commentator, he specialized in criticism of what he regarded as the inaccuracy and misrepresentation of the press. But he ceased to be news. He was met with almost complete silence.

If the shortcomings of the American press can best be overcome by the efforts of the press itself, the abandonment of the practice of refraining from mutual comment and the adoption instead of a resolute policy of criticism of the press by the press are indicated. . . .

THE NEED AND THE PERFORMANCE: QUALITY

Our society needs an accurate, truthful account of the day's events. We need to know what goes on in our own locality, region, and nation. We need reliable information about all other countries. We need to supply other countries with such information about ourselves. We need a market place for the exchange of comment and criticism regarding public affairs. We need to reproduce on a gigantic scale the open argument which characterized the village gathering two centuries ago. We need to project across all groups, regions, and nations a picture of the constituent elements of the modern world. We need to clarify the aims and ideals of our community and every other.

These needs are not being met. The news is twisted by the emphasis on firstness, on the novel and sensational; by the personal interests of owners; and by pressure groups. Too much of the regular output of the press consists of a miscellaneous succession of stories and images which have no relation to the typical lives of real people anywhere. Too often the result is meaninglessness, flatness, distortion, and the perpetuation of misunderstanding among widely scattered groups whose only contact is through these media.

As we have said, the American press has great technical achievements to its credit. It has displayed remarkable ingenuity in gathering its raw material and in manufacturing and distributing its finished product. Nor would we deny that extraordinarily high quality of performance has been achieved by the leaders in each field of mass communications. When we look at the press as a whole, however, we must conclude that it is not meeting the needs of our society. The Commission believes that this failure of the press is the greatest danger to its freedom.

19.   WHAT'S HAPPENING TO OUR NEWSPAPERS?

by Louis Seltzer *

Newspaper circulation is now at all-time peaks. Advertising volume is incredible; the goose hangs high. Profits in spite of costs and taxes are pretty good. We in our business are well fed, well clothed, well sheltered, and anxious to let well enough alone. We think we are good, because business and circulation are good. In the last decades the phenomena of science have thrown multiple competition at us; not only are we surviving but we are expanding almost everywhere and in some places fabulously. It is quite true that over the years there has been a high mortality rate among newspapers, but even that, at least for the moment, appears to be suspended.

Despite all the happy omens, however, it may be useful to step out of the sunshine for a few minutes in order to observe some scattered clouds.

A lot has happened in the roughly forty years I have been in the business. For one thing, forty years ago newspapers were virtually alone as the principal medium of fact and opinion. There were some magazines, but they were mainly concerned with fiction and entertainment. Newspapers were vital, enterprising, resourceful, audacious. They dug. They tolerated no intermediaries. They went to original sources. They were courageous. They were dedicated, devoted, determined.

Along came Bigness—Bigness begot by mass production. Instantly, as is the way of such things, it affected, influenced, and catalyzed the newspaper business. Gradually, along with almost everything and everybody else, we changed character if not form. Original reporting, crusading, individual investigative reporting began to subside, almost in proportion as features, fiction, comics, departments, and entertainment flowed into our columns.

* Editor of the Cleveland Press since 1928 and editor-in-chief of the Scripps-Howard newspapers of Ohio since 1937. Author of *The Years Were Good*. This selection is from *The Saturday Review*, vol. 39, no. 17, Apr. 28, 1956, pp. 7-8 and 30. By permission of the author and publisher.

It seemed logical, even inevitable. Circulation was the big thing; increased advertising volume was important. And as costs rose in a fabulously expanding economy there was created an economic cycle. It couldn't have been otherwise. Probably it shouldn't have been otherwise. But this cycle did, nonetheless, produce some changes—and it is with these changes, both good and bad, with which I now propose to deal.

It is a fact, evidence for which literally abounds on newsstands, that, whereas newspapers were once primarily concerned with fact and opinion, and magazines with fiction and features, an abrupt, significant, and interesting reversal has taken place. The magazines of America gradually became the instruments of original reporting, crusading, investigative reporting. The newspapers of America gradually took on the former coloration of the magazines with their fiction, features, crossword puzzles, panels, columnists, comics, and other entertainments.

It is important to consider this shift as between newspapers and magazines. For one thing, in newspaper offices a realignment of relative staff importance has taken place. It is a shift from emphasis upon original and investigative reporting to the columnist or clever, sprightly writer—the personality with turned phrase or ingeniously contrived approach. For another, de-emphasis of what once was the newspaper's essential strength has occurred at precisely the wrong time. When it is needed most its absence is most conspicuously noted and felt. It is especially needed today in order to deal with the big changes of our age.

Across the nation, in every community no matter what size or economic condition, there are sweeping social, economic, political, and physical changes that literally cry out for the attention, leadership, counsel, guidance of American newspapers. If, as I am personally convinced, there is a paradoxical frustration and impotence felt by the individual in America in the presence of unprecedented plenty, then how much more this paradoxical feeling afflicts our communities—overwhelmed as they are by tremendous change, industrial expansion, educational inadequacies, housing shortages, racial frictions, business realignments, deterioration of inner cores, by the fierce sociological and psychological winds which blow across the whole American landscape.

Knowing their present is prosperous, and convinced and believing, therefore, their future relatively secure, too many editors believe their newspapers need not change. It's much easier to hire wire services than to gather, write, and print local news. The wire news is already there, ready to pick up and set. You don't have to hire a lot of men and women to round it up. You don't get into arguments with your readers over it.

Local situations are the conversation pieces for nine-tenths of the talk among newspaper readers. Most papers, however, give nine-tenths of Page One to news from remoter and less controversial areas. They then check with *The New York Times* to see if their judgments are upheld.

When most papers *do* turn to their local scenes what do they cover? In too many cities and on too many papers it's the easy way out that editors seek. They take the news the press agents bring in. They cover meetings and speeches and good causes that come easy and that no one can find any fault with. They blurb the friend of a friend at the Union Club, where the editor eats his lunch every day.

I take my hat off to the few newspapers in this country whose editors are going out and getting the local stories which are hard to get—and which sometimes loose all hell on the editorial offices—but these papers are very, very scarce. I can count them on the fingers of my two hands, maybe one. It's easy to cover the annual meeting of the Welfare Federation, but it's tough to tell about the veteran probate judge who is stealing from the estates in his trust. It's easy to reprint the police chief's report on how crime has declined each year, but rugged when you set out to document and illustrate how policemen are mooching from the refrigerators of brothels. It's easy to talk about desegregation far away, but not right at home.

The magazines, to repeat, are doing some of the best digging for facts going on in this country today. And newspapers, many of them built a greatness on the tradition of fearless reporting, are only going through the motions of covering beats or waiting for the news releases to be thrown through the transom. I feel certain that big stories, tremendous situations are lying undiscovered and untouched in almost every large city in the country waiting for alert reporters directed by energetic and fearless editors to dig them out. How much livelier some of our dailies would be, and how much the great majority of readers would love them for it, if these big stories could be brought to the surface.

It takes courage to do that. It takes experienced and competent direction of such assignments, for readers are more sensitive and more vocal than ever if you go off half-cocked on a job of investigative reporting. It takes staff—good men, well-paid, specialized reporters. It takes money. The newspaper today *has* the money. To wait until circulation or advertising revenue drops and then attempt to turn the trend is futile. That would be too much like the advertiser who quits spending money when times are good and wonders why he doesn't survive when trouble hits.

Nobody's going to do the local digging-reporting if newspapers don't. Some of the good magazines may do the job in national or international situations. But they probably won't come into the smaller towns for obvious reasons. Nor will radio and television do it. Their field has settled down to be mostly entertainment (and in the process they have considerably reduced the demand of newspaper readers for entertainment in the paper). All this makes the newspaper more important than ever locally. . .

20. THE "MONOPOLY" NEWSPAPER
by Paul Block, Jr.*

In 90 per cent of American cities there is only one newspaper, or there are two under single ownership. It's high time the men who publish these newspapers acknowledged these facts, time they quit apologizing for them.

* Copublisher of *The Toledo Blade* and *Pittsburgh Post-Gazette*. The selection is from "Facing up to the 'Monopoly' Charge," *Nieman Reports,* vol. 9, no. 3, July, 1955, pp. 3-7. By permission of the publisher.

Newspaper publishers ought to be explaining why there has been a strong trend to consolidation. They should be showing the public how the trend actually has produced better newspapers. They should be exchanging knowledge and experience on how to deal with the special problems single ownership creates. If they don't do these things, critics of the press will have a free field in which to sell people the idea that American newspapers are vicious monopolies acting against the best interests of our free society.

What is needed most is forthright discussion of the trend toward single ownership. This kind of exchange can, I believe, help the public better understand the benefits single ownership offers readers. It can illustrate the fact that this trend is the best hope to improve the quality of journalism and reduce the abuses which flourish in all but the largest cities, where newspapers can compete for different groups of readers instead of trying to be all things to all people.

New approaches, new techniques must be developed by newspapers in single ownership cities. Their advancement would be more rapid if publishers, and editors, and the professional societies they belong to would discuss them freely.

Yet they never have been talked about by the American Newspaper Publishers Association, the American Society of Newspaper Editors, or the Associated Press Managing Editors. Why not?

One notion which has no substance is that the trend to newspaper consolidation results from efforts to accumulate wealth or power, say in the manner of the utility or railroad combines of the Era of the Moguls. Too much prestige in the community is involved in publishing a newspaper to permit a motive for sale of a prosperous one, in the way a prosperous plastics factory might be disposed of to turn a quick profit. If one does come on the market, an estate or an elderly widow usually is involved. Even unprofitable papers struggle on for years because there is more satisfaction in being a publisher poor in the world's goods than in the peace and comfort of retirement in Florida. When one of these finally is sold to its competitor, it must be clear that the causes of single ownership preceded its consummation by years.

Nor can the tendency toward concentration be wholly credited to "rising costs." It's true that technological advances haven't kept pace with demands by newspaper unions for higher standards of living. But to find the cause of the merger trend, one must add to the pressure of costs the effect of factors leading to the disappearance of the two-party press in this country.

The two-party system itself, the increasing similarity of the parties as the Civil War faded into the past—easily demonstrated by the similarity of their election-year platforms, the American people's lack of interest in political doctrine—here is where reasons are to be found why the press of this country could label itself "independent" so it could bid for mass readership, while the press in most other countries remained tied to the party system.

Large-scale advertising emerged in this same period and helped kill off the party press. Advertisers provided a larger share of newspaper revenue.

The party-minded reader became less important. Then the advertiser found he got more customers from dollars spent in newspapers whose readers had high purchasing power, normally the more conservative newspapers. These prospered at the expense of others, finally swallowing them up. Strong party views were tempered to make them less offensive to the readers of the defunct paper, who were potential new subscribers. Meanwhile, retailers found that, with fewer newspapers, they could cover their market at lower cost.

Critics of the press have wasted few tears on the passing of the party pamphlet era of journalism. They agree it is a better informed reader who is exposed to opposing views than the one who is cheered on by repetition of ideas he already holds, even though the critics wouldn't admit that this process has gone far enough. What they don't realize is that once newspapers become more or less independent, competing newspapers acquired a strong resemblance to competing telephone companies.

The validity of this comparison will be protested, not unnaturally, by those students of the press who are steeped in journalistic principle and more or less familiar with how newspapers operate. The student is deeply interested in all phases of newspaper content. He will recognize differences in treatment by different papers and will measure them against his own set of professional standards. But most readers have no such critical eye for all parts of their daily paper (although most readers have real and critical concern for some part which represents a field of their own intense interest). The avid sports fan will argue the virtues of one sports writer as compared with another; the average reader is largely satisfied to know who won the game, by what score. Some will appreciate the choice of interesting detail and the skill required to write a good obituary; most will be satisfied to learn who died. And most readers, confronted by two newspapers, neither of which is an out-and-out political organ, will find the news of national and world affairs looking pretty much the same in either paper.

So it has been that newspapers, as they have become more responsible and more independent, inevitably have come to resemble each other more and more. Where news is concerned, they tend to give the reader duplicating services. That's where the comparison with competing telephone companies comes in. Most people, needing to conserve time or money, will subscribe to only one. Which of several competing newspapers are they likely to choose? Normally, the one with the most pages, which usually is to say the one containing the most local retail advertising.

Men don't realize the part retail advertising plays in appeal to women readers. To the woman keeping house and raising a family, the offerings of the stores, the bargains available from day to day, make the most important news of all. I do not mean to suggest that retail advertising alone can make a newspaper. If it could, the shopping news formula would be much more successful than it is. Advertising is a form of news for the newspaper, but the newspaper lends some of its character and credibility to advertising. Thus, advertisers seek those newspapers which give their advertising greater prestige, as well as those with the most readers, and the trend toward consolidation feeds itself.

Having become more responsible, more independent, single ownership newspapers reflect advantages which are only possible because they have no competition. They are able to give the reader a better, a more dependable product.

For one thing, a newspaper which isn't competing against a rival can present news in better balance. There is no need to sensationalize. A headline doesn't have to say any more than the story warrants. The temptation to over-emphasize, or under-emphasize, has been removed. The sin of exaggeration is committed less often.

Competing newspapers live in fear of each other. They may be stampeded into excesses by their fear of losing circulation to a competitor less burdened with conscience, or even one who might this once be less conscientious than he usually has been. Underplaying news is another result of competition. An editor not uncommonly omits or plays down a story his opposition has uncovered and developed exclusively. Having been caught short, he may try to give his readers the impression it never was much of a story anyhow.

The unopposed newspaper can give its reader the benefit of another tremendous advantage—relief from the pressure of time. Deadlines no longer loom like avenging angels just this side of the next edition. Editor and reporter may be as anxious as ever to get the news fast, and get it right. But they will put more emphasis on getting it right. Where a few more hours broadening the background, or rounding out final details, can prevent inadequacy or inaccuracy, time is there for the taking. The need to make the next edition ceases to be the excuse for giving readers a half-developed story.

Pressure no longer promotes premature and hazardous publication of stories about business negotiations not yet closed, or governmental action not yet taken. The newspaper can print the record of what has occurred, without interfering unintentionally in the occurrence.

There's relief from a peculiar newspaper nuisance—the pyramiding story —in the lessening of time pressure, too. A big story is in progress. It has been carefully and understandably reported for the first edition. Along comes a new development—the latest, but not necessarily the most important. The mechanics of printing conspire with the tradition of vigorous competition to place that new development at the top of the story, ahead of all the detail, all the background, everything that helps the reader put the whole event in proper perspective. Any other course would require extensive rewriting and resetting of type, making it impossible to meet edition deadline. The newspaper without local competition need not pile bulletin on top of bulletin; it can postpone for the sake of balance and clarity. The newspaper bucking competitors usually equates latest with most important, obscuring the whole continuity of the story, the whole emphasis of the story, and frequently the whole meaning of the story.

But not all advantages of single ownership are in news treatment. There is more freedom from financial pressure on the business side. A single ownership newspaper can better afford to take an unpopular stand. It can better absorb the loss of money in support of a principle. For what other institution is called on to antagonize its customers, even as it solicits business from them?

Such a newspaper has more freedom to reject questionable advertising. It can better accept advertising from out-of-town retailers who compete with local merchants. Scarcely six newspapers in the country had no rules against this type of business at last count.

There are objections to single ownership—some valid, some not. Surely the commonest of them is the highly emotional aversion to the word "monopoly." Americans instinctively oppose monopoly. The very word conjures up horrendous images and thoughts. Monopolists frequently are arbitrary, if not downright criminal. These antagonisms have largely been overcome by some utilities through intelligent public relations. Newspapers, trying to ignore the problem, haven't directed their public relations programs specifically to this point, contenting themselves to emphasize their public service, their features, or the magnitude of their circulation.

Yet clearly a single ownership newspaper isn't a monopoly in the same sense as an electric utility. It has competition from television, radio, out-of-town newspapers, neighborhood newspapers, weekly news periodicals, monthly interpretive periodicals—even, if you wish, comic books. And a shopping news in some cases, too.

The public hardly knows about one truly valid complaint against single ownership. It is the difficulty of keeping a newspaper's departments on their toes—editorial staff as well as solicitors of advertising and circulation. Solutions will be found, but they will not be so obvious or so direct as the constant race against an energetic competitor. Here an exchange of information and of practices between newspapers which share the problem surely would help.

There's an especially ominous ring to the complaint that single ownership provides the reader only one local editorial point of view. This does sound like monopoly. A critic of single control may grant that national and international news and opinion can be obtained from many sources, staking his case on the supposedly appalling situation of having only one voice in local affairs. And who will deny that in any controversial situation, the more "voices" expounding and opining, the better? Unfortunately for this complaint, competing newspapers don't always mean competing ideas and competing opinions. The very fact of competition may make it more difficult to espouse causes that are unpopular with community leaders. The art of playing off one competitor against another is as old in the newspaper business as in any other.

This line of reasoning finally falls, however, when actual cases are considered. No cities are known to the writer where competing newspapers consistently take opposing sides of controversial questions, giving readers a clear-cut choice. A rapid survey indicates that a sharp difference of opinion between two newspapers on a local matter doesn't occur as often as once a year on the average.

Here it is tempting to illustrate by use of specific examples. The writer is familiar with single ownership newspapers which are keenly aware of their public responsibility on all issues, and with others which acknowledge no interest but their own. Similar contrasts can be cited between newspapers which have real competition, and also between those with only nominal opposition. How better illustrate that this is not a problem confined to single ownership newspapers?

Yet I am going to forego this opportunity to take my place among the judges of American newspapers, who issue periodic lists of the best and worst, because I do not believe any one not actually a resident of the city in which a newspaper is published can pass judgment on it in this day and age when most national and world news comes by wire into the offices of all newspapers. What determines the merit of a newspaper today isn't the way it shovels this wire copy into its pages. It is the enterprise and skill it shows in handling those things closest to it, the fortitude it displays in standing up to local pressures.

No maker of lists, dropping into a city for a few days or reading its newspaper from afar off, can begin to assess this effectiveness. So the list-makers, who almost invariably are of liberal political persuasion, turn to newspapers with editorial pages of liberal inclination, which keep showing up there year after year. Such newspapers deserve commendation for editorial courage. They are not necessarily what the listmakers represent them to be. So some of the best newspapers in the country go unrecognized, while some of the "Best 10" are living on their reputations.

In every city except New York and probably Chicago, all daily newspapers try to appeal to all people. The effect of competition, then, is for all viewpoints to draw closer together.

Here newspapers have followed the trend already described with respect to political parties. Politicians now agree that the way to win elections is to be as much alike as possible, managing to lean just a little to one side or the other. Thus the extremists know which candidates they must vote for. It's middle-of-the-road voters who are confused. . . .

There is one more traditional complaint against monopolies in general that doesn't apply to single ownership newspaper fields. It is the charge that monopolies inevitably tend to grow bigger and bigger. Some single ownership newspapers are, in fact, very small. And all of them are limited by the size of the community in which they operate.

Not all differences between single ownership and competitive newspaper situations can be classified as advantages or disadvantages. Some are problems created by the trend toward consolidation which challenge the ingenuity of all newspapers which occupy the field by themselves.

An important psychological change takes place in the relationship between a newspaper and its readers in single ownership cities. The newspaper becomes the "voice" of the city and, by a kind of ventriloquist's technique, the "voice" of all its component parts.

Being the "voice" of a community can raise hob with traditional newspaper standards. Joseph Pulitzer once wrote: "An able, disinterested, public-spirited press with trained intelligence to know the right and courage to do it, can preserve that public virtue without which popular government is a sham and a mockery." Pulitzer was a wise man and a great journalist. He undoubtedly would have been one of the first to recognize that under single ownership the significance of "disinterested" is so intensified that it over-shadows "public-spirited." How can you be both disinterested and public-spirited? To be public-spirited is by nature to be partial, to be a proselyter, to press for something; whereas the man who is wholly disinterested becomes an umpire. And this role is not compatible with partisanship and zeal required of the public-spirited citizen.

Trying to reconcile these opposing roles, the single ownership newspaper must make compromises from day to day. The "one voice" must support major community projects; must sometimes furnish much of the drive behind a public undertaking. In generating energy it sometimes must be less than the disinterested community umpire, but never to the point of forgetting that every project, no matter how worthwhile it may appear, conflicts with some interests who will expect and be entitled to a "voice."

Where it is the only voice, a newspaper must be independent of any civic faction, any social set, any economic interest, just as it must be independent of any political party or philosophy. Fortunately, as has been pointed out, the same single ownership which demands such independence makes it economically feasible.

On the Toledo *Blade*, we have found it necessary to adjust our approach and some of our news techniques to this "one voice" psychology. One of the first of these adjustments has to do with the story that would ordinarily be rejected because it will interest too few readers—in other words, is not "newsworthy." Where there are competing newspapers, the rejection would be accepted as a matter of judgment. Where there is single ownership, rejection frequently brings the charge of discrimination. It's hard on the well-trained city editor at first, but standards of what is "newsworthy" have to change in cities with but one newspaper "voice."

Some techniques adopted under single ownership will seem to the newspaper in competition to be leaning over backwards to avoid even the most foolish accusation of unfairness. Good journalists would squirm at the way the Toledo *Blade* edits political news during election campaigns. It's done with a ruler—partly in deference to the political prejudices of readers, partly to protect the *Blade* from that type of post-election survey which implies that a newspaper was grossly unfair because the speeches of one party's candidate received more space than those of the other.

Then there's the matter of letters to the editor. Competitive newspapers as a rule carefully screen them, printing only the better ones. Where there is only one "voice," the newspaper can't be so fastidious. The *Blade* cheerfully prints letters that are merely illiterate or idiotic, drawing the line only at blasphemy, pornography, or sedition.

Another way single ownership newspapers may do things differently is in the use of syndicated columnists, who offer a chance to present conflicting political points of view. On the Toledo *Blade*, these columnists are used without regard for their popular appeal, solely in the belief that its politically variegated readers are entitled to every viewpoint that can be had, provided it is an honest one. Contrary to the practice of appraising each column on the basis of what it has to say and how well it says it, recognizing that no writer can be good every day, the *Blade* carries its hands-off policy to the point of refusing to edit or omit the copy of any of its regular columnists (however much forbearance it sometimes may require).

Single ownership newspapers can demonstrate their concern with the public interest in the most practical pecuniary way. Public appeal advertising and that of charities gets the lowest possible rate in the *Blade* (the same rate earned by those retail stores which do the largest amount of advertising in a year's time). The *Blade* also keeps its rate for political advertising low, in contrast with the rather general practice of charging a premium rate. In a single ownership field, it is more important to encourage the fullest expression of political opinion than to set a high price on it, even though political advertising—being irregular and uncertain—will not otherwise carry its share of the cost load.

These are only a few of the ways single ownership newspapers may use to vary their approach and change their techniques. More will be developed as publishers are willing to stand up for the journalistic advantages of single ownership. With the opportunity in their grasp to prove to readers that single ownership newspapers can be—usually are—better newspapers, why try to ignore or hide the fact that single ownership is the dominant form of American journalism?

Failure to acknowledge what is a fact, failure to act boldly, intelligently, and without apology on this knowledge, can only increase public misunderstanding and encourage agitation for government interference in the newspaper business. If the men who edit and publish American newspapers fail to counteract this misunderstanding and this agitation, if they let the government come into the news room, the editorial conference, and the business office through an opening created by unreasoning fear of monopoly, the First Amendment soon will be as meaningless as the Second, which actually declares that ". . . the right of the people to keep and bear arms shall not be infringed."

21. THE POWER OF THE PRESS: THE CASE OF *THE TOLEDO BLADE*
by Reo M. Christenson*

Ever since Franklin D. Roosevelt and Harry S. Truman overcame the massed opposition of the nation's newspapers, observers have wagged their heads over the political impotence of the press. The dominant position of *The Toledo Blade* in Toledo politics, however, suggests that the power of the press has other dimensions than that of electing presidents. It also suggests that writers of municipal textbooks and students of municipal government might prudently pay more attention to the newspaper—from the standpoint both of description and evaluation—than they have been wont to do in the past.

* Editorial writer for *The Toledo Blade* (1953-1956) prior to joining the staff of the department of government, Miami University, Oxford, Ohio. Author of *The Brannan Plan: A Study in Farm Politics and Policy*. This selection is from the *Midwest Journal of Political Science*, vol. 3, no. 3, August, 1959, pp. 227-240. By permission of the publisher.

The press renders an invaluable service to self-government by reporting upon men and organizations who possess political influence and power, and by passing judgment on them. On the other hand, the press exercises power of its own which is largely unreported and unexamined. In the interests of both public enlightenment and a more responsible press, this vacuum needs to be filled.

Although Publisher Paul Block, Jr. (who also owns the only other newspaper in town, the morning *Times*),[1] would win no popularity contest in Toledo, *The Blade* is by all odds the most potent political force in Toledo. It certainly does not run the city in arbitrary, single-handed fashion. No newspaper could. But it wields immense influence. It has made, broken and chastened many a politician. It has pushed through or blocked many a public policy. When it gives the word and applies the heat, Council is normally quick to respond. When it adopts a Sphinx-like pose, Council squirms uneasily. Day in and day out, Council acts with one eye cocked on *The Blade*.[2]

Editor Mike Bradshaw, no man to boast, put *The Blade's* position in these words a few years ago. "[I would] shudder to think what the responsibility [of the editorial page] must have been if [its influence] was ever greater . . . the political influence of our independent newspaper in our independent community is so strong that we are not so much concerned with the power of the press as with our responsibility to use it wisely." Bradshaw added that

> . . . unavoidably the editorial page has become the arbiter of community affairs in many of our single ownership cities. When Democrats and Republicans have at each other, it is our responsibility to say which party has offered the better candidates—to choose between them.
>
> But the same thing happens in a less measurable way in other civic controversies. If the Chamber of Commerce and the CIO get into a hassle, if the milk drivers strike for higher wages, if the judge of our Domestic Relations Court insists that a building for the Child Study Institute, and his chambers, should cost a million dollars and the real-estate board contends that $750,000 will be enough, we are supposed to weigh the arguments and say which side is right. The newspaper is to be the referee.

The power of *The Blade* (circulation about 190,000 compared to about 40,000 for *The Times*) flows from various sources:

(1) Toledo's electorate has a tradition of voting independently rather than along party lines. This tradition, apparently rooted in the reform period of Mayor "Golden Rule" Jones almost sixty years ago, has weakened the parties as a community force and played into the hands of the independent *Blade*.

[1] Block keeps *The Times* in existence at least partially to blunt the persistent community complaint that Toledo is a "one newspaper town." Even though *Times'* editorial positions differ from *The Blade's* at least as much as in the average city with separately owned newspapers, the common knowledge that Block owns both papers leads citizens to discount the *Times*—probably unduly—as a competitive medium.

[2] This piece draws upon the writer's experience as an editorial writer for *The Blade* from 1953 to 1956 and upon interviews in 1958 with Toledo's mayor, three ex-mayors, several councilmen and a number of other prominent Toledo figures.

(2) *The Blade* has had little effective competition from other private groups bent on controlling municipal decisions.[3] The political parties just about fold up between elections (except where patronage is concerned), and neither the unions, the Chamber of Commerce nor other private power blocs are geared up to seriously challenge *The Blade* in this sphere.

The reasons for the comparative weakness of other groups are not entirely clear to the writer, although some of the factors will emerge from the description of *The Blade's* activities which follows. Certainly no other group can match the staff and research facilities of *The Blade,* or has access to the kind of background intelligence reports supplied its editor by his reporters, or is equipped with such a variety of tools for influencing public opinion, or can devote itself so continuously to the job of community leadership, or has such ready access to the public mind. It *may* be that no community group or no person—except a strong mayor, perhaps— can successfully contend with a newspaper which has won community respect, which *wants* to lead as well as mirror, which uses its power judiciously and is careful not to overplay its hand.

(3) A further contributing factor is to be found in Council's lack of really strong leadership since able Mike Di Salle left the mayoralty post in 1950. Lacking direction from within, Council has reflected leadership from without—principally that of *The Blade.*

(4) The skill with which editor Mike Bradshaw handles local issues and candidates is widely acknowledged. One of Bradshaw's favorite adjectives is "deft," and deft is the word for his own shrewdly constructed editorials. A man who loves the game of politics with a passion, Bradshaw combines an artistically homely style (which rarely sacrifices editorial dignity) with rapier-like thrusts at an enemy's most vulnerable point. Nor does he lose sight of the fact that the approaches to the public mind are often penetrated most effectively through an appeal to the emotions woven within a fabric of reasonableness—or at least the appearance of reasonableness.

Because of Bradshaw's near-flawless sense of timing, his gift for discerning the public mood, and his acute awareness that politics is the art of the possible, the publisher relies heavily on his editor's well-honed political instincts. A paper which would be powerful, after all, is a paper which does not lose too many political bouts. A reputation for power confers power, and this *The Blade* never forgets.

(5) So far as national politics and policies are concerned, Toledo residents are of course exposed to the reports and interpretations of a wide variety of sources—national TV and radio networks, news magazines, journals of opinion, and syndicated newspaper columnists, for example. In this hotly competitive field, *The Blade's* news and editorial columns must contend with numerous other voices.

But about the only picture most Toledoans get of Toledo is that supplied by *The Blade.* From the way that picture is focused and developed in the news columns, certain conclusions will often suggest themselves to the reader even if he ignores the editorial page.

[3] Whether a developing City Manager League will supply some stiff competition remains to be seen.

If *The Blade* chooses to promote or discredit or simply call community attention to a development or proposal in which it is interested, it may detail a reporter to do a special story, or series of stories, on that subject. For example, it was able to arouse community support for a more vigorous enforcement of the city's housing regulations by printing a series of reports describing the squalid conditions existing in certain rental units, naming the owners and spelling out their resistance to previous law-enforcement pressures. This maneuver, skillfully executed by a first-class reporter, had an editorial impact greater than the editorial page could hope to achieve.

Again, when the Conant report on secondary schools made twenty-one recommendations for achieving sound high school programs, *The Blade* commissioned a reporter to see how well Toledo's schools measured up to the Conant criteria. The feature articles which followed undoubtedly helped stimulate a reappraisal of Toledo schools by its educational leaders, and there are indications that this reappraisal will bear fruit.

On the other hand, like every other newspaper, *The Blade* may play down developments it frowns upon, or which do not contribute to the community picture it prefers to reflect. Because of the lack of reader sophistication in these matters, selectivity and emphasis in reporting the news can be employed quite freely to help shape desired community attitudes without unduly arousing community suspicions. *The Blade*, it should be added, uses this strategy within the framework of a relatively high standard of journalistic ethics.

(6) *The Blade* is recognized by many Toledoans—especially those who have travelled extensively—as a first-rate newspaper. Its coverage of national and international affairs is remarkable for a city of Toledo's size. *The Blade* has its own foreign correspondent, something no paper in a comparable city can boast. . . . Reflecting the publisher's scientific bent (he has a Ph.D. in chemistry from Columbia University), *The Blade* employs a competent science writer to give to its readers a better than average account of current scientific developments. Its superior coverage of religious news developments has won it the approval of many readers.

Furthermore, Block rejects the notion that a paper can be judged by the amount of wire copy that is shovelled into its columns. A good newspaper, he says, is one which gives its readers information in depth on local issues and which digs tirelessly and fearlessly into every crook and cranny of municipal affairs. While *The Blade's* performance does not always measure up to the ideal,[4] the performance is good enough to keep Toledo citizens

[4] For years *The Blade* chose to ignore gambling activities in the Toledo area of a fairly extensive character. When Detroit newspapers began carrying stories that gamblers and racketeers were drifting back to Toledo (a racketeer haven during the early 1930's), *The Blade* took fright, demanded and got strict enforcement of existing anti-gambling statutes. It also successfully urged a somewhat reluctant Council to outlaw pinball machines. (This reluctance is perhaps accounted for by the well-founded suspicion that gambling interests had for years been chipping into the campaign coffers of both political parties in return for a tolerant Council attitude.)

If illicit gambling or red-light operations thrive in a city (at least in middle-sized cities or smaller), it is usually a safe bet that the press has taken a worldly view of human nature and the police understand that they need undertake no more enforcement than is necessary to put on a good front.

unusually well-informed on local problems, and their public officials commendably prudent.

Thus, part of *The Blade's* power stems from public recognition of the paper's journalistic excellence and its sober sense of responsibility—on most occasions.

Block, who inherited the paper from his father in 1941, has demonstrated a number of qualities which admirably fit him for running a newspaper. A man of considerable intellectual distinction, he has a lightning-quick mind and occasional flashes of insight which admirers think border on genius. He is no man's, or group's, cat's-paw. He has an instinctive concern for the underdog and is a steady champion of civil liberties. He is a patron of the arts. Even his enemies concede his dedication to the progress and prosperity of Toledo.

Why, then, is Block regarded with something short of affection in Toledo —at least in political, professional and business circles?

The answer is a story in itself. Briefly, Block is a lone wolf who holds himself aloof from the social circles in which a publisher normally moves. Abrupt, tactless, sometimes rude, he doesn't appear to care whether he is liked or not. Rather, he seems to prefer being respected and, perhaps, feared.

Abnormally suspicious of the motives of others, and quick to take offense over imagined slights, Block is frequently governed by his passions and prejudices where personalities are concerned. And, as one shrewd Toledoan observed, "When personalities enter Block's picture (as they so often do), it almost never means Block likes a man. It means he dislikes him."

Once Block's animosity is aroused, its objects are likely to be condemned to the editorial doghouse for years to come, if not for good.

This fate can befall organizations as well as individuals. *The Blade,* which keeps a sharp eye on persons or groups which may be seeking a larger leadership role than it thinks proper, keeps its guns perpetually trained on the Toledo Municipal League. The League, a perfectly respectable, responsible and useful research and "good government" body, has been exposed to a prolonged succession of withering attacks by *The Blade.* The latter has repeatedly gone out of its way to belittle the League, all too often by distorting its position or by attributing improper motives or chicanery to it which the paper is able to sustain only by innuendo.

Block's ingrained reluctance to give Toledo officials a hand for work well done has also contributed to his unpopularity. So has his editor's propensity, once his *Blade* is drawn and its editorial point inserted in an adversary, to twist it a bit before withdrawal. Characteristics such as these have not only exposed the publisher to bitter private criticism but, more important, have tended to make higher echelon public service relatively unattractive in Toledo. The shortage of able candidates for Council in no small measure reflects *The Blade's* singularly ungenerous attitude toward public officials. Such, at least, is a widely held view. . . .

The Blade has a notable long-run record of supporting local candidates who turn out to be winners. . . .

[Its] record in this respect might indicate no more than its possession of the gift of prophecy. But while some political veterans can undoubtedly win without *Blade* support, more obscure political figures, including younger men trying to get a foothold on the city's political ladder, are critically dependent on *The Blade's* favor. An editorial or two lambasting or lauding a relatively unknown man can affect his fortunes crucially. And if *The Blade* makes a really determined effort to defeat a councilman who won by a narrow margin in the previous election, it is more than likely to succeed. As for judicial candidates running on a nonpartisan ballot, *The Blade's* verdict carries its heaviest punch in these contests.

Generally speaking, strong editorial support for a candidate is believed by experienced Toledo politicians to be worth three or four thousand votes out of a total city vote of around 70,000 to 90,000. Of course *The Blade's* vote-wielding power varies from candidate to candidate, and from election to election, depending on a host of factors.

The Blade's control over Council has occasioned both wry amusement and considerable irritation among those who follow municipal affairs closely. When the local Gridiron Club's program committee is working out its skits, it rarely passes up the chance to roast councilmen for their readiness to dance to the tune of *The Blade*. (Piqued by some of their satire, Block has retaliated in recent years by denying the Club's annual dinner more than the barest of mention in *The Blade's* news columns.)

Council normally shrinks from taking a firm stand on any major civic measure until *The Blade* has tipped its hand. Once the latter has given its marching orders, Council knows the path of safety and the path of peril and almost invariably chooses the former. A number of occasions could be cited, in fact, in which Council, after voting one way in Committee of the Whole, reversed itself in regular session following an editorial blast by *The Blade*.

When *The Blade* feels that Council is not up to its job, it may seize the wheel and steer out on its own. Shortly after World War II, Block imported Norman Bel Geddes to draw up an imaginative plan for long-range Toledo expansion and development. Personally financing an attractive and impressive model of "Toledo Tomorrow," Block sought to stimulate public support by putting it on display in the popular Toledo Zoo. Visited by tens of thousands, it fanned public interest and prepared the way for a series of major municipal improvements.

The Blade, of course, gave ample publicity to "Toledo Tomorrow" and vigorous support for a proposed one per cent city income tax with which to finance a municipal capital improvements program modelled roughly along "Toledo Tomorrow" lines. The tax was promptly enacted, the first of its kind in Ohio and the second in any American city.

Again, when Block concluded that Council lacked the drive, imagination, and discipline to take advantage of the opportunities created by the passage of the St. Lawrence Seaway, *The Blade* peremptorily brushed aside the fumbling and squabbling Toledo-Lucas County Port Commission which had borne responsibility for the area's port development program. One fine Sunday morning Toledo citizens awoke to find a front page editorial announcing the creation of a committee of prominent Toledoans (including

Block) prepared to take full charge of port planning—temporarily, at least.

Faced with this tour-de-force, the Port Commission gulped, grumbled a bit, and then obediently abandoned the field, leaving Block's committee with a virtually free hand to draw up the blueprint for this most important of city responsibilities. . . .

Perhaps *The Blade's* finest achievement has been its role as a sleepless watchdog for civil liberties and individual rights in Toledo. It has insisted, for example, that the local police force grant arrested persons their full constitutional rights rather than resort to the short-cuts which perennially tempt law enforcement agencies. It has declined to identify criminal suspects by race, except under most unusual circumstances. And by steady editorial nourishment of a spirit of tolerance and fair play, by consistent support of persons and organizations who have fought for or exemplified those principles, and by unsparing attacks on those who fall short of the mark, *The Blade* has done much—far more than any other organization in the city—to create an atmosphere in which civil liberties have flourished.

Toledo passed through the McCarthy period relatively unscathed, so far as local eruptions of misguided patriotic zeal were concerned. On several occasions McCarthy-ish persons launched crusades to "purify" the schools or arouse the community to the "dangers" of allegedly subversive elements in its midst. By exposing their character and implications, and by the kind of editorial irony which can be shattering in cases of this kind, *The Blade* caused these movements to collapse before they could get well underway.

One of *The Blade's* prouder accomplishments was its part in damping down a major racial flare-up which threatened public housing desegregation in East Toledo in 1953. Although desegregation had proceeded uneventfully in public housing elsewhere in the city, residents of East Toledo had promptly taken alarm at the prospect of its happening there.

Mass protest meetings were held, local agitators urged defiance, and proposals were advanced for the secession of East Toledo from Toledo proper. (Since it was a federal housing project, secession would have been fruitless, as *The Blade* was quick to point out.) As threats of violence cropped up with increasing frequency, fear of possible race riots spread throughout the city.

After an initial bruising attack on the leaders of the anti-integration movement, *The Blade* soon veered off to a different course. It emphasized the imperative need for lawful procedures, praised those who were demanding them, and then proceeded to play down the whole affair, putting a public ravenous for information on the shortest possible rations.

The Blade felt, no doubt rightly, that the coverage usually given an issue of consuming public interest would in this case only inflame public passions, prolong an atmosphere of "crisis" and delay the cooling-off period which it regarded as essential. In line with this general policy, *The Blade* also excluded from its "Daily Forum" letters which dealt with the issue.

Obviously *The Blade* was using its columns as an instrument of community control rather than as a mirror of community sentiment and action. The implications of such a course, used under different circumstances and for a different purpose, are sobering. In this instance, however, it apparently paid off. The threat of violence gradually subsided (partly because a local federal judge read the riot act to one of the principal agitators), the community settled back to watchful waiting, and the whole issue eventually blew over. When desegregation actually began, many months later, it took place without incident and with a calculated minimum of newspaper publicity.

Councilmen who had toadied to the segregation forces were later marked out for political extermination by *The Blade*. All went down to defeat in the next election.

If *The Blade's* power for weal and woe has impressive local dimensions, *The Blade* would be the first to concede the limitations of its influence. Although it favored the substitution of the strong-mayor for the city-manager form of municipal government in 1957, it made only a feeble pitch for the former because it sensed the deep-rooted community opposition which later erupted at the polls. When a property tax boost to provide capital improvement funds was proposed on the heels of a reassessment which had raised property taxes considerably, *Blade* pleas for its passage were met by a negative avalanche of tax-weary votes. A second try in the spring of 1958, with the increased levies limited to financing expressways, was also beaten despite *Blade* support.

Thus even a shrewd and generally respected monopoly newspaper appears unable to shape local opinions when voters are strongly predisposed to favor a given course of action or inaction. But where they are closely divided, or more commonly, apathetic, *The Blade's* experience suggests that a newspaper which knows what it's about can often carry the day.

Although the power of the press in local affairs is a largely unexplored area of America's political anatomy, the writer is under no illusion that the power of *The Blade* in municipal affairs is typical of the power of the press on the local scene. Possibly a majority of publishers look upon the newspaper as a strictly commercial enterprise, and make little or no serious effort to convert it into a vehicle for acquiring and exercising the maximum political power. Many of them lack the instinct to do battle, shrink from giving offense to any important group in the city, or lack the political finesse which effective leadership demands. Some newspapers apparently have a negative political impact—their endorsement of a candidate or a proposal constitutes the kiss of death.

But if *The Blade's* power is not representative of American newspapers, the role of papers like the *Milwaukee Journal*, the *Louisville Courier-Journal*, the *Cleveland Press*, the *Akron Beacon-Journal*, and the *Los Angeles Times* suggests that *The Blade's* experience is by no means unique. Thus even if the press can't elect presidents at will, it is time to challenge the notion that its political influence has largely withered away.

Under these circumstances, two valuable purposes would be served by focusing more research on the political functions of newspapers. First, public knowledge of the power structure in a community is prerequisite to public understanding and control of government, and to effective political action by individuals and groups. Second, any institution is prone to conduct itself in a more responsible manner if it knows its performance will be subjected to periodic evaluation in the public interest. While no informed person would assert that newspapers escape certain disciplining influences which are inherent in a free political community, these influences are not always adequate in themselves to keep newspapers on their best behavior. Since the press is often an active participant in the political struggle, as well as an observer, it is all the more essential that the watchers be watched. Journalists and political scientists share this responsibility.

22.   CHAIN-STORE JOURNALISM
by Louis M. Lyons *

. . . The dissolution of our metropolitan communities has been both a cause and an effect of the increasing tendency to run newspapers like chain stores, by their balance sheets. Just as the sense of community will have to be restored to maintain the vitality of a mass society, so the newspaper that is to survive as a viable institution will have to rediscover its relation to a true community. [Mark] Ethridge [*Louisville Courier-Journal*] suggests this may work out in smaller papers, of a quality the reader will pay more for. The ultimate answer may lie "in the English pattern of small papers with high advertising and circulation rates," he says. ". . . We are going to have to . . . charge what newspapers are worth."

Somehow it does prove possible for distinguished papers to survive to serve a small clientele in England, as has not happened here. Time and space in America, we are told, prevent such a national reach for a natural community of readers. But if the *Wall Street Journal* and now the *Christian Science Monitor*, can distribute nationally from several printing plants, it is hard to see why some other papers of distinction might not seek a sufficient circulation at large.

The limitation most usually cited is the necessity of a local advertising base, which is another way of saying it can be done only if the reader will pay more of the cost. He should; it would insure the independence of his paper. It is too easy to blame the readers for the ills of our mass media, as Frank Luther Mott seems to in his recent *Saturday Review* article, "A Twentieth-Century Monster: The Mass Audience." In most places the reader has no choice. Mark Ethridge finds that in twenty states no city has competing papers and eleven more have only one city with competition.

Newspapers are not thriving under these conditions. Ethridge shows that newspaper circulation has gained only half as much as population in thirty years. The eleven largest Sunday papers have lost two and a half million circulation the past ten years. These years have seen both a sharp decline in the number of separate newspapers and a sharp rise in the num-

* Editor of *Nieman Reports* and curator of the Nieman fellowship program (under which selected newsmen receive fellowships to attend Harvard University). A former news commentator who won the Peabody award for local news broadcasts in 1958 and the Lauterbach award for civil liberties in 1957. Coauthor of *Our Fair City* and author of numerous magazine articles. This selection is from *The Reporter,* vol. 23, no. 10, Dec. 8, 1960, pp. 60-63. By permission of the author and the publisher.

ber of chains, until the chains now control more than half the daily circulation. We saw one consequence of chain operation in early October. One
night an order from Hearst headquarters voted all fifteen of the Hearst
papers for Mr. Nixon; the editorial was dictated over the wire, the same
words in Mr. Kennedy's home town of Boston as in Mr. Nixon's California.
A week later a similar wire voted all the nineteen Scripps-Howard papers
the same way. This is not precisely local autonomy.

Ethridge doesn't believe that competition from the entertainment world
of TV need be fatal to newspapers if they work at the solid information
and interpretation job that TV is less equipped to do. Ethridge sees nothing
mysterious in what ails the press: "Give me a newspaper that prints the
news fully, fairly, and fearlessly, interprets it intelligently and comments
upon it vigorously, and I will take my chances that those other things for
which publishers are responsible—fiscal soundness, economic independence
and public acceptance—will be added in satisfactory measure."

But he is concerned, as are the schools of journalism, over the leakage
of top talent from the press to TV and other communications fields. The
schools should worry more, as some do, about the failure of the newspaper
to attract its share of talent from the campuses each June. Few newspapers
do any recruiting, as all the modern industries do; fewer have any training
program to offer recruits. For the most part there is no intelligible approach for the college graduate to seek newspaper employment. Many who
explore it give up in bewilderment. Others who had imbibed the legend of
crusading zeal of old-time editors are disillusioned by the limited outlook
of the people they would be working for. If journalism is just a job, they
can do better in public relations. Some journalism schools have changed
their name to recognize the more remunerative allied fields. This is easier
than accepting their long-deferred responsibility of leadership and professional criticism.

The conformity of the chains to a central-office pattern is of course only
the most obvious indicator of the conformity that runs through almost all
of the big newspapers on all basic issues. It is an invisible thread in our
national consciousness. James Reston of the New York *Times*, well situated
to know, has noted the absence of criticism in the press of the Eisenhower
administration. This is a constant in our public opinion, a conforming to
conservatism that has become so habitual as to be unconscious.

If a certain singleness of editorial outlook seems riveted on the press by
its business control, it is nevertheless offset in degree by the box-office value
of the syndicated columnist, who may be independent and may be liberal.
Such columnists as Walter Lippmann and Joseph Alsop doubtless have
more impact on the readers of many newspapers than do the editorials.
This provides some balance.

Very many publishers, however, buy only columnists who echo their own
views. This is a serious damper on American public opinion, which is
further handicapped by the inadequacy of our foreign correspondence in an
ever more difficult and confusing world. And even in domestic affairs, few
papers have specialists capable of analyzing the increasing complexity of
issues.

Family ownership of the American newspaper, which long resisted the familiar corporate structure of most business, had seemed the surest guarantee of the continuance of the character of independent newspapers. This is still true in notable instances, and these newspapers treat their readers seriously. It is true of the successors of Adolph Ochs in the New York *Times*, of the Pulitzers in the St. Louis *Post-Dispatch*, the Danielses in Raleigh, the Cowleses in Minneapolis, the Binghams in Louisville, the heirs of Lucius Nieman in the Milwaukee *Journal*, of Charles H. Taylor in the Boston *Globe*, the publishers of the Washington *Star* and the Washington *Post*, and some others. They exhibit a sense of responsibility for the character of the newspaper as an institution of the community. Until recently it seemed possible that their example would lead other publishers increasingly to accept a relationship to their papers similar to that of trustees to a university, to protect its independence and build its strength to serve.

But family ownership has proved vulnerable, due to the consequences of our common mortality. Control has sometimes been vested in trustees, and divisions have risen within owning families. These conditions have opened the way for outside purchase by entrepreneurs like Newhouse. But in some other places the local heirs to family-held newspapers seem just to have grown tired. It is hard to imagine the Tafts and their neighbors letting control of all the newspapers of Cincinnati pass to the outside ownership of the Scripps-Howard chain. But it did happen there, as it has in other cities.

Of course the standardization of the press has not been the only factor diluting the individual characteristics of our community life. But a newspaper is such a strategic institution that what devitalizes its character weakens its community.

It is probably true that most of the newspapers that have survived the pressures to merge have been strengthened by the elimination of competition. How that is to be balanced against the loss of diversity of viewpoint and the constriction of our channels of communication depends on your priority of values. It is true that under responsible control, the "monopoly" newspapers have been freed from the downpull of competition in sensationalism and have been able to present the news in the perspective of their own professional editorial judgment, uninhibited by fear of what "that yellow rag across the street" may do. But with all the news and its interpretation under one control, the community is terribly dependent on the kind of publisher it gets.

Readers are most conscious of the publisher's absolute control of "public opinion" at election time. The publisher in his political attitude represents what the British call "the Establishment," or our sociologists "the local power setup." It is usually not advertiser influence that presses him to the conservative side, or even wholly his own economic stake as big taxpayer and big employer. Rather it is his consciousness of representing the part of the community closest to him, the Downtown Club, his fellow trustees and directors and vestrymen of the institutions he supports. Few big-business publishers are mavericks, as many of our picturesque old-time editors were. The newspaper in their hands becomes a conventional institution, parallel to the Chamber of Commerce, the Community Fund Council, and the First National Bank, to which they are usually in hock for twenty years for that $18-million new plant they were forced to put up outside the traffic jams that strangled distribution from their old plant. "How many people have got $18 million?" a big publisher plaintively asks.

The commitment to the bank for such enormous new capital outlay is a reason often given for failure to launch new editorial enterprises. Revenues have reached a peak, in the publisher's mind, because he feels unable to raise advertising rates, lest he lose an even larger slice of the advertisers' dollar to the more dramatic competition of television. He has raised the reader price to five, seven, eight cents, and looks to the dime as an attainable ceiling. But this is only to catch up, not to finance a foreign service, to strengthen staff resources, or to set standards of taste in his community by informed criticism of books, music, theater, the arts, or even of public planning.

The publisher feels in a bind that forces him to make whatever savings can be secured by relying more on syndicated features and wire-service news, which shrink the individuality and enterprise of the paper.

The current trend is toward ever more mergers—some have occurred while this piece was on the typewriter—and thus to increasing concentration of control. The ultimate economy the publisher sees is a round-the-clock operation, publishing a morning and evening paper in the same plant, with no local competition. This is indeed the primary objective of mergers, and in all but a handful of cities it is already achieved, or on the drawing boards.

The American sentiment against monopoly or near-monopoly has not got us very far in other fields, even though the government is armed with anti-trust weapons. It is not apt to be effective in the newspaper business until there are technological developments, not now in sight, to cut down the tremendous capital requirement. Or else there will have to be a public awareness of the importance of diversity and independence—not in sight either—that will bring support of smaller newspapers that can be more representative of the diverse elements in American life. For these the reader will have to pay a higher price—the price of independence from the revenues of mass advertising. Until then, except in rarely fortunate communities, the reader will have to look beyond the daily press, as many have learned to do, for fuller dimensions and more independence of discussion of public issues.

This is not at all to say that the daily paper has no vital function or that it is not in many instances performing it competently; only that it is limiting its role to less than the readers' needs.

23. THE ONE-PARTY PRESS
by Adlai Stevenson*

It is very pleasant to consider today that I have a group of editors and publishers temporarily at my mercy. I know it won't last long. But, since

* Chief United States delegate to the United Nations. Ran for the Presidency on the Democratic ticket in 1952 and 1956. This selection is from a speech delivered to newspapermen at Portland, Oregon, Sept. 8, 1952.

the press—some of it—keeps describing me as a captive candidate, I particularly enjoy speaking to a captive audience.

In addition, I have had a strange feeling these past weeks that people are following me. They all seem to be friendly, inquisitive and rumpled; they wear hats and keep writing things down on pieces of paper. I cannot drink a milk-shake or put on a pair of shoes without their friendly but implacable surveillance. Given this relentless observation, I find it an agreeable change to stand here and look straight back at such a distinguished group of what I believe are called "opinion molders."

If ignorance, apathy and excessive partisanship are still the greatest enemies of democracy—as I believe Bryce said some forty or fifty years ago—then of course it is up to a free press to help us on all three counts and all the time. Otherwise neither democratic government nor a free press can be sure of permanency.

In short, government—our brand of representative government—depends on you, and, something which I think your profession sometimes overlooks, you depend on government, for the ultimate protection of a free press is in the Constitution.

That is why the rock-bottom foundation of a free press is the integrity of the people who run it. Our press may make a million mistakes of judgment without doing itself permanent harm so long as its proprietors are steadfast in their adherence to truth. I have no doubt whatever that the bulk of owners and publishers and editors are doing an honest job with the news.

I ought to know, because I am straining the impartiality of the press to the limit these days. Yet, as a candidate in a hard-fought campaign, I have been well impressed by the fair treatment accorded me by most newspapers, including most of those aligned editorially with the opposition. I am convinced that nearly all publishers are doing their honest best, according to their lights—even if I must confess that sometimes their lights seem to me a little dim.

I am glad to pay this tribute to the press. It is true, and I think it should be said. I am grateful for the impartiality and fullness of your news columns. Yet I am not recommending complacency. And, from my vantage point, certain defects are apparent. If I were still an editorial writer I suppose I would say that there are some ominous tendencies, or even that these tendencies could weaken the fabric of the Republic.

In my new role in life, I can't help noticing from time to time—I want to put it as delicately as I can—that the overwhelming majority of the newspapers of the country are supporting the opposition candidate. This is something, I find, that even my best friends *will* tell me! And I certainly don't take it personally. In fact, I would have been somewhat startled and unhappy if I received much press support after the reception given my Democratic predecessors, Mr. Truman and Mr. Roosevelt. Some people might even have considered such support an ill omen.

It would seem that the overwhelming majority of the press is just against Democrats. And it is against Democrats, so far as I can see, not after a sober and considered review of the alternatives, but automatically, as dogs are against cats. As soon as a newspaper—I speak of the great majority, not of the enlightened ten per cent—sees a Democratic candidate it is filled with an unconquerable yen to chase him up an alley.

I still haven't got over the way some of our nation's great papers rushed to commit themselves to a candidate last spring, long before they knew what that candidate stood for, or what his party platform would be, or who his opponent was, or what would be the issues of the campaign. I know where a young publisher's fancy turns in that season of the year, and I don't blame them for a moment. But I feel that some of them may yet regret the impetuosity of their wooing now that autumn is here.

I am touched when I read in these papers solicitous editorials about the survival of the two-party system. Now I really can't bring myself to believe that the Republican Party is about to fade away, even if it loses in 1952. If so, it is staging one of the longest and loudest deathbed scenes in history. How can the Republican Party disappear when about 90 per cent of the press for ten or fifteen years has been telling the American people day in and day out that the Republican Party alone can save the Republic? Surely Republican publishers and editors don't honestly believe that they have so little influence!

I am in favor of a two-party system in politics. And I think we have a pretty healthy two-party system at this moment. But I am in favor of a two-party system in our press too. And I am, frankly, considerably concerned when I see the extent to which we are developing a one-party press in a two-party country.

I earnestly wish that the newspapers so highly agitated over the two-party system in politics would contemplate the very real dangers of the one-party system in the press. I don't say this because of any concern over the coming election. My party has done all right in recent elections in spite of the country's editorial pages, and I have a hunch we will do all right this year too.

But, as an ex-newspaperman and as a citizen, I am gravely concerned about the implications of this one-party system for our American press and our free society.

A free society means a society based on free competition and there is no more important competition than competition in ideas, competition in opinion. This form of competition is essential to the preservation of a free press. Indeed, I think the press should set an example of the nation in increasing opposition to uniformity.

What I think I detect is a growing uniformity of outlook among publishers—a tendency toward the trade-association mentality of uniformity of attitude toward the public, the customer, if not toward one another as producers of consumer goods. I doubt if this shoe fits the peculiar function of the newspaper.

I think you will agree that we cannot risk complacency. We need to be rededicated every day to the unfinished task of keeping our free press truly free. We need to work even harder for the time when all editors will honor their profession, when all publishers will have a sense of responsibility equal to their power and thus regain their power, if I may put it that way.

It's not honest convictions honestly stated that concern me. Rather, it is the tendency of many papers, and I include columnists, commentators, analysts, feature writers, and so on, to argue editorially from the personal objective, rather than from the whole truth. As the old jury lawyer said: "And these, gentlemen, are the conclusions on which I base my facts."

In short, it seems to me that facts, truth, should be just as sacred in the editorial column as the news column. And, as I have said, happily most papers, but by no means all, do struggle with sincerity for accuracy in the news. Coming from Chicago, of course, I am not unfamiliar with the phenomenon of an editorial in every news column!

What I am saying is that the press cannot condemn demagoguery, claptrap, distortion and falsehood in politicians and public life on the one hand and practice the same abuses on the public themselves, on the other. I know the people are smarter than many politicians think and sometimes I suspect that even editors underestimate them.

The free press is the mother of all our liberties and of our progress under liberty. That's easy to say, but while saying it, it is well to remember what it means. . . .

I would like to conclude with the warning that we must not let [the campaign] obscure the outlines of the world crisis in which we are involved. This generation has been summoned to a great battle—the battle to determine whether we are equal to the task of world leadership. I am deeply persuaded that the press can be our shield and our spear in this battle. I believe Jefferson said, "If a nation expects to be ignorant and free in a state of civilization it expects what never was and never will be."

We must look largely to the press for the enlightenment that will arm us for this conflict. We should be able to look to the press for much of the sober certainty that will carry us to victory and peace. Our government and our arms and our wealth will avail us little if the editors do not accept this invitation to greatness. The agents of confusion and fear must not usurp the seats of the custodians of truth and patriotism.

In saying this, I want to emphasize my belief that the leadership for this development of a free press must come entirely from the profession itself. Government has its co-operative part to play. It must do everything possible to oppose censorship and to free the channels of communication. Beyond that point, it cannot safely go. The basic job can be done only within and by the free press itself, by you gentlemen. I know you can do it superbly. We have solemn reason to pray it will be done that way.

24. IS TV OVERTAKING THE NEWSPAPERS?
by Marya Mannes*

. . . Newspapers have two great advantages over television. They can be used by men as barriers against their wives. It is still the only effective screen against the morning features of the loved one, and, as such, performs a unique human service. The second advantage is that you can't line a garbage pail with a television set . . . it's usually the other way around.

I think I can also make you happy by bringing to your attention a recent little survey by Mr. Roper called "The Public's Reaction to Television Following the Quiz Investigations." In it he asks everybody but me this question: Suppose you could continue to have only one of the following—radio, television, newspapers, or magazines? And do you know what—you came in second: Forty-two per cent said if they could only have one, they would keep television. Thirty-two per cent said if they could only have one, they would keep newspapers. Isn't that wonderful? You should, I think, be much happier than the magazine people, because only four per cent said they needed them as against nineteen per cent for radio. So much for weeklies—the Clapps Baby Food of the nation's news diet—specially processed for quick digestion.

And listen to this, gentlemen. Mr. Roper asked these same harried people: "If you get conflicting or different reports of the same news story from radio, television, the magazines, and the newspapers, which of the four versions would you be most inclined to believe?" Can you bear the suspense? You win. Just. Thirty-two per cent believe newspaper as against thirty per cent television. But then something really strange happens, which should give you pause. When Mr. Roper asked his guinea pigs *which* of these media they would be *least* inclined to believe, you—the newspapers—topped the list. In a big way, too. Twenty-four per cent don't believe you as against nine per cent who don't believe television. And though I'm as leery of certain polls as you must be, I think this margin of credibility—in your *dis*favor—is too wide to be discounted.

And this leads me to the defense of certain practices in television which may astound those who have read my views of the medium—eight years of pretty unsparing criticism of the many TV *mal*practices. . . . But I must say this: although network television still allots far too little time to the vital service of informing the public, it does a better job in that little time than the nation's press as a whole. And when I speak of the nation's press as a whole, I am *not* speaking of the five or six splendid newspapers—and the one great newspaper—which serve the world as models of responsible public

* Staff writer for *The Reporter*. Author of *More in Anger* and *Subverse: Rhymes of Our Times*. This selection is from a speech delivered before the Women's National Press Club, Apr. 21, 1960. By permission of Miss Mannes.

information. I am speaking of the local press which in hundreds of American communities is the *only* news available, aside from those recitals of ticker tape that pass for radio news, and which defaults on its public.

Why do I think network TV does a better job of informing than these papers? Well, let's get the partisan bit over with. Television lives on advertising to an even greater extent than you do, and since advertising is big business, advertising is by nature Republican. Yet nowhere in network newscasts or network commentaries on current events have I encountered the intense partisanship—the often rabid bias that colors the editorial pages of the majority of newspapers in this country. My distinguished colleague, on *The Reporter*, Douglass Cater, in his book *The Fourth Branch of Government*, confines himself to only one pungent footnote on this subject. "I have deliberately avoided," he writes, "getting into the predominantly one-party nature of newspaper ownership. It is a fact of life. Quite frankly," he goes on, "I have no new ideas or information to add to the subject." No new information is necessary. This particular fact of life is a shameful fact; that the newspapers whose duty it is to inform the American public give them only one side of the issues that affect them profoundly: the Republican side. This is shameful not only for Democrats—we have survived it before and we will survive it again—but for the maturity of our people. Some of the same papers which loudly extol the virtues of free enterprise and a free press are consistently failing to print the facts on which a people can form a balanced and independent opinion. That balanced and independent opinion is our only real security as a nation.

Now, very often, television coverage of news is superficial and inadequate. Very often the picture takes precedence over the point. But by and large the news reports and commentaries on CBS and NBC and ABC make every effort to present viewers with more than one aspect of an issue, either by letting opposing spokesmen have their say or by outlining the positions held by both major parties on the subject involved.

Television also provides a wide range of opinion by setting up four or five experts and letting them knock each other down. What have you in your local press of this nature? Are you discharging your duty to diversity by printing snippets of opinion from unqualified readers? Is this exploring an issue?

Television may not have a Lippmann or a Reston, but then, what papers in America can claim a Sevareid and Murrow, a Huntley and Brinkley, and —although he is invisible—an Edward Morgan?

Another thing. Among the leading commentators on television, you find no Pegler—no O'Donnell—no David Lawrence. Fortunately for the American public, television will not tolerate the kind of distortion of fact, the kind of psychotic partisan virulence and personal peeve—that many newspapers not only welcome but encourage. In its entertainment, television caters far too much to the lowest instincts of man—particularly the lust for violence, or—at the opposite end of the spectrum—the urge to escape from reality into sedation. But there is one appetite it does not feed and which the partisan newspapers of the nation do: the appetite for hate . . . hate of whatever is different. I do not find on television the kind of editorials chronic in the New York tabloids as well as in, say, the Manchester *Union* where the techniques of demagoguery prevail: rouse the rabble by routing reason. With smear, by innuendo and sideshow, attack the viscera and obscure the fact.

A newspaper has the right—the duty even—to assume an attitude, to take a position. But it has an equally sacred right to explain that position in the light of the opposing one, to document that position and to bolster that position not with emotion but with fact. In television a man like Murrow has often taken a position, but never without presenting, as completely and factually as possible, the alternate opinion.

Here, of course, is where background information helps the public to draw its conclusions. TV does a great deal of this in the form of documentaries, and you can of course say that they have the time and the money to do this and you haven't. Yet across this wide country, and with the exception of a handful of syndicate columns, I fail to find in any local paper any attempt, however minimal, to strengthen this muscle of digestion—without which news can neither nourish nor inform. It can only stuff. Between the opinions of the editor and the bare statements of the wire services there is nothing . . . nothing, that is, except a collection of snippets used as fillers between the ads and picked at random.

One of the greatest and most justified criticisms of television has been that, in appealing to the largest audience possible, it neglects minority audiences and minority tastes. This is still largely true. But there is, perhaps, one program a day and many, of course, on Sunday which an intelligent man or woman can enjoy and derive interest from. In my trips east or west or north or south, I pick up the local paper to find this enjoyment or interest . . . in vain. Now, surely there's something wrong here. Many of these places I've visited—and I'm sure this is true of the whole country— have college communities where highly intelligent and talented people live, whether they are teachers or doctors or lawyers or musicians or scientists. What is there for them in the paper—usually the only paper—of their town? What features do you provide for these people? What stimulation? How many times have I heard them say: "If you want to see what a really bad paper is like, read our sheet." When you have a monopoly in a region —as most of you do—why is it necessary to aim at the lowest common denominator?

I also wonder just what you do for women. Your women's pages exist on the assumption that women are interested only in clothes, food, diet, and personal problems. This is an old and tired assumption . . . a form of segregation that has less and less bearing on the life we live. Surely we have reached the stage where food can interest men just as nuclear tests can interest women. Television has discovered this. But have you? Admittedly, television has its lady gossipers who call themselves journalists. But it has the sense to use them as performers in parlor games instead of as pundits. And so far as I know, there is on network television no vapidity equal to that of your most beloved syndicated babbler, Louella Parsons. Is this really the best the nation's press can offer its women? This and upside-down-pineapple-fudge cake?

I don't think so. And I am quite sure most of you don't think so. But I believe that over a period of decades newspapers have become a habit rather than a function. You have held your franchise so long that change has become inadmissible. I do not know, in fact, of any medium that has changed as little in the last twenty years as the daily press. And this resistance to change is the end of growth—which, in turn, marks the end of usefulness. In twelve short years television was about to approach this condition. It had become a habit and the networks rested complacently on their giant franchise. And it was only when, through a series of scandals and exposures, it became apparent that television was putting the advertising dollar ahead of the public interest that some change, some growth became not only advisable but imperative. The parallel is obvious.

What is more, I believe that this resistance to change in your field is the product of two factors: laziness and conservatism. And hold on now, gentlemen . . . before the tomatoes fly, let me say that you are the most harried, beset, and overworked men in the nation, and I would not be in your shoes for anything. Think what you have to contend with! Your publishers! Your deadlines! Your unions! Your advertisers! The State of the World! And above all, the relentless daily chore of selecting items from that giant supermarket of processed news composed of wire services' and government handouts! What a terrible life you lead!

No, the laziness and the conservatism go much deeper, and they derive from the same source. By conservatism I mean something much broader than a Republican bias, though there is some connection. I mean a fear of change. "This is the way things always have been, this is the way they'll be." Change means trouble, change means work, change means money, and here is where the laziness creeps in. It is easier to print wire services' dispatches than have a reporter on the beat. It is easier to buy syndicated columns than find—and train—your own local talent. It is easier to let the ads dictate the format than develop a format that elevates news above dog-food. It is easier to write editorial copy that appeals to emotion rather than reason. And in handling straight news, it is easier to assume the pious mantle of objectivity than to edit. To quote Eric Sevareid: "Our rigid formulae of so-called objectivity, beginning with the wire agency bulletins and reports—the warp and woof of what the papers print . . . our flat, one-dimensional handling of news, have given the lie the same prominence and impact that truth is given. They have elevated the influence of fools to that of wise men; the ignorant to the level of the learned; the evil to the level of the good." This featureless objectivity is nothing less than the editor's abdication of responsibility, is just as dangerous as the long and subtle processing of fact to fit a policy that characterizes a magazine like *Time*. The one is dereliction; the other is dishonesty. And both may provide a reason for the decline of public confidence in their press.

This is, to me, a tragedy. I am a printed-word woman myself, and I still think the word was not only in the beginning but will be in the end. No picture can ever be an adequate substitute. The word will prevail, that is, if you, who are its guardians, treat it with the respect it deserves. For if you degrade and cheapen the word too long, the people will turn to the picture. They are beginning to turn to the picture now. Not in New York, maybe, not in Washington, D.C., or St. Louis or two or three other cities . . . but in hundreds of towns across the country. Oh, they will buy your papers —to hold up at breakfast or to line the trash can or light a fire. But not to learn. And you may wake up one day to find you have lost the greatest power entrusted to men: to inform a free people.

25. BIAS IN THE WEEKLY NEWSMAGAZINES
by Ben H. Bagdikian*

1. *U.S. NEWS & WORLD REPORT*

Each week a politically crucial bloc of American voters—perhaps as many as 10 million men and women—have arranged before their eyes a neatly reconstructed picture of the nation and the world. This arrangement is through the pages of the Big Three among newsmagazines: *Time, Newsweek* and *U.S. News & World Report.*

Each magazine tells its readers it is devoted mainly to news.

Time's subtitle is: "The Weekly Newsmagazine."

Newsweek's name is augmented by its motto: "A Well-Informed Public Is America's Greatest Security."

And the encyclopedic title, *U.S. News & World Report,* is embellished with the legend: "The Complete News Magazine."

The 4 million copies of newsmagazines that are picked off newsstands and delivered by mailmen go into homes and are read chiefly for what they have to report of the news of the world. But their function is not the same as newspapers. The 58 million copies of newspapers that circulate every day among Americans record as quickly as possible the hard bricks of events flying through the air minute-by-minute, hour-by-hour, and day-by-day.

The magazines look back at the end of the week, pick up the random blocks where they lie, rearrange them into an architecture, add their own backdrops, landscaping, climate and sound effects.

How accurate is this weekly re-creation? How close to real life does it look a year afterward, five years afterward? How often are the bricks placed where they fit? How often are they left alone when, for the moment, they don't seem to fit anywhere? How often are the bricks of real events reshaped to build a scene more comforting to the public eye or more satisfying to a publisher's taste than the scenery of real life?

It is one of the ironies of the Big Three newsmagazines that the proprietor with a reputation for the most extreme political bias—David Law-

* Reporter for the Providence *Journal-Bulletin.* The selections are from the *Providence Journal and Evening Bulletin,* Oct. 6-8 and 13-16, 1958. By permission of the author and publisher.

rence—publishes a newsmagazine with a reputation for being the least biased of the three—*U.S. News & World Report.*

How justified is that reputation?

On the last page of *U.S. News & World Report* one finds in small print: "This page presents the opinions of the Editor." A study of six months of *U.S. News & World Report* shows that these opinions run to the need to expel Russia from the United Nations and attack it militarily, the "illegality" (his quotation marks) of the Supreme Court decision on racial integration, the dangers of "New Deal experimentalism," the "dictatorship" of big unions, the "immorality" of stopping H-bomb tests, and the general perfidy of the Kremlin and left-wing Supreme Court justices.

On this same page is printed another sentence:

"The news pages are written by other staff members independently of these editorial views."

Are they?

One newspaper editor, answering a poll, referred to "Lawrence's reactionary weekly." Yet the survey of 144 editorial page editors, by Carol Donley of the Department of Journalism, University of Wyoming, resulted in easy first place in usefulness for Lawrence's magazine. *Time* was a poor second, *Newsweek* third. . . .

Among the features of this growing giant are:

Lengthy tape-recorded interviews with important news sources, printed verbatim in question-and-answer form without comment.

Generous use of full texts of important public declarations, speeches by politicians, and other spoken news, also without comment within the text. These plus the interviews may constitute as much as one-third of any one issue.

Competent, on-the-scene reports by the magazine's correspondents.

Full-scale analytical pieces on a single theme, with heavy emphasis on economic reporting.

Outstanding use of graphic illustration to clarify economic and other complex news.

These all include many presentations plainly contrary to the opinions of David Lawrence himself.

In terms of quantity of reporting, *U.S. News & World Report* is far ahead of its two major competitors. In 1957 it averaged 90 pages a week of news, double *Time* and *Newsweek.* In the first six months of 1958 it printed 297 pages on business outlook (*Newsweek,* 82; *Time,* 36); 103 pages on education (*Time* and *Newsweek* each 34 pages); and 91 pages on science and space (*Newsweek,* 74, *Time,* 54). Total news pages so far this year average 69 pages a week for *U.S. News & World Report,* 52 for *Newsweek,* and 46 for *Time.*

This by itself is no measure of net value to the reader. *Time* and *Newsweek* summarize, which could conceivably be more useful than the lengthy primary documents published by *U.S. News & World Report.* And *Time* and *Newsweek* devote considerable space to cultural-intellectual-entertainment life, but *U.S. News & World Report* almost none.

But for political and economic reporting, *Time* and *Newsweek* plainly are outdistanced in space and detail by their younger rival. A study at the University of Syracuse School of Journalism of the 1956 political campaign showed that *Time* printed 34,000 words of campaign news, *Newsweek* some 14,000 and *U.S. News & World Report* 150,000 words. Searching for bias, the survey said *Time's* words were 75 percent biased toward the Republicans, *Newsweek's* 28 percent toward the Republicans, *U.S. News & World Report* only one percent toward the Republicans, the rest neutral.

But this study evidently looked only for editorially inserted words of bias. *U.S. News & World Report* deals heavily in exact reproduction of the words of others. The Syracuse survey did not measure a pertinent factor: how balanced and fair was the selection of persons whose words were accurately reported? And in what editorial surroundings were these words placed?

A study of 1958's *U.S. News & World Report* shows that it uses sources who are individually legitimate and interesting focal points of news and opinion. But it also shows that taken together they do not form a balanced picture of informed opinion.

In the first six months of 1958, for example, there were verbatim interviews with 27 representatives of large corporations. There were almost none from labor or the opposite wing of domestic economics. On autoworkers' demands there were textual reprints from heads of the car manufacturing corporations, none from the union. On prices, wages and profits there were full texts from Harlow Curtice, head of General Motors; Roger M. Blough, chairman of US Steel; and Benjamin F. Fairless, president of the American Iron and Steel Institute; but none from the opposite side.

Where the magazine searched out unusual sources, they tended to be on the side of the editor's opinions. For example, on March 21, 1958, the magazine reprinted as news the monthly newsletter of the First National City Bank of New York. Its message was that Germany is more prosperous than England because Germany has a free enterprise economy and England a semi-socialist one. No presentation was made of the obvious additional or even contrary factors in understanding the two economies.

Politically, the personalities and space are biased toward the Lawrence view. Of speech texts from 12 politicians, 11 are conservatives or conservative-moderates. (Styles Bridges, Harry Byrd, Lyndon Johnson, John Stennis) and only one (Hubert Humphrey) from the other side of the Congressional spectrum.

On January 21 a series of texts on the '58 political campaign formed a Republican-versus-Democratic debate by way of speeches selected by the editors. The three Republicans (President Eisenhower, Nixon and Sherman Adams) started off with three and three-tenths pages; the three Democrats (Sam Rayburn, Humphrey and Dean Acheson) were at the end with seven-tenths of one page, or only 18 percent of the total space for that feature.

This is not to say that anti-Lawrence opinions are excluded. In actual wordage, there are probably more in *U.S. News & World Report* than in *Time, Newsweek,* or, indeed, in the liberal *New Republic* and *The Nation.* But in balance and net impact, the total effect is heavily weighted in his favor....

Many years ago, Delbert Clark said: "In some ways Lawrence is the most skillful of all the Washington columnists: he has the ability to appear sweetly reasonable while making the most highly prejudiced statements of opinion. . . ." Clark was talking of Lawrence's personal column, but a study of *U.S. News & World Report* leads one to much the same conclusion. It also causes doubt as to the validity of the claim:

"The news pages are written by other staff members independently of these editorial views."

In the June 13, 1952, issue the editors of the fastest-growing American newsmagazine inserted a special display that took two-thirds of a page. A tinted inspirational photograph of the United States Supreme Court building plainly showed the legend: EQUAL JUSTICE UNDER LAW.

The display celebrated the Court's declaration that President Truman's seizure of the steel industry during a labor dispute was unconstitutional. In undisguised admiration of the Court, the display said that no dictatorship is possible in the United States because the Court is a "Barrier to Dictatorship," and in order for tyrants to reign: ". . . the Supreme Court must be challenged . . . or its dictum defied."

In small print at the bottom it said: "Copyright, 1952, U.S. News Pub. Corp."

A study of the magazine in 1958 makes the 1952 display hard to believe. In issue after issue the Supreme Court and its Justices are attacked, articles are published implying that it is dominated by "left-wing" law clerks, the editor refers to its pronouncements as "illegal" and the results as "law" (his quotation marks), and features headlines such as "COURT IS GIVING 'COMFORT' TO COMMUNISTS," and says Chief Justice Earl Warren shows "indifference to human suffering."

What happened to change the Court—in the eyes of *U.S. News & World Report*—from a dictator's "barrier" in 1952 to a Communist "comfort" in 1958? And to change the editor, who in 1936 wrote a book, *Nine Honest Men*, in fervent praise of the United States Supreme Court?

A study of the magazine leads one to the conclusion that it was the single act of the 1954 decision declaring racial segregation in public schools unconstitutional. The impression is that this decision caused a profound trauma and that the magazine picks at the wound every week. Not one week passed in the first six months of 1958 without a reference to racial integration. The references were sometimes straight news, sometimes highly pertinent opinions accurately recorded, but often a reaching out by the editors for material—accurately reproduced—which in its net impact carried out the feeling against the Supreme Court decision.

The usual reference in headlines and stories was not to "integration," but the most emotional term, "racial mixing." ". . . President Eisenhower sent troops to force the mixing of the races" (Dec. 27, 1957); ". . . racial mixing in schools in 1958" (Jan. 3, 1958); "to force racial mixing" (Jan. 10, 1958); and so on during the year.

The high incidence of integration news is by no means poor news judgment. Many would agree that Negro-white relations are the major domestic problem in the United States in our time. Exposure of news, opinion and

study fills a real need. Advocacy of one side or the other is in the tradition
of free discussion. But the quiet loading of "news" presentation is not.

It is "quiet" in *U.S. News & World Report* because it is largely by use
of the words of others and because it is by means of the weight of space
and emphasis, rather than outright opposition, as is done quite appropriately in the editor's page. Recently on his editorial page, David Lawrence expressed his personal view of reality in the South when he wrote:

> . . . something the South understands and wishes the North could understand
> too—that racial bitterness between whites and Negroes has never been char-
> acteristic of the South.—DAVID LAWRENCE, *Editor*.

As in political and economic items, there are large quantities of anti-
Lawrence views published. In the past—though not in the first six months
of 1958—there have been long interviews with integrationist leaders, long
textual excerpts from Negro sources. In addition, the argument can be
made that the most dramatic news has been made by the segregationists
and the most vocal arguments made by the South. Despite these factors,
there is evidence that *U.S. News & World Report* reaches out for segregationist views. And in absolute measure, the magazine tells the reader more
of the segregationist view than of the integrationist.

In the first six months of 1958, the equivalent of 80 pages of race relations or critical Court material appeared in the magazine, at least one item
every week. More than 75 percent of these items treated integration critically, either showing it to be a failure or as causing trouble. Thirteen percent was neutral in tone or impact. Six percent was approving (one example: in an interview with the commandant of the US Marines the
magazine asked if racial integration is a problem; the magazine published
in straightforward manner the reply that it had worked well).

Race relations show up obsessively in the most unlikely places. On
January 3, 1958, the magazine reported that in Uganda schools are to start
"racial mixing." Two weeks later, "Racial Problems a New Headache for
Red Chinese." The week after, an item on violence in Kansas City schools
with the quick reference: "The trouble has centered at Central Junior High
School, which is 60 percent Negro. . . ." On February 7 a three-page article
on New York school crimes gravitates rapidly to "schools that are heavily
populated by Negro and Puerto Rican pupils. . . ."; the week after that, a
two-page article on Washington, D. C., where it reported major crimes by
Negroes and the opinion that the Supreme Court has crippled law enforcement; the next week another New York City school story—"Is race tension
behind the surge of crime in New York City's integrated schools?"

On April 4 "Worldgram, From the Capitals of the World":

> Moscow . . . Beirut . . . Paris . . . Bonn . . . Singapore . . . Here's the Red
> strategy for US. . . . Talk peace, whip up the "peace at any price" drive. Stir
> up Negroes to fight segregation.

In the same issue, another article on Washington, D. C., where "Officials
estimate that one-fourth of Washington's Negro children are illegitimate."
A couple of weeks later a sympathetic account of the election of Prime
Minister Strijdom, "Mr. Afrikaner . . . Lion of the Transvaal," in South

Africa where there is "strictly enforced racial segregation," and a few weeks later another item on the Union of South Africa, "Where Racial Barriers Keep Going Higher . . . South Africa is now turning to more and more segregation as the answer to its racial problems," quoting only pro-Strijdom sources.

While a reasonable reader would not dispute any one item on integration, the tone and direction of the pattern of coverage is almost obsessively anti-integrationist. Friends of David Lawrence say this is out of character with him, though he is a long-time resident of Washington and Virginia. He has printed material against "group prejudices." Yet the magazine's treatment of the issue, while never excluding integrationist views completely, is overwhelmingly against the Supreme Court decision.

Two-thirds of the October 4, 1957, issue was devoted to the Little Rock crisis, with almost every department of the magazine suffused with emotion. The confidential sounding page, "Washington Whispers," is filled with such items as:

> Earl Warren . . . who sold the Supreme Court on ordering . . . Mr. Eisenhower . . . has acted upon his own without consulting his Cabinet . . . Newspapermen in Little Rock noted that the town was swarming with FBI agents who were reported to be the advance guards of agents who will move into the South to police the new civil rights law.

The step-by-step formal chronology of events leading to the crisis, ostensibly as unbiased as a calendar, has 66 percent of its three pages devoted to direct and indirect quotations of Gov. Orval Faubus.

A five-page layout, "Political Leaders and Editors Size Up Little Rock Crisis," is 80 percent against integration moves, with 30 percent of the total devoted to Sen. Richard Russell of Georgia. The opinion of a Southern Governor, supporting President Eisenhower, is not quoted. Two full pages quote a bitter segregationist and are entitled: "How James F. Byrnes Sizes Up Integration Troubles." There is no contrary view presented.

An example of the far-reaching enterprise of the magazine to find texts to support its view is the full page in the same issue quoting an editorial from an English Roman Catholic newspaper questioning whether the Roman Catholic Church should regard segregation in schools as "morally wrong and sinful." It is entitled, "A Catholic View on Segregation" (although the overwhelming official Catholic view has been against segregation).

Of all editorial and news material in that issue, 77 percent was essentially anti-integrationist in tone, substance or presentation; 19 percent was neutral; and 4 percent was pro-integration. The 4 percent was the text of the President's television address to the nation.

While segregationists did make news that week, so did those supporting the Supreme Court and integration. The magazine did not publish the text of the federal judge's injunction against violence in Little Rock; nor the President's proclamation before he ordered in troops; nor the speech of the federal Army commander to the high school students; nor the words of J. Edgar Hoover, who said Governor Faubus was lying; nor the text of a statement by the Rev. Billy Graham, a Southerner, condemning the violence and favoring integration, even though *U.S. News & World Report* had devoted a cover story to Billy Graham the week before.

Thus, if one characterized the treatment by *U.S. News & World Report* of integration—and of other issues with which the editor strongly disagrees —one could say that it records dutifully the official news and some of the opposition. And it pursues with enthusiasm, imagination and overwhelming space the ideas dearest to his heart. . . .

2. *TIME*, THE WEEKLY NEWSMAGAZINE

Henry R. Luce, co-founder, editor-in-chief and largest single stockholder of *Time* magazine, once told a school of journalism: "The owner-editor cannot honorably evade his personal confrontation with every aspect of truth in every aspect of his paper."

The problem of Truth in the news is an old one. In the process of struggling with it, *Time* magazine has, at least, solved the problem of success. It is the biggest, brightest and most powerful of the Big Three newsmagazines. It has a paid circulation of 2,250,000. It is the foundation for the publishing empire of Time, Inc.: *Time, Life, Fortune, Sports Illustrated, Time International, Life International, Life en Espanol, House & Home, Architectural Forum* and a complex of paper mills and radio-TV stations.

For millions of middle-class Americans it is the interpreter of national and world affairs. Thousands of foreigners get their major impression of the United States from it. The United States Information Agency last year distributed 1.8 million copies free in 56 foreign countries as part of the American propaganda effort.

The magazine has 500 carefully selected, well-paid staff members capable of the most skilled performance of almost any publication in the country. It has the most effective network of information gatherers in the United States, in terms of extensive coverage of particular subjects. On occasion its work is distinguished, showing by contrast the superficial coverage of other magazines and of many newspapers.

When it has a mind to, *Time* can develop the possibilities of a news event more imaginatively than almost any other news organization in the world; its writing and editing is bright, sometimes brilliant. But is it the Truth?

The elusiveness of Truth must have worried the editors of *Time* occasionally. But if so, they have spared the reader this human doubt. Each week the world is created absolute and dogmatic, the good guys on one side, the bad guys on the other, with *Time* holding the only scorecard. Only when the reader checks back does he discover that the good guy of October may be the bad guy of January, that Truth and *Time* change.

For example, was it the Truth, when *Time* reported Dwight Eisenhower's appearance at the start of his 1952 campaign in Abilene in the June 16, 1952, issue:

They saw Ike, and they liked what they saw.
They liked him because he turned out to be an amazingly good cam-

paigner. . . . They liked him for his strong, vigorous manner of speech, for his quiet control. . . . It was a crashing conquest.

Or was it the Truth when, after the campaign was over, *Time* in its issue of November 3, 1952, described that same week in Abilene:

At first the echoes were not strong. Ike . . . as a political candidate . . . did not quite "come across" . . . his voice was flat; he looked like an old man on TV. . . .

Time, during the 1952 campaign:

. . . Stevenson tore into this straw man . . . the Democratic candidate made a careful pitch. . . . In the same speech, Stevenson got in a reference to aid to India, which is getting to be the stock Democratic way of changing the subject on China.

Time, four years later: "Stevenson of 1952, a man meticulously concerned with the facts. . . ."

Time, before Adlai Stevenson became a Presidential candidate:

. . . Illinois has a good governor now: Adlai Ewing Stevenson. . . . In his three years . . . Stevenson has . . . sent state police out to stop commercial gambling downstate . . . lopped 1,300 political hangers-on off the state payroll . . . he didn't think State's Attorney John Boyle of Chicago was a good candidate. Stevenson has largely kept hands off law enforcement in Cook County, on the theory that local authorities are better staffed to handle it. But he didn't like the way Boyle had done the job . . . promptly dumped Boyle. . . . If Lincoln Steffens was right, corruption is the norm of US political life. . . . But men like Adlai Stevenson have dedicated themselves to a more hopeful and dynamic proposition: that the US is not a static pattern but an experiment, among other things—in good government.

Time, after Stevenson became a Presidential candidate, eight days before election:

Stevenson . . . has himself cited his record as governor to support his argument that he can deal with corruption; he tells his audience that he knows about corruption because he followed "eight years of Republican rascality." He never so much as slapped the wrist of the Cook County Democratic organization, the most corrupt and powerful of existing big-city machines. . . .

Time, August 1, 1955, on President Eisenhower's accomplishment at Geneva:

. . . If Geneva was to be measured by the spirit, as all the participants insisted it should be, then quite a bit was achieved . . . the chances of war started by the Russians is continuing to diminish. This was the reading of Geneva.

Time, May 19, 1958, quoting Dean Acheson approvingly to support *Time's* thesis that a Summit conference should not be held:

From former (1949-53) US Secretary of State Dean Acheson came two forceful, well-argued statements on US foreign policy. . . . The 1955 Geneva Conference, said Dean Acheson, "was not merely a failure; it was a fraud and positive harm. . . . "

The changeability of Truth in the pages of *Time* was noted in 1955 by a Harvard student, Milton S. Gwirtzman, who listed in the *Harvard Crimson* some *Time* Truths which seemed to change with Administrations.

Time, March 10, 1952, on the income tax under a Democratic Administration:

> This week, once again, the American taxpayer . . . was working over his income tax return. He did not do the job happily. . . . The blow, in full and crushing measure, now lands each March 15 on the chin of a fellow named John Q.

Time, April 18, 1955, on the income tax during a Republican Administration:

> . . . 60 million Americans have by this week signed their 1954 income tax forms. . . . They did this, wonderful to tell, without riots or protest. . . . It has become more and more unfashionable to criticize the income tax level.

Time, August 12, 1946, on the character of George E. Allen under a Democratic Administration:

> Last week . . . the President [Truman] eased his croniest crony, George E. Allen, into the Board of Directors of the Reconstruction Finance Corporation.

And on January 28, 1946: "George is all the more remarkable because to the naked eye, he is a clown."

Time, December 14, 1954, on the character of George E. Allen under a Republican Administration: "Last week . . . the President [Eisenhower] chatted quietly with . . . golfing companion George E. Allen, Washington lawyer and friend of Presidents."

Time throughout the 1956 campaign ridiculed public questions about the risk of having a sick President in office; or as it said in the July 22, 1956, issue on the President's decision to run again: ". . . Settled the issue with the simplicity and finality of a one-foot putt." And 16 months after the campaign, *Time* raised the question, in its March 3, 1958, issue:

> President Eisenhower is 67; the cumulative effect of his three major illnesses has sapped his second-term strengths. . . . Most of the work curtailment has come in the field of domestic affairs . . . if allowed to slide, small problems can snowball into major cases, *e.g.*, the present economic recession, and it is in this area that the President's inability to ride constant herd is most often felt.

The late William Allen White once wrote:

> I think on the whole, sooner or later, the American people do get the truth. But they often get it when it is cold potatoes and does them no good.

Time once claimed that the top men in their fields of work in America vote *Time* their favorite magazine: "They depend on its accuracy." Yet, "accuracy" is not always easy to judge in journalism. It may be a matter of judgment, knowledge and the integrity of the reporter. The dominant rule is objectivity, or the reporting of facts with a minimum of the reporter's own opinions about them. This, too, has difficulties. As *Time* once said in its Press section in a piece entitled, "The Fetish of Objectivity":

One of the most treacherous journalistic clichés is that a news story should always "let the facts speak for themselves." Thoughtful newspapermen know that the facts alone seldom can, that they speak clearly only when they are told in proper order and perspective—and thus interpreted by an honest journalist.

The question is: does the reporter collect all the facts he can and then draw a picture based on the facts? Or does he have a preconceived idea and collect only the facts that bear it out?

In American politics and foreign news, *Time's* reporting appears to be governed by an iron rule: when the facts fit the mold of *Time's* wishes, the reporting can be superb; when they do not fit the mold, *Time's* reporting can be so distorted as to raise serious questions about responsibility in mass communications. . . .

The key to *Time* reportage is not the hard news reported to it by the *New York Times*, the *New York Herald Tribune*, the Associated Press, United Press International and its own staff in the field. The key is how it is written in the high reaches of the offices in Rockefeller Center, New York.

Noel Busch, cousin of the late Briton Hadden, the man who co-founded *Time* magazine in 1923 with Henry R. Luce, says of his experience on the magazine that *Time* regards as ideal that: "Writers should not witness the events they write about." It is the writer away from the scene, passing the story back and forth among the editors, who gives to the *Time* story the impact it will have on the reader.

If one isolates the facts from the tone words added by *Time's* editors, the pattern appears. It is typical of *Time's* political reporting that the political world is generally divided into the forces of evil and the forces of virtue. If a political figure is a devil—in *Time's* perdition—he helps an elderly lady across the street just to impress the neighbors. If he is a political angel—floating in *Time's* heaven—his hand at the aged elbow is a sign of innate kindness.

In 1951, the Secretary of State, Dean Acheson, was a *Time* devil, an outstanding culprit of the Truman-Acheson Gang. While *Time* was not alone in characterizing Acheson as a menace, it was perhaps the most sophisticated and effective organ in destroying public confidence in Acheson. It did this not so much with rational argument and fact, as with the tone of words added in Rockefeller Center. Such words from its cover story on Acheson on January 8, 1951, include:

> . . . This week . . . he expanded his gloomy note. . . . What people thought of Dean Gooderham Acheson ranged from the proposition that he was a fellow-traveler, or a wool-brained sower of "seeds of jackassery" or an abysmally uncomprehending man, or an appeaser or a warmonger who was taking the US into a world war, to the warm if not so audible defense that he was a great secretary of state, a brilliant executor of the best of all foreign programs. . . . In his fifth floor office in Foggy Bottom he tried not to listen to the criticism . . . with his blue, slightly protuberant eyes studied his foreign policy. It was not a very encouraging study . . . to what extent was Acheson to blame . . . Acheson therefore inherited some of the policies and problems which he had helped create . . . was well on the way to becoming

an immeasurable disaster . . . one of the major decisions and disastrous
phases that have boomeranged to plague him. . . . The one reason . . . was
to provide Acheson's State Department with an alibi for its share in China's
tragic disaster . . . State Department, by its acts and by its failure to act
. . . had bribed . . . thrown China's door open to Russia. . . . Acheson's State
Department continued hopefully to stroke the fur of the Red leader . . . most
notable survivor among the architects of the "China mistake" is Secretary
Acheson. . . . The case against Dean Acheson . . . policy has disastrously
failed in Asia. The misreading of the Red Chinese . . . he must take full
responsibility . . . the old animus against Chiang Kai-shek. . . . On the
record, US policy in Europe is in a crucial state of hesitation. . . . Acheson
and the Administration . . , could not get around the fact of Western Europe's
anguished resignation. . . . Acheson has been invariably punctilious and polite
. . . in the end . . . he had too frequently let himself be pulled down to the level
of his hem-hawing, tiptoeing fellow-conferees. . . . The question was whether
a different secretary of state might have done more. . . . He possesses some
of the intellectual arrogance . . . a highly civilized man, an intellectual snob.
. . . No blood, no sweat, no tears ever smudge the neat laundering of
Acheson's sentences, or the mannerisms of his theories . . . the US people . . .
cannot quite tune in on him. . . . Has Dean Acheson become . . . a national
danger? . . .

In its January 3, 1955, issue, *Time* did a cover story on Secretary of
State John Foster Dulles. Like Acheson, Dulles had become a matter of
bitter dispute in the United States. The tone, words and phrases from that
story:

. . . John Foster Dulles looked squarely at the man . . . pressed Molotov
with greater skill and force than any US diplomat had ever shown . . . one
sharp stroke after another . . . Dulles rescued other millions from gullibility
. . . trips to re-inforce the free world outposts . . . develop cohesion and
strength . . . Dulles played the key role . . . Dulles' patient year of work
and travel . . . Dulles both drew upon and nourished US confidence . . . this
emphasis on US interests had a wholesome effect of stimulating the national
prides of other Western nations . . . he played the year's most effective role
. . . he was nimble in disentangling himself from his errors . . . after long and
careful negotiation . . . Dulles . . . played goalkeeper in the free world's two
major setbacks. . . . A smaller man than Dulles might have insisted . . . had
a brilliant career . . . applied Christian principles to historic realities . . .
soundest bit of diplomacy . . . Dulles' restraint was deliberate . . . his highly
practical analysis . . . Dulles analyzed . . . was all the more forceful because
Dulles' line had already been proved right . . . At that kind of diplomatic
opinion-molding, John Foster Dulles is a master. . . . He recognizes the importance . . . works hard . . . tries again, tirelessly . . . gained new confidence
. . . remarkable for their sweep and clarity . . . goes tirelessly about that
business . . . displays a tremendous capacity for concentration and work
. . . depth of the concentration. . . . Dulles is providing direction . . . cleared
the ground . . . stop epidemics of fear . . . Dulles disregarded the cries of
those . . .

It would be unrealistic in the extreme to expect any news to make a
mathematically or emotionally precise division pro-and-con. And in commentary one is dealing with opinion and judgment. But it is interesting

that of about 640 lines on Acheson in the *Time* story, about 74 percent is directly negative and critical; in the 670 lines on Dulles, only 4 percent. *Time* did not repeat directly the common anti-Acheson phrase of the time recalling that Acheson had said he would not turn his back on Alger Hiss. But it did use the phrase obliquely twice in the story: "Although he might have preferred to turn his back on the East" . . . and "Asia on which he had turned his back."

A major method of loading the story is to mention the positive arguments for a devil and follow with material wiping it out. Thus, of the 640 lines on Acheson, 23 are devoted to the major achievements which *Time* attributed to Acheson's regime, which on reflection, appear considerable: Lend-Lease, UNRRA, World Bank, Export-Import Bank, Truman Doctrine, Marshall Plan, NATO. But though it took 17 words to describe that "Acheson presided over the signing of the North Atlantic Treaty creating (on paper) a collective defense system," it then took 22 words immediately afterward to say, "The idea had not been his; it had originated in a resolution presented by Senator Arthur Vandenberg, approved by a Republican Senate. . . ." Again, when it mentioned his "new anti-Russian policy," it followed by saying that it fell short of the need.

In the case of Dulles, some 96 percent is devoted to approving and positive declarations. Curiously, it made some damning statements—but these consisted of 14 lines followed by 210 lines of more praise, then 12 lines of criticism, and a final conclusion of high approval. The two small negative insertions might strike a reader as somewhat underemphasized: "Despite these attempts . . . the free world came to a year's end with a net loss and a troubled outlook in Asia." And "After two years in office, the Eisenhower Administration has failed to plug the yawning gap in its foreign policy. . . ."

Time did not exclude unpleasant facts completely. In the case of a man it condemned, Acheson, it buried 62 lines of his considerable achievements in an avalanche—477 lines—of emotionally loaded words that stained the image. In the case of a man it approved of, Dulles, it buried 26 lines of grave and fundamental criticism, in an avalanche, 617 lines, of words that glowed with heroic praise.

Underneath it all, the reader could extract the basic facts if he worked at it. But the basic facts could conceivably come in a form which does the *Time* reader—a citizen who votes—no good. If, on the other hand, one grants that *Time* has a right to its opinions, one may judge how the opinions hold up.

In the Dulles profile, *Time's* opinion was:

> Regionally, 1954's greatest area of success for American diplomacy and the man who runs it was the Middle East. There, a number of old problems were solved by new approaches . . . the status of the Suez Canal area was settled more firmly than ever before . . . the settlement was skillfully midwifed by the US State Department.

According to some observers, Suez resulted in one of the gravest disasters for the West and for American diplomacy in this decade, and Hungary brought a disillusionment with America's "liberation" policy. Yet during this period, *Time*, on December 13, 1956, told the reader that things were never better for the United States position abroad: "The world's gaze and the world's hopes were directed toward Washington as rarely before. . . . In time of crisis and threat of World War III, President Eisenhower had cast US policy in a role to reflect the US's basic character. . . ."

Walter Lippmann that same week said ". . . the initiative and the power are not in our hands, and we found ourselves doing what we did not want to do. . . ."

James Reston, chief of the *New York Times* Washington bureau, said that the general feeling in Washington was that "the Soviet Union and Egypt have scored a tremendous victory."

Obviously, *Time* disagreed with both. The magazine said Reston "reported nonsensically." Later, Editor-in-Chief Henry R. Luce of *Time* wrote to Reston apologizing. Mr. Luce wrote that Reston was not nonsensical, he was only wrong.

A symbolic word for the discriminating reader of *Time* magazine is "cry." In the normal vocabulary it is a verb meaning to make a loud call, to utter lamentations, or to weep. But in the lexicon of *Time* style it means: A Fool Is Shouting Hysterical Nonsense. For in *Time* villains "cry"; the heroes "solemnly state."

There are other words the student of *Time* learns. The modern Republican President of the United States when irritated "snaps" back an answer. "Snap" means that the question has been in bad taste or stupid and the President is showing manly spirit. But a New Deal-Fair Deal Democratic President "snarls" or "sputters" or "spouts."

Stylistically, the result is the most dramatic, crisp and evocative language in the news profession. But politically it is a vapor of bias that seeps into the text, clouding facts and bypassing the normal critical judgment of the reader. It is a highly artistic technique, but a study of *Time's* behavior in recent political campaigns shows that it is used as a partisan political weapon.

A study of the magazine during the 1952 and 1956 Presidential campaigns leaves the impression that *Time* was the most effective propaganda printed for the benefit of the Republican National Committee. The bias appeared in the balance of space, in the selection of facts, and in the use of pictures and illustrations. But the chief weapon was the emotional prejudgment with which it surrounded the news. A reader cannot argue long over a strictly personal selection of adjectives by a writer. But if these selections fall into a clear political pattern, the reader has a right to know it.

In the September 1, 1952, issue under "REPUBLICANS, The Rediscovery," a story about General Dwight Eisenhower—leaving out the news core—began:

> A great American soldier disclosed political greatness—rediscovered courage as a policy for a nation. Out of his own wide experience with the fateful issues of the 20th Century, Dwight D. Eisenhower phrased a definition of the peril besetting the US . . . a definition so compelling . . . it displayed . . . his credentials as a candidate for President . . . a good speech, in both the moral

and political sense . . . Ike calculated with grim arithmetic . . . turned to the kind of shrewd analysis . . . which the US seldom hears from its officials. . . .

In the same issue, under "DEMOCRATS, Away From It All," a story about Adlai Stevenson—leaving out the news core—began:

> Candidate Adlai Stevenson climbed into his state-owned, two-engined Beechcraft last week and flew off to the Wisconsin woods . . . hours loafing . . . a little half-hearted casting. . . . Evenings he lolled in the bearskin-draped living room before a fieldstone fireplace big enough to take 7-foot logs, which were hauled automatically from the basement at the touch of a button . . . he did little work. . . .

On October 10, 1956, *Time* reported the appearance of both Stevenson and Eisenhower at a farmers' gathering:

> Here, on rolling land near Newton, Iowa, some 8,000 American farmers and townsmen, their wives, kids and relatives assembled . . . giving their attention to their honorary chairman—President Dwight Eisenhower—honed to intellectual sharpness . . . dwelt on a theme . . . his own inner peace. . . .
>
> From the same giant platform . . . Adlai Stevenson made a major bid for the farm vote at Newton. . . . Stevenson promised the farmers everything but the moon on behalf of the Democrats. . . . From the past, Stevenson dragged out a familiar Democratic tactic . . . contended Adlai, in an astonishing defense of . . .

The title of the Eisenhower story was: "Ike's Promise."

The title of the Stevenson story was: "Adlai's Pitch."

This relatively subtle technique does not mean that *Time* neglected the blunt instrument of loaded pictures. In the 13 issues covering the 1952 campaign, *Time* printed 21 photographs of Eisenhower, all of them showing him in a favorable light—heroic, or friendly, or earnest. Stevenson's face in these issues appeared only 13 times, the two largest facial shots from photographs taken 30 years before, and 40 percent of the total showed Stevenson in unflattering poses eating, drinking or grimacing.

Eisenhower's picture appeared on Page One of National Affairs in *Time* three times, on Page Two four times during the campaign period. Stevenson's never appeared on Page One of National Affairs.

In 1956, *Time* dealt heavily in cartoons. In the 13 pre-election issues it showed 10 cartoons involving the personal figure of Stevenson, all of them derogatory. It showed none that portrayed Eisenhower personally in a derogatory way. While Eisenhower regularly "dwelt" on subjects or stated them, Stevenson "cried" or, as *Time* said October 8, 1956: ". . . Adlai Stevenson went whirling across the US landscape last week, spouting sparks and smoke. . . ."

Time's severest distortions are in the area of national politics and China policy. Both appear to be matters of deep conviction on the part of Editor-in-Chief Henry R. Luce. He is involved more deeply in the present Administration than any other American publisher. And as the son of missionaries in China, where Luce grew up, it is said that the Editor-in-Chief retains the dream of Christianizing China and insists on unflagging support of Christian Chiang Kai-shek.

The bias does not usually keep important facts out of the magazine. But sympathetic facts are presented with dignity and joy; unsympathetic ones with ridicule and contempt. Describing visiting dignitaries at the 1952 Republican convention, *Time* said:

> And there was former President Herbert Hoover . . . the old gentleman smiled a cautious smile. . . . Time had whitened his hair . . . and softened the lines of his face. For 20 years he had suffered with dignity and without complaint an *auto da fe* of criticism such as few men . . . have ever endured. . . . But this was his night among friends. . . .

Describing the visiting dignitaries at the 1952 Democratic convention:

> Hefty, hearty India Edwards . . . a woman with an eye on the vice presidency . . . tramped to the speaker's stand splendidly corseted . . . fogged in some fast opening lines. . . . Mrs. Franklin D. Roosevelt, whose new frizzy hairdo made her look like a genial golliwog. . . .

The difference in the descriptions of these two persons in *Time* is unimportant. What is important is that the corset-golliwog content of Democratic stories was always high during the campaigns and practically absent in Republican stories; and the "suffered with dignity" content was high in Republican stories, absent in Democratic.

Nor need one be pro-Democratic or anti-Republican to question the ethics of such political reporting in a publication that tells the reader he is getting news in *Time, The Weekly Newsmagazine*. *Time* pursues its political enemies and boosts its friends by another technique. If facts are damaging to friends, it mentions the facts briefly and then rebuts them at length or dismisses them with editorial contempt. If they are damaging to enemies, *Time* dwells on them at length, may even base its entire reportage on them and accepts them as proved conclusions. When, for example, the 1952 Republican convention compromised the civil rights issue, *Time* reported:

> . . . one of the convention's youngest and prettiest delegates was the central figure in a struggle over civil rights. Mrs. Mildred Younger, a 31-year-old Los Angeles housewife, presided over the civil rights subcommittee with an intelligent, calm hand. . . . The subcommittee was bitterly divided. . . . As a result . . . came out with a plank that each side could construe as it wished.

A short time later the Democrats did the same thing: "To satisfy two men with such divergent views on civil rights as Russell and Harriman was a real triumph in fence-straddling for Stevenson."

Pretty Mrs. Younger presided with an intelligent hand; Stevenson fence-straddled.

Often during the campaign, *Time* did not trust the Republicans to make their own arguments, but provided the reader with its own. When television viewers saw that the Republican delegates at the convention paid no attention whatever to the platform, *Time* volunteered: "The delegates' inattention was not necessarily evidence that they did not care what was in the platform. They knew that the resolutions committee. . . ."

Another technique is to concentrate on the mechanics or the messy details of an enemy operation, but to dwell on the spiritual side of a friend.

When Sen. John Sparkman was nominated Democratic Vice Presidential candidate in 1952:

> John Jackson Sparkman, who had just been nominated for Vice President of the United States, stopped grinning, fished a cough drop out of his mouth and slipped it through a crack in the platform floor. "There," commented an unsympathetic observer bitterly, "is a man who has every quality a Democratic candidate for Veep needs: he's from the South." This comment contained considerable truth. . . . Sparkman, in fact, is so resolute a compromiser that it takes a political micrometer to tell just where he stands. . . .

But apparently *Time* had no unsympathetic observers at the Republican convention: "The meeting quickly settled on California's Richard Nixon. No deal was involved. Nixon was a logical choice. . . ." Its description of Sparkman during the campaign was minimal but repeated many criticisms made by others. Its treatment of Nixon did not, although Nixon had been bitterly criticized by many Americans:

> . . . the most up-to-date attraction at the Illinois State Fair last week was a goodlooking, dark-haired young man with a manner both aggressive and modest, and a personality to delight any political barker. He seemed to have everything—a fine TV manner, an attractive family, a good war record, deep sincerity and religious faith . . . He was Richard Milhous (pronounced mill house) Nixon, Republican nominee for Vice President. . . .

Time tended to take Republican statements at face value, and where the Republicans failed to say things, *Time* volunteered them; if the Republicans said embarrassing things, *Time* explained them away. Yet what Democrats said usually was looked at critically, or cynically, and then rebutted. During the 1956 campaign, for example:

> One day last week Stevenson . . . was disturbed, he said, that the Republicans might be trying to fob off Eisenhower upon a "docile, complacent, carefree people all happily chanting, 'Peace, Prosperity and Progress—ain't it wonderful' . . . Candidate Stevenson obviously felt he had a point. . . ."

Time then went on to explain on its own—in a report of Democratic campaign activities—

> The US has learned to live with its crises with equanimity . . . if there seems to be little interest in it as an election-year issue, it is only because the search is constant and the US is always new.

Time regularly in the campaign drifted from Republican statements into heroic prose affirming those statements. And it regularly devoted part of the space under its heading "DEMOCRATS" to Republican [or its own] attacks on Democrats.

In a cover story on Vice Presidential candidate Kefauver it started with a reference to Kefauver pitching manure and thereafter put the words "shovel" and "pitch" in the text describing his speeches. Aside from this, directly derogatory material constituted 30 percent of the story, with *Time* adding editorial agreement. The story on Nixon was an almost unbroken epic of approval, brushing past criticisms to even higher praise:

. . . while he is a politician to his fingertips, Nixon is a man of consistent principle, whose values are as sound and fundamental as any in US politics today. . . . Had Nixon been the weak, unprincipled character that his more choleric enemies make him out to be, he might well have given up. . . .

In an October, 1952, profile of Stevenson, 55 percent was unflattering, derogatory or otherwise damaging, much of that 55 percent being used to counter or nullify positive material. The Eisenhower cover story had only three percent derogatory lines and with these *Time* took the initiative to answer: "One of the Democratic charges against Eisenhower is that he is vague on issues. Actually, while Ike's prose is vague in style, his speeches are highly specific in content. . . ."

An analysis of its behavior during the 1952 and 1956 political campaigns casts serious doubts on its own early prospectus:

"There will be no editorial page in *Time*.

"No article will be written to prove any special case."

CHAPTER IV

The Mass Media:
Television, Radio, and Movies

Traditionally, we have thought of the home, the school, and the church as the major molders of the attitudes, values, and opinions of our people. They remain so today. But when we speak of the home these days, we refer to more than the family members. An invited guest with an astonishing capacity to make himself welcome has joined the family circle for 35 to 40 hours per week. This visitor leaves a very considerable imprint upon the parents and subtly yet powerfully challenges their formerly dominant influence upon the minds and emotions of their children. Although television is commonly thought of as a medium of entertainment, it is obviously much more than that. The pervasiveness of advertising and its values, of news and occasional educational programs, as well as the *kind* of entertainment it offers, inevitably has a major (if immeasurable) effect on those whose attention is gripped by the video screen.

From the first, TV's potentialities as a national cultural force were recognized by thoughtful people. It was recognized, too, that in its early and experimental stages TV would grope toward a pattern compatible with its status as a truly *mass* medium, with its native compulsions to maximize its profits, and with its minimum sense of obligations to serve educational as well as monetary ends.

But just what the mix would turn out to be, how effective the Federal Communications Commission could be as a representative of the public interest (with an eye on the First Amendment), how high or low the industry's estimate of the public taste and of its public responsibilities, and how demanding or acquiescent the viewing public would be—these developments could not be foreseen.

Although television has been the object of more or less continuous attacks since the industry's inception, the volume of criticism probably reached a peak in 1959 and early 1960, touched off by the TV quiz scandal revelations.

Edward R. Murrow, who has done as much as anyone to raise the standards of TV, leads off the selections in this chapter with the blunt charge (in a speech before the broadcasting industry, no less!) that, if historians a hundred years hence were to watch a typical week of TV kinescopes, they would find "recorded in black and white, or color, evidence of decadence, escapism, and insulation from the realities of the world in which we live." Contending that the American people are "more reasonable, restrained, and more mature than most of our industry's program planners believe," he cites his own experience with controversial programs as supporting evidence. America's major corporations, he says, would neither impair their corporate images nor hopelessly antagonize their stockholders if they occasionally accepted the opportunity to "exalt the importance of ideas and information."

The ever-pungent John Fischer, editor of the ever-lively *Harper's Magazine,* joins in Mr. Murrow's strictures, while granting that TV is better than some of its critics concede. He questions the practicability of Mr. Murrow's recommendation, preferring to require the networks to foot the bill for the effort required to improve TV programming. He proposes the establishment of a National Broadcasting Authority to be financed from broadcasting profits derived from their lucrative privilege of using the *public's* air waves. The Authority would prepare triweekly programs of high quality for prime-time network showings.

Mr. Fischer's plan draws a satirical counterattack from National Broadcasting Company's Robert Sarnoff. Reasoning on a sauce-goose-gander basis, Mr. Sarnoff suggests that a similar proposal should first be given a trial run in the publishing industry. Senator Monroney's comment on Mr. Fischer's plan reflects the typical American fear of permitting further governmental influence in the communications industries.

The penetrating study of the harsh economics of TV by Robert Horton shifts attention to the costs of obtaining and operating a TV franchise, the decisive role of the advertisers, the tyranny of the rating systems, the impotence of the FCC, and the growing dominance of the networks over local station programming. (The latter presumably reduces the capacity of stations to carry programs of special local interest, although the experience of many observers has been that local autonomy all too often leads to the canceling of the network public service programs in favor of local trivia.)

The article by *Consumer Reports* sums up the recommendations made by many critics of TV and calls for a series of reforms which will doubtless receive serious consideration by the FCC during the Kennedy Administration.

Newton Minow's straightforward blast at TV's "wasteland" left the broadcasting industry in a state of temporary shock. In his first major address as chairman of the Federal Communications Commission, he made clear his intention to revive the withered powers of the commission and to hold the industry to a higher standard of public responsibility than his predecessors. His remarks about children's programs were regarded with particular interest by many critics of TV.

TV, of course, is not the only entertainment medium which has vastly more than hedonistic significance. Social and political philosopher Max Lerner regards the movies as "a crucial American popular art," which, because it deals with "the stuff American dreams are made of," plays a vital part in the emotional economy of the American people. Lerner believes the movies, as an art form, have outclassed their competitors, but he notes their tendency to lapse into stereotypes, implicitly to overvalue the importance of mammon. and to express "not sex or love but sexiness."

When "genuine love and sexuality are crowded out of any literary or dramatic production, whether by censorship or timidity, violence comes in to fill the vacuum." Violence, he adds, is "grotesquely inflated" in relation to its significance in our society and presumably in relation to its necessary and proper role as a dramatic theme. That these characteristics of the cinema cannot fail to leave their mark on the conscious and subconscious attitudes of its consumers need not be argued.

That the mass media also has persuasive and thoughtful supporters is demonstrated by Leo Rosten's judicious and down-to-earth analysis of the media's performance and problems. Mr. Rosten is in no whitewashing mood, but as he ticks off the particulars of the bill of indictment drawn against the mass media, he offers specific evidence that the critics overstate their case, fail to recognize adequately the inevitable limitations of mass media, and apply unrealistic evaluative criteria. Above all, he contends that American intellectuals have failed to make peace with the fact that, as intellectuals, they are a breed apart, with special needs and tastes and a chronic tendency to exaggerate the capacity of most people to enjoy and appreciate that which proves gratifying to them. They are members of an elite, he says, who as democrats shrink from acknowledging their membership and drawing the logical conclusions therefrom.

Our concluding contributor, Charles Siepmann, calls upon university professors to reckon with the potency of mass communications and to accept their responsibilities to help discipline and guide them into more constructive channels. It is not enough to berate their performance in the cloister; scholars must be prepared to "speak out loud and bold," to apply to mass communications their scholarly judgment, perspectives, and vision, and to remind society of the "tradition of civility" which separates civilized man from barbarian.

As we go to press, there are indications that the sustained critical barrage leveled against TV is having a salutary effect, at least temporarily. All the major networks are devoting more time—at better viewing periods—to educational programs. Whether the industry will lapse into its old habits now that the uproar has subsided is the major unanswered question.

26. A BROADCASTER TALKS TO HIS COLLEAGUES
by Edward R. Murrow*

This just might do nobody any good. At the end of this discourse a few people may accuse this reporter of fouling his own comfortable nest; and your organization may be accused of having given hospitality to heretical and even dangerous thoughts.

But the elaborate structure of networks, advertising agencies, and spon-

* Director of the United States Information Agency. Formerly conducted *Person to Person* and *See It Now*. War correspondent for CBS from 1939 to 1945 and director of public affairs for CBS from 1945 to 1960. The selection is from *The Reporter*, vol. 19, no. 8, Nov. 13, 1958, pp. 32-36. By permission of the author and publisher. This selection is a speech delivered before the Radio and Television News Directors' Association.

sors will not be shaken or altered. It is my desire, if not my duty, to try to talk to you journeymen with some candor about what is happening to radio and television in this generous and capacious land.

I have no technical advice or counsel to offer those of you who labor in this vineyard that produces words and pictures. You will forgive me for not telling you that the instruments with which you work are miraculous; that your responsibility is unprecedented; or that your aspirations are frequently frustrated. It is not necessary to remind you—the fact that your voice is amplified to the degree where it reaches from one end of the country to the other does not confer upon you greater wisdom or understanding than you possessed when your voice reached only from one end of the bar to the other. All of these things you know.

You should also know at the outset that, in the manner of witnesses before Congressional committees, I appear here voluntarily—by invitation —that I am an employee of the Columbia Broadcasting System, that I am neither an officer nor a director of that corporation, and that these remarks are of a "do-it-yourself" nature. If what I have to say is responsible, then I alone am responsible for the saying of it. Seeking neither approbation from my employers, nor new sponsors, nor acclaim from the critics of radio and television, I cannot well be disappointed. Believing that potentially the commercial system of broadcasting as practiced in this country is the best and freest yet devised, I have decided to express my concern about what I believe to be happening to radio and television. These instruments have been good to me beyond my due. There exist in my mind no reasonable grounds for personal complaint. I have no feud, either with my employers, any sponsors, or with the professional critics of radio and television. But I am seized with an abiding fear regarding what these two instruments are doing to our society, our culture, and our heritage.

"Shield the Sensitive Citizens"

Our history will be what we make it. And if there are any historians about fifty or a hundred years from now, and there should be preserved the kinescopes for one week of all three networks, they will there find recorded in black-and-white, or color, evidence of decadence, escapism, and insulation from the realities of the world in which we live. I invite your attention to the television schedules of all networks between the hours of eight and eleven P.M. Eastern Time. Here you will find only fleeting and spasmodic reference to the fact that this nation is in mortal danger. There are, it is true, occasional informative programs presented in that intellectual ghetto on Sunday afternoons. But during the daily peak viewing periods, television in the main insulates us from the realities of the world in which we live. If this state of affairs continues, we may alter an advertising slogan to read: "Look Now, Pay Later." For surely we shall pay for using this most powerful instrument of communication to insulate the citizenry from the hard and demanding realities which must be faced if we are to survive. I mean the word—"survive"—literally. If there were to be a competition in indifference, or perhaps in insulation from reality, then Nero and his fiddle, Chamberlain and his umbrella, could not find a place on an early-afternoon sustaining show. If Hollywood were to run out of Indians, the program schedules would be mangled beyond all recognition. Then some courageous soul with a small budget might be able to do a documentary telling what, in fact, we have done—and are still doing—to the Indians in this country. But that would be unpleasant. And we must at all costs shield the sensitive citizens from anything that is unpleasant.

I am entirely persuaded that the American public is more reasonable, restrained, and more mature than most of our industry's program planners believe. Their fear of controversy is not warranted by the evidence. I have reason to know, as do many of you, that when the evidence on a controversial subject is fairly and calmly presented, the public recognizes it for what it is—an effort to illuminate rather than to agitate.

Several years ago, when we undertook to do a program on Egypt and Israel, well-meaning, experienced, and intelligent friends shook their heads and said: "This you cannot do—you will be handed your head—it is an emotion-packed controversy, and there is no room for reason in it." We did the program. Zionists, anti-Zionists, the Friends of the Middle East, Egyptian and Israeli officials said, with a faint note of surprise: "It was a fair count. The information was there. We have no complaints."

Our experience was similar with two half-hour programs dealing with cigarette smoking and lung cancer. Both the medical profession and the tobacco industry co-operated in a rather wary fashion. But in the end of the day they were both reasonably content. The subject of radioactive fallout and the banning of nuclear tests was and is highly controversial. But according to what little evidence there is, viewers were prepared to listen to both sides with reason and restraint. This is not said to claim any special or unusual competence in the presentation of controversial subjects, but rather to indicate that timidity in these areas is not warranted—by the evidence.

Recently, network spokesmen have been disposed to complain that the professional critics of television have been "rather beastly." There have been hints that somehow competition for the advertising dollar has caused the critics of print to gang up on television and radio. This reporter has no desire to defend the critics. They have space in which to do that on their own behalf. But it remains a fact that the newspapers and magazines are the only instruments of mass communication which remain free from sustained and regular critical comment. If the network spokesmen are so anguished about what appears in print, let them come forth and engage in a little sustained and regular comment regarding newspapers and magazines. It is an ancient and sad fact that most people in network television and radio have an exaggerated regard for what appears in print. And there have been cases where executives have refused to make even private comment on a program for which they were responsible until they had read the reviews in print. This is hardly an exhibition of confidence.

The oldest excuse of the networks for their timidity is their youth. Their spokesmen say: "We are young; we have not developed the traditions nor acquired the experience of the older media." If they but knew it, they are building those traditions, creating those precedents every day. Each time they yield to a voice from Washington or any political pressure, each time they eliminate something that might offend some section of the community, they are creating their own body of precedent and tradition. They are, in fact, not content to be "half safe."

Nowhere is this better illustrated than by the fact that the chairman of the Federal Communications Commission publicly prods broadcasters to engage in their legal right to editorialize. Of course, to undertake an editorial policy, overt and clearly labeled, and obviously unsponsored, requires a station or a network to be responsible. Most stations today probably do not have the manpower to assume this responsibility, but the manpower could be recruited. Editorials would not be profitable; if they had a cutting edge they might even offend. It is much easier, much less troublesome, to use the money-making machine of television and radio merely as a conduit through which to channel anything that is not libelous, obscene, or defamatory. In that way one has the illusion of power without responsibility.

"I Say It Isn't News"

So far as radio—that most satisfying and rewarding instrument—is concerned, the diagnosis of its difficulties is rather easy. And obviously I speak only of news and information. In order to progress it need only go backward—to the time when singing commercials were not allowed on news reports, when there was no middle commercial in a fifteen-minute news report; when radio was rather proud, alert, and fast. I recently asked a network official, "Why this great rash of five-minute news reports (including three commercials) on week ends?" He replied: "Because that seems to be the only thing we can sell."

In this kind of complex and confusing world, you can't tell very much about the *why* of the news in broadcasts where only three minutes is available for news. The only man who could do that was Elmer Davis, and his kind aren't about any more. If radio news is to be regarded as a commodity, only acceptable when salable, and only when packaged to fit the advertising appropriation of a sponsor, then I don't care what you call it—I say it isn't news.

My memory also goes back to the time when the fear of a slight reduction in business did not result in an immediate cutback in bodies in the News and Public Affairs Department, at a time when network profits had just reached an all-time high. We would all agree, I think, that whether on a station or a network, the stapling machine is a poor substitute for a newsroom typewriter.

One of the minor tragedies of television news and information is that the networks will not even defend their vital interests. When my employer, CBS, through a combination of enterprise and good luck, did an interview with Nikita Khrushchev, the President [Mr. Eisenhower] uttered a few ill-chosen, uninformed words on the subject, and the network practically apologized. This produced a rarity. Many newspapers defended the CBS right to produce the program and commended it for initiative. But the other networks remained silent.

Likewise when John Foster Dulles, by personal decree, banned American journalists from going to Communist China and subsequently offered contradictory explanations. For his fiat the networks entered only a mild protest. Then they apparently forgot the unpleasantness. Can it be that this national industry is content to serve the public interest only with the trickle of news that comes out of Hong Kong? to leave its viewers in ignorance of the cataclysmic changes that are occurring in a nation of six hundred million people? I have no illusions about the difficulties of reporting from a dictatorship; but our British and French allies have been better served—in their public interest—with some very useful information from their reporters in Communist China.

Dollars vs. Duty

One of the basic troubles with radio and television news is that both instruments have grown up as an incompatible combination of show business, advertising, and news. Each of the three is a rather bizarre and demanding profession. And when you get all three under one roof, the dust never settles. The top management of the networks, with a few notable exceptions, has been trained in advertising, research, sales, or show business. But by the nature of the corporate structure, they also make the final and crucial decisions having to do with news and public affairs. Frequently they have neither the time nor the competence to do this. It is not easy for the same small group of men to decide whether to buy a new station for millions of dollars, build a new building, alter the rate card, buy a new Western, sell a soap opera, decide what defensive line to take in connection with the latest Congressional inquiry, how much money to spend on promoting a new program, what additions or deletions should be made in the existing covey or clutch of vice-presidents, and at the same time—frequently on the same long day—to give mature, thoughtful consideration to the manifold problems that confront those who are charged with the responsibility for news and public affairs.

Sometimes there is a clash between the public interest and the corporate interest. A telephone call or a letter from the proper quarter in Washington is treated rather more seriously than a communication from an irate but not politically potent viewer. It is tempting enough to give away a little air time for frequently irresponsible and unwarranted utterances in an effort to temper the wind of criticism.

Upon occasion, economics and editorial judgment are in conflict. And there is no law which says that dollars will be defeated by duty. Not so long ago the President [Mr. Eisenhower] delivered a television address to the nation. He was discoursing on the possibility or probability of war between this nation and the Soviet Union and Communist China—a reasonably compelling subject. Two networks—CBS and NBC—delayed that broadcast for an hour and fifteen minutes. If this decision was dictated by anything other than financial reasons, the networks didn't deign to explain those reasons. That hour-and-fifteen-minute delay, by the way, is about twice the time required for an ICBM to travel from the Soviet Union to major targets in the United States. It is difficult to believe that this decision was made by men who love, respect, and understand news.

"Both Free and Enterprising"

So far I have been dealing largely with the deficit side of the ledger, and the items could be expanded. But I have said, and I believe, that potentially we have in this country a free-enterprise system of radio and television which is superior to any other. But to achieve its promise, it must be both free and enterprising. There is no suggestion here that networks or individual stations should operate as philanthropies. But I can find nothing in the Bill of Rights or the Communications Act which says that they must increase their net profits each year, lest the Republic collapse. I do not suggest that news and information should be subsidized by foundations or private subscriptions. I am aware that the networks have expended and are expending very considerable sums of money on public affairs programs from which they cannot hope to receive any financial reward. I have had the privilege at CBS of presiding over a considerable number of such programs. I testify and am able to stand here and say that I have never had a program turned down by my superiors because of the money it would cost.

But we all know that you cannot reach the potential maximum audience in marginal time with a sustaining program. This is so because so many stations on the network—any network—will decline to carry it. Every licensee who applies for a grant to operate in the public interest, convenience, and necessity makes certain promises as to what he will do in terms of program content. Many recipients of licenses have, in blunt language, welshed on those promises. The money-making machine somehow blunts their memories. The only remedy for this is closer inspection and punitive action by the FCC. But in the view of many this would come perilously close to supervision of program content by a Federal agency.

So it seems that we cannot rely on philanthropic support or foundation subsidies, we cannot follow the "sustaining route," the networks cannot pay all the freight, and the FCC cannot or will not discipline those who abuse the facilities that belong to the public.

What then is the answer? Do we merely stay in our comfortable nests, concluding that the obligation of these instruments has been discharged when we work at the job of informing the public for a minimum of time? Or do we believe that the preservation of the Republic is a seven-day-a-week job, demanding more awareness, better skills, and more perseverance than we have yet contemplated?

I am frightened by the imbalance, the constant striving to reach the largest possible audience for everything; by the absence of a sustained study of the state of the nation. Heywood Broun once said, "No body politic is healthy until it begins to itch." I would like television to produce some itching pills rather than this endless outpouring of tranquilizers. It can be done. Maybe it won't be, but it could. Let us not shoot the wrong piano player. Do not be deluded into believing that the titular heads of the networks control what appears on their networks. They all have better taste. All are responsible to stockholders, and in my experience all are honorable men. But they must schedule what they can sell in the public market. And this brings us to the nub of the question.

Tithe Time

In one sense it rather revolves around the phrase heard frequently along Madison Avenue: "The Corporate Image." I am not precisely sure what this phrase means, but I would imagine that it reflects a desire on the part of the corporations who pay the advertising bills to have the public imagine, or believe, that they are not merely bodies with no souls, panting in pursuit of elusive dollars. They would like us to believe that they can distinguish between the public good and the private or corporate gain. So the question is this: Are the big corporations who pay the freight for radio and television programs wise to use that time *exclusively* for the sale of goods and services? Is it in their own interest and that of the stockholders so to do? The sponsor of an hour's television program is not buying merely the six minutes devoted to his commercial message. He is determining, within broad limits, the sum total of the impact of the entire hour. If he always, invariably, reaches for the largest possible audience, then this process of insulation, of escape from reality, will continue to be massively financed, and its apologists will continue to make winsome speeches about giving the public what it wants, or "letting the public decide."

I refuse to believe that the presidents and chairmen of the boards of these big corporations want their "corporate image" to consist exclusively of a solemn voice in an echo chamber, or a pretty girl opening the door of a refrigerator, or a horse that talks. They want something better, and on occasion some of them have demonstrated it. But most of the men whose legal and moral responsibility it is to spend the stockholders' money for advertising are removed from the realities of the mass media by five, six, or a dozen contraceptive layers of vice-presidents, public-relations counsel, and advertising agencies. Their business is to sell goods, and the competition is pretty tough.

But this nation is now in competition with malignant forces of evil who are using every instrument at their command to empty the minds of their subjects, and fill those minds with slogans, determination, and faith in the future. If we go on as we are, we are protecting the mind of the American public from any real contact with the menacing world that squeezes in upon us. We are engaged in a great experiment to discover whether a free public opinion can devise and direct methods of managing the affairs of the nation. We may fail. But we are handicapping ourselves needlessly.

Let us have a little competition. Not only in selling soap, cigarettes, and automobiles, but in informing a troubled, apprehensive, but receptive public. Why should not each of the twenty or thirty big corporations which dominate radio and television decide that they will give up one or two of their regularly scheduled programs each year, turn the time over to the networks, and say in effect: "This is a tiny tithe, just a little bit of our profits. On this particular night we aren't going to try to sell cigarettes or automobiles; this is merely a gesture to indicate our belief in the importance of ideas." The networks should, and I think would, pay for the cost of producing the program. The advertiser, the sponsor, would get name credit, but would have nothing to do with the content of the program. Would this blemish the corporate image? Would the stockholders object? I think not. For if the premise upon which our pluralistic society rests—which as I understand it is that if the people are given sufficient undiluted information, they will then somehow, even after long, sober second thoughts, reach the right decision—if that premise is wrong, then not only the corporate image but the corporations are done for.

There used to be an old phrase in this country employed when someone talked too much. It was "Go hire a hall." Under this proposal the sponsor would have hired the hall; he has bought the time; the local station operator, no matter how indifferent, is going to carry the program—he has to. Then it's up to the networks to fill the hall. I am not here talking about editorializing, but about straightaway exposition as direct, unadorned, and impartial as fallible human beings can make it. Just once in a while let us exalt the importance of ideas and information. Let us dream to the extent of saying that on a given Sunday night the time normally occupied by Ed Sullivan is given over to a clinical survey of the state of American education, and a week or two later the time normally used by Steve Allen is devoted to a thoroughgoing study of American policy in the Middle East. Would the corporate image of their respective sponsors be damaged? Would the stockholders rise up in their wrath and complain? Would anything happen other than that a few million people would have received a little illumination on subjects that may well determine the future of this country, and therefore the future of the corporations? This method would also provide real competition between the networks as to which could outdo the others in the palatable presentation of information. It would provide an outlet for the young men of skill—and there are some even of dedication— who would like to do something other than devise methods of insulating while selling.

There may be other and simpler methods of utilizing these instruments of radio and television in the interests of a free society. But I know of none that could be so easily accomplished inside the framework of the existing commercial system. I don't know how you would measure the success or failure of a given program. And it would be hard to prove the magnitude of the benefit accruing to the corporation which gave up one night of a variety or quiz show in order that the network might marshal its skills to do a thoroughgoing job on the present status of NATO or plans for controlling nuclear tests. But I would reckon that the president, and indeed the majority of shareholders of the corporation who sponsored such a venture, would feel just a little bit better about the corporation and the country.

"Fat, Comfortable, Complacent"

It may be that the present system, with no modifications and no experiments, can survive. Perhaps the money-making machine has some kind of built-in perpetual motion, but I do not think so. To a very considerable extent the media of mass communications in a given country reflect the political, economic, and social climate in which they flourish. That is the reason ours differ from the British and French, or the Russian and Chinese. We are currently wealthy, fat, comfortable, and complacent. We have currently a built-in allergy to unpleasant or disturbing information. Our mass media reflect this. But unless we get up off our fat surpluses and recognize that television in the main is being used to distract, delude, amuse, and insulate us, then television and those who finance it, those who look at it and those who work at it, may see a totally different picture too late.

I do not advocate that we turn television into a twenty-seven-inch wailing wall, where longhairs constantly moan about the state of our culture and our defense. But I would just like to see it reflect occasionally the hard, unyielding realities of the world in which we live. I would like to see it done inside the existing framework, and I would like to see the doing of it redound to the credit of those who finance and program it. Measure the results by Neilsen, Trendex, or Silex—it doesn't matter, the main thing is to try. The responsibility can be easily placed, in spite of all the mouthings about giving the public what it wants. It rests on big business, and on big television, and it rests at the top. Responsibility is not something that can be assigned or delegated. And it promises its own reward: good business and good television.

Perhaps no one will do anything about it. I have ventured to outline it against a background of criticism that may have been too harsh, only because I could think of nothing better.

Someone once said—I think it was Max Eastman—that "That publisher serves his advertiser best who best serves his readers." I cannot believe that radio and television, or the corporations that finance the programs, are serving well or truly their viewers or listeners, or themselves.

I began by saying that our history will be what we make it. If we go on as we are, then history will take its revenge, and retribution will not limp in catching up with us.

We are to a large extent an imitative society. If one or two or three corporations would undertake to devote just a small fraction of their advertising appropriation along the lines that I have suggested, the procedure would grow by contagion, the economic burden would be bearable; and there might ensue a most exciting adventure—exposure to ideas, and the bringing of reality into the homes of the nation.

To those who say, "People wouldn't look, they wouldn't be interested, they're too complacent, indifferent and insulated," I can only reply: "There is, in one reporter's opinion, considerable evidence against that contention." But even if they are right, what have they got to lose? Because if they are right, and this instrument is good for nothing but to entertain, amuse, and insulate, then the tube is flickering now and we will soon see that the whole struggle is lost.

This instrument can teach, it can illuminate; yes, and it can even inspire. But it can do so only to the extent that humans are determined to use it to those ends. Otherwise it is merely wires and lights in a box. There is a great and perhaps decisive battle to be fought against ignorance, intolerance, and indifference. This weapon of television could be useful.

Stonewall Jackson, who knew something about the use of weapons, is reported to have said: "When war comes, you must draw the sword and throw away the scabbard." The trouble with television is that it is rusting in the scabbard during a battle for survival.

27. TV AND ITS CRITICS
by John Fischer*

In the hurt tones of a misunderstood man, Robert W. Sarnoff recently complained that television is getting a raw deal. Its critics, he said, are calling it bad names—"mediocre" . . . "unworthy" . . . "time-wasting."

This, he intimated, is both unfair and damaging to the industry. TV is giving the public what it wants, and the public loves it. Its critics are either misinformed, or they have a selfish interest in discrediting TV; or they are intolerant intellectuals who despise the mass taste and want to impose their own arcane standards on a reluctant America.

If this keeps up, he warned, TV will face two hideous dangers. Its audience and advertisers may drift away, because they are constantly being told that watching their favorite programs is "a shameful act." Worse yet, the government might start meddling with TV programing.

So Mr. Sarnoff urged his industry to launch "a massive communications effort" to answer its critics. It should explain that "a principal function" is to serve up light entertainment—to "meet the need of most active Americans for relaxation." (Well, all right, maybe it ought to provide something for "minority tastes" as well—but that is secondary.) And the industry ought to make clear that it finds no conflict between serving the public and serving advertisers; what is good for the sponsor is good for the United States.

Since Mr. Sarnoff is boss of NBC and since he was talking to the broadcasters' trade association, he got action. Committees were set up, money was raised, and the industry is now planning a heavy-caliber campaign to defend itself.

Mr. Sarnoff has a point. Four points, to be precise.

Much criticism of TV *has* been misinformed. Some of it has come from professional intellectuals whose main stock in trade is lament over the malodorous decay of American culture. (A classic example is Gunther Anders' essay in *Mass Culture: The Popular Arts in America*,[1] in which he deplores TV for 4,500 words without once touching on anything so vulgar as a fact. One of his conclusions is that "because the world is brought into

---

* Former newspaperman who served with the U.S. Department of Agriculture from 1937 to 1942 and with various war agencies during World War II. Editor of *Harper's Magazine* and author of *Why They Behave like Russians* and *Master Plan: USA*. This selection is from *Harper's Magazine*, vol. 219, no. 1310, July, 1959, pp. 10-14. Reprinted by permission of the author.

[1] Edited by Bernard Rosenberg and David Manning White; published in 1957 by the Free Press, Glencoe, Illinois.

our homes, we do not have to explore it . . . modern man travels only as a last resort." To preserve his intellectual purity, Dr. Anders evidently avoids not only TV, but also highways, airports, trains, and docks.)

Perhaps it is also true—though hard to prove—that some of the newspaper and magazine criticism of TV has been snide and hostile, because TV is a strong competitor for audience and advertising.

Surely, Mr. Sarnoff is right in fearing that government domination would be a bad thing. The Federal Communications Commission has made sorry use of what power over broadcasting it now has; and foreign experience—notably in England—suggests that government-operated TV has about as many (though different) failings as the American system. Then, too, it is always dangerous to let politicians or bureaucrats get their fingers on *any* channel of communication. The temptation to use it for propaganda is too great a strain to put on any conscience.

Finally, for whatever one man's opinion is worth, it seeems to me that TV is better than many of its critics are willing to admit. In a slow and spotty way, it may actually be improving. At least in the New York area, where the network programs usually originate, anybody willing to hunt a little can now find one or two worthwhile programs almost every day— ranging from history lectures to Eugene O'Neill, from first-rate jazz to Leonard Bernstein. (True enough, local stations in the hinterland often refuse to carry the best of the network offerings; they can make more money by running ancient movies.) In the household I know best, TV has caused none of the disasters predicted by the gloomier sociologists. My children haven't turned into videots, or even neglected their homework much. And if my own brain is softening, I can't honestly blame it on my watching an occasional prize-fight, baseball game, or Phil Silvers comedy.

But if we grant all this, the fact remains that Mr. Sarnoff and many of his fellow broadcasters don't seem to understand what their responsible critics are really saying. These critics too have some valid points—and they cannot be answered by any "communications effort," however massive. The only possible answer would be a basic change in the organization of the industry.

The true indictment against TV is not that it is all bad, but rather that it is not nearly as good as it could be—nor as good as the public has a right to expect. The public is now paying a high price for something it has been promised, and is not getting. With the best will in the world, the industry *in its present form* evidently is powerless to deliver what it has promised—solemnly and legally—that it would deliver.

Some specifications of this charge were set forth most vigorously, not by a cloistered intellectual, but by one of the most respected and successful executives in broadcasting, Edward R. Murrow. Last October he scandalized the industry by saying, right out loud, that its performance is timid, trivial, and escapist. . . .

Shortly after [Mr. Sarnoff's] speech about the critics, I talked to him at some length, and have no doubt that he is a conscientious and intelligent man, eager to do what he can to improve his industry. So too with the responsible executives at CBS—notably its president, Dr. Frank Stanton, a former professor who is at least as thoughtful as any of his intellectual critics; and its TV chief, Louis Cowan, a former aide of Adlai Stevenson.

The trouble is they can't do much.

As the industry is now organized, *nobody*—neither networks, nor local stations, nor sponsors—has much leeway to attempt anything more than marginal improvements.

Some such modest improvements already are in prospect. Mr. Sarnoff recently announced that NBC is planning seven hour-long informational programs, plus some operas and original plays, to be presented at peak viewing periods. Dr. Stanton has said that next year CBS will schedule "regular hour-long informational broadcasts once a month in prime evening time," and that later he hopes to offer such programs twice a month and eventually every week.

These are remarkably courageous steps. Even if the network chiefs get away with them, however, that will still mean that only about one twenty-eighth of the prime hours will be salvaged from the froth. And to judge from past experience, many of the networks' affiliated stations will refuse to carry such programs.

The reason why such improvements are so daring and difficult is, in a word: Money. Those prime hours are enormously valuable. Their sale to advertisers brings in most of the network's income. From this profit it pays for unsponsored programs, for its costly news service, and for those cultural items which appear at dawn and on Sunday afternoon. From this same profit it must pay its dividends. If the networks give away too many of these golden hours for "informational broadcasts," the stockholders will soon want to know why. They may even want a new president. After all, TV is not a philanthropic enterprise.

Each local station is under similar pressure. When it carries an unsponsored network public-service program it is actually out of pocket; but if it rejects that program and sells the time to half a dozen local sponsors, it makes a tempting profit. What would you do if you were the station manager?

Why, then, don't some of the big corporations sponsor an occasional program dealing with "ideas and information," as Mr. Murrow suggested? Again, because they feel they can't afford to. It costs a sizable fortune to put an evening program on a national network. The sponsor will get his money back only if he draws the largest possible audience. If horse opera sells more autos than Ed Murrow—as it does—then the advertiser has to go for horse opera. The fact that he, personally, may prefer Murrow makes no difference. If he should yield to such a whim, his harder-headed competitors will soon run him out of the market.

Actually the sponsor doesn't even have the freedom to take that chance. Once in a long while some advertiser may be rich enough—or stubborn enough—to put on a program which strikes his fancy, even though it does not fetch a whopping audience. One such was Firestone. Until recently it presented a program of semi-serious music—not great art, but certainly a high cut above the quality of most evening shows. Although its audience was relatively small, Firestone was content.

The ABC network was not. It was afraid to carry a low-rating show at 9:00 P.M., because millions of viewers might switch to a competing channel —and stay there for the rest of the evening. So ABC told Firestone that it would have to shift to a less strategic hour or get off the air. No other network could find a place for "The Voice of Firestone" in prime time either— and at this writing the program apparently is doomed.

Everybody feels awfully sorry about this—and everybody is helpless. Them, as Jimmy Durante used to say, is the conditions which prevail.

Our system of broadcasting was not meant to work that way. When it got started, a generation ago, everybody recognized that radio (and later TV) could serve as an immensely powerful instrument of public education and enlightenment. In theory, every station is supposed to put that purpose first. It is licensed to broadcast, under the Federal Communications Act, in order to serve "the public convenience and necessity."

Such a license is a gold mine. It gives the lucky applicant a monopoly on the use of a particular piece of public property—a radio wave-length or TV channel. It costs him nothing, though it may earn him a fortune. Some licenses have been sold, shortly after they were granted by the FCC, for as much as $8 million.

In return for this magnificent gift of public property, the station owner is supposed to devote a considerable part of his air time to public service programs. Naturally the competition is keen for every one of the available channels, and each of the competing applicants makes impressive promises about the public service he will provide. (Sometimes, as the Harris Committee discovered, he also tries to bribe an FCC commissioner.)

These promises are seldom, if ever, kept. The Federal Communications Commission has made no serious effort to enforce them. No station's license has ever been revoked, or refused renewal, because the operator broke his pledge. In practice, therefore, most stations simply ignore this obligation, and sell every hour they can for as much money as they can get. Much of their programing consists of showing old movies in fifteen-minute slices— with as many as six consecutive commercials sandwiched in between all the segments. (Watching one of these mutilated dramas is enough to make a man wonder about Mr. Sarnoff's conviction that "broadcasting's responsibility to the public is harmonious with its responsibility to advertisers.")

If some undesirable time remains unsold, then the station may use it as a cheap gesture toward the public service—often by running a sermon by some local minister.

The upshot is that we are all paying dearly for something we don't get. We are letting the broadcasters use valuable public property, for free— and they are not delivering in return the public service which they promised.

Can anything be done to stop this scandal? Well, of course, the FCC might try to enforce its own rules—but that seems most unlikely with the caliber of men now on the commission and the political atmosphere in which it operates.

There is, however, another possible solution. It would, I think, meet most of the points raised by the responsible critics of broadcasting. It would give the public real freedom of choice in programs. It would avoid the dangers of government control. Finally, it would remove the economic pressures which now bear down so painfully on people like Sarnoff, Stanton, Murrow, and others who would like to improve TV and radio, but can do so only with great difficulty and risk.

In bare outline, it might work something like this:

(1) Instead of giving away its air channels, from now on the government would rent them. Each local TV and radio station would pay a modest percentage of its annual earnings—say 10 or 15 per cent. This would be no great hardship, since most broadcasters are now making very comfortable profits. For example, CBS earned $7 million in the first quarter of the year, a gain of nearly 8 per cent over the same period in 1958. Radio Corporation of America, the parent company of NBC, reported first quarter earnings of nearly $13 million, for a 44 per cent gain; but some of this came from the sale of TV sets and other equipment, rather than from broadcasting.

The earnings of all the hundreds of local stations are hard to discover, so I have no idea how much money such rentals might bring in. Certainly it would be substantial. For the sake of illustration, let's assume that they might total $50 million a year.

(2) This money would be turned over to a National Broadcasting Authority—a public body chartered by Congress but carefully insulated from politics. Its directors would be five men who already hold responsible positions in the fields of education, culture, and information. They must not be governmental appointees; they must be free from economic and political pressures; they must not represent any competing media; they should represent a broad spectrum of the public interest; and they must command respect.

Such a board might include the president of Harvard, the heads of the Carnegie and Rockefeller foundations, the director of the Metropolitan Museum, and the chief of the National Radio and Television Center. . . . (Again, this list is merely illustrative; no doubt it could be improved upon.) The essential point is that the men who hold such jobs at any given moment would *ex officio* become directors of the National Broadcasting Authority. They should be well paid for their part-time services. I can think of no better method to select a board of assured competence, and above suspicion of any interest except the public welfare.

(3) The board would hire a Program Manager, and would give him general policy directives—much as a corporation board of directors deals with the company's president. This manager would, of course, be an experienced broadcasting executive. Mr. Murrow, for example.

(4) The main job of the Authority and its manager would be to produce public-service programs—news-in-depth, top-quality music and theater, documentaries dealing with science, the arts, and public affairs, plus any kind of experimental features they might want to try. In the beginning, they might attempt three hour-long programs each week for TV and an equal number for radio.

(5) Each program would have to be carried by one of the major networks and all of its affiliated stations, in prime evening time. Monday's

program, for example, might be assigned to NBC, Wednesday's to CBS, and Friday's to ABC. This hour would be an additional rental-in-kind, demanded of the broadcasters in part-payment for the privilege of using the public's air waves. (Unaffiliated stations might be required to devote an equal amount of time to showing the Authority's kinescopes.)

Thus the viewer would have genuine freedom of choice. If he is not interested in the Authority's report on the Berlin crisis, scheduled for 9:00 P.M. Monday on NBC, then he can turn to a western on CBS or a song-and-dance act on ABC. And *vice versa*. (He would even get a chance to see an occasional program uninterrupted by commercials, since the Authority would have no need for advertising.) Such an arrangement would, moreover, expose the Authority's program producers to the bracing effects of competition for their audience.

(6) This system would cost the broadcasters far less than you might think. For the networks and the few conscientious local stations would be relieved of the painful and expensive duty of producing public-service programs. And those stations which now evade this duty would be forced to bear their fair share of the Authority's cost.

All broadcasters could then go merrily about their primary business of selling advertising—undistracted by the present conflict between their duty to their stockholders and their duty to the public service. Nagging consciences would be stilled, snarling critics would be silenced—or, at least, largely diverted to watching the Authority's programs—and ulcers might no longer be the TV man's occupational disease.

(7) The Authority would open up a stimulating new opportunity for broadcasting talent. I personally know a dozen top-flight producers, writers, and actors who would jump at the chance to work for such an outfit, even if it meant a cut in salary—simply because they are tired, as one of them put it, of "producing garbage."

(8) The plan would not cost the taxpayer a penny; it could be put into effect with a simple piece of legislation; and it would require no governmental machinery to operate it. . . .

28. NBC AND A UNITED STATES SENATOR ADVISE AND DISSENT

Robert Sarnoff and Senator A. S. Mike Monroney*

From Senator A. S. Mike Monroney of Oklahoma

To the Editors:

Congratulations to the editor of the Easy Chair on his criticism of the current dismal diet of TV programming. I have tried my best many times in the Senate to express my resentment against this underestimation of

* Mr. Sarnoff is president of the National Broadcasting Company, and Mr. Monroney is a United States Senator from Oklahoma. The selection is from "Letters," *Harper's Magazine*, vol. 219, no. 1312, September, 1959, pp. 4, 6, and 8. By permission of the authors and publisher.

American intelligence and good taste. I applaud and concur in your diagnosis of the case.

I must respectfully dissent violently from your proposed treatment for the removal of the fungus my TV screen has developed. . . . I do not wish ever to see the control of public service programing turned over to any quasi-public group of censors, keepers, planners, or psychologists. No matter how eminent such men may be in their fields, government-sponsored intrusion into this field smacks of state control of the dissemination of information in this most important medium. During my years in Washington, I have not seen any great masterpieces come from such commissions, boards, or authorities. As poor as the current run of TV programs is, I'd rather go on leaving my screen dark than abandon the concept that a competitive system of TV offers the best long-range hope for decent programing. I would hope that, instead of transferring public-service programing to an artificial brain of government authority, the TV industry eventually will mature. After all, the newspapers and the magazines weren't so hot twenty years after Gutenberg invented movable type.

Some day, our commercial TV programers will divorce that nagging old crone, audience ratings, and show some adult initiative. There is a TV audience for quality programs that advertisers of quality products need to reach. Perhaps the big-show sponsor may be displaced by joint ventures of advertisers who now use quality media in the journalistic field. The very existence of *Harper's*, the *New Yorker*, and other fine magazines, as well as many distinguished newspapers, proves it can be done. Even newspapers with screeching headlines of crime and violence still devote some space to book reviews, art and music columns, sports, and financial news.

The best corrective eventually will prove to be the TV viewer. When intelligent people begin to write the sponsor telling him what they really think of this program, heads will begin to roll along Madison Avenue and in the network programing departments. Public opinion is slow to be aroused, but once it awakens, it's better than a stampede of buffalo in any current Western drama. It is, thank God, the most important force of all in a democracy.

From Robert Sarnoff

To the Editors:

I am much intrigued by John Fischer's proposal for a National Broadcasting Authority, which would be supported by an ingenious double levy of time and money on American broadcasters and, as a *quid pro quo*, would relieve these same broadcasters of "the painful and expensive duty of producing public-service programs."

That I, as a broadcaster, might disagree with some aspects of the proposal does not lessen my appreciation of Mr. Fischer's very earnest and sincere effort to solve a problem that has bothered us for many years. We are still groping for solutions, and his thoughtful attempt to provide them should be cause for gratitude, not irate reproach.

My principal quarrel with Mr. Fischer's idea relates to its area of application and to the fact that he nowhere suggests that it be pre-tested. The very name National Broadcasting Authority has a ring of granitic permanence; and before anything so radically and challengingly different is imposed on the infant, sprawling, enormously complex television industry, I would like to see a trial run in a more mature, more stable branch of the mass communications family.

I suggest magazines for the test, and I believe the data developed through a National Magazine Authority would be enormously useful in fashioning any future NBA—far more, in fact, than might at first blush be apparent.

It is hardly necessary, in proposing this to *Harper's* readers, to elaborate on the imbalance of mass-appeal magazines. In 1958, for example, nearly one-third of all weekly magazine serials (as well as mass-market paperbound fiction) consisted of Westerns—a ratio several times greater than the ratio of Westerns to other programs on the NBC Television Network.

Why should the great mass of American magazine readers—those who read *Look, Playboy,* the *Saturday Evening Post,* to say nothing of such chastised brethren as *Confidential*—never be exposed to Alfred Kazin's analysis of the fiction of the 'fifties [coming in October in *Harper's*] or a piece by the Bolshoi Ballet's Galina Ulanova on how she created the role of Juliet [July]? Why not give readers of *Time, Life,* and *Fortune* a crack at articles with such titles as "The Hidden Affair Between Big Business and Big Labor" [July]?

As with television, there are two valid reasons to promote greater cultural, educational, and "public-service" content in our mass magazines. One is that it would help to raise public taste and broaden public interests. The other affects readers who already count themselves among the cultural elite. Why should a member of this elite who happens to find some amusement in *Reader's Digest* be saddled with the expense and trouble of finding more specialized fare in smaller publications, any more than the *avant-garde* television viewer should undergo the inconvenience of tuning to his special preferences at hours or on days when he may want to be doing something else?

Mr. Fischer has pointed the way to the remedy. In proposing that television and radio stations and networks be taxed twice (once in funds and again in segments of choice time) to underwrite an NBA, he noted that the broadcasters are commercial beneficiaries of the free public air, obliged by law to operate in the public interest, convenience, and necessity.

Magazines too are on the receiving end of substantial public bounty, although a more old-fashioned type: money. In 1958, the U. S. Post Office put the subsidy represented by second-class mailing privileges at $272,096,464.[1] The largest group beneficiary was magazines, with the most popular, mass-appeal magazines naturally benefiting to the greatest extent. Moreover, Congress clearly intended this privilege to encourage the spread of public enlightenment; the law grants it expressly "for the dissemination

---

[1] As Mr. Sarnoff states, these are Post Office figures; in fact they are highly controversial interpretations of cost accounting.—The Editors [of *Harper's Magazine*]

of information of a public character, or devoted to literature, the sciences, arts, or some special industry."

Nothing could be more in keeping with the spirit of this clause, and with the thrust of Mr. Fischer's idea, than to tax the recipients of this public largesse to implement the very ends it was intended to serve. A nominal levy on the profits of each magazine, even less than the "modest percentage" of 10 per cent or 15 per cent that Mr. Fischer would impose on broadcasters, could underwrite the costs of a National Magazine Authority, a public body chartered by Congress but carefully insulated from politics.

The five directors of this Authority should meet all the exacting criteria that Mr. Fischer has prescribed for the NBA. They should be men of impeccable professional competence, high intellectual stature, and detachment. Under their general policy directives, exemplary articles, fiction, reviews, and verse would be solicited, and conceived, assigned and written, and generously paid for. These efforts would be placed regularly, on a staggered basis, in the commandeered pages of national magazines of vast circulation.

Thus, for example, every other issue of the *Ladies' Home Journal* would be required to devote, say, six pages in the front of the magazine to the kind of worthwhile prose and poetry that ripens almost unnoticed in such esoteric periodicals as *Hudson Review*, *Sewanee Review*, and *Commentary*. Or if J. D. Salinger wants to undertake another extraordinary effort such as the 34,000-word story "Seymour," which appeared in a single issue of the *New Yorker* last June, the NMA could place it for him in a magazine of far greater circulation, say the *Reader's Digest*.

Just consider what a refreshing and uplifting change of pace, what a stimulus to further creativity, this procedure promises for those literary figures who now scorn the mass magazines because they dislike being forced to write "garbage."

My NMA plan would cost magazines far less than they might fear. Conscientious editors and publishers would be largely relieved of the painful and expensive duty of ferreting out, encouraging, and publishing obscure works of genuine distinction. All that would be taken care of for them by the NMA, and they could concentrate instead on income-producing Western and private-eye serials for the millions. And those magazines which totally evade their moral obligation under the second-class mail privilege—for example, the semipornographic magazines that dominate so many newsstands—would be forced to bear their fair share of the Authority's cost.

For the NMA to serve as an adequate test of Mr. Fischer's basic idea, at least two years might be needed, and I do not think it ought to be rushed just to get at television. Indeed, he has my assurance that the one-hour weekly quota of prime-time, prime-quality programs assigned under his plan to the NBC Television Network will in fact be fulfilled two to three times over in the forthcoming season, and without the help of any Authority. Among these programs, during peak evening viewing hours, will be original dramas by such playwrights as Archibald MacLeish and James Costigan; news-in-depth specials on such subjects as the rise of African nationalism; adaptations of outstanding works, *e.g.*, Maugham's "The Moon and Sixpence," starring Sir Laurence Olivier, "What Makes Sammy Run" by Budd Schulberg, and Shakespeare's "The Tempest"; historical dramas filmed on the actual scenes of the events, *e.g.*, Jefferson at Monticello, and numerous music specials with artists of the caliber of Renata Tebaldi, Harry Belafonte, Isaac Stern, Eileen Farrell, and the New York City Center Ballet.

Since these projects and many others like them involve lengthy contractual commitments by NBC, it seems only fair that we have the opportunity to fulfill our contracts before we are relieved of the painful and expensive duty of presenting any further programs of this kind.

29. THE ECONOMIC SQUEEZE ON MASS TV
by Robert Horton *

Unique among American industries, broadcasting was conceived by its founders not as an adventure in profit-making but as a new opportunity for high public service. In 1926 David Sarnoff, who had come to RCA from American Marconi, saw the role of broadcasting "as a public institution in the same sense that a library, for example, is regarded." He was flatly opposed to "direct advertising on the air" and fondly believed that radio manufacturers would in their own interest pay some of the costs of station operation.

Such views were not peculiar to Sarnoff. The first annual conference of commercial broadcasters, held in 1922, solemnly resolved not only that direct advertising be absolutely prohibited but "that indirect advertising be limited to the announcements of the call letters of the station and of the name of the concern responsible for the matter broadcasted, subject to such regulations as the Secretary of Commerce may impose." Herbert Hoover, then Secretary of Commerce, had already made it clear where he stood: "It is inconceivable that we should allow so great a possibility for service, for news, for entertainment, for education, and for vital commercial purposes to be drowned in advertising chatter."

Some thirty years later, Richard Salant, a CBS vice-president, was to give an accurate statement of the philosophy and practice that had evolved. Describing television as "just about this quarter century's brashest entry on the American industrial scene," he urged his colleagues to admit frankly and "out loud that ours is a business which depends on revenue—dollars— from advertisers for survival."

Because radio used the public domain—that is, the air waves—it was understood from the start to have some of the character and responsibility of a public utility, a principle embodied in the original Communications Act of 1927 and carried over to the 1934 act, which established the Federal Communications Commission. The spirit of the basic law lay in "the assertion

* Free lance writer who specializes in communications. This selection from *The Reporter*, vol. 22, no. 9, Apr. 28, 1960, pp. 14–19. By permission of the author and publisher.

. . . that the right of the public to service is superior to the right of any individual to use the ether." The FCC, accordingly, was directed to regulate broadcasting in the public interest, pass on the nature of the service to be rendered by each station, determine the qualifications of those licensed to operate them, and generally to discipline the industry. TV is obligated by law to place public service over private profit, and to serve "the public interest, convenience and necessity."

Broadcasting has acknowledged its responsibilities to the public with impeccably stated precepts, all recognizing the public stake in the air waves. In the absence of other income, however, commercial broadcasting has had to rely exclusively on advertising for its revenue. It is also the only mass-market industry to which the mass consumer *directly* pays not a single cent. To stay in business and flourish, it must sell not its own end products, its programs, but the product of other industries—the soaps and the cereals, the drugs and the cigarettes, the coffee and the dog foods.

Richard Salant makes the point that "We in broadcasting have never really sat down to think out what our story really is. We have never stopped to figure out what we are and what we are trying to do." Any attempt to make good on this failure will have to begin by examining the economics of the industry. For the most striking aspect of TV's plight is that the economics of broadcasting, as presently organized, run directly counter to the basic law that governs the industry.

Gargantua Takes Over

Detailed figures on the finances of television are not easy to come by, but even a sampling of those available shows how the industry grew.

As recently as 1949 the networks and the fourteen stations they owned outright had modest revenues of $19.3 million and showed a loss of $12.1 million for the year. The other eighty-four television stations combined had total revenues of only $15 million and reported to the FCC aggregate losses of $13.5 million. In 1958, by contrast, some 520 stations, practically all affiliated with the networks by then, grossed more than $1.25 *billion*, realized profits estimated at $170 million before taxes, employed about thirty thousand people, and were able to show a seventeen per cent return as compared with the twelve per cent average for American industry. That is an impressive nine-year record for any industry. Of the total gross revenues, moreover, the three networks and the fifteen stations they owned outright in 1958 accounted for fully forty-four per cent.

Of those who keep the screen aglow, the biggest spenders are the food companies, which laid out $109.2 million in 1958 to promote their goodies, from coffier coffee to instant dog food. Next in the order of their patronage of the arts via television came the makers of toiletries and toilet goods, $98.9 million; smoking materials, $62 million; medicine and patent medicines, $58 million; automotive accessories and equipment, $52.5 million. The list then tapered down to agriculture and farming, which contributed a mere $63,454.

To these advertisers the cost of using the air waves is formidable. To plug the drug Anacin, for example, $740,627 was spent in a single month just for the time on the air, apart from talent and production costs. One competitor, Bayer Aspirin, spent $527,855 and another, Bufferin, $455,934.

The cost of TV time, like that of any other advertising, is based on the size of the audience, or what is believed to be the size of the audience, and such are the estimates on this score that time has never had so high a dollar value placed upon it. According to the statistical outfits, bred by the TV industry to produce figures for the ad agencies and the sponsors, about fifty million TV sets in forty-five million American homes are tuned in for thirty-five to forty hours a week. As if that were not awesome enough, Sindlinger & Co., one of the busiest statistical bureaus, came up with the finding that during a single week last year, 126,564,000 Americans over twelve years of age spent 2,231,600,000 hours watching television and only 474,000,000 hours reading newspapers.

However sound these figures may be, the public must in truth make a staggering use of its television sets, since it pours out a vast fortune just to keep them in working order. Trade statistics show that in 1958 Americans spent $2.5 billion for parts and services, which was roughly five times the investment of the industry itself in broadcasting facilities. In addition, enough sets are on enough of the time to run up a year's bill of some $300 million for electricity.

Free Licenses Cost Big Money

Television's massive structure of public and private investment rests in the first instance on two devices: the Federal license, without which a station cannot operate; and the networks, which by their nation-wide coverage open the door to the mass markets required by the advertisers. The pressure on those responsible for both these features of the business is stupendous and begins to operate from the moment a prospective station owner applies for a license.

In the early days of TV it was possible for a reasonably well-heeled citizen to present himself to the FCC, to pledge himself, as required by law, to operate his station for the "public interest, convenience and necessity," and after submitting a prospective schedule showing a satisfactory balance between public service and entertainment, to walk off with the precious license. Sometimes, however, he faced stiff competition from another investor applying for the same channel, and rather than enter a prolonged contest that could only encourage the FCC to probe deeper into his qualifications, he arranged to buy off his competitor and even charge the expense against future profits. Such payoffs were usually substantial. In Providence a few years ago, one of these disappearing competitors collected $200,000 for just such co-operation.

With 520 TV stations now on the air and very few unassigned channels left, licenses are harder to come by. For the most part they are acquired by transfer, a transaction in which the station is sold without the new owner's having to undergo the scrutiny imposed on an original licensee by the FCC.

Among the bigger deals of recent years was the transfer of a CBS-affiliated property in Philadelphia that cost some $5.5 million and was sold for $20 million (radio station included). Another CBS affiliate in Sacramento, California, that had cost $750,000 brought $1.5 million. And an NBC-affiliated station in Kansas City that had cost $2 million sold for $7.6 million.

In most of these transfer cases only some twenty-five to thirty per cent of the sale represents the physical properties of a station, such as tower transmitters and studios. The question then arises, What is the remainder of the money paid for? A good slice of it, of course, is the inflated cost of buying into a seemingly sure-fire growth industry with the prospect of a high rate of return and large capital gains. Another substantial slice goes to pay for the network affiliation, without which, as we shall see, a TV station can hardly hope to break even.

Not least, a sizable, though unspecified, part of the purchase price must be considered by any realistic judgment as payment for the transferred license, without which there could be no deal at all. For a broadcaster's basic stock in trade is the public air, which he sells, along with program and talent, to the advertisers, and he can do that only by virtue of holding a Federal license. According to the law this should be good for only three years, but in reality, as former FCC Chairman James Lawrence Fly observed, a TV license has gradually become "just as permanent as a fee simple deed to the Empire State Building." Under the law it is revocable for violations of FCC orders and regulations, but even in cases of open defiance the commission has taken no such drastic action.

Then You Need a Network

Next to its physical facilities and its license, the most valuable asset a station can have is a contract with one of the three major networks. According to FCC figures, nine out of ten stations depend on network affiliation for survival. Except for a few independents in big metropolitan areas, stations with such contracts can also figure on enjoying the steepest markups over the original price when their owners put them up for sale on the transfer market. An independent station in Milwaukee that cost $700,000 and was barely breaking even sold recently for $5 million just because the seller knew that the buyer already had a CBS affiliation contract in his pocket. Conversely, a half interest in a CBS affiliate in Charleston that had cost more than a million dollars brought only $650,000 when it became known that the network was withdrawing its affiliation.

Behind these fluctuations lies the simple fact that network affiliation often means the difference between healthy profit for a station and intolerable loss. Government figures show, for example, that while thirty affiliated stations in markets with four or more outlets enjoyed an average income of $1,462,000, sixteen independent stations in the same market were suffering losses averaging $78,000.

With an average broadcasting week of one hundred hours, an independent local station could not possibly afford to fill its schedule with live shows even if the material and talent were available, and they are not. Signing a contract with one of the networks, it agrees to turn over its best viewing hours, usually in the form of an "option" on nine or more hours of its best time divided into three daily periods. In return it gets a steady supply of sponsored and sustaining programs free of charge; a guaranteed income from national advertisers, usually about thirty per cent of the total time charges; and big-name shows that greatly enhance the value of its non-network hours, which it sells to local and national advertisers for spot commercials.

True, by the FCC's interpretation, a station is required to devote a reasonable part of its schedule to sustaining programs and to "local live programs" of direct benefit and interest to the community in which it operates. The FCC has further directed that "such programs should not be crowded out of the best listening hours." And it has ordered that the individual broadcaster or licensee must maintain control over his own programming and may not surrender this responsibility to networks, agencies, or other program-producing organizations. Yet this is precisely what has happened. The same pressures that force the individual station to rely on the network for survival force the networks into an incessant scramble to control more time in more markets in order to be able to offer the national advertiser the biggest possible audience at any given hour.

At hearings held in New York last summer the FCC heard some blunt testimony on this score. Robert L. Foreman, executive vice president of Batten, Barton, Durstine & Osborn, replied when asked about the individual broadcaster's responsibility for programming: "I am afraid that is an unrealistic situation. My understanding is that that onus was placed upon the local stations many years ago and the situation today is such that the individual stations really do not have that authority, and if they really exercised it the economics of the situation is such that they would not long be in business."

The Tyranny of Ratings

The three networks have in effect taken over the programming of all but a handful of the 520 TV stations scattered about the country. The networks' overriding concern from the start was, and probably had to be, incessant pursuit of the fickle mass audience. Mr. Salant put it clearly enough in a talk last year to the St. Louis Rotary Club:

... the fact is that broadcasting is a truly mass medium; it has to be. Unless it can enlist and hold the interest of most of the people a good part of the time, it is just too expensive a medium to survive. It must, in its spectrum of programming, have something—even the great majority of its material—that will appeal to not just thousands or hundreds of thousands but to millions and tens of millions.

Coinciding by chance with the emergence of polling techniques, the preoccupation with numbers has given birth to an esoteric science that purports to tell a sponsor all about his television "market"—its size, location, and composition—along with comparable data about his competitors.

TV marketing has a basic unit of measurement, called the CPM, which is the cost of presenting the sponsor's message in a thousand homes. Since the total cost of a program is fixed, the greater the number of sets tuned in to it, the lower the CPM. A cost of $3.50 per thousand should not make the average sponsor wince—unless he discovers that a competitor is getting good sales results at $1.95. In that case, the first show will have a very short life, and the chances are good that what replaces it will be a close imitation of the $1.95 show. So it turns out that fifty to sixty per cent of each season's weekly shows are failures and are dropped at the first opportunity available under the contract.

To arrive at the vital CPM, advertisers and networks must first determine the "circulation" of a given program. Unlike newspapers and magazines, which have specific figures on copies sold (though not on total readership), the broadcasting industry must rely on market-research organizations and the rating services they provide. These firms, which have developed into flourishing enterprises in their own right, compile the fateful circulation statistics that determine the nature of TV programming. Using sampling techniques, the rating services obtain their raw information from telephone interviews, from "diaries" listing the programs viewed by a small number of persons selected as a cross section, by meters recording the operation of sets in selected homes, or by a combination of these methods. The rest is done by projection, extrapolation, analysis, and other techniques of the services' special art. Besides circulation estimates, they offer data and advice on almost any aspect of the TV audience—total viewing time, reaction to programs and products, social and physical appetites, and statistical breakdowns by age, sex, and size of family.

Like all pollsters, they appear to be dancing on the head of a pin, basing their findings on microscopic samples. The Nielsen TV Index, largest of the rating services, with a gross business of more than $20 million annually, uses a sample of approximately a thousand homes. The American Research Bureau checks 2,200 and Trendex from 600 to 1,500 homes, depending on the time period involved. So frequently and extensively do they differ that the industry commissioned a two-year study of the problem by qualified specialists, who in 1954 reported that none of the rating services could pass muster.

The rating systems have been questioned on several counts. With nearly fifty million TV sets in operation, a sampling of less than a thousand may or may not put undue strain on the valid theory of the microcosm, but it is certainly questionable when conditions vary greatly from area to area. There is wide choice of programs in some cities, very little in others; geography imposes variations in time; and local programs may account for differing degrees of competition. Moreover, it is charged, insufficient allowance is made for range of error, and the measuring techniques themselves are vulnerable. A man who feels that he ought to be looking at *Amahl and the Night Visitors* may well hesitate to tell a questioner over the telephone that he is actually watching the Terrible Turk doing mayhem on the Hairy Giant. A diary can have an even more inhibiting effect on the viewer's choice of programs. And a monitoring device is unable to measure the all-important factor of attention. There is no way of telling from the tape whether at a given time the set was playing to a roomful of interested viewers or merely droning on in an empty room because no one in the house was energetic enough to turn it off.

Whatever their technical validity, the sensitivity to this data in the industry is all-pervasive. If a sponsor's goal is a family of five or more in which the age of the adults ranges from thirty-four to forty-nine, he is acutely upset to learn that his show is probably attracting youthful parents with one or two children and with blood that is not yet tired enough to require the sponsor's product. If the Audimeter tape indicates that the audience is increasing toward the end of the show, the sponsor interprets this to mean that people are tuning in for the next program. His best bet, therefore, is to save his hardest sales pitch for the closing commercial in order to take advantage of an augmented audience that wasn't interested in his program in the first place.

It is such considerations as this that spur the networks to acquire what is called "audience flow." This involves the corraling of a whopping audience for an evening show at seven o'clock and holding it, with whatever is thought to be required for mass attention, right up to ten-thirty or eleven. Hence all the blood and thunder in what is considered prime evening time. The current season has featured twenty-five Westerns, three more than last year, and crime shows have increased from ten to thirteen. Two years ago, when quizzes were at their height, there were sixty-four of them, by day and by night. Hence, too, the illustrative fate of "The Firestone Hour."

It was believed, from the ratings, that as soon as this music hour started, several million viewers regularly switched their dials for lustier fare and failed to return to NBC. Accordingly, the sponsor, who was paying for the time, the talent, and the production, was told in 1954 that NBC could no longer accommodate the show in the Monday evening slot to which its established minority audience had long been accustomed. The network, he was told, was losing about a million dollars a year from the program's comparatively low rating and had to "maintain a competitive position in the fight for circulation." ABC, then a struggling network trying to catch up, considered Monday a "throwaway" day, and gladly signed the Firestone show for its accustomed hour. But four years later, ABC was prospering enough to compete with the other networks on Monday evening and with "audience flow" in mind, contrived to rout Firestone's music hour once more—and this time the music never came back on.

He Who Pays the Piper

Worse than the outright extinction of shows is the insidious effect of ratings on programs that survive. It is strange indeed for broadcasting officials to raise the fear of government censorship when they permit private business to exercise a steady and unremitting censorship of its own. At last summer's hearings held by the FCC, Dan Seymour, vice-president of J. Walter Thompson, was explicit on this point:

> . . . we will object to controversial matter in dramatic shows from time to time on the basis that our clients are investing millions and millions of dollars in the TV medium. They are doing this to create good will and where we find

there is the possibility that ill-will will be reflected on the sponsor . . . by and large we have been able to delete the controversial line.

A few examples suggest the level of taste and imagination sometimes involved in such deletions. One executive of an ad agency handling a major cigarette manufacturer previewed a pilot show on the Hungarian revolt and recommended: ". . . this is our feeling. Don't have too many Russian officers smoking cigarettes." Another agency, handling a filter cigarette, demanded that villains be shown smoking only nonfilters. And still another on reading a script based on the Emmett Till lynching in Mississippi insisted that the scene be shifted to New England, that all mention of Coca-Cola (a "Southern drink") be eliminated, and that ringing Yankee "g's" be restored to the dialogue.

Even the Dead Sea Scrolls came in for tampering. When nervous executives realized that the cast of characters in a dramatic show about their discovery was almost exclusively Jewish, they arranged to cast an actress identified with Irish roles as the Jewish mother and a Scandinavian boy as the Jewish son.

When the Associated Gas & Electric sponsored a stirring CBS production of the Nuremberg trials a year ago, nobody foresaw any hitches. But an alert ad-agency man, following the script at the control panel, noted the upcoming words "gas chambers," quickly cut the sound, and treated TV viewers across the country to a split second of mysterious silence. "Even though it was a different kind of gas," said Nicholas E. Keesley, president of the agency involved, "it would have been stupid for us to have let that mention stay in the program." On the same level was the Ford man who ordered a shot of the New York skyline eliminated because it gave prominence to the Chrysler Building.

If there is any doubt about the reasons behind such pressures or about what television can mean to a sponsor, a few examples of TV's advertising potency should dispel it. Among several cases cited in *Television and Radio,* a standard textbook on the subject by Chester and Garrison, is that of Saran Wrap, a long-neglected product that the Dow Chemical Company started to promote on network television in November, 1953. By October of the following year, sales had jumped from twenty thousand cases to six hundred thousand. Another instance was the boom enjoyed by the Hazel Bishop lipstick manufacturers once they took to the air waves with a drippy show called "This Is Your Life." From a gross annual take of $50,000 in 1950, sales rose to $4.5 million in 1952, to $10 million a year later, and to $12 million in 1954, by which time the company was spending $6 million a year on television advertising and doing twenty-five per cent of the nation's lipstick business.

The war that followed between Hazel Bishop and Revlon was one of the more sordid classics of advertising history. When Hazel Bishop's contract for "This Is Your Life" expired in 1955, Raymond Spector, who handled its advertising, hit upon the new "$64,000 Question" as a likely successor. In the cloak-and-dagger atmosphere then prevailing in the cosmetics trade Charles Revson and his colleagues contrived to seize

"Question" for Revlon before Spector could close a deal. In three years that show boosted Revlon's cosmetic sales from a sizable volume of $33 million in 1954 when the "Question" went on the air to $110 million and some forty per cent of the entire market by the end of 1958. Hazel Bishop lost most of the gains it had made, and Coty, an innocent bystander, was forced into the red.

Testimony at Congressional hearings on the quiz shows made it plain that their corruption flowed from the single-minded attempt to stimulate ratings. To do that they had to have "attractive personalities," and, having obtained them, they had to be very sure of keeping them week after week, building up personality, audience, and suspense all at the same time. Regular rating services were too slow to satisfy Revlon executives on how well the stimulation was working. According to the testimony of George Abrahams, then Revlon's top advertising man, the company also "purchased overnight telephone-survey reports, which were charted on a regular basis, along with the names of contestants appearing coincident with the recorded ratings."

As the ratings fluctuated, so did the feeding of questions to the star player. As the stakes increased, he had to be given questions in rehearsal that by the merest chance turned up on the program. And finally, without a qualm, he was given questions and answers ahead of time, rehearsed in his answers, and trained down to the last gesture of agonized thought. "The tacit assumption of all concerned in this process," according to a report prepared by Attorney General William P. Rogers, "was the direct connection between a highly rated program and increased product sales."

Passing the Buck

The history of television is the history of a responsibility that never came to rest. The law appeared to distribute it in unequal measure between the FCC and the station owners. But neither has proved capable of dealing with the unforeseen economic pressures generated by the industry's dizzy growth. The individual stations were committed, by the terms of their license, to serve the public interest, but in order to survive, as we have shown, they soon surrendered the best of their time to the networks. And along with the buck on programming, they passed the financial squeeze.

For the network that squeeze comes, quite simply, from the cost of producing entertainment and the advertiser's judgment of what a program is worth in selling his wares. Nothing much can be done about "below-the-line" costs—studio, stage, sets, equipment, crew, and the like—which are fixed, but the price of talent can vary from the low-cost quiz shows to the "spectacular." Last season's most ambitious venture, the Ford series of thirty-nine spectaculars running ninety minutes each, cost $15 million. Ingrid Bergman's services in just one of these shows, *The Turn of the Screw*, cost $100,000 plus European rights. But it is worth noting that Miss Bergman's price would have been modest for a Hollywood movie, which is a comparatively stable commodity compared with a one-shot performance on television. The networks constantly face the fact that, with Hollywood paying $500,000 or even $1 million for a dramatic lead and Las Vegas paying comedians $25,000 a week, prominent stars are going to exact the maximum that television can afford to pay.

At the same time, with sponsors demanding high ratings, and ratings supposedly demanding stars, the squeeze continues with mounting pressure. "In the case of broadcast operations there is an exceedingly slender margin between satisfactory profit and devastating loss," CBS President Frank Stanton told a Congressional committee in 1956. "The balance between profit and loss in the case of networks is so delicate that the failure to sell one hour between 7:30 and 10:30 each night for a year . . . would, in 1955, have turned the CBS Television Network's profit into a loss." Last year Stanton testified at FCC hearings that failure to sell a single half hour a week had cost the network close to $3 million—$1.3 million in time revenue and $1.6 million to fill the gap with sustaining programs.

Sheep and Golden Geese

According to Stanton's testimony in 1956, "Anything that is done that puts an inordinate burden on the advertiser could kill the goose that lays the golden egg." Given this dependence on the advertising sponsor, the next question, obviously, is how far the network can afford to insist on program control in spite of Stanton's statement that "We and we alone will decide not only what is to appear on the CBS Television Network, but how it is to appear." The simple fact is that if an advertiser does not care for the particular shows offered by a network, he can buy one from an independent packager or even have one produced, and then simply buy the network's time, although the networks are showing increasing resistance to this practice. If neither CBS nor NBC cares to run the show he wants to put on, he can go to ABC, which has made it clear that it is out for ratings rather than the compliments of television critics. And what if a show rejected by CBS should turn out on another network to have the drawing power of the "$64,000 Question"—capable of killing off competing shows not only in the same time period but in the half-hour slots preceding and following?

The rewards and costs of TV advertising being what they are, it is inevitable that the sponsor will want a considerable say in the use of the time, talent, and production for which he has paid. The motive is plain enough, but its translation via the ad agencies into everyday practice is a highly complex affair. This much was learned at hearings in New York last June, when "after twenty-five years," as *Broadcasting* magazine acidly commented, the FCC "finally got around to trying to find out what an advertising agency has to do with programming."

Robert L. Foreman, executive vice-president of B.B.D.O., has said: "I think this is the only advertising medium today in which the advertiser has any say over the editorial content." He was right, of course. Advertising agencies have not dared to poach on the editorial preserves of newspapers and magazines to anything like the same extent. The admitted seduction of TV should give pause to those who have taken at face value the broadcasting industry's plea to be allowed to stand equally with the press under the protection of the First Amendment. The fact is that the tussle between the network and the sponsor (together with his ad agency) for the final say-so on programming has for years been a standard feature of the industry's family life. The one commands the dollars, the other the time on the air, and the balance of power has oscillated between them roughly according to the laws of supply and demand. Put more brutally in the words of no less a person than Robert S. Kintner, president of NBC: "The ultimate responsibility is ours, but the ultimate power has to be the sponsor's because without him you couldn't afford to run a network."

30. A PROGRAM FOR THE FCC
Consumer Reports *

Early in December, the Federal Communications Commission held hearings in Washington, D.C., to which representatives of various consumer and professional groups were invited. The Commission asked for expressions of opinion on current TV programming and suggestions for improvements. CU was among those requested to testify. A summary of CU's proposals made at the hearing are presented below, and on two counts CU wishes to call special attention to the details of its program:

In the opinion of the best-informed members of the press who have been following the TV scandals, neither the FCC nor the Congress will take significant remedial action unless consumers—that is, TV set owners— bring insistent and consistent pressure for reform. Congress is expected to turn soft on the issue because this is an election year, during which TV time for office seekers will be sought, and also because a number of Congressmen are reported to have close financial ties to the broadcasting industry.

Although there was no previous consultation among the various groups and individuals invited to testify, many of the suggestions outlined in the CU testimony also were made by other witnesses. Thus, the most important revelation to come out of the FCC's recent hearings was evidence of a broad agreement, among groups interested in the public welfare, about what must be done to guard against the abuse of broadcasting privileges and against corruption in the Governmental regulatory agency, the FCC.

A 12-Step Proposal

In its testimony, CU took a positive tone, spent no time reviewing the recent and multiplying exposures of malpractice on the part of both the broadcasting industry and the FCC, but put emphasis rather on what might be done to build into the FCC's operations a living concept of the public interest. The 12 steps outlined in CU's testimony would require no changes in legislation, only a change of heart, ethics, and point-of-view on the part of the Commission. They were:

1) Set up, as advisory to the Commission, a Television and Radio Con-

* This selection is from *Consumer Reports*, vol. 25, no. 2, February, 1960, pp. 93-95.

sumers Council with full power: a) to review all FCC licensing decisions; b) to request, if necessary, additional data on a licensee's performance; and c) to publicize its findings.

Neither the FCC nor the Congress gives evidence of being aware of the importance of the TV- and radio-set owner in the economics of broadcasting. Nor are most consumers fully cognizant of the central role they play when they purchase receiving sets, or of their rights and obligations as set-owners to exercise a dominant influence over programming and advertising policies.

So far as investment goes, the consumer's stake in the radio and television industry outranks that of any other segment. Conservatively figured, consumers have paid out $10,000,000,000 for the 50,000,000 TV sets they own. Another $10,000,000,000 has been spent on repair and maintenance of these sets. The power that operates them an average of four to five hours a day also comes out of consumers' pockets. Furthermore, when they buy the goods advertised over the air, consumers pay all the costs of the programs as well as the operating costs and earnings on investment of the broadcasting stations.

For its 100,000,000 or more radio sets, the public has spent, roughly, another $2,000,000,000.

Thus, leaving out the cost of power to run the receivers and taking only $15,000,000,000 as a conservative estimate of what was spent for TV and radio advertising in the past six to ten years, we find that consumers have invested the impressive total of $37,000,000,000 in this industry.

2) Make hearings mandatory in all license renewals.

This point was emphasized a number of times at the hearings. To obtain its highly prized license to operate—the right to use the public domain: an air channel—a TV or radio station vies with other contestants by, among other things, promising programs of quality. Every three years, according to law, a broadcasting license must be renewed. Although the FCC has the power to hold a renewal hearing to determine how well the licensee has carried out his promises, it has been most lax on this score. In 1958, for example, out of the 1500 or so radio and TV renewals granted, only two renewal hearings were held. . . .

3) Hold all such renewal hearings, as well as new license hearings, in the locale of the broadcasting station, so that the community to be served may be heard.

Since community tastes and interests may differ, local set-owners are, obviously, the ones best situated not only to know what they want over the air, but what the actual program content has been. It makes little sense, therefore, to hold license hearings in Washington, D.C., where attendance is limited, practically speaking, to the industry's lobbyists, attorneys, and public relations personnel.

4) Publicize the renewal hearings over the stations involved for a given number of days at fixed hours, and invite public participation in the proceedings.

A public hearing of which the public is unaware is hardly public.

5) Require each broadcaster to maintain for public investigation the

commitments he made with regard to programming and advertising when he was granted his license.

The promises made by the broadcaster as a condition to his receipt of a license are not, practically speaking, a matter of public record unless access to such commitments is made easily available to the particular consumers whose sets receive the particular licensee's broadcasts.

6) Require each broadcaster to carry, at least once a week during prime time, a statement of the basis upon which he holds his exclusive privilege to the public domain. And as a part of this weekly announcement, licensees should be required to invite set-owner comment on the station's program content, advertising policy, etc. To receive this continuing public check on performance, the FCC should maintain in each broadcasting area a local Post Office box to which set owners would be invited to mail their comments.

Advertisers and their agencies are now exercising a rigid censorship over program content. The fact that this is a private censorship exercised for private ends renders it doubly hazardous to the public welfare.

Only when avenues are opened up for *free* and *considered* response from set owners and their organizations oriented to the public welfare can we design a means by which to escape the rigid commercial censorship now exercised over this all-important medium.

7) Establish in each of the FCC's 24 district offices a consumer review staff to read and classify public responses, and then to further the material to the Consumer Advisory Council of the Commission. After review, this material should become a matter of record with the Commission and the broadcaster concerned. Both at FCC headquarters in Washington, D.C., and at the place of business of the station involved, a continuing account of these consumer responses should be maintained for public inspection.

The misuse of commercial program ratings to dictate program content long has bedeviled the efforts of the conscientious creative talent engaged in preparing TV and radio programs. These commercial checks on listener response are far from reliable. The results of one such poll will not infrequently contradict the findings of another. Furthermore, the method of collecting reactions via spot telephone calls is not only irritating to householders but cannot produce any *considered judgment* of program quality from listeners and viewers.

A function as important as the reflection of public reaction to program content should under no circumstances be left in the hands of the advertisers, whose first interest is not program content but competitive sales pressure. Further, because an accurate and reliable report of public reactions is vital to the conduct of broadcasting in the public interest, CU recommended that the first review of that response be done in regional offices in order to minimize the possibility of misinterpretation or misrepresentation of reactions. The comparisons and contrasts of response between and among the regional offices can serve as a partial defense against manipulation of the record. As a further spot-check, the Consumer Advisory Council should be empowered to conduct telephone polls periodically if the Council feels a counter-check is required.

8) Require that all Federal Trade Commission and Food and Drug Administration citations against advertising carried over each station be on file and available to the public at both the FCC's Washington headquarters and at the licensee's place of business; and make these citations a part of any licensee's record submitted at renewal hearings.

A broadcasting licensee cannot, in the conduct of his business, be compared to most other private-enterprise ventures. The broadcaster's most valuable holding, his license, is given to him by the Congress via the Federal Communications Commission. He is, therefore, a trustee, a manager of public property.

Furthermore, this particular trusteeship over the public domain carries with it the unique opportunity to enter the home of every set owner and to use the householder's private property, his TV or radio set, as a source of revenue for himself, the broadcaster. What a broadcaster sells to advertisers is not transmission of a program but its reception. It is the consumer's set which, basically, earns the broadcaster's advertising revenue.

Thus, the licensee has a special responsibility for the ethical standards of the advertising he transmits, since his license grants him a monopoly privilege to capitalize on the consumer investment in receiving sets.

9) Require of all licensees, as a condition for obtaining either an original license or a renewal, a declaration of advertising policy which shall contain: a) the standards by which the contents of commercials shall be evaluated by the licensee—standards to screen not only false and misleading statements but also bad taste; b) a limit of both the number of commercials to be permitted in an hour and the total amount of time to be given over to commercials in each separate hour of broadcasting; and c) a review of the means by which the broadcaster will screen from both advertising and programs all sources of commercial corruption such as "freebies" and "payola," etc.

A "freebie" is a pictorial boost for a non-sponsoring product, provided via a gratuitous display in either the program or commercial. And a "payola" is, as everybody knows, payment made to play particular records. These two examples do not exhaust the sources of commercial bribery in TV and radio, but they do serve to illustrate the nature of the problem.

Above and beyond such huckster pay-offs, however, TV and radio advertising suffers from almost a total lack of control at the local level because the Federal Trade Commission (the agency empowered to enforce the truth-in-advertising law) has power only over inter-state commerce. When the offensive ad for a local product or service is broadcast over a station whose signal strength does not exceed state boundaries, the FTC has no jurisdiction. Of course, through its licensing power, the FCC could exercise control over local commercials; but it has failed to do so, with the result that TV and radio consistently carry much of the worst "bait and switch" advertising.

In addition to local frauds, TV commercials in particular, even those of national advertisers, frequently are both irritating and repulsive—the gamy statues in the body-odor ads, some of the words and postures used in soap and toothpaste ads, the blaring forth in the living room about hemorrhoids or constipation.

The fact that bad taste in advertising is not illegal does not mean that set owners should be forced to endure it.

10) Require the declarations of advertising policy to be posted for public inspection in each licensee's place of business and also to be available on file at the FCC's Washington headquarters. Include in renewal hearings a review of the effectiveness of a licensee's advertising control as well as his fulfillment of promises on program content.

The difficult problem of monitoring radio and TV commercials might be mitigated by volunteer viewers if advertising codes of ethics were made available to them.

11) Prohibit the sale of any license without a full-scale re-hearing on the transfer of the privilege.

Under present FCC rules and regulations, a license granted to one party on a given set of promises made at an official public hearing may be transferred through private sale to another party. Frequently, such transfers earn great sums for the original holder, who obtains his license absolutely free but who sells it for thousands, and hundreds of thousands, of dollars. If full-scale re-hearings before permitting such a transfer were required— hearings where competitive bids could be entertained—the use of this transfer privilege as an avenue of corruption could be limited.

12) Set up a graduated system of licensing fees based on two considerations: station signal-strength and advertising revenues.

The licenses which the FCC grants are, under present rules and regulations, absolutely free gifts to their holders. The high dollar-value of these gifts is obvious in the fantastic earnings of the networks and many of the stations. In most other industries operating under Government license, the cost of regulation is borne not by the taxpayers, as it is now in the case of broadcasting, but by the licensees themselves, who pay a fee for their privileges.

The cost of putting the whole of the program recommended here into effect could be financed by such fees without hindering the development of TV and radio services.

The Blue Book

One additional suggestion made by several witnesses at the FCC hearings, but not included in CU's testimony due to lack of time allocated for presentation, dealt with the famed Blue Book, a statement of basic principle made by the FCC in 1946 to guide broadcasters in their determination of public interest in programming. Although no heed has been paid to those principles for many years now and the Blue Book is out of print, it never has been repudiated. Its immediate revival and re-issuance were urgently called for at the hearings and CU agrees that, in addition to opening up the FCC to public response, it also is important that both the broadcasters and the set owners be made aware of what good broadcasting practice means.

One of the most respected newspaper commentators on the problems now besetting TV, Jack Gould of the *New York Times*, had the following to say about the Blue Book:

A slim pamphlet called "The Blue Book," now out of print but once the target of violent abuse by the nation's brodcasters, may yet turn out to be something of a prize volume—thirteen years late. . . . The history of "The Blue Book" might well be used as a summary of today's controversy over television; all that remains to be seen is whether the ending is going to be different.

31. FCC CHAIRMAN EXPLORES TV "WASTELAND"
by Newton N. Minow*

The following are excerpts from the speech of Newton N. Minow, chairman of the Federal Communications Commission, before the National Association of Broadcasters, May 9, 1961.

I have confidence in your health. But not in your product.

When television is good, nothing—not the theatre, not the magazine or newspapers—nothing is better. But when television is bad, nothing is worse. I invite you to sit down in front of your television set when your station goes on the air and stay there without a book, magazine, newspaper, profit-and-loss sheet or rating book to distract you and keep your eyes glued to that set until the station signs off. I can assure you that you will observe a vast wasteland.

You will see a procession of game shows, violence, audience participation shows, formula comedies about totally unbelievable families, blood and thunder, mayhem, violence, sadism, murder, Western badmen, Western goodmen, private eyes, gangsters, more violence, and cartoons. And end-lessly, commercials—many screaming, cajoling and offending. And most of all, boredom. True, you will see a few things you will enjoy. But they will be very, very few. And if you think I exaggerate, try it.

Is there one person in this room who claims that broadcasting can't do better?

Well, a glance at next season's proposed programming can give us little heart. Of seventy-three and one-half hours of prime evening time, the net-works have tentatively scheduled fifty-nine hours to categories of "action adventure," situation comedy, variety, quiz and movies.

Gentlemen, your trust accounting with your beneficiaries is overdue. Never have so few owed so much to so many.

MANY REASONS OFFERED

Why is so much of television so bad? I have heard many answers: De-mands of your advertisers; competition for ever-higher ratings; the need

* Chairman, Federal Communications Commission. By permission of Mr. Minow. Excerpted from the *New York Times,* May 10, 1961, p. 79.

always to attract a mass audience; the high cost of television programs; the insatiable appetite for programming materials—these are some of them. Unquestionably, these are tough problems not susceptible to easy answers.

But I am not convinced that you have tried hard enough to solve them.

I do not accept the idea that the present over-all programming is aimed accurately at the public taste. The ratings tell us only that some people have their television sets turned on, and of that number, so many are tuned to one channel and so many to another. They don't tell us what the public might watch if they were offered half a dozen additional choices. A rating, at best, is an indication of how many people saw what you gave them.

Unfortunately, it does not reveal the depth of the penetration, or the intensity of reaction and it never reveals what the acceptance would have been if what you gave them had been better—if all the forces of art and creativity and daring and imagination had been unleashed. I believe in the people's good sense and good taste, and I am not convinced that the people's taste is as low as some of you assume.

If parents, teachers and ministers conducted their responsibilities by following the ratings, children would have a steady diet of ice cream, school holidays and no Sunday school. What about your responsibilities? Is there no room on television to teach, to inform, to uplift, to stretch, to enlarge the capacities of our children? Is there no room for programs deepening their understanding of children in other lands? Is there no room for a children's news show explaining something about the world for them at their level of understanding? Is there no room for reading the great literature of the past, teaching them the great traditions of freedom? There are some fine children's shows, but they are drowned out in the massive doses of cartoons, violence and more violence. Must these be your trademarks? Search your conscience and see if you cannot offer more to your young beneficiaries whose future you guard so many hours each and every day.

MANY INTERESTS SERVED

Let me make clear what I am talking about is balance. I believe that the public interest is made up of many interests. There are many people in this great country, and you must serve all of us. You will get no argument from me if you say that, given a choice between a Westerner and symphony, more people will watch the Western. I like Westerns and private eyes, too—but a steady diet for the whole country is obviously not in the public interest.

We all know that people would more often prefer to be entertained than stimulated or informed. But your obligations are not satisfied if you look only to popularity as a test of what to broadcast. You are not only in show business; you are free to communicate ideas as well as relaxation. You must provide a wider range of choices, more diversity, more alternatives. It is not enough to cater to the nation's whims—you must also serve the nation's needs.

The people own the air. They own it as much in prime evening time as they do 6 o'clock Sunday morning. For every hour that the people give you—you owe them something. I intend to see that your debt is paid with service.

Educational television has an enormous contribution to make to the future and I intend to give it a hand along the way. If there is not a nation-wide educational television system in this country, it will not be the fault of the F. C. C.

I am unalterably opposed to governmental censorship. There will be no suppression of programming which does not meet with bureaucratic tastes. Censorship strikes at the tap root of our free society.

SEES RESOURCES SQUANDERED

I did not come to Washington to idly observe this squandering of the public's airwaves. The squandering of our airwaves is no less important than the lavish waste of any precious natural resource.

As you know, when your license comes up for renewal, your performance is compared with your promises. I understand that many people feel that in the past licenses were often renewed pro forma. I say to you now: renewal will not be pro forma in the future. There is nothing permanent or sacred about a broadcast license.

But simply matching promises and performance is not enough. I intend to do more. I intend to find out whether the people care. I intend to find out whether the community which each broadcaster serves believes he has been serving the public interest. When a renewal is set down for hearing, I intend—wherever possible—to hold a well-advertised public hearing, right in the community you have promised to serve.

I want the people who own the air and the homes that television enters to tell you and the F. C. C. what's been going on. I want the people—if they are truly interested in the service you give them—to make notes, document cases, tell us the facts. For those few of you who really believe that the public interest is merely what interests the public—I hope that these hearings will arouse no little interest.

The F. C. C. has a fine reserve of monitors—almost 180,000,000 Americans gathered around 56,000,000 sets. If you want those monitors to be your friends at court—it's up to you.

BERATES NETWORK CONCENTRATION

I can tell you right now that I am deeply concerned with concentration of power in the hands of the networks. As a result, too many local stations have foregone any efforts at local programming, with little use of live talent and local service. Too many local stations operate with one hand on the network switch and the other on a projector loaded with old movies.

Tell your sponsors to be less concerned with cost per thousand and more concerned with understanding per millions. And remind your stockholders that an investment in broadcasting is buying a share in public responsibility.

I know the problems networks face in trying to clear some of their best programs—the informational programs that exemplify public service. They are your finest hours, whether sustaining or commercial, whether regularly scheduled or special—these are the signs that broadcasting knows the way to leadership.

I believe that stations taking network service should also be required to report the extent of the local clearance of network public service programming and when they fail to clear them they should explain why. If it is to put on some outstanding local program, this is one reason. But if it is simply to run an old movie, that is an entirely different matter.

What will the people of other countries think of us when they see our Western badmen and good men punching each other in the jaw in between the shooting? What will the Latin American or African child learn of America from our great communications industry? We cannot permit television in its present form to be our voice overseas.

32. THE MOVIES: ROLE AND PERFORMANCE

by Max Lerner*

. . . Never in history has so great an industry as the movies been so nakedly and directly built out of the dreams of a people. Any hour of the day or the evening you can go into a darkened theater (the darkness is in itself like a dream withdrawal) and as the figures move across the wide screen you sail off on storm-tossed seas of sex, action, and violence, crime and death. The "super-colossal" is at your disposal. The loveliest girls (voluptuously feminine), the most "romantic" men (blatantly masculine), the most stylish clothes, the shapeliest legs and most prominent bosoms—these are yours with an explicitness that leaves nothing subtle to be supplied. When you come home to sleep, your dreams are woven around the symbols which themselves have been woven out of your dreams, for the movies are the stuff American dreams are made of.

New standards of living and taste have leveled up the masses and leveled down the elite into a vast movie-going audience that is more complex emotionally than the movie makers suspect, but homogeneous enough to serve as an abstract "average man" in their calculations. This audience has the thin taste of experience that marks the new American middle classes. They go to the movies not so much to get a compensation for what they have lost emotionally as to get a surrogate for what they have not yet achieved but know to be possible in their world. Thus, the movies are dreams but not necessarily "escape" dreams; they may also be ambition-and-attainment dreams. It is impossible that a people should reach for new living standards without at the same time reaching for new emotional experiences.

*Professor of American civilization at Brandeis University and columnist for the *New York Post.* Author of *It Is Later than You Think, Ideas Are Weapons, The Mind and Faith of Justice Holmes, The Portable Veblen,* and other works. This selection is from *America as a Civilization,* Simon and Schuster, Inc., New York, 1957, pp. 820-821 and 828-832. © Copyright 1957 by Max Lerner. Reprinted by permission of Simon and Schuster, Inc.

The trouble is that emotional richness and depth cannot be attained mechanically, especially in a civilization dominated by the practical and the pecuniary. You cannot distribute it as you might distribute Pepsi-Cola, the electric light, radio, comic books, or universal suffrage. The thirst for it is there, and when thousands of screens offer to slake the thirst the people are receptive. But they are not "escaping" from anything; they are reaching out. By their essential technique the movies make this possible: the camera picks out for the audience the elements of a scene, getting its emotional effects by selection and sequence of shots and by their pace and rhythm as they unfold a story; it can weave together past and present, annihilate time and bridge space; by varying "close-ups" with long shots, by showing the individual face and framing the total scene, it builds up tension and evokes a continuous flow of absorption; it reaches to the instinctual in man, cutting across nations and cultures; it appeals to the emotional and imaginative elements in our make-up as no other popular art has ever done.

This is what makes the movies a crucial American popular art, although in economic terms the industry is slipping. The press is stronger in shaping attitudes, and radio in reaching more people more quickly, TV in bringing a more varied world into their homes. But because they alone deal in a sustained way with dreams and fables, the movies maintain their role in America. If TV is to displace them it must first take over this dream function they possess. . . .

There is obviously a strong relation between the themes of the American movies and the psychological drives in American life. Certainly the masters of Hollywood have tried to probe into the American personality pattern, playing up whatever gets a deep response. Unfortunately, while they mirror well the life values of the culture, they present them often with only a surface fidelity and repeatedly fall into stereotypes which can appeal only to the immature. All the traits of the culture are there in the movies, but dressed up, foreshortened, softened up, made more contrived by indirections and glossiness.

To start with, of course, the movies mirror the value and power of money. "There was money in her voice," said Scott Fitzgerald, and money continues to speak through most of the Hollywood products. There is money in Hollywood's voice, in the way the camera dwells on surfaces and textures. There is money in the lavish settings, whether of estate or hotel or penthouse suite: every picture says dutifully and explicitly that money is not everything, that money (in fact) doesn't count, that love and self-respect and happiness are better than money; but every picture continues to say implicitly, by all the things it takes for granted and by its own example, that nothing really counts quite as much as money.

As for sex, what the movies express (as Gilbert Seldes documented it) is not sex or love but sexiness. In formal terms an elaborate contrivance of self-censorship, called "The Code," bans the exposure of too large a surface of the female breast, or a male and female embrace in a horizontal posture. Yet obviously there is ample leeway for blatant sexiness set against

provocative backdrops, or subtle sexiness encased in the silkiest adorn-
ments. Sometimes the battle of the censorship makes the producer ingenious
in suggesting more than the picture seems to say, and inventive in seeing
what he can get away with. The movies rarely express the passionate attraction of mature people for each other, such as may be found in some of the
foreign films. This would be difficult in a Hollywood product, extramarital
liaisons being forbidden on the screen. Since movie characters cannot be
caught in any strong passion, since they have babies only for humorous
effect, since divorces cannot be carried through and cannot be shown as
having a valid base, since marital difficulties cannot be described in the
full-blooded terms of people grappling with the genuine problems of a
marriage, the result is that life is presented as a series of pretend entangle-
ments which are resolved by pretend solutions, both of them applying to
people whose lives are drained of emotional meaning.

In the absence of three-dimensional figures with strong emotions, the
movies must turn to action as substitute. The movies do move fast. The art
of cutting sees to it that each scene slips into the next and there is never a
pause for contemplation. Things must be happening all the time—threats,
quarrels, dangers, traps, narrow escapes, flights, reconciliations, falling in
love, misunderstandings, courtroom scenes, gun battles, mob scenes, bar-
room brawls, escapes from moving trains, shipwrecks, death in the skies,
automobile chases, the discovery of unexpected corpses, conspiracies, skul-
duggery, the confusing and unmasking of identities, deathbed confessions,
the triumph of virtue. Rarely do they offer an internal exploration, and
then it may be the tracing out of a split personality in connection with
some mystery thriller. The American conquers as a man of action, he puts
his faith in action, and he expects action in his movies.

To these ingredients must be added violence. It may be that the movies
reflect the strain of interior violence and tension in the culture, yet it is
grotesquely inflated. When genuine love and sexuality are crowded out of
any literary or dramatic production, whether by censorship or timidity,
violence comes in to fill the vacuum. Where there is no mature expression
of the relation between the sexes, the "battle of the sexes" is presented in
a bantering way, with strong overtones of masculine dominance. The
earlier movies had treated women mainly as prize and idol, as temptress
and siren. A landmark in the history of the movies came in the classic
episode in *Public Enemy* when James Cagney pushed a grapefruit into the
face of his girl. It was greeted as the reassertion of manly power in a
society beset by female values. The violence theme also finds other outlets
—the tyranny of a hard parent, a sadistic jail warden or ship captain, a
gangland leader.

The strain of violence is reinforced by the toughness of the detective-
hero in the crime and mystery thrillers, where the girl—although spoiled
and sophisticated at the start—recognizes his strength in the end. The
ingredients of the murder thriller, as of the racketeer or prize-fight movie,
are slickness, pace, fast dialogue, and continuous violence. The movie detective does not have to be a mastermind. His story has become that of a

hard-boiled Tom Jones who is no great shakes as a detector but who shows he can take whatever punishment is in store for him. Even his ordeals are physical rather than psychological. He meets with a succession of adventures that crowd in breathlessly, he is warned but persists, he is ambushed, slugged, kicked, tortured, given up for dead, he endures all with fortitude, and in the end he gets his man and—in another sense—gets his girl. His story is a picaresque of death. In the course of his adventures he discovers or creates as many as a half dozen corpses. Every death is an unevocative event—an item rather than a tragedy. It has neither psychic roots nor psychic consequences, just as the crimes themselves have no moral roots or consequences. This pervasive violence, with its need for ever stronger stimulation to produce a "thrill," may be a portent of the desensitizing of the society itself.

Wolfenstein and Leites, in their *Movies: A Psychological Study*, did a content-analysis by searching out not the overt but the covert meanings of American movies, not what was manifest in them but what was psychologically latent. While this can be stretched to the point of burlesque, it does rest on the sound proposition that the important relation of the movies is to the daydreams and the fantasy world of Americans. The producer may guess only blunderingly at these daydreams and is severely limited by censorship and his own timidity, so that the pattern that emerges may not represent his considered judgment of what the audience is like. He may not be knowing or cynical, but only a man who wants to make a lot of movies and a lot of money, and is deeply troubled—as David Selznick was—because the movie critics approach films as an art form. To succeed, Selznick argued, a movie producer must aim not only at the "common denominator" of the people but at their "lowest common denominator."

This does not mean that the movie industry has not produced some great pictures. Actually it is the only one of the American popular arts which has thus far built up a heritage of great artistic products to leave to future generations. One may include among these classics such diverse pictures as Griffith's *The Birth of a Nation*, Chaplin's *City Lights*, *Monsieur Verdoux*, and *The Gold Rush*, the Westerns like *High Noon* and *Bad Day at Black Rock*, comedies like *Born Yesterday*, *It Happened One Night*, and *Nothing Sacred*, detective mysteries like *The Thin Man*, and *The Maltese Falcon*, murder stories like *Double Indemnity*, gangster pictures like *Public Enemy* and *Earl of Chicago*, terror movies like *Night Must Fall*, documentary pictures of urban life like *The Asphalt Jungle*, war pictures like *Hell's Angels* and *The Red Badge of Courage*, social documentaries like *Home of the Brave*, *The Men*, *Not as a Stranger*, and *The Wild One*, movies of character and adventure like *The Treasure of Sierra Madre* and *The African Queen*, character studies like *The Informer* and *Citizen Kane*. The list could be greatly extended without lowering the quality of what it includes. And no list would be complete without the inclusion of the wonderfully inventive cartoon pictures of Walt Disney, one of the geniuses of the popular arts, who created a world of his own in his nature studies as well as his animated cartoons.

It is curious that a medium capable of such work should be confronted by the fact of a declining audience. Yet thousands of movie theaters have recently had to close up, and the audiences are heavily weighted toward those under thirty-five and especially adolescents. A number of critics put the blame on the movie products, saying that movie fare presented on a higher intellectual and emotional level would tap an unreached audience of adult minds. David Riesman feels, however, that the older people may be staying away from the movies because they don't understand them and have not yet caught up with the younger ones who do. The argument is that recent changes in American society have changed the nuances of living together, bringing in new aspects of social experience which the movies express and which the young can grasp but the old must sweat for, since their minds are turned toward the past.

I agree that young Americans go to the movies not just to be amused but (more or less consciously) to get guidance in "interpersonal relations." But this only makes more urgent the question of what kind of guidance they get. It is hard not to conclude that the worlds of feeling and thought presented to them are imaginary worlds, using that phrase in the synthetic sense. There is little feeling for growth of personality and the painful groping for identity which the best novels give, and from which young Americans do get clues to their dilemmas. I suspect that the movies stereotype not only the solutions but even the problems, and that the young people who see them get even their dilemmas from them. In time such a process could result in real emotional matching of movies and audience, but it would be one in which the audience had been first corrupted and conditioned into such a matching.

The validity of Hollywood's view of man's nature and man's fate would not be so important if it did not rule an imperial domain. What Hollywood does, and how, becomes a way of life for millions throughout the world. Hollywood produces, distributes, exports, more than pictures. People take their philosophy, their clothes style, their manners, their walk, their talk, their worldly wisdom, from the pictures they see and the Hollywood fan magazines and gossip columns they read. For the movie fan, what is called the "entertainment" value of the movies is an inextricable mixture of magic, mores, and morals. The lavishness which is meant to dazzle him remains to guide him. The action and power that are meant to thrill him remain to set his tempo. The sexual glamour that is meant to lure him remains to embellish his dreams. The violence that is meant to give him "a wallop" remains to desensitize him.

There have been great movies and movie directors . . . who have gone against the grain and tried for different values. I hold firm to my belief that the movies as art form—despite the cynicism of some of the Hollywood businessmen—have achieved a far higher level than any of the other American big-audience media. My criticism of the movie makers is based on the gap between the reality and the potential. However great this gap is in the case of the movies, it is a good deal greater . . . in the case of the popular arts of radio and TV.

33. THE INTELLECTUAL AND THE MASS MEDIA
by Leo Rosten*

Most intellectuals do not understand the inherent nature of the mass media. They do not understand the process by which a newspaper or magazine, movie or television show is created. They project their own tastes, yearnings, and values upon the masses—who do not, unfortunately, share them. They attribute over-simplified motivations to those who own or operate the mass media. They assume that changes in ownership or control would necessarily improve the product. They presume the existence of a vast reservoir of talent, competence, and material which does not in fact exist.

A great deal of what appears in the mass media is dreadful tripe and treacle; inane in content, banal in style, muddy in reasoning, mawkish in sentiment, vulgar, naïve, and offensive to men of learning or refinement. I am both depressed and distressed by the bombardment of our eyes, our ears, and our brains by meretricious material designed for a populace whose paramount preferences involve the narcotic pursuit of "fun."

Why is this so? Are the media operated by cynical men motivated solely by profit? Are they controlled by debasers of culture—by ignorant, vulgar, irresponsible men?

Many intellectuals think so and say so. They think so and say so in the face of evidence they either do not examine or cannot bring themselves to accept: that when the public is free to choose among various products, it chooses—again and again and again—the frivolous as against the serious, "escape" as against reality, the lurid as against the tragic, the trivial as against the serious, fiction as against fact, the diverting as against the significant. To conclude otherwise is to deny the data: circulation figures for the press, box-office receipts for the movies and the theater, audience measurement for radio and television programs.

The sad truth seems to be this: that relatively few people in any society, not excluding Periclean Athens, have reasonably good taste or care deeply about ideas. Fewer still seem equipped—by temperament and capacity, rather than education—to handle ideas with both skill and pleasure.

The deficiencies of mass media are a function, in part at least, of the deficiencies of the masses. Is it unfair to ask that responsibility for mental laziness and deplorable taste be distributed—to include the schools, the churches, the parents, the social institutions which produce those masses who persist in preferring pin-ball games to anything remotely resembling philosophy?

* Author of *The Washington Correspondents*, *The Education of Hyman Kaplan*, and other books (pseudonym: Leonard Q. Ross). Has taught at New York University, Stanford, The New School for Social Research, the University of California, and Yale University. This selection is reprinted by permission from Leo Rosten, "The Intellectual and the Mass Media: Some Rigorously Random Remarks," *Daedalus* (The Journal of the American Academy of Arts and Sciences), Spring, 1960, pp. 333-346, and in Norman Jacobs (ed.), *Culture for the Millions?* D. Van Nostrand Company, Inc., Princeton, N.J., 1961. By permission of the author.

Intellectuals seem unable to reconcile themselves to the fact that their hunger for more news, better plays, more serious debate, deeper involvement in ideas is not a hunger characteristic of many. They cannot believe that the subjects dear to their hearts bore or repel or overtax the capacities of their fellow citizens. Why this is so I shall try to explore later. At this point, let me remark that the intellectual, who examines his society with unyielding and antiseptic detachment, must liberate himself from the myths (or, in Plato's term, the royal lies) by which any social system operates. It is ironic that intellectuals often destroy old myths to erect and reverence special myths of their own. A striking example is found in the clichés with which they both characterize and indict the mass media. Let us consider the principal particulars in that indictment.[1]

"The mass media lack originality."

They certainly do. Most of what appears in print, or on film, or on the air, lacks originality. But is there any area of human endeavor of which this is not true? Is not the original as rare in science or philosophy or painting as it is in magazines? Is not the original "original" precisely because it is rare? Is it not self-evident that the more that is produced of anything, the smaller the proportion of originality is likely to be? But is the absolute number of novel creative products thereby reduced? Are we dealing with Gresham's Law—or with imperfect observation?

The mass media are not characterized by endless inventiveness and variation. But they are considerably more varied and inventive, given their built-in limitations, than we give them credit for. Consider these limitations: neither life nor truth nor fiction offers infinite choices: there is only a limited number of plots or stories or themes; there is only a limited number of ways of communicating the limited body of material; audiences develop a cumulative awareness of resemblances and an augmented resistance to the stylized and the predictable; and even the freshest departures from routine soon become familiar and routine. Besides, originality is often achieved at the price of "balance" or proportion: the most arresting features in, say, *The New Yorker* or *Time* often incur the displeasure of scholars precisely because they prefer vitality to a judicious ordering of "all the facts."

The artist, of course, wrests freshness and new insight from the most familiar material; but true artists, in any field at any given time, are so rare that their singularity requires a special word—"genius."

The mass media are cursed by four deadly requirements: a gargantuan amount of space (in magazines and newspapers) and time (in television and radio) *has* to be filled; talent—on every level, in every technique—is scarce; the public votes, i.e., is free to decide what it prefers (and it is the deplorable results of this voting that intellectuals might spend more time confronting); and a magazine, paper, television or radio program is committed to periodic and unalterable publication. Content would be markedly improved if publications or programs appeared only when superior material

---

[1] For the best general summary, and critical comment, see Chapter XV in *The Fabric of Society*, by Ralph Ross and Ernest van den Haag (Harcourt, Brace & Co., 1957), a work of remarkable lucidity and good sense.

was available. This applies to academic journals no less than to publications or programs with massive audiences.

"The mass media do not use the best brains or freshest talents."

Surely the burden of proof is on those who make this assertion. The evidence is quite clear that talent in the popular arts is searched for and courted in ways that do not apply in other fields: seniority is ignored, tenure is virtually nonexistent, youth is prized. In few areas is failure so swiftly and ruthlessly punished, or success so swiftly and extravagantly rewarded.

And still—talent is scarce. It is a woeful fact that despite several generations of free education, our land has produced relatively few first-rate minds; and of those with first-rate brains, fewer have imagination; of those with brains and imagination, fewer still possess judgment. If we ask, in addition, for the special skills and experience involved in the art of communicating, the total amount of talent available to the media is not impressive.

"The best brains" in the land do not gravitate to the media—if by brains we mean skill in analyzing complexities, or sustaining abstract propositions for prolonged intellectual operations. But the best brains would not necessarily make the best editors, or writers, or producers, or publishers—at least they would not long survive in a competitive market.

The media are enterprises, not IQ tests. They feed on inventiveness, not analytic discipline. They require creative skills and non-standardized competences. Their content has, thus far at least, resisted the standardized and accumulative statement of propositions of a Euclid or an Adam Smith.

"The mass media do not print or broadcast the best
material that is submitted to them."

To edit is to judge; to judge is, inevitably, to reward some and disappoint others.

The assumption that a vast flow of material pours into the editorial offices of the media—from which publishers or producers simply select the worst—is simply incorrect. A huge proportion of what finally appears in magazines, radio, and television was "dreamed up" inside the media offices, and ordered from the staff or from free-lance writers. And as often as not, even when the best talent is employed, at the highest prices, and given complete freedom, the results disappoint expectations. Excellence is not necessarily achieved because it is sought.[2]

"The mass media cannot afford to step on anyone's toes."

The following recent articles in popular magazines most conspicuously stepped on quite powerful toes: What Protestants Fear about Catholics;

---

[2] Yet consider that the mass media have recently presented to the public such indubitable highbrows as, say, Jacques Maritain, Reinhold Niebuhr, Robert Oppenheimer, Edith Hamilton, Aldous Huxley, Warren Weaver, Edith Sitwell, Jacques Barzun, James Bryant Conant, and Julian Huxley.

Cigarettes and Lung Cancer; Birth Control; The Disgrace of Our Hospitals; Fee-Splitting by Doctors; Agnosticism; Financial Shenanigans and Stock Manipulations; A Mercy Killing; The Murder of Negroes in the South.

The movies and television recently offered all but the deaf and blind these scarcely soporific themes: miscegenation; adultery; dope addiction; white-Negro tensions; the venality of television; the vulgarity of movie executives; the cowardice of a minister, a banker; hypocrisy in business and advertising; big business and call girls; the degeneracy of Southern whites.

It was long assumed that the most sacred of sacred cows in a capitalist society is the Businessman or Big Business as an institution. But in recent years we have been exposed to a striking number of revelations about Business. Advertising men and methods, presumably too "powerful" to expose, much less deride, have been raked with coals of fire—in media which depend upon advertisers and advertising. "The Man in the Grey Flannel Suit" became a symbol of conformity to the masses, no less than the intellectual, through the mass media.

It is worth noticing that the sheer size of an audience crucially influences the content of what is communicated to it. Taboos, in movies or television, are not simply the fruit of cowardice among producers (though their anxiety is often disproportionate, and their candor unnecessarily hampered by pessimistic assumptions of what public reaction will be). Taboos are often functions of audience size, age-range, and heterogeneity. Things can be communicated to the few which cannot be communicated (at least not in the same way) to the many.

Books, magazines, and newspapers can discuss sex, homosexuality, masturbation, venereal disease, abortion, dope addiction, in ways not so easily undertaken on television or film. The reader reads alone—and this is a fact of great importance to those who write for him.

"The mass media do not give the public enough or adequate information about the serious problems of our time."

Never in history has the public been offered so much, so often, in such detail, for so little. I do not mean that Americans know as much as intellectuals think they ought to know, or wish they did know, about the problems which confront us. I do mean that the media already offer the public far more news, facts, information, and interpretations than the public takes the trouble to digest. I find it impossible to escape the conclusion that, apart from periods of acute crisis, most people do not want to be *involved*, in precisely those areas which the intellectual finds most absorbing and meaningful.

Consider these recent authors and subjects in popular journalism: Winston Churchill on the war; Harry S. Truman on the presidency; Geoffrey Crowther on United States-British relations; William O. Douglas on Russia; Dean Acheson on Berlin; Joseph Alsop on Suez; George Kennan on Europe; Henry Kissinger on nuclear weapons; Adlai Stevenson on nine different countries and their problems; Nehru on India and the West; Ben-Gurion on the Middle East.

I wonder how many academic journals have been more relevant or edifying.

Do intellectuals find it unnoteworthy that, year after year, four to five times as many citizens in New York City choose the *Daily News* as against the New York *Times* or *Herald Tribune*? Or that for decades the citizens of Chicago have preferred the Chicago *Tribune* to competitors closer to the intellectuals' heart? Or that for decades the people of Los Angeles have voted in favor of the Los Angeles *Times*, at the expense of less parochial competitors?

*"The aesthetic level of the mass media is appalling: truth is
sacrificed to the happy ending, escapism is exalted, romance,
violence, melodrama prevail."*

The mass media do not attempt to please intellectuals, on either the aesthetic or the conceptual plane. Some commentators believe that if the media offered the public less trivia, the taste of the public would perforce be improved. But if the media give the public too little of what they want, and too much of what they don't want (too soon), they would simply cease to be mass media—and would be replaced by either "massier" competitors or would drive the public to increased expenditures of time on sports, parlor games, gambling, and other familiar methods of protecting the self from the ardors of thought or the terrors of solitude.

The question of proportion (how much "light stuff" or staple insipidity to include as against how much heavy or "uplifting" material) is one of the more perplexing problems any editor faces. It is far from uncommon to hear an editor remark that he will run a feature which he knows will be read by "less than 5 per cent of our readers."

I suspect that intellectuals tend to judge the highbrow by its peaks and the nonhighbrow by its average. If we look at the peaks in both cases, how much do the mass media suffer by comparison? American movies, for instance, caught in staggering costs (and, therefore, risks), have produced, in a short span of time, such films as *The Bridge on the River Kwai, Marty, The African Queen, Twelve Angry Men, The Defiant Ones, High Noon, The Sheepman, Seven Brides for Seven Brothers,* etc.

Television, beset by the problem of a heterogeneous audience, and submitting to the disgraceful practice of advertisers permitted to exercise editorial censorship, has produced some extraordinary news and documentary programs, and such dramas as: *Middle of the Night, Patterns, Little Moon of Alban, Days of Wine and Roses, The Bridge of San Luis Rey, The Winslow Boy, Requiem for a Heavyweight.* CBS's "Camera Three" recently presented, with both skill and taste, three programs dramatizing Dostoevski's *Notes from the Underground, A File for Fathers* (scenes from Lord Chesterfield, Lewis Carroll, Oscar Wilde), *Père Goriot,* Chekhov's *The Proposal.*

In my opinion, some of the more insightful work of our time can be found in the mass media, for example, the comic strip *Peanuts,* which throws an original and enchanting light on children; the comic strip *Li'l Abner,* which is often both as illuminating and as savage as social satire should be; the movies of, say, William Wyler, George Stevens, Jules Dassin, John Huston, David Lean, Delbert Mann.

Intellectuals generally discover "artists" in the popular arts long after the public, with less rarefied aesthetic categories, has discovered them. Perhaps there is rooted in the character structure of intellectuals an aversion, or an inability, to participate in certain sectors of life; they do seem blind to the fact that the popular can be meritorious. This changes with time (e.g., consider the reputations of Twain, Dickens, Dumas, Balzac, Lardner). And a Jack Benny or Phil Silvers may yet achieve the classic dimension now permitted the Marx Brothers, who—once despised as broad vaudevillians—have become the eggheads' delight.

"The mass media corrupt and debase public taste;
they create the kind of audience that enjoys
cheap and trivial entertainment."

This implies that demand (public taste or preference) has become a spurious function of manipulated supply. Here the evidence from Great Britain is illuminating: for years the government-owned BBC and the admirable Third Program offered the British public superior fare: excellent music, learned talks, literate discussions. For years, the noncommercial radio defended the bastions of culture. Yet when the British public was offered choices on television, it dismayed Anglophiles by taking to its heart the same silly quiz shows, panel shows, Westerns, melodramas, and "situation comedies" which the critics of daily newspapers deplore both in London and New York.

Or consider what happened in March 1959 when the Granada TV network, a British commercial chain, presented *The Skin of Our Teeth* with no less a star than Vivien Leigh—and in her first appearance on television. The noncommercial BBC ran, opposite the Wilder play and Lady Vivien, a twenty-five-year-old American movie, *Follow the Fleet*, with Ginger Rogers and Fred Astaire. The English critics sang rare hosannahs for Thornton Wilder's play, its glamorous star, the script, the direction, the production. But for every seventeen homes in London that chose the Pulitzer Prize play, sixty-six preferred the twenty-five-year-old musical. Outside of London, the ratio was even more depressing. Viewers by the millions, reported Reuters, switched their dials away from Wilder and Leigh to Fred and Ginger. The head of the Granada network even castigated the BBC in the press, urging that it be "ashamed of itself" for seducing a public that might have adored Art by offering it Entertainment. (A similar *contretemps* occurred on American television when the magnificent production of *Green Pastures* lost viewers by the millions to the ghastly *Mike Todd Party* in Madison Square Garden.) The final and crushing irony lies in the fact that *Follow the Fleet* put a BBC program among the first ten, in popularity, for the first time in the year.

Doubtless the mass media can do more, much more, to elevate what the public reads, sees, and hears. But the media cannot do this as easily or as rapidly as is often assumed. Indeed, they cannot get too far in front of their audiences without suffering the fate of predecessors who tried just that.

There is considerable evidence to support the deflating view that the media, on the whole, are considerably *ahead* of the masses—in intelligence, in taste, in values, e.g., the vocabulary in almost any popular journal, not excluding fan magazines, is often too "highbrow" for its readers.

It seems to me a fair question to ask whether the intelligence or taste of the public is really worse today than it was before the mass media came along.

"The mass media are what they are because they are
operated solely as money-making enterprises."

Publishers and producers are undoubtedly motivated by a desire for profits. But this is not *all* that motivates them. Publishers and producers are no less responsive than intellectuals to "ego values"; they are no less eager to win respect and respectability from their peers; they respond to both internalized and external "reference groups"; they seek esteem—from the self and from others.

Besides, producers know that a significant percentage of what they present in the mass media will not be as popular as what might be substituted —but it is presented nonetheless. Why? Partly because of nonpecuniary values, and partly because of what critics of the crass profit-motive seem blind to: the fact that part of the competitive process involves a continuous search for products which can win favor with audiences not attracted to, or satisfied by, the prevailing output. New and minority audiences are constantly courted by the media, e.g., the strictly "egghead" programs on television, the new magazines which arise, and flourish, because they fill a need, as *Scientific American, American Heritage.*

Whenever profits, used as either a carrot or a stick, are criticized, it is tacitly assumed that reliance on other human impulses would serve man better. Is this so? Do virtue, probity, self-sacrifice guarantee excellence? It seems to me that most of the horrors of human history have been the work not of skeptical or cynical or realistic men, but of those persuaded of their superior virtue.

To replace publication for profit by publication via subsidy would of course be to exchange one set of imperfections for another.[3] The postal system offers scant support to those who assume that nonprofit enterprise is necessarily better than private competition (I hasten to add that in some fields, e.g., public health, it clearly is).

It should be noted, parenthetically, that anyone who enters the magazine or newspaper field in the expectation of high profits is either singularly naïve, extremely optimistic, or poorly informed: few areas of American business show so high a mortality rate, are plagued by such unpredictabilities, promise so many headaches, and return so low a net profit. Successful

---

[3] It is unthinkable, for instance, that any open competitive system would have barred from the air someone like Winston Churchill—who was not given access to BBC, for his then-maverick opinions, from 1934 to 1939. Nor is it likely that a government-controlled network would be able to withstand the furore that followed CBS's initial interview with Nikita Khrushchev. Nor would a governmentally supervised program dare to present a show such as *The Plot to Kill Stalin.*

magazines earn as modest a profit as three percent on invested capital. To the purely profit-minded, business has long offered innumerable opportunities outside of publishing which far surpass it in profitability, security, or potential.

"The mass media are dominated—or too much influenced— by advertisers."

The influence of advertising is often too great—even if that influence is one-tenth as potent as many assume it to be. The editorial function should be as entirely free of non-editorial influences as possible.

But publishers, producers, and editors would respond to power or influence *even if all advertising were abolished.* It is an inescapable fact of human organization that men adjust to power (that, indeed, is one of power's attributes); that men consider, or try to anticipate, the effect of their acts on those who hold most of whatever is most prized in a society.

There is a reverse and paradoxical angle to advertising: when a newspaper or magazine, a radio or television station becomes successful, the advertiser needs it as much as the other way around. Revenues from many advertisers increase the capacity to resist pressure from individual advertisers. Organs which can be "bought" nearly always decline in prosperity and influence.

Purely professional calculations often override vested interest. Some news or stories are so significant that it is impossible to prevent their publication.

The instance of the cigarette industry, mentioned above, is worth notice. Tobacco companies represent one of the largest and most consistent sources of national advertising revenue. Yet within an hour after medical reports appeared linking cigarette smoking to lung cancer, they were fully and dramatically presented to the public—not only on the front pages of newspapers but in radio and television reporting as well. The news was simply too big, too "newsworthy" to be suppressed (even though several discussion programs shied away from the subject). The deficiencies of automobiles, where safety is concerned, have been analyzed in magazines which receive huge advertising revenues from automobile companies.

This is not to say that all truths which threaten power—in business, in the arts, even in the groves of academe—always gain as swift and public an airing as they deserve. They often do not. They do not because men, even men in power, are often timid, or weak, or frightened, or avaricious, or opportunistic, or unwise, or short-sighted. Some media operators, like some politicians, some clergymen, some labor leaders, some economists, are overly sensitive to the side on which their bread is buttered.

There is another and telling body of evidence about advertising on which no one, so far as I know, has commented: motion pictures accept no advertisements, never did, never depended on it, and were never "at the mercy of advertisers."[4] Yet of all the mass media, it is the movies which have been most parochial and timorous. Is it because movies do depend

---

[4] Some movie theaters show advertisements on their screens before and after a feature, but advertising is not to be found *in* movies.

entirely on box-office receipts, and have no advertising revenues to subsidize independence?

Advertisers seem to me to exercise their most pernicious influence in television. For in television, advertisers are permitted to decide what shall or shall not appear in the programs they sponsor. This seems to me insupportable. An advertiser in a newspaper or magazine buys a piece of space in which to advertise his product. He does not buy a voice on the news desk or at the editorial table. But the television advertiser buys time both for his commercials and for *the time between commercials;* he becomes a producer and publisher himself. I am convinced that this is bad for the public, bad for television, and (ultimately) bad for the sponsors.[5]

"The mass media do not provide an adequate forum for minority views—the dissident and unorthodox."

Producers and publishers give more space and time to minority views (which include the *avant-garde*) than numerical proportions require. They feel that it is the function of specialized journals to carry specialized content. The popular media carry far more material of this kind than anyone would have predicted two decades ago.

The democratic society must insure a viable public forum for the dissenter—in politics, morals, arts. That forum will never be as large as the dissenters themselves want. But I know of no perfect way to determine who shall have what access to how many—at the expense of whom else—except to keep pressing for as free a market as we can achieve.

It may seem to some readers that I have substituted an indictment of the masses for an indictment of the mass media; that I have assigned the role of villain to the masses in a social drama in which human welfare and public enlightenment are hamstrung by the mediocrity, laziness, and indifference of the populace. I hope that detachment will not be mistaken for cynicism.

I should be the first to stress the immensity of the social gains which public education and literacy alone have made possible. The rising public appreciation of music, painting, ballet; the growth of libraries; the fantastic sales of paperback books (however much they are skewed by *Peyton Place* or the works of Mickey Spillane), the striking diffusion of "cultural activities" in communities throughout the land, the momentous fact that popular magazines *can* offer the public the ruminations of such nonpopular minds as Paul Tillich or Sir George Thomson—the dimensions of these changes are a tribute to the achievements of that society which has removed from men the chains of caste and class that hampered human achievement through the centuries. I, for one, do not lament the passing of epochs in which "high culture" flourished while the majority of mankind lived in ignorance and indignity.

What I have been emphasizing here is the inevitable gap between the common and the superior. More particularly, I have been embroidering the

[5] When I wrote a similar criticism in *Harper's Magazine* in 1958, certain television executives hotly denied this. That was eighteen months before the recent and sensational revelations of advertiser-control over quiz shows.

theme of the intellectual's curious reluctance to accept evidence. Modern intellectuals seem *guilty* about reaching conclusions that were once the *a priori* convictions of the aristocrat. It is understandable that twentieth-century intellectuals should dread snobbery, at one end of the social scale, as much as they shun mob favor at the other. But the intellectual's snobbery is of another order, and involves a tantalizing paradox: a contempt for what *hoi polloi* enjoy, and a kind of proletarian ethos that tacitly denies inequalities of talent and taste.

The recognition of facts has little bearing on motivations and should surely not impute preferences. The validity of an idea has nothing to do with who propounds it—or whom it outrages. The author is aware that he is inviting charges of Brahminism, misanthropy, a reactionary "unconscious," or heaven knows what else. But is it really heresy to the democratic credo for intellectuals to admit, if only in the privacy of professional confessionals, that they are, in fact, more literate and more skillful—in diagnosis, induction, and generalization, if in nothing else—than their fellow-passengers on the ship of state?

Perhaps the intellectual's guilt, when he senses incipient snobbery within himself, stems from his uneasiness at being part of an elite, moreover, a new elite which is not shored up by ancient and historic sanctions. For intellectualism has been divorced from its traditional *cachet* and from the majesty with which earlier societies invested their elites: a classical education, Latin or Greek (in any case, a language not comprehensible to the untutored), a carefully cultivated accent, the inflection of the well born, the well bred, or the priestly. One of the painful experiences spared intellectuals in the past was hearing Ideas discussed—with profundity or insight —in accents which attest to birth on "the other side of the tracks."

It may be difficult for shopkeepers' sons to admit their manifest superiority over the world they left: parents, siblings, comrades. But the intellectual who struggles with a sinful sense of superiority, and who feel admirable sentiments of loyalty to his non-U origins, must still explain why it was that his playmates and classmates did not join him in the noble dedication to learning and the hallowed pursuit of truth. The triumph of mass education is to be found not simply in the increment of those who can read, write, add, and subtract. It is to be found in a much more profound and enduring revolution: the provision of opportunities to express the self, and pursue the self's values, opportunities not limited to the children of a leisure class, or an aristocracy, or a landed gentry, or a well-heeled bourgeoisie. The true miracle of public education is that no elite can decide where the next intellectual will come from.

Each generation creates its own devils, and meets its own Waterloo on the heartless field of reality. The Christian Fathers blamed the Prince of Darkness for preventing perfectible man from reaching Paradise. Anarchists blamed the state. Marxists blame the class system. Pacifists blame the militarists. And our latter-day intellectuals seem to blame the mass media for the lamentable failure of more people to attain the bliss of intellectual grace. This is a rank disservice to intellectuals themselves, for it dismisses those attributes of character and ability—discipline, curiosity, persistence, the renunciation of worldly rewards—which make intellectuals possible at all. The compulsive egalitarianism of eggheads even seems to lure them into a conspicuous disinterest in the possible determinism of heredity.

Responsibility increases with capacity, and should be demanded of those in positions of power. Just as I hold the intellectual more responsible than others for the rigorous exploration of phenomena and the courageous enunciation of truths, so, too, do I ask for better and still better performance from those who have the awesome power to shape men's minds.

34. THE PROFESSOR'S RESPONSIBILITY TO THE MASS MEDIA
by Charles A. Siepmann *

Of the major revolutionary forces that have overtaken us during the last 40 years, that of mass communication is surely the most pervasive, if not the most powerful in its influence on our culture. In these four decades the circulation, the content, and the managerial control of newspapers have changed radically. No less radical has been the evolution of the film, as an art, as an influence, as a business. Over this same period, the character and status of radio have suffered a significant change. In the last decade, TV has developed from an expensive toy to the dominant influence in many people's leisure life. Social scientists have sought to appraise the cultural effect of this massive revolution but have scarcely scratched the surface of what we need to know—as pointed to what we need to do.

This is a formidable record of developments and changes, each and all of them fraught with profound social and cultural implications. Yet is it not true that, with some distinguished exceptions, scholars and teachers in our institutions of higher learning have failed to give these revolutionary forces the critical appraisal that they would seem to deserve? In recent months, what with the quiz scandals and the disclosures on payola, radio and TV have enjoyed the dubious privilege of widespread publicity, raising questions transcending the role of broadcasting and its relation to the public interest, and embracing the moral health of our society. Yet here again, in the strident controversy that has raged in the columns of the press, as in the private conversations of millions, the voice of the scholar and the teacher, as of the proud institutions of which they are members, has been scarcely heard.

Should these voices have been heard? My own answer is an emphatic yes. It was a member of our profession who, to my thinking, gave one reason why. In analyzing the endemic moral squalor revealed and merely instanced by the quiz scandals, Professor Frankel suggested that part of its

* Chairman of the department of communications and professor of education at New York University. This selection is from "What Should Be the Role of Higher Education in Social Criticism of the Mass Media?" in *Current Issues in Higher Education: 1960*, Association for Higher Education, Chicago, 1960, pp. 216-219. By permission of the publisher.

occasion was the absence in our society of any countervailing institutional forces challenging the relativist philosophy, so widely prevalent, that anything goes for a fast buck. Is it unreasonable to suggest that our institutions of higher learning might have been, and should be, such a force? This obviously depends on our view of the distinctive role of our colleges and universities in our society.

To me the transcendent task of education is to sharpen the minds and refine the sensibilities of students to a proper appreciation of the meaning of life and their own vital part in it, to responsible understanding of themselves in relation to their fellows, to a passion for freedom and grasp of its true meaning, and above all to a passion for excellence in all its manifestations. Students will not learn of these things other than as, in our teaching, we give them primacy of place, as *we* bespeak and as we exemplify them, as we elicit enthusiasm for them, in A. N. Whitehead's words, by resonance from our own personality.

Note that I speak of these as the *primary* goals of education, not as exclusive of the acquisition of skills and specialties of knowledge. I claim only that it is vital that you and I learn, first, to be a person and only thereafter to be a specialist—that, indeed, it is dangerous to be a specialist before one is a person. The truly educated man is one trained to sensitive and civilized choices, based on knowledge and reason, to participation in affairs, and to a sense of duty. It all amounts to self-discovery in the context of abiding values; in short, to character. Thus, our first and last commitment in higher education is to what Walter Lippmann has termed the tradition of civility. As we subordinate our elucidation of its meaning to the claims of specialized job training and practical know-how, to the utilitarian demands and distracting aims so often implicit in fat grants from government, we commit ourselves to *further*, not to *higher* education. Both are necessary, but the latter subordinated to the former spells disaster as it warps our purposes and results in lowered standards.

Our first allegiance is to the only kind of aristocracy compatible with our democratic faith, the aristocracy of mind. As we desert the heights of knowledge, of reason and refined sensibility that we are appointed to defend, we shall see the flood waters of ignorance and vulgarity, of crude and self-regarding motives, rise about the valley floor. I recognize that to many so-called practical minded men this is head in air stuff, impracticable, because idealist. But then I am committed to, as I find purpose and delight in, the pursuit of the impossible. If life is to have any meaning, the only practical purpose of a wagon that I know of is to hitch it to a star. It is, anyhow, the only premise on which my following conclusions may be held, logically, to depend.

It is in such a context that I see the need for critical concern with the mass media of communication. The interests of our profession and (though this matters little) our own self-interest demand it. The monopoly that we have shared with the churches over centuries as transmitters and interpreters of culture is ended. Today there are two voices in the land. Strident, omnipresent, endowed with the authority of high popular prestige, eager to make friends, if unconcerned to influence people, the voice of mass communication disputes and rivals, as it tends to drown our voice. Its values are not ours, but are of the market place, subordinate to profit without end, making popular demand the sole measure of supply and head counting the determinant of quality, catering to what people want in defiance of what reason demonstrates to be their need, wielding vast power without a commensurate sense of social responsibility. "Civilization," as Cyril Connolly has said, "is maintained by a very few people in a small number of places." Its advances are precarious and slow. Its torch needs to be held high, for there are those, and they are not few, who would dash it to the ground. Thus, it is in the context of civilized survival that I judge mass communication to warrant the scrutiny and challenge that we have failed to give it.

Our critical, vociferous concern is warranted in a related context. We live in an age of crisis. Unless I am vastly mistaken we are running a race against time. The demands on our intelligence and moral insight are unprecedented in the book of history. And the fact is that we in the teaching profession muster neither the strength nor the numbers to help win the race that we are running. Nothing short of the joint, harmonious use of every medium of communication, harnessed to rapid and widespread advance in the intelligence and insight of our entire population is likely to save the day. Conflicting voices in the context of values and priorities of need spell ruin for us. In this matter, too, have we been heard to "speak out loud and bold"? How far have we wrested the resources of mass communication to our needs and purposes? How far have we provided the antibodies in the bloodstream of our students to whatever is corrosive and debilitating in the flow of mass communication? Discount my judgment of the media as you think fit, displace it with your own, yet will you at least admit that here are forces to be reckoned with? The mere fact of mass communication challenges our critical appraisal by the standards of value that we should have learned to honor.

Such evaluation, if it is to be more than subjective, depends upon knowledge, as knowledge depends upon study and research. If we are to be responsible critics of this rival voice, we need knowledge and facts as the basis of such criticism. Who but we can furnish such knowledge and such objective facts as the springboard of decision and of action? And what of our teaching? How far are we guilty of default in failing to avail ourselves of the field of mass communication as a frame of reference illustrative of the principles and values to which, in our teaching, we owe first allegiance? "The only subject matter of education," says A. N. Whitehead, "is life in all its manifestations." The interpretation of life's meaning in a context of such familiarity as that of mass communication seems to some of us a heaven-sent means, as it is a sure-fire technique, for relating the abstract principles and theories that we seek to clarify to concrete realities.

We live in communication's golden age. Why, with such resources at our command, have we not moved faster and farther toward the golden age of culture? The answer, it seems to me, is implicit in the considerations I have mentioned above. Mass communication, to the extent that it retards or obstructs general enlightenment, casts on us an added burden of responsibility.

Today, as in the past, higher education is like a lighthouse, casting its solitary beam over dark seas of ignorance and confused, erratic values. The darkness today is aggravated by dense fog as the mass media obscure for ships at sea the direction of their true destination. To the extent that this is true, the mass media should concern us deeply. For he that is not with us is against us. Our voice was never strong. We could never boast of great numbers. Yet the tradition of civility has been precariously maintained. As, for prudential or other reasons, we cease to honor and bespeak it, we betray more than ourselves. God knows our hands are full. Yet we must learn to make our grasp more comprehensive. We may live in ivory towers, but our work is out in the world where we must jostle with the crowd, arguing for victory and exemplifying (to quote Cyril Connolly again) "a sense of perfection and a faith in human dignity, combined with a tragic apprehending of the human situation and its nearness to the abyss."

CHAPTER V

The Mass Mind: Fact or Fiction?

Are the mass media and mass education and mass production and mass advertising and mass amusements and mass travel and mass urban living and mass politics creating a mass mind—a mind which finds its standards in a collective looking glass, which is both jealous and intolerant of the superior man, which demands therefore that superiority be interpreted as eccentricity or mere pretentiousness, and which, drunk with a vision of equality, casts a smothering blight of mediocrity, monotony, and meanness over the social landscape?

Over the past century this question has agitated Western thinkers, ranging from such gloomy observers as de Tocqueville, Ortega y Gasset, Philip Wylie, and Joseph Wood Krutch to the more sanguine Walt Whitman, Denis Brogan, Joyce Cary, and Russell Lynes. It will continue to disturb thoughtful men as long as democracy survives, for in any society without formal class distinctions the natural aristocracy of mind and talent, as well as the historic aristocracy of wealth and family, are bound to be uneasy about certain assumptions and trends within a professedly equalitarian society.

No one has delivered a more scorching attack on the common man than Philip Wylie in his *Generation of Vipers*. Although he reluctantly concedes that "what makes common man worthy of note is his occasional, individual rise above the commonplace," Mr. Wylie typically gags at the greed, the ignorance, the vulgarity, the smugness, and the thinly crusted-over primeval qualities of common man. The only thing more contemptible than the average man, in Wylie's opinion, is that same man as part of a mob. Here the "one-molecule oil scum over the deep abyss of our instinctual nature" falls away, revealing man in all his bestiality.

Wylie's *supreme* contempt, however, is reserved not for common man but for those who idealize him. Those who equate the voice of the common man with the voice of God nauseate Wylie as only he can be nauseated.

Wylie's shock treatment is followed by Joyce Cary's calm and reasoned optimism. Many of the qualities Wylie attributes to contemporary "civilized" man Cary finds much more pronounced in primitive modern societies. The improvement is explained by education, which Cary believes has altogether beneficent effects, even in totalitarian societies. As for Western man, Cary finds that the oft-deplored appearance of sameness and conformity and "common" tastes obscures a growing individualism, a broadening of interests, and a rising of standards which augur well for the future.

Joseph Wood Krutch emphasizes the depressing effects of American egalitarianism on the artistic and the cultural performance of the nation.

Surveying the latter, he finds us lacking in genuine creativity while engaging in an orgy of self-congratulation over the growth of our "cultural" statistics. Our tendency to measure excellence by a popularity yardstick can only result, he is convinced, in the cheapening of the arts. Rather than drag art down to the appreciative level of the masses, we should encourage as many common men as possible to develop uncommon tastes.

Russell Lynes, judicious observer that he is, finds ours a "you-name-it-we-have-it" culture. He cheerfully concedes much that the critics say but finds evidence on all sides that artistic creativity is increasing and that a new vitality is in the air. "Out of the crowd that the *voyeurs* of culture call 'the mass,'" he says, "many single voices are heard." Having recognized that tastes are legitimately various, he asserts that America provides a growing opportunity for many appetites to find satisfaction.

So runs the controversy—in an area where facts and value judgments are often indistinguishable. The existence of the mass mind is surely moot, but few would deny that the character of a nation's cultural enterprises both reflects and influences the vigor and creativity of its intellectual achievements on the social, economic, and political planes. There is an indivisibility about the intellectual atmosphere of a society. Thus, where stagnation and mediocrity prevail in the arts, stagnation and mediocrity are likely to permeate political thought and political institutions as well. Since the opposite is also true, friends of democracy will hope Mr. Lynes is as perceptive as he is persuasive.

35. THE COMMON MAN: THE HERO'S BACKSIDE
by Philip Wylie*

"God must have loved the common people because He made so many of them."

I have noticed that when people hear that saw repeated, they generally snigger with a warm sense of self-appreciation, and grow a little less watchful of themselves—more overt—and, all in all, commoner. It is indeed a bland and balmy assumption that, intrinsically, the common man is a wonder beyond all other wonders, possessed of indwelling virtue, and automatically endowed by God with marvelousness. Anybody, stopping to think, knows the idea is rot—a sentimental, fatuous, and absurd expression of zero.

Common man has in his lump the good qualities of uncommon men.

* Former editor and newspaper columnist. Author of *An Essay on Morals, As They Revelled, The Best of Crunch and Des,* and other works. This selection is from Philip Wylie, *Generation of Vipers,* by Holt, Rinehart and Winston Company, New York, pp. 95-105, copyright 1942, copyright 1955, by Philip Wylie, by permission of the publisher.

What makes common man worthy of note is his occasional, individual rise
above the commonplace. His ignorances and vulgarities are tolerated only
because they may be supposed to overlie better qualities. Thus, in spite of
our betrayal of every instinct we have, even American common men and
women are still capable, in extremes, of rising to heights of courage, re-
sourcefulness, and self-sacrifice, albeit grudgingly. At least, some of them
are, and most of the rest can be frightened into a show of compliance.

There was, at the beginning of this war, a grave doubt in the minds of
many intelligent men concerning the loyalty and generosity of the common
man. If the war lasts for any number of years, common man will unquestionably give many reasons for a recurrence of the doubt.

But common men are not, in any particular group, at any particular
time, given as a whole to nobility of thought or of deed. Common men
spend the majority of their free time and most of their excess energy in
small, unpleasant activities which, in the aggregate, stay the advance of
common man himself. Common men are greedy and superstitious, self-
seeking and without trust—because they are not especially trustworthy
themselves. They are clannish, narrow-minded anthropoids, hating work,
hating novelty—but hating monotony also—backbiting, mean, cruel, grasp-
ing, insolent where they dare to be, and sullen, if not craven, in the
presence of that which impresses them. The vast and vomitous outpouring
of their vulgarity appalls and nauseates even themselves, at times, and
hardly any common man is able to live with the others, even for a few
hours, without some violent complaint, criticism, or reproach of his associates. The world of common men is worse than a monkey-world, because
common men know better than what they do, to their consequent endless,
bitter guiltiness.

This Bourbon passage, taken from context, would be invaluable to my
opponent if I were ever to run for political office. A politician, be he president or county clerk, must forever blather about the virtues and mag-
nificence of common men. For practical purposes, and not in public hearing, he curses and reviles common man more than most. The universal
American custom of spouting the apotheosis of common man is, at best, a
dangerous form of flattery, and more often a fearsomely hazardous form
of universal, self-deceit.

Poops and prickamice of every description have got themselves public
offices, fortunes, and even what passes for literary reputations, by this
tetanic exaltation of common men. People who should know better melt
into a dither of sentimentality at the mere utterance of "common man."
Indeed, in my lifetime I believe I have seen more facial expressions of
sanctity follow the mention of common man than I have the mention of
God. God, to most people who mention him seriously at all, is a professional
subject, a stock in trade, and as such has a name to be bandied about. But
the same voices shake with the sound of the words "common man." And
that—is real vanity!

Now the words, to me, conjure up the fine things that have been said
honestly about some common people and the fine deeds that certain common people have done. But they also suggest the terrible capacity that

common people possess to be wrong and to do evil. It is common people who run off our many annual lynchings. It is common people who scream for blood at prize fights. It is common people who, acting concertedly, vote fools into Congress and the state legislatures. It is common people who fill the insane asylums. Common people massacre each other on our highways. Common people, mostly, fill our penitentiaries. Common people run our rackets. Common, no-good sons of bitches.

"God," the saying might also read, "must *hate* the common people because he made them so common."

Both constructs of the aphorism hold true. But, because it is an American convention to adore common people without restriction, I elect here to criticize them, as a lesson. A society which cannot criticize its masses is hamstrung—as ours is. For it is our American common people, and not the highly educated ones, who have chucked overboard the critical method and thereby cut loose the ship of state from its sounding machinery, its rudder, its glass, and its keel, leaving the whole business to drift where the blather of common men blows it.

Love of liberty is laudable and logically the chief political end of man, so long as it is hitched to responsibleness. Eighteenth century man, politically educated and understanding the major implications of what was going on in his environment, made a fairly responsible voter. Today, common man insists on his right to vote and insists, equally, on the right not to have to know what he is voting about. This folly is pitching all common men rapidly toward the rocks. The current war is a mere reef we are now grating over. What lies beyond may be the greater disaster. . . .

The urge toward liberty is, of course, an instinct. Like every instinct, it has its obverse side. The obverse side of this particular coin is the absolute responsibility of each free man for every single use to which he puts his freedom. All the legends that represent liberty—or freedom of choice—show the punishment for its abuse: Pandora and her box, the servants and the silver talents, Phaëthon and the sun chariot and so on endlessly. Man knows he can't get away with anything. He, as an individual, may appear to—but his fellow man always pays his debts at compound interest. We are, indeed, part of the *Maine*—as John Donne said—irrevocably bound up in it, and the commonness of common man, his baseness, his tawdry attempts at self-deception, and his deceit of others steadily erodes the ground that sustains us all.

Everywhere I see common people suffering for this knowledge of their willful, private shortcomings; I see them tormenting themselves and abusing their families because of their pain. However, fear of the prison wall—fear, even, of the hot squat, as the criminal often points out—is not deterrent to antisocial behavior, which is to say, behavior that lacks integrity of concept, motive, and execution. All the rotten little men around us in this world, embezzling dimes, lifting the scales as the grocer pours sugar, cheating their customers, lying about their assets, taking the money of the helpless, beating their wives, mauling their kids, wearing on their faces as fiercely as possible all the while a look of smug arrogance—all these are afraid of themselves and live in queasy terror. They may deny fear and scorn fear, but the blackness of it shoots around inside them somewhere. For man's instincts are more powerful than his pretensions; they will *not* be cheated. And the common man of this nation has, as a rule, by the time he reaches middle age, a carcass that is an engraving of internal penalties paid in part or in full.

Few men, indeed, are so mad that they do not know when they are doing wrong. But so avid is their pursuit of goods that wrongdoing has become an element of all they do. To protest that fact is idle. Our politics, our business—little and big, our professions, our labor, are smitten in every facet with a corruption occasioned by reckless determination to make not just a reasonable profit but all the profit that can be wrung from every enterprise. Our commonest man, emulating his superiors, forges ahead with a brick on the safety valve of his conscience. Think over *your* morning newspaper in that light.

It never seems to occur to people that, so far in history, the common men of every nation that has arisen on the face of the earth have, somehow, run it into the ground. It is not a lack of leadership that creates ruin where there was once a city, but failure, at last, of common men to heed their leaders or, at the least, to elect to follow wise ones. Apparently, as soon as a society, or a state, or a city, achieves sufficient organization to make its existence profitable in money to large numbers of its people a process of deterioration sets in among them. They turn from the hard idealism of the founders to the golden pursuits of the incumbents and, presently, there is not enough discipline, or integrity, or asceticism, in the whole entity to maintain the positive forces and prohibitions essential for collective life.

Sometimes, as this process begins, the halls of state quibble while the common people ride around in chariots, and lo!, the slaves rebel. Sometimes a barbarian horde descends and sacks the debilitated community. Sometimes a technological disruption brings a plague that kills the inhabitants: the engineers have no longer been able to build the proper sewers because of prior land claims of the merchants. Occasionally a hardier nearby race on the upswing of honest endeavor, sickened or sullied by a decadent neighbor, moves in and cleans up. Sometimes a nation merely passes stalely into nothingness, so that its population moves from well-engineered cities to huts, and lives forever in view of the ruins of what it once was.

In all these cycles of decay, common man plays the only significant role. The humanitarian impulses of his first leaders spur him to more idealistic efforts—which, presently, become mere economic efforts. Less humanitarian colleagues then exploit him. Common man, catching on, learns to exploit others. In a primitive economy the exploitation of human beings, except by direct enslavement, is a limited possibility. In a city, or a state filled with cities, it becomes an enterprise of great diversification. Common man, forever confusing progress with material gain, exploited and exploiting, begins at that point to undermine his own community. State quibbles are more fun for him than hard orders—so he promotes quibbling. He keeps down his slaves, if he has any, by savage persecution, even as we keep down our half slaves, the Negroes. He buys a chariot he cannot well afford and

rides around in it when he ought to be patching up the cloaca maxima.
Then the Germans attack him. Or, perhaps, he just decays, like the people
left in some New England towns or certain rural areas in the Appalachians,
who bob and nod and leer and scratch for corn around the rattling shells of
the homes of their eighteenth century forebears....

Men collectively, for instance, never have a joint creative impulse, and
rarely, any kind of joint positive impulse, except when it is instilled into
them by one man. A crowd of people never painted a picture, wrote a
book, composed a song, or spontaneously hit upon the idea of doing much
of anything else that was constructive. Even in primitive societies, doing
or building is the result of conferences in which individuals speak their
minds. The acts of crowds, when crowds act at all, are almost wholly
negative. Lynching and murder, torture, arson, stampede, stoning, persecution, heckling, fugue, rage, and other destructive processes are the frequent
manifestations of gatherings of common people that, often enough, start for
other purposes. True, mass rape and orgy could be construed as a creative
act, but aside from that it is axiomatic that crowd behavior, if it takes any
objective form, will take a fiendish one.

It is axiomatic, but nobody bothers to investigate the axiom. Most of
the treatises on what is called "mob psychology" are the work of nitwits,
largely either Marxists or Columbia Ph.D.'s. I have perused several sham-
bling documents on the topic, and what they show, mainly, is that I am
right to contend that we do not apply the methods of science to ourselves.
To treat a crowd as an entity for the purpose of its study, as most self-
made authorities do, is to take a very gross attitude toward subjectivity.
It is a process equivalent to alchemy, which recognized a few elements of
matter, in a rough way, but had not yet considered molecules, let alone
atoms.

A crowd, of course, consists of individuals. The behavior of a crowd is
the behavior of many individuals. The net effect of a mob act may appear
to be due to one impulse possessed by all alike. There is a contagion of the
spirit that is almost tangible when "Fire!" is shouted in a packed theater.
"In a matter of seconds," subsequent reports will say, "the audience became a raging, hysterical mob." For practical purposes, it did. Anyone who
has felt the rise of any violent mob emotion knows that it is a real quantity,
perceptible to senses not yet catalogued by the wizards of science, and difficult to resist. But, in the face of mob uproar, there are usually individuals
who try to quell the panic, or hysteria, or fear, or hate; there are usually
other individuals who get under things or behind things and by keeping
cool heads save themselves from being trampled to death.

The ability of plain, ordinary, self-respecting, controlled, godly, decent,
patriotic, home-loving men and women to turn, suddenly, into fiends of
hell—killing one another without remorse, dragging live people through
the streets behind automobiles, cutting off their testes and making the
victims eat them and then burning them to death—this quantum, which
may be commonly observed in many a town or city in the U.S.A. in this
year of grace, should make economists think a thousand times, and
sociologists a hundred thousand, before they spend any precious energy

laying out collectivist plans for the future happiness, or abundance, or what not, of humanity. Because in the samples of collective behavior which it exhibits the mob or crowd exposes not a phenomenon appertaining only to mobs, but a basic characteristic of the individual man.

Before its revelation, all the pretty schemes of governments and statesmen crumble to dust. Until the individual man has made himself a sufficient master of his own personality to be secure in the face of such temptations as that to which the "mob" falls victim, no society, no state, no economic system, no social program, will be safe. All will be subject to violent and horrible overthrow at the hands of common men.

The action of mobs is another exquisite proof of the argument of this book—that man is not yet the captain of his soul and that his destiny is therefore in grave doubt. What an individual can do in a mob shows many things. It shows that we live, always, side by side with our brute ancestors, and that all they have done we can do, plus refinements we are able to add by employing science. It shows that common man is still a fiend. It shows that good Americans are scarce because good people are scarce. It shows a need to reckon with ourselves on this bestial plane, collectively and individually, now and always. It shows that everything we call civilization, religion, enlightenment, modernity, knowledge, and hope is as thin as a one-molecule oil scum over the deep abyss of our instinctual nature. . . .

36. THE MASS MIND: OUR FAVORITE FOLLY
by Joyce Cary*

Every age, they say, has its special bit of nonsense. The eighteenth century had its noble savage, and the nineteenth, its automatic progress. Now we have this modern nonsense about the "mass man." We are all told constantly that people are becoming more and more standardized. That mass education, mass amusements, mass production, ready-made clothes, and a popular press are destroying all individuality—turning civilization into a nice, warmed, sterilized orphan asylum where all the little lost souls wear the same uniforms, eat the same meals, think the same thoughts, and play the same games.

This belief is now so completely accepted that it underlies half the writing and thinking of the time, like chalk under the downs. You don't see it but it gives shape to what you do see. If you deny it you will get exactly the same response as Galileo when he said that the earth moved through the sky. You will be told, "Use your eyes. And don't talk nonsense. Look at the crowds in the street or at any football match. Go to the films, read the newspapers. Consider the disappearance of national dress

* Irish author of *The African Witch, The Captive and the Free, Art and Reality, A Fearful Joy,* and numerous other works. This selection is from *Harper's Magazine,* vol. 204, no. 1222, March, 1952, pp. 25-27. By permission of the publisher.

all over the world—the immense development of laws restricting individual liberty, standardizing our lives. Go on a tour to famous sights—year by year there will be bigger crowds of morons gaping at them and listening to the spiel of some bored guide—a piece nicely designed to satisfy the mass mind."

And you will be referred to history and old travel accounts to learn how various and delightful the world was, in dress and thought and individuality, one hundred or even fifty years ago.

I was convinced of all this myself till I went to administer the affairs of a primitive tribe in Africa. There I found that the tribal mind was much more truly a mass mind than anything I had known in Europe. The nearest approximation to it was among illiterate peasantry in remote country districts. Tribesmen and primitive peasants are intensely narrow and conservative. Their very simple ideas and reactions guide them in a mysterious and dangerous world.

I found that young chiefs with enterprise and ambition were keen to learn about the world outside the tribe. If they got away from it, they tended to put on European dress. To them, European dress was not a mark of the mass mind, but of the free and independent mind.

Likewise, when a European peasantry becomes educated and enterprising, it breaks away from the national dress which seems a badge of servitude and backwardness. To tourists, no doubt, this is a misfortune. As a keen tourist and sight-seer, I wish all Scotsmen would wear the kilt and all Turks the tarboosh. I'm delighted that some are beginning to do so again. But these are individualists, eccentrics, nationalists—national dress is not a tribal uniform to them, but a proclamation of difference, an assertion of self.

Education, contact with other peoples, breaks up tribal uniformity of thought and custom, brings in new ideas. That is, it makes for difference. The celebrated eccentrics of former centuries were either lunatics—or educated men.

New ideas also make for conflict. Old African chiefs hated roads and railways: they said they brought in strangers who corrupted the young people with new ideas and made them rebellious. They were quite right. It is far easier to rule a primitive tribe than a modern democracy where every individual is ready to criticize the government, where everyone has his own ideas about politics and religion, and where dozens of societies, unions, religious sects claim independence and support ambitious leaders who are ready to fight at any time for their "rights."

The more education a man has the more likely he is to be independent in his views and obstinate in sticking to them. A committee of professors, I can assure you, is much harder to manage than a council of African chiefs.

And this throws light on another argument brought forward to prove that individuality is vanishing from the world—the enormous increase of law and regulation, the growing power of the police. In my primitive African tribe, law enforcement was in the hands of village chiefs. There was very little theft. I could leave my bungalow wide open and unguarded for three weeks at a time and nothing was ever taken. We had crimes of passion and crimes of witchcraft, but no criminal class, no crooks as you know them in the big city, no cranks, no anarchists—so we did not require an elaborate structure of law.

You do not need traffic police where there is no wheeled traffic. You do not need postal bylaws where no one knows how to write. But the modern state, simply because of the independence of its citizens, the complication of their demands, needs a huge machine of law and police. This is not a proof of the mass mind but the exact opposite—of a growing number of people who think and act for themselves, and, rightly or wrongly, are ready to defy the old simple rules founded on custom.

Thus, the modern state has lost its mass mind in getting education. But, you will say, this education destroys the primitive mass mind only to replace it with a number of mob minds: in the crowds which queue for the films or a match, read the same newspapers, and shout for the same spellbinders. Mass education is driving out the sound, traditional culture to bring in a lot of half-baked slogans. It produces the shallow brain seeking only to be distracted from serious reflection.

But these "mobs" have no resemblance to those of the tribal world where every individual does the same thing at the same time—hunts, dances, drinks in the mass. Even if he had the will to do anything else, it would not be there to do. The modern individual has an immense choice of occupation and amusement. So that the "mass" of sight-seers at any show place today is actually composed of individuals who have freely chosen to join that crowd and will join a different one tomorrow. What looks like a proof of the mob mind is really evidence of spreading interests among the people and a variety of occupations. And if some of these interests are "popular," aimed at a crowd which is not very critical or reflective, they are a good deal more so than interests which were the only recourse of their ancestors—dog-fighting, bear-baiting, the fit-up melodrama or one-night stand, once a year, and booze.

In the best educated countries, you find the biggest demand for something new in amusement as well as for instruction. Education enlarges all the interests of a man. Apart from what he learns, he acquires a general curiosity and a wider taste.

Compare the press of today with that of a hundred or even fifty years ago. You will find a far greater variety of subjects appealing to a greater variety of tastes. You will find instructive articles on matters formerly dealt with only in the special magazines. Perhaps they don't aim at a learned audience, but they help the general reader to get some idea of what the experts are doing in atomic research or medicine or even astronomy. If you want to write a best seller, your best subject nowadays is probably cosmology.

But if a hundred thousand people are ready to buy a book on the nature of the universe, you have a mass demand at the bookshops. The mass demand is not a proof of falling standards: it means that millions are being educated who would formerly have been left in the illiterate mass. There are "masses" reading learned works just as there are other "masses" going to popular films. The number of people with a good university education is many hundred times what it was fifty years ago, and that explains the immense development of arts and literature in experimental forms that would have had no chance of appreciation before. And in the millions in the next category who have just become literate in the last generation, whose reactions to education have given rise to this illusion of an increasing "mass mind," what we are seeing is not a collapse of standards, but a very rapid improvement. The crowds at the cinemas and the bus loads on the sight-seeing tours are on the way up. They have already left the mass; they are individuals seeking ideas for themselves.

The mass mind idea is not only a bit of nonsense, it is dangerous nonsense. It leads to a profound defeatism, to the secret and unacknowledged belief that the dictators hold all the trumps.

The reasoning, when you bring it to light, is something like this. There are two kinds of education in the world: the free, which develops the individual according to his nature, and the specialized, which turns out doctors, scientists, mechanics—useful servants of the state or of industry. In a democracy each individual has both types. In the Soviet he gets only the specialized—the whole plan is to make him a state slave.

But it seems that free education merely debases the standards of thought and life by producing mob minds without spiritual strength. Meanwhile the Soviet acquires millions of workers, docile as serfs, yet skillful as our own craftsmen. Aiming deliberately at the creation of a mass mind it will easily defeat the free world, where opinions are shallow and divided.

But this is based on bad psychology. The West is not producing a mass mind, but a variety of strong minds with the richest sense of adventure and will for discovery. The East is not succeeding in obtaining a mass mind either—it is going in the opposite direction. Merely by process of education, it is producing every year people who can at least think a little more freely than illiterate peasants, who are very likely therefore to think critical thoughts, however much they may hide them. That is why the task of the dictatorship becomes constantly more difficult, why it is obliged to stiffen its grip, to hire more police, to bribe more spies, and to purge its own party, every year or so, of "deviators."

What I suggest is that no kind of education, however narrow, can produce the mass mind. The reason is that minds are creative, that thoughts wander by themselves and cannot be controlled by the cleverest police. All education is free in this sense; it cannot be shut up within walls. To teach people to think, if only to make them more useful as soldiers and mechanics, is to open all thoughts to them—a whole world of new ideas. And though the dictator may wish to think of them as a proletariat they have already begun to leave the proletariat.

The "mass mind" is a delusion. How many dictators have been amazed when their rule, which seemed so strong, has collapsed in a few hours, without a friend?

37. IS OUR COMMON MAN TOO COMMON?
by Joseph Wood Krutch*

The Age of the Common Man is not merely a phrase; it is also a fact. Already we are definitely entered upon it, and in all probability it is destined to continue for a long time to come, intensifying its characteristics as it develops in some of the directions which it has already begun to take.

Most people welcome the fact, but we have only begun to assess it or even to ask ourselves what choices are still open to us once the grand decision has been made, as by now it has. How common does the common man need to be? Does his dominance necessarily mean that the uncommon man will cease to be tolerated or that the world will become less suited to his needs, less favorable to the development of his talents, than it now is? Will excellence be looked upon as in itself unworthy or "undemocratic"? Can we have an Age of the Common Man without making it an Age of the Common Denominator? Do any dangers lie ahead?

One way to approach these questions is, of course, to ask what has happened already, what changes in attitudes have demonstrably taken place, how the culture of the first era of the Age of the Common Man differs from that which preceded it. What, in other words, is the culture of present-day America like, and are there aspects of it, directly traceable to the emphasis on the common man and his tastes, which are not wholly reassuring? And if there are, then to what extent are the defects corrigible, to what extent are they necessary consequences of the premises we have already accepted?

Unfortunately, but not surprisingly, there is no general agreement concerning the real nature of the situation at the present moment, though it does seem clear enough that most Americans judge both the present and the future a good deal more favorably than many observers from the Old World do.

Thus, in his recent book "The Big Change," Frederick Lewis Allen summed up very cogently the case for contemporary American culture. Hundreds of thousands read the selections of the book clubs; hundreds of thousands more attend concerts of serious music; millions listen to debates, symphonies, and operas on the radio. Never before in the history of the world has so large a proportion of any population been so interested in and so alert to intellectual and artistic activities. Ours is the most cultured nation which ever existed.

Compare this with any one of the typical fulminations which proceed at regular intervals from European commentators and the result is both astonishing and disturbing. In Europe the prevalent opinion seems to be

* Former member of the board of editors of *The Nation* from 1932 to 1937 and dramatic critic for *The Nation* from 1937 to 1952. Taught at Vassar, Columbia, and The New School for Social Research. Author of *Human Nature and the Human Condition*, *The Measure of Man*, *The Twelve Seasons*, and other works. This selection is from *The Saturday Review*, vol. 36, no. 2, Jan. 10, 1953, pp. 8-9, 35-37. By permission of the author and publisher.

that this same civilization of ours constitutes a serious threat to the very existence of anything which can properly be called a culture.

We are told, in the first place, that for every American who does read the Book of the Month and attend a symphony concert there are a dozen who live in a vulgar dream-world induced by a perpetual diet of soap operas, comic books, torch songs, and "B" movies. Moreover, the material prosperity and political power of this majority of sick barbarians enable them to become, as no cultural proletariat ever was before, a threat to every civilized minority. They rule the roost, and they are becoming less and less tolerant of anyone or anything superior to them.

In the second place—and perhaps even more importantly—the culture of even the minority is described as largely an imitation. It consumes but does not produce art. The best of the books it reads and the music it listens to is imported. Its members are really only parasites feeding upon European culture, and their sterility will in time kill it completely. Even their power to "appreciate" is essentially shallow—the result of superficial education, propaganda, advertisement, and a general pro-cultural hoop-la, all of which produce something very different indeed from that deep, personal, demanding passion for Truth and Beauty which has always been the dynamic force in the production of any genuine culture.

Now it is easy enough to dismiss this European view as merely the product of ignorance, prejudice, and envy. But it is dangerous to do so. To look candidly at the two pictures is to perceive something recognizable in both of them. Nobody really knows what the American phenomenon means or what it portends. And the reason is that it is actually something genuinely new. Whether you call it the Dawn of the First Democratic Culture or call it the Triumph of Mediocrity, the fact remains that there is no obvious parallel in human history. Mr. Allen and those who agree with him are obviously right as far as they go. But the unique phenomenon which they describe can stand further analysis.

A college education for everybody and two cars in every garage are ideals not wholly unrelated. An even closer analogy can be drawn with the earlier, more modest ideal of universal literacy. America was the first country to teach nearly everybody to read. Whether we are quite aware of it or not, we are now embarked upon the pursuit of what is really an extension of the same ideal, namely, a minimum cultural literacy for all. There is a vast difference between being barely able to spell out a newspaper and being able to read in the full sense of what the term implies. There is a similar and probably no greater difference between, say, being able to get something out of the movie "The Great Caruso" or the latest volume dispatched to the members of a book club by editors who have trained themselves to understand the limitations of their average subscriber, and a genuine grasp of either music or literature. The term "literacy" covers a large area whether we are using it in its limited sense or extending it to include what I have called "cultural literacy." A few generations ago we pointed with pride to the fact that most Americans "could read"; we now point with pride to the fact that an astonishing proportion of them "read serious books" or "listen to serious music," and in both cases we take satisfaction in a mass capacity which exists only if we define it in minimum terms. In neither case does the phenomenon mean quite as much as those who celebrate it most enthusiastically sometimes seem to assume.

But, what, one may ask, is either disturbing or surprising about that? The minimum remains something more than any people as a whole ever before achieved. Is it likely that fewer people will read well just because a larger number can read a little? Is not, indeed, the opposite likely to be true? Is anything but good likely to come from the establishment of a broad base of even a minimum cultural literacy?

Any hesitation in answering "no" to the last question might seem at first sight to spring inevitably from nothing except arrogance, snobbishness, and a desire to preserve the privileges of an aristocracy. Yet a good many Europeans and an occasional American do seem inclined to take the negative position. The wide spread of our minimum culture does seem to them to constitute some sort of threat.

At least one fact or alleged fact they can cite as possible evidence on their side of the argument. So far, the number of recognized masterpieces produced by native-born Americans does seem disappointingly small when compared with the number of literate citizens we have produced. Is that because American art is inadequately recognized, or because we just haven't had time yet to mature? Or is it, perhaps, somehow connected—as some would say it is—with mass culture itself. Is the Good always the friend of the Best or is it sometimes and somehow the enemy? Is Excellence more likely to lose out to Mediocrity than it is to mere Ignorance or Nullity?

The line being taken in Europe today has a good deal in common with that of the American intellectual of the Twenties. To some extent indeed it may have been learned from our post-World War I intellectuals; the disdainful European conception of American society is a good deal like Mencken's Boobocracy. At the present moment, however, the current of opinion at home is running in the opposite direction, and it is no longer unusual for the confessed intellectual to defend the culture which his predecessor of a generation ago despised and rejected. But complacency has its dangers too, and it may be worth while to examine a little further what can be said in support of the European's thesis.

This, he hears us say, is the Age of the Common Man. But we as well as he are not quite certain what we mean by that. In so far as we mean only the age of universal opportunity, what was once called simply "the career open to talents," nothing but good could seem to come of it. But many people do, sometimes without being entirely aware of it, mean something more. When we make ourselves the champion of any particular group we almost inevitably begin to idealize that group. From defending the common man we pass on to exalting him, and we find ourselves beginning to imply, not merely that he is as good as anybody else, but that he is actually better. Instead of demanding only that the common man be given an opportunity to become as uncommon as possible, we make his commonness a virtue, and, even in the case of candidates for high office, we sometimes praise them for being nearly indistinguishable from the average man in the street. Secretly, no doubt, we hope that they are somehow superior, but we feel at the same time that a kind of decency requires them to conceal the fact as completely as possible.

The logical extreme of this opinion would be the conviction that any deviation in either direction from the statistical average is unadmirable; even, to take a concrete example, that the ideal man or woman could best be represented, not by an artist's dream, but by a composite photograph of the entire population. And though few would explicitly acknowledge their acceptance of this extreme position, there is a very strong tendency to emphasize quantitative rather than qualitative standards in estimating achievement. We are, for instance, more inclined to boast how many Americans go to college than to ask how much the average college education amounts to; how many people read books rather than how good the books are; how many listen to the radio rather than how good what they hear from it really is.

Argue, as I myself have argued, that more can be learned about almost any subject from ten minutes with a printed page than from half an hour with even one of the better educational programs and you will be met with the reply: "Perhaps. But so many *more* people will listen to the radio." In a democracy quantity is important. But when the stress upon it becomes too nearly exclusive, then democracy itself threatens to lose its promise of moving on to higher levels. Thus the Good really can become the enemy of the Best if one insists upon exclusively quantitative standards.

Certainly one of the striking—some would say one of the inevitable—characteristics of our society is its penchant for making widely and easily accessible either substitutes for, or inferior versions of, a vast number of good things, like the vile substitute for bread available at any grocers. That bread can be come by without effort, and it may be true that fewer people are in want of bread of some kind than ever were in want of it in any society before. But that does not change the fact that it is a very inferior product.

Another and related tendency of this same society is its encouragement of passivity. A generation ago moralists viewed with alarm the popularity of "spectator sports": the fact that people gathered in stadia to watch others play games for them. But we have gone far beyond that and today the baseball fan who takes the trouble to make a journey to the Polo Grounds instead of watching the game on his TV set has almost earned the right to call himself an athlete. One wonders, sometimes, if the popularity of "discussion" programs does not mean very much the same thing; if most people have not now decided to let others hold remote conversations for them—as well as play remote games—even though the conversations are often no better than those they could hold for themselves.

As John Stuart Mill—certainly no anti-democrat—wrote a century ago:

> Capacity for the nobler feeling is in most natures a very tender plant. . . .
> Men lose their high aspirations as they lose their intellectual tastes, because
> they have not time or opportunity for indulging them; and they addict them-

selves to inferior pleasures, not because they deliberately prefer them, but because they are either the only ones to which they have access, or the only ones which they are any longer capable of enjoying.

In the history books of the future this age of ours may come to be known as the Age of Statistics. In the biological and physical as well as the sociological sciences, statistics have become, as they never were before, the most important tool of investigation. But as every philosophical scientist knows, the conclusions drawn by a science depend to a considerable extent upon the tools used. And it is in the nature of statistics not only that they deal with quantity but that they emphasize the significance of averages and medians. What usually exists or usually happens establishes The Law, and The Law is soon thought of as identical with The Truth. In all the arts, nevertheless, it is the exceptional and the unpredictable which really count. It is the excellent, not the average, which is really important. And there is, therefore, one aspect of the cultural condition of a civilization to which statistical study is curiously inappropriate.

No one, it may be said, needs to accept the inferior substitute or hold himself down to the average level. But simple and complete as that answer may seem to be, there are facts and forces which do tend to encourage an almost unconscious acceptance of mediocrity. One, of course, is that the inferior substitute—whether it be baker's bread or the movie show playing at the neighborhood house—is so readily accessible and so forced upon one's attention by all the arts of advertising as well as by the very way in which our lives have been organized. Another and more serious one is the tendency of the mass media to force out of the field every enterprise which is not based upon mass appeal. Whatever the reason may be, it is a generally recognized fact that it is becoming increasingly difficult, economically, to publish a book which is not a best seller or produce a play which is not a smash hit. More and more, therefore, artistic enterprise must be abandoned to the movies and to television where the mass audience is sufficient to defray the staggering cost.

Besides these economic reasons why the new media tend to concern themselves only with mass appeal, there is the additional technical reason why the two newest of such media tend to confine themselves to it. Since TV and radio channels are limited in number, all the arguments in favor of democracy as it is sometimes defined justify the existing fact that these channels should be used to communicate what the greatest number of people seem to want. That is the argument of the great broadcasting chains, and on the premise assumed it is a valid one.

The only mechanical instrument of communication which can make a reasonable case for the claim that it has actually served to increase the popularity of the thing communicated on its highest level of excellence is the phonograph, and it is significant that the phonograph is the only such device for communication which—especially since the invention of tape recording and LP—has found it economically feasible to cater to relatively small minorities. The fact that it does not cost much to produce a record may well have an incalculably great effect upon American musical taste.

What the question comes down to in the simplest possible terms is one of those which we asked at the very beginning of this discussion: Can we have an Age of the Common Man without having also an Age of the Common Denominator? That question has not been answered, probably cannot be convincingly answered, at the present moment. But it is a fateful question and the one with which this discussion is concerned.

One must not, of course, idealize the past to the extent of assuming that the best works were always, inevitably, and immediately the most popular. Two years ago James D. Hart's thorough and amusing "The Popular Book" (Oxford University Press) demonstrated conclusively that since colonial times there have always been absurd best sellers. The year that Hawthorne earned $144.09 royalty in six months was the year his own publisher paid Susan Warner $4,500 for the same period and another publisher sold 70,000 copies of one of Fanny Fern's several works.

Neither, I think, should it be supposed that any society ever has been or ever will be so organized as to favor exclusively the highest artistic excellence. As a system, aristocratic patronage is absurdly capricious; capitalistic democracy tends to favor vulgarity; Socialism would probably favor official mediocrity. The question here is not whether contemporary America provides ideal conditions for cultural developments on the highest level, but whether it renders such development unusually difficult instead of making it, as the optimists insist, almost inevitable.

Of the unfavorable influences which I have mentioned, it seems to me that the most serious is the tendency to confuse the Common Denominator with a standard of excellence. The mechanical and economic facts which tend to give the purveyors of mediocrity a monopoly—highly developed in the case of radio and TV, probably growing in the publishing business—may possibly be changed by new developments, as they have already been changed in the case of the phonograph. But to confuse The Best with the most widely and the most generally acceptable is to reveal a spiritual confusion which is subtle and insidious as well as fundamental. It could easily nullify any solution of the mechanical and economic problems created by the age of mass production.

How real and how general does this confusion seem actually to be?

More than one sociologist has recently pointed out that as technology integrates larger and larger populations into tighter and tighter groups the members of these groups tend inevitably to work, live, and recreate themselves in the same way and in accordance with the standardized patterns which the facilities provided for these various activities lay down. For ill as well as for good, "community living" becomes more and more nearly inevitable and individual temperament or taste finds less and less opportunity to express itself.

One result of this is that the natural tendency of the adolescent to practice a desperate conformity is prolonged into adult life and the grown man continues to want what his neighbors have, to do what his neighbors do, to enjoy what his neighbors enjoy. This is one of the things which the European may have in mind when he calls us a nation of adolescents, and commercial interests take advantage of our adolescent characteristics by stressing, through all sorts of publicity, the fact that this is the kind of cigarette most people smoke, the kind of breakfast food most people eat,

and the torch singer or crooner most people like. The best-selling book is
not only the one easiest to buy, but it is also the one we must read unless
we are willing to be made to seem somehow inferior. What is most popular
must be best. As a broadcast official recently said, to call the most popular
radio programs vulgar is to call the American people vulgar. And that, he
seemed to imply, was not merely nonsense but pretty close to treason. The
voice of the people is the voice of God. God loves the common man. If the
common man loves Bob Hope then God must love Bob Hope also. In musical taste as in everything else the common man is divine. . . .

What is obviously called for is a public opinion less ready than it now is
to excuse the failure to meet even minimal responsibilities; but that public
opinion is not likely to arise unless those responsible for public thinking
play their own parts, and there is a tendency for them to yield rather than
protest. Unfortunately, the fanatical exaltation of the common denominator
has been taken up not only by the common man himself and by those who
hope to profit by his exploitation but also and increasingly by those who
are supposed to be educators and intellectual leaders. Instead of asking
"What would a good education consist of?" many professors of education
are asking "What do most college students want?"; instead of asking
"What books are wisest and best and most beautiful?" they conduct polls
to determine which the largest number of students have read with least
pain. Examination papers are marked, not in accordance with any fixed
standard, but in accordance with a usual level of achievement; the amount
of work required is fixed by the amount the average student does; even the
words with which the average student is not familiar are edited out of the
books he is given to read. How, granted such methods, is it other than
inevitable both that the average will seldom be exceeded and that the
average itself will gradually drop?

As David Reisman and his collaborators pointed out two years ago in
their brilliant analysis called "The Lonely Crowd" (Yale University Press),
the ideal now persistently held before the American citizen from the
moment he enters kindergarten to the time when he is buried under the
auspices of a recognized funeral parlor is a kind of conformity more or less
disguised under the term "adjustment." "Normality" has almost completely
replaced "Excellence" as an ideal. It has also rendered all but obsolescent
such terms as "Righteousness," "Integrity," and "Truth." The question is
no longer how a boy ought to behave but how most boys do behave; not
how honest a man ought to be but how honest men usually are. Even the
Robber Baron, who represented an evil manifestation of the determination
to excel, gives way to the moneymaker who wants only to be rich according
to the accepted standards of his group. Or, as Mr. Reisman sums it up, the
American who used to be conspicuously "inner-directed" is now conspicuously "outer-directed."

According to the anthropologists, many primitive societies are based
almost exclusively upon the idea of conformity and generate what are, in
the anthropologist's meaning of the term, remarkable cultures. It may, of
course, be argued that America and the whole world which follows in
America's wake is evolving in the direction of this kind of culture. But if
by "culture" we mean something more narrowly defined, if we mean a

culture which is continuous with that of the Western world since the Renaissance, then it is my contention that it cannot flourish where the stress is as nearly exclusively as it threatens to become upon "adjustment," "normality," or any of the other concepts which, in the end, come down to mean that the Common Denominator is identical with the Ideal. Especially, it cannot flourish under those conditions if the result which they tend to produce is intensified by the fact that ingenious methods of mass production and mass propaganda help impose upon all the tyranny of the average.

Salvation, if salvation is possible, may be made so by technological developments like those in the phonograph industry which tend to break monopoly and permit the individual to assert his preferences and his tastes. But the possible will not become the actual if in the meantime the desire for excellence has been lost and those who should be leaders have willingly become followers instead. If the Age of the Common Man is not to become the Age of the Common Denominator rather than what it was originally intended to be—namely an age in which every man had the opportunity to become as superior as he could—then the cultural as well as the political rights of minorities must somehow be acknowledged. There is not really anything undemocratic about either the desire for, or the recognition of, excellence. To prove that ours is the most cultured nation which ever existed will constitute only a barren victory if we must, to prove our point, use nothing but quantitative standards and reconcile ourselves to the common denominator as a measure of excellence.

One might sum up the situation in a series of propositions. (1) The Age of the Common Man has begun. (2) Despite all the gains that it may legitimately claim, they are threatened by those confusions which arise when the common denominator is consciously or unconsciously allowed to function as a standard of excellence. (3) The dominance of mass media almost exclusively under the control of those who are little concerned with anything except immediate financial gain does tend to debase taste. (4) Ultimate responsibility for the future rests with the thinkers and the educators whose most important social task at the moment is to define democratic culture in some fashion which will both reserve a place for uncommon excellence and, even in connection with the largest masses, emphasize the highest rather than the lowest common denominator.

38. PROOF THAT WE ARE NOT BARBARIANS
by Russell Lynes*

"Culture" in America is a fighting word. At the mention of the state of American culture people choose up sides, for it is unlikely that there has ever been a nation as concerned about its cultural facade as ours.

Listen, for instance, to what the returning traveler says about our pavilion at the Brussels Fair: It makes a mockery of what we are pleased

* Managing editor of *Harper's Magazine.* Author of *Highbrow, Lowbrow, Middlebrow, The Taste-makers, A Surfeit of Honey,* and other works. This selection is from *The New York Times Magazine,* July 6, 1958, pp. 5 and 21-22. By permission of the author and publisher.

to call the American Way of Life or it inspires confidence in our concept of the pursuit of happiness. To one traveler it is imaginative and inspired, to another it is frivolous and misleading. It is the same with every attempt to define our culture. We argue and we complain; we pat ourselves on the back and we heap ashes on our heads. But no one could say we are indifferent, and we are very likely to be partisan. The fact is that for a long time we have been trying to make our culture fit a pattern. We are now beginning to discover that we must find a pattern to fit it.

Take an example. Not long ago, I sat next to an attractive woman at dinner who could have been the prototype for what Jacques Barzun has called "the professional European." "I don't understand you Americans," she said, though she is married to an American and by now is presumably one herself. "You give money to rebuild European opera houses destroyed in the war, and yet you have no national opera company of your own."

I suggested that in America we believe that cultural institutions are the responsibility of the community, not of the Federal Government, and that the strength of our culture is the diversity of its support. "Ah," she said, "but Americans have no culture."

Americans should be used to hearing such statements from Europeans; they have been saying that we have no culture since they first started coming here as tourists nearly a century and a half ago. In the vocabulary of European clichés used to describe America, there are all sorts of words and phrases for our industry and adventurousness, for our ingenuity, classlessness and casual manners. But the European is reluctant to admit that we have any culture or any cultural institutions worth his attention.

It has long been fashionable in certain intellectual circles in America to look at our culture through European eyes and to measure what goes on here in terms of what used to go on there. Each generation, for a century and more, has had its share of expatriates who went to Europe to absorb the older culture and who came home in hopes of making European standards our standards. It is only quite recently that the study of American culture as a phenomenon distinct from European culture has become intellectually respectable.

This respectability takes two principal forms of expression. There are those who deplore our culture as "mass culture," geared to the lowest common denominator of taste and education; they believe that everything that is precious and "serious" is sacrificed to the commercial maw of the communications media. This attitude is popular in university and college circles at the faculty level—especially in the language, English and art departments. You will also find it in some highbrow coteries, though by no means in all.

There is, in fact, an increasingly sharp distinction between those who deplore American mass culture, its size, shape, texture and quality, and those whom John Kouwenhoven has defined as the "neo-Pollyanna" school of cultural observers. This is a group of intellectuals who are determined to find something good or something interesting in all things American. The two groups might be called the "Oh-the-pain-of-it" and the "Oh-the-joy-of-it" schools of thought.

The Pain and Joy groups have most Americans somewhere in between. Many of them merely shrug their shoulders and say that good old America is all right with them. But there are many others who are fascinated by the seeming contradictions in our culture. They deplore some of it and delight in some of it. But whatever the quality, of one thing we may be sure: America is on a sort of cultural bender.

In his preface to "The Meaning of Culture," John Cowper Powys quoted this definition: "Culture is what is left over after you have forgotten all you have definitely set out to learn." By this definition, it is the residue and not the effort that matters, whereas the only way that we have of measuring American culture at this moment is in the amount of effort that we, as a nation, are putting into it. It will take several generations before we will know whether the residue was worth the effort.

Culture does not lend itself to statistical analysis, but cultural effort does. We know how many new books are published each year in America (about 10,000) and how this compares with publishing twenty-five years ago (about 7,000). We know that some 350,000,000 books (of which 275,000,000 are paperbacks) are bought by Americans each year. This is about three books to each person. We are told that 17 per cent of Americans now read books today compared with 22 per cent before television.

On the other hand, a quarter of a century ago there were some 600 museums serving the public; now there are 2,500. We now have thirty major symphony orchestras and 650 professional and semiprofessional orchestras, not including those in colleges. There are 2,300 community and civic theatres in America and some 100,000 theatrical groups in social clubs and industrial organizations, in addition to some 25,000 high schools that produce plays.

Looked at in these terms, it seems a wonder that we have any time left over from culture to get any work done. Add to these figures the explosion that has taken place in college and university populations since World War II (I grant you it's like adding apples and oranges), and more Americans seem to be involved in cultural activities than there are Americans. Such is the way of statistics.

But statistics aside, one need look only at his own community to see the cultural pot seething with activity. Those who ride the New York subways cannot but be struck with the number of people reading books ranging from Mickey Spillane to difficult philosophical treatises. A trip to the Metropolitan Museum of Art on a Sunday afternoon finds you there with as many as 30,000 people who also thought it a good idea to expose themselves to art. Look at the number of off-Broadway theatres experimenting with unconventional plays, and look, too, at their account books; if they are not rich, they are at least not broke.

You will find the same kinds of things wherever you travel in America. You will find a successful opera company in Santa Fé and a distinguished experimental theatre in Dallas. You will find suburban groups organizing art exhibitions. You will find music festivals in Aspen, Colo., and Newport, R. I., and Lenox, Mass., and a dozen other places. And everywhere people are taking cultural courses.

There is no question that our cultural statistics are impressive, but then so are those of other nations. The English publish twice as many books a year as we do and the Russians claim to publish three times as many. It is always easier to be impressed with one's own statistics than with somebody else's and comparisons can be misleading. We, for example, read a great many more magazines than the British who publish a great many more "dime-novels" (to use a pre-inflationary phrase) than we do. But the danger with statistics of this sort is that they are likely to make us complacent (if they happen to be on our side) or competitive (if they happen to favor our rivals). In neither case do they really have anything to do with quality, and culture is a qualitative and not a quantitative word.

The real culture of America must be measured by its feel and not by its weight, by its texture and not by its size. And in the long run (to change the metaphor), it is the echo, not the shout, that matters.

Fortunately, the state of our culture is subjected to constant criticism from within. It doesn't (or at least it shouldn't) make much difference to us what the professional Europeans say about our culture; they certainly aren't interested in what we say about theirs. But the attacks that are leveled at American culture from those who are part of it and are most concerned with its directions keep our culture lively.

Just as in our body politic the conflicting interests of our minorities assure a kind of vital, if sometimes aggravatingly slow, progress, so the minorities in our body cultural assure intellectual vitality which is not likely to stagnate or become smug. Nor does it allow any one group of self-styled arbiters of culture to take over and tell the rest of us what we ought to like.

Let's look at some of these conflicting opinions, at what the pain-of-it-all and the joy-of-it-all groups find dismaying and encouraging about the state of our cultural health.

The Pain group, as I have already suggested, is primarily concerned with the debilitating effects of "mass culture." Mass culture, the argument runs, is the result of the commercial hunger of mass communications. It is culture controlled by "ratings" and popularity polls. It shuns the experimental in the arts (especially where television and the movies are the media involved) because the investment of money is too great to risk on anything but tested formulas. The result is that we have a sort of mail-order-catalogue culture in which every style for every taste is pre-tested in the market place to assure acceptance by the largest possible number of people.

Mass culture is culture that will offend no one, surprise no one, raise no one's sights and stir no one's emotions, whatever it may do to his sentiments. Such are the demands for entertainment of this sort that even what is proved to be foolproof (or, to put it another way, proved to be surefire with fools) soon wears itself out. But the media cannot be stopped and to assure a continuous flow of the innocuous to the public, the media seduce the potentially "serious" writer from his proper work and, with blandishments of cash, make him turn to producing "tripe."

The result of this commercialization of culture, the argument goes, is to lull the public into a kind of cultural coma and to cheapen and prostitute the creative artist. The middleman in this "pandering to popular taste" is the editor of the mass magazine, the agency that handles the account of the big television sponsor and the network and movie moguls who, out of greed, encourage such cheapening of standards.

The Joy group looks at mass culture from a quite different point of view. In the past, they say, most Americans had no opportunity whatever to enjoy the talents of our most able performers, dramatic artists and musicians. Not only do the mass media bring to millions of Americans first-rate talent and exposure to the arts (as, for example, in mass magazines that publish our ablest writers and all sort of paintings, including the most *avant-garde*), but they also provide a certain amount of exposure to the experimental and the exotic through such television shows as "Omnibus," "Sunrise Semester" and an increasing number of unsponsored educational programs and stations.

The fact that such shows do not have the ratings of Ed Sullivan and Steve Allen is not a reflection on American taste. The fine arts have never commanded the same audiences as the popular arts and the wonder of it is that there are so many millions of Americans who enjoy the good things set before them.

Somewhere in every discussion about American culture today the word "conformity" is bandied about. The Pain group views with alarm the conformity which it sees everywhere—in dress, in the kinds of houses people live in, in the kinds of food they buy from supermarkets, in their cars and in their consciences. The Joy group construes the same manifestations of our culture in a diametrically opposite manner. There is a difference, they say, between conformity and individualism. Conformity of a sort is essential to making the wheels of our civilization turn; people must conform somewhat or they wouldn't be able to work together in harmony.

Individualism, on the other hand, is in evidence everywhere. Look, they say, at what is happening in the mass-produced suburbs; everyone is making changes in his house to defeat the established patterns. Look at the supermarkets and the odd and interesting kinds of food that they make available to everyone who wants to experiment. And so on. The coin of conformity seems to have heads on both sides.

The promise of our culture seems to lie somewhere between the alarm of the Pain group and the euphoria of the Joy group. In my opinion, and in the opinion of a good many other observers, if you add up the pro and con columns of our cultural effort, the pro column has the edge.

In the con column, in addition to the attacks against mass culture that I have mentioned, you will find wasted educational effort. You will find cluttering up our educational institutions many thousands of young men and women to whom education is not an intellectual exercise or an expansion of horizons but a waiting game. B.A. and Ph.D. degrees, instead of being intellectual achievements, are only job tickets.

In this same column, you will find "projectitis" among scholars: that is, the scholar with the biggest project involving the most people and for which he can get the most money from a foundation achieves a kind of preferred academic status. It substitutes group-thinking for individual exploration. You will find, in spite of concerted effort to the contrary in recent months, the sacrifice of the bright, eccentric student to the standards of achievement of the average and below-average student. The premium is on "well-roundedness." You will find group journalism in which "slant" takes the place of opinion and is passed off as truth. You will find a great deal of what passes for cultural activity to be merely social climbing.

But in the pro column you will find genuine enthusiasm, excitement and curiosity. People have been getting up at the crack of dawn to listen to television lectures on literature. They have been going out evenings to extension courses in everything from the Art of the Short Story to Paleontology. Record companies can scarcely find enough music, new or old, to satisfy the tremendous range (from pre-Palestrina to post-Bartók) of the public taste.

In much the same kind of dilemma, publishers of paperback books comb libraries for more "significant" books of philosophy, sociology, history, the physical sciences and the arts with which to satisfy a public that is hungry for something more than whodunits.

The current boom in the art market is more than just a hedge against inflation; it reflects a reaction against what sometimes seems like the tyranny of machine-made materialism. The growth of our colleges and universities is not just a demographic phenomenon; at least part of it is a genuine search by the young for intellectual values in an era when such values seem to have been overrun by what the sociologists call status symbols. Three-hundred-horsepower parlors bedecked with tinsel are not enough.

There is no question that we create much that is tawdry, flashy and phony—as what nation doesn't? But there is also no question that our arts —fine and popular—are enjoying a new kind of vitality. It comes, I believe, from a new self-confidence. We no longer worry about being the stepchild of Europe. For a long time it seemed as though we were connected with European culture by a one-way street with all the ideas coming our way.

Now ideas seem to flow out rather more than they flow in. Our novelists are eagerly read everywhere. Our painting and sculpture and our architecture not only command respect but strongly influence the visual arts of other countries. Our playwrights fill foreign theatres and our musicians fill foreign concert halls and opera houses. Our ballet plays to respectful and enthusiastic audiences, and above all, our jazz has become a universal language. Our present danger is not that we underestimate the vitality of our cultural production as we once did, but that we become complacent and chauvinist about it.

Anyone can add his own items to the pro and con columns and arrive by his own arithmetic at almost any conclusions he pleases about the state of our culture. But he cannot truthfully say that our culture is any one thing or that it is dominated by any one group. No one can honestly contend that materialism has driven out humanism or that science in one of its greatest ages of exploration has slammed the door on the arts. No one can say that mass audiences have silenced the intellectuals any more than he can demonstrate that highbrows control the public taste.

Ours is a "You-name-it-we-have-it" kind of culture. It is a vast market place of conflicting tastes, conflicting ambitions and conflicting needs. In guaranteeing "the pursuit of happiness," we recognize that not every man's happiness is measured by the same yardstick. We may do our damnedest to convince him that our yardstick is better than his, but we do not beat him over the head with it.

We cajole and seduce, but we do not coerce or command. Out of the crowd that the *voyeurs* of culture call "the mass," many single voices are heard. So long as this is true, what we have is not a "mass culture," but neither is it an aristocratic culture. It is a highly competitive culture, perhaps the first of its kind, and unless it succeeds, perhaps the last.

CHAPTER VI

The Tyranny of Majority Opinion

When the Supreme Court, emboldened by the events at Appomattox four years previously, announced in April of 1869 that "the Constitution, in all its provisions, looks to an indestructible Union, composed of indestructible states,"[1] the doctrine of secession was legally laid to rest. The doctrine of nullification, however, has shown greater resistance to interment. We need only consider Southern reaction to the 1954 public school desegregation decisions[2] to realize that such legal theories in support of minorities against majorities have not disappeared from the American political scene. True, the theories have been updated as the "doctrine of interposition," but their intent and effects are the same.

We propose to examine in this chapter the perennial concern of democrats over the possibility of majority tyranny. There are two distinct but obviously related aspects to this problem: First, what is the propensity of *political majorities* to tyrannize, and how may we protect ourselves from such a danger? Second, to what extent are we tyrannized by *social majorities*, and what are the defenses against this type of oppression? Only beleaguered political minorities are likely to feel that the former problem is still very much with us; the consensus in America today would appear to be that the Founding Fathers were appropriately attentive to this issue and provided adequate safeguards. Many Americans currently feel greater concern over the possibility of political majorities being victimized by resolute and formidable minorities who have the resources, the dedication, and the manipulative skills than over the possible peril of despotic majorities. There is merit, however, in reviewing our remedies for the older of these two problems, while awaiting the prescriptions of the philosophers who are still busily diagnosing the minority malady.

But if the modern scholar is comforted by such governmental arrangements as separation of powers and federalism and by such legislative procedures as the filibuster and by extraordinarily difficult constitutional-amending procedures, he does not exhibit the same kind of complacency with regard to imperious *social* majorities. When he reads de Tocqueville's impassioned defense of personal autonomy ("for myself, when I feel the hand of power lie heavy on my brow, I care but little to know who oppresses me; and I am not the more disposed to pass beneath the yoke because it is held out to me by the arms of millions of men"[3]) and when he considers the influence of public opinion on the arts, on fashions, on

---

[1] *Texas v. White,* 7 Wall. 700, 725 (1869).

[2] *Brown et al. v. Board of Education,* 347 U.S. 483; *Bolling et al. v. Sharpe,* 347 U.S. 497.

[3] Alexis de Tocqueville, *Democracy in America* (trans. Henry Reeve), Appleton-Century-Crofts, Inc., New York, 1904, vol. II, p. 494.

morals, on leisure, and on the significant artifacts of our culture, he is likely to conclude that a situation which was already alarming in the Jacksonian era has only worsened with the passage of time.

We begin with a brief but eloquent definition by Bryce of the expression "tyranny of the majority." It is a definition written with governmental majorities in mind, but its strictures are no less applicable to social majorities. John Stuart Mill then discusses how majority tyranny emerges as a by-product of the evolution of democracy, and he shows himself to be equally concerned with both varieties of tyranny: "Protection, therefore, against the tyranny of the magistrate is not enough; there needs protection also against the tyranny of prevailing opinion and feeling. . . ."

Alexis de Tocqueville follows with a sobering account of the immanent tendencies toward majority despotism in American society. He contrasts the individual tyrant who breaks bodies to bend the will with the collective tyrant who leaves the body intact but uses such weapons as ostracism and moral suasion to enslave the soul. De Tocqueville was writing of conditions as he viewed them in the United States in the 1830s. Lest one conclude that these observations were seriously overdrawn or that they were applicable only to the temporary excesses of Jacksonian democracy, we have also included a brief excerpt from one of the more perceptive analysts of mid-twentieth-century America, William H. Whyte, Jr. In his remarkably articulate and cogent book, *The Organization Man*, he deals with one important aspect of the problem: the stifling effects upon individual initiative, freedom and creativity of an excessive commitment to the group, of an exaggerated belief in the virtues and values of belongingness—in short, of what he calls the Social Ethic. In this selection, Mr. Whyte summarizes his case against the social ethic, an ethic which, as he states, seeks to justify our "imprisonment in brotherhood."

Mill and Bryce return to offer their thoughts on possible safeguards against the tyranny of majority opinion. Mill urges upon those who have power an attitude of *noblesse oblige*. Against this kind of despotism he would erect "a strong barrier of moral conviction": a firmly held belief that democratic society is endangered unless the proper limits to societal interference with personal conduct are recognized and observed. Bryce, on the other hand, speaks of a variety of defenses: those which arise from the temper of the people, from vigilant statesmen, from a heterogeneous population, and from a system of limited government and of shared government. Lastly, the Founding Fathers have their say, through the medium of a portion of the fifty-first *Federalist* paper, on the contributions of federalism to our security.

There are, of course, those who find little cause to fear either our majorities or our minorities. To a Max Lerner neither appear to present a "clear and present" danger. In a selection from his monumental study of *America as a Civilization*, he concludes that the pluralistic nature of our society affords substantial protection against the forces of tyranny. The abuse of power by *any* group—of whatever size—is surely to be resisted, but Lerner believes that we have developed a "talent for equilibrium" which minimizes the possibility of such abuse.

Having chosen to explore the problems of conformity in some detail does not mean that we are unaware of the possible excesses of *non*conformity. Morris Freedman has written perceptively on this subject and is, therefore, invited to share his observations with the reader.

39. "TYRANNY OF THE MAJORITY" DEFINED
by James Bryce*

The expression "tyranny of the majority" is commonly used to denote any abuse by the majority of the powers which it enjoys in free countries under and through the law, and in all countries outside the law. Such abuse will not be tyrannous in the sense of being illegal, as men called a usurper like Dionysius of Syracuse or Louis Napoleon in France a tyrant, for in free countries whatever the majority chooses to do in the prescribed constitutional way will be legal. It will be tyrannous in the sense of the lines

> O it is excellent
> To have a giant's strength, but it is tyrannous
> To use it like a giant.

That is to say, tyranny consists in the wanton and improper use of strength by the stronger, in the use of it to do things which one equal would not attempt against another. A majority is tyrannical when it decides without hearing the minority, when it suppresses fair and temperate criticism on its own acts, when it insists on restraining men in matters where restraint is not required by the common interest, when it forces men to contribute money to objects which they disapprove, and which the common interest does not demand. The element of tyranny lies in the wantonness of the act, a wantonness springing from the sense of overwhelming power, or in the fact that it is a misuse for one purpose of power granted for another. It consists not in the form of the act, which may be perfectly legal, but in the spirit and temper it reveals, and in the sense of injustice and oppression which it evokes in the minority.

40. THE EVOLUTION OF MAJORITY TYRANNY AND THE TYRANNY OF PUBLIC OPINION
by John Stuart Mill†

The struggle between Liberty and Authority is the most conspicuous feature in the portions of history with which we are earliest familiar, par-

* British lawyer, professor of law, member of Parliament, and diplomat. British Ambassador to the United States, 1907-1913. This selection is from James Bryce, *The American Commonwealth*, Macmillan and Co., Ltd., London, 1889, vol. II, p. 307.

† Nineteenth-century (1806-1873) English philosopher and political economist. Author of *System of Logic, Principles of Political Economy, On Liberty, Representative Government, Utilitarianism*, and other works. This selection is from John Stuart Mill, *On Liberty*, 3d ed., Ticknor & Fields, Boston, 1864, pp. 8-15.

ticularly in that of Greece, Rome, and England. But in old times this contest was between subjects, or some classes of subjects, and the government. By liberty, was meant protection against the tyranny of the political rulers. The rulers were conceived (except in some of the popular governments of Greece) as in a necessarily antagonistic position to the people whom they ruled. They consisted of a governing One, or a governing tribe or caste, who derived their authority from inheritance or conquest; who, at all events, did not hold it at the pleasure of the governed, and whose supremacy men did not venture, perhaps did not desire, to contest, whatever precautions might be taken against its oppressive exercise. Their power was regarded as necessary, but also as highly dangerous; as a weapon which they would attempt to use against their subjects, no less than against external enemies. To prevent the weaker members of the community from being preyed upon by innumerable vultures, it was needful that there should be an animal of prey stronger than the rest, commissioned to keep them down. But as the king of the vultures would be no less bent upon preying on the flock than any of the minor harpies, it was indispensable to be in a perpetual attitude of defence against his beak and claws. The aim, therefore, of patriots, was to set limits to the power which the ruler should be suffered to exercise over the community; and this limitation was what they meant by liberty. It was attempted in two ways. First, by obtaining a recognition of certain immunities, called political liberties or rights, which it was to be regarded as a breach of duty in the ruler to infringe, and which, if he did infringe, specific resistance, or general rebellion, was held to be justifiable. A second, and generally a later expedient, was the establishment of constitutional checks; by which the consent of the community, or of a body of some sort supposed to represent its interests, was made a necessary condition to some of the more important acts of the governing power. To the first of these modes of limitation, the ruling power, in most European countries, was compelled, more or less, to submit. It was not so with the second; and to attain this, or when already in some degree possessed, to attain it more completely, became everywhere the principal object of the lovers of liberty. And so long as mankind were content to combat one enemy by another, and to be ruled by a master, on condition of being guaranteed more or less efficaciously against his tyranny, they did not carry their aspirations beyond this point.

A time, however, came, in the progress of human affairs, when men ceased to think it a necessity of nature that their governors should be an independent power, opposed in interest to themselves. It appeared to them much better that the various magistrates of the State should be their tenants or delegates, revocable at their pleasure. In that way alone, it seemed, could they have complete security that the powers of government would never be abused to their disadvantage. By degrees, this new demand for elective and temporary rulers became the prominent object of the exertions of the popular party, wherever any such party existed; and superseded, to a considerable extent, the previous efforts to limit the powers of rulers. As the struggle proceeded for making the ruling power emanate from the periodical choice of the ruled, some persons began to think that too much importance had been attached to the limitation of the power itself. *That* (it might seem) was a resource against rulers whose interests were habitually opposed to those of the people. What was now wanted was, that the rulers should be identified with the people; that their interest and will should be the interest and will of the nation. The nation did not need to be protected against its own will. There was no fear of its tyrannizing over itself. Let the rulers be effectually responsible to it, promptly removable by it, and it could afford to trust them with power of which it could itself dictate the use to be made. Their power was but the nation's own power, concentrated, and in a form convenient for exercise. This mode of thought, or rather perhaps of feeling, was common among the last generation of European liberalism, in the Continental section of which, it still apparently predominates. Those who admit any limit to what a government may do, except in the case of such governments as they think ought not to exist, stand out as brilliant exceptions among the political thinkers of the Continent. A similar tone of sentiment might by this time have been prevalent in our own country, if the circumstances which for a time encouraged it had continued unaltered.

But, in political and philosophical theories, as well as in persons, success discloses faults and infirmities which failure might have concealed from observation. The notion, that the people have no need to limit their power over themselves, might seem axiomatic, when popular government was a thing only dreamed about, or read of as having existed at some distant period of the past. Neither was that notion necessarily disturbed by such temporary aberrations as those of the French Revolution, the worst of which were the work of an usurping few, and which, in any case, belonged, not to the permanent working of popular institutions, but to a sudden and convulsive outbreak against monarchical and aristocratic despotism. In time, however, a democratic republic came to occupy a large portion of the earth's surface, and made itself felt as one of the most powerful members of the community of nations; and elective and responsible government became subject to the observations and criticisms which wait upon a great existing fact. It was now perceived that such phrases as "self-government," and "the power of the people over themselves," do not express the true state of the case. The "people" who exercise the power, are not always the same people with those over whom it is exercised, and the "self-government" spoken of, is not the government of each by himself, but of each by all the rest. The will of the people, moreover, practically means, the will of the most numerous or the most active *part* of the people; the majority, or those who succeed in making themselves accepted as the majority: the people, consequently, *may* desire to oppress a part of their number; and precautions are as much needed against this, as against any other abuse of power. The limitation, therefore, of the power of government over individuals, loses none of its importance when the holders of power are regularly accountable to the community, that is, to the strongest party therein. This view of things, recommending itself equally to the intelligence of thinkers and to the inclination of those important classes in European society to whose real or supposed interests democracy is adverse, has had no difficulty in establishing itself; and in political speculations— "the tyranny of the majority" is now generally included among the evils against which society requires to be on its guard.

Like other tyrannies, the tyranny of the majority was at first, and is still vulgarly, held in dread, chiefly as operating through the acts of the public authorities. But reflecting persons perceived that when society is itself the tyrant—society collectively, over the separate individuals who compose it—its means of tyrannizing are not restricted to the acts which it may do by the hands of its political functionaries. Society can and does execute its own mandates: and if it issues wrong mandates instead of right, or any mandates at all in things with which it ought not to meddle, it practises a social tyranny more formidable than many kinds of political oppression, since, though not usually upheld by such extreme penalties, it leaves fewer means of escape, penetrating much more deeply into the details of life, and enslaving the soul itself. Protection, therefore, against the tyranny of the magistrate is not enough; there needs protection also against the tyranny of the prevailing opinion and feeling; against the tendency of society to impose, by other means than civil penalties, its own ideas and practices as rules of conduct on those who dissent from them; to fetter the development, and, if possible, prevent the formation, of any individuality not in harmony with its ways, and compel all characters to fashion themselves upon the model of its own. There is a limit to the legitimate interference of collective opinion with individual independence; and to find that limit, and maintain it against encroachment, is as indispensable to a good condition of human affairs, as protection against political despotism.

But though this proposition is not likely to be contested in general terms, the practical question, where to place the limit—how to make the fitting adjustment between individual independence and social control—is a subject on which nearly everything remains to be done. All that makes existence valuable to any one, depends on the enforcement of restraints upon the actions of other people. Some rules of conduct, therefore, must be imposed, by law in the first place, and by opinion on many things which are not fit subjects for the operation of law. What these rules should be, is the principal question in human affairs; but if we except a few of the most obvious cases, it is one of those which least progress has been made in resolving.

41. THE IMMANENCE OF MAJORITY TYRANNY IN NINETEENTH-CENTURY AMERICA

by Alexis de Tocqueville*

It is in the examination of the display of public opinion in the United States that we clearly perceive how far the power of the majority surpasses

* Nineteenth-century (1805-1859) French political writer and statesman. Author of *Democracy in America* and several other works. This selection is from Alexis de Tocqueville, *Democracy in America* (trans. Henry Reeve), Appleton-Century-Crofts, Inc., New York, 1904, vol. I, pp. 279-287.

all the powers with which we are acquainted in Europe. Intellectual principles exercise an influence which is so invisible, and often so inappreciable, that they baffle the toils of oppression. At the present time the most absolute monarchs in Europe are unable to prevent certain notions, which are opposed to their authority, from circulating in secret throughout their dominions, and even in their courts. Such is not the case in America; as long as the majority is still undecided, discussion is carried on; but as soon as its decision is irrevocably pronounced, a submissive silence is observed, and the friends, as well as the opponents, of the measure unite in assenting to its propriety. The reason of this is perfectly clear: no monarch is so absolute as to combine all the powers of society in his own hands, and to conquer all opposition with the energy of a majority which is invested with the right of making and of executing the laws.

The authority of a king is purely physical, and it controls the actions of the subject without subduing his private will; but the majority possesses a power which is physical and moral at the same time; it acts upon the will as well as upon the actions of men, and it represses not only all contest, but all controversy.

I know no country in which there is so little true independence of mind and freedom of discussion as in America. In any constitutional state in Europe every sort of religious and political theory may be advocated and propagated abroad; for there is no country in Europe so subdued by any single authority as not to contain citizens who are ready to protect the man who raises his voice in the cause of truth from the consequences of his hardihood. If he is unfortunate enough to live under an absolute government, the people is upon his side; if he inhabits a free country, he may find a shelter behind the authority of the throne, if he require one. The aristocratic part of society supports him in some countries, and the democracy in others. But in a nation where democratic institutions exist, organized like those of the United States, there is but one sole authority, one single element of strength and of success, with nothing beyond it. . . .

Fetters and headsmen were the coarse instruments which tyranny formerly employed; but the civilization of our age has refined the arts of despotism, which seemed, however, to have been sufficiently perfected before. The excesses of monarchical power had devised a variety of physical means of oppression: the democratic republics of the present day have rendered it as entirely an affair of the mind as that will which it is intended to coerce. Under the absolute sway of an individual despot the body was attacked in order to subdue the soul, and the soul escaped the blows which were directed against it and rose superior to the attempt; but such is not the course adopted by tyranny in democratic republics; there the body is left free, and the soul is enslaved. The sovereign can no longer say, "You shall think as I do on pain of death"; but he says: "You are free to think differently from me, and to retain your life, your property, and all that you possess; but if such be your determination, you are henceforth an alien among your people. You may retain your civil rights, but they will be useless to you, for you will never be chosen by your fellow-citizens if you solicit their suffrages, and they will affect to scorn you if you solicit their esteem. You will remain among men, but you will be deprived of the rights of mankind. Your fellow-creatures will shun you like an impure being, and those who are most persuaded of your innocence will abandon you too, lest they should be shunned in their turn. Go in peace! I have given you your life, but it is an existence incomparably worse than death."

Monarchical institutions have thrown an odium upon despotism; let us beware lest democratic republics should restore oppression, and should render it less odious and less degrading in the eyes of the many, by making it still more onerous to the few. . . .

The tendencies to which I have just alluded are as yet very slightly perceptible in political society, but they already begin to exercise an unfavourable influence upon the national character of the Americans. I am inclined to attribute the singular paucity of distinguished political characters to the ever-increasing activity of the despotism of the majority in the United States. When the American Revolution broke out they arose in great numbers, for public opinion then served, not to tyrannize over, but to direct the exertions of individuals. Those celebrated men took a full part in the general agitation of mind common at that period, and they attained a high degree of personal fame, which was reflected back upon the nation, but which was by no means borrowed from it.

In absolute governments the great nobles who are nearest to the throne flatter the passions of the sovereign, and voluntarily truckle to his caprices. But the mass of the nation does not degrade itself by servitude: it often submits from weakness, from habit, or from ignorance, and sometimes from loyalty. Some nations have been known to sacrifice their own desires to those of the sovereign with pleasure and with pride, thus exhibiting a sort of independence in the very act of submission. These peoples are miserable, but they are not degraded. There is a great difference between doing what one does not approve and feigning to approve what one does; the one is the necessary case of a weak person, the other befits the temper of a lackey.

In free countries, where every one is more or less called upon to give his opinion in the affairs of state; in democratic republics, where public life is incessantly commingled with domestic affairs, where the sovereign authority is accessible on every side, and where its attention can almost always be attracted by vociferation, more persons are to be met with who speculate upon its foibles and live at the cost of its passions than in absolute monarchies. Not because men are naturally worse in these States than elsewhere, but the temptation is stronger, and of easier access at the same time. The result is a far more extensive debasement of the characters of citizens.

Democratic republics extend the practice of currying favour with the many, and they introduce it into a greater number of classes at once: this is one of the most serious reproaches that can be addressed to them. In democratic States organized on the principles of the American republics, this is more especially the case, where the authority of the majority is so absolute and so irresistible that a man must give up his rights as a citizen, and almost abjure his quality as a human being, if he intends to stray from the track which it lays down.

In that immense crowd which throngs the avenues to power in the United States I found very few men who displayed any of that manly candour and that masculine independence of opinion which frequently distinguished the Americans in former times, and which constitutes the leading feature in distinguished characters, wheresoever they may be found. It seems, at first sight, as if all the minds of the Americans were formed upon one model, so accurately do they correspond in their manner of judging. A stranger does, indeed, sometimes meet with Americans who dissent from these rigorous formularies; with men who deplore the defects of the laws, the mutability and the ignorance of democracy; who even go so far as to observe the evil tendencies which impair the national character, and to point out such remedies as it might be possible to apply; but no one is there to hear these things besides yourself, and you, to whom these secret reflections are confided, are a stranger and a bird of passage. They are very ready to communicate truths which are useless to you, but they continue to hold a different language in public. . . .

Despotism debases the oppressed much more than the oppressor: in absolute monarchies the king has often great virtues, but the courtiers are invariably servile. It is true that the American courtiers do not say "Sire," or "Your Majesty"—a distinction without a difference. They are forever talking of the natural intelligence of the populace they serve; they do not debate the question as to which of the virtues of their master is preeminently worthy of admiration, for they assure him that he possesses all the virtues under heaven without having acquired them, or without caring to acquire them; they do not give him their daughters and their wives to be raised at his pleasure to the rank of his concubines, but, by sacrificing their opinions, they prostitute themselves. Moralists and philosophers in America are not obliged to conceal their opinions under the veil of allegory; but, before they venture upon a harsh truth, they say: "We are aware that the people which we are addressing is too superior to all the weaknesses of human nature to lose the command of its temper for an instant; and we should not hold this language if we were not speaking to men whom their virtues and their intelligence render more worthy of freedom than all the rest of the world." It would have been impossible for the sycophants of Louis XIV to flatter more dexterously. For my part, I am persuaded that in all governments, whatever their nature may be, servility will cower to force, and adulation will cling to power. The only means of preventing men from degrading themselves is to invest no one with that unlimited authority which is the surest method of debasing them.

Governments usually fall a sacrifice to impotence or to tyranny. In the former case their power escapes from them; it is wrested from their grasp in the latter. Many observers, who have witnessed the anarchy of democratic States, have imagined that the government of those States was naturally weak and impotent. The truth is, that when once hostilities are begun between parties, the government loses its control over society. But I do not think that a democratic power is naturally without force or without resources: say, rather, that it is almost always by the abuse of its force and the misemployment of its resources that a democratic government fails. Anarchy is almost always produced by its tyranny or its mistakes, but not by its want of strength.

It is important not to confound stability with force, or the greatness of a thing with its duration. In democratic republics, the power which directs society is not stable; for it often changes hands and assumes a new direction. But whichever way it turns, its force is almost irresistible. The governments of the American republics appear to me to be as much centralized as those of the absolute monarchies of Europe, and more energetic than they are. I do not, therefore, imagine that they will perish from weakness.

If ever the free institutions of America are destroyed, that event may be attributed to the unlimited authority of the majority, which may at some future time urge the minorities to desperation, and oblige them to have recourse to physical force. Anarchy will then be the result, but it will have been brought about by despotism.

42. THE SOCIAL ETHIC AND MAJORITY TYRANNY
by William H. Whyte, Jr.*

"The more equal social conditions become," De Tocqueville, no friend of conformity, presciently observed, "the more men display this reciprocal disposition to oblige each other."

And there is the crux, when De Tocqueville wrote this a century ago it was the double-edged nature of this disposition that haunted him. He understood its virtue; he was an aristocrat and he confessed that he missed the excellence of the few in the good of the many, but he saw clearly that our egalitarianism and our ease of social co-operation were the great fruits of democracy. We could not sustain these virtues without suffering their defects. But could we keep them in balance? De Tocqueville made a prophecy. If America ever destroyed its genius it would be by intensifying the social virtues at the expense of others, by making the individual come to regard himself as a hostage to prevailing opinion, by creating, in sum, a tyranny of the majority.

And this is what the organization man is doing. He is doing it for what he feels are good reasons, but this only makes the tyranny more powerful, not less. At the very time when the pressures of our highly organized society make so stringent a demand on the individual, he is himself compounding the impact. He is not only other-directed, to borrow David Riesman's concept, he is articulating a philosophy which tells him it is right to be that way.

My charge against the Social Ethic, then, is on precisely the grounds of contemporary usefulness it so venerates. It is not, I submit, suited to the

* Writer and assistant managing editor of *Fortune*. Author of *Is Anybody Listening?* and *The Organization Man*. This selection is from William H. Whyte, Jr., *The Organization Man*, Simon and Schuster, Inc., New York, 1956, pp. 395-398. © Copyright 1956 by William H. Whyte, Jr. Reprinted by permission of Simon and Schuster, Inc.

needs of "modern man," but is instead, reinforcing precisely that which least needs to be emphasized, and at the expense of that which does. Here is my bill of particulars.

It is redundant. In some societies individualism has been carried to such extremes as to endanger the society itself, and there exist today examples of individualism corrupted into a narrow egoism which prevents effective co-operation. This is a danger, there is no question of that. But is it today as pressing a danger as the obverse—a climate which inhibits individual initiative and imagination, and the courage to exercise it against group opinion? Society is itself an education in the extrovert values, and I think it can be rightfully argued that rarely has there been a society which has preached them so hard. No man is an island unto himself, but how John Donne would writhe to hear how often, and for what reasons, the thought is so tiresomely repeated.

It is premature. To preach technique before content, the skills of getting along isolated from why and to what end the getting along is for, does not produce maturity. It produces a sort of permanent prematurity, and this is true not only of the child being taught life adjustment but of the organization man being taught well-roundedness. This is a sterile concept, and those who believe that they have mastered human relations can blind themselves to the true bases of co-operation. People don't co-operate just to co-operate; they co-operate for substantive reasons, to achieve certain goals, and unless these are comprehended the little manipulations for morale, team spirit, and such are fruitless.

And they can be worse than fruitless. Held up as the end-all of organization leadership, the skills of human relations easily tempt the new administrator into the practice of a tyranny more subtle and more pervasive than that which he means to supplant. No one wants to see the old authoritarian return, but at least it could be said of him that what he wanted primarily from you was your sweat. The new man wants your soul.

It is delusory. It is easy to fight obvious tyranny; it is not easy to fight benevolence, and few things are more calculated to rob the individual of his defenses than the idea that his interests and those of society can be wholly compatible. The good society is the one in which they are most compatible, but they never can be completely so, and one who lets The Organization be the judge ultimately sacrifices himself. Like the good society, the good organization encourages individual expression, and many have done so. But there always remains some conflict between the individual and The Organization. Is The Organization to be the arbiter? The Organization will look to its own interests, but it will look to the individual's *only as The Organization interprets them.*

It is static. Organization of itself has no dynamic. The dynamic is in the individual and thus he must not only question how The Organization interprets his interests, he must question how it interprets its own. The bold new plan he feels is necessary, for example. He cannot trust that The Organization will recognize this. Most probably, it will not. It is the nature of a new idea to confound current consensus—even the mildly new idea. It might be patently in order, but, unfortunately, the group has a vested interest in its miseries as well as its pleasures, and irrational as this may be, many a member of organization life can recall instances where the group clung to known disadvantages rather than risk the anarchies of change.

It is self-destructive. The quest for normalcy, as we have seen in suburbia, is one of the great breeders of neuroses, and the Social Ethic only serves to exacerbate them. What is normalcy? We practice a great mutual deception. Everyone knows that they themselves are different—that they are shy in company, perhaps, or dislike many things most people seem to like—but they are not sure that other people are different too. Like the norms of personality testing, they see about them the sum of efforts of people like themselves to seem as normal as others and possibly a little more so. It is hard enough to learn to live with our inadequacies, and we need not make ourselves more miserable by a spurious ideal of middle-class adjustment. Adjustment to what? Nobody really knows—and the tragedy is that they don't realize that the so-confident-seeming other people don't know either.

43. A POSSIBLE SAFEGUARD AGAINST MAJORITY TYRANNY

by John Stuart Mill*

The object of this Essay is to assert one very simple principle, as entitled to govern absolutely the dealings of society with the individual in the way of compulsion and control, whether the means used be physical force in the form of legal penalties, or the moral coercion of public opinion. That principle is, that the sole end for which mankind are warranted, individually or collectively, in interfering with the liberty of action of any of their number, is self-protection. That the only purpose for which power can be rightfully exercised over any member of a civilized community, against his will, is to prevent harm to others. His own good, either physical or moral, is not a sufficient warrant. He cannot rightfully be compelled to do or forbear because it will be better for him to do so, because it will make him happier, because, in the opinions of others, to do so would be wise, or even right. These are good reasons for remonstrating with him, or reasoning with him, or persuading him, or entreating him, but not for compelling him, or visiting him with any evil, in case he do otherwise. To justify that, the conduct from which it is desired to deter him must be calculated to produce evil to some one else. The only part of the conduct of any one, for which he is amenable to society, is that which concerns others. In the part which merely concerns himself, his independence is, of right, absolute. Over himself, over his own body and mind, the individual is sovereign. . . .

This, then, is the appropriate region of human liberty. It comprises, first, the inward domain of consciousness; demanding liberty of conscience, in

* Nineteenth-century English philosopher and political economist. This selection is from John Stuart Mill, *On Liberty*, 3d ed., Ticknor & Fields, Boston, 1864, pp. 22-23 and 27-31.

the most comprehensive sense; liberty of thought and feeling; absolute freedom of opinion and sentiment on all subjects, practical or speculative, scientific, moral, or theological. The liberty of expressing and publishing opinions may seem to fall under a different principle, since it belongs to that part of the conduct of an individual which concerns other people; but, being almost of as much importance as the liberty of thought itself, and resting in great part on the same reasons, is practically inseparable from it. Secondly, the principle requires liberty of tastes and pursuits; of framing the plan of our life to suit our own character; of doing as we like, subject to such consequences as may follow; without impediment from our fellow-creatures, so long as what we do does not harm them, even though they should think our conduct foolish, perverse, or wrong. Thirdly, from this liberty of each individual, follows the liberty, within the same limits, of combination among individuals; freedom to unite, for any purpose not involving harm to others: the persons combining being supposed to be of full age, and not forced or deceived.

No society in which these liberties are not, on the whole, respected, is free, whatever may be its form of government; and none is completely free in which they do not exist absolute and unqualified. The only freedom which deserves the name, is that of pursuing our own good in our own way, so long as we do not attempt to deprive others of theirs, or impede their efforts to obtain it. Each is the proper guardian of his own health, whether bodily, or mental and spiritual. Mankind are greater gainers by suffering each other to live as seems good to themselves, than by compelling each to live as seems good to the rest.

Though this doctrine is anything but new, and, to some persons, may have the air of a truism, there is no doctrine which stands more directly opposed to the general tendency of existing opinion and practice. Society has expended fully as much effort in the attempt (according to its lights) to compel people to conform to its notions of personal, as of social excellence. The ancient commonwealths thought themselves entitled to practise, and the ancient philosophers countenanced, the regulation of every part of private conduct by public authority, on the ground that the State had a deep interest in the whole bodily and mental discipline of every one of its citizens; a mode of thinking which may have been admissible in small republics surrounded by powerful enemies, in constant peril of being subverted by foreign attack or internal commotion, and to which even a short interval of relaxed energy and self-command might so easily be fatal, that they could not afford to wait for the salutary permanent effects of freedom. In the modern world, the greater size of political communities, and above all, the separation between the spiritual and temporal authority (which placed the direction of men's consciences in other hands than those which controlled their worldly affairs), prevented so great an interference by law in the details of private life; but the engines of moral repression have been wielded more strenuously against divergence from the reigning opinion in self-regarding, than even in social matters. . . .

Apart from the peculiar tenets of individual thinkers, there is also in the world at large an increasing inclination to stretch unduly the powers of society over the individual, both by the force of opinion and even by that of legislation: and as the tendency of all the changes taking place in the world is to strengthen society, and diminish the power of the individual, this encroachment is not one of the evils which tend spontaneously to disappear, but, on the contrary, to grow more and more formidable. The disposition of mankind, whether as rulers or as fellow-citizens, to impose their own opinions and inclinations as a rule of conduct on others, is so energetically supported by some of the best and by some of the worst feelings incident to human nature, that it is hardly ever kept under restraint by anything but want of power; and as the power is not declining, but growing, unless a strong barrier of moral conviction can be raised against the mischief, we must expect, in the present circumstances of the world, to see it increase.

44. FURTHER SAFEGUARDS AGAINST MAJORITY TYRANNY

by James Bryce *

Where a majority has erred, the only remedy against the prolongation or repetition of its error is in the continued protests and agitation of the minority, an agitation which ought to be peaceably conducted, carried on by voice and pen, but which must be vehement enough to rouse the people and deliver them from the consequences of their blunders. But the more complete the sway of majorities is, so much the less disposed is a minority to maintain the contest. It loses faith in its cause and in itself, and allows its voice to be silenced by the triumphant cries of its opponents. How are men to acquiesce promptly and loyally in the decision of a majority, and yet to go on arguing against it? how can they be at once submissive and aggressive? That conceit of his own goodness and greatness which intoxicates an absolute monarch besets a sovereign people also, and the slavishness with which his ministers approach an Oriental despot may reappear in the politicians of a Western democracy. The duty therefore of a patriotic states- man in a country where public opinion rules, would seem to be rather to resist and correct than to encourage the dominant sentiment. He will not be content with trying to form and mould and lead it, but he will confront it, lecture it, remind it that it is fallible, rouse it out of its self-complacency. Unfortunately, courage and independence are plants which a soil impreg- nated with the belief in the wisdom of numbers does not tend to produce: nor is there any art known to statesmen whereby their growth can be fostered.

Experience has, however, suggested plans for lessening the risks incident to the dominance of one particular set of opinions. One plan is for the people themselves to limit their powers, i.e. to surround their own action and the action of their agents with restrictions of time and method which

* British lawyer, professor of law, member of Parliament, and diplomat. British Ambassador to the United States, 1907-1913. This selection is from James Bryce, *The American Commonwealth*, Macmillan and Co., Ltd., London, 1889, vol. II, pp. 222-224.

compel delay. Another is for them so to parcel out functions among many agents that no single one chosen indiscreetly, or obeying his mandate over-zealously, can do much mischief, and that out of the multiplicity of agents differences of view may spring which will catch the attention of the citizens.

The temper and character of a people may supply more valuable safe-guards. The country which has worked out for itself a truly free govern-ment must have done so in virtue of the vigorous individuality of its chil-dren. Such an individuality does not soon yield even to the pressure of democratic conditions. In a nation with a keen moral sense and a capacity for strong emotions, opinion based on a love of what is deemed just or good will resist the multitude when bent on evil: and if there be a great variety of social conditions, of modes of life, of religious beliefs, these will prove centres of resistance to a dominant tendency, like rocks standing up in a river, at which he whom the current sweeps downwards may clutch. In-stances might be cited even from countries where the majority has had every source of strength at its command—physical force, tradition, the all but universal persuasions and prejudices of the lower as well as of the higher classes—in which small minorities have triumphed, first by startling and then by leavening and convincing the majority. This they have done in virtue of that intensity of belief which is oftenest found in a small sect or group, not because it is small, but because if its belief were not intense it would not venture to hold out at all against the adverse mass. The energy of each individual in the minority makes it in the long run a match for a majority huger but less instinct with vitality. In a free country more especially, ten men who care are worth a hundred who do not.

Such natural compensations as this occur in the physical as well as in the spiritual and moral world, and preserve both. But they are compensa-tions on which the practical statesman cannot safely rely, for they are partial, they are uncertain, and they probably tend to diminish with the progress of democracy. The longer public opinion has ruled, the more abso-lute is the authority of the majority likely to become, the less likely are energetic minorities to arise, the more are politicians likely to occupy them-selves, not in forming opinion, but in discovering and hastening to obey it.

45. FEDERALISM AS A SAFEGUARD AGAINST MAJORITY TYRANNY

by James Madison *

There are, moreover, two considerations particularly applicable to the federal system of America, which place that system in a very interesting point of view.

* Member of the Continental Congress, the Constitutional Convention, and the United States House of Representatives; United States Secretary of State, 1801-1809; President of the United States, 1809-1817. Coauthor (with Alexander Hamilton and John Jay) of *The Federalist*. This selection is from *The Federalist*, no. 51 (Everyman's Library Edition), E. P. Dutton & Co., Inc., New York, 1911, pp. 265-267.

First. In a single republic all the power surrendered by the people is submitted to the administration of a single government; and the usurpations are guarded against by a division of the government into distinct and separate departments. In the compound republic of America, the power surrendered by the people is first divided between two distinct governments, and then the portion allotted to each subdivided among distinct and separate departments. Hence a double security arises to the rights of the people. The different governments will control each other, at the same time that each will be controlled by itself.

Second. It is of great importance in a republic not only to guard the society against the oppression of its rulers, but to guard one part of the society against the injustice of the other part. Different interests necessarily exist in different classes of citizens. If a majority be united by a common interest, the rights of the minority will be insecure. There are but two methods of providing against this evil: the one by creating a will in the community independent of the majority—that is, of the society itself; the other, by comprehending in the society so many separate descriptions of citizens as will render an unjust combination of a majority of the whole very improbable, if not impracticable. The first method prevails in all governments possessing an hereditary or self-appointed authority. This, at best, is but a precarious security; because a power independent of the society may as well espouse the unjust views of the major, as the rightful interests of the minor party, and may possibly be turned against both parties. The second method will be exemplified in the federal republic of the United States. Whilst all authority in it will be derived from and dependent on the society, the society itself will be broken into so many parts, interests, and classes of citizens, that the rights of individuals, or of the minority, will be in little danger from interested combinations of the majority. In a free government the security for civil rights must be the same as that for religious rights. It consists in the one case in the multiplicity of interests, and in the other in the multiplicity of sects. The degree of security in both cases will depend on the number of interests and sects; and this may be presumed to depend on the extent of country and number of people comprehended under the same government. This view of the subject must particularly recommend a proper federal system to all the sincere and considerate friends of republican government, since it shows that in exact proportion as the territory of the Union may be formed into more circumscribed Confederacies, or States, oppressive combination of a majority will be facilitated; the best security, under the republican forms, for the rights of every class of citizens will be diminished; and consequently the stability and independence of some member of the government, the only other security, must be proportionally increased. Justice is the end of government. It is the end of civil society. It ever has been and ever will be pursued until it be obtained, or until liberty be lost in the pursuit. In a society under the forms of which the stronger faction can readily unite and oppress the weaker, anarchy may as truly be said to reign as in a state of nature, where the weaker individual is not secured against the violence of the stronger; and as, in the latter state, even the stronger individuals are prompted, by the uncertainty of their condition, to submit to a government which may protect the weak as well as themselves; so, in the former state, will the more powerful factions or parties be gradually induced, by a like motive, to wish for a government which will protect all parties, the weaker as well as the more powerful. It can be little doubted that if the State of Rhode Island was separated from the Confederacy and left to itself, the insecurity of rights under the popular form of government within such narrow limits would be displayed by such reiterated oppressions of factious majorities that some power altogether independent of the people would soon be called for by the voice of the very factions whose misrule had proved the necessity of it. In the extended republic of the United States, and among the great variety of interests, parties, and sects which it embraces, a coalition of a majority of the whole society could seldom take place on any other principles than those of justice and the general good; whilst there being thus less danger to a minor from the will of a major party, there must be less pretext, also, to provide for the security of the former, by introducing into the government a will not dependent on the latter, or, in other words, a will independent of the society itself. It is no less certain than it is important, notwithstanding the contrary opinions which have been entertained, that the larger the society, provided it lie within a practical sphere, the more duly capable it will be of self-government. And happily for the *republican cause*, the practicable sphere may be carried to a very great extent by a judicious modification and mixture of the *federal principle*.

46. VETO GROUPS AND MINORITY TYRANNY
by Max Lerner*

Power in America cannot be understood by looking only at the governmental structure. American historians and social thinkers have sometimes overvalued and sometimes undervalued the role of political power in the American story, depending on their own angle of vision and their theory of history and human nature. The conservatives, secure in their economic power, have stressed the dangers of the political. The liberals have inveighed against economic power, while counting on the political most heavily for modes of change and reform. The radicals have stressed economic power because of their class approach to history, while (as shown in the case of Veblen and Beard) they have grossly undervalued political power and its use as an instrument for change.

Mostly, however, the run-of-the-mill American has shown a healthy concern for all phases of power: as a practical matter he has pursued purchasing power, admiring intensely its accumulation in the hands of the rich. While focusing his political interest on the Presidency as the core

* Author, newspaper columnist, and professor of American civilization at Brandeis University. The selection is from Max Lerner, *America as a Civilization*, Simon and Schuster, Inc., New York, 1957, pp. 397-400 and 405-407. © Copyright 1957 by Max Lerner. Reprinted by permission of Simon and Schuster, Inc.

and symbol of the government, he has been wary of the Federal power and its administrative arm as too complicated for the mind to grasp. He has been suspicious of trade-union power and church power even more than of corporate power, and suspicious also of military power—at least until the period of the world wars and cold wars.

Recent American history has witnessed important changes in the distribution of power. There has been a shift from Congressional to Presidential and administrative power, a shift from formal policy-making to budget-making power which often has carried policy-making with it, a shift from local and state power to Federal power. Similarly there has been a shift of power from the churches, the universities, and the lawyers to the Big Press and the opinion industries, from the farmers and small-industry groups to the big corporate industries, from the owners to the managers of industry, from civilians to the military.

The fact about American power, as about so many other phases of American life, is that it is plural and fluid. It is many-faceted rather than uniform; it is dispersed among a number of groups; it has shifted geographically and in its class distribution. There has been, to be sure, a steady movement toward concentration in every form of power. Yet the agencies of power have multiplied, as witness the growing distribution of economic power among the corporation, the trade-union, and the government.

Since the beginning of the nation the whole American atmosphere has been saturated with power—technological, economic, political, religious, military, financial. From the cop and the precinct boss to the foreman and trade-union leader and corporate executive, from sergeant to general, from bureau clerk to President, the sense of power has been pervasive in the American experience, and the sense of the limits of power has also been constantly present. In contrast with aristocratic or military societies, America has had no elite groups of birth or status trained to the exercise of power. There has been enough diffusion to give the nation as a whole the chance to revel in the feeling of abundant power. The Americans as a nation have been relatively parvenus in its use and have therefore distrusted its users, but what is remarkable is that this nation of parvenus has not carried the abuse of power further than it has.

The reason may perhaps be found in a distinction drawn by Santayana between *power* as a generative force and *domination* as a frustrating and destructive one. The atmosphere in which American life has developed has been one of a continued expansiveness which has kept America relatively free of the frustrations of power that more constricted cultures have incurred. This offers a clue to the fact that while there has often been corruption in American political life, there has never been a serious attempt at dictatorship. The dangers of tyranny are greatest in a society where power has never been widely diffused. As Santayana again points out, in a comment on Lord Acton's great epigram on power, only those unaccustomed to power are corrupted by it. While Santayana means it to be an argument for aristocratic societies and against popular democracies, it has actually worked differently in America, where the corruption is likely to be in the lure of the Big Money rather than of absolute political power.

This raises the question of what De Tocqueville stressed and Aristotle foresaw long before him—the dangers of a majority tyranny on the one hand and on the other the servility of the democratic mob to a demagogue-dictator. As one of the great innovations of world history, majority rule powerfully attracted De Tocqueville and other commentators to the American experiment while it raised in their minds profound doubts and fears. These doubts and fears have a real base, as shown by the popular hysterias that have swept over American opinion. Yet the power of the demagogue-dictator has worked itself out to a grim sequel not in America, where mob rule had been most anticipated and feared, but in Germany, Italy, Russia, China, and the "People's democracies" of eastern Europe.

What was wrong with the calculations of the fearers and predictors? Partly they failed to reckon with the strength of the constitutional tradition, but mainly they failed to take into account the pluralist character of power in America—its many loci, its widespread diffusion in one form or another, the heterogeneous quality of American society, and the talent for equilibrium it has shown.

The tyranny of the mob is a very real tyranny. It shows itself notably in America in periods after wars, when tensions have come to the breaking point, and on the brink of war, when the cult of the nation-state gives an opportunity to the loyalty hunters and the professional accusers. Yet it would be hard to point to any period in American history and say, "Here is where the majority ran riot in America and trampled upon freedom." A close student of American power is more apt to study not the majority but the minorities—the lobbies, the pressure groups, the sectional interests, the corporate and trade-union leaders, the heads of the Congressional investigations. Even in the case of the loyalty hunts and the search for "subversives," the effective stimulus has not been majority hysteria but a cold campaign by pressure groups in the hunt for some particular quarry. A new feature on the landscape of American power is the "veto group," which pretends to act in the name of the majority but actually terrorizes it.

To understand the American pressure groups, one must understand that to move a huge and unwieldy mass, such as the American leviathan, you have to push very hard. The strength and variety of these pressure groups, the brazenness of their lobbyists, the vast sums they have spent on propaganda, their use of techniques as diverse as the corruption of government officials on the one hand and large-scale direct mailing on the other hand: these have often been described. The number of registered lobbyists in Washington, not taking account of those who operate under cover, exceeds the number of Congressmen. They are paid more than the President and the Supreme Court justices, and they have the big money at their disposal. There is little doubt that they influence legislation, in many cases help draft the laws; they are especially active in a war economy where big contracts are at stake; they often succeed in reaching and sometimes even supplying strategic members of the government.

The political theorists of the early twentieth century, including some Americans, used to write a good deal about guilds and hanker for a society in which a network of them would hold the power and perform the functions of government. In a sense there is a network of American pressure groups—from the farm bloc, the trade-unions, the churches militant, the ethnic groups and the patriotic societies down to protective associations for birds and historic shrines—that form a kind of *guildism* in American life. Sometimes they are merely a nuisance with which Congressmen and bureaucrats have learned to deal, sometimes they represent permanent group interests which they do not allow the legislators and administrators to forget. Always they express the individual's sense that he is powerless alone in so huge a society and must therefore band with others to exert pressure; they also express the principle of the right of free association gone berserk. Alongside this guildism there is also what has been called a *clientelism* that has developed in America, meaning that when a man has some particular interest at stake and wants to exert his power to protect or advance it, he turns as a client to a professional influence technician who knows—for a fee or a percentage—how to get what, where, when, and from whom.

I doubt whether any of these—interest groups, pressure groups or veto groups, guildism or clientelism, lobbyists or per-centers—will undermine the American Republic. Just as the tyranny of the majority in American life has been overrated, so also more recently has the destructiveness of minorities. Both have been facets of the effort to balance the principle of popular sovereignty with the fact of a richly diverse and pluralistic society. America's enemies nourished the hope of a nation so fragmented that it would succumb to a concerted attack, whether by arms or propaganda. The hope has proved wrong. So have the fears of those who felt that it was ripe for tyranny. . . .

The pluralist, pragmatist, and federalist character of American politics has compelled it to develop the arts of compromise and to achieve an equilibrium of conflicting powers in motion. Yet the fact is that Americans did not always succeed in settling their conflicts of authority or escape disaster. At one point the frame of both federalism and the party system could not contain the tensions, and the result was a Civil War. To be sure, America was not alone in its tensions, and the quarter century between 1840 and 1865, which saw the gathering forces and the explosion in America, witnessed in Europe also a series of bitter class conflicts and revolutions. The contemporary writings of Marx and Engels on the American Civil War interpret it as part of this world revolutionary surge toward freedom. Yet Lincoln saw it more realistically as a challenge to national unity—that is, to the traditional Federal balance. At the time of the Gettysburg Address he was using the Federal power to ride herd on the state governors who challenged it. "Government, of, by, and for the people" under American conditions could not dispense with an adequate degree of unity at the center.

The doctrinal struggle involved in the Civil War was Calhoun's doctrine of the "concurrent majorities"—actually a doctrine of minority power through veto—as arrayed against Lincoln's doctrine of national unity. Lincoln won, and by that fact the sovereignty of the minority was squeezed out of the American system: since the Federal system allows for autonomy enough in the constituent parts and at the rim, along with enough effective power at the center, it was unnecessary to make a fetish of the minority's veto power. It is this knack for framing their crucial problems in terms of equilibrium ("both/and") rather than of doctrinal struggle to the death ("either/or") which has helped Americans give continuity and survival to their history.

This is illustrated by the relative absence of class struggle in America. Actually the power of the contending classes, both of business and of labor, has been greater than in most European countries which have shown more class conflict. But Americans have perforce learned the arts of balancing their classes in the equilibrium as they have learned to balance their sections. This is true not only of the economy but of the society as a whole. The gigantism that has afflicted American life could long ago have destroyed it had not some sort of balance been achieved between the contending forms of bigness. Thus America developed not only Big Government but also Big Business, Big Labor, Big Distribution, the Big Press, the Big Church, and the Big Army. No one of these is monolithic: each of them in turn is a tangle of conflicting forces, and each in turn has had to achieve an equilibrium within itself. Thus the American system of power has become like a system of nebulae held together by reciprocal tensions in intergalactic space.

But, unlike the nebulae of the physical universe, the dangers of disrupting the equilibrium are a constant concern. It is not only the traditional fear that one of the Bigs may overshadow and finally annex the others, and with them the principle of freedom, or that a combination of them might become imperialist and destroy the equilibrium. There is also the danger of a fetishism of the equilibrium principle itself, which could give each of the new forces the veto power that Calhoun once sought for each of the sections. Because of the problem of reaching a consensus among the giant structures that dominate American society, a number of "veto groups" have emerged—minorities with a strategic position, whose psychic intensity takes advantage of the equilibrium and draws a confining line around the diversity of American life. The problem of reaching a consensus has always been hard in America, yet it has always had to be solved. Otherwise government would be deadlocked and society stagnant, and the carving out of a line of direction for American growth would be frustrated.

47. THE DANGERS OF NONCONFORMISM
by Morris Freedman *

Not long ago I heard one of this country's professional intellectuals— a former university president, a present foundation president—address a university gathering of several hundred persons. The gentleman attacked

* Professor of English at the University of New Mexico and former associate editor of *Commentary*. This selection is from Morris Freedman, "The Dangers of Nonconformism," *American Scholar*, vol. 28, issue no. 1, pp. 25-32, Winter, 1958-1959. By permission of the author.

the blight of conformism in the United States; he deplored the fact that men in gray flannel suits had become "interchangeable"; he lamented the loss of true individualism. I do not mention his name, for I agreed with much of what he said, and what I did not agree with is not quite my point at present. What struck me while listening to his urbane talk was his own "interchangeable" appearance: neat, three-button blue suit, plain tie, precisely coiffured graying hair, erect carriage: the very model of a model executive, not only interchangeable with dozens of men in similar positions and in "gentlemen of distinction" ads, but ready to be played in the movies by a dozen or so actors—Walter Pidgeon, Cary Grant, Gregory Peck, Ray Milland. It struck me as somewhat odd, too, that several hundred persons should applaud in unison a speech urging nonconformity, and that during the question period one of the questions that did not "conform" with the speaker's views should be greeted with derision.

Of course one man's conformism may be another man's heresy. But what seems to have taken place in American intellectual life in recent years is the rising of just about any nonconformity to the status of respectable orthodoxy. It is even more strange that it has become as risky to attack these nonconformist orthodoxies as it ever was to attack a conformist one. These days the best protection is to become a nonconformist. In Mary McCarthy's novel about academic life, *The Groves of Academe*, the central character withstands an attempt by the liberal college administration to fire him for incompetence by falsely claiming to be a Communist. The nonconformist orthodoxy in that environment clearly required being more than fair with Communists, and the professor changed color accordingly. Indeed, it is probably more comfortable today on many campuses to be politically radical than politically conservative. One sure way of getting a job in an advertising agency, I have been told, is to insist that you are an angry young rebel.

The question of conformity, of course, exercises only those certain portions of the American population that loosely may be called the "intellectual" circles. College communities undoubtedly form the largest of these, although the publishing, advertising and entertainment circles are not insubstantial. The issue of conformity scarcely exists for others, the majority, who conform automatically and happily, without giving the question a second thought. Nonconformists have this majority in mind when they attack conformity. They condemn this majority for deriding individual differences, for responding in herd-fashion to the blandishments of advertising and public relations experts, for being responsible for mass taste and mass opinion. No doubt the nonconformists are right in all of these charges. Yet it may easily be shown that the self-elected nonconformists are culpable on every count on which they attack conformists.

It has been well established that nonconformists, instead of responding to the values of tabloid newspaper, subway car or television advertisements, respond to a no less specific and no less rigid set, particularly those in the advertisements of the New York *Times*, the *New Yorker*, the *Saturday Review* and the like, or of the commercials of FM stations that broadcast classical music all day. Although the nonconformist may refuse, with a shudder, to engage in the barbaric practice of drinking instant coffee, he will no less eagerly sip *expresso*. If you can construct a stereotype of the man in the street, you can build an equally plausible one of the man out of the street. Of course, as I say, this proposition is not new, as was definitively demonstrated by Russell Lynes's wickedly clever classifications some while ago in *Life* of the habits of low-brow, middle-brow and high-brow (classifications which themselves no doubt helped establish new laws of how not to conform).

Were all this merely a matter of an amusing sociological pastime—observing and arranging the eating, drinking, dressing, entertainment, furniture buying, political and general ideological habits of low-, middle- and high-brows, or of conformists and nonconformists—there would not be much point in bringing up the matter again after Lynes, Riesman and others have settled it so exhaustively. Actually, however, much more is involved. It seems to me that the orthodoxy of the nonconformists is especially dangerous since it claims to be the result of free investigation and free thought, the product of the uncontrolled, individual mind. Orthodoxy clearly related to some conformist dogma we can so much more easily accept or reject on its own basis.

Let me cite the subject of education from among a number I might have chosen. The country is engaged in a major debate on the problem: the debate is quite limited, on one side, to the professional educators, referred to as "educationists" by the opposition; and, on the other, to what might be called the humanists, many of whom would also proudly claim the title of nonconformists (for they refuse to accept the majority attitude toward education). Now I like to think of myself as among the humanists; and I am certainly appalled by the more extreme notions of educators who believe in teaching the "whole child" (presumably to the suppression of any talented part of him), who believe in teaching "life adjustment" rather than subject matter, who believe in "social promotion," et cetera, et cetera, ad nauseam. I hold that persons who believe such things without qualification should be opposed vigorously; I believe that they should not have final or exclusive say about the schooling of American children, as they now do in many places. But having said this, I must also say that I do not think that the professional educators are to a man villains or idiots—as many critics of them do say or come close to saying.

I probably would not have come to this last conclusion, mild as it may seem, except for the excess and inconsistency of the professional nonconformists on the subject of education. Like nonconformists elsewhere, the nonconformists here prefers to deal with abstractions rather than with reality. One of the many realities of the problem of American education is surely the immense compulsion for universal schooling. Most states have some kind of law compelling attendance in school of every young person up to a certain age regardless of his willingness to learn. I do not say that such laws offer a blanket excuse to educators for their positions, but these laws, the result of great community pressures in the past, are almost always neglected by extremist critics of the schools who insist on an across-the-board raising of standards. Nor have I seen critics of the schools consider the broader pressures in American life that tend to make American education the very special thing that it is.

Consider *Life* magazine's much-publicized first issue in a series on the "Crisis in Education." It blasts the casual diffuseness of American schools by contrast with the concentrated seriousness of Russian ones. The day of a Russian boy and the day of an American boy of the same age are compared, both in school and after. As one might expect, the American boy is inept at mathematics, which he takes as a joke; he tosses off his homework; he is adept only at rock-and-roll and swimming. In short, the American boy is typical of many American young people, who, among other things, are interested in finding out about the making of a movie, or looking at scantily dressed young actresses changing costumes, or reading about horse racing and the latest trend in cars, or going to church to see their minister perform tricks of magic, or looking at the new fashions in clothes and carpets—or reading the latest *Life*, which, in addition to criticizing American education, devoted that same issue to covering all of these edifying and instructive aspects of the broad American scene for its readers. *Life* magazine itself is certainly one of the main forces in making American life what it is; yet the editors, I am sure, would never think of blaming themselves for emphasizing values possibly inimical to seriousness in education. (Perhaps I ought to mention that I do not belong to the nonconformist faction which criticizes *Life;* all in all, if anyone cares, I think the magazine is all right.)

It was not so long ago that a position taken by a Luce publication would have been instinctively opposed by large numbers of nonconformists; but *Life* in recent years has so well caught the importance of being fashionably nonconformist that it is now a leader in establishing accepted nonconformist thought, which, of course, some while ago spilled over from the highbrow crest onto the extensive middle-brow plateaus. On the matter of education, *Life* and other media shaping mass nonconformist ideology have now laid down the party line, making it intellectually suicidal to suggest that possibly the educators have their own peculiar problems to solve before they can reshape their curricula to respond to the present pressures. On most campuses, I venture, a professor in liberal arts would be read out of the ranks if he said a good word about colleges of education, let alone about educational television, which combines two bogeys. The pressure of nonconformists to force an unmodulated conformity to their present position on education makes it extremely difficult for humanists of good will to conduct that "dialogue" with the educators which the foundation president I spoke of earlier insisted is necessary for understanding and progress. Perhaps it is an exaggeration, even a distortion, to say that nonconformists, like Communists of old, insist on free speech for themselves but not for their opponents; certainly one is tempted to think this when a woman in the audience I mentioned made a remark favorable to the schools and was answered with a quip from the speaker and jeers from the audience.

I have spent this much time on education because the danger of intransigent nonconformism seems to me greatest at this moment in that area; nonconformist opposition may yet do as much damage to American education as the educators themselves have done—although I concede it would probably take nonconformism a long time to establish a record of equal harm. The dangers of nonconformism are to be found wherever opinions, tastes, standards, judgments and beliefs are operative. Let me catalogue from my own recent experience a number of positions, attitudes and habits of behavior and thought no nonconformist in good standing can hold these days. These are, of course, subject to rapid change, like fashions in ladies' dress. Also, I should say, it is not essential to reject *all* to remain a respectable nonconformist—only most of them.

It is impossible, then, for the nonconformist to say a good word about Dulles, Nixon, Lyndon Johnson or (since Dwight MacDonald's critique in *Commentary*) James Gould Cozzens, or a bad one about Henry James, Adlai Stevenson, Lionel Trilling or Freud; to express approval of any television show (except *Omnibus*, Ed Murrow or Sid Caesar) or of any American movie (except the inexpensive and badly lighted ones, or the solemn westerns, like *High Noon*); to dislike any foreign films (except those imitating American ones); to believe that you can buy ready-made a good hi-fi set; to wear a non-Ivy-league suit or long hair if a man, or to wear or not wear a sack dress if a woman (I am not sure what feminine nonconformism calls for at the moment); to prefer American cars, for any reason, to European; to believe that there may be any justice in the official position on Oppenheimer; to defend Western diplomacy on any basis; to invite company to dinner without candles on the table and without chamber music in the background; to criticize Arthur Miller or Tennessee Williams as playwrights or otherwise (of course, the shifting popularity of each is constantly causing nonconformist adjustments); to like Tschaikovsky or Irving Berlin, or to dislike Leonard Bernstein or Mozart; to express admiration for Marilyn Monroe or any other American movie star; to disparage Alec Guiness; and so on and on. Since some of the items I list are clearly considered heinous heresies in some quarters and likely to cost individuals professing them their jobs or at least their reputations, I hasten to add that I know no one guilty of more than one of them; as for myself, I plead the fifth. Nor is this altogether frivolous, for I do know of one college teacher who did not have his contract renewed at least in part for his persistent advocacy of the conformist Southern position on segregation; and I know of one junior executive in advertising who will always remain junior because he occasionally wears a double-breasted, navy-blue Cheviot suit with brown shoes—"like a subway rider reading the *Daily News*," he was described to me by a disapproving colleague.

There is no more self-righteously, high-mindedly closed a mind than that of a nonconformist. It is likely that he will begin every conversation with some such gambit as "I know this isn't a popular position, but. . . ." He will insist that no one since Galileo or Joan of Arc has had as much courage as he. Challenge him, and he will dismiss you as a peasant not worth his attention. "If you don't know what's wrong with American

culture," I heard one champion nonconformist say down his nose to someone who mildly demurred on the subject, "then there's no point even talking with you." You can never ask about the emperor's clothes lest you
prove at once in the nonconformist's eyes to be a monumental repository
of naïveté.

Obviously, neither conformity nor nonconformity is to be accepted or
rejected per se. What is to be rejected is the nonconformity that is so sure
it is right that it is going to cram itself down your throat. No doubt the
heresy of today may well become the orthodoxy of tomorrow, but we
should not hurry the process any more than we have to; heresies of worth
are quite capable of making their own way. If we have anything to fear
from the conformists who wish to change the world in accordance with
their ideologies, as we no doubt do, then we have equally much to fear
from the phalanxes of the nonconformists—and perhaps more, for I sense
an aggressive belligerence among nonconformist sects that seems as zealous
as olden W.C.T.U. fanaticism. I am thinking, for example, of the San
Francisco howlers for whom anything conventional is to be denigrated for
the reason of conventionality alone. There are also those chronic nonconformists who do not have even a principle to guide them; they rebel in
every direction at once for the sheer sake of perverseness. College campuses
have become populated lately with bearded, anarchic mediocrities who
blackmail their fellows and their professors into accepting them for more
than their worth by trading on the current high value of nonconformity.

Nonconformism today, whatever particular form it takes, appears to be
a legitimate enough descendant of the soft liberalism of the thirties. Like
the Stalinist creed with which it was often allied, this liberalism saw the
world through glasses that never quite focused on things in themselves. It
saw things only as fuzzy abstractions that fitted a variety of inflexible
needs of the mind. I recall the argument, for instance, that "decent" people
were simply not aware of ethnic differences. An ingredient, too, of this soft
liberalism was that puritanism which has always been a part of American
intellectual life. It is inclined, a priori, to deny any pleasures or successes
in popular culture and to look for its satisfactions in more rarefied atmos-
pheres. (American movies are only a recent subject for serious nonconformist discussion.) I suppose, too, that mass production, which was invading
every aspect of American life in the twenties and the thirties, had to be
resisted by a determined seeking out and idealizing of the unique, the
handmade product or thought.

One would have expected, however, or at least hoped, that the impulses
that turned "thinking" persons away from the passive acceptance of mass-
produced things and ideas would have also brought them to the enlightenment of approaching any thing or idea on its own merits rather than
through a conditioned reflex. Certainly something like the Museum of
Modern Art's tireless, wholesome independence in considering machine-
produced objects as worthy of aesthetic attention should have helped nonconformism to develop more broadly, for the Museum is one of the wor-
shiping places of New York nonconformists (although one should never

underestimate the power of a nonconformist to compartmentalize). Certainly, too, one would have liked to think that nonconformism, once it cast off the shackles of Communist dogma, would not harden into similarly thoughtless patterns of response to fixed stimuli.

If nonconformity is to have its rightful say in American life, as it did with Emerson, Thoreau, Whitman and Veblen, it must stop making a fetish of itself. Conformity with its range of established, nonevangelical possibilities may, in the end, prove to have the greater attraction for those genuinely seeking a free and full life. After all, unrestricted amateur nonconformism is one of the honorable paths in American history. In the meanwhile, we must oppose all efforts of the dedicated nonconformists to make us not conform according to their rules.

CHAPTER VII

Censorship and Freedom

It is commonplace to recognize that social pressures within institutions, the community, and the state frequently limit free expression far more than statutory prohibitions do. The schoolteacher who skirts controversial subjects or avoids controversial expressions is responding to his or her estimate of the hazards of offending community sentiment. Consider also the rising young executive who discreetly conceals his preference for the Democratic party, the Southern racial moderate who hides his deepest feelings about desegregation, the student who declines to challenge the dogmatic professor's views in the classroom, the young pastor who soft-pedals some of his more liberal theological views when addressing his congregation, and the prudent wife who steers clear of subjects known to raise her husband's hackles. Examples could be cited ad infinitum to illustrate the point that freedom often has more to fear from general or localized climates of opinion than from law and the courts.

In the realm of speech which directly concerns the state, few men and no society would dispute the proposition that liberty can become license. But identifying the kinds of speech which inflict more injury on society than the injury of suppression itself—that calls for the best wisdom a society can muster.

There is general agreement that politicians are not free to solicit votes in hospital wards or use sound trucks at 3 A.M. Persons are not free to divulge military secrets in wartime. Libel and slander are outlawed by unanimous consent. Direct and immediate incitement to violence finds few defenders despite the First Amendment's unequivocal declaration that Congress shall make *no* law abridging the freedom of speech or of the press.

But other restrictions meet with more resistance. Although the Supreme Court held that obscenity is without social significance and not entitled to constitutional protection, a minority of the Court sharply dissented.[1] Again, when the Court declared that Congress could make the advocacy of violence a Federal offense, the minority attacked this view as a shocking departure from the First Amendment.[2] On the issue of freedom for "subversive" speech and publications, the cleavage between Americans is deep, bitter, and enduring.

[1] *Roth v. United States,* 354 U.S. 489 (1957).
[2] *Dennis v. United States,* 341 U.S. 494 (1951). In *Yates v. United States,* 354 U.S. 298 (1957) the Court in effect reversed the Dennis decision by declaring that the *abstract* advocacy of violence was not illegal under the Smith Act of 1940. The majority went so far as to imply that such advocacy fell under the protection of the Constitution. On June 5, 1961, however, the Court confused the picture by upholding the conviction of a former Communist leader under a Smith Act provision making it a crime to be a member of a party advocating the forceful overthrow of the government when a person is aware of the organization's purpose.

This cleavage was apparent in the conflict over library policies during the McCarthy era. Many libraries were exposed to heavy pressures either to remove "subversive" books and works by "subversive" authors from their shelves or to identify them for the protection of readers "weak in the faith." Fighting back with something akin to intellectual passion, the American Library Association's "The Freedom to Read" stoutly defends the citizen's right to read, unhampered by official interpretation, guidance, or proscription.

John Stuart Mill's *On Liberty* remains, perhaps, Western man's most eloquent affirmation of the values of free speech and press. His well-documented reminder that no man or group can infallibly interpret truth is always timely, as is his insistence that even grossly erroneous views serve a useful purpose. Realist that he is, Mill believes truth cannot be extinguished but can be put to rout and reduced to hiding for long periods of time.

John Fischer takes exception to some of the tactics of the National Organization for Decent Literature, a Catholic organization which (in 1956, at least), in addition to advising its supporters to boycott certain books and booksellers, sought to coerce the latter into removing offending volumes from their shelves. Mr. Fischer regarded the NODL's attitude as incompatible not only with the general principles of liberty but also with the views of more liberal Catholics.

For decades American courts had adjudged allegedly obscene books by Victorian standards and by the supposed effect of even isolated portions of such works on persons susceptible to improper influences. Characteristically, the courts were slow to catch up with the developing view that (1) candor represents a moral value as well as a popular preference, and (2) authors should be permitted to address audiences of mature, emotionally stable individuals in the literary style they find appropriate to the accurate portrayal of some of life's more earthy aspects. In affirming these principles, the *Ulysses* decision (in a Federal district court) represented a historic landmark in the struggle for literary freedom. "Dirt for dirt's sake" was still beyond the pale of judicial protection, but the writer's scope was otherwise notably expanded.

(The *Ulysses* decision was confirmed and broadened somewhat by the Supreme Court in *Roth v. United States*. In this case the Court declared the test of obscenity was "whether to the average person, applying contemporary community standards, the dominant theme of the material taken as a whole appeals to prurient interest.")

The Supreme Court pushed on from here, in the *Miracle* case,[3] to the conclusion that movies—as well as literature—can carry on the battle against censorship behind the shield of the First Amendment. In 1915 the Court had ruled otherwise, holding that the movies were a means of entertainment rather than of information.[4] But by 1951 the Court had come to the more defensible view that they were both. As such, they could not be outlawed on grounds of sacrilege, partly because of the imprecision of that term and partly because "powerful orthodoxies" may not, in a free society, wall off their cherished views from critical or even irreverent comment.

[3] *Burstyn v. Wilson*, 343 U.S. 495 (1952).
[4] *Mutual Film Corp. v. Ohio Industrial Commission*, 263 U.S. 230 (1915).

Although the Court later expanded its decision to forbid censorship of movies on grounds that they are "harmful" or "tend to corrupt morals" or "present acts of sexual immorality as desirable, acceptable, or proper patterns of behavior,"[5] the direction of the Court's course was reversed early in 1961 when it announced that municipalities could legally require a permit before movie house operators could exhibit motion pictures. There is no constitutional right, stated the Court, to "exhibit at least once, any and every kind of motion picture." Standards of censorship were not at issue in the case, only the right to require advance approval before showing a film. Regarding any form of "prior censorship" as a disturbing step backward, the minority was not reassured by the fact that exhibitors could appeal an arbitrary or ill-advised verdict. Delays could involve "irreparable damage" to both litigants and public, it warned. The minority further inquired if the decision did not create a precedent permitting licensing requirements for "every form of communication, be it newspapers, journals, books, magazines, television, radio, or public speeches."[6]

Is entertainment which interminably exploits themes of violence, brutality, and sadism an important contributing factor to the multiplying cases of teen-age violence America is experiencing? Many observers, citing the multiplicity of factors which influence individual behavior and the near impossibility of identifying direct causal relationships, either deny the charge or regard it as merely speculative. Walter Lippmann, however, makes bold to assert that "there can be no reasonable doubt" that a causal relationship does exist between juvenile crime and the vogue of sadistic entertainment. He concludes, reluctantly, that censorship of entertainment for the young is a legitimate and necessary national goal.

Congress has indicated an interest in the possibly adverse effects of excessive violence on TV, but the prospects of congressional action appear exceedingly slim. If its expression of concern seems genuine, of course, Congress might be able to persuade the broadcasting industry to alter its program content somewhat in order to forestall formal regulatory action in the future.

When New York, however, sought in an earlier day to ban literature describing scenes of violence so massed as to incite violent and depraved crimes, the Supreme Court (*Winters v. New York*, 1948) refused to uphold its authority to so act. The majority stressed the unconstitutional vagueness of the standard of guilt, while Justice Frankfurter supported the right of the state to use necessarily inexact but broadly descriptive criteria banning literature which reasonable men might believe would foster delinquency. The rights of a free press would not be unduly abused, in his judgment, so long as the courts were prepared to overturn arbitrary interpretations of the law.

The problems of censorship in a free society involve a continuous balancing of the right of government to withhold certain information which cannot be divulged in the public interest and the right of the people to know those facts essential to government by the informed consent of the people. There can be no doubt, for example, that there are occasions when public

[5] *Kingsley Pictures Corp. v. Regents,* 360 U.S. 684 (1959).
[6] *Times Film Corp. v. City of Chicago,* 365 U.S. 43 (1961).

officials need to exchange views with a frankness impossible in the presence of representatives of the press. This is particularly true when negotiations are taking place between governments or where information vital to national security is involved. It also applies, however, to numerous situations in which decisions must be made on touchy public matters. At the same time, the temptation is almost irresistible for public officers to abuse this privilege by concealing information which, although embarrassing to the officials involved, is in the legitimate province of public information.

Francis E. Rourke discusses various manifestations of "executive privilege" and public informational policies in "How Much Should the Government Tell?" He observes that "there are those who argue that the influence which democratic government has come to exert over the communications process, particularly in the area of foreign affairs, has given it possibilities for manipulating public opinion not altogether different from those enjoyed by governments on the other side of the Iron Curtain." He further notes that governmental publicity, although often essential to public understanding, can also be used as a weapon to punish individuals whose expressed views or activities are offensive to the government.

Governmental censorship is one thing, and the deliberate falsification of facts by government is another. A *New York Times* editorial of May 10, 1961, insists that free government demands an informed people and that official falsehoods are ethically unacceptable, foolish, and incompatible with the precepts and requirements of free government. "A democracy—our democracy—cannot be lied to."

Formal American censorship, irritating and unnecessary as it often is, is nonetheless a pallid creature compared to that which prevails in totalitarian societies. William Jorden's article explains why the West believes a society like Russia's is compulsively driven to maintain rigid controls over the approaches to the minds of its people. Emphasizing the continuity of Russian censorship from Czarist to Communist times, he sees this closed society as the victim of its own propaganda and its censorship as a reflection of its own weakness.

Arthur Schlesinger, Jr., on the other hand, explains Russian barriers against alien literature as an outgrowth of Soviet certainty that the decadent West has nothing constructive (outside the realm of science) to offer a society which has extricated itself from the mire of commercialism and moral corruption which envelops bourgeois capitalist societies.

48.   THE CASE FOR FREEDOM
by John Stuart Mill *

. . . Let us suppose, therefore, that the government is entirely at one with the people, and never thinks of exerting any power of coercion unless in

* Nineteenth-century English philosopher and political economist. This selection is from John Stuart Mill, *On Liberty*, 3d ed., Ticknor & Fields, Boston, 1864, pp. 35-44 and 49-58.

agreement with what it conceives to be their voice. But I deny the right of the people to exercise such coercion, either by themselves or by their government. The power itself is illegitimate. The best government has no more title to it than the worst. It is as noxious, or more noxious, when exerted in accordance with public opinion, than when in opposition to it. If all mankind minus one, were of one opinion, and only one person were of the contrary opinion, mankind would be no more justified in silencing that one person, than he, if he had the power, would be justified in silencing mankind. Were an opinion a personal possession of no value except to the owner; if to be obstructed in the enjoyment of it were simply a private injury, it would make some difference whether the injury was inflicted only on a few persons or on many. But the peculiar evil of silencing the expression of an opinion is, that it is robbing the human race; posterity as well as the existing generation; those who dissent from the opinion, still more than those who hold it. If the opinion is right, they are deprived of the opportunity of exchanging error for truth: if wrong, they lose, what is almost as great a benefit, the clearer perception and livelier impression of truth, produced by its collision with error.

It is necessary to consider separately these two hypotheses, each of which has a distinct branch of the argument corresponding to it. We can never be sure that the opinion we are endeavoring to stifle is a false opinion; and if we were sure, stifling it would be an evil still.

First: the opinion which it is attempted to suppress by authority may possibly be true. Those who desire to suppress it, of course deny its truth; but they are not infallible. They have no authority to decide the question for all mankind, and exclude every other person from the means of judging. To refuse a hearing to an opinion, because they are sure that it is false, is to assume that *their* certainty is the same thing as *absolute* certainty. All silencing of discussion is an assumption of infallibility. Its condemnation may be allowed to rest on this common argument, not the worse for being common.

Unfortunately for the good sense of mankind, the fact of their fallibility is far from carrying the weight in their practical judgment, which is always allowed to it in theory; for while every one well knows himself to be fallible, few think it necessary to take any precautions against their own fallibility, or admit the supposition that any opinion, of which they feel very certain, may be one of the examples of the error to which they acknowledge themselves to be liable. Absolute princes, or others who are accustomed to unlimited deference, usually feel this complete confidence in their own opinions on nearly all subjects. People more happily situated, who sometimes hear their opinions disputed, and are not wholly unused to be set right when they are wrong, place the same unbounded reliance only on such of their opinions as are shared by all who surround them, or to whom they habitually defer: for in proportion to a man's want of confidence in his own solitary judgment, does he usually repose, with implicit trust, on the infallibility of "the world" in general. And the world, to each individual, means the part of it with which he comes in contact; his party, his sect, his church, his class of society: the man may be called, by comparison, almost liberal and large-minded to whom it means anything so comprehensive as his own country or his own age. Nor is his faith in this collective authority at all shaken by his being aware that other ages, countries, sects, churches, classes, and parties have thought, and even now think, the exact reverse. He devolves upon his own world the responsibility of being in the right against the dissentient worlds of other people; and it never troubles him that mere accident has decided which of these numerous worlds is the object of his reliance, and that the same causes which make him a Churchman in London, would have made him a Buddhist or a Confucian in Pekin. Yet it is as evident in itself, as any amount of argument can make it, that ages are no more infallible than individuals; every age having held many opinions which subsequent ages have deemed not only false but absurd; and it is as certain that many opinions, now general, will be rejected by future ages, as it is that many, once general, are rejected by the present.

The objection likely to be made to this argument, would probably take some such form as the following. There is no greater assumption of infallibility in forbidding the propagation of error, than in any other thing which is done by public authority on its own judgment and responsibility. Judgment is given to men that they may use it. Because it may be used erroneously, are men to be told that they ought not to use it at all? To prohibit what they think pernicious, is not claiming exemption from error, but fulfilling the duty incumbent on them, although fallible, of acting on their conscientious conviction. If we were never to act on our opinions, because those opinions may be wrong, we should leave all our interests uncared for, and all our duties unperformed. An objection which applies to all conduct, can be no valid objection to any conduct in particular. It is the duty of governments, and of individuals, to form the truest opinions they can; to form them carefully, and never impose them upon others unless they are quite sure of being right. But when they are sure (such reasoners may say), it is not conscientiousness but cowardice to shrink from acting on their opinions, and allow doctrines which they honestly think dangerous to the welfare of mankind, either in this life or in another, to be scattered abroad without restraint, because other people, in less enlightened times, have persecuted opinions now believed to be true. Let us take care, it may be said, not to make the same mistake: but governments and nations have made mistakes in other things, which are not denied to be fit subjects for the exercise of authority: they have laid on bad taxes, made unjust wars. Ought we therefore to lay on no taxes, and, under whatever provocation, make no wars? Men, and governments, must act to the best of their ability. There is no such thing as absolute certainty, but there is assurance sufficient for the purposes of human life. We may, and must, assume our opinion to be true for the guidance of our own conduct: and it is assuming no more when we forbid bad men to pervert society by the propagation of opinions which we regard as false and pernicious.

I answer, that it is assuming very much more. There is the greatest difference between presuming an opinion to be true, because, with every opportunity for contesting it, it has not been refuted, and assuming its truth for the purpose of not permitting its refutation. Complete liberty of contradicting and disproving our opinion, is the very condition which justifies us in assuming its truth for purposes of action; and on no other terms can a being with human faculties have any rational assurance of being right.

When we consider either the history of opinion, or the ordinary conduct of human life, to what is it to be ascribed that the one and the other are no worse than they are? Not certainly to the inherent force of the human understanding; for, on any matter not self-evident, there are ninety-nine persons totally incapable of judging of it, for one who is capable; and the capacity of the hundredth person is only comparative; for the majority of the eminent men of every past generation held many opinions now known to be erroneous, and did or approved numerous things which no one will now justify. Why is it, then, that there is on the whole a preponderance among mankind of rational opinions and rational conduct? If there really is this preponderance—which there must be, unless human affairs are, and have always been, in an almost desperate state—it is owing to a quality of the human mind, the source of everything respectable in man either as an intellectual or as a moral being, namely, that his errors are corrigible. He is capable of rectifying his mistakes, by discussion and experience. Not by experience alone. There must be discussion, to show how experience is to be interpreted. Wrong opinions and practices gradually yield to fact and argument: but facts and arguments, to produce any effect on the mind, must be brought before it. Very few facts are able to tell their own story, without comments to bring out their meaning. The whole strength and value, then, of human judgment, depending on the one property, that it can be set right when it is wrong, reliance can be placed on it only when the means of setting it right are kept constantly at hand. In the case of any person whose judgment is really deserving of confidence, how has it become so? Because he has kept his mind open to criticism of his opinions and conduct. Because it has been his practice to listen to all that could be said against him; to profit by as much of it as was just, and expound himself, and upon occasion to others, the fallacy of what was fallacious. Because he has felt, that the only way in which a human being can make some approach to knowing the whole of a subject, is by hearing what can be said about it by persons of every variety of opinion, and studying all modes in which it can be looked at by every character of mind. No wise man ever acquired his wisdom in any mode but this; nor is it in the nature of human intellect to become wise in any other manner. The steady habit of correcting and completing his own opinion by collating it with those of others, so far from causing doubt and hesitation in carrying it into practice, is the only stable foundation for a just reliance on it: for, being cognizant of all that can, at least obviously, be said against him, and having taken up his position against all gainsayers—knowing that he has sought for objections and difficulties, instead of avoiding them, and has shut out no light which can be thrown upon the subject from any quarter—he has a right to think his judgment better than that of any person, or any multitude, who have not gone through a similar process.

It is not too much to require that what the wisest of mankind, those who are best entitled to trust their own judgment, find necessary to warrant their relying on it, should be submitted to by that miscellaneous collection of a few wise and many foolish individuals, called the public. . . . The Roman Catholic Church, even at the canonization of a saint, admits, and listens patiently to, a "devil's advocate." The holiest of men, it appears, cannot be admitted to posthumous honors, until all that the devil could say against him is known and weighed. If even the Newtonian philosophy were not permitted to be questioned, mankind could not feel as complete assurance of its truth as they now do. The beliefs which we have most warrant for, have no safeguard to rest on, but a standing invitation to the whole world to prove them unfounded. If the challenge is not accepted, or, is accepted and the attempt fails, we are far enough from certainty still; but we have done the best that the existing state of human reason admits of; we have neglected nothing that could give the truth a chance of reaching us: if the lists are kept open, we may hope that if there be a better truth, it will be found when the human mind is capable of receiving it; and in the mean time we may rely on having attained such approach to truth, as is possible in our own day. This is the amount of certainty attainable by a fallible being, and this the sole way of attaining it.

Strange it is, that men should admit the validity of the arguments for free discussion, but object to their being "pushed to an extreme"; not seeing that unless the reasons are good for an extreme case, they are not good for any case. Strange that they should imagine that they are not assuming infallibility, when they acknowledge that there should be free discussion on all subjects which can possibly be *doubtful,* but think that some particular principle or doctrine should be forbidden to be questioned because it is *so certain,* that is, because *they are certain* that it is certain. To call any proposition certain, while there is any one who would deny its certainty if permitted, but who is not permitted, is to assume that we ourselves, and those who agree with us, are the judges of certainty, and judges without hearing the other side. . . .

Mankind can hardly be too often reminded, that there was once a man named Socrates, between whom and the legal authorities and public opinion of his time, there took place a memorable collision. Born in an age and country abounding in individual greatness, this man has been handed down to us by those who best knew both him and the age, as the most virtuous man in it; while *we* know him as the head and prototype of all subsequent teachers of virtue, the source equally of the lofty inspiration of Plato and the judicious utilitarianism of Aristotle, *"i maëstri di color che sanno,"* the two headsprings of ethical as of all other philosophy. This acknowledged master of all the eminent thinkers who have since lived—whose fame, still growing after more than two thousand years, all but outweighs the whole remainder of the names which make his native city illustrious—was put to death by his countrymen, after a judicial conviction, for impiety and immorality. Impiety, in denying the gods recognized by the State; indeed his accuser asserted (see the "Apologia") that he believed in no gods at all. Immorality, in being, by his doctrines and instructions, a "corruptor of youth." Of these charges the tribunal, there is every ground for believing, honestly found him guilty, and condemned the man who probably of all then born had deserved best of mankind, to be put to death as a criminal.

To pass from this to the only other instance of judicial iniquity, the mention of which, after the condemnation of Socrates, would not be an anti-climax: the event which took place on Calvary rather more than eighteen hundred years ago. The man who left on the memory of those who witnessed his life and conversation, such an impression of his moral grandeur, that eighteen subsequent centuries have done homage to him as the Almighty in person, was ignominiously put to death, as what? As a blasphemer. Men did not merely mistake their benefactor; they mistook him for the exact contrary of what he was, and treated him as that prodigy of impiety, which they themselves are now held to be, for their treatment of him. The feelings with which mankind now regard these lamentable transactions, especially the later of the two, render them extremely unjust in their judgment of the unhappy actors. These were, to all appearance, not bad men—not worse than men commonly are, but rather the contrary; men who possessed in a full, or somewhat more than a full measure, the religious, moral, and patriotic feelings of their time and people: the very kind of men who, in all times, our own included, have every chance of passing through life blameless and respected. The high-priest who rent his garments when the words were pronounced, which, according to all the ideas of his country, constituted the blackest guilt, was in all probability quite as sincere in his horror and indignation, as the generality of respectable and pious men now are in the religious and moral sentiments they profess; and most of those who now shudder at his conduct, if they had lived in his time, and been born Jews, would have acted precisely as he did. Orthodox Christians who are tempted to think that those who stoned to death the first martyrs must have been worse men than they themselves are, ought to remember that one of those persecutors was Saint Paul.

Let us add one more example, the most striking of all, if the impressiveness of an error is measured by the wisdom and virtue of him who falls into it. If ever any one, possessed of power, had grounds for thinking himself the best and most enlightened among his contemporaries, it was the Emperor Marcus Aurelius. Absolute monarch of the whole civilized world, he preserved through life not only the most unblemished justice, but what was less to be expected from his Stoical breeding, the tenderest heart. The few failings which are attributed to him, were all on the side of indulgence: while his writings, the highest ethical product of the ancient mind, differ scarcely perceptibly, if they differ at all, from the most characteristic teachings of Christ. This man, a better Christian in all but the dogmatic sense of the word, than almost any of the ostensibly Christian sovereigns who have since reigned, persecuted Christianity. Placed at the summit of all the previous attainments of humanity, with an open, unfettered intellect, and a character which led him of himself to embody in his moral writings the Christian ideal, he yet failed to see that Christianity was to be a good and not an evil to the world, with his duties to which he was so deeply penetrated. Existing society he knew to be in a deplorable state. But such

as it was, he saw, or thought he saw, that it was held together, and prevented from being worse, by belief and reverence of the received divinities.
As a ruler of mankind, he deemed it his duty not to suffer society to fall in
pieces; and saw not how, if its existing ties were removed, any others
could be formed which could again knit it together. The new religion openly
aimed at dissolving these ties: unless, therefore, it was his duty to adopt
that religion, it seemed to be his duty to put it down. Inasmuch then as the
theology of Christianity did not appear to him true or of divine origin;
inasmuch as this strange history of a crucified God was not credible to
him, and a system which purported to rest entirely upon a foundation to
him so wholly unbelievable, could not be foreseen by him to be that reno-
vating agency which, after all abatements, it has in fact proved to be; the
gentlest and most amiable of philosophers and rulers, under a solemn sense
of duty, authorized the persecution of Christianity. To my mind this is
one of the most tragical facts in all history. It is a bitter thought, how
different a thing the Christianity of the world might have been, if the
Christian faith had been adopted as the religion of the empire under the
auspices of Marcus Aurelius instead of those of Constantine. But it would
be equally unjust to him and false to truth, to deny, that no one plea
which can be urged for punishing anti-Christian teaching, was wanting to
Marcus Aurelius for punishing, as he did, the propagation of Christianity.
No Christian more firmly believes that Atheism is false, and tends to the
dissolution of society, than Marcus Aurelius believed the same things of
Christianity; he who, of all men then living, might have been thought the
most capable of appreciating it. Unless any one who approves of punishment for the promulgation of opinions, flatters himself that he is a wiser
and better man than Marcus Aurelius—more deeply versed in the wisdom
of his time, more elevated in his intellect above it—more earnest in his
search for truth, or more single-minded in his devotion to it when found;—
let him abstain from that assumption of the joint infallibility of himself
and the multitude, which the great Antoninus made with so unfortunate
a result.

Aware of the impossibility of defending the use of punishment for restraining irreligious opinions, by any argument which will not justify Marcus Antoninus, the enemies of religious freedom, when hard pressed, occasionally accept this consequence, and say, with Dr. Johnson, that the
persecutors of Christianity were in the right; that persecution is an ordeal
through which truth ought to pass, and always passes successfully, legal
penalties being, in the end, powerless against truth, though sometimes
beneficially effective against mischievous errors. This is a form of the argument for religious intolerance, sufficiently remarkable not to be passed without notice.

A theory which maintains that truth may justifiably be persecuted because persecution cannot possibly do it any harm, cannot be charged with
being intentionally hostile to the reception of new truths; but we cannot
commend the generosity of its dealing with the persons to whom mankind
are indebted for them. To discover to the world something which deeply

concerns it, and of which it was previously ignorant; to prove to it that it had been mistaken on some vital point of temporal or spiritual interest, is as important a service as a human being can render to his fellow-creatures, and in certain cases, as in those of the early Christians and of the Reformers, those who think with Dr. Johnson believe it to have been the most precious gift which could be bestowed on mankind. That the authors of such splendid benefits should be requited by martyrdom; that their reward should be to be dealt with as the vilest of criminals, is not, upon this theory, a deplorable error and misfortune, for which humanity should mourn in sackcloth and ashes, but the normal and justifiable state of things. The propounder of a new truth, according to this doctrine, should stand, as stood, in the legislation of the Locrians, the proposer of a new law, with a halter round his neck, to be instantly tightened if the public assembly did not, on hearing his reasons, then and there adopt his proposition. People who defend this mode of treating benefactors, cannot be supposed to set much value on the benefit; and I believe this view of the subject is mostly confined to the sort of persons who think that new truths may have been desirable once, but that we have had enough of them now.

But, indeed, the dictum that truth always triumphs over persecution, is one of those pleasant falsehoods which men repeat after one another till they pass into commonplaces, but which all experience refutes. History teems with instances of truth put down by persecution. If not suppressed forever, it may be thrown back for centuries. To speak only of religious opinions: the Reformation broke out at least twenty times before Luther, and was put down. Arnold of Brescia was put down. Fra Dolcino was put down. Savonarola was put down. The Albigeois were put down. The Vaudois were put down. The Lollards were put down. The Hussites were put down. Even after the era of Luther, wherever persecution was persisted in, it was successful. In Spain, Italy, Flanders, the Austrian empire, Protestanism was rooted out; and, most likely, would have been so in England, had Queen Mary lived, or Queen Elizabeth died. Persecution has always succeeded, save where the heretics were too strong a party to be effectually persecuted. No reasonable person can doubt that Christianity might have been extirpated in the Roman empire. It spread, and became predominant, because the persecutions were only occasional, lasting but a short time, and separated by long intervals of almost undisturbed propagandism. It is a piece of idle sentimentality that truth, merely as truth, has any inherent power denied to error, of prevailing against the dungeon and the stake. Men are not more zealous for truth than they often are for error, and a sufficient application of legal or even of social penalties will generally succeed in stopping the propagation of either. The real advantage which truth has, consists in this, that when an opinion is true, it may be extinguished once, twice, or many times, but in the course of ages there will generally be found persons to rediscover it, until some one of its reappearances falls on a time when from favorable circumstances it escapes persecution until it has made such head as to withstand all subsequent attempts to suppress it. . . .

49. THE HARM GOOD PEOPLE DO
by John Fischer*

A little band of Catholics is now conducing a shocking attack on the rights of their fellow citizens. They are engaged in an un-American activity which is as flagrant as anything the Communist party ever attempted— and which is, in fact, very similar to Communist tactics. They are harming their country, their Church, and the cause of freedom.

Their campaign is particularly dangerous because few people realize what they are up to. It can hurt you—indeed, it already has—without your knowing it. It is spreading rapidly but quietly; and so far no effective steps have been taken to halt it.

Even the members of this organization probably do not recognize the damage they are doing. They are well-meaning people, acting from deeply moral impulses. They are trying, in a misguided way, to cope with a real national problem, and presumably they think of themselves as patriots and servants of the Lord. Perhaps a majority of Americans, of all faiths, would sympathize with their motives—though not with their methods.

They do not, of course, speak for all Catholics. On the contrary, they are defying the warnings of some of their Church's most respected teachers and theologians. The Catholic Church as a whole certainly cannot be blamed for their actions, any more than it could be held responsible a generation ago for the political operations of Father Coughlin.

This group calls itself the National Organization for Decent Literature. Its headquarters are in Chicago; its director is the Very Reverend Monsignor Thomas Fitzgerald. Its main purpose is to make it impossible for anybody to buy books and other publications which it does not like. Among them are the works of some of the most distinguished authors now alive— for example, winners of the Nobel Prize, the Pulitzer Prize, and the National Book Award.

Its chief method is to put pressure on news dealers, drug stores, and booksellers, to force them to remove from their stocks every item on the NODL blacklist. Included on this list are reprint editions of books by Ernest Hemingway, William Faulkner, John Dos Passos, George Orwell, John O'Hara, Paul Hyde Bonner, Emile Zola, Arthur Koestler, and Joyce Cary. In some places—notably Detroit, Peoria, and the suburbs of Boston —the organization has enlisted the local police to threaten booksellers who are slow to "co-operate."

This campaign of intimidation has no legal basis. The books so listed have not been banned from the mails, and in the overwhelming majority of cases no legal charges have ever been brought against them. Indeed, it seems that the National Organization for Decent Literature deliberately prefers to ignore the established legal channels for proceedings against

* Editor of *Harper's Magazine*. Author of *Why They Behave like Russians* and *Master Plan: USA*. This selection is from John Fischer, "The Harm Good People Do," *Harper's Magazine*, vol. 213, October, 1956, pp. 14, 16-18, and 20. By permission of the author.

books which it thinks improper. Its chosen weapons are boycott and literary lynching.

For example, early last year committees of laymen from Catholic churches in the four northern counties of New Jersey—Union, Hudson, Essex, and Bergen—began to call on local merchants. These teams were armed with the NODL lists. They offered "certificates," to be renewed each month, to those storekeepers who would agree to remove from sale all of the listed publications. To enforce their demands, they warned the merchants that their parishioners would be advised to patronize only those stores displaying a certificate.

Contact, a bulletin published by the Sacred Heart Parish Societies of Orange, New Jersey, listed fourteen merchants in its March 1955 issue. "The following stores," it said, "have agreed to co-operate with the Parish Decency Committee in not displaying or selling literature disapproved by the National Organization for Decent Literature. . . . Please patronize these stores only. They may be identified by the certificate which is for one month only."

Similar tactics have been followed in scores of other communities. Even in Nevada—a state not noted for Puritanical temper—the Council of Catholic Men has asked booksellers to purge from their shelves a list of books which included such widely read novels as *Mr. Roberts* and *From Here to Eternity.* When an Associated Press reporter pointed out that millions of people already were familiar with these works, in print and on film, the state chairman of the campaign, Paul Laxalt of Carson City, replied:

"We've got to stand by the list. If we make one exception the list would be chopped up."

Such tactics are highly effective. Most news dealers, druggists, and similar merchants carry paper-bound books only as a minor side line. Moreover, they receive from the wholesalers more books than they have space for; if they remove one title from their racks, there are plenty of others to take its place. They don't want trouble. It is never good business to argue with a customer—so most of them readily comply with this form of private censorship. After all, their other customers, who might want to read a book by Faulkner or Hemingway or Zola, will never know that it has been suppressed, and when they don't find it on the shelves they probably will buy something else.

For these reasons it was possible for the Archdiocesan Council of Catholic Men in St. Louis to report recently that it had "obtained the consent of about one-third of the store owners approached in a campaign to ask merchants to submit to voluntary screening. . . ."

Something—but not much—can be said in defense of the National Organization for Decent Literature and its local campaigners. A good many tawdry and disreputable magazines, paper-bound reprints, and comic books have been offered for sale on a lot of newsstands. A few publishers unquestionably have tried to base their sales appeal on sex and violence; the pictures and text on the covers of their publications often hint that the contents are far more salacious than they are in fact. (Such misrepresentation, however, is less common now than it was a few years ago, and both the contents and the covers of most pocket-size books seem to be growing less lurid.)

It can be argued, too, that law enforcement agencies in some cities have not been vigorous in enforcing the statutes against obscene publications. Finally, the "decent literature" campaigners apparently feel that their main mission is to protect young people, whose judgment is unformed and who might be attracted to sleazy reading matter by a provocative newsstand display; they seem to take far less interest in the hard-bound editions of the same books available in libraries or regular book stores. The Detroit NODL, for example, states that its list is "not intended as a restrictive list for adults"—though it does not explain how adults could purchase the books if merchants have been persuaded not to stock them.

But the motives of these zealous people are not the issue. The real issue is whether any private group—however well-meaning—has a right to dictate what other people may read.

Clearly any church, or any sub-group within a church, has a right to advise its own members about their reading matter.

Clearly, too, anybody has a right to try to *persuade* other people to read or to refrain from reading anything he sees fit.

The National Organization for Decent Literature, however, goes much further. Its campaign is not aimed at Catholics alone, and it is not attempting to *persuade* readers to follow its views. It is *compelling* readers, of all faiths, to bow to its dislikes, by denying them a free choice in what they buy.

This principle is of course unacceptable to Catholics—as it is to all Americans—if they take the trouble to think about it for a moment. How would Catholics react if, say, a group of Jewish laymen were to threaten merchants with boycott unless they banned from their shops all publications which referred to the divinity of Christ? Some religious denominations believe that gambling is immoral; most Catholics do not, and many of their parishes raise considerable sums by means of bingo games and raffles. What if some Protestant sect were to try to clean out of the stores all publications which spoke tolerantly of gambling, and to boycott every merchant who bought a raffle ticket?

The principle at stake was set forth with admirable clarity by Father John Courtney Murray, S.J., professor of moral theology at Woodstock College, Maryland, in a recent address on "Literature and Censorship." He listed four rules, which ought to command the enthusiastic support of all Americans regardless of religious belief:

(1) "Each minority group has the right to censor for its own members, if it so chooses, the contents of the various media of communication, and to protect them, by means of its own choosing, from materials considered harmful according to its standards." (He also pointed out that in the United States "all religious groups . . . are minority groups.")

(2) "No minority group has the right to demand that government should impose a general censorship" on material "judged to be harmful according to the special standards held within one group."

(3) "Any minority group has the right to work toward the elevation of

standards of public morality . . . through the use of the methods of persuasion and pacific argument."

(4) "No minority group has the right to impose its own religious or moral views on other groups, through the use of methods of force, coercion, or violence."

And Father Murray went on to warn that methods of coercion are especially imprudent for Catholic associations.

"The chief danger," he said, "is lest the Church itself be identified in the public mind as a power-association. The identification is injurious; it turns into hatred of the faith. And it has the disastrous effect of obscuring from the public view the true visage of the Church as God's kingdom of truth and freedom, justice and love."

He quoted from Jacques Leclercq "of the Catholic University of Louvain, who is no slight authority" the dictum that "no government has ever succeeded in finding a balanced policy of combating unhealthy sexual propaganda without injuring legitimate freedom or provoking other equally grave or worse disorders."

Finally, Father Murray emphasized that "censorship in the civil order must be a judicial process," carried out under the statutes and according to the due processes of law.

The conclusions which flow from Father Murray's teachings seem plain enough:

(1) *For the National Organization for Decent Literature.* It should stop immediately its campaign of threats, blacklisting, and boycott. It should then pursue its aims by the legitimate methods of persuasion, propaganda, and action through the courts. Most states have adequate laws against the publication and sale of indecent literature. In cases where the law seems inadequate, the legislature can be persuaded to amend it, by the normal means of lobbying and petition. In cases where the law is not enforced, public officials should certainly be reminded of their duty—and opposed at the polls, in the democratic way, if they fall down on their jobs.

Above all, the NODL ought to consider the possibility of guiding young readers by positive rather than negative techniques. Youngsters are not likely to read trash whenever they have good books readily available. If they are brought up in homes where good literature is a constant part of their environment—where parents read to them from infancy, and encourage them to build up their own libraries—then there is scant chance that they will be attracted by comics or two-bit horrors.

What has the NODL done to urge parents to give their children such basic moral training? Has it done all it can to foster topnotch libraries—public, school, church, and family? In how many communities has it sponsored campaigns to stimulate good reading?

(2) *For news dealers, booksellers, and other merchants.* They should muster the courage to defy any group of private citizens which tries to impose its own brand of censorship on the publications they offer for sale. And, with equal courage, they should set their own house in order; they should refuse to sell any publication which—in their own untrammeled judgment—falls below their own standards as responsible business men.

(3) *For the patriotic citizen.* He should protest against the lynching of books just as vigorously as against the lynching of people. He should go out of his way to support the merchants who resist such coercion. He should point out to the members of the National Organization for Decent Literature (and to any other self-appointed censors in his community) the immeasurable damage they are doing to the American way of life, to the very foundations of democratic government.

For the gravest harm done here is not to the Catholic Church—though as Father Murray noted, that is dangerous enough—or to the individual who is denied the right to choose his own books. The great peril is to the fabric of orderly government. It is always injured when any group takes the law into its own hands. And whenever such a band of vigilantes succeeds in imposing its will by force, some other—and perhaps more sinister—group is encouraged to try the same thing.

Dean Joseph O'Meara of the Notre Dame Law School recently put it like this:

> Unfortunately many sincere people do not comprehend the genius of our democracy . . . such people would deny free speech to those with whom they are in fundamental disagreement. . . . They would establish a party line in America—*their* party line, of course. This is an alien concept, a totalitarian concept; it is not consonant with the American tradition; it is antidemocratic; it is, in short, subversive and it should be recognized for what it is.

Still another eminent Catholic—Senator Joseph Kennedy of Massachusetts—summed up the case in even more prophetic terms.

"The lock on the door of the legislature, the parliament, or the assembly hall," he said, "by order of the King, the Commissar, or the Führer—has historically been followed or preceded by a lock on the door of the printer's, the publisher's, or the bookseller's."

50. THE *ULYSSES* CASE:
OBSCENITY AND THE COURTS*

. . . II. I have read "Ulysses" once in its entirety and I have read those passages of which the Government particularly complains several times. In fact, for many weeks, my spare time has been devoted to the consideration of the decision which my duty would require me to make in this matter.

"Ulysses" is not an easy book to read or to understand. But there has been much written about it, and in order properly to approach the consideration of it it is advisable to read a number of other books which have now become its satellites. The study of "Ulysses" is, therefore, a heavy task.

III. The reputation of "Ulysses" in the literary world, however, warranted my taking such time as was necessary to enable me to satisfy myself as to the intent with which the book was written, for, of course, in any case where a book is claimed to be obscene it must first be determined,

---

* *United States v. One Book Called "Ulysses,"* 5 F. Supp. 182 (1933).

whether the intent with which it was written was what is called, according to the usual phrase, pornographic,—that is, written for the purpose of exploiting obscenity.

If the conclusion is that the book is pornographic that is the end of the inquiry and forfeiture must follow.

But in "Ulysses," in spite of its unusual frankness, I do not detect anywhere the leer of the sensualist. I hold, therefore, that it is not pornographic.

IV. In writing "Ulysses," Joyce sought to make a serious experiment in a new, if not wholly novel, literary genre. He takes persons of the lower middle class living in Dublin in 1904 and seeks not only to describe what they did on a certain day early in June of that year as they went about the City bent on their usual occupations, but also to tell what many of them thought about the while.

Joyce has attempted—it seems to me, with astonishing success—to show how the screen of consciousness with its ever-shifting kaleidoscopic impressions carries, as it were on a plastic palimpsest, not only what is in the focus of each man's observation of the actual things about him, but also in a penumbral zone residua of past impressions, some recent and some drawn up by association from the domain of the subconscious. He shows how each of these impressions affects the life and behavior of the character which he is describing.

What he seeks to get is not unlike the result of a double or, if that is possible, a multiple exposure on a cinema film which would give a clear foreground with a background visible but somewhat blurred and out of focus in varying degrees.

To convey by words an effect which obviously lends itself more appropriately to a graphic technique, accounts, it seems to me, for much of the obscurity which meets a reader of "Ulysses." And it also explains another aspect of the book, which I have further to consider, namely, Joyce's sincerity and his honest effort to show exactly how the minds of his characters operate.

If Joyce did not attempt to be honest in developing the technique which he has adopted in "Ulysses" the result would be psychologically misleading and thus unfaithful to his chosen technique. Such an attitude would be artistically inexcusable.

It is because Joyce has been loyal to his technique and has not funked its necessary implications, but has honestly attempted to tell fully what his characters think about, that he has been the subject of so many attacks and that his purpose has been so often misunderstood and misrepresented. For his attempt sincerely and honestly to realize his objective has required him incidentally to use certain words which are generally considered dirty words and has led at times to what many think is a too poignant preoccupation with sex in the thoughts of his characters.

The words which are criticized as dirty are old Saxon words known to almost all men and, I venture, to many women, and are such words as would be naturally and habitually used, I believe, by the types of folk whose life, physical and mental, Joyce is seeking to describe. In respect of the recurrent emergence of the theme of sex in the minds of his characters, it must always be remembered that his locale was Celtic and his season Spring.

Whether or not one enjoys such a technique as Joyce uses is a matter of taste on which disagreement or argument is futile, but to subject that technique to the standards of some other technique seems to me to be little short of absurd.

Accordingly, I hold that "Ulysses" is a sincere and honest book and I think that the criticisms of it are entirely disposed of by its rationale.

V. Furthermore, "Ulysses" is an amazing *tour de force* when one considers the success which has been in the main achieved with such a difficult objective as Joyce set for himself. As I have stated, "Ulysses" is not an easy book to read. It is brilliant and dull, intelligible and obscure by turns. In many places it seems to me to be disgusting, but although it contains, as I have mentioned above, many words usually considered dirty, I have not found anything that I consider to be dirt for dirt's sake. Each word of the book contributes like a bit of mosaic to the detail of the picture which Joyce is seeking to construct for his readers.

If one does not wish to associate with such folk as Joyce describes, that is one's own choice. In order to avoid indirect contact with them one may not wish to read "Ulysses"; that is quite understandable. But when such a real artist in words, as Joyce undoubtedly is, seeks to draw a true picture of the lower middle class in a European city, ought it to be impossible for the American public legally to see that picture?

To answer this question it is not sufficient merely to find, as I have found above, that Joyce did not write "Ulysses" with what is commonly called pornographic intent, I must endeavor to apply a more objective standard to his book in order to determine its effect in the result, irrespective of the intent with which it was written.

VI. The statute under which the libel is filed only denounces, in so far as we are here concerned, the importation into the United States from any foreign country of "any obscene book." Section 305 of the Tariff Act of 1930, Title 19 United States Code, Section 1305. It does not marshal against books the spectrum of condemnatory adjectives found, commonly, in laws dealing with matters of this kind. I am, therefore, only required to determine whether "Ulysses" is obscene within the legal definition of that word.

The meaning of the word "obscene" as legally defined by the Courts is: tending to stir the sex impulses or to lead to sexually impure and lustful thoughts. . . .

I am quite aware that owing to some of its scenes "Ulysses" is a rather strong draught to ask some sensitive, though normal, persons to take. But my considered opinion, after long reflection, is that whilst in many places the effect of "Ulysses" on the reader undoubtedly is somewhat emetic, nowhere does it tend to be an aphrodisiac.

"Ulysses" may, therefore, be admitted into the United States.

John M. Woolsey
United States District Judge

December 6, 1933

51. THE *MIRACLE* CASE:
MOVIES AND THE FIRST AMENDMENT*

Mr. Justice Clark delivered the opinion of the Court.

The issue here is the constitutionality, under the First and Fourteenth Amendments, of a New York statute which permits the banning of motion picture films on the ground that they are "sacrilegious." That statute makes it unlawful

> to exhibit, or to sell, lease or lend for exhibition at any place of amuse-
> ment for pay or in connection with any business in the state of New York,
> any motion picture film or reel [with specified exceptions not relevant here],
> unless there is at the time in full force and effect a valid license or permit
> therefor of the education department. . . .

The statute further provides:

> The director of the [motion picture] division [of the education depart-
> ment] or, when authorized by the regents, the officers of a local office or
> bureau shall cause to be promptly examined every motion picture film sub-
> mitted to them as herein required, and unless such film or a part thereof is
> obscene, indecent, immoral, inhuman, sacrilegious, or is of such a character
> that its exhibition would tend to corrupt morals or incite to crime, shall issue
> a license therefor. If such director or, when so authorized, such officer shall
> not license any film submitted, he shall furnish to the applicant therefor a
> written report of the reasons for his refusal and a description of each rejected
> part of a film not rejected in toto.

Appellant is a corporation engaged in the business of distributing motion pictures. It owns the exclusive rights to distribute throughout the United States a film produced in Italy entitled "The Miracle." On November 30, 1950, after having examined the picture, the motion picture division of the New York education department, acting under the statute quoted above, issued to appellant a license authorizing exhibition of "The Miracle," with English subtitles, as one part of a trilogy called "Ways of Love." There-after, for a period of approximately eight weeks, "Ways of Love" was exhibited publicly in a motion picture theater in New York City under an agreement between appellant and the owner of the theater whereby ap-pellant received a stated percentage of the admission price.

During this period, the New York State Board of Regents, which by statute is made the head of the education department, received "hundreds of letters, telegrams, post cards, affidavits and other communications" both protesting against and defending the public exhibition of "The Miracle." The Chancellor of the Board of Regents requested three members of the Board to view the picture and to make a report to the entire Board. After viewing the film, this committee reported to the Board that in its opinion there was basis for the claim that the picture was "sacrilegious. . . ."

* *Burstyn v. Wilson*, 343 U.S. 495 (1952).

As we view the case, we need consider only appellant's contention that the New York statute is an unconstitutional abridgment of free speech and a free press. . . .

It cannot be doubted that motion pictures are a significant medium for the communication of ideas. They may affect public attitudes and behavior in a variety of ways, ranging from direct espousal of a political or social doctrine to the subtle shaping of thought which characterizes all artistic expression. The importance of motion pictures as an organ of public opinion is not lessened by the fact that they are designed to entertain as well as to inform. As was said in *Winters* v. *New York:*

> The line between the informing and the entertaining is too elusive for the protection of that basic right [a free press]. Everyone is familiar with instances of propaganda through fiction. What is one man's amusement, teaches another's doctrine.

It is urged that motion pictures do not fall within the First Amendment's aegis because their production, distribution, and exhibition is a large-scale business conducted for private profit. We cannot agree. That books, newspapers, and magazines are published and sold for profit does not prevent them from being a form of expression whose liberty is safeguarded by the First Amendment. We fail to see why operation for profit should have any different effect in the case of motion pictures.

It is further urged that motion pictures possess a greater capacity for evil, particularly among the youth of a community, than other modes of expression. Even if one were to accept this hypothesis, it does not follow that motion pictures should be disqualified from First Amendment protection. If there be capacity for evil it may be relevant in determining the permissible scope of community control, but it does not authorize substantially unbridled censorship such as we have here.

For the foregoing reasons, we conclude that expression by means of motion pictures is included within the free speech and free press guaranty of the First and Fourteenth Amendments. . . .

To hold that liberty of expression by means of motion pictures is guaranteed by the First and Fourteenth Amendments, however, is not the end of our problem. It does not follow that the Constitution requires absolute freedom to exhibit every motion picture of every kind at all times and all places. That much is evident from the series of decisions of this Court with respect to other media of communication of ideas. Nor does it follow that motion pictures are necessarily subject to the precise rules governing any other particular method of expression. Each method tends to present its own peculiar problems. But the basic principles of freedom of speech and the press, like the First Amendment's command, do not vary. Those principles, as they have frequently been enunciated by this Court, make freedom of expression the rule. There is no justification in this case for making an exception to that rule.

The statute involved here does not seek to punish, as a past offense, speech or writing falling within the permissible scope of subsequent punishment. On the contrary, New York requires that permission to communicate ideas be obtained in advance from state officials who judge the content of the words and pictures sought to be communicated. This Court recognized many years ago that such a previous restraint is a form of infringement upon freedom of expression to be especially condemned. *Near* v. *Minnesota ex rel. Olson,* 283 U.S. 697 (1931). The Court there recounted the history which indicates that a major purpose of the First Amendment guaranty of a free press was to prevent prior restraints upon publication, although it was carefully pointed out that the liberty of the press is not limited to that protection. It was further stated that "the protection even as to previous restraint is not absolutely unlimited. But the limitation has been recognized only in exceptional cases. . . ." In the light of the First Amendment's history and of the *Near* decision, the State has a heavy burden to demonstrate that the limitation challenged here presents such an exceptional case.

New York's highest court says there is "nothing mysterious" about the statutory provision applied in this case: "It is simply this: that no religion, as that word is understood by the ordinary, reasonable person, shall be treated with contempt, mockery, scorn and ridicule. . . ." This is far from the kind of narrow exception to freedom of expression which a state may carve out to satisfy the adverse demands of other interests of society. In seeking to apply the broad and all-inclusive definition of "sacrilegious" given by the New York courts, the censor is set adrift upon a boundless sea amid a myriad of conflicting currents of religious views, with no charts but those provided by the most vocal and powerful orthodoxies. New York cannot vest such unlimited restraining control over motion pictures in a censor. . . . Under such a standard the most careful and tolerant censor would find it virtually impossible to avoid favoring one religion over another, and he would be subject to an inevitable tendency to ban the expression of unpopular sentiments sacred to a religious minority. Application of the "sacrilegious" test, in these or other respects, might raise substantial questions under the First Amendment's guaranty of separate church and state with freedom of worship for all. However, from the standpoint of freedom of speech and the press, it is enough to point out that the state has no legitimate interest in protecting any or all religions from views distasteful to them which is sufficient to justify prior restraints upon the expression of those views. It is not the business of government in our nation to suppress real or imagined attacks upon a particular religious doctrine, whether they appear in publications, speeches, or motion pictures.

Since the term "sacrilegious" is the sole standard under attack here, it is not necessary for us to decide, for example, whether a state may censor motion pictures under a clearly drawn statute designed and applied to prevent the showing of obscene films. That is a very different question from the one now before us. We hold only that under the First and Fourteenth Amendments a state may not ban a film on the basis of a censor's conclusion that it is "sacrilegious."

Reversed

52. VIOLENT ENTERTAINMENT: STIMULUS TO VIOLENCE?

by Walter Lippmann*

Statistics collected by the F.B.I. confirm the impression made by the recent newspaper stories of horrifying crimes committed by very young men. The figures show not only a sudden increase in the number of these crimes but also in their viciousness. In a survey of 200 cities the F.B.I. found that last year the crime rate of adults rose by 1.9 per cent while among youths eighteen years and under it rose by 7.9 per cent. From 1952 to 1953 the number of assaults committed by youths was doubled and there was a sharp rise in murders, rapes, burglaries, auto thefts, weapons carrying and liquor violations.

It is depressing and alarming, and a lot will have to be done about it. When we ask ourselves what can be done about it, we must not, however, look for the impossible. We must not expect a "solution" of the problem in the sense that vaccination is a solution of the problem of smallpox. The criminal tendencies will always be there, reborn in each new generation, and the question is how much these tendencies can be kept under control and how far they can be domesticated. The teen-agers of 1954 are not differently constituted from the teen-agers of the past or of the future. If there is more crime and vice among them today than there used to be, it is not because there is suddenly a more criminal and vicious generation. It must be because there is less discipline, more excitement, and more tempting opportunities for vice and crime. The tendencies which are latent in every generation are in this post-war generation less effectively restrained and more actively stimulated.

When we ask ourselves what "we" can do about the under-restraint and the over-stimulation, I am not venturing to think about advising parents with direct, immediate, and specific responsibility for growing children. I am thinking of the general public which, of course, includes the parents as citizens, but is concerned with general measures.

The problem is one for which public remedies are most likely to be found by choosing the more obvious issues, and tackling them experimentally in various communities. The commissions of study which will no doubt be set up are likely to be more productive if they can study the effects of practical experiments.

Enough is known about the problem, so it seems to me, to justify our picking three lines of action for the experiment. Not every one will agree, I realize, with the proposals for action. But no one can deny, I think, that action of some kind is called for along these three lines.

* Author, newspaper columnist, and former editor. This selection is from a column by Walter Lippmann, "The Young Criminals," *New York Herald Tribune*, Sept. 7, 1954, © 1954 New York Herald Tribune, Inc. By permission of the author and publisher.

One is to increase parental responsibility. The second is to augment the disciplinary power of the schools. The third is to intervene to protect the country, and particularly the adolescents, against the morbid stimulation they now get from comic books, and much of the movies and of television. The best we can do along these three lines will not solve the problem in the sense that it will make juvenile delinquency negligible. But along these lines a beginning can be made toward bringing the lawlessness under control.

First—The law should be amended so as to hold parents liable to punishment and fines for crimes committed by their children. This is stern doctrine. But it need not and it should not be, nor is it likely to be, administered too harshly. These children are committing adult crimes, and if they are too immature to be held responsible then the adults who are responsible for them should be held responsible for the offenses. This liability should do something to make the wayward parents who are letting their children run wild amenable to the teaching and the preaching which they now ignore.

Second—The schools are the public institutions which have to do with the formation of character and the learning of discipline. In many American communities, owing to the weakening of the family ties and of the authority of the church and of public opinion in the social order, the public schools have had thrust upon them very nearly the whole burden of civilizing the new generation.

They are not equal to the very heavy and difficult burden of performing the function not only of a school of learning but also the older function of the closely-knit family and of the powerful church. A shortage of our public education is grave but this is too big a subject for this article. This much can, however, be said briefly. If the schools are to instill the discipline that the family and the church are not instilling, they must be given much larger disciplinary powers than they now have.

Third—There can be no real doubt, it seems to me, that the movies and television and the comic books are purveying violence and lust to a vicious and intolerable degree. There can be no real doubt that public exhibitions of sadism tend to excite sadistic desires and to teach the audience how to gratify sadistic desires. Nor can there be any real doubt that there is a close connection between the suddenness of the increase in sadistic crimes and the new vogue of sadism among the mass media of entertainment.

Censorship is no doubt a clumsy and usually a stupid and self-defeating remedy for such evils. But a continual exposure of a generation to the commercial exploitation of the enjoyment of violence and cruelty is one way to corrode the foundations of a civilized society. For my own part, believing as I do in freedom of speech and thought, I see no objection in principle to censorship of the mass entertainment of the young. Until some more refined way is worked out of controlling this evil thing, the risks to our liberties are, I believe, decidedly less than the risks of unmanageable violence.

53. WINTERS v. NEW YORK:
"MASSED VIOLENCE" IN LITERATURE
VERSUS LEGISLATIVE POWER*

MR. JUSTICE REED delivered the opinion of the Court.

Appellant is a New York City bookdealer, convicted . . . of a misdemeanor for having in his possession with intent to sell certain magazines charged to violate . . . the New York Penal Law. It reads as follows:

§ 1141. Obscene prints and articles
  1. A person . . . who,
  2. Prints, utters, publishes, sells, lends, gives away, distributes, or shows, or has in his possession with intent to sell, lend, give away, distribute or show, or otherwise offers for sale, loan, gift or distribution, any book, pamphlet, magazine, newspaper or other printed paper devoted to the publication, and principally made up of criminal news, police reports, or accounts of criminal deeds, or pictures, or stories of deeds of bloodshed, lust or crime; . . .
  Is guilty of a misdemeanor, . . .

The validity of the statute was drawn in question in the state courts as repugnant to the Fourteenth Amendment to the Constitution of the United States in that it denied the accused the right of freedom of speech and press, protected against state interference by the Fourteenth Amendment....

The appellant contends that the subsection violates the right of free speech and press because it is vague and indefinite. It is settled that a statute so vague and indefinite, in form and as interpreted, as to permit within the scope of its language the punishment of incidents fairly within the protection of the guarantee of free speech is void, on its face, as contrary to the Fourteenth Amendment. . . . A failure of a statute limiting freedom of expression to give fair notice of what acts will be punished and such a statute's inclusion of prohibitions against expressions, protected by the principles of the First Amendment, violates an accused's rights under procedural due process and freedom of speech or press. . . .

We recognize the importance of the exercise of a state's police power to minimize all incentives to crime, particularly in the field of sanguinary or salacious publications with their stimulation of juvenile delinquency. Although we are dealing with an aspect of a free press in its relation to public morals, the principles of unrestricted distribution of publications admonish us of the particular importance of a maintenance of standards of certainty in the field of criminal prosecution for violation of statutory prohibitions against distribution. We do not accede to appellee's suggestion that the constitutional protection for a free press applies only to the exposition of ideas. The line between the informing and the entertaining is too elusive for the protection of that basic right. Everyone is familiar with instances of propaganda through fiction. What is one man's amusement, teaches another's doctrine. Though we can see nothing of any possible value to society

* Winters v. New York, 333 U.S. 507 (1948).

in these magazines, they are as much entitled to the protection of free speech as the best of literature. . . . They are equally subject to control if they are lewd, indecent, obscene or profane. . . .

The subsection of the New York Penal Law, as now interpreted by the Court of Appeals, prohibits distribution of a magazine principally made up of criminal news or stories of deeds of bloodshed or lust, so massed as to become vehicles for inciting violent and depraved crimes against the person. But even considering the gloss put upon the literal meaning by the Court of Appeals' restriction of the statute to collections of stories "so massed as to become vehicles for inciting violent and depraved crimes against the person . . . not necessarily . . . sexual passion," we find the specification of publications, prohibited from distribution, too uncertain and indefinite to justify the conviction of this petitioner. Even though all detective tales and treatises on criminology are not forbidden, and though publications made up of criminal deeds not characterized by bloodshed or lust are omitted from the interpretation of the Court of Appeals, we think fair use of collections of pictures and stories would be interdicted because of the utter impossibility of the actor or the trier to know where this new standard of guilt would draw the line between the allowable and the forbidden publications. No intent or purpose is required—no indecency or obscenity in any sense heretofore known to the law. "So massed as to incite to crime" can become meaningful only by concrete instances. This one example is not enough. The clause proposes to punish the printing and circulation of publications that courts or juries may think influence generally persons to commit crimes of violence against the person. No conspiracy to commit a crime is required. . . . It is not an effective notice of new crime. The clause has no technical or common law meaning. Nor can light as to the meaning be gained from the section as a whole or the Article of the Penal Law under which it appears. As said in the *Cohen Grocery Company* case . . .

> It leaves open, therefore, the widest conceivable inquiry, the scope of which no one can foresee and the result of which no one can foreshadow or adequately guard against.

The statute as construed by the Court of Appeals does not limit punishment to the indecent and obscene, as formerly understood. When stories of deeds of bloodshed, such as many in the accused magazines, are massed so as to incite to violent crimes, the statute is violated. It does not seem to us that an honest distributor of publications could know when he might be held to have ignored such a prohibition. Collections of tales of war horrors, otherwise unexceptionable, might well be found to be "massed" so as to become "vehicles for inciting violent and depraved crimes." Where a statute is so vague as to make criminal an innocent act, a conviction under it cannot be sustained. . . .

To say that a state may not punish by such a vague statute carries no implication that it may not punish circulation of objectionable printed matter, assuming that it is not protected by the principles of the First Amendment, by the use of apt words to describe the prohibited publica-

tions. . . . Neither the states nor Congress are prevented by the requirement
of specificity from carrying out their duty of eliminating evils to which, in
their judgment, such publications give rise.

Reversed

MR. JUSTICE FRANKFURTER, joined by MR. JUSTICE JACKSON and MR.
JUSTICE BURTON, dissenting.

By today's decision the Court strikes down an enactment that has been
part of the laws of New York for more than sixty years, and New York
is but one of twenty States having such legislation. Four more States have
statutes of like tenor which are brought into question by this decision, but
variations of nicety preclude one from saying that these four enactments
necessarily fall within the condemnation of this decision. Most of this legislation is also more than sixty years old. . . .

This body of laws represents but one of the many attempts by legislatures to solve what is perhaps the most persistent, intractable, elusive, and
demanding of all problems of society—the problem of crime, and, more
particularly, of its prevention. By this decision the Court invalidates such
legislation of almost half the States of the Union. The destructiveness of
the decision is even more far-reaching. This is not one of those situations
where power is denied to the States because it belongs to the Nation. These
enactments are invalidated on the ground that they fall within the prohibitions of the "vague contours" of the Due Process Clause. The decision thus
operates equally as a limitation upon Congressional authority to deal with
crime, and, more especially, with juvenile delinquency. These far-reaching
consequences result from the Court's belief that what New York, among a
score of States, has prohibited, is so empty of meaning that no one desirous
of obeying the law could fairly be aware that he was doing that which was
prohibited. . . .

In these matters legislatures are confronted with a dilemma. If a law is
framed with narrow particularity, too easy opportunities are afforded to
nullify the purposes of the legislation. If the legislation is drafted in terms
so vague that no ascertainable line is drawn in advance between innocent
and condemned conduct, the purpose of the legislation cannot be enforced
because no purpose is defined. It is not merely in the enactment of tax
measures that the task of reconciling these extremes—of avoiding throttling
particularity or unfair generality—is one of the most delicate and difficult
confronting legislators. The reconciliation of these two contradictories is
necessarily an empiric enterprise largely depending on the nature of the
particular legislative problem.

What risks do the innocent run of being caught in a net not designed for
them? How important is the policy of the legislation, so that those who
really like to pursue innocent conduct are not likely to be caught unaware?
How easy is it to be explicitly particular? How necessary is it to leave a
somewhat penumbral margin but sufficiently revealed by what is condemned to those who do not want to sail close to the shore of questionable
conduct? These and like questions confront legislative draftsmen. Answers

to these questions are not to be found in any legislative manual nor in the work of great legislative draftsmen. They are not to be found in the opinions of this Court. These are questions of judgment, peculiarly within the responsibility and the competence of legislatures. The discharge of that responsibility should not be set at naught by abstract notions about "indefiniteness...."

This brings our immediate problem into focus. No one would deny, I assume, that New York may punish crimes of lust and violence. Presumably also, it may take appropriate measures to lower the crime rate. But he must be a bold man indeed who is confident that he knows what causes crime. Those whose lives are devoted to an understanding of the problem are certain only that they are uncertain regarding the role of the various alleged "causes" of crime. Bibliographies of criminology reveal a depressing volume of writings on theories of causation. . . . Is it to be seriously questioned, however, that the State of New York, or the Congress of the United States, may make incitement to crime itself an offense? He too would indeed be a bold man who denied that incitement may be caused by the written word no less than by the spoken. If "the Fourteenth Amendment does not enact Mr. Herbert Spencer's Social Statics . . ." neither does it enact the psychological dogmas of the Spencerian era. The painful experience which resulted from confusing economic dogmas with constitutional edicts ought not to be repeated by finding constitutional barriers to a State's policy regarding crime, because it may run counter to our inexpert psychological assumptions or offend our presuppositions regarding incitements to crime in relation to the curtailment of utterance. This Court is not ready, I assume, to pronounce on causative factors of mental disturbance and their relation to crime. Without formally professing to do so, it may actually do so by invalidating legislation dealing with these problems as too "indefinite."

Not to make the magazines with which this case is concerned part of the Court's opinion is to play "Hamlet" without Hamlet. But the Court sufficiently summarizes one aspect of what the State of New York here condemned when it says "we can see nothing of any possible value to society in these magazines." From which it jumps to the conclusion that, nevertheless, "they are as much entitled to the protection of free speech as the best of literature." Wholly neutral futilities, of course, come under the protection of free speech as fully as do Keats' poems or Donne's sermons. But to say that these magazines have "nothing of any possible value to society" is only half the truth. This merely denies them goodness. It disregards their mischief. As a result of appropriate judicial determination, these magazines were found to come within the prohibition of the law against inciting "violent and depraved crimes against the person," and the defendant was convicted because he exposed for sale such materials. The essence of the Court's decision is that it gives publications which have "nothing of any possible value to society" constitutional protection but denies to the States the power to prevent the grave evils to which, in their rational judgment, such publications give rise. The legislatures of New York and the other States were concerned with these evils and not with neutral abstractions of harmlessness. Nor was the New York Court of Appeals merely resting, as it might have done, on a deep-seated conviction as to the existence of an evil and as to the appropriate means for checking it. That court drew on its experience, as revealed by "many recent records" of criminal convictions before it, for its understanding of the practical concrete reasons that led the legislatures of a score of States to pass the enactments now here struck down.

The New York Court of Appeals thus spoke out of extensive knowledge regarding incitements to crimes of violence. In such matters, local experience, as this Court has said again and again, should carry the greatest weight against our denying a State authority to adjust its legislation to local needs. . . .

"Magazine thrillers" hardly characterizes what New York has outlawed. New York does not lay hold of publications merely because they are "devoted to and principally made up of criminal news or police reports or accounts of criminal deeds, regardless of the manner of treatment." So the Court of Appeals has authoritatively informed us. . . . The aim of the publication must be incitation to "violent and depraved crimes against the person" by so massing "pictures and stories of criminal deeds of bloodshed or lust" as to encourage like deeds in others. It would be sheer dogmatism in a field not within the professional competence of judges to deny to the New York legislature the right to believe that the intent of the type of publications which it has proscribed is to cater to morbid and immature minds—whether chronologically or permanently immature. It would be sheer dogmatism to deny that in some instances . . . deeply embedded, unconscious impulses may be discharged into destructive and often fatal action. . . .

But we are told that New York has not expressed a policy, that what looks like a law is not a law because it is so vague as to be meaningless. Suppose then that the New York legislature now wishes to meet the objection of the Court. What standard of definiteness does the Court furnish the New York legislature in finding indefiniteness in the present law? Should the New York legislature enumerate by name the publications which in its judgment are "inciting violent and depraved crimes"? Should the New York legislature spell out in detail the ingredients of stories or pictures which accomplish such "inciting"? What is there in the condemned law that leaves men in the dark as to what is meant by publications that exploit "criminal deeds of bloodshed or lust" thereby "inciting violent and depraved crimes"? What real risk do the Conan Doyles, the Edgar Allan Poes, the William Rougheads, the ordinary tribe of detective story writers, their publishers, or their booksellers run?

Insofar as there is uncertainty, the uncertainty derives not from the terms of condemnation, but from the application of a standard of conduct to the varying circumstances of different cases. The Due Process Clause does not preclude such fallibilities of judgment in the administration of justice by men. Our penal codes are loaded with prohibitions of conduct depending on ascertainment through fallible judges and juries of a man's intent or motive—on ascertainment, that is, from without of a man's inner thoughts, feelings and purposes. Of course a man runs the risk of having a jury of his peers misjudge him. Mr. Justice Holmes has given the conclusive answer to the suggestion that the Due Process Clause protects against such a hazard: "the law is full of instances where a man's fate depends on his estimating rightly, that is, as the jury subsequently estimates it, some matter of degree. If his judgment is wrong, not only may he incur a fine or a short imprisonment, as here; he may incur the penalty of death. . . ."

And so I conclude that New York, in the legislation before us, has not exceeded its constitutional power to control crime. The Court strikes down laws that forbid publications inciting to crime, and as such not within the constitutional immunity of free speech, because in effect it does not trust State tribunals, nor ultimately this Court, to safeguard inoffensive publications from condemnation under this legislation. Every legislative limitation upon utterance, however valid, may in a particular case serve as an inroad upon the freedom of speech which the Constitution protects. . . .

54. THE FREEDOM TO READ

American Library Association and American Book Publishers Council *

The freedom to read is essential to our democracy. It is under attack. Private groups and public authorities in various parts of the country are working to remove books from sale, to censor textbooks, to label "controversial" books, to distribute lists of "objectionable" books or authors, and to purge libraries. These actions apparently rise from a view that our national tradition of free expression is no longer valid; that censorship and suppression are needed to avoid the subversion of politics and the corruption of morals. We, as citizens devoted to the use of books and as librarians and publishers responsible for disseminating them, wish to assert the public interest in the preservation of the freedom to read.

We are deeply concerned about these attempts at suppression. Most such attempts rest on a denial of the fundamental premise of democracy: that the ordinary citizen, by exercising his critical judgment, will accept the good and reject the bad. The censors, public and private, assume that they should determine what is good and what is bad for their fellow-citizens.

We trust Americans to recognize propaganda, and to reject obscenity. We do not believe they need the help of censors to assist them in this task. We do not believe they are prepared to sacrifice their heritage of a free press in order to be "protected" against what others think may be bad for them. We believe they still favor free enterprise in ideas and expression.

We are aware, of course, that books are not alone in being subjected to efforts at suppression. We are aware that these efforts are related to a larger pattern of pressures being brought against education, the press, films, radio and television. The problem is not only one of actual censorship. The

* This selection is from *The Freedom to Read,* American Library Association and American Book Publishers Council, May, 1953.

shadow of fear cast by these pressures leads, we suspect, to an even larger voluntary curtailment of expression by those who seek to avoid controversy.

Such pressure toward conformity is perhaps natural to a time of uneasy change and pervading fear. Especially when so many of our apprehensions are directed against an ideology, the expression of a dissident idea becomes a thing feared in itself, and we tend to move against it as against a hostile deed, with suppression.

And yet suppression is never more dangerous than in such a time of social tension. Freedom has given the United States the elasticity to endure strain. Freedom keeps open the path of novel and creative solutions and enables change to come by choice. Every silencing of a heresy, every enforcement of an orthodoxy, diminishes the toughness and resilience of our society and leaves it the less able to deal with stress.

Now as always in our history, books are among our greatest instruments of freedom. They are almost the only means for making generally available ideas or manners of expression that can initially command only a small audience. They are the natural medium for the new idea and the untried voice from which come the original contributions to social growth. They are essential to the extended discussion which serious thought requires, and to the accumulation of knowledge and ideas into organized collections.

We believe that free communication is essential to the preservation of a free society and a creative culture. We believe that these pressures towards conformity present the danger of limiting the range and variety of inquiry and expression on which our democracy and our culture depend. We believe that every American community must jealously guard the freedom to publish and to circulate, in order to preserve its own freedom to read. We believe that publishers and librarians have a profound responsibility to give validity to that freedom to read by making it possible for the reader to choose freely from a variety of offerings.

The freedom to read is guaranteed by the Constitution. Those with faith in free men will stand firm on these constitutional guarantees of essential rights and will exercise the responsibilities that accompany these rights.

We therefore affirm these propositions:

1. *It is in the public interest for publishers and librarians to make available the widest diversity of views and expressions, including those which are unorthodox or unpopular with the majority.*

Creative thought is by definition new, and what is new is different. The bearer of every new thought is a rebel until his idea is refined and tested. Totalitarian systems attempt to maintain themselves in power by the ruthless suppression of any concept which challenges the established orthodoxy. The power of a democratic system to adapt to change is vastly strengthened by the freedom of its citizens to choose widely from among conflicting opinions offered freely to them. To stifle every nonconformist idea at birth would mark the end of the democratic process. Furthermore, only through the constant activity of weighing and selecting can the democratic mind attain the strength demanded by times like these. We need to know not only what we believe but why we believe it.

2. *Publishers and librarians do not need to endorse every idea or presentation contained in the books they make available. It would conflict with*

the public interest for them to establish their own political, moral or aesthetic views as the sole standard for determining what books should be published or circulated.

Publishers and librarians serve the educational process by helping to make available knowledge and ideas required for the growth of the mind and the increase of learning. They do not foster education by imposing as mentors the patterns of their own thought. The people should have the freedom to read and consider a broader range of ideas than those that may be held by any single librarian or publisher or government or church. It is wrong that what one man can read should be confined to what another thinks proper.

3. *It is contrary to the public interest for publishers or librarians to determine the acceptability of a book solely on the basis of the personal history or political affiliations of the author.*

A book should be judged as a book. No art or literature can flourish if it is to be measured by the political views or private lives of its creators. No society of free men can flourish which draws up lists of writers to whom it will not listen, whatever they may have to say.

4. *The present laws dealing with obscenity should be vigorously enforced. Beyond that, there is no place in our society for extra-legal efforts to coerce the taste of others, to confine adults to the reading matter deemed suitable for adolescents, or to inhibit the efforts of writers to achieve artistic expression.*

To some, much of modern literature is shocking. But is not much of life itself shocking? We cut off literature at the source if we prevent serious artists from dealing with the stuff of life. Parents and teachers have a responsibility to prepare the young to meet the diversity of experiences in life to which they will be exposed, as they have a responsibility to help them learn to think critically for themselves. These are affirmative responsibilities, not to be discharged simply by preventing them from reading works for which they are not yet prepared. In these matters taste differs, and taste cannot be legislated; nor can machinery be devised which will suit the demands of one group without limiting the freedom of others. We deplore the catering to the immature, the retarded or the maladjusted taste. But those concerned with freedom have the responsibility of seeing to it that each individual book or publication, whatever its contents, price or method of distribution, is dealt with in accordance with due process of law.

5. *It is not in the public interest to force a reader to accept with any book the prejudgment of a label characterizing the book or author as subversive or dangerous.*

The idea of labeling presupposes the existence of individuals or groups with wisdom to determine by authority what is good or bad for the citizen. It presupposes that each individual must be directed in making up his mind about the ideas he examines. But Americans do not need others to do their thinking for them.

6. *It is the responsibility of publishers and librarians, as guardians of the people's freedom to read, to contest encroachments upon that freedom by individuals or groups seeking to impose their own standards or tastes upon the community at large.*

It is inevitable in the give and take of the democratic process that the political, the moral, or the aesthetic concepts of an individual or group will occasionally collide with those of another individual or group. In a free society each individual is free to determine for himself what he wishes to read, and each group is free to determine what it will recommend to its freely associated members. But no group has the right to take the law into its own hands, and to impose its own concept of politics or morality upon other members of a democratic society. Freedom is no freedom if it is accorded only to the accepted and the inoffensive.

7. *It is the responsibility of publishers and librarians to give full meaning to the freedom to read by providing books that enrich the quality of thought and expression. By the exercise of this affirmative responsibility, bookmen can demonstrate that the answer to a bad book is a good one, the answer to a bad idea is a good one.*

The freedom to read is of little consequence when expended on the trivial; it is frustrated when the reader cannot obtain matter fit for his purpose. What is needed is not only the absence of restraint, but the positive provision of opportunity for the people to read the best that has been thought and said. Books are the major channel by which the intellectual inheritance is handed down, and the principal means of its testing and growth. The defense of their freedom and integrity, and the enlargement of their service to society, requires of all bookmen the utmost of their faculties, and deserves of all citizens the fullest of their support.

We state these propositions neither lightly nor as easy generalizations. We here stake out a lofty claim for the value of books. We do so because we believe that they are good, possessed of enormous variety and usefulness, worthy of cherishing and keeping free. We realize that the application of these propositions may mean the dissemination of ideas and manners of expression that are repugnant to many persons. We do not state these propositions in the comfortable belief that what people read is unimportant. We believe rather that what people read is deeply important; that ideas can be dangerous; but that the suppression of ideas is fatal to a democratic society. Freedom itself is a dangerous way of life, but it is ours.

55. HOW MUCH SHOULD
THE GOVERNMENT TELL?

by Francis E. Rourke*

President John F. Kennedy has raised some basic questions about the role of the press in a free society. It is difficult to think of an American President in the past century who did not express a similar concern.

* Professor of political science at the Johns Hopkins University. Author of *Secrecy and Publicity: Dilemmas of Democracy* and *Intergovernmental Relations in Employment Security* and coauthor of *The Campus and the State*. This selection is from "How Much Should the Government Tell?" *Saturday Review,* vol. 44, issue no. 19, May 13, 1961, pp. 17-19 and 31. Reprinted by permission of the Johns Hopkins Press, Baltimore.

If the question is a historic one, at least it has never been more insistent than it is today. In particular, the events in Cuba and Laos call for decisions affecting the future of the United States. Yet the American people have been groping for adequate information about these events. It would seem that President Kennedy, in addition to issuing a call to the press for greater responsibility, might also have indicated the willingness of the government itself to engage in essential soul-searching about its policies in the arena of public information and opinion. Democracy has always rested —in philosophical assumption if not in practical fact—upon the support of public opinion. Even so, however, there is no question but that over the past century the role of public opinion in the operations of democratic states has come to assume increasing importance—with the growth of population, the elimination of suffrage restrictions, the organization of political parties and pressure groups, and the emergence of a milieu in which politicians find it increasingly expedient to cater to the tastes and preferences of the masses.

What is infinitely more striking is the passion modern despotism has now acquired for the art of public relations, for nothing more clearly separates modern from traditional authoritarian government than the stress contemporary dictatorship puts upon arousing and maintaining public support, even though technological development has long since given it instruments for putting down opposition by force immensely superior to anything the monarchs of old ever enjoyed. But the plain fact of the matter is that the new-style despotism depends upon public enthusiasm for its policies, both domestic and foreign, because these policies so often require cooperation or even sacrifices on the part of the citizen for their success. No five-year plan can achieve its goals in the face of public lethargy.

A principal effect of this heightened governmental interest in the character of public opinion is a heavy involvement by the state in the process by which the community forms its opinions. As far as dictatorships are concerned, this commitment is indispensable to the maintenance of authoritarian control. The ministry of information is an ideological focal point.

In the case of modern democratic states, the role of government in the communications process is necessarily more circumscribed. The existence of a free press and broadcasting industry would alone tend to insure this result, since these media are understandably jealous of governmental competition in their efforts to report current events. But even in a democracy, the influence of government upon the process of opinion formation is nonetheless very great, since the operations of the private media of communications are subject to some degree of influence by public agencies and government itself is the source of much of the information upon which the community's political opinions are ultimately based. There are those who argue that the influence which democratic government has come to exert over the communications process, particularly in the area of foreign affairs, has given it possibilities for manipulating public opinion not altogether different from those enjoyed by governments on the other side of the Iron Curtain.

Long before the secrecy crises involving Laos and Cuba, this possibility was given dramatic emphasis by the events surrounding the U-2 affair. The fact that a plane had been shot down was first announced by Premier Khrushchev on May 5, 1960. For two days following this announcement, the American government stoutly insisted that the aircraft was a weather observation plane that had accidently blundered over the Turkish-Soviet border when the pilot's oxygen supply gave out.

Then, on May 7, Khrushchev sprang his trap: the plane had been shot down 1,200 miles inside the Soviet Union; the pilot had been captured; and he had confessed to being an employee of the Central Intelligence Agency sent aloft on the mission of photographing Soviet military installations. At this point the Eisenhower Administration was forced into a rapid about-face. It confirmed and eventually defended the fact that the U-2 had been on an intelligence mission. After the subsequent breakup of the summit conference, President Eisenhower explained that the false account of the U-2 incident originally issued by the government represented "what is known in intelligence circles as a covering statement," designed to conceal our intelligence operations from the enemy.

The implications of this event for American democracy are as yet not altogether clear. Insofar as a reaction was visible, the public did not seem greatly disturbed by this official effort to conceal the facts with "covering statements" when it proved expedient to do so. But the original fabrication was followed so quickly by a true account, and so many other events were coupled in the public mind with the release of false information, including Premier Khrushchev's violent personal attacks upon President Eisenhower, that it is difficult to identify the precise public response to that part of the U-2 affair which involved the deliberate misrepresentation of facts by high government officials. It is too early to say that the public is prepared to give unqualified acceptance to governmental falsehoods as long as they seem to serve the security interests of the United States, but the U-2 affair certainly presents the possibility that this is now the case.

In any event, the incident provides a clear indication of the power that has come to rest in the hands of government officials. For some forty-eight hours at least, public opinion on the U-2 affair was shaped by information at variance with the facts—information that responsible officials knew to be false when it was released. While cases in which such deception occurs may be the exception rather than the rule in any healthy democracy, the possibility of their occurrence has been heightened by the increased importance of military and diplomatic affairs—areas in which it is difficult to obtain access to the facts except through official channels, and where official activities themselves are often shrouded in secrecy.

Concern over the impact of government upon public opinion is by no means a new phenomenon in American politics. It found expression very early in the history of this country in the inclusion in early state constitutions, as well as in the national Constitution, of strict guarantees of freedom of speech and of the press. These guarantees reflected a strong determination that the power of government should never be used to impede the free expression and exchange of private opinion.

But it was also recognized at a very early date that while government should not impede, it could do a great deal to facilitate the process of communication within society. When the post office and the system of post roads were first established, one of their primary functions was that of improving the community's ability to inform itself. The dissemination of accurate information among the citizens on public affairs had implications for some statesmen that were as much political as educational, for it was believed that people in isolated areas could be misled into sedition or insurrection only if they were prevented by poor communications from obtaining access to the truth.

But the fact that such an instrument of education could also serve as a vehicle for influencing political belief did not escape attention. In 1790, for example, a Federalist proposal to give the President the right to determine where post offices and post roads should be located was bitterly opposed in Congress on the grounds that it would give the chief executive extraordinary power over the shape of public opinion.

There were other areas in which government information activity assumed early importance. Executive reports to Congress provided much of the information on which legislative decisions were based during this period. The influence that the reports and proposals of Alexander Hamilton exerted while he was serving as Secretary of the Treasury has become legendary, but executive influence over legislative action was not restricted to his tenure of office. In summing up the careers of the Jeffersonian Presidents who succeeded to power after Hamilton's retirement, Leonard White has noted:

> Substantially all major legislation and much minor legislation were based on administrative reports, giving facts and opinions for the guidance of Congress . . . requests for facts represented a normal part of the interplay between Congress and the executive departments. The latter acted in this respect somewhat in the capacity of staff aides to committees of Congress, none of which had any assistance of their own.

This period also saw the first use of governmental publicity for punitive purposes. Even though it led to some embarrassment for executive officials, Congress at this time inaugurated the practice of publicizing all unsettled accounts in the executive branch, a requirement which revealed that two of the chief accounts on which books had not yet been closed were with ex-Presidents John Adams and James Monroe. Jefferson also insisted upon disclosing the salaries of all executive officials, on the grounds that this publicity would help check any undue expansion in the size of the executive branch.

This employment of the power of publicity as a deterrent to malpractice was one of the many ways in which contemporary issues in information policy were foreshadowed at the very beginning of our history, as the power of government over public opinion stirred widespread concern in the law and practice of early American politics. However, these apprehensions have been greatly magnified during this century, and particularly in the period since World War II. For the issues that have arisen on the contemporary scene stem in good part from the steady expansion in the scope of state activity that has occurred during recent decades—a development that has opened up avenues for governmental influence over public opinion that could scarcely have been anticipated when this nation was established.

Today, for example, it is widely believed that governmental secrecy has now reached the point where it so seriously constricts the availability of information about public affairs as to threaten the vitality of democracy itself, or at least the opportunity for informed discussion that is the essence of free government.

The growth of secrecy within present-day American government reflects in large measure the presence of international tensions. In this respect as in many others, the current development of American life has taken its cue from the force of Soviet pressure. In the missile race, for example, the advantages of secrecy as a tactical asset have been increasingly underlined by emerging events. It is the means by which the Soviets have concealed their plans, hidden their blunders, and prevented comparisons unfavorable to them. The U-2 affair provides a compelling indication of the length to which we will go to overcome Soviet secrecy, even risking, as in this case, the initiation of a chain of events that might end in thermonuclear war.

To be sure, the development of secrecy in American government had its origins long before the first satellite was put into orbit, and before Khrushchev or Marx himself was actually born. Even apart from military matters, Presidents and other high executive officials have always argued that a certain measure of privacy is essential for the effective conduct of civilian affairs, principally on the grounds that it invigorates executive deliberations by protecting career officials from political reprisal for incautious remarks or proposals they may offer. This is the foundation upon which has been erected a doctrine of "executive privilege"—the notion that executive officials have an inherent right to withhold information from the public and the legislature. But down through the years, this effort to preserve a degree of privacy in the conduct of executive activities has stirred repeated conflict, and on more than one occasion has triggered a major crisis in the relations between President and Congress.

What is distinctive about governmental secrecy today is the vast range of information that is now subject to laws prohibiting the disclosure of official data. Apart from the classification system in national defense, which attempts to conceal a wide variety of military and diplomatic secrets from foreign espionage, there have been a great number of statutes enacted and executive regulations promulgated that attempt to prevent the unauthorized release of non-defense but nevertheless confidential information. And in areas where secrecy is not sanctioned by such specific legal safeguards, Presidents can always invoke their executive privilege to withhold information when they choose to do so. As a result there is virtually no area of the administrative process that has been left untouched by the claims of secrecy in modern American government.

The difficulties that governmental secrecy presents in contemporary American politics have been enormously complicated by the fact that they coexist with and are related to a formidable range of questions that have been raised by the growing role of government in the field of publicity.

This problem looms largest in the field of military and diplomatic affairs. But Congress has long been highly alarmed by the role of informational activity in the work of all executive agencies. These apprehensions over administrative press agentry have swelled rather than receded with time, as new instruments of persuasion have been added to the weaponry of government public relations. The advent of radio and television and the growing orientation of the entire community around national affairs have now brought brainwashing on a nationwide scale within the range of at least technical possibility.

But the manipulation of official information to control community opinion is by no means the only danger that governmental use of publicity today presents. For it has become increasingly clear that the weapon of publicity can be used not only for the purpose of engineering consent on the part of the community, but also to punish individuals when the government chooses to do so. Publicity as a punitive sanction has come to be recognized as a serious problem only in comparatively recent times, with the vast expansion that has occurred in government regulatory activity and the extension of Congressional investigations from governmental affairs into areas of social and economic activity outside of government itself. During recent years, Congressional inquiries into subversion, gambling, drug prices, television quiz shows, and a host of other subjects have brought home the fact that the power of publicity can be used with telling effect.

The power of publicity as a technique of governmental coercion has presented perplexing problems of civil liberties, insofar as its use is not hedged about with the same restraints that are attached to such traditional legal sanctions as fines or imprisonment. The damage the cranberry industry suffered in 1959 as a result of an official statement released by the Food and Drug Administration just before Thanksgiving warning the public against the purchase of contaminated berries provided a clear indication of both the effectiveness of official publicity as a technique of control and the adverse effect publicity may have upon those against whom it is used.

In 1960, Protestant clergymen associated with the National Council of Churches of Christ were also exposed to the punitive side of government publicity as a result of the publication of an Air Force training manual linking the Council (as well as Protestant churches generally) with Communism. Although the Secretary of the Air Force subsequently ordered the manual withdrawn from circulation, he did so "without any determination as to whether the charges were true or false." Indeed, the council never was able to obtain a satisfactory retraction from the government, in spite of the fact that publication of these charges by an official agency was, in the council's view, "a patent violation of the free exercise of religion as guaranteed by the First Amendment to the Constitution of the United States."

But while official use of publicity often results in injury to private citizens, the fact remains that government information activities can serve the health and welfare of the community in an infinite variety of ways. It is necessary only to cite the educational program carried on by the Social Security Administration to inform beneficiaries of the old-age and survivors insurance system of their pension rights, or the efforts of local public health authorities to convince residents of their communities to avail themselves of the Salk vaccine against polio outbreaks, or the never-ending, if none too fruitful, attempts of highway commissions to cut down the number of motor vehicle accidents through widely publicized safety campaigns. The truth of the matter is that publicity is the Promethean gift with which modern government has been both blessed and cursed.

No aspect of the subject of government information activity can be dealt with adequately, however, except in conjunction with the whole range of problems presented by publicity and secrecy in government. Criticism of governmental secrecy, for example, cannot ignore the role that restrictions upon the release of official information may play in protecting private individuals against needless damage from adverse publicity. This is not to suggest that measures intended to shield private persons from unfavorable attention are always immune from criticism even if they result in a serious reduction in the availability of information about public affairs. It is only to point out that the need for disclosure is not the sole yardstick by which government information activity can be appraised.

Similarly, concern over government publicity needs to focus not only upon the dangers of an official propaganda machine, but also upon the fact that there are respects in which the public interest can easily suffer more from the weakness than it does from the strength of government publicity. This may be a special problem in the case of activities such as civil defense and urban rehabilitation—programs that have high priority in terms of community welfare but low standing as far as public interest is concerned. Thus, no study of government information activity is complete if it entirely neglects the possibility that in some areas we may suffer not from "brainwashing" but from the inability of government to gain the attention of the community.

It would not, perhaps, be necessary to make these observations were it not for the fact that public discussion of government information activity is so largely shaped by journalists and others associated with the communications media. As a result, there has been a tendency to place great emphasis upon those aspects of the problem of information policy that threaten the valid interests of the newspaper and television industry. These interests are challenged primarily by excessive publicity, which presents the spectre of governmental competition in reporting the news, and executive secrecy, which threatens to block off access to news. It has not always been as forcefully pointed out that the public interest may also suffer damage from ineffective publicity or insufficient privacy in the affairs of government.

Here as elsewhere in matters of public policy, the problem is one of striking a balance. And in arriving at such a point of equilibrium in the field of government information practices, it is important to consider not only the claims that need to be weighed in the balance, such as the need to stimulate the maximum flow of information to the community and to prevent the disclosure of state secrets to a national adversary, but also the degree to which each of these conflicting interests is effectively represented in the process of pressure and counterpressure through which public policy in a democracy is so largely hammered out.

It is, in other words, a matter of estimating the practical likelihood that any of the dangers with which we are confronted in the field of information activity may occur. There can be no doubt, for example, that there are vitally important issues of public policy where practices of governmental secrecy are carried so far as seriously to impede public scrutiny and appraisal of official performance. In the past these issues have included the adequacy of national defense, the practical limits and possibilities of disarmament, and the effectiveness of American foreign policy. Here the prestige and authority of military agencies weigh so heavily in the scales, or considerations of national self-interest appear to be so overriding, that resort to gross practices of secrecy may go unchallenged, while newsmen and legislators are bending every effort to force a more vulnerable civilian agency to disclose some petty detail.

At the same time, however, there are other areas in which it has become increasingly difficult to prevent pressures for publicity from getting out of hand. "Exposure for exposure's sake," as the Supreme Court has noted, is by no means a political necessity in a free society, since the values of democracy permit and even encourage a large measure of privacy at the polling place, in the jury room, and elsewhere. And it may be far from prudent, in view of the substantial contribution privacy often makes to the efficiency of democratic government, not only in diplomacy but in domestic administration as well. There is no more difficult task facing the modern democratic state than that of containing pressures toward excessive publicity, without at the same time encouraging practices of secrecy that choke off the flow of information about public affairs upon which the vitality of government by discussion essentially depends.

56. THE RIGHT NOT TO BE LIED TO*

The Cuban tragedy has raised a domestic question that is likely to come up again and again until it is solved. The cause may be something that is happening in Laos, in Central Africa or in Latin America, but the question remains the same: is a democratic government in an open society such as ours ever justified in deceiving its own people?

In this period of cold war, with its nightmares of hot war just around the corner, there must be secrets kept from the American public in order to preserve them from our adversaries. The Central Intelligence Agency is specifically authorized to "correlate and evaluate intelligence relating to the national security and provide for the appropriate dissemination of such intelligence within the Government." The existence of the cold war implies secret operations on our side in self-defense against the normal subversive

* Reprinted from the editorial page, *New York Times,* May 10, 1961, p. 44. By permission of the publisher.

operations of the other side that cannot be revealed, nor would the responsible American press want to reveal them.

But the Government has a duty also. Neither prudence nor ethics can justify any administration in telling the public things that are not so. A year ago this month, when an American plane was shot down over Russia, the State Department said that "there was no deliberate attempt to violate Soviet space and there never has been." This wasn't true. It was not even usefully untrue, for the Russians already held the pilot, Francis Gary Powers, and had secured a confession from him.

The recent Cuban episode has not been so clear. As has been reported in this and other newspapers, there is no doubt that men were recruited in this country for the projected attack on Cuba. The fact was well known in and around Miami prior to the attack and could not be kept secret from Castro's own spies.

What some leaders of our Government stated in this regard did not square with the facts. If they could not reveal the facts, they would have done better to remain silent. A democracy—our democracy—cannot be lied to. This is one of the factors that make it more precious, more delicate, more difficult and yet essentially stronger than any other form of government in the world.

The basic principle involved is that of confidence. A dictatorship can get along without an informed public opinion. A democracy cannot. Not only is it unethical to deceive one's own public as part of a system of deceiving an adversary government; it is also foolish. Our executive officers and our national legislators are elected on stated days, but actually they must be re-elected day by day by popular understanding and support.

This is what is signified by a government by consent.

57. A WESTERN VIEW
OF RUSSIAN CENSORSHIP
by William J. Jorden*

. . . Before we try to judge whether the Iron Curtain is being lifted, let us have in mind what it is—beyond its purely physical and military implications. It is the sum of all the many methods used by the Soviet leaders to control information about their country that reaches the outside world. More important, it includes the varied methods used to insure that the Russian people hear nothing, see nothing and read nothing that might run counter to the values and beliefs the Kremlin has been trying for forty-one years to inculcate in them.

Every word about the Soviet Union that reaches us in our daily news-

* Member of the U.S. State Department, Policy Planning Council. Former member of *New York Times,* Washington bureau. Headed the *New York Times'* Moscow office from 1956 to 1958. This selection is from William J. Jorden, "Why Russia Needs an Iron Curtain," *New York Times Magazine,* May 3, 1959, pp. 2 and 99-100. By permission of the author and publisher.

papers or on radio and television broadcasts, if it came from Moscow, has passed the scrutiny of the Soviet censors. In addition to controlling the reporters' stories, the Soviet authorities also carefully regulate the raw material of news. Most of it comes from official publications. Moreover, the Soviet Government controls the travel of newsmen and insists on acting as middleman for all official contacts, interviews and the like.

There are rigorous travel limitations for foreigners in the Soviet Union, particularly for those who live and work there as diplomats or newspaper correspondents. Vast areas of the Soviet land are closed to foreigners and numerous cities even in so-called "open areas" are "off limits."

Ordinary tourists to Russia are under controls not always evident. Most follow the carefully regulated routine worked out for them by Intourist, the official travel agency. They see what has been selected for them to see. As a result they have no way of making meaningful contacts with the Russian people.

For the Russians, controls are far more rigid. The Communist party, either directly or through the Governmental, trade union or other organizations it dominates, runs all the newspapers, publishing houses, radio and television stations. Censors approve everything that is printed or broadcast. When mistakes are made, as they sometimes are in the case of book publishing, the authorities are able to withdraw the offending work from circulation, promptly and without opposition.

The most elaborate system of radio jamming known keeps the Russian people from hearing news or "propaganda" from the outside world. When it comes to going abroad, the barriers are almost insurmountable. The average Russian cannot get a passport without special authorization, nor can he get the necessary foreign exchange. All of these things and more add up to what we call the Iron Curtain.

It is not strange to anyone who knows a little of the long and devious history of Russia that the present rulers in Moscow should be following this kind of program. It would be an error to ascribe what has happened, and is happening today, to the Communists alone. The fact is that traditions of secrecy and suspicion are as old as Russia herself, part of the warp and woof of that nation's entire recorded history.

Lenin and his Bolsheviks seized power in a land that never had known real freedom. For centuries, autocratic rulers had held the reins of power. The people were a largely peasant mass, released from serfdom only fifty years before the October Revolution. Illiteracy, superstition and fear held in check most impulses toward liberalism and change.

The written word was controlled by censors from the time of Catherine the Great to the collapse of czarism. We sometimes forget that the giants of Russian literature, men like Pushkin, Gogol, Dostoyevsky and Tolstoy, all struggled against the pencil wielders in the censor's office. And, like the Communist rulers today, the czars insisted that they were not denying literary freedom but only keeping writers within the bounds of accuracy and truth.

The statute on censorship submitted to Alexander I in 1804 bore the following comment: "These regulations do in no sense infringe upon the freedom of thought and of writing, they merely institute appropriate measures against the abuse of this freedom."

That sounds not very different from the comment I once heard Premier Khrushchev make—that the censor's only job was "to prevent the spreading of lies and distortions." Writers, under the czars or under the Communists, found, and find, vast differences between their "truth" and the censors' "truth."

There are other points of striking similarity between the Soviet state and its czarist antecedents. The secret police was not a Soviet innovation. The police had always been an important element in czarist rule, but the secret police were reorganized and vastly expanded under Nicholas I in the first half of the nineteenth century, becoming the notorious Third Section of the Imperial Chancellery.

Men like Lenin and Stalin who suffered arrest and imprisonment under the czars merely adopted and refined the police system, using it against their enemies with far more efficiency and immeasurably greater cruelty than it had been used against them. Today's autocrats of the Kremlin, like their predecessors, find it necessary to use the police, official spies, the closest observance of individuals, the threat—if not always the actuality—of terror, arrest and oblivion as weapons to maintain themselves in complete power. The historical line from the Third Section of Nicholas' time to today's K. G. B. (Committee for State Security) is an unbroken one.

Suspicion of foreign influences is still another of the constants that runs through the history of czarist Russia and the Soviet regime. Russian xenophobia is a blending of many factors—the natural insecurity of a people subjected to periodic foreign invasions and conquest, an allegiance to Byzantine orthodoxy in contrast to the Roman affiliation of Catholicism in Western Europe in an earlier era, a feeling of inferiority in its backwardness as compared with the West, a belief in the essential superiority of Russian culture, a messianic strain producing a drive to carry Russian culture—and now the essentials of the Soviet system—to others less favored. These and more are mixed in the Russian nature and in Soviet attitudes.

An American diplomat in Russia once wrote:

> Secrecy and mystery characterize everything. Nothing is made public that is worth knowing. You will find no two individuals agreeing in the strength of the army and navy, in the amount of public debt, or the annual revenue. In my opinion it is not intended by the Government that these things should be known.

That was in 1852.

Parallels between the Russia of the Czars and the Soviet Union of the Communists can be carried too far, of course. At its worst, the repression of liberty under czardom was not carried to the extremes it reached under Stalin. Moreover, it is noteworthy that in the years immediately before the Revolution, political opposition was permitted and parties of varying hues could work in the open.

Certainly, men like Lenin and Stalin who plotted to overthrow the established order suffered amazingly light penalties compared with those they later meted out to their foes. There can be no question that any organizers of political opposition to communism in the Soviet Union today would be dealt with ruthlessly. On another plane, can there be any doubt that Dostoyevsky was freer to write as he pleased than Boris Pasternak is today?

It is difficult for most people in the West to understand why the Soviet leaders find it necessary to continue to insulate themselves and their people so thoroughly from the outside world. It was perhaps comprehensible in the early days of the Soviet state when they were physically weak and had a larger hostile world opposing them. But now the Soviet Union has risen to a position of imposing power and influence. Why does such a nation need to limit its contacts with the rest of the world, to prevent its own people from traveling freely, to keep out every bit of information it can, to maintain an Iron Curtain?

Authorities on Soviet affairs have pointed out some of the answers. Those who know the Soviet Union well—including, above all, the Soviet leaders themselves—realize how much of a facade has been erected there to conceal reality. Soviet claims to have found a system for providing the average man and his family with a decent standard of living take on a new meaning for anyone who has seen the generally low living standards that prevail through most of the Soviet Union.

More important than keeping foreigners from seeing too much of Soviet life, it is necessary for the Kremlin leaders to prevent any considerable number of their own people from seeing the reality of life in other lands. The average Russian thinks his living conditions are not quite as good as those of Americans, but he has no conception of how different they are. Nor does he realize that he enjoys far less of the good things of life than do the people of almost every country in Europe, including some Communist countries.

I met a farmer in the Ukraine who proudly showed me his new home, three modest rooms for four people. I could understand his pride when I compared his quarters with those of the average Russian. Like most of his fellow-countrymen, he was comparing what he had now with the housing he had been living in previously. He saw nothing strange in the fact he had no refrigerator to keep his food, no bathroom, no car, no radio, nor that he had to carry all the water used for cooking, drinking, bathing and washing from a well.

I kept thinking how surprised he would be to visit the average well-equipped American farmhouse. And what a shock it would be to him to see how little he had, compared with a farmer in Denmark, Holland, France or even in satellite East Germany.

The Russians have heard so much about the advances they are making and so many lies about the poverty, unemployment and economic distress in the United States and other countries that they have no realistic frame of reference for judging their living conditions.

"When you go to Helsinki from Paris," a French diplomat once said to me, "it is a small, pleasant but rather provincial capital. But when you go there from Moscow, it is paradise, paradise!"

Unfortunately the average Russian has never been to Helsinki or anywhere else outside his homeland. Nor will he ever get there. Those who do go outside generally look for evidence they can cite on their return home to prove the official case the Soviet Government has made about the superiority of its system. It is part of the price for being selected.

Freer contacts with other countries and peoples probably would reduce many of the suspicions and fears deliberately stimulated among the Soviet people by their leaders. That would make it more difficult for the regime to maintain its periodic campaigns of vigilance and fear, which in turn are designed to make the people forget some of their more personal grievances against the system.

I recall a conversation I had with a Moscow cab driver just after the violent mass demonstration in front of the American Embassy protesting the sending of American troops to Lebanon. I asked him whether that was the way all Russians felt about the United States.

"Well," he said, "if Nikita Sergeyevich [Khrushchev] tells them to do that, they do it. Besides, if they are worried about what you are doing, they are not thinking about their own problems."

Milovan Djilas, who is paying for his heresy to the Communist movement by his imprisonment in a Yugoslav jail, wrote in his book, "The New Class":

> The most important reason why there was no organized resistance to communism lies deep in the all-inclusiveness and totalitarianism of the Communist state. It had penetrated into all the pores of society and of the personality—into the vision of the scientists, the inspiration of poets and the dreams of lovers. To rise against it meant not only to die the death of a desperate individual, but to be branded and excommunicated from society. There is no air or light under the Communist government's iron fist.

But, of all the many reasons advanced to explain the quarantine doctrine of the Soviet Government, probably the most important is fear of the inevitable consequences. Despite all their proud boasts and their superficial confidence, the leaders of the Communist world know they could not win in any open contest with the political ideals that prevail in most of the Western world. The Bolsheviks lost the only free election ever held in Russia after the Revolution and they have never exposed themselves to that kind of test again. In the rest of the world, no well-informed people has ever deliberately chosen to saddle itself with a Communist regime on a national scale.

The Soviet Communists are simply not interested in any real exchange of ideas or in any large-scale traffic in information, except of a technical nature from which they expect to benefit. The prospect of any considerable number of Russians discussing the merits of political opposition or free elections is one that could only generate terror in the minds of the Kremlin leaders.

They long ago declared war on all "bourgeois ideas" and "survivals of the past" and there is no reason to think they now are prepared to admit such ideas, let alone help in their introduction. Nor are they eager that their people should hear details of the West's viewpoint on such issues as the German problem or disarmament, unless they appear as a footnote to an elaborate official refutation. . . .

We will know that the Russians are sincere about freer exchange with the West when a citizen of Moscow or Kiev can walk down the street and buy a foreign newspaper, when he can tune in his radio to London or New York without jamming and without fear, when he can go to a travel agency and buy tickets for himself and his family to Paris or Chicago.

That day is a long way off. Developments like this would mean that Soviet communism had undergone fundamental changes, changes the leadership of the party has indicated it would never tolerate.

We should welcome the signs we have seen of late of modest relaxation and do what we can to encourage them. But it would be a grave error to overestimate or misinterpret them. In this matter, as in everything else, the Soviet Union seeks to gain as much as it can by paying as small a price as possible.

Elimination of the Iron Curtain would mean the end of the Soviet system as we know it today, and that is a price the Kremlin will never willingly pay.

58. CENSORSHIP: THE RUSSIAN RATIONALE

by Arthur Schlesinger, Jr.*

. . . The Soviet conception of the writer as a gunner, an engineer of the soul, a mass educator—as almost anything except a writer—has to be understood if we are to grasp what the Soviet Union means by cultural exchange. It does not mean free trade in ideas. It means rather a series of reciprocal trade agreements, in which usable ideas of one country are bartered for usable ideas of another. The editor of *October* explained to us that any impression of Soviet indifference to Western ideas was all wrong. "We are eager to take everything constructive and good you have to offer," he said, and went on to instance agronomy, metallurgy, and engineering as fields in which the West had something to contribute.

The implication, in a statement addressed to the American writers' delegation, was plain enough: the Soviet Union had nothing to learn from literary critics, editors, or historians. So the visiting scientist or engineer is assured of a warm welcome and an interested hearing. Even the visiting economist finds a ready audience for a discussion of technical problems of economic management. But the Soviet elite is not much interested in the visiting humanist, who, after all, has no techniques to communicate—has, indeed, nothing to lose but his ideas.

* Special assistant to the President. Professor of history at Harvard University. Winner of Pulitzer, Francis Parkman, and Bancroft prizes and author of *The Age of Jackson*, *The Vital Center*, *The Coming of the New Deal*, *The Politics of Upheaval*, and numerous other books and magazine articles. This selection is from Arthur Schlesinger, Jr., "The Many Faces of Communism," *Harper's Magazine*, vol. 220, no. 1316, January, 1960, pp. 57-58. By permission of the author and publisher.

The hard fact is that the last thing the Soviet Union cares about is a free exchange of ideas. Nothing is more puzzling, for example, given the blazing self-confidence of the Soviet regime, than the distress, even fear, with which Soviet citizens confront the thought of the sale within the U.S.S.R. of foreign books, magazines, and newspapers.

The foreigner in Moscow, going slowly mad as he tries to figure out what is happening in the world from the pages of the London *Daily Worker* and *Humanité*, soon begins to inquire why he cannot buy the *Times* or the *Telegraph* of London, or the *Times* or *Herald Tribune* of New York. Embassies, government offices, and a few libraries receive copies of foreign magazines and newspapers; but, for all practical purposes, the ordinary foreign visitor or Soviet citizen has no access to non-Communist publications. Why? We used to tell Soviet writers that we would be glad to take them to bookshops in Washington, New York, and London where they could buy *Pravda, Izvestia,* and Soviet magazines and books. Why, we would ask, could they not take us to similar places in Moscow? This appeal left them singularly unmoved. The present one-way passage apparently strikes most of them as perfectly right and natural.

Pressing the question further produced curious results. A couple of eminent writers, separately explaining why Moscow could not put the *Times* of London or *New York Times* on sale, cited what they represented as typical Western news kiosks, one in Nice, the other on Broadway. From the lurid and somewhat lip-smacking descriptions one learned that these stands offered nothing but sex and pornography.

"That is what you want to do with us," we were told in grandiloquent tones. "You want to make us accept your Western obscenity and filth. But we say to you that we will not accept it. We will not corrupt our people the way the capitalists have corrupted yours."

To this, one replies that the Soviet Union can keep out all the pornography it wants, but that the London *Times* is not usually regarded as primarily a medium for pornography. One says plaintively: Let us please talk about serious magazines and books and newspapers. Why can't such be sold? The reply comes in increasingly angry and incoherent tones:

"We have told you that we do not want your filth. You want to force your Western ideas upon us. We are going to keep them out. You had better understand that. Etc., etc."

The other argument invoked to defend the ban is that the time is not ripe—the Soviet people are still like a growing child, who has to have its reading selected for it. When one replies that the theory of the forty-two-year-old infant is not convincing and that the Soviet regime is surely so well established that it has little to fear from permitting a few hundred copies of the *New York Times* to be sold each day, one only elicits new bursts of incoherence and anger.

How is one to interpret this? Do people become angry because they realize how stupid and feeble their arguments sound? Or do they really feel that Western newspapers and magazines constitute a threat to the regime? I doubt whether it is either.

What they do feel, I believe, is a sense of infallibility about their own ideas and a despair at the incomprehension of Westerners or a rage at their Machiavellianism. "Our people do not want to eat bad food poisoned with the venom of bourgeois ideas," as Khrushchev put it the other day. ". . . Let us take from each other only what is best, exchange what is best, and eat yourselves your rotten goods."

So long as the Soviet Union remains a theological society, based on the principle of infallibility, it will not permit the circulation of Western skepticism and heresy—and it will remain proud in its prohibition. . . .

CHAPTER VIII

The Nature of Propaganda

What relationship exists between public opinion and propaganda which justifies their joint consideration? And how do the mass media fit into the picture? Analysts of mass communications have conceptualized the process in a manner which sheds some light upon these two questions. They inform us that five elements are distinguishable in the process: the communicator, the message, the medium or channel of communication, the audience, and the effects of the message.[1] In these terms, the propagandist is the communicator who uses the mass media to disseminate his message (propaganda) to the public as his audience with a particular kind of public opinion as the result.

Obviously, this formulation somewhat oversimplifies the matter. Propagandists do not always have publics as their targets, for frequently they seek to influence masses (the members of which interact little or not at all) rather than publics (which are defined in terms of interaction). Moreover, not all communicators are propagandists. And, further, the mass media are more than mere conduits through which information and exhortation flow. As we have already seen, their role is often neither neutral nor passive. Finally, as we have also seen, public opinion is the product of many other factors besides propaganda. But, certainly, public opinion, propaganda, and the mass media are basically interrelated in the manner indicated.

This chapter is designed merely to introduce the subject of propaganda. It remains to the succeeding four chapters to elaborate on the matter. In Chapters IX and X we investigate two contrasting types of governmental or political propaganda: democratic and totalitarian, and two of the major species of the genus "pitchman" (PR experts and admen) are examined in Chapters XI and XII.

Harold Lasswell leads off with a definition of propaganda which clearly distinguishes it from other types of communication. America's debt to propaganda is the topic of the next excerpt—again by Professor Lasswell. He contends that "propaganda has been one of the most powerful contributors to the growth of civilization on the North American continent" and then proceeds effectively to document this statement.

In his "Notes on Propaganda" Aldous Huxley speaks on a subject which has engaged his attention for many years. He compares social and political propaganda with commercial advertising and indicates why the latter is more likely to be successful. Ideology as a rationalization of desires, the differential success of writers equally skilled as propagandists, the cyclical

---

[1] Cf. Bruce L. Smith, Harold D. Lasswell, and Ralph D. Casey, *Propaganda, Communication, and Public Opinion: A Comprehensive Reference Guide,* Princeton University Press, Princeton, N.J., 1946, p. 3.

nature of history, and the function of dictatorial propaganda are among the other topics covered in this article.

If "propaganda" is the label applied to efforts by the few to manage the opinions and/or behavior of the many, the term would appear to cover an almost infinite variety of techniques. And such is the case. Dr. Joseph Goebbels, Hitler's Minister of Propaganda, has stated that "propaganda in itself has no fundamental method. It has only purpose—the conquest of the masses. Every means that serves this end is good." Aside from its candid acceptance of the proposition that the ends justify the means— with which, alas, too many propagandists concur—this statement serves to support the assertion that the techniques of propaganda are varied and numerous. In the chapters to follow we shall examine some of these techniques as they have been adapted to particular situations, but in this chapter we provide a convenient summary of the more common propaganda devices. The excerpt selected for this purpose is from Charles Siepmann's *Radio, Television, and Society* and draws its examples, therefore, primarily from the electronic media.

Most propagandists do not ply their trade solely from a sense of compulsion; rather, they expect to achieve results. They are hopeful of convincing or converting or reinforcing or dissuading or of goading into action. But what are the conditions under which the propagandist is likely to accomplish these objectives, and when, on the other hand, can we predict that his efforts will be unavailing? For Lazarsfeld and Merton propaganda effectiveness requires the conjoint satisfaction of the conditions of canalization, monopolization, and supplementation. In an excerpt from their writings these concepts are defined and illustrated.

The morally indignant are legion, but few of their ranks are more articulate than Aldous Huxley. He returns in the concluding selection of this chapter with some general remarks from *Brave New World Revisited* on the chances for survival of freedom and democratic institutions in a propaganda-oriented world.

59. A DEFINITION OF "PROPAGANDA"
by Harold D. Lasswell *

And what do I mean by propaganda? It serves no useful purpose to conceive of propaganda so broadly that it becomes a synonym for every form of communication—from the furtive whisper between neighbors at a lecture to the Voice of America or the circulation of a book purporting to

* Professor of law and political science at Yale University. Author and coauthor of numerous works including *Propaganda Techniques in the World War, Psychopathology and Politics, World Politics and Personal Insecurity, Politics: Who Gets What, When, How, Democracy through Public Opinion, Power and Personality, Language of Politics, Power and Society, National Security and Individual Freedom,* and *The Policy Sciences.* This selection is from Harold D. Lasswell, "Propaganda and Mass Insecurity," *Psychiatry,* vol. 13, issue no. 3, August, 1950, pp. 284-285. By permission of the author and publisher.

show how the planet Venus influenced human destiny. There is a need for a word which means the making of deliberately one-sided statements to a mass audience. Let us choose "propaganda" as such a word. It is an act of advocacy in mass communication. I am thinking, in particular, of communications with a direct bearing on public policy, such as the campaign speeches of party candidates or the special pleading of pressure groups.

It is unquestionably propaganda to editorialize or to select the content of channels of communication for the purpose of influencing attitudes on controversial issues. When the government distributes a pamphlet on the care and feeding of babies, the act is *informative* and *instructive,* not propagandistic, unless there is doubt about the authenticity of what is said or unless the desirability of babies is in dispute. It is an act of *inquiry* and not of propaganda to analyze controversial doctrines for the sake of promoting critical judgment. It is an act of *ceremony* to intone the sentiment-encrusted phrases of the creed in an assemblage of believers. It is an act of *incitement* to climax an impassioned harangue with a cry to burn the courthouse, or lynch the prisoner, or smash the windows of the unbeliever.

The stream of propaganda is one among the many streams of communication characterizing the interpersonal relationships of society. Where it is found it proceeds within a framework of information, instruction, ceremony, and incitement; and these categories do not begin to exhaust the richness of the communicative context. In one direction propaganda grades into overt action; in another direction, into private discourse.

The most striking marginal case is *propaganda of the deed.* Since propaganda is an act of communication, it uses the instruments which are ordinarily specialized to the carrying on of communication, such as words, gestures, pictures, and written characters. Yet communication effects can also be obtained by physical devices which are not ordinarily specialized to the function. Most people would agree that the act of killing is no ordinary channel for the making of communications. It is, however, proper to speak of killing as propaganda of the deed when political assassinations are carried out for the purpose of influencing social attitudes. . . .

Propaganda involves the mass audience. The most important trait of such an audience is not size. It is the shallowness and impersonality of the tie between communicator and audience. It is a sense of this distinction which precludes terming private arguments among intimates as propaganda, unless they are part of a campaign to spread controversial viewpoints throughout a considerable group, which indeed they often are. The shallowness of the bond binding the mass audience does not imply that the bond is weak—often the contrary. . . .

60. AMERICA'S DEBT TO PROPAGANDA
by Harold D. Lasswell*

. . . There is some virtue in recalling the debt of America to propaganda. Far from being a recent affliction, propaganda has been one of the most powerful contributors to the growth of civilization on the North American continent. The propagandist of religion walked beside or a little in advance of the explorer, trader, and occupier of the broad acres of the New World. The natural reluctance of men to pull up stakes and settle overseas was partially overcome by the incessant use of propaganda.

It is true, as we are often reminded by disillusioned observers of the American scene, that the early bearers of European culture to this continent were often recruited from the debtor's prisons of the Old World, and dispatched to the New World under constraint. Gradually, however, the lure of the West caught the imagination of Europe and sturdy citizens trooped by the millions to these shores. The alluring slogan, "the land of opportunity" is in itself a tribute to the tireless propaganda of the colonizing and shipping interests on both sides of the Atlantic Ocean. Without the seminal touch of capital investment, the abundant resources of the New World would have remained unused. The task of attracting capital to a fallow continent was undertaken by promoters who made use of every device in the propaganda repertory of their day. All in all, there is no doubt of the efficacy of propaganda in overcoming the hesitation of men to move themselves and to risk their capital in America. This, perhaps, is America's greatest debt to propaganda.

The internal consolidation of America proceeded with the specialized use of propaganda. From an early day the propaganda of religion, in the form of home and foreign missions, was a powerful outlet for American energy. The ingenious Committees of Correspondence bound together the men of action among the several colonies and welded them into a battering ram of freedom from England. Benjamin Franklin did a superlative propaganda campaign in Paris on behalf of the seceding colonies.

With the democratization of the suffrage and the westward bulge of the nation, America developed remarkable devices of electoral propaganda. Torchlight processions, barbecues, and all the paraphernalia of popular excitement stirred the rank and file of the American people to a virile sense of participation in the great decisions of the hour. Even the secret societies, anti-democratic and intolerant as some of them were, stimulated the self-confidence of the masses in the truth that they, among all men in the world of their day, had a hand on the tiller of destiny. The great agitations —against slavery, against the liquor traffic, against monopoly, for women's rights—were psychic waves that swept across successive generations. In

*Professor of law and political science at Yale University. This selection is from Harold D. Lasswell, *Democracy through Public Opinion*, published as no. 1, part 2 of vol. 43 of *The Eleusis of Chi Omega*, 1941, pp. 35-37. By permission of the author and publisher.

war—whether war with Britain, with Mexico, or between the States, or against Spain or the Central Powers—propaganda rallied the energies of the nation. Great humanitarian causes—educational, recreational, curative —depended upon skillful appeals for gifts.

The main stream of American propaganda, however, was neither religious, partisan, reformist, official nor philanthropic. It was commercial. It was advertising. Its purpose was to control buying habits. In a world of spectacular technical advances in the creation of new goods, where ancient habits were upset by migration, advertising bounded to undreamed-of heights. With rhetorical license one might say that if Columbus found the continent, the advertiser formed the nation.

61. NOTES ON PROPAGANDA
by Aldous Huxley*

I

They were always numerous; but now their name is legion. All over the world thousands upon thousands of men and women pass their whole lives denouncing, instructing, commanding, cajoling, imploring their fellows. With what results? One finds it rather hard to say. Most propagandists do their work in the dark, draw bows at a venture. They write; but they don't know how far they will succeed in influencing their readers, nor what are the best means for influencing them, nor how long their influence will last. There is, as yet, no science of propaganda.

This fact may seem the more surprising when we reflect that there is something not far removed from a science of advertising. In the course of years advertisers have come to be fairly expert at selling things to the public. They know accurately enough the potentialities and limitations of different kinds of propaganda—what you can do, for example, by mere statement and repetition; by appeals to such well-organized sentiments as snobbery and the urge toward social conformity; by playing on the animal instincts such as greed, lust, and especially fear in all its forms, from the fear of sickness and death to the fear of being ugly, absurd, or physically repugnant to one's fellows.

If then commercial propagandists know their business so well, why is it that ethical and political propagandists should know theirs on the whole so badly? The answer is that the problems with which the advertisers have to deal are fundamentally unlike the problems which confront moralists and, in most cases, politicians. A great deal of advertising is concerned with matters of no importance whatsoever. Thus I need soap; but it makes not the smallest difference to me whether I buy soap manufactured by X or

* Novelist and essayist. Author of *Chrome Yellow, Point Counter Point, Brave New World, After Many a Summer Dies the Swan, The Perennial Philosophy, Ape and Essence, Brave New World Revisited,* and numerous other works. This selection is from Aldous Huxley, "Notes on Propaganda," *Harper's Magazine,* vol. 174, December, 1936, pp. 32-41. By permission of the author.

soap manufactured by Y. This being so, I can allow myself to be influenced in my choice by such entirely irrelevant considerations as the sex appeal of the girl who smiles so alluringly from X's posters, or the puns on Y's and his comic drawings. In many cases of course I do not need the commodity at all. But as I have a certain amount of money to spare and am possessed by the strange desire to collect unnecessary objects, I succumb easily to anyone who asks me to buy superfluities and luxuries. In these cases commercial propaganda is an invitation to give into a natural or acquired craving. In no circumstances does it ever call upon the reader to resist a temptation; always it begs him to succumb. It is not very difficult to persuade people to do what they are all longing to do.

When readers are asked to buy luxuries and superfluities or to choose between two brands of the same indispensable necessity nothing serious is at stake. Advertising is concerned in these cases with secondary and marginal values. In other cases, however, it matters or seems to matter a great deal whether the reader allows himself to be influenced by the commercial propagandist or no. Suffering from some pain or physical disability, he is told of the extraordinary cures effected by M's pills or N's lotion. Naturally he buys at once. In such cases the advertiser has only to make the article persuasively known; the reader's urgent need does the rest.

Ethical and political propagandists have a very different task. The business of the moralist is to persuade people to overcome their egotism and their personal cravings, in the interest either of a supernatural order or of their own higher selves or of society. The philosophies underlying the ethical teaching may vary; but the practical advice remains in all cases the same—and this advice is in the main unpleasant; whereas the advice given by commercial propagandists is in the main thoroughly pleasant. There is only one fly in the ointment offered by commercial propagandists: they want your money.

Some political propagandists are also moralists; they invite their readers to repress their cravings and set limits to their egotistical impulses for the sake of some political cause which is to bring happiness in the future. Others demand no personal effort from their readers—merely their adherence to a cause, whose success will save the world automatically and, so to speak, from the outside. The first has to persuade people to do something which is on the whole disagreeable. The second has to persuade them of the correctness of a policy which, though it imposes no immediate discomforts, admittedly brings no immediate rewards. Both must compete with other propagandists. The art of political propaganda is much less highly developed than the art of commercial propaganda; it is not surprising.

Long experience has taught the moralists that the mere advertising of virtue is not enough to make people virtuous. During the past few thousands of years incalculable quantities of hortatory literature have been produced in every civilized country of the world. The moral standard remains, none the less, pretty low. True, if all this ethical propaganda had never been made the standard might be even lower. We can't tell. I suspect, however, that if we could measure it, we should find that the mechanical efficiency of ethical propaganda through literature was seldom in excess of one per cent. In individual cases and where, for some reason, circumstances are peculiarly favorable, written propaganda may be more efficient than in others. But, in general, if people behave as well as they do it is not because they have read about good behavior and the social or metaphysical reasons for being virtuous; it is because they have been subjected during childhood, to a more or less intensive, more or less systematic training in good behavior. The propagandists of morality do not rely exclusively or even mainly, on the written word.

Unlike the advertisers, political and social propagandists generally work in the dark and are quite uncertain as to the kind of effects they will be able to produce upon their readers. Propagandists themselves seldom admit this fact. Like all the rest of us, they like to insist upon their own importance. Moreover, there has been a tendency among historians and political theorists to lend support to their claims. This is not surprising. Being themselves professional writers, historians and political theorists are naturally prone to exaggerate the significance of literature. In most studies of modern history a great deal of space is devoted to the analysis of different political and economic theories; and it is tacitly or explicitly assumed that the propagation of these theories in the writings of literary men had a more or less decisive influence on the course of history. In other and more reverberant words, the literary men are credited with having "built Nineveh with our sighing and Babel itself in our mirth." Let us try to discover how far the facts confirm or invalidate this proud claim.

II

Consider, to begin with, the periodical press. Rich men and politicians have a fixed belief that if they can control the press they will be able to control public opinion—to control it even in a country where democratic institutions are allowed to function without gross interference. They buy up newspapers, partly in order to make money (for the production of newspapers is a very profitable industry), but mainly in the confident hope of being able to persuade the electorate to do what they want it to do. But in fact, as recent history proves, they fail just as often as they succeed. . . . We are led to two conclusions: first, that most people choose their daily paper not for its opinions but for its entertainingness, its capacity to amuse and fill the vacancies of leisure. Second, that written propaganda is less efficacious than the habits and prejudices, the class loyalties and professional interests of the readers.

Nor must we forget that propaganda is largely at the mercy of circumstances. Sometimes circumstances fight against propaganda; at other times they fight no less effectively on its side. . . . Significant in this context is the case of Allied propaganda during the World War. Up till the summer of 1918 the propaganda designed to undermine the will-to-fight of the German troops was almost perfectly ineffective. During and after that summer, when hunger and a series of unsuccessful battles had prepared the ground for it, this propaganda achieved its purpose. But the leaflets which Lord Northcliffe's organization scattered with such good effect during July and August could have done absolutely nothing to discourage the German troops during their victorious offensive against Saint Quentin in the month of March.

Propaganda by even the greatest masters of style is as much at the mercy of circumstances as propaganda by the worst journalists. Ruskin's diatribes against machinery and the factory system influenced only those who were in an economic position similar to his own; on those who profited by machinery and the factory system they had no influence whatever. From the beginning of the twelfth century to the time of the Council of Trent, denunciations of ecclesiastical and monastic abuses were poured forth almost without intermission. And yet, in spite of the eloquence of great writers and great churchmen, like St. Bernard and St. Bonaventura, nothing was done. It needed the circumstances of the Reformation to produce the Counter-Reformation. Upon his contemporaries the influence of Voltaire was enormous. Lucian had as much talent as Voltaire and wrote of religion with the same disintegrating irony. And yet, so far as we can judge, his writings were completely without effect. The Syrians of the second century were busily engaged in converting themselves to Christianity and a number of other Oriental religions; Lucian's irony fell on ears that were deaf to everything but theology and occultism. In France during the first half of the eighteenth century a peculiar combination of historical circumstances had predisposed the educated to a certain religious and political skepticism; people were ready and eager to welcome Voltaire's attacks on the existing order of things. Political and religious propaganda is effective, it would seem, only upon those who are already partly or entirely convinced of its truth. . . .

III

. . . In other words, social and political propaganda is influential only when it is a rationalization of the desires, sentiments, prejudices, or interests of those to whom it is addressed. A theology or a political theory may be defined as an intellectual device for enabling people to do in cold blood things which, without the theology or the theory, they could only do in the heat of passion. Circumstances, whether external or internal and purely psychological, produce in certain persons a state of discontent, for example, a desire for change, a passionate aspiration for something new. These emotional states may find occasional outlet in violent but undirected activity. But now comes the writer with a theology or a political theory in terms of which these vague feelings can be rationalized. The energy developed by the prevailing passions of the masses is given a direction and at the same time strengthened and made continuous. Sporadic outbursts of feeling are converted by the rationalization into purposive and unremitting activity. The mechanism of successful propaganda may be roughly summed up as follows: Men accept the propagandist's theology or political theory because it apparently justifies and explains the sentiments and desires evoked in them by circumstances. The theory may, of course, be completely absurd from a scientific point of view; but this is of no importance so long as men believe it to be true. Having accepted the theory, men will work in obedience to its precepts even in times of emotional tranquillity. Moreover, the theory will often cause them to perform in cold blood acts which they would hardly have performed even in a state of emotional excitement.

Our nature abhors a moral and intellectual vacuum. Passion and self-interest may be our chief motives; but we hate to admit the fact even to ourselves. We are not happy unless our acts of passion can be made to look as though they were dictated by reason, unless self-interest be explained and embellished so as to seem to be idealistic. Particular grievances call not only for redress but also for the formulation of universally valid reasons why they should be redressed. Particular cravings cry aloud to be legitimized in terms of a rational philosophy and a traditionally acceptable ethic. The moral and intellectual vacuum is perpetually in process of formation, and it sucks into itself whatever explanatory or justificatory writing happens at the moment to be available. Clean or dirty, brackish or sweet, any water will serve the turn of a pump that has been emptied of its air. And analogously, any philosophical writing, good, bad, or indifferent, will serve the turn of people who are under the compulsion of desire or of self-interest, and who consequently feel the need of intellectual and moral justification. Hence the extraordinary success at a particular historical moment of books that to a later generation seem almost completely valueless; hence the temporary importance and power of manifestly second-rate and negligible writers.

Let us consider a concrete example. The organization of eighteenth-century French society was hopelessly inefficient, and its pattern so anachronistic that great numbers of individual Frenchmen, unable to fit into the scheme of things, suffered acute discomfort. The sense of grievance and the desire for change were intense; and correspondingly intense was the desire for a philosophy that should rationalize this desire and legitimize this grievance in terms of pure reason and absolute justice. Yearning to be filled, the moral and intellectual vacuum sucked into itself whatever writings were available. Among these was the *De l'Esprit* of Helvétius. This is a thoroughly bad book, full of preposterous stuff. But, though obviously untrue, some of its theses (such as that which affirmed the equality of all intellects and the consequent possibility of transforming any child at will into a Newton or a Raphael) were well suited to rationalize and justify the contemporary claims for political, religious and economic reform. During a few years the book was invested with a significance and exercised an influence which its intrinsic literary and philosophical merits could not justify. Its fortune was made not by the ability of its author but by the needs of its readers. . . .

At every period of history certain writings are regarded by all or some members of a given society as being *ex hypothesi* true. They are, therefore, charged with an unquestionable authority. To show that this authority is on the side of the cause he supports has always been one of the propagandist's tasks. Where it is not possible for him to make them serve his purposes, the propagandist has to discredit the existing authorities. The devil opens the attack by quoting Scripture; then, when the quotations fail him, trots out the Higher Criticism and shows that Scripture has no more authority than the *Pickwick Papers*. At any given moment there are certain fixed landmarks of authority; the propaganda of the period has to orientate itself in relation to these landmarks. Correct orientation to existing authority is one of the conditions making for success of propaganda.

IV

We see, then, that the effectiveness of propaganda is determined by the circumstances of the time when it is written. These circumstances are of two kinds—circumstances external to the individual, and internal or psychological circumstances. External circumstances may change catastrophically, as during a war; or gradually, as when means of production are altered and economic prosperity is increased or diminished. Changes in external circumstances are of course accompanied by changes in internal circumstances. But internal circumstances may also change on their own account, independently, to a certain extent, of external circumstances and according to an autonomous rhythm of their own. History pursues an undulatory course; and these undulations are the result, to some extent at least, of the tendency displayed by human beings to react after a certain time away from the prevailing habits of thought and feeling toward other habits. (This process is greatly complicated by the fact that in modern heterogeneous societies there are numerous coexisting groups with different habits of thought and feeling. But it is unnecessary to discuss these complications here.) The autonomous nature of psychological undulations is confirmed by the facts of history. Thus the ardor of all violently active religious and political movements has generally given place to relative indifference and worldliness after a period of anything from a few months to twenty-five years. . . .

The mistake of all propagandists has been to suppose that the psychological movement which they observe in the society around them is destined to go on continuously in the same direction. Thus we see that in a time of skepticism, skeptical propagandists announce with triumph that superstition is dead and reason triumphant. In a time of religious reaction Christian and nationalistic propagandists announce with equal satisfaction and certainty that skepticism has for ever been destroyed. Both, it is hardly necessary to say, are wrong. The course of history is undulatory, because (among other reasons) self-conscious men and women easily grow tired of a mode of thought and feeling which has lasted for more than a certain time. Propaganda gives force and direction to the successive movements of popular feeling and desire; but it does not do much to create those movements. The propagandist is a man who canalizes an already existing stream. In a land where there is no water, he digs in vain.

V

In a democratic state any propagandist will have rivals competing with him for the support of the public. In totalitarian states there is no liberty of expression for writers and no liberty of choice for their readers. There is only one propagandist—the state.

That all-powerful rulers who make a regular use of terrorism should also be the most active propagandists known to history seems at first sight paradoxical. But you can do anything with bayonets except sit on them. Even a despot cannot govern for any length of time without the consent of his subjects.

Dictatorial propaganda aims first of all at the legitimizing in popular estimation of the dictator's government. Old-established governments do not need to produce certificates of legitimacy. Long habit makes it seem "natural" to people that they should be ruled by an absolute or constitutional monarch, by a republican president, by a prince bishop, by an oligarchy of senatorial families—whichever the case may be. New rulers have to prove that they have not usurped their title, but possess some higher right to govern than the mere fact of having grabbed power. Usurpation, like any other crime, has to justify itself in terms of the prevailing code of values—in terms, that is to say, of the very system which brands it as a crime. For example, in Italy during the fourteenth and fifteenth centuries there were two acknowledged sources of political power: the Empire and the Church. For this reason the men who had succeeded, by fraud or violence, in seizing the government of a city, generally hastened to have themselves appointed Vicars of the Church or Hereditary Captains of the Empire. To be able to tyrannize effectively they needed the title and appearance of constitutional authority. Since the French Revolution the recognized sources of power have been the People and the Nation.

When modern despots have to legitimize their usurpations, they do so in terms of nationalism and of that humanitarian democracy they themselves have overthrown. They issue propaganda to prove that their regime is for the good of the people or else, if the economic facts make nonsense of such a claim, for the good of that mystical entity, different from and superior to the mere individuals composing it, the Nation. But the general acknowledgment that his government is legitimate is not enough for the totalitarian dictator; he demands from his subjects that they shall all think and feel alike, and he uses every device of propaganda in order to make them think and feel alike. Complete psychological homogeneity occurs among primitive peoples. But the conditions of such homogeneity are, first, that the population shall be small; second that it shall live in an isolation due either to geography or to the exclusiveness of the local religion; and, third, that its system of production shall be more or less completely unspecialized. European dictators may wish and try to make their peoples as homogeneous as a tribe of Melanesians, to impose upon them a conformity as complete as that which exists among the Australian aborigines. But circumstances must finally prove too strong for them. Fifty million professionally specialized men and women cannot live together without emphasizing one another's natural diversities. Nor, with the best will in the world, can the dictator isolate himself from all contact with the outside world. This is one of the reasons why, in the long run, he is bound to fail.

Meanwhile he is sure of at least a partial and temporary success. Dictatorial propaganda demands obedience and even considerable financial and other sacrifices; but by way of compensation it assures the individual that, as a member of a chosen nation, race, or class, he is superior to all other individuals in the world; it dissipates his sense of personal inferiority by investing him with the vicarious glory of the community; it gives him reasons for thinking well of himself; it provides him with enemies whom he may blame for his own shortcomings and upon whom he may vent his latent brutality and love of bullying. Commercial propaganda is acceptable because it encourages men and women to satisfy their sensuous cravings and offers them escapes from their physical pains and discomforts. Dictatorial propaganda, which is always nationalistic or revolutionary propaganda, is acceptable because it encourages men and women to give free rein to their pride, vanity, and other egotistical tendencies, and because it provides them with psychological devices for overcoming their sense of personal inferiority. Dictatorial propaganda promotes the ugly reality of prejudice and passion to the rank of an ideal. Dictators are the popes of nationalism; and the creed of nationalism is that what ought to be is merely what is, only a good deal more so. All individuals seek justifications for such passions as envy, hatred, avarice, and cruelty; by means of nationalistic and revolutionary propaganda dictators provide them with such justifications. It follows, therefore, that this propaganda of the dictators is certain to enjoy a certain temporary popularity.

In the long run, as I have said, the impossibility of reducing a huge, educated population to the spiritual homogeneity of a savage tribe will tell against it. Furthermore, human beings have a strong tendency toward rationality and decency. (If they had not they would not desire to legitimize their prejudices and their passions.) A doctrine that identifies what ought to be with the lowest elements of actual reality cannot remain acceptable for long. Finally, policies based upon a tribal morality simply won't work in the modern world. The danger is that in process of proving that they don't work the dictators may destroy that world.

Dictatorial propaganda may be classified under two heads: negative and positive. Positive propaganda consists of all that is written, negative propaganda, of all that is not written. In all dictatorial propaganda silence is at least as important as speech, *suppressio veri* as important as *suggestio falsi*. Indeed, the negative propaganda of silence is probably more effective as an instrument of persuasion and mental regimentation than speech. Silence creates the conditions in which such words as are spoken or written take most effect.

An excess of positive propaganda evokes boredom and exasperation in the minds of those to whom it is addressed. Advertising experts are well aware that after a certain point an increase in the pressure of salesmanship produces rapidly diminishing and finally negative returns. What is true of commercial propaganda seems to be equally true, in this respect, of political propaganda. . . . *Suppressio veri* has one enormous advantage over *suggestio falsi:* in order to say nothing, you do not have to be a great stylist. People may get bored with positive propaganda; but where negative propaganda is so effective that there is no alternative to the spoken and written suggestions that come to them, all but the most independent end by accepting those suggestions.

62.   PROPAGANDA TECHNIQUES
by Charles A. Siepmann*

Aristotle, in his treatise on Rhetoric (Book 1, Chapter 2), tells us where to look if we seek to identify and to distinguish between propagandists true and false, good and bad. "Of the modes of persuasion provided by the spoken word there are three kinds. The first kind depends on the personal character of the speaker, the second on putting the audience into a certain frame of mind, the third on the proof, or apparent proof, provided by the words of the speech themselves." In other words, honest propaganda (and we must here insist again that honest propaganda is not only possible but peculiarly urgent today) demands integrity in the propagandist, a reverence for the integrity of those whom he addresses, and valid argument substantiated as far as possible by evidence. As the propagandist is usually unknown to us, we are driven to assessing his integrity either by reference to his general reputation or, more certainly, by observing his approach to us and his use, or manipulation, of language. His resources here are manifold. Among the many available tricks of the trade we select the following, partly because they are so frequently exemplified in practice (and therefore can be checked) and partly because they bear on those traits of character and outlook that we have identified as widely prevalent among us. The following are pitfalls for the unwary.

1. Repetition

If we want to register an impression, we must use repetition. The mere currency of a statement lends it credibility. Even a lie can often thus be made to "stick." (Hitler insolently claimed and, alas, demonstrated that the bigger the lie, the better it could sometimes be made to register.) Our readiness to accept at its face value what is commonly asserted by others is a pathetic manifestation not merely or even primarily of our lack of independent judgment, but of the narrow limits of what we know (or can know) by firsthand experience. Most of what we know must be accepted on the authority of others. It is thus that a child "grows in knowledge." From childhood we carry into adult life this habit of unquestioning acceptance of what is commonly asserted. It is a dangerous habit.[1]

The most familiar example of the use of repetition is commercial advertising. The sponsor of a radio program buys time, if he can, in large chunks. Thirteen weeks is a frequent minimum. Apart from the persuasive frills of the advertising copy, his objective is generally to register a brand name with the public. Each "plug," therefore, contains repeated reference to his

* Chairman of the department of communications and professor of education at New York University. Author of *Radio, Television, and Society* and other works. This selection is from Charles A. Siepmann, *Radio, Television, and Society,* Oxford University Press, New York, 1950, pp. 181-193. Copyright 1950 by Oxford University Press. Reprinted by permission.

[1] For a brilliant elaboration of this theme see Lippmann, Walter, *Public Opinion,* The Macmillan Co., New York, 1922.

product, and the plugs continue, with only minor variations, over the whole period of his sponsorship. "Sponsor-identification recall" is his clue to the success or failure of his campaign.

2. Insistent Exaggeration

Exaggeration, too, is most commonly exemplified in commercial advertising. The reason is worthy of examination. No one can question the importance and usefulness of commercial advertising; it lubricates, as it were, the machinery of commerce. But there are two kinds of advertising, the one legitimate and useful, the other, as frequently employed, illegitimate and harmful. The first consists of straight publicity—the announcement of the availability of goods and of relevant facts (price, size, where available, and so on) about them. A good example is the Sears Roebuck catalogue which tells you where you can get what, and at what price.

The second consists of competitive bidding for the consumer's patronage. At issue here is the availability not simply of goods but of competing brands of the same goods; not soap or cigarettes but different kinds of soap and cigarettes. Advertising of this kind is peculiar to the private-enterprise system. It, too, is legitimate—unless and until the advertiser allows his competitive zeal to master his integrity and his respect for the integrity of the consumer. The more highly competitive a society (the more predominantly it is "a nation of shopkeepers"), the greater the danger of abuse in advertising of this nature. In his eagerness to outbid his competitor the advertiser proceeds to advance fantastic or unsubstantiated claims for his product. It is "better" (the Federal Trade Commission forbids him to complete the sentence and specifically name his rivals), or it is "best." Persistent exaggeration permeates his claims (and in radio creeps into the very tone of voice of the announcer) to such an extent that language and reality itself become confounded. We are invited to live in a world where almost everything is "best"—which is, of course, a contradiction in terms. And yet many accept the invitation, as one radio listener reveals in her comment, "I think all the soap ads are good. I used to buy a different kind every day when I could get it."[2] All of us enjoy the best and want to possess it. It is on this impulse that the unscrupulous propagandist can play effectively.

3. Identification

We are hardly persuaded by a stranger. We are easily impressed by those with whom we are familiar and with whom we feel closely identified. This fact presents the propagandist who uses modern media of communication (which operate by "remote control") with a problem. How is he to overcome the twofold obstacle of being generally unknown to the listeners as well as physically remote? Paradoxically, radio, at least (by virtue of that mysterious alchemy to which we have referred), converts this seeming liability into an asset, lending itself to the creation of a sense of intimacy that can be as real as it is often false. Perhaps because the broadcaster can

[2] Lazarsfeld, *The People Look at Radio*, Chapel Hill, 1946, p. 21.

convey his personality, not only by style (i.e., his choice of language) but also by the tone and inflections of his voice, the discriminating listener can gather a fuller and fairer impression of him than can the reader of the author of a book or article. Thus the personal integrity of such commentators as Raymond Swing, Edward Murrow, and Howard K. Smith seems clearly established—and quite independently of the validity of what they say. They may be "wrong" but they cannot, we say, be false. Now, personal integrity cannot be assumed, as we dress ourselves with clothes. Therefore, it is not strictly speaking, a "technique." Yet integrity remains the hallmark of wholesome and useful propaganda, just as its opposite constitutes propaganda's most insidious and vicious attribute.

There are several contributory ways of achieving identification. (a) The most obvious is to clothe our thoughts in the language—even the jargon and local idiom—of those we seek to persuade. (All wartime propaganda did so. The German short-wave radio, concentrating on the Middle West, advisedly employed a man with a distinct Iowan accent.) (b) Another is to exhibit familiarity with the listener's (or reader's) environment, to use "local incidents" to illustrate our point. To be concrete and not abstract is, indeed, a cardinal point in all effective propaganda. (c) The subtlest way, the hardest—and, in its spurious form, the most contemptible—is to identify ourselves sympathetically with the true interests, perplexities, fears, and hopes of those we address and to relate these to our propaganda objective. It is in this regard that good and bad propaganda are to be most sharply differentiated, and that we can identify bad propaganda as specifically undemocratic in that it exploits innocence and credulity and violates the dignity and integrity of the individual.

A wartime example of abuse was the propaganda to Britain of Lord Haw Haw, whose subversive arguments were the more highly charged for stemming from an intimate knowledge and perverted understanding of disaffected elements among the British public. Fortunately for all of us, this renegade was outrivaled by another propagandist—Winston Churchill —whose more comprehensive and sympathetic understanding of the British character secured him a truer and more compelling identification with the people.

But we have our own wartime[3] and peacetime examples in the widespread abuse of privilege by commercial advertisers. Perhaps in no particular is the abuse more flagrant than in this matter of spurious identification—the more sickening in radio for the hired propagandist's tonal implications of false devotion (either to the listener or to the product or to both) associated with the script. "Radio announcers and featured stars repeatedly

---

[3] A general executive of one of the largest advertising firms in the country sums up the situation since Pearl Harbor: "Copy written on war themes has not been generally thoughtful or inspiring. 'Almost as a pattern,' writes a distinguished advertising man, 'it features glamorous, colorful, schoolboy pictures of zooming American bombers winning the war thanks to Zilch's Bolts & Nuts. . . . *The chance to swing on the trapeze of war emotion has also been grasped by unworthy hands.* Many a cheap circular or advertisement in a low grade paper has urged the public to hoard, through variations of the "Buy Now" and "Only 50 left in stock," appeals.'" Quoted in Merton, *Mass Persuasion,* Harper & Brothers, New York, 1946, p. 83.

assert their enthusiasm for the products of their sponsors; they are said (by some listeners) to exhibit a warm personal interest in people they neither know nor take pains to know. . . ."[4]

If, irrespective of the context, such abuse is widely prevalent, what, we must ask, is its cumulative effect? To what extent is the very understanding of what intimacy means affected? Is the regard for it in personal relations reduced by such travesty in public? Does invasion of our privacy in such terms drain us, for very lassitude under such constant bludgeoning, of the desire, even, to be private and by a kind of mass mesmerism habituate us to indulge in those forms of "mass ecstasy" Karl Mannheim believes to be characteristic of our age? And if so, whether it be in major or minor degree, is not the very citadel we claim to be defending in process of being at once undermined and progressively deserted? How can we now claim to be the champions of freedom of the person and of institutions dedicated to its growth? And what, finally, of that hallmark of healthy propaganda—the integrity of a sincere person? For how many (of those, for instance, who have read *The Hucksters*) can the word sincerity be any longer used without an accompanying sense of nausea or at least an awareness of the practice and tolerance of its opposite?

4. The Appeal to Authority

As already mentioned, most of what we know has to be accepted on the authority of others. As the amount of what we need to know for life in the modern world increases, so does our dependence on outside authority. A corollary consequence is that increased prestige tends to attach to the channels through which knowledge of all kinds comes to us. A sensational example of this truth is the famous Orson Welles broadcast, "The Invasion from Mars" (an ironical example, incidentally, of unwitting "organized persuasion"!). Among the many contributory causes of the panic this program precipitated, perhaps the most decisive was the listener's belief in the authenticity of radio. For millions, radio speaks with the voice of authority.[5]

This almost inevitable "deference" on our part easily lends itself to exploitation—both good and bad—by propagandists. Proper substantiation of an argument, as Aristotle said, requires the citing of evidence, the appeal to authority. Improper substantiation aids and abets an undiscriminating and credulous subservience, tractable *mass*-mindedness, not an exacting, critical, and individual awareness.

Here, too, commercial advertising is a convenient and accessible source of evidence, providing ample proof of the effectiveness of this technique and examples both of its legitimate and of its more questionable uses. The reader is urged to identify samples of both kinds. In the process, he will discover interesting clues to where, in popular estimation, authority nowadays resides. Commonly found are appeals, both valid and invalid, to statistics, science, and so-called "experts," sometimes identified but often not.

---

[4] *Ibid.*, p. 83.
[5] For analysis of the fear, presuppositions, and susceptibilities that occasioned the Martian panic see Cantril, Hadley, *The Invasion from Mars*, Princeton University Press, Princeton, 1940.

Whatever the reference, the wary listener or reader is advised always to ask himself two questions: (1) Is the appeal to authority strictly relevant to the claim made? (2) Can the authority quoted be checked? Thus, if statistics are cited, are we told or can we discover their origin? If a personal authority is given, is he named? Is it, for instance, adequate to claim that "many doctors" or "medical experts" vouch for this or that?

5. False Association

In our daily intercourse we meet and deal with one another seemingly in the light of day. But our true life flows underground; it is a subterranean stream. Were we to "unearth" this stream of consciousness, we should discover it to be composed of currents and eddies, distinct in origin but converging, in due course, and running into one another. In their totality they constitute the uneven flow of our life's passage.

Much that has meaning for us (things and persons cared for, remembered incidents), our reaction to and behavior in a given situation, our hates and fears, our envy and sense of guilt—all have origins. All stem from these once-distinct currents and eddies of our past. Though mostly unremembered at the conscious level, facets of our experience are thus linked in an intricate web of inextricable threads. This is what is meant by association.

It is by subconscious association of ideas far more than by reason (which is a disciplined and cultivated faculty) that many of us come by our value judgments. It follows, therefore, that we are peculiarly susceptible to associations of ideas suggested to us and are the less prone to subject them to reasoned scrutiny. Because we are moved, we "feel" justified and do not pause to ask if we are being rational. Indeed we sometimes fortify ourselves against reason by clothing our emotional attitudes with a seeming rationale, which we achieve by a process of false reasoning known as "rationalization." This is instinctual man's grudging concession to the faculty of reason.

Much of the beauty and ambivalent power of language is concerned with its associative significance. Certain words become highly charged by virtue of their associations. The skilful propagandist knows how to exploit the use of such words and thus to tap sources of deep feeling in us and to attach them, as it were, to attitudes or actions he seeks to promote. For instance, we have seen how Kate Smith used the associative value of patriotic symbols. Sex and religion (and their verbal and pictorial symbols) are other sources of evocative association. We have only to turn the pages of any popular magazine to observe the false associations connected with sex. A subtle example of religious association, the more insidious for relying only on its stylistic overtones of association with Biblical writing, is an advertisement that appeared some years ago in *Life* magazine. It was in the early years of the war. A full-page illustration depicted a man prostrate in an armchair in his living room, the floor littered with newspapers, all of them with war headlines. In the man's limp hand was one such paper bearing the banner headline INVASION. Under the picture, in modest type, was this caption: "In times of conflict there is Peace in beer. In these bewildered times where shall a man turn to replenish the wells of his courage, to repair the walls of his faith?"

Wartime admittedly provided unusual opportunity for such insensitive and false association of ideas.

> During the war, imagination triumphed over conscience among advertisers who "ingeniously" related their products to the war effort. Radio commercials were not immune from this technique. A commercial dentist, for example, suggests that a victory smile helps boost morale and that we can have that smile by purchasing our dentures from him. So, too, a clothing manufacturer reminds listeners that morale is a precious asset in time of war and that smart clothes, more particularly Selfridge Lane Clothes, give a man confidence, and courage . . . and a manufacturer of cosmetics becomes solicitous about the imbalance in the sex ratio resulting from the war. "Fewer men around because of war? Competition keen? Keep your skin smooth. Keep attractive for the boys in the service when they come marching home."[6]

The public's romantic sentiments associated with stars of radio and screen likewise result in strange distortions of logical thinking. Whatever the obscure and complex origins in our disorganized and troubled psyche of this form of "mass ecstasy," its associative value is too well-known to be overlooked. Even the government now pays obsequious court to these modern idols of the public in the hope that they will "associate" their personality—and voice or face—with the furtherance of some public appeal. The war years provided countless examples. But in peace, too, all manner of actions and attitudes are thus canvassed. We are influenced to "transfer" (irrationally) our admiration, for instance, for a radio star to an admiration of all he says. That he should say something becomes of itself the guarantee of its validity. The inherent logic, or lack of logic, of what he says escapes us. This is the height of unreason.

The use of words with a low boiling point of emotional association is one of the great dangers of current propaganda. It is a ready means of smearing decent people and of short-circuiting true evidence of guilt. To the anti-Semite the word "Jew" is sufficient in itself to condemn those to whom it is applied. In Russia the word "capitalist" and with us "communist" have become "umbrella" terms by which to arouse general prejudice and antagonisms—ahead of or even without specific evidence. For this reason propaganda is particularly dangerous in times of strain and tension. We are emotionally "trigger happy" and tend to the prejudgment of issues. Fire a shot, and the whole herd starts off in panic.

The many ramifications of false association defy detailed analysis. Again the reader is urged to unearth his own examples and to ponder their implications. How have we come to be this way? How can we safeguard our independence, the freedom of our personality? How does all this bear on our chances for victory in the struggle for men's minds?

[6] *Broadcasting the War*, Office of Radio Research, Bureau of Intelligence, Office of War Information, 1943, p. 37.

6. Herd Instinct

We may mention one final example of propaganda techniques, which is in some respects related to false association. Clyde Miller calls it the "Band Wagon" device and thus defines it:

> . . . a technique to make us follow the crowd, to accept the propagandist's program *en masse*. Here the theme is: "Everybody's doing it. . . ." Because he wants us to follow the crowd in masses, the propagandist directs his appeal to groups held together by common ties of religion, race, environment, sex, vocation, nationality. . . . All the artifices of flattery are used to harness the fears and hatreds, prejudices and biases, convictions and ideals common to the group; thus emotion is made to push and pull the group on to the Band Wagon.[7]

The appeal to the herd instinct has obvious virtues and equally obvious defects. How we differentiate these depends on our attitude to the nature and destiny of man. Is he, as we believe, individual, distinct, to be reverenced in his own right? Or is he, as in collectivist societies, merely significant and only to be tolerated as he functions as a member of the group or mass? The answer, of course, is that he is neither—in his entirety. Man is individual and he is also a social animal. Our own view of life, however, stresses the former and aspires to a system of society that provides the fullest scope for individuality compatible with the overriding needs of the collective group.

Many kinds of conformity are necessary and desirable. But we must be clear in each instance why they are so. There is nothing virtuous, *per se*, in climbing on the bandwagon; we need to be there only when we must go places together. But because we are all in a degree lonely and diffident and often uncertain of our purpose, the temptation is great to save ourselves the effort of individual decision and go with the crowd. Some are even fearful of standing out from the herd—even when strongly motivated to do so. It often takes courage to be different. As a nation we are, on the whole, rather markedly conformist. We tend to look askance at the eccentric, the man who is "off center." How and why we are so, as compared with some other nations, merits considerable thought. It is a characteristic to beware of, lest we unwittingly convert it into an unreasonable and restrictive tyranny over the individual's right to be himself.

The pressure to conform is today greater, in some respects, than it used to be, because of exploitation of the herd instinct by means of the mass media of communication. It thus behooves us all the more to subject such appeals to the question "What for?" To stimulate further inquiry, a few examples may be cited: (1) Is the fact that many equate success in life with making money sufficient reason for us to do likewise? Much advertising suggests that it is. There are those, even, who equate it with the American way of life. (2) Is the fact that "more people" smoke a certain brand of cigarette reasonable grounds for us to follow their example?

---

[7] Miller, Clyde R., "What Everybody Should Know about Propaganda," Commission for Propaganda Analysis, New York, 25¢, p. 19.

(3) Because some fashion designer lowers the skirt line three inches, is it necessary or expedient (it may be—but we should be clear why!) for women to restock their wardrobe? The accumulation of further instances will serve to clarify not only the variety of false assumptions implicit in such appeals, but the extent to which we are nowadays subjected to appeals, warnings, and guidance by people and agencies both truly and falsely solicitous for our welfare. Never were there so many anglers for men's souls, men's purses, men's political allegiance.

We have thus far stressed the ubiquitous reach and the refined techniques of modern propaganda and the peculiar degree of our susceptibility to its appeals. But we shall have misled the reader if we have induced the thought that we are consequently as straws in the wind, helplessly blown about by the gusts of organized persuasion. For this is not so. Paradoxically, indeed, the very psychology that renders us susceptible under certain conditions makes us almost obstinately resistant under others. What are the variant conditions that produce such antithetical results? . . .

The essential fact to grasp is that propaganda is effective only when its seeds are dropped on fertile soil. *Susceptibility must precede response.* No propagandist, good or bad, who fails to understand this point and to adapt his techniques accordingly can hope to succeed. Propaganda is not magic but manipulation.

Consider three examples that prove this point. Hitler and Goebbels could not have succeeded had not the German people desired in some sense to hear the lies and half-truths that were told them. A complex of prior factors in the German situation created predispositions without which Nazism could not have triumphed. Or consider, by way of contrast, the 1948 Presidential election here in the United States. Despite a formidable barrage of largely one-sided propaganda, the people stood their ground and appeared impervious to organized persuasion. Consider, likewise, the growth and ultimate triumph at the polls of the Labour party in Great Britain, achieved over many years with relatively meager campaign funds and in face of an almost consistently hostile press. These and similar examples should rid us of the notion that even in an age of mass communication men are mere driftwood. Indeed, we are in some respects less open to conviction than we ought to be. What, then, is the true conclusion to be drawn about the power of propaganda?

We might say, for a start, that men are not easily budged when deep convictions (whether rational or irrational) or what they feel to be their primary interests are involved. We might go on to claim that where habits of thought or ways of life are solidly entrenched, resistance to propaganda will be strong. Habit, indeed, is frequently more powerful than thought as an influence on attitude or action. We might add, too, that men will be more independent, and therefore less susceptible, where propaganda has reference to circumstances or issues with which they have first hand acquaintance. They will be more susceptible where the issues are such as they themselves cannot verify.

The 1948 Presidential election offers a case in point. The main issues, which were domestic, were clear to the people and touched off deep convictions and clear needs from which the great majority of citizens could not, therefore, be distracted. On the other hand, if the main issue had had reference to Russia, for instance, their susceptibility would have been greater, for few had firsthand evidence on Russia. Thus, propaganda will be the more effective—and the more dangerous—as it relates to matters beyond people's immediate ken, though seemingly relevant to their main interests or convictions. Here the propagandist will have the advantage of being able to manipulate facts that people cannot check, while playing upon sentiments all too easily aroused.

Destructive propaganda has this advantage: it can manipulate habitual attitudes by unscrupulously playing on people's ill-developed powers of discrimination. It can associate true needs with false or irrelevant ends. Much commercial advertising is of this kind. Constructive propaganda, where it involves appeal to reason or the subordination of self-centered interests, is likely to run foul of habitual and selfish modes of outlook and the dominance of these over reason. All social reform involves the breaking of adhesions of the mind and the loosening of the hold of habit on our outlook. Thus with respect to organized persuasion, it is, on one side at least, less our susceptibility than our accumulated powers of resistance of which we should become aware. Conservatism resists conquest.

63. REQUISITE CONDITIONS
FOR PROPAGANDA SUCCESS
by Paul F. Lazarsfeld and Robert K. Merton *

What are the conditions for the effective use of mass media for what might be called "propaganda for social objectives"—the promotion, let us say, of non-discriminatory race relations, or of educational reforms, or of positive attitudes toward organized labor? Research indicates that, at least, one or more of three conditions must be satisfied if this propaganda is to prove effective. These conditions may be briefly designated as (1) monopolization (2) canalization rather than change of basic values and (3) supplementary face to face contact. Each of these conditions merit some discussion.

* Paul F. Lazarsfeld, professor of sociology and director of the Bureau of Applied Social Research at Columbia University, author and coauthor of numerous books including *Radio and the Printed Page, Radio Listening in America, Continuities in Social Research, The People's Choice, Voting,* and *Personal Influence.* Robert K. Merton, professor of sociology and associate director of the Bureau of Applied Social Research at Columbia University, author and coauthor of numerous works including *Mass Persuasion* and *Social Theory and Social Structure,* and coeditor of *Continuities in Social Research, Reader in Bureaucracy,* and *Sociology Today.* This selection is from Paul F. Lazarsfeld and Robert K. Merton, "Mass Communication, Popular Taste and Organized Social Action," in Lyman Bryson (ed.), *The Communication of Ideas,* Institute for Religious and Social Studies, New York, 1948, pp. 113-118. By permission of the publisher.

MONOPOLIZATION

This situation obtains when there is little or no opposition in the mass media to the diffusion of values, policies or public images. That is to say, monopolization of the mass media occurs in the absence of counter propaganda.

In this restricted sense, monopolization of the mass media is found in diverse circumstances. It is, of course, indigenous to the political structure of authoritarian society, where access to the media of communication is wholly closed to those who oppose the official ideology. The evidence suggests that this monopoly played some part in enabling the Nazis to maintain their control of the German people.

But this same situation is approximated in other social systems. During the war, for example, our government utilized the radio, with some success, to promote and to maintain identification with the war effort. The effectiveness of these morale building efforts was in large measure due to the virtually complete absence of counter propaganda. . . .

Neutralization occurs, for example, as a result of preelection campaigns by Republicans and Democrats. By and large . . . the propaganda issued by each of these parties neutralizes the effect of the other's propaganda. Were both parties to forego their campaigning through the mass media entirely, it is altogether likely that the net effect would be to reproduce the present distribution of votes.

This general pattern has been described by Kenneth Burke in his *Attitudes Toward History* ". . . businessmen compete with one another by trying to *praise their own commodity* more persuasively than their rivals, whereas politicians compete by slandering the *opposition*. When you add it all up, you get a grand total of absolute praise for business and grand total of absolute slander for politics."

To the extent that opposing political propaganda in the mass media are balanced, the net effect is negligible. The virtual monopolization of the media for given social objectives, however, will produce discernible effects upon audiences.

CANALIZATION

Prevailing beliefs in the enormous power of mass communications appear to stem from successful cases of monopolistic propaganda or from advertising. But the leap from the efficacy of advertising to the assumed efficacy of propaganda aimed at deeprooted attitudes and ego involved behavior is as unwarranted as it is dangerous. Advertising is typically directed toward the canalizing of preexisting behavior patterns or attitudes. It seldom seeks to instil new attitudes or to create significantly new behavior patterns. "Advertising pays" because it generally deals with a simple psychological situation. For Americans who have been socialized in the use of a toothbrush, it makes relatively little difference which brand of toothbrush they use. Once the gross pattern of behavior or the generic attitude has been established, it can be canalized in one direction or another. Resistance is slight. But mass propaganda typically meets a more complex situation. It may seek objectives which are at odds with deeplying attitudes. It may seek to reshape rather than to canalize current systems of values. And the successes of advertising may only highlight the failures of propaganda. Much of the current propaganda which is aimed at abolishing deepseated ethnic and racial prejudices, for example, seems to have had little effectiveness.

Media of mass communication, then, have been effectively used to canalize basic attitudes but there is little evidence of their having served to change these attitudes.

SUPPLEMENTATION

Mass propaganda which is neither monopolistic nor canalizing in character may, nonetheless, prove effective if it meets a third condition: supplementation through face to face contacts.

A case in point will illustrate the interplay between mass media and face to face influences. The seeming propagandistic success achieved some years ago by Father Coughlin does not appear, upon inspection, to have resulted primarily from the propaganda content of his radio talks. It was, rather, the product of these centralized propaganda talks *and* widespread local organizations which arranged for their members to listen to him, followed by discussions among themselves concerning the social views he had expressed. This combination of a central supply of propaganda (Coughlin's addresses on a nationwide network), the coordinated distribution of newspapers and pamphlets and locally organized face to face discussions among relatively small groups—this complex of reciprocal reinforcement by mass media and personal relations proved spectacularly successful.

Students of mass movements have come to repudiate the view that mass propaganda in and of itself creates or maintains the movement. Nazism did not attain its brief moment of hegemony by capturing the mass media of communication. The media played an ancillary role, supplementing the use of organized violence, organized distribution of rewards for conformity and organized centers of local indoctrination. The Soviet Union has also made large and impressive use of mass media for indoctrinating enormous populations with appropriate ideologies. But the organizers of indoctrination saw to it that the mass media did not operate alone. "Red corners," "reading huts" and "listening stations" comprised meeting places in which groups of citizens were exposed to the mass media in common. The fifty-five thousand reading rooms and clubs which had come into being by 1933 enabled the local ideological elite to talk over with rank and file readers the content of what they read. The relative scarcity of radios in private homes again made for group listening and group discussions of what had been heard.

In these instances, the machinery of mass persuasion included face to face contact in local organizations as an adjunct to the mass media. The privatized individual response to the materials presented through the channels of mass communication was considered inadequate for transforming exposure to propaganda into effectiveness of propaganda. In a society such as our own, where the pattern of bureaucratization has not yet become so pervasive or, at least, not so clearly crystallized, it has likewise been found that mass media prove most effective in conjunction with local centers of organized face to face contact.

Several factors contribute to the enhanced effectiveness of this joining of mass media and direct personal contact. Most clearly, the local discussions serve to reinforce the content of mass propaganda. Such mutual confirmation produces a "clinching effect." Secondly, the central media lessen the task of the local organizer, and the personnel requirements for such subalterns need not be as rigorous in a popular movement. The subalterns need not set forth the propaganda content for themselves, but need only pilot potential converts to the radio where the doctrine is being expounded. Thirdly, the appearance of a representative of the movement on a nationwide network, or his mention in the national press, serves to symbolize the legitimacy and significance of the movement. It is no powerless, inconsequential enterprise. The mass media, as we have seen, confer status. And the status of the national movement reflects back on the status of the local cells, thus consolidating the tentative decisions of its members. In this interlocking arrangement, the local organizer ensures an audience for the national speaker and the national speaker validates the status of the local organizer. . . .

The mass media prove most effective when they operate in a situation of virtual "psychological monopoly," or when the objective is one of canalizing rather than modifying basic attitudes or when they operate in conjunction with face to face contacts.

But these three conditions are rarely satisfied conjointly in propaganda for social objectives. To the degree that monopolization of attention is rare, opposing propagandas have free play in a democracy. And, by and large, basic social issues involve more than a mere canalizing of preexistent basic attitudes; they call, rather, for substantial changes in attitude and behavior. Finally, for the most obvious of reasons, the close collaboration of mass media and locally organized centers for face to face contact has seldom been achieved by groups striving for planned social change. Such programs are expensive. And it is precisely these groups which seldom have the large resources needed for these expensive programs. The forward looking groups at the edges of the power structure do not ordinarily have the large financial means of the contented groups at the center.

As a result of this threefold situation, the present role of mass media is largely confined to peripheral social concerns and the media do not exhibit the degree of social power commonly attributed to them.

By the same token, and in view of the present organization of business ownership and control of the mass media, they have served to cement the structure of our society. Organized business does approach a virtual "psychological monopoly" of the mass media. Radio commercials and newspaper advertisements are, of course, premised on a system which has been termed free enterprise. Moreover, the world of commerce is primarily concerned with canalizing rather than radically changing basic attitudes; it seeks only to create preferences for one rather than another brand of product. Face to face contacts with those who have been socialized in our culture serve primarily to reinforce the prevailing culture patterns.

Thus, the very conditions which make for the maximum effectiveness of the mass media of communication operate toward the maintenance of the going social and cultural structure rather than toward its change.

64. PROPAGANDA IN A DEMOCRATIC SOCIETY
by Aldous Huxley*

"The doctrines of Europe," Jefferson wrote, "were that men in numerous associations cannot be restrained within the limits of order and justice, except by forces physical and moral wielded over them by authorities independent of their will. . . . We (the founders of the new American democracy) believe that man was a rational animal, endowed by nature with rights, and with an innate sense of justice, and that he could be restrained from wrong, and protected in right, by moderate powers, confided to persons of his own choice and held to their duties by dependence on his own will." To post-Freudian ears, this kind of language seems touchingly quaint and ingenuous. Human beings are a good deal less rational and innately just than the optimists of the eighteenth century supposed. On the other hand they are neither so morally blind nor so hopelessly unreasonable as the pessimists of the twentieth would have us believe. In spite of the Id and the Unconscious, in spite of endemic neurosis and the prevalence of low IQ's, most men and women are probably decent enough and sensible enough to be trusted with the direction of their own destinies.

Democratic institutions are devices for reconciling social order with individual freedom and initiative, and for making the immediate power of a country's rulers subject to the ultimate power of the ruled. The fact that, in western Europe and America, these devices have worked, all things considered, not too badly is proof enough that the eighteenth-century optimists were not entirely wrong. Given a fair chance, human beings can govern themselves, and govern themselves better, though perhaps with less mechanical efficiency, than they can be governed by "authorities independent of their will." Given a fair chance, I repeat; for the fair chance is an indispensable prerequisite. No people that passes abruptly from a state of subservience under the rule of a despot to the completely unfamiliar state of political independence can be said to have a fair chance of making democratic institutions work. Again, no people in a precarious economic condition has a fair chance of being able to govern itself democratically. Liberalism flourishes in an atmosphere of prosperity and declines as declining prosperity makes it necessary for the government to intervene ever

* Novelist and essayist. This selection is from Aldous Huxley, "Propaganda in a Democratic Society," *Brave New World Revisited,* Harper & Brothers, New York, 1958, pp. 37-46. Copyright © 1958 by Aldous Huxley. Reprinted by permission of Harper & Brothers and the author.

more frequently and drastically in the affairs of its subjects. Over-population and over-organization are two conditions which . . . deprive a society of a fair chance of making democratic institutions work effectively. We see, then, that there are certain historical, economic, demographic and technological conditions which make it very hard for Jefferson's rational animals, endowed by nature with inalienable rights and an innate sense of justice, to exercise their reason, claim their rights and act justly within a democratically organized society. We in the West have been supremely fortunate in having been given our fair chance of making the great experiment in self-government. Unfortunately it now looks as though, owing to recent changes in our circumstances, this infinitely precious fair chance were being, little by little, taken away from us. And this, of course, is not the whole story. These blind impersonal forces are not the only enemies of individual liberty and democratic institutions. There are also forces of another, less abstract character, forces that can be deliberately used by power-seeking individuals whose aim is to establish partial or complete control over their fellows. Fifty years ago, when I was a boy, it seemed completely self-evident that the bad old days were over, that torture and massacre, slavery, and the persecution of heretics, were things of the past. Among people who wore top hats, traveled in trains, and took a bath every morning such horrors were simply out of the question. After all, we were living in the twentieth century. A few years later these people who took daily baths and went to church in top hats were committing atrocities on a scale undreamed of by the benighted Africans and Asiatics. In the light of recent history it would be foolish to suppose that this sort of thing cannot happen again. It can and, no doubt, it will. But in the immediate future there is some reason to believe that the punitive methods of *1984* will give place to the reinforcements and manipulations of *Brave New World*.

There are two kinds of propaganda—rational propaganda in favor of action that is consonant with the enlightened self-interest of those who make it and those to whom it is addressed, and non-rational propaganda that is not consonant with anybody's enlightened self-interest, but is dictated by, and appeals to, passion. Where the actions of individuals are concerned there are motives more exalted than enlightened self-interest, but where collective action has to be taken in the fields of politics and economics, enlightened self-interest is probably the highest of effective motives. If politicians and their constituents always acted to promote their own or their country's long-range self-interest, this world would be an earthly paradise. As it is, they often act against their own interests, merely to gratify their least creditable passions; the world, in consequence, is a place of misery. Propaganda in favor of action that is consonant with enlightened self-interest appeals to reason by means of logical arguments based upon the best available evidence fully and honestly set forth. Propaganda in favor of action dictated by the impulses that are below self-interest offers false, garbled or incomplete evidence, avoids logical argument and seeks to influence its victims by the mere repetition of catchwords, by the furious denunciation of foreign or domestic scapegoats, and by cunningly associating the lowest passions with the highest ideals, so that atrocities come to be perpetrated in the name of God and the most cynical kind of *Realpolitik* is treated as a matter of religious principle and patriotic duty.

In John Dewey's words, "a renewal of faith in common human nature, in its potentialities in general, and in its power in particular to respond to reason and truth, is a surer bulwark against totalitarianism than a demonstration of material success or a devout worship of special legal and political forms." The power to respond to reason and truth exists in all of us. But so, unfortunately, does the tendency to respond to unreason and falsehood—particularly in those cases where the falsehood evokes some enjoyable emotion, or where the appeal to unreason strikes some answering chord in the primitive, subhuman depths of our being. In certain fields of activity men have learned to respond to reason and truth pretty consistently. The authors of learned articles do not appeal to the passions of their fellow scientists and technologists. They set forth what, to the best of their knowledge, is the truth about some particular aspect of reality, they use reason to explain the facts they have observed and they support their point of view with arguments that appeal to reason in other people. All this is fairly easy in the fields of physical science and technology. It is much more difficult in the fields of politics and religion and ethics. Here the relevant facts often elude us. As for the meaning of the facts, that of course depends upon the particular system of ideas, in terms of which you choose to interpret them. And these are not the only difficulties that confront the rational truth-seeker. In public and in private life, it often happens that there is simply no time to collect the relevant facts or to weigh their significance. We are forced to act on insufficient evidence and by a light considerably less steady than that of logic. With the best will in the world, we cannot always be completely truthful or consistently rational. All that is in our power is to be as truthful and rational as circumstances permit us to be, and to respond as well as we can to the limited truth and imperfect reasonings offered for our consideration by others.

"If a nation expects to be ignorant and free," said Jefferson, "it expects what never was and never will be. . . . The people cannot be safe without information. Where the press is free, and every man able to read, all is safe." Across the Atlantic another passionate believer in reason was thinking about the same time, in almost precisely similar terms. Here is what John Stuart Mill wrote of his father, the utilitarian philosopher, James Mill: "So complete was his reliance upon the influence of reason over the minds of mankind, whenever it is allowed to reach them, that he felt as if all would be gained, if the whole population were able to read, and if all sorts of opinions were allowed to be addressed to them by word or in writing, and if by the suffrage they could nominate a legislature to give effect to the opinions they had adopted." *All is safe, all would be gained!* Once more we hear the note of eighteen-century optimism. Jefferson, it is true, was a realist as well as an optimist. He knew by bitter experience that the freedom of the press can be shamefully abused. "Nothing," he declared, "can now be believed which is seen in a newspaper." And yet, he insisted (and we can only agree with him), "within the pale of truth, the

press is a noble institution, equally the friend of science and civil liberty."
Mass communication, in a word, is neither good nor bad; it is simply a
force and, like any other force, it can be used either well or ill. Used in one
way, the press, the radio and the cinema are indispensable to the survival
of democracy. Used in another way, they are among the most powerful
weapons in the dictator's armory. In the field of mass communications as in
almost every other field of enterprise, technological progress has hurt the
Little Man and helped the Big Man. As lately as fifty years ago, every
democratic country could boast of a great number of small journals and
local newspapers. Thousands of country editors expressed thousands of
independent opinions. Somewhere or other almost anybody could get almost
anything printed. Today the press is still legally free; but most of the
little papers have disappeared. The cost of woodpulp, of modern printing
machinery and of syndicated news is too high for the Little Man. In the
totalitarian East there is political censorship, and the media of mass communication are controlled by the State. In the democratic West there is
economic censorship and the media of mass communication are controlled
by members of the Power Elite. Censorship by rising costs and the concentration of communication power in the hands of a few big concerns is
less objectionable than State ownership and government propaganda; but
certainly it is not something of which a Jeffersonian democrat could possibly approve.

In regard to propaganda the early advocates of universal literacy and
a free press envisaged only two possibilities: the propaganda might be
true, or it might be false. They did not foresee what in fact has happened,
above all in our Western capitalist democracies—the development of a vast
mass communications industry, concerned in the main neither with the true
nor the false, but with the unreal, the more or less totally irrelevant. In a
word, they failed to take into account man's almost infinite appetite for
distractions.

In the past most people never got a chance of fully satisfying this
appetite. They might long for distractions, but the distractions were not
provided. Christmas came but once a year, feasts were "solemn and rare,"
there were few readers and very little to read, and the nearest approach
to a neighborhood movie theater was the parish church, where the performances, though frequent, were somewhat monotonous. For conditions even
remotely comparable to those now prevailing we must return to imperial
Rome, where the populace was kept in good humor by frequent, gratuitous
doses of many kinds of entertainment—from poetical dramas to gladiatorial
fights, from recitations of Virgil to all-out boxing, from concerts to military
reviews and public executions. But even in Rome there was nothing like the
non-stop distraction now provided by newspapers and magazines, by radio,
television and the cinema. In *Brave New World* non-stop distractions of
the most fascinating nature (the feelies, orgy-porgy, centrifugal bumble-
puppy) are deliberately used as instruments of policy, for the purpose of
preventing people from paying too much attention to the realities of the
social and political situation. The other world of religion is different from
the other world of entertainment; but they resemble one another in being

most decidedly "not of this world." Both are distractions and, if lived in too continuously, both can become, in Marx's phrase, "the opium of the people" and so a threat to freedom. Only the vigilant can maintain their liberties, and only those who are constantly and intelligently on the spot can hope to govern themselves effectively by democratic procedures. A society, most of whose members spend a great part of their time, not on the spot, not here and now and in the calculable future, but somewhere else, in the irrelevant other worlds of sport and soap opera, of mythology and metaphysical fantasy, will find it hard to resist the encroachments of those who would manipulate and control it.

In their propaganda today's dictators rely for the most part on repetition, suppression and rationalization—the repetition of catchwords which they wish to be accepted as true, the suppression of facts which they wish to be ignored, the arousal and rationalization of passions which may be used in the interests of the Party or the State. As the art and science of manipulation come to be better understood, the dictators of the future will doubtless learn to combine these techniques with the non-stop distractions which, in the West, are now threatening to drown in a sea of irrelevance the rational propaganda essential to the maintenance of individual liberty and the survival of democratic institutions.

CHAPTER IX

Political Propaganda:
American Election Campaigns

As any reasonably sophisticated observer must have noted during the last presidential campaign, hammering out a voting majority on the national level has become one of the more highly skilled public arts. There is no single "right way" to achieve success, since each candidate must adapt his technique to his own personality and style, to the nature of the party which supports him, and to a variety of conditions unique to each campaign. But there are innumerable wrong ways, which candidates instinctively sense or learn through painful trial and error.

Although popular tastes in American political oratory have changed drastically in the past century, certain prerequisites for successful political campaigning endure. The campaigner must appear well informed, he must possess the common touch, and above all, he must strike the magic note of sincerity.

But if an ambitious candidate has difficulty projecting "sincerity," some people believe this deficiency can be overcome by sufficient coaching. Murray Chotiner represents the school of thought which holds that politicking is principally a matter of learning the tricks of the trade and trusting to the credulity of the public. Paul Douglas, on the other hand, takes a more hopeful and balanced view of campaigning, holding to the more liberal rationalistic view that campaigns can illuminate both the candidate and his views, thereby making a healthy contribution to the democratic process. If democracy succeeds, it will be because Mr. Douglas's views (and Adlai Stevenson's) represent a more realistic estimate of the electorate and its capacities than do Mr. Chotiner's.

Harry Truman's campaign style reflected his conviction that people are usually more interested in the personality and "human" aspects of a candidate than in any detailed exposition of his views. Mr. Rovere's brief account gives more than a little insight into Mr. Truman's successful campaign in 1948—successful in part because Mr. Dewey seemed somewhat too cool, too aloof, too impersonal, and—perhaps—too slick.

No one can be sure how influential the contrasting campaign approaches of Richard Nixon and John Kennedy were in the 1960 campaign, but there can be no doubt that they revealed something significant about the candidates and about the American public. The aristocratic flavor as well as the intensity of Mr. Kennedy's nature were reflected in his mode of persuasion; Mr. Nixon's approach, on the other hand, seemed to tell more about his appraisal of the American public than about Mr. Nixon. Various commentators observed that Mr. Nixon projected a folksy, optimistic, somewhat saccharine image of himself which was in marked contrast with the basically reserved, coolly realistic, hardheaded politician most journalists have found him to be when off the hustings.

It is now generally conceded that TV helped Mr. Kennedy win the 1960 election (although other factors such as the recession, the big Democratic registration drive, Mr. Kennedy's call to Martin Luther King's family, etc., were also important) by helping dispel popular skepticism about his Presidential capacities growing out of his youthfulness and alleged inexperience. However this may be, there is no agreement that the over-all political impact of TV represents a hopeful factor for democracy.

Writing before the Kennedy-Nixon TV debates, Emmett Hughes cast a sweeping eye on the political consequences of TV and its potentialities for good and ill. While granting that TV, like every new communication medium, can either render a national service or debase the public opinion process, Mr. Hughes tends to a pessimistic outlook. He doubts that TV debates will enable voters to form a more intelligent judgment of candidates' qualifications or even obtain a clearer picture of their political views. Rather, he fears that the temptations to resort to forensic trickery and to seek to project a favorable public "image" rather than truly illuminate the issues or the man will prove hard to resist. Some of this pessimism was shared by Douglass Cater after his experience as a member of a panel of newsmen which questioned the two candidates.

On the other hand, Philip Stern feels that, compared to the alternatives, there is much to be said for the educational and informational values of the debates. Obviously, no final judgment can be formed from one campaign. Whether Mr. Kennedy will risk his presidential prestige in 1964 by submitting to another series of "Great Debates" remains to be seen. Certainly the pressures to continue these performances, considering the public interest which was aroused in 1960, will be great.

Several speeches are included in this section for propaganda analysis purposes. Richard Nixon's defense of his "secret" $18,000 political fund in 1952 has won a place alongside Bryan's "Cross of Gold" speech as one of the classic pieces of salesmanship in American political history. Charged with accepting funds which would unduly obligate him to the contributors and the interests they represented, Mr. Nixon's carefully staged defense showed a shrewd awareness of the susceptibilities of a variety of American groups and demonstrated an unerring instinct for the symbols and values cherished by most Americans.

Harry Truman's free-swinging, roundhouse style of attack, perhaps representative of a passing generation of politicians, was well adapted to arousing the partisan fervor of party regulars—and to raising the hackles of his foes.

Governor J. Lindsay Almond's last-gasp oratorical effort, just before yielding to judicial pressure for integrated schools in Virginia, doubtless left few listeners unmoved—one way or another! Students of propaganda techniques will find a gold mine of illustrations in this sample of a certain type of Southern oratory.

65. CAMPAIGNING: "SCIENTIFIC" CYNICISM
by Robert Bendiner*

Just a year ago this fall pupils attending the Republican Party's three-day seminar in political campaigning sat at the feet of Murray Chotiner. . . .

Although for several reasons that needn't be probed here I am not a Republican state chairman, it has been my privilege to absorb the Chotiner Lectures, and I am ready to testify that they are to the ambitious office seeker what the Boy Scout Handbook is to the cub.

Here you learn, in simple precepts, the heart of a profession. For example, people want to feel that they are selecting the candidate of their party, Professor Chotiner says, "rather than having the candidate tell them 'I am going to run, hell or high water.'" Very well, let them feel it. "It is really quite simple. . . . All you have to do is to get a number of the people talking, 'Now if we can only get so and so to run for the office.'" In no time at all, the Professor assures us, you will find the party drafting so-and-so as the people's choice.

It may be that if Harold Stassen had studied under Dr. Chotiner instead of fooling around with disarmament all these months, Christian Herter would have been the people's choice for Vice-President instead of winding up as just one of the people.

BE CONSTRUCTIVE, BE IRRELEVANT

Be constructive, of course, Dr. Chotiner advises, but get this straight: You must start "deflating" a possible opponent as much as a year before you even launch your own campaign. "If you do not . . . the odds are that you are going to be doomed to defeat."

If he starts to deflate *you,* just keep quiet. Maybe no one is listening and you will only "call it to the attention of the voting public." Should you find the attack really getting home, however, and you are forced to reply, "do so with an attack of your own against the opposition for having launched it in the first place." The famous "Checkers" speech of Richard Nixon, Dr. Chotiner's star pupil, is a "classic" example of what can be done and one "that will live in all political history." Once you have made this kind of response, painfully sincere and wholly irrelevant, drop the whole thing. Because if you don't, your opponent will say things like " 'Well, he didn't answer this part' and your whole campaign will be put on the defensive." Just say, instead, "That subject has been answered. Let us go on to the next issue."

The lectures are full of this homey wisdom. "We never put out the complete voting record of our candidate," Dr. Chotiner explains, because a

*Free-lance writer on politics and public affairs, former magazine editor, and American correspondent of *The New Statesman of London.* Author of *The Riddle of the State Department, White House Fever,* and numerous articles. This selection is from Robert Bendiner, "Chotiner Academy of Scientific Vote-catching," *The Reporter,* vol. 15, no. 4, Sept. 20, 1956, pp. 28-29. By permission of the author and publisher.

prospective voter doesn't look at the number of times the candidate was right but only at the times he was wrong. So just give the record "in general terms," like "Voted for reduction of taxes," "Voted for military preparedness," etc. Let the voter dig out the details for himself if he has the time and the know-how.

Courage is always appealing, and a good way to establish it is to have your candidate "get up in front of a meeting and say, 'I have been told that I must not talk about this subject but I am going to tell the people of our State just exactly what is going on.'" Chotiner had Mr. Nixon use this packaged courage when he ran for the Senate, and it worked wonders. Try it, the Professor advises; "you will be amazed at what happens." Rush down to your local soapbox now!

PROSPECTUS FOR PREVARICATION

There are many such tips and helpful hints in the Lectures, like letting an editor know very early in the game that you intend to do political advertising in his paper—"It may help on some of our stories."

It is a pity that such simple wisdom should be confined to so narrow a circle. What we obviously need is a full-blown graduate school, to be known, let's say, as the Machiavelli Institute of Public Affairs, bipartisan of course and open to students of all political persuasions. The catalogue might run something like this:

Handshaking and General Cordiality. Practice in the earnest grasp, the hearty pump, and the affectionate hold. Special attention to development of the warm smile and the boyish grin. How to be charming without being witty.

Flattery for Beginners. All the standard techniques, starting with infant kissing and the appropriate introduction of apple-blossom queens, beet-sugar queens, sand-and-gravel queens, and other domestic royalty. Practice in the fulsome complimenting of audiences on their absolutely unique intelligence and courage.

Elementary Slander. Basic instruction in hit-and-run tactics, innuendo, and the raising of the big doubt. Emphasis on the charitable touch, such as suggesting that an opponent is not a crook, ladies and gentlemen, but merely the willing dupe of crooks.

Advanced Slander (admission only to candidates for Senator and up). A rigid course in treason spotting, graft charging, and wholesale damnation. Field exercises in Red hunting, with or without hounds and with or without Reds.

Photography for Campaigners. Course in posing with golf club, family, and other essential props. Full-dress rehearsals as cowboy, train engineer, Sioux Indian, and Davy Crockett.

Television Techniques. Instruction in reading a speech from the tele-prompter, or "idiot board," as though the talk is being delivered off the cuff. Hollywood coaches on hand to teach prepared spontaneity, studied sincerity, and camera angles.

Political Geography. A quick course on the features and products of any local area in which the candidate expects to mount the stump: Enables the speaker to "feel especially good in these familiar surroundings which are a second home" to him, whether he is in Bilious Bluff, Ark., Upper Crust, N. Y., or Apple Core, Vt. The survey should also serve to keep him from pledging to lower tariff on slivovitz, for example, to an audience that thrives only on local bourbon.

Political Folklore. A companion course intended to help the student avoid such pitfalls as praising the British in Chicago, President Nasser in the Bronx, or Eleanor Roosevelt in Mississippi.

Pledging and Counterpledging. Advanced work in the art of promising everything to everybody all at once. Credit given only when student can offer, in one sentence and without blinking an eye, to increase government spending on public welfare, strengthen national defense, lower taxes, keep the peace, scare hell out of Russia, and balance the budget.

Double Talk and Rhetoric. Rigorous course in the use of the cliché and the ringing appeal to the Founding Fathers, along with lessons in the personal wearing of the flag. Designed to enable the pupil to sustain forty-minute flights of eloquence without preparation and without taking a position on anything.

66. CAMPAIGNING:
TRUMAN AND THE "FOLKSY" TOUCH
by Richard Rovere*

. . . The show, as a rule, gets under way after "Hail to the Chief" has been rendered by the local high-school band. Next, a local beauty, a local union man, or a local Kiwanis man hands the President, depending on where we are, a bag of peaches, a mess of celery, a miner's hat, or just the key to the city. He has become quite adept at accepting these offerings graciously and then shoving them the hell inside his car. It takes, by my unofficial clocking, one and three-quarters minutes to give the mayor, the governor, and the Democratic candidate for Congress—the two last are likely to ride along with us through their state—their cracks at the audience. Whoever comes at the end of the procession has, as they say, the unparalleled honor and glorious privilege of introducing the President. During the ten-minute layovers, Truman limits his part of the act to five minutes. He begins with local scenery, local industry, local agriculture, and local intelligence; leads from this into a description of the contempt in which the Republican Party holds the region he is passing through; goes on to a preview of the Good Society that he, given another term and the kind of Congress he wants, will create; and, penultimately, makes his plea for votes. Then, with a surer sense of timing than he shows in major addresses, he

* Staff writer for *The New Yorker* since 1944 and United States correspondent for *The Spectator.* Contributing editor, *Harper's Magazine,* 1949-1954. Author of *The Eisenhower Years* and *Senator Joe McCarthy* and coauthor (with Arthur Schlesinger, Jr.) of *The General and the President.* This selection is from Richard H. Rovere, "Letter from a Campaign Train," © 1948 *The New Yorker Magazine, Inc.,* vol. 24, no. 33, Oct. 9, 1948, pp. 69-71. By permission of the author and publisher.

pauses a moment, looks quizzically at the crowd, smiles, and asks, very humbly, "And now, howja like to meet ma family?" He cocks his head slightly to catch the response; he has the appealing look of a man who wouldn't be surprised if the answer was no but would be terribly hurt. The crowd's desire to meet the Truman women, however, never fails to exceed by a good deal its desire for repeal of the Taft-Hartley Act. When he has caught the favorable response, he says, "First, Mizz Truman," and the First Lady, who, like her husband, is more relaxed before small crowds than before large ones or photographers, parts the curtain and takes her place at his right side. Sometimes, when the crowd is very small and friendly, the President identifies Mrs. Truman as "the boss" and winks knowingly at the men in the audience. After Mrs. Truman and her admirers have exchanged greetings, the President says, "And now I'd like to have you meet my daughter, Margaret." (I thought it a nice touch that, down in the border states, he said, whether artfully or not I am unable to decide, "And now I'd like for you to meet Miss Margaret.") It involves no disrespect for Mrs. Truman to say that her daughter gets a bigger hand than she does; this country may be run by and for mothers, but its goddesses are daughters. Margaret's entrance comes closer than anything else to bringing down the house.

As soon as the Truman womenfolk have flanked the President, a railroad official, generally a vice-president of the line, who sits at a telephone in the car ahead of the President's, calls the locomotive engineer—fifteen cars, or a quarter of a mile, down the track—and tells him to get slowly under way. As the train pulls out from the station, the family waves goodbye. Mrs. Truman and Margaret then go back into the car to fix their hair for the next curtain call, leaving the President alone on the platform until the last switchman in the yards has had his look. I am certain that, no matter what the fate of the Truman administration, millions of Americans will, for the rest of their lives, have framed in their mind's eye a vivid image of the Three Travelling Trumans highballing off into the black nights of Colorado or Arizona, blending with the tall pines in the Sierras, or being slowly enveloped by the dust of the Midwestern plains. It will be a picture to cherish, and it will stand Harry Truman in good stead for the rest of his life. Travelling with him, you get the feeling that the American people who have seen him and heard him at his best would be willing to give him just about anything he wants except the Presidency.

67. CAMPAIGNING:
EXHAUSTION AND EXHILARATION
by Adlai E. Stevenson*

... In all I find in my files whole or partial texts of some 250 speeches, to as many groups, large and small, in almost as many places. How many more times I spoke I shudder now to think, and that no record remains disturbs me not at all.

What *does* disturb me is what remains! Reading them over hurriedly recalls uncomfortably some words of Froude in his life of Bunyan: "The excitement of perpetual speechmaking is fatal to the exercise of the highest powers." To "excitement" I would add "exhaustion," for sheer physical exhaustion was for me a continuous and disquieting menace to equilibrium, judgment and creative concentration. "Sleep is stealing me away" is a lovely West Indian phrase, and that wretched, blessed thief was ever at my weary elbow while I tried to think and read and write in interrupted intervals in planes and trains and hotel rooms for almost three interminable months.

But it was a glorious, heart-filling, head-filling odyssey for which I shall be forever grateful to my party, to my staff and to my fellow Americans. Their faces are a friendly, smiling sea of memory stretching from coast to coast. Bitter, ugly, false things were said and written during the campaign, I know, but not by those people. Millions of them believed in me and my party and voted for Senator Sparkman and me. Thousands even wrote gracious, flattering letters, after the election, explaining why they did *not* vote for me. They seemed to feel they owed me an explanation. I was touched and flattered, but I confess the thought occurred to me now and then that a little "X" in the right place on the ballot would have been so much easier than a long, thoughtful letter.

At least for an inexperienced candidate, I suppose we have contrived few more exacting ordeals than a Presidential campaign. You must emerge, bright and bubbling with wisdom and well-being, every morning at 8 o'clock, just in time for a charming and profound breakfast talk, shake hands with hundreds, often literally thousands, of people, make several inspiring, "newsworthy" speeches during the day, confer with political leaders along the way and with your staff all the time, write at every chance, think if possible, read mail and newspapers, talk on the telephone, talk to everybody, dictate, receive delegations, eat, with decorum—and discretion!—and ride through city after city on the back of an open car, smiling until your mouth is dehydrated by the wind, waving until the blood runs out of your arm, and then bounce gaily, confidently, masterfully into great howling halls, shaved and all made up for television with the right color shirt and tie—I always forgot—and a manuscript so defaced with

* Chief United States delegate to the United Nations. Former governor of Illinois and twice the Democratic Party candidate for the Presidency (1952 and 1956). This selection is from Adlai Stevenson, *Major Campaign Speeches of Adlai E. Stevenson*, Random House, Inc., New York, 1953, pp. xi-xiii. By permission of the publisher.

chicken tracks and last-minute jottings that you couldn't follow it, even if the spotlights weren't blinding and even if the still photographers didn't shoot you in the eye every time you looked at them. (I've often wondered what happened to all those pictures!) Then all you have to do is make a great, imperishable speech, get out through the pressing crowds with a few score autographs, your clothes intact, your hands bruised, and back to the hotel—in time to see a few important people.

But the real work has just commenced—two or three, sometimes four hours of frenzied writing and editing of the next day's immortal mouthings so you can get something to the stenographers, so they can get something to the mimeograph machines, so they can get something to the reporters, so they can get something to their papers by deadline time. (And I quickly concluded that all deadlines were yesterday!) Finally sleep, sweet sleep, steals you away, unless you worry—which I do.

The next day is the same.

But I gained weight on it. And it's as tenacious as a campaign deficit! Somehow the people sustain you, the people and a constant, sobering reminder that you are asking them to entrust to you the most awesome responsibility on earth. And, too, there is mirth mingled with the misery all along the way. They shout, "Good old Ad-lie!" If you run for office and have a slightly unusual name, let me advise you to either change it before you start, or be prepared to take other people's word for it. And I shall not soon forget about the woman in the crowd in San Francisco who reached into the car to shake hands with me, and not long after discovered that she had lost her diamond ring. Nor will I forget the warm welcome I received on a whistle stop in Bethlehem and my thanks to "the people of Allentown." My only hope is that *they* forget it! Again, out West, I warmly endorsed the impressive chairman of a meeting as a candidate for Congress, only to discover that he was not running for Congress or anything else. . . .

68. "SPOT" ANNOUNCEMENTS IN THE 1952 CAMPAIGN
by Martin Mayer*

Two men, one of them an acquaintance of the General's and the other a complete outsider, were primarily responsible for advertising by means of 20-second television spot announcements the presidential candidacy of Dwight D. Eisenhower in 1952. The acquaintance was Alfred Hollender, a slight, rather shy man then a broadcasting station manager and now head of the television department at Grey Advertising, who had met the General while supervising the U.S. propaganda radio to Germany during the war; the stranger was Rosser Reeves of Ted Bates. Hollender had come into the

* Author of *The Experts, Wall Street: Men and Money,* and numerous magazine articles. This selection is from Martin Mayer, *Madison Avenue: U.S.A.,* Harper & Brothers, New York, 1958, pp. 293-297. Copyright © 1958 by Martin Prager Mayer. Reprinted by permission of Harper & Brothers.

campaign through a letter which he wrote the General, offering his services, shortly after Eisenhower had announced that he would accept the Republican nomination if it was offered. Reeves, too, was a volunteer, though the process in his case had been more complicated: good friends from the oil business had called him up from a country club locker room and asked him to come up with a slogan which would counteract what they considered the strong effect of the Democrats' "You Never Had It So Good." Reeves told them they didn't need a slogan, they needed a plan. "If you want to elect Eisenhower," he said, "you go after maximum penetration: use spots."

Radio spot announcements, cast very much in the form of regular commercials, had been used in national elections since the Liberty League spots for Landon in 1936. Their purpose, however, had been strictly supplementary, and they were concentrated in areas where the candidate's formal speeches were broadcast at low-audience hours. If they presented any personality, it was usually a local figure endorsing the candidate rather than the candidate himself. The idea of spending a large part of the campaign budget on spot announcements, with the candidate himself as featured player, and using these spots to some extent as a substitute for broadcast campaign speeches, had never been formally suggested by anyone until 1948, when E. H. Little, chairman of Colgate-Palmolive, had the Bates agency prepare sample radio spots for Thomas E. Dewey. With the full approval of BBDO, which had handled the New York State Republican party advertising effort for some years and was planning the advertising program for the 1948 national campaign, Dewey turned down Little's suggestion.

The three basic arguments in favor of spot announcements to promote the Eisenhower candidacy were the low cost per thousand homes reached; the fact that spots, unlike full-length programs, would reach people not already prejudiced in favor of the candidate; and the opportunity to concentrate fire in the relatively few critical states which could not certainly be counted in either candidate's column. Using these arguments, Hollender had convinced the General and his brother Milton Eisenhower that spots should be employed and had put together from newsreel clippings a few spot announcements for use in the Republican primaries, even before Reeves mentioned the idea to his friends. But it was the telephone call from the clubhouse that closed the deal: Reeves's companions, among them oilman James Snowden, promised that they would raise the necessary money for the campaign if Reeves would handle the advertising end.

A few weeks later Reeves gave a dinner in a private room at "21" to show suggested scripts and story boards to his friends and a few of their friends. The next step was formal contact with Citizens for Eisenhower, the secular arm of the Republican party for 1952, at which point Hollender and Reeves came together. A second dinner at "21" sold the spots approach to Walter Williams, chairman of C-for-E, and to John Hay Whitney, who was C-for-E's chief fund raiser. A committee including Williams, Whitney and Reeves then waited on Sherman Adams, chief of staff at central Eisenhower headquarters, and convinced Adams that the General himself should appear in the spot campaign. The formal Republican 1952 "Campaign

Plan," presented to Eisenhower and Nixon and their staffs on August 7 by Robert Humphreys, Republican National Committee public relations director, stated that "The use of radio and TV station-break 'spots' during the last ten days of the campaign is a *must* for stimulating the voters to go to the polls and vote for the candidates."

By that time Reeves was already at work on the spots. Though he had arranged for assistance if he needed it (several agencies offered "the whole copy department"), in the end he wrote all the scripts himself, without help. "Every word of them," he says today, "and very tedious work it was." Taking a six-week leave of absence from Bates without pay, he established himself in a suite at the St. Regis Hotel, and researched by reading the newspapers. "I took Eisenhower's speeches," he recalls, "and read them all. He was talking about three thousand things, and you don't do that in advertising. You lose penetration." In the end, he picked something more than a dozen over-all themes out of the Eisenhower campaign argument and set up an appointment for himself with George Gallup, whom he had never met. He asked Gallup what issues were most important with the public, and received the reply that people were most disturbed about the Korean War, corruption in Washington, taxes and the high cost of living, in that order. Reeves prepared a few scripts and had an artist draw story boards for spots on each of these themes. He used in all the spots the same introduction, an announcer saying, with suppressed excitement, "Eisenhower Answers the Nation!" Then the voice of "an ordinary citizen" would ask a question, such as, "Mr. Eisenhower, what about the high cost of living?" And the General would reply, in this instance, "My wife, Mamie, worries about the same thing. I tell her it's our job to change that on November fourth." A formal disclaimer from the television station (of the "What you have just heard is a paid political announcement" variety) would end the spot and in each home the television set would then return to its usual fare.

As an advertising man, Reeves felt that just one issue should be chosen, and should be hammered home in all the spots. He presented his arguments to Walter Williams and representatives from the Republican National Committee at a meeting in the Hotel Plaza toward the end of August, and was turned down. Instead, the Republicans told him to hit at all the issues Gallup had described as important, and to get all the scripts ready for September 13, when Eisenhower would be in New York and would be able to take a day to make his part of the films. Reeves had hoped for more time to get the spots written, and more time with the candidates to get the films right—one does not make fifty television spots in a single day, even with professional actors—but he was destined in this venture to work under orders.

By the time September 13 came Reeves was just as pleased he had just the one day with Eisenhower before the cameras: only twenty-two spots were ready, approved by Citizens for Eisenhower and waiting for the General. Reeves and Eisenhower met, for the first time, at the Transfilm studios in midtown Manhattan, and the Bates make-up department prepared the candidate for the cameras. Reeves was particularly anxious to have Eisenhower appear in the spots without his glasses, but without his glasses the General was unable to read the prompt cards. The head of Bates's radio-TV department personally took a brush and hand-lettered huge prompt cards for Eisenhower to read without glasses.

The first few spots went like the wind, and Reeves realized that Eisenhower probably could go through the planned fifty in a single day. So he sat down at his typewriter and wrote twenty-eight spots in a few hours, under forced draft. As he finished each spot he would take it to Milton Eisenhower, who would either okay or reject it. Sometimes Reeves, who was pulling most of Eisenhower's lines straight out of already delivered speeches, would protest against the rejection; to which the invariable answer would be, "I don't care if he said it in Texas in June, the General isn't going to say it now." Accepted scripts would be read quickly by the candidate, then passed on to be lettered on the prompt cards.

Eventually, $1,500,000 were spent to put these television spots on the air, and echoes of the controversy which they caused can still be heard. They were regarded as an important and in many quarters as an undesirable innovation in American political campaigning, and they will be worth a footnote in the history books someday. Part of that footnote should be a vignette of the scene in Transfilm's studios as recalled by Reeves: Hollender working with the camera crew, Reeves himself pounding a typewriter in a back room, a high-priced executive hand-lettering prompt cards, and Milton Eisenhower keeping up the spirits of the next President of the United States, who sat in a hard chair between takes, shaking his head and saying, "To think that an old soldier should come to this!"

69. NIXON AND KENNEDY
HIT THE CAMPAIGN TRAIL
by Richard Rovere*

. . . Despite jets and television, the 1960 campaign is running on an 1860 schedule, and although "maximum exposure"—indeed, almost complete exposure—may be obtained in a few television appearances, the time between these appearances must be filled in the classic ways. By far the greater part of each candidate's time goes into cultivating the favor of groups that are infinitesimal parts of the electorate. Both men are speaking several times a day; making themselves and their prestige available to candidates for local offices; enduring endless chicken-and-green-pea lunches, with endless introductions and endless oratory by their hosts; building morale in ladies' auxiliaries by saying they can see at a glance how splendid morale already is; and taking the most roundabout routes to the civic auditoriums, so that they can wave at the largest number of curbside watchers. If these ancient rites are obsolete, they retain a certain charm,

* Staff writer for The New Yorker since 1944. This selection is from Richard H. Rovere, "Letter from Chicago," © 1960 The New Yorker Magazine, Inc., vol. 36, no. 34, Oct. 8, 1960, pp. 171-172. By permission of the author and publisher.

and they yield some insights into the candidates and their different methods.

There is no doubt in any observer's mind that the Vice-President is far in the lead when it comes to using the devices of traditional campaigning. The experience he has had as Vice-President may or may not make him a worthy successor to Mr. Eisenhower, but the experience he has had in national campaigns—more than anyone since Franklin Roosevelt—has made him a hard man to beat in a courthouse square. Even without experience, he would be a hard man to beat, for if his style is not the best for monitored debates, it is ideal for the traditional political rally. Senator Kennedy can now and then set fire to an audience, and some ralliers apparently find it impossible to keep their hands off him, but the art of mass flattery seems completely beyond him, and he cannot bring himself to say the sort of thing that is supposed to give a crowd a sense of close identification with the candidate. Mr. Nixon on the stump is a storehouse of anecdotes and homely phrases. He talks about Mrs. Nixon and their life together, about his boyhood and his parents, about the exciting life a Vice-President leads, about funny things that happened to him on the way to the meeting, and—on this he never misses—about the time he spent with that devilish and devilishly clever Khrushchev. He can speak of a candidate for the state senate whom he met only five minutes earlier as though the man were a lifelong chum. The audiences devour it all. Senator Kennedy has lately taken to making an occasional mention of the fact that he has a home and a wife who is having a child, but he will go no further, and he would not go even that far until members of his staff, who had talked themselves hoarse imploring him not to plunge directly into political discourse before audiences that mainly wanted to take his measure as a human being, forced him to listen to some friendly newspapermen who endorsed the staff's proposals. . . .

70. IS CAMPAIGN ORATORY A WASTE OF BREATH?

by Paul Douglas*

This fall I have had the chance to compare current political speeches with those of past generations and to consider once again their relative effectiveness. For I am following my annual custom of reporting in person to the voters of my state and, as this is an election year, although I am not running myself, I am also making many speeches in behalf of my party and our candidates. At the same time, since we are celebrating in Illinois

* Former professor of economics at the University of Chicago. Served in the United States Senate since 1948 (except for a wartime stint with the United States Marine Corps). Author of *The Theory of Wages, Controlling Depressions, Ethics in Government,* and other works. This selection is from Paul Douglas, "Is Campaign Oratory a Waste of Breath?" *New York Times Magazine,* Oct. 19, 1958, pp. 26 and 72-73. By permission of the author and publisher.

the centennial of the famous Lincoln-Douglas debates of 1858, I have gone back over the records of those historic contests.

The first and most obvious difference between the political speeches of today and those of a century ago is that today's are much shorter. Television and radio have no doubt limited the tolerance of the listeners. When Lincoln and Douglas crossed words, each was allotted an hour and a half, and, if the contemporary accounts can be believed, the crowds listened with close attention throughout the three hours' struggle. It was not unusual then for orators to speak for two or three hours. In my youth I can remember how "Old Bob" LaFollette would frequently exceed even this limit and once, the legend goes, he started as the moon rose and only stopped as the sun appeared over the Wisconsin prairies!

Today no one dares to speak an hour. If you go over thirty-five minutes you are unpopular, while twenty minutes is considered about right. This is especially hard for those of us who are Senators and accustomed to develop our arguments in some detail. My wife, who served in Congress before me, sometimes remarks, a little wryly, that a Senator can condense into an hour what an ordinary man can say in five minutes. Certainly a political speech today, if it is to bear fruit, needs a lot of pruning.

A second great difference between the speeches of today and those heard by our grandfathers is that the crowds are now much smaller. In the days of Lincoln and Douglas there were few, if any, competing attractions. Politics and religion were the chief intellectual interests of the people and orators and politicians attracted almost as much attention as do the movie stars and television personalities of today. A Lincoln-Douglas debate in 1958 would not draw the 12,000 who a century ago came to Charleston, or the still greater numbers who listened through a chilling October day at Galesburg. Outside the big cities a gathering of 200 is respectable today and an attendance of 500 is really heartwarming.

Another notable change is in the places of public meetings. County rallies were formerly held in the courthouses, while the rural precinct meetings were held in the schools. But since the seats were hard, the rooms poorly lighted and either too hot or too cold and always at the top of long flights of stairs, attendance at these meetings declined rapidly during the Forties. Today a more common gathering is the potluck supper put on by women. In warmer weather, the men often take over with their fish fries. At these meetings, good food and sociability give a great lift to political morale.

Because of the decline of the courthouse meetings, I introduced an innovation in Illinois politics when I first ran for the United States Senate in 1948. Since the voters would not come to the meetings, I took the meetings to the voters. I bought a station wagon that I equipped with a loudspeaker (some have called it a "noise wagon") and took to the road. I held my meetings out of doors wherever people gathered. I spoke in the business districts of towns, at shopping centers, traffic intersections and factory gates. Sometimes, indeed, I spoke where no one came despite all my advance publicity. But knowing that there were listeners behind the windows, I would persist with my speech. (At least two of the towns which thus gave me the absent treatment have since invited me back and accorded me tumultuous welcomes.)

In the course of that campaign I made more than 1,100 brief speeches, talked out of doors to about 250,000 people and shook hands with about an equal number. That the program was effective is shown by the election results as well as by the number of candidates who have since adopted it.

Still a third difference between the speeches of today and those of a century or more ago lies in their style. The great pre-Civil War orators in this country, such as Webster, Clay, Calhoun, Benton and Douglas, were schooled in the literary traditions of the eighteenth century. Their oratory was involved and magniloquent. In the mouth of a Winston Churchill or a Bryan this manner of speaking has, even in modern times, thrilled millions. But it is today almost obsolete. The late Senator Neely of West Virginia was probably its last great exemplar.

Today the emphasis is upon exposition rather than oratory. And here again radio and television have had their effect. Clarity, directness and logic are the qualities which the public wants in a speaker. Short words of Anglo-Saxon origin are preferred to Latinisms, and to be effective the sentences and paragraphs should be brief and to the point.

Finally, the tone of modern speaking is far more moderate than it was. We have had some vituperative speakers in Congress during the last two decades but even at their height these men could not match the stinging bitterness and personal abuse that marked the speeches of John Randolph and Charles Sumner. Even the victims of McCarthyism were not heaped with the poisonous epithets that were showered upon William Jennings Bryan when he first ran for the Presidency in 1896.

There is today an increasing desire for fair play and a recognition that no one party or cause is either wholly good or evil. The result is that the bitter demagogue, who seeks to stir up hatred, generally and in the long run destroys himself. Joyce Cary's political character who stated that his aim was not to inform, but to arouse, still has his followers, but I believe they are far fewer than before.

But perhaps the simplicity of style and the greater moderation in tone have reduced the excitement in politics. The rise of competing interests for men's time and attention has certainly shifted the attention of the public away from questions of foreign and domestic policy. If bitterness and vituperation have fortunately decreased, the search for moderation and a middle ground have produced a rather tepid attitude toward public affairs.

People are interested in these subjects—but not very much! The controversies of sixty years ago over imperialism, free silver, the tariff and the trusts may have been more inflamed but they reflected and produced a greater degree of concern than do the modern discussions about foreign aid, the United Nations, monetary policy and gas rates. It is not quite good form to discuss these issues publicly or to take a deep interest in them.

Despite the valiant efforts of such organizations as the League of Women Voters, numerous public forums and a handful of great newspapers, I am forced to the melancholy conclusion that we, as a people, have slipped in our concern about public affairs.

This helps to answer a frequent question: namely, do we really need political speaking and does it have any effect upon the public mind or upon the final results? There are writers who argue that it does not, since one talks primarily to those already converted. Face-to-face meetings, they say, should be largely cast aside and one should turn instead to other media. The pollsters and the advertising men are the foremost exponents of this point of view.

The pollsters encourage the doctrine of inevitability and hold that the course of an election is set early and that any later talk cannot alter its direction in any appreciable way. All this in spite of 1948! The advertising and public relations men are the expositors of the theory that they can "sell" a candidate or a party in the same way they can sell soap or a beauty lotion. There is, of course, a great deal of truth in this last contention and advertising men are playing an increasing part in political campaigns.

But reliance on such methods at the expense of political argument is unfortunate and not in the public interest. In the first place, such methods seek to exploit the emotional and nonrational and what the mass-motivation group labels "subliminal" factors, rather than the conscious and rational. The progress of humanity has been largely caused by the increasing use of reason and logic and for us to subordinate these qualities to the darker and more emotional sentiments that lie beneath the surface of the mind leads to wrong decisions. Hitler's advice to his fellow Nazis to "think with your blood" claimed tens of millions for its victims. It would have been better to have had free and rational discussion.

The second objection to the mass-communication techniques is that their sheer cost makes them available only to those candidates and parties which have large funds. An evening half-hour nation-wide telecast on one of the national chains costs from $50,000 to $60,000 and a similar statewide hookup in Illinois costs about $4,000. Printing costs are also now almost astronomical and the new postage rates make wide-scale mailing nearly prohibitive.

The contention that there is equal treatment on the airwaves because there is a requirement that if one party buys time the other must be offered equal time completely misses the point. The other side can have such equal time only if it can pay the price. The whole situation reminds one of Anatole France's remark in "The Red Lily" about "the majestic equality of the law which forbids the rich as well as the poor to sleep under bridges and beg in the streets for bread."

The result is that the well-financed candidate or party will be able to deluge the airwaves with propaganda while those with only meager resources will lack the entrance fee which is required to reply.

In such circumstances public meetings and speeches, along with the hand-to-hand distribution of literature, are about the only means that financially impoverished candidates and parties have by which to put their cases before the public.

There remains the question of how effective political speeches are. On the basis of many years' experience, I am convinced that they are far more effective than the skeptics believe. In a political campaign, the central problem of candidates and parties is to get their own adherents aroused, working and voting—and to win over as many of the independent voters as possible. Neither side has any real chance of winning over the supporters of the other side and it is really a waste of effort during campaign time to try to do so. But one should try with all one's strength to hold one's own supporters and to make great inroads upon the uncommitted voters.

Except in overwhelmingly one-party districts, unless a speaking campaign is staged the members of one's own party will lose heart, decide that the battle has been lost and will either cease to work or do so in very low gear. Public meetings are therefore necessary to animate the faithful so that they will spread their interest to others. While not many independent and undecided voters come to the formal party meetings, there are generally some and there should be more. These, too, can be influenced by a good speech or repelled by a bad one.

This is one of the reasons I like informal out-of-doors meetings at places where crowds gather for other purposes. For here one finds a true cross-section and can often elicit honest and thoughtful questions as well as the bracing experience of standing up under a barrage of heckling.

One of the biennial campaign meetings which I most enjoy is such an out-door gathering during the noon hour at the Western Electric Plant in Cicero. Although I am never sure how many converts I have made, men frequently come up and tell me how much they have enjoyed the questions and answers.

The indirect influence of campaign speeches is of course greater than their direct effect upon listeners. The message gets around by word of mouth and by newspaper accounts and radio and television newscasts. There are a few newspapers in my state, however, that practice systematic blackouts on all local meetings of my party. But, even when biased publishers tend to slight our news, there are generally some members of the working press who will write accounts of our meetings and try to get them printed. That is why an experienced campaigner will always have press releases with him to pass on to the local papers and stations. And if he is wise, he will take pains to keep these releases both lively and current.

In any event, by a subtle process of osmosis, the arguments of the orators do enter the intellectual life of the community. Public appearances invest those arguments with the flesh and blood of personality and hence dramatize the issues. Thus, with all their imperfections, campaign speeches contribute to the open dialogue on questions upon which wise public decisions depend. Certainly they are far more worth-while from the public point of view than the one-minute spot announcements that the advertising men tell us are the most effective in "selling" a candidate. And they allow the voters to see a candidate "in the round" without the highly artificial and contrived impression that is commonly given on radio and television.

Harry Truman's speaking tour through the country in 1948 against what seemed to be overwhelming odds, was what turned the tide in that election. The voters came to admire the plucky fighter and were convinced he had been badly misrepresented by the press.

My conclusion is that we should strengthen rather than discard our political meetings; that speakers, without sacrificing legitimate emotion, should strive for ever greater accuracy and closer logic, and that meetings should be made more colorful by the injection of more music and greater audience participation. The meetings and speeches can thus be made still more effective instruments for helping Mr. and Mrs. Voter to winnow out the truth in the free competition of ideas.

71. WHAT TRENDEX FOR LINCOLN?
by Sidney Hyman*

. . . Should a man's TV manner be a determinant of whether he is fit for high public office? One wonders in this connection whether any of our Presidential "greats" would have come off well on television.

George Washington had ill-fitting false teeth that not only came unstuck but also made it hard for him to speak without uttering a whistling sound. Besides, he showed signs of smallpox. Thomas Jefferson was frequently described as having "shifty eyes." Abraham Lincoln, with his heavy features and warts, was compared to a "baboon." Theodore Roosevelt was all dentures. And television would have shown Franklin D. Roosevelt moving haltingly toward a rostrum.

Perhaps but one recent President would have come off brilliantly on television, and the mere mention of his name should be enough to remind voters that their business is to know what goes on inside a candidate's head and heart—provided they can get at it without the tricks of lighting. That President was handsome, warm, friendly, sincere Warren G. Harding.

72. THE IMPACT OF TV
ON AMERICAN POLITICS
by Emmett Hughes†

. . . Has the power of television—now dramatized by the device of debate—really revolutionized the democratic process? Is the change more apparent than real? For better or for worse?

So stunning are the factors of size of audience and speed of communication on the grand scale that the very rhythm of political life does seem revolutionized. And a case can be at least plausibly argued that American

* Author of *The American President* and numerous articles on the Presidency. This selection is from Sidney Hyman, "What Trendex for Lincoln?" *New York Times Magazine*, Jan. 17, 1960, p. 36. By permission of the author and publisher.

† Formerly associated with the Luce publications (*Time, Life, Fortune*) as foreign correspondent and editorial writer. Speech writer for President Eisenhower. Author of *America the Vincible, The Church and the Liberal Society,* and *Report from Spain.* This selection is from Emmett Hughes, "52,000,000 TV Sets: How Many Votes?" *New York Times Magazine*, Sept. 25, 1960, pp. 23 and 78-80. By permission of the author and publisher.

political history has been decisively affected, these last eight years, by this revolution in technique.

Three witnesses—three of America's political giants—can be summoned to lend evidence to that case.

Richard M. Nixon in 1952 dramatically appeared on national television to explain to all the homes of America how he had financed his home, his career, his whole life—in a performance that made Checkers the nation's most famous dog since F. D. R.'s Fala. Hours, even minutes before that telecast, Mr. Nixon stood an excellent chance of making history as the first candidate on a national ticket ever to be stricken from the lists in mid-campaign as an insufferable embarrassment to his own party.

So nearly definite was this stern verdict of the party leaders that it is not enough to note that television remarkably served the man: it saved him. No other kind of apologia—nothing but television, with impact both massive and instantaneous—could have spared Mr. Nixon swift retirement to the little town of Whittier, Calif., whose residents thronged the streets, just a few weeks ago, to hail the 1960 Presidential nominee.

Dwight D. Eisenhower in 1956 spent an agonizing late spring in slow recovery from major surgery, following his earlier heart attack. His decision to run for re-election trembled in doubt for weeks; even the thought of it would have made a weaker man tremble. But it is hardly conceivable that even he would have elected to wage a national campaign were it not for the fabulous facilities of television to ease and simplify the ordeal.

John F. Kennedy in 1960 found his spring offensive for the Democratic nomination fatefully committed to the primary battle for West Virginia. His most ominous problem was the state's massive and pervasive hostility to a Catholic candidate. Only the most full and personal kind of campaign —directly reaching and affecting tens of thousands—could counter popular passions so diffuse, so widespread. And only television made such an effort conceivable.

Three different men, in three different years: for all of them, the road to this political moment took its crucial turning around the same extraordinary fact.

Towering personalities and dramatic incidents aside, the impact of television on American political life can be reckoned in a number of other ways. These are ways less crisply clear, yet perhaps more seriously historic and lasting.

First, TV makes political life itself more fluid and more volatile. Men can surge or stumble with astonishing speed—either triumphing over obscurity or tripping over a hasty or graceless public word or gesture. And issues can become as mercurial as individuals: A single performance before a sufficiently massive audience can virtually end an issue or precipitate one.

In the golden days of radio, the nightmare of performers in the studio was the mumbling of some indiscretion or vulgarity a moment before the microphone was dead. Now the politician almost lives before a live "mike" and camera. His world is tapped.

Second, TV forces much of the backstage machinery of political life to endure the same exposure. Conventions tend to become not national caucuses of politicians, but public spectacles, designed less for deliberation (or dealing) among the participants than the delight (or entertainment) of an audience. It is at least debatable whether this makes the event itself more sober or merely more contrived.

It is equally debatable whether the effect upon the audience is one of visual education, in a serious sense, or one of visual enjoyment just a notch or two above the level of the peepshow. What is not in doubt is the fact that the people *see* more.

Third, TV dramatically tends to nationalize political life. The citizen who can watch and hear Presidential candidates from his easy chair feels understandably less excitement than his father at the prospect of a "live" appearance in the local auditorium of a Congressman or even a Senator. Local political clubs—as centers of political life—tend to suffer and sag in appeal.

The firing of local partisan zeal, then, requires ever more prestigious names—as close to the top of the ticket as one dare demand. Ultimately, this could dictate, of course, greater dependence of all local tickets upon the national ticket.

Fourth, TV can strikingly shift political advantage toward those office-holders with easiest access to a national medium; these are national office-holders. It seems hardly an accident that 1960 has been notable for the fact that three of the four candidates on the national tickets come from the U. S. Senate—traditionally inferior to state governorships as sources of national candidates—while the fourth candidate, Henry Cabot Lodge, has enjoyed unique exposure on national television.

In the future of television, it would seem doubtful if the most distinguished governor, whatever his record or his personality, could come close to national candidacy without finding a way, first, to establish his identity as nationally as Washington leaders.

Fifth, accenting the person and the personal, TV both imposes new demands and offers new opportunity to the individual politician. This transcends the level of a Kennedy's concern with his hair or a Nixon's anxiety about his eyebrows (both appropriately adjusted for the current campaign). In the meeting—or the muffing—of issues, it puts new and heavy stress on the man himself.

Thus, for example, one astute political commentator, watching last spring's West Virginia primary, anticipated Senator Kennedy's massive victory on the basis of one response, discovered universally among all citizens queried a fortnight before election. This was the simple fact that all who had seen the Senator on television had reacted favorably, even if grudgingly. Enough television, then, logically would prevail. It did. But it underscored the fact that there could have been no effective substitute for this entirely personal attack on the political problem.

Sixth, TV obviously quickens the tendency of big politics to resemble big business. The cost of campaigning, of course, soars: the relatively easy political struggle of 1956 cost the G. O. P. some $2 million for television and radio. The eager novice, in this televised political life, can afford to start unknown—but not unfinanced.

And more and more, the higher he aspires politically, the candidate must equip himself, like a corporation, with advisers, specialists, public relations experts and every kind of retainer with ideas and words, counsels and cautions, to guide him in his almost totally exposed existence. Paradoxically, the "product" who alone must sell himself—by his person, his living presence—cannot be left alone.

Are all these not marks of a new age in American politics? Oddly, in the face of such evidence, the answer would seem to be only perhaps, in part, and in still quite uncertain measure. This becomes most clear when one assesses realistically the more extreme judgments—the laments and the eulogies—that have attended the advent of the new technique.

The laments are sharp and familiar. Television exalts the factor of personality. It invites, even demands, appeal to emotion rather than intellect. It commercializes, savagely hammering political discourses into capsule banalities to fit one-minute, thirty-second, ten-second "spots." It cheapens the value of the spoken word since one does not *listen* to television (and it is no accident that surveys showed Adlai Stevenson far more highly esteemed by radio listeners than by televiewers).

It compels candidates for the highest political office in the world to fret anxiously, self-consciously, over minutiae of personal grooming, as if they were agonized ingenues. And—most depressing of all—it introduces them to the intellectual companionship of Jack Paar, with or without Zsa Zsa. What manner of farce is this? Sideshow-for-free—for a free people—or dress rehearsal for national tragedy?

For all the fragments of truth in this kind of lament, it hardly states the whole truth. Personality (or "the image") has always mattered critically in politics—back through the age of radio to the street-corner rally and the doorbell-ringing campaigns. Nor is television the *cause* of the fact that few citizens of 1960 have time, even if the occasion arose, to listen leisurely to exquisitely constructed, grandiloquently delivered orations—the sort hailed as classics in the nineteenth century.

Nor is there much new in the importance of deliberate artifice, calculated technique, studious striving for effect. Many of those great orators of a century ago were wont to rehearse their dramatic addresses for weeks. Bryan was able to talk his way to a Presidential nomination no less than three times—and the dramatic "Cross of Gold" speech had been given careful trial-runs at the crossroads many times before it stunned, swept and exalted his party in convention.

At another extreme, the tributes paid to the power of television—to enrich and mature the democratic process—have been hardly less emphatic than the indictments. It promises (so the optimists proclaim) fuller popular awareness and sense of participation, even intimacy. It inevitably educates—visually and vividly. No method of communication could make governors and governed more close, more mutually responsible and responsive.

This benign vision could, some day, become a little real. But the living signs of it are few. There is not a shred of evidence to date, for example, to suggest that television has increased the size of the politically active and concerned populace. As for the general notion of television bringing the politician "closer" to the average citizen, this pleasing estimate jars against the clear fact that TV costs compel this politician to command financial resources further than ever beyond the means of this average citizen.

And as for enabling public affairs to compete with entertainment for attention in the American home, the classic, curt disproof came in a telegram from a televiewer to Adlai Stevenson in 1956, not long after a message of his had pre-empted five minutes from the season's most popular show: "I like Ike and I love Lucy. Drop dead."

Above all such extreme judgments, pro and con, perhaps one illusion seems to thrust itself most menacingly. For this is an illusion widely entertained not by experts or critics (who tend to affect a democracy's workings rather little) but by the people (who affect those workings rather decisively). This is the general belief, only partly conscious and rarely articulate, that the sight seen on the television screen boasts some special authenticity. It somehow seems much more "the real thing" than, for example, a formal speech or statement. Seeing is believing—or disbelieving.

This notion itself might eventually mark and measure the gravest impact of television on America's political life, and it may be doubted whether any such result would be for the good. For any popular illusion of "authenticity" or "purity" could be a grotesque self-deception.

The fact that national conventions are elaborately televised, for example, does not remotely assure their being "open"—though the camera eye implies the contrary. And the implicit invitation to judge a man by the accident of the camera's glimpse of him could only encourage in the national mind a political world populated by caricatures and stereotypes, demons, and angels—a world in which great leaders always shave cleanly, smile easily, and look one right in the eye, while all villainous bosses are caught whispering mysterious secrets and wearing dark glasses.

Caution—for an alert and thoughtful citizenry—extends with no less force to television at its most "serious." Television will be serious—portentously so—as it presents the debates, in the weeks ahead, between Vice President Nixon and Senator Kennedy. These will be provocative encounters. They may be exciting. They might be illuminating. So far, so good, for the democratic process.

But, how good this will prove to be will not finally depend upon the debaters themselves. It will depend upon how wisely the nation of viewers appraise this debate—or *any* debate.

Such an appraisal turns on the simple question: How logical and reasonable a way is this to determine a man's qualifications for the Presidency? A useful and pertinent addition to other evidence—this it surely is. A convenient and quick substitute for either other evidence or any thought—this it surely is not.

It is not true that a large volume of serious words, earnestly spoken, even before an interrogator or an adversary, are necessarily revealing of even a candidate's views, much less his qualifications. Thus, last spring,

Vice President Nixon subjected himself—stoically and shrewdly—to the verbal endurance test of a televised interview that lasted three hours and forty-five minutes.

The result (no fault of the Vice President, but a measure of the vapidity of the questioning) was summarized accurately by one reviewer as an interview that "had such depth it almost disappeared." For the newspapers of the following morning could report, from all the verbiage, not a single notable item of news—other than the news of so much "serious" time being spent making no news.

It is not true, of course, that the historical recollection (so cavalierly made) of the Lincoln-Douglas debates has the slightest relevance. Those debates turned upon a single, clear and universally understood issue—slavery. And most of them lasted almost three hours—a good enough time for truly serious argument.

Finally—and most important—it is manifestly not true that a good debater clearly qualifies as a good President or, for that matter, as anything but a good debater. By way of analogy, the Washington press knows (without wishing to publicize the fact too clearly) that, as often as not, a good government official happens to conduct a poor press conference, while his mediocre colleague may happen to have a most felicitous talent for the occasion.

It is perfectly true that a "debate" can be singularly revealing: a rude grimace, a brusque gesture, a hasty retort can suddenly color the whole event. But the discovery of one of these phenomena suggests a quixotic, if not reckless, test of capacity for high office.

And as for the great issues, the unfortunate fact is that far less skill is required to blur them than to clarify them ("I have been concerned a great deal about that myself. . . . You have stated one point of view most persuasively, but. . . . Frankly, I once held that view myself, but. . . . There is much to be said for what you have said, but I honestly think that a broader perspective. . . .").

If and when such smoke and fog films the nation's television screens, only a most credulous people could imagine the wispy, curling clouds of words are magically going to assume the shape and form of a national leader.

There are quite a few Americans who have worried, for some time now, about the slow, steady degrading of the democratic dialogue—by cliché and sophistry, loud euphemism and pompous platitude, cheap symbol and sly slogan. They have worried because the way men talk must both reflect and affect the way they think—the process of thought that, ultimately, *is* the process of democracy.

Will the revolution in surface method and technique, brought to political life by television, make this life-giving process more true and profound?

If the people who watch (and manage) this visual feast sense and admit its limitations as a diet for the brain; if its vast range opens the exchange of ideas to a truly national scale; if its sustained reportage of the fate of men and nations makes a larger public better informed; if it affords to new men in public affairs a unique forum for swiftly conveying new and urgent understanding to the citizenry; if its full power serves to make the democratic dialogue between men and parties, between people and government, more full and free, more precise and more purposeful—the answer will be yes.

If it is imagined to serve not in the search for truth but as a substitute for truth; if it drives politics towards theatrics, so that the number of politicians who imagine themselves entertainers swells to match the number of entertainers who imagine themselves politicians; if it ruthlessly practises a kind of intellectual payola that rewards the man who can reduce the most complex issue to the silliest simplification; if it effectively invites a whole people to foreswear the labor of reading for the ease of gaping; if the merchandising of tranquilizers and sedatives is imitated or surpassed by a concept of leadership that pits party against party, orator against orator, in rival stroking and soothing of the complacencies of the citizen; if the pungent slogan asserts such sovereignty that disarmament is discussed on the level of deodorants; if all impulses conspire to glut the channels with what sells rather than with what matters; if, by all these lapses and deceits, a whole people lets itself become mentally trapped in a suffocating kind of isolation booth from which no sound can be heard but the voice of the huckster—the answer will be no.

The hope is obvious—that a marvelous voice will be used, by free men talking to free men, in syllables of fit majesty.

The ultimate test is what the philosopher has called "the chastity of the mind," uncovetous of the impure answer, unseduced by the simple solution.

The final result will be dictated as with every great resource or device in the hands of a free people—be it fire, be it water, be it nuclear power. It will serve or it will damage—it will dignify, or it will degrade—as the wisdom and will of free men, fervent or feckless, decide.

73. A NEGATIVE REPORT
ON THE NIXON–KENNEDY TV DEBATES
by Douglass Cater*

. . . One thing was quite clear: as they approached this brave new frontier of television, the two candidates were far more concerned about their images than their arguments.

Both candidates proved themselves remarkably adaptable to the new art form. They were marvels at extemporization, wasting none of the precious media time in reflective pauses, never having to grasp for the elusive word, able in the peculiar alternation of reply and rebuttal to switch topics smoothly and without a hitch. Each could discuss anything within the allotted two and a half minutes for reply and one and a half for rebuttal.

* Washington editor for *The Reporter*. Coauthor of *Ethics in a Business Society* (with Marquis Childs) and author of *The Fourth Branch of Government*. This selection is from Douglass Cater, "Notes from Backstage," *The Reporter*, vol. 23, no. 8, Nov. 10, 1960, pp. 19-20. By permission of the author and publisher.

To anyone who spent much time on tour with the two men, this was no great surprise. The dialogue was largely a paste-up job containing bits and snippets from campaign rhetoric already used many times. As the series wore on, the protagonists were like two weary wrestlers who kept trying to get the same holds. What became clear was how limited the vocabulary of the debate really was and how vague were the candidates' ideas about what to do. Kennedy, we learned over and over, wants to get America moving again. Nixon argues that it is moving, and, in an unfortunate phrase, "We can't stand pat."

Nobody around the candidates seemed to think that clarity of argument was the objective. For the sidelines observer trying to judge this new contest without benefit of rules or score card, it raised more questions than it answered.

Kennedy's trainers pointed out that he won an important victory simply by closing the maturity gap separating him from a rival four years his elder. He proved himself able to stand up to the man who stood up to Khrushchev. It was an accomplishment, they claimed, that no other means of communication could have effected so well and so quickly.

It may be so. But one kept wondering about those silent millions who sat before their television sets. Did they come any closer to a knowledge of their candidates? Not even a trained political observer could keep up with the crossfire of fact and counterfact, of the rapid references to Rockefeller Reports, Lehman amendments, prestige analyses, G.N.P., and a potpourri of other so-called facts. Or was the knack of merely seeming well informed what counted with the viewer? If so, Mr. Nixon did all right despite an amazing capacity to twist facts to suit his convenience. ("Now, as a result of our taking the strong stand that we did [on Indo-China], the civil war there was ended and today, at least in the south of Indo-China, the Communists have moved out and we do have a strong free bastion there.") Eventually, it seemed as if Kennedy gave up the Herculean effort to sweep up his opponent's fictions.

Who was judged more sincere? What may have been a major test was Nixon's soliloquy on Harry Truman's language and little children. It provoked loud guffaws among the press corps at the studio. But maybe other good Americans were deeply stirred by this pious man who promised, if elected, not to utter strong words in the White House. (He did, however, utter a few in the studio directly after the program, when he accused Kennedy of violating his no-notes proviso; afterward he told reporters that his spontaneous expressions were off the record.)

Last but not least, was the viewer really edified by the frantic clash on foreign policy? Neither of the men showed any regard for the fact that some things are better left unsaid if one of them expects to conduct that foreign policy next January. It was like a bastardized version of Art Linkletter's "People Are Funny" in which the contestant had to tell how he would deal with Castro in 150 seconds flat.

In closing what he thought was the last of the series, moderator Quincy Howe remarked, "As members of a new political generation, Vice-President Nixon and Senator Kennedy have used new means of communication to pioneer a new type of political debate. . . . Perhaps they have established a new tradition." Howe may or may not be right in his prediction. But before this particular tradition becomes firmly rooted in American politics, it needs the kind of examination it never got before it started. The next time around, one of these pioneers will almost certainly be talking as our President.

74. A POSITIVE REPORT ON THE NIXON–KENNEDY TV DEBATES
by Philip Stern*

Even before the campaign was over, leading Democrats, whose candidate was generally agreed to have benefited decisively from the joint TV appearances, were carefully non-committal about any debates in 1964. Robert Kennedy said the decision would have to be made when the next campaign rolls around, and National Chairman Jackson said the debates pose difficult problems when one of the candidates is President of the United States.

Indeed they do, for a great deal more rides on the off-the-cuff words of *the* President than on those of *a* prospective President. But the debates can be credited with so many identifiable contributions to the edification of the electorate that every effort should be made to assure the President's participation in them in 1964.

First and foremost, the debates, televised, as they were, by all the major networks simultaneously, exposed the candidates to tens of millions of voters who might otherwise never have seen or heard them. What is more, those who viewed the debate were treated to an unusually candid and accurate portrait. How much better for the voters to see the two standing on their own feet, without benefit of ghost-written script, than to be primarily exposed, as in past campaigns, to half-hour views of one candidate or the other reading a speech (prepared in whole or in large part by somebody else), unquestioned and unchallenged.

Granted that the strictures of time imposed by the debates prevented them from being the perfect medium for the detailed exposition of programs and policies. But two months of steady campaigning afforded many opportunities for that, amply used by both candidates, through speeches and "position papers." The unique provision of the debates was an opportunity for the voters to get "the feel" of the two men.

Not only did the debates expose the candidates to millions; they did so without cost to the candidates or their parties. By thus lessening the enormous party outlays for half-hours of expensive TV time, they thereby lessened the dependence of the parties on the special interests from which both largely derive their support. Anything that reduces the financial obligations of the two parties and thus enhances the President's freedom of action once he is in office is in the public interest.

* This selection is from Philip Stern, "The Debates in Retrospect," *New Republic*, vol. 143, no. 22, Nov. 21, 1960, pp. 18-19. By permission of the publisher.

One critic has pointed out that the "dialogue was largely a paste-up job, containing bits and snippets from campaign rhetoric already used many times." To be sure, this fact, not readily apparent to the average viewer, did artificially create the impression of remarkable articulateness on the part of both men. But isn't it far better that "bits and snippets" are heard by 60 to 70 million people, rather than by a smaller number who might catch them at a street corner or a railway station?

Another important contribution of the debates was their deterrent effect on hyperbole and unfounded statements. The knowledge that any off-base charge or statement might be questioned either by a newsman or one's opponent in full view of 60 or 70 million people must have made both candidates more wary of what they said. Doubtless, the much-discussed fifth debate would have covered some old ground. But it would probably also have served the useful purpose of toning down some of the haymakers both candidates were throwing in the final heated days, such as Mr. Nixon's wild charge that Senator Kennedy was threatening the cut-off of social security if Nixon won.

What of the format of future debates?

Walter Lippmann and others have criticized the interpolation of questions of newsmen as possibly jeopardizing the integrity of the debates: it has also been suggested that if the questions were formulated by the candidates themselves, they might be sharper, and one could make a judgment about the respective contenders not only on the basis of their answers but on the basis of the questions they asked.

Another more basic criticism is that the 1960 debates afforded no opportunity for follow-up questions, as does *Meet the Press* or *Face the Nation*. This is a serious drawback to the present format, mitigated to some extent by the fact that, owing to the repeal of the "equal time" stricture of the Communications Act, the networks were able to present each of the four top candidates on *Meet the Press* type shows for at least one hour during the campaign.

There might be some advantages, in 1964, to having the questions prepared by the candidates, rather than by newsmen, possibly to be posed by a network announcer so as to respect the dignity of the candidates. But whether the questions are posed thus, or by newsmen, the question-answer-rebuttal pattern has a number of advantages.

Like it or not, an hour is a long time to hold audience attention, especially for a discussion of public affairs. The 1960 format was well-suited to keep the viewer watching; it made the debates move quickly; it encouraged conciseness and discouraged rambling; it assured coverage of a variety of issues; and it prevented the discussion from becoming bogged down in wrangling, beyond the point of diminishing returns, on any single point; and it tended to focus both candidates' attention on a single subject at a given time.

The future of this new form of campaigning will be decided by President Kennedy. It will take courage and firmness for him to participate in such encounters, if he is his party's candidate again in '64, for he will be besieged by advisors who will point out to him, quite correctly, that he will be handing his lesser known opponent an unnecessary advantage. It would be ironic if John F. Kennedy, who, second only to the American public, was the greatest beneficiary of the 1960 debates, should deal the death blow to a spectacularly successful use of the television medium, whose enormous educational potential has heretofore been so largely wasted.

75. THE "CHECKERS" SPEECH
Richard M. Nixon*

My Fellow Americans:

I come before you tonight as a candidate for the Vice Presidency and as a man whose honesty and integrity have been questioned.

The usual political thing to do when charges are made against you is to either ignore them or to deny them without giving details.

I believe we've had enough of that in the United States, particularly with the present Administration in Washington, D.C. To me the office of the Vice Presidency of the United States is a great office, and I feel that the people have got to have confidence in the integrity of the men who run for that office and who might obtain it.

I have a theory, too, that the best and only answer to a smear or to an honest misunderstanding of the facts is to tell the truth. And that's why I'm here tonight. I want to tell you my side of the case.

I am sure that you have read the charge and you've heard it that I, Senator Nixon, took $18,000 from a group of my supporters.

WAS IT WRONG?

Now, was that wrong? And let me say that it was wrong—I'm saying, incidentally, that it was wrong and not just illegal. Because it isn't a question of whether it was legal or illegal, that isn't enough. The question is, was it morally wrong?

I say that it was morally wrong if any of that $18,000 went to Senator Nixon for my personal use. I say that it was morally wrong if it was secretly given and secretly handled. And I say that it was morally wrong if any of the contributors got special favors for the contributions that they made.

And now to answer those questions let me say this:

Not one cent of the $18,000 or any other money of that type ever went to me for my personal use. Every penny of it was used to pay for political expenses that I did not think should be charged to the taxpayers of the United States.

It was not a secret fund. As a matter of fact, when I was on "Meet the

*Vice President of the United States from 1953 to 1961. Republican candidate for President in 1960. Speech was delivered Sept. 23, 1952. Reprinted from the *New York Times*.

Press," some of you may have seen it last Sunday—Peter Edson came up to me after the program and said, "Dick, what about this fund we hear about?" And I said, Well, there's no secret about it. Go out and see Dana Smith, who was the administrator of the fund. And I gave him his address, and I said that you will find that the purpose of the fund simply was to defray political expenses that I did not feel should be charged to the Government.

And third, let me point out, and I want to make this particularly clear, that no contributor to this fund, no contributor to any of my campaign, has ever received any consideration that he would not have received as an ordinary constituent.

I just don't believe in that and I can say that never, while I have been in the Senate of the United States, as far as the people that contributed to this fund are concerned, have I made a telephone call for them to an agency, or have I gone down to an agency in their behalf. And the record will show that, the records which are in the hands of the Administration.

WHAT FOR AND WHY?

But then some of you will say and rightly, "Well, what did you use the fund for, Senator? Why did you have to have it?"

Let me tell you in just a word how a Senate office operates. First of all, a Senator gets $15,000 a year in salary. He gets enough money to pay for one trip a year, a round trip that is, for himself and his family between his home and Washington, D.C.

And then he gets an allowance to handle the people that work in his office, to handle his mail. And the allowance for my State of California is enough to hire thirteen people.

And let me say, incidentally, that that allowance is not paid to the Senator—it's paid directly to the individuals that the Senator puts on his payroll, that all of these people and all of these allowances are for strictly official business. Business, for example, when a constituent writes in and wants you to go down to the Veterans Administration and get some information about his GI policy. Items of that type for example.

But there are other expenses which are not covered by the Government. And I think I can best discuss those expenses by asking you some questions. Do you think that when I or any other Senator makes a political speech, has it printed, should charge the printing of that speech and the mailing of that speech to the taxpayers?

Do you think, for example, when I or any other Senator makes a trip to his home state to make a purely political speech that the cost of that trip should be charged to the taxpayers?

Do you think when a Senator makes political broadcasts or political television broadcasts, radio or television, that the expense of those broadcasts should be charged to the taxpayers?

Well, I know what your answer is. The same answer that audiences give me whenever I discuss this particular problem. The answer is, "no." The taxpayer shouldn't be required to finance items which are not official business but which are primarily political business.

But then the question arises, you say, "Well, how do you pay for these and how can you do it legally?"

And there are several ways that it can be done, incidentally, and that it is done legally in the United States Senate and in the Congress.

The first way is to be a rich man. I don't happen to be a rich man so I couldn't use that.

Another way that is used is to put your wife on the payroll. Let me say, incidentally, my opponent, my opposite number for the Vice Presidency on the Democratic ticket, does have his wife on the payroll. And has had her on his payroll for the ten years—the past ten years.

Now just let me say this. That's his business and I'm not critical of him for doing that. You will have to pass judgment on that particular point. But I have never done that for this reason. I have found that there are so many deserving stenographers and secretaries in Washington that needed the work that I just didn't feel it was right to put my wife on the payroll.

My wife's sitting over here. She's a wonderful stenographer. She used to teach stenography and she used to teach shorthand in high school. That was when I met her. And I can tell you folks that she's worked many hours at night and many hours on Saturdays and Sundays in my office and she's done a fine job. And I'm proud to say tonight that in the six years I've been in the House and the Senate of the United States, Pat Nixon has never been on the Government payroll.

There are other ways that these finances can be taken care of. Some who are lawyers, and I happen to be a lawyer, continue to practice law. But I haven't been able to do that. I'm so far away from California that I've been so busy with my Senatorial work that I have not engaged in any legal practice.

And also as far as law practice is concerned, it seemed to me that the relationship between an attorney and the client was so personal that you couldn't possibly represent a man as an attorney and then have an unbiased view when he presented his case to you in the event that he had one before the Government.

And so I felt that the best way to handle these necessary political expenses of getting my message to the American people and the speeches I made, the speeches that I had printed, for the most part, concerned this one message—of exposing this Administration, the communism in it, the corruption in it—the only way that I could do that was to accept the aid which people in my home state of California who contributed to my campaign and who continued to make these contributions after I was elected were glad to make.

NO SPECIAL FAVORS

And let me say I am proud of the fact that not one of them has ever asked me for a special favor. I'm proud of the fact that not one of them has ever asked me to vote on a bill other than as my own conscience would dictate. And I am proud of the fact that the taxpayers by subterfuge or otherwise have never paid one dime for expenses which I thought were political and shouldn't be charged to the taxpayers.

Let me say, incidentally, that some of you may say, "Well, that's all right, Senator; that's your explanation, but have you got any proof?"

And I'd like to tell you this evening that just about an hour ago we received an independent audit of this entire fund.

I suggested to Gov. Sherman Adams, who is the chief of staff of the Dwight Eisenhower campaign, that an independent audit and legal report be obtained. And I have that audit here in my hand.

It's an audit made by the Price Waterhouse & Co. firm, and the legal opinion by Gibson, Dunn & Crutcher, lawyers in Los Angeles, the biggest law firm and incidentally one of the best ones in Los Angeles.

I'm proud to be able to report to you tonight that this audit and this legal opinion is being forwarded to General Eisenhower. And I'd like to read you the opinion that was prepared by Gibson, Dunn & Crutcher and based on all the pertinent laws and statutes, together with the audit report prepared by the certified public accountants.

> It is our conclusion that Senator Nixon did not obtain any financial gain from the collection and disbursement of the fund by Dana Smith; that Senator Nixon did not violate any Federal or state law by reason of the operation of the fund, and that neither the portion of the fund paid by Dana Smith directly to third persons nor the portion paid to Senator Nixon to reimburse him for designated office expenses constituted income to the Senator which was either reportable or taxable as income under applicable tax laws. (signed) Gibson, Dunn & Crutcher by Alma H. Conway.

Now that, my friends, is not Nixon speaking, but that's an independent audit which was requested because I want the American people to know all the facts and I'm not afraid of having independent people go in and check the facts, and that is exactly what they did.

But then I realize that there are still some who may say, and rightly so, and let me say that I recognize that some will continue to smear regardless of what the truth may be, but that there has been understandably some honest misunderstanding on this matter, and there's some that will say: "Well, maybe you were able, Senator, to fake this thing. How can we believe what you say? After all, is there a possibility that maybe you got some sums in cash? Is there a possibility that you may have feathered your own nest?"

THE FAMILY STORE

And so now what I am going to do—and incidentally this is unprecedented in the history of American politics—I am going at this time to give to this television and radio audience a complete financial history; everything I've earned; everything I've spent; everything I owe. And I want you to know the facts. I'll have to start early.

I was born in 1913. Our family was one of modest circumstances and most of my early life was spent in a store out in East Whittier. It was a grocery store—one of those family enterprises. The only reason we were able to make it go was because my mother and dad had five boys and we all worked in the store.

I worked my way through college and to a great extent through law school. And then, in 1940, probably the best thing that ever happened to me happened. I married Pat—sitting over here. We had a rather difficult time after we were married, like so many of the young couples who may be listening to us. I practiced law; she continued to teach school. I went into the service.

Let me say that my service record was not a particularly unusual one. I went to the South Pacific. I guess I'm entitled to a couple of battle stars. I got a couple of letters of commendation but I was just there when the bombs were falling and then I returned. I returned to the United States and in 1946 I ran for the Congress.

When we came out of the war, Pat and I—Pat during the war had worked as a stenographer and in a bank and as an economist for a Government agency—and when we came out the total of our savings from both my law practice, her teaching and all the time that I was in the war—the total for that entire period was just a little less than $10,000. Every cent of that, incidentally, was in Government bonds.

Well that's where we start when I go into politics. Now what have I earned since I went into politics? Well here it is—I jotted it down, let me read the notes. First of all I've had my salary as a Congressman and as a Senator. Second, I have received a total in this past six years of $1,600 from estates which were in my law firm at the time that I severed my connection with it.

SAVED TO BUY HOUSE

And, incidentally, as I said before, I have not engaged in any legal practice and have not accepted any fees from business that came into the firm after I went into politics. I have made an average of approximately $1,500 a year from non-political speaking engagements and lectures. And then, fortunately, we've inherited a little money. Pat sold her interest in her father's estate for $3,000 and I inherited $1,500 from my grandfather.

We live rather modestly. For four years we lived in an apartment in Park Fairfax, in Alexandria, Va. The rent was $80 a month. And we saved for the time that we could buy a house.

Now, that was what we took in. What did we do with this money? What do we have today to show for it? This will surprise you, because it is so little, I suppose, as standards generally go, of people in public life. First of all, we've got a house in Washington which cost $41,000 and on which we owe $20,000.

We have a house in Whittier, Calif., which cost $13,000 and on which we owe $3,000. My folks are living there at the present time.

I have just $4,000 in life insurance, plus my G.I. policy which I've never been able to convert and which will run out in two years. I have no life insurance whatever on Pat. I have no life insurance on our two youngsters, Patricia and Julie. I own a 1950 Oldsmobile car. We have our furniture. We have no stocks and bonds of any type. We have no interest of any kind, direct or indirect, in any business.

WHAT DO WE OWE?

Now, that's what we have. What do we owe? Well, in addition to the mortgage, the $20,000 mortgage on the house in Washington, the $10,000 one on the house in Whittier, I owe $4,500 to the Riggs Bank in Washington, D.C., with interest 4½ per cent.

I owe $3,500 to my parents and the interest on that loan which I pay regularly, because it's the part of the savings they made through the years they were working so hard. I pay regularly 4 per cent interest. And then I have a $500 loan which I have on my life insurance.

Well, that's about it. That's what we have and that's what we owe. It isn't very much but Pat and I have the satisfaction that every dime that we've got is honestly ours. I should say this—that Pat doesn't have a mink coat. But she does have a respectable Republican cloth coat. And I always tell her that she'd look good in anything.

One other thing I probably should tell you, because if I don't they'll probably be saying this about me too, we did get something—a gift—after the election. A man down in Texas heard Pat on the radio mention the fact that our two youngsters would like to have a dog. And, believe it or not, the day before we left on this campaign trip we got a message from Union Station in Baltimore saying they had a package for us. We went down to get it. You know what it was?

DISAGREES WITH MITCHELL

It was a little cocker spaniel dog in a crate that he sent all the way from Texas. Black and white spotted. And our little girl—Trisha, the 6-year-old—named it Checkers. And you know the kids love the dog and I just want to say this right now, that regardless of what they say about it, we're gonna keep it.

It isn't easy to come before a nation-wide audience and air your life as I've done. But I want to say some things before I conclude that I think most of you will agree on. Mr. Mitchell, the chairman of the Democratic National Committee, made the statement that if a man couldn't afford to be in the United States Senate he shouldn't run for the Senate.

And I just want to make my position clear. I don't agree with Mr. Mitchell when he says that only a rich man should serve his Government in the United States Senate or in the Congress.

I don't believe that represents the thinking of the Democratic party, and I know that it doesn't represent the thinking of the Republican party.

I believe that it's fine that a man like Governor Stevenson who inherited a fortune from his father can run for President. But I also feel that it's essential in this country of ours that a man of modest means can also run for President. Because, you know, remember Abraham Lincoln, you remember what he said: "God must have loved the common people—he made so many of them."

And now I'm going to suggest some courses of conduct.

First of all, you have read in the papers about other funds now. Mr.

Stevenson, apparently, had a couple. One of them in which a group of business people paid and helped to supplement the salaries of state employees. Here is where the money went directly into their pockets.

And I think that what Mr. Stevenson should do should be to come before the American people as I have, give the names of the people that have contributed to that fund; give the names of the people who put this money into their pockets at the same time that they were receiving money from their state government, and see what favors, if any, they gave out for that.

URGES SPARKMAN STATEMENT

I don't condemn Mr. Stevenson for what he did. But until the facts are in there, there is a doubt that will be raised.

And as far as Mr. Sparkman is concerned, I would suggest the same thing. He's had his wife on the payroll. I don't condemn him for that. But I think that he should come before the American people and indicate what outside sources of income he has had.

I would suggest that under the circumstances both Mr. Sparkman and Mr. Stevenson should come before the American people as I have and make a complete financial statement as to their financial history. And if they don't it will be an admission that they have something to hide. And I think you will agree with me.

Because folks, remember, a man that's to be President of the United States, a man that's to be Vice President of the United States must have the confidence of all the people. And that's why I'm doing what I'm doing, and that's why I suggest that Mr. Stevenson and Mr. Sparkman since they are under attack should do what I am doing.

Now, let me say this: I know that this is not the last of the smears. In spite of my explanation tonight other smears will be made; others have been made in the past. And the purpose of the smears, I know, is this—to silence me, to make me let up.

Well, they just don't know who they're dealing with. I'm going to tell you this: I remember in the dark days of the Hiss case some of the same columnists, some of the same radio commentators who are attacking me now and misrepresenting my position were violently opposing me at the time I was after Alger Hiss.

But I continued the fight because I knew I was right. And I can say to this great television and radio audience that I have no apologies to the American people for my part in putting Alger Hiss where he is today.

And as far as this is concerned, I intend to continue the fight.

Why do I feel so deeply? Why do I feel that in spite of the smears, the misunderstandings, the necessities for a man to come up here and bare his soul as I have? Why is it necessary for me to continue this fight?

And I want to tell you why. Because, you see, I love my country. And I think my country is in danger. And I think that the only man that can save America at this time is the man that's running for President on my ticket—Dwight Eisenhower.

ATTACKS STATE DEPARTMENT

You say, "Why do I think it's in danger?" and I say look at the record. Seven years of the Truman-Acheson Administration and what's happened? Six hundred million people lost to the Communists, and a war in Korea in which we have lost 117,000 American casualties.

And I say to all of you that a policy that results in a loss of 600,000,000 to the Communists and a war which costs us 117,000 American casualties isn't good enough for America.

And I say that those in the State Department that made the mistakes which caused that war and which resulted in those losses should be kicked out of the State Department just as fast as we can get 'em out of there.

And let me say that I know Mr. Stevenson won't do that. Because he defends the Truman policy and I know that Dwight Eisenhower will do that, and that he will give America the leadership that it needs.

Take the problem of corruption. You've read about the mess in Washington. Mr. Stevenson can't clean it up because he was picked by the man, Truman, under whose Administration the mess was made. You wouldn't trust a man who made the mess to clean it up—that's Truman. And by the same token you can't trust the man who was picked by the man that made the mess to clean it up—and that's Stevenson.

And so I say, Eisenhower, who owes nothing to Truman, nothing to the big city bosses, he is the man that can clean up the mess in Washington.

Take communism. I say that as far as that subject is concerned, the danger is great to America. In the Hiss case they got the secrets which enabled them to break the American secret State Department code. They got secrets in the atomic bomb case which enabled 'em to get the secret of the atomic bomb five years before they would have gotten it by their own devices.

And I say that any man who called the Alger Hiss case a "red herring" isn't fit to be President of the United States. I say that a man like Mr. Stevenson has pooh-poohed and ridiculed the Communist threat in the United States—he said that they are phantoms among ourselves; he's accused us that have attempted to expose the Communists of looking for Communists in the Bureau of Fisheries and Wildlife—I say that a man who says that isn't qualified to be President of the United States.

And I say that the only man who can lead us in the fight to rid the Government of both those who are Communists and those who have corrupted this Government is Eisenhower, because Eisenhower, you can be sure, recognizes the problem and he knows how to deal with it.

Now let me say that, finally, this evening I want to read to you just briefly excerpts from a letter which I received, a letter which, after all this is over, no one can take away from me. It reads as follows:

Dear Senator Nixon,
    Since I'm only 19 years of age I can't vote in this Presidential election but believe me if I could you and General Eisenhower would certainly get my vote. My husband is in the Fleet Marines in Korea. He's a corpsman on the front lines and we have a two-month-old son he's never seen. And I feel con-

fident that with great Americans like you and General Eisenhower in the White House, lonely Americans like myself will be united with their loved ones now in Korea.

I only pray to God that you won't be too late. Enclosed is a small check to help you in your campaign. Living on $85 a month it is all I can afford at present. But let me know what else I can do.

Folks, it's a check for $10, and it's one that I will never cash.

And just let me say this. We hear a lot about prosperity these days but I say, why can't we have prosperity built on peace rather than prosperity built on war? Why can't we have prosperity and an honest government in Washington, D.C., at the same time. Believe me, we can. And Eisenhower is the man that can lead this crusade to bring us that kind of prosperity.

And, now, finally, I know that you wonder whether or not I am going to stay on the Republican ticket or resign.

Let me say this: I don't believe that I ought to quit because I'm not a quitter. And, incidentally, Pat's not a quitter. After all, her name was Patricia Ryan and she was born on St. Patrick's Day, and you know the Irish never quit.

But the decision, my friends, is not mine. I would do nothing that would harm the possibilities of Dwight Eisenhower to become President of the United States. And for that reason I am submitting to the Republican National Committee tonight through this television broadcast the decision which it is theirs to make.

Let them decide whether my position on the ticket will help or hurt. And I am going to ask you to help them decide. Wire and write the Republican National Committee whether you think I should stay on or whether I should get off. And whatever their decision is, I will abide by it.

But just let me say this last word. Regardless of what happens I'm going to continue this fight. I'm going to campaign up and down America until we drive the crooks and the Communists and those that defend them out of Washington. And remember, folks, Eisenhower is a great man. Believe me. He's a great man. And a vote for Eisenhower is a vote for what's good for America.

76. HARRY GIVES 'EM HELL

Harry S. Truman*

... Now, I suppose the Republicans will raise a great hullabaloo because I have come to this hall on Labor Day and said that the Democratic candidates are friends of labor. According to the Republicans, there seems to be something bad about being a friend of labor, something bad about Democrats being friends of the farmer, something bad about our party being interested in the welfare of all the people.

Well, let me say this to you. The Democratic party has a long, long

* President of the United States from 1945 to 1953. Speech was delivered in Milwaukee, Wisc., Sept. 2, 1952. Reprinted from the *New York Times*.

record of friendship and support for the working men and women of America and a long, long record of friendship for all the 150,000,000 people who cannot afford a paid lobbyist at the capital.

You know, the only lobbyist that that 150,000,000 people has is the President of the United States, and when he turns 'em down they're in a bad fix, sure enough.

We have tried to improve working conditions and living standards. And we have succeeded. What's more, we shall keep it up. The Democratic party is going right ahead, fighting for the welfare of all the people of this great Republic.

The record makes very plain what we have done and what we shall continue to do.

We've fought for the farmer just as hard as we fought for labor. We've done the same thing for all groups in our population. We have done this because we know that our national welfare cannot be divided. We know that the welfare of each group is dependent upon the welfare of all the others. And that makes a great country.

We are proud that the Democratic party is the party of the people. That's the way it has been and that's the way it will be under the new leadership of Adlai Stevenson.

It's a mighty good thing that the people have a Democratic party to count on. For it's a sure thing they can't count on the Republican party. The Republicans are still the party of special interests, still the errand boys of the big lobbies, still the ones who want to exploit labor, and the farmers and the consumers. The only thing different about them this year is that they are trying to hide behind a new face—their lonely, captive candidate.

Now, my friends, they have tried disguises before. They always try to put on a new face, put a new face on the elephant at election time. But the disguise never works because the rest of the elephant is too big to hide— and the rest of that major elephant has the record of the Republican reaction written all over him.

Now, the Republicans are trying very hard to cover up their record. They are campaigning on the idea that it is time for a change. But they don't come right out and tell you the kind of a change they really want. That's what I think you ought to know and that's what I'm going to tell you. And I'm going to prove it by the Republican record.

ASSAILS "NAGGING OPPOSITION"

The Republican record is one of constant, nagging opposition to all the great progressive measures that our country has adopted in the past twenty years. They fought these things every step of the way; they don't want to admit it now, they don't want to admit at all that any good has been accomplished; they don't want to admit that they are going to undo these things and turn the clock back if they get a chance—and that's just what they'd do.

Take the matter of providing jobs for people who want them. We have full employment now—62,000,000 jobs, more and better job opportunities than ever before in history. No republic, no monarchy, no empire ever had such a record. Not only are the jobs available, but wages are good, too. In fact, wages are at an all time high.

Now, is that what the Republicans want to change? I'm afraid it is. The Republicans in the House of Representatives voted against the full employment bill almost two to one.

Actually, the big money boys like a little unemployment and they also like low wages. Remember the last time they held office—they steered this country into the worst depression we ever had. And there's nothing in their record to give us any confidence that they wouldn't do it again if they had a chance.

Now, my friends, I want you to remember back in 1933 there were less than 3,000,000 union members in this country. Jobs were scarce, and wages were poor, and the working man was getting a raw deal all across the board. Today, the situation is very different. Our American trade unions have more than 16,000,000 members and the working man is getting a fair deal all across the board.

Now, do the Republicans want to change that? I'll say they do. A lot of 'em would get a big kick out of doing just a little union busting. They would be glad to go right back to the days of the "yellow dog" contracts and the labor spies.

It was the Republicans who fought the Wagner Act in 1935. It was the Republicans who fought the Minimum Wage Law in 1938. It was the Republicans who dreamed up and put across the Taft-Hartley Act in 1947. A grand record—you ought to remember it.

You would think they might have learned something in 1948. But they didn't. Look at the record of the last four years. In 1949, almost every single Republican in Congress voted against the repeal of the Taft-Hartley Act. Then they tried to keep us from raising the minimum wage to 75 cents.

And just three months ago almost every one of them lined up on the side of the steel corporations against labor in the steel case.

A "DRED SCOTT" OPINION

I'll tell you all about the steel case one of these days and analyze this modern Dred Scott opinion that the six justices put out. And I'll tell you all about it and then you'll know exactly what's behind all this.

When you look at the record, I don't think there's much doubt about the kind of change the Republicans want so far as labor is concerned.

Now look for a moment at Social Security. Under Democratic leadership, the Government has recognized that it has a responsibility for the general welfare of its citizens. We've passed Social Security laws to provide unemployment insurance and old-age insurance, and to help needy old people and dependent children and to provide aid for the blind.

When the Republicans say it's time for a change, do they mean they are going to take your Social Security benefits away? I wonder if they do.

That's not what they're telling you now, but look at the record.

Almost to a man, the Republicans in Congress opposed the original

Social Security Law in 1935. And I was in that Congress and I know. They fought against improving it in 1939. And in that terrible do-nothing Eightieth Congress, they even took insurance protection away from nearly 1,000,000 people. Now that's the record of Social Security.

STEPPED INTO "HORNET'S NEST"

In the last four years, it's been the same way. The House Republicans voted ten to one to block the great Social Security improvements of 1949.

And just last May they did it again. They lined up two to one against increasing old age insurance benefits and public assistance payments to meet the increased cost of living. A lot of them found out they had stepped into a hornet's nest on this one, and they had to change their votes when the bill was brought up at a later date.

The Republican candidate for President made a speech the other day and said that all Americans of all parties now support Social Security. I guess he didn't know about the Republican record in Congress. He could find out a lot of things by examining that record. He ought to give it some study.

We ought to give it study too—you and all other Americans. That's the way you find out what the Republicans really mean when they say it's time for a change.

Apparently they mean that it's time to change our policy of building decent homes for low-income families. Eighty per cent of the Republican Congress voted this spring to cut the public housing program—and they almost succeeded in doing it.

Apparently they mean it's time to change our policy of developing the power from our rivers for the benefit of all the people. Over 80 per cent of the Republican Congress have voted time after time, at the bidding of the private power lobby, to sabotage our public power program in any way they can.

Apparently they mean it's time to change our policy on rural electrification. Over 80 per cent of the Republican Senators went on record three separate times last year in favor of cutting funds for R. E. A. [Rural Electrification Administration] cooperatives.

ALMOST ALWAYS VOTED WRONG

Apparently they mean it's time to change our policy on soil conservation. Seventy-five per cent of the Republican Senators voted just three months ago for a crippling slash in our soil conservation program.

Apparently they mean it's time to change our policy of stabilizing prices to prevent runaway inflation. Seventy-nine per cent of the Republicans in the House voted this year to scuttle price control.

Every time I hear the Republicans moan about high prices I get angry. They ganged up in Congress in 1946 and voted to ruin O. P. A. and kill price controls. In 1947, 1948 and 1949, they opposed every effort to get controls restored even on a standby basis.

Then in 1950 when Korea came along, they tried their best to cripple the new controls bill at the start. And what they weren't able to accomplish the first time around, they tried hard to put across in 1951 and again this year.

These are some of the things the Republicans would like to change. They may tell you something different, but the Republican party has writtten its record in Congress where it is plain to see. In my whole experience as President, a great majority of the Republicans in Congress have almost always voted wrong—that is against the welfare of the people and for special interests.

I am glad for my country's sake and for the sake of my party that the Democratic record is different. During these ten years, a sizable majority of the Democrats in Congress have almost always voted right.

Take the great issues of the last seven years, foreign and domestic. You will find as I have, that 60, 70 and 80 per cent of the Democrats have been on the right side, the liberal side, the side of the people.

You'll also find—and it follows naturally—that with more Democrats in Congress, and fewer Republicans, more good legislation gets adopted. You all know what happened in the do-nothing, good-for-nothing Eightieth Congress. And I think you can agree that in the last Congress, the Eighty-second Congress where there were almost as many Republicans as Democrats—our liberal programs had very tough sledding.

But in the Eighty-first Congress—the one elected in 1948—in 1948, you remember that's when I had a wonderful campaign—where the Democrats had a real majority—we passed more progressive legislation than was passed during the entire past ten years.

Now, this little bit of history makes it clear to you what the problem is in the Congressional elections this year. We don't need just a few more Democrats than Republicans in Congress, we need a lot more Democrats so that the liberal majority in our party will be big enough to outvote the overwhelming number of reactionaries in the Republican party.

MIGHT NOT WIN AGAIN

Now listen to me, my friends, listen carefully. It is not time and it never will be time for the kind of change that would hit this country if the Republicans should win in November. The record shows what they stand for and what they want to do. The people of America just cannot afford to take a risk like that.

You know, if the Republicans don't wake up and reform, it wouldn't surprise me if they never did win another election. That seems to worry some people these days. There are those who are going around saying that no matter what the Republicans are like, you'd better vote them into office this time. Otherwise, the Republican party might disappear. And that, they say, would ruin the two-party system.

Well, now, those people who say that don't know anything about history. You remember the old Federalist party went out of business when it tried to turn the Government over to old man Biddle and the United States Bank and Andrew Jackson wouldn't let them. That ended the Federalist party.

Then along in 1852, if I remember correctly, the Whigs, successors to the Republican party, nominated a general of the Army by the name of Winfield Scott. In 1852 the Whigs got the best licking any party ever got until Franklin Roosevelt gave the Republicans a licking in 1936.

NO PARTY DESERVES CHARITY

Well, that ended the Whig party. Now when people say that if the Republican party disappears it might injure the two-party system, that's an appeal to charity.

It reminds me of a panhandler outside of a tavern asking for a dime.

And the answer to that should be simple:

I want you to say to them that you'll vote the Republicans in when they reform. That you'll vote for 'em when they prove to you that they can run the country for the good of the people and that you won't vote for 'em before that time.

I'm not talking about reform just before election for campaign purposes. I'm talking about the kind that shows up on the record between elections in the Congress of the United States.

No party deserves to be kept alive just out of the kindness of charity. We don't run our country to keep political parties alive, we run our parties to keep the country alive, and strong and growing.

Please don't misunderstand me. There's one thing that I'm in agreement with the Republicans about. It is time for a change. But not the kind of change they're thinking about. It's time for a change from the endless campaign of Republican opposition to progress.

It's time for a change from the big lie—from the brazen Republican efforts to falsify history, to smear and ruin innocent individuals, to trample on the basic liberties of American citizens.

It's time for a change, all right, for a change to a situation where our Government will not be so hamstrung by Republican opposition in building a better America and a safe and peaceful world.

Now, to bring that about, we have to send enough Democrats to Congress to give the new Democratic President a real working majority that will carry out the Democratic platform, which is the best platform any party ever adopted. There is not a weasel word in that platform and our Democratic candidates are standing squarely upon it.

Now, my friends, this is the way to get a change in Washington—the kind of a change that helps the workers of our country and all the people. So when the Republicans urge you that you ought to have a change, don't hesitate to take 'em up on it. Take 'em at their word and vote the Democratic ticket.

Don't be deceived. Don't be deceived by anything the Republicans may tell you this election year. Remember who they are and what they are. Remember their record.

If you do that, I have no doubt about how this election will come out.

Then this country, which we all love so much, will be starting on a bright new chapter in the history of progress for us all. The Congress will be firmly Democratic. And our next President will be Adlai Stevenson.

77. A SOUTHERN GOVERNOR ON DESEGREGATION

J. Lindsay Almond *

My fellow Virginians:

I am grateful for the privilege of this brief appearance to discuss with you some aspects of the constitutional crisis shackled upon us by a judicial oligarchy and its shocking and terrible impact on our public school system.

Throughout this struggle Virginia has fought to preserve and defend her rights vouchsafed to her under and within the framework of the Constitution of the United States. On the highest plane of honor, inherent conviction and loftiness of ideals and principle she has sought only to maintain those rights reserved by her and her sister states, and which have never been delegated, forfeited or surrendered to the Federal Government. Her loyalty to our federated system of govern as ordained by the Constitution is woven with indestructible thread into the heart and fiber of her people.

A combination of forces motivated by political expediency, armed with arrogated power and inimical to our constitutional system, has advanced with ruthless tread to strike down and destroy the right of the people of this State to have a voice in the education of their children.

This is lamentably true, notwithstanding the indisputable fact that the fundamental law of the land embraced and protected the use and enjoyment of this right for nearly a century. The right is now denied through the process of judicial legislation amendatory of the Constitution in contravention thereof, and in violation of the oath to uphold and defend it.

RAPS SUPREME COURT

Without reference to the people as the Constitution requires, it is demanded of Virginia by the executive and judicial departments of the Federal Government that she forsake honor, abandon principle and eschew her loyalty to the Constitution by slavish acceptance of this travesty upon the Constitution, and grace the violated oath with a modicum of decency.

Virginia will not weaken in her allegiance to the compact which forms the basic structure of this "indissoluble union of indestructible states"; she will not dilute and desecrate her concept of honor; she will not abandon or compromise with principle to have it lost never to be regained.

To those of faint heart; to those whose purpose and design is to blend and amalgamate the white and Negro races and destroy the integrity of both races; to those who disclaim that they are integrationists but are working day and night to integrate our schools; to those who don't care what happens to the children of Virginia; to those false prophets of a "little or token integration"; to those in high places and elsewhere who advocate integration for your children and send their own to private or public segre-

* Former Governor of Virginia from 1958 to 1960. Speech was delivered in Richmond, Va., Jan. 19, 1959. Reprinted from the *Washington Post.*

gated schools; to those who defend or close their eyes to the livid stench of
sadism, sex, immorality and juvenile pregnancy infesting the mixed schools
of the District of Columbia and elsewhere; to those who would overthrow
the customs, mores and traditions of a way of life which has endured in
honor and decency for centuries and embrace a new moral code prepared
by nine men in Washington whose moral concepts they know nothing about;
to those who would substitute strife, bitterness, turmoil and chaos for the
tranquillity and happiness of an orderly society; to those who would destroy our way of life because of their pretended concern over what Soviet
Russia may think of us—to all of these and their confederates, comrades
and allies let me make it abundantly clear for the record now and here-
after, as Governor of this State, I will not yield to that which I know to be
wrong and will destroy every rational semblance of public education for
thousands of the children of Virginia.

FIRM STAND ASKED

I call upon the people of Virginia to stand firmly with me in this struggle.
Be not dismayed by recent judicial deliverances.

I propose to restore the tax revenues of this Commonwealth to the control of the people. They and they alone will decide these issues. United in
the common purpose of defending constitutional government and advancing
the welfare of our children—with determination more relentless than ever
before—we have just begun to fight.

No price is too high to pay; no burden too heavy to bear; no consequence too grave to endure in defense of the right and duty of this Commonwealth to protect the people of Virginia in the proper enjoyment of
their right and obligation to mold the character and promote the welfare
of their children through the exercise of their voice and judgment in their
education and development.

The grave constitutional crisis which has been thrust upon us makes
it imperative that our energy, resources and efforts be launched and applied on a state-wide basis. Abandonment of the principles involved anywhere is to forsake them everywhere.

The inevitable result will be total engulfment with the progress of dissolution and chaos measured by the combination of forces confederated and
arrayed to divide, conquer, rule and ruin.

WILL NOT BREAK FAITH

The people of Virginia through their elected representatives and by
registering their convictions in the exercise of their franchise have repeatedly made it crystal clear that they cannot and will not support a
system of public education on a racially integrated basis. I make it equally
clear that I cannot and that I will not break faith with them.

No parent or guardian is under any legal compulsion from any source
to send a child to a racially mixed school. In certain areas affected by
adverse Federal decrees the people have responded magnificently to the

emergency created through the closing of schools. Thousands of our children have adjusted to the situation.

The processes of education are being admirably and effectively administered. The hardships and sacrifices have constituted a challenge to overcome obstacles with the result that fundamentally sound educational progress is being made without chaos or undue confusion.

Amid the agony of these trying days I have been heartened and inspired by the profound spirit of dedication and determination of these citizens and their children, as well as the teachers, who have comported themselves so as to reflect immeasurable credit on the highest qualities of patriotic citizenship.

It is my purpose to appoint and convene with all practical expedition a commission composed of members of the General Assembly for the purpose of assessing and evaluating the entire situation in the light of existing conditions.

SPECIAL LEGISLATIVE SESSION

It is my earnest hope and desire that we may be able to formulate a sound and constructive program for submission to a special session of the General Assembly.

The problem is not one lending itself to an easy solution. It is most grave and difficult. It will require hard work, patience and a deep sense of dedication.

To prevent the pyramiding of chaos, confusion and disruption, I urgently request that private instruction now obtaining, and wherever it may become necessary, continue to go forward without interruption.

I urge the wholehearted cooperation of all concerned to this end. It is my firm belief that to break the chain of continuity in the administering of private instruction and the consequent confusion of a transition which may involve conditions justifying its termination would be productive of incalculable harm.

I shall not hesitate to use every available and proper means at my command to keep the peace and good order of this Commonwealth. I call upon our people to comport themselves with dignity and restraint to the end that the honor and name of Virginia be not defamed.

I have implicit faith and confidence in the genius of the people to cope with any emergency, and their loyalty and dedication to the preservation of their inherent and inalienable rights.

Our cause is sound, right and just. With your unwavering loyalty under the guidance of almighty God we shall go forward to higher and greater accomplishments.

CHAPTER X

Political Propaganda:
Totalitarian Indoctrination

In a democratic society, the voice of the government must compete not only with the voice of the opposition but also with innumerable other voices speaking through privately owned media of communication. The public can thus choose between propaganda and counterpropaganda, thereby retaining that power of decision which is essential to free and popular government.

This is not so, of course, in a totalitarian system. One of the most ominous developments of the twentieth century has been the demonstrated capacity of despotic governments to gain a stranglehold on the means of communication and to use those means for the rigorous indoctrination of a whole people. With alternative sources of information and opinion unavailable (except by word of mouth or bootleg channels), it becomes more and more difficult for the people to evaluate the information they receive or the dogmas they are fed. When propaganda is belied by their personal experiences and observations, they can continue to form an independent judgment as well as develop a healthy skepticism about the official media. When the information supplied concerns matters outside the purview of their experience, however, and when political doctrines ever more closely identified with patriotism and nationalism are dinned into people's eyes and ears day in and day out, year in and year out, propaganda often becomes a potent force for mobilizing mass support for a regime and its goals.

In the Soviet Union, propaganda is said to be the second biggest national enterprise—second only to defense. It is carried on by millions of educators, by every member of the Communist Party (theoretically at least), by the far-flung system of agitators (whose job is not to agitate as Westerners use the term but to peddle the party line), by radio and television, by plant managers and foremen, artists and entertainers, sloganeers, army officers, trade union officials, agricultural foremen and technicians, and by the entire publishing industry.

The latter is examined by Leo Gruliow, who provides an illuminating commentary on the organization, purposes, attitudes, controls, and techniques of the Soviet press. "Writers are gunners," Nikita Khrushchev once said, in the fight against the enemy and in the struggle for the construction of a "socialist" society. As such, newspaper editors take their cue from GHQ, represented by the Communist Party in general and *Pravda* in particular. The editors never forget for a moment that their task is to tell people what they ought to know, i.e., what will help them more effectively to serve the interests of the state, rather than frivolously to print what the people might merely want to read. The Party is also unequivocal in its rejection of either the possibility or the desirability of "objective" news reporting.

Marya Mannes discusses the medium which may be taking first rank in the Soviet propaganda arsenal—television. While noting the primitive artistic techniques of Soviet TV and its characteristic obsession with political doctrines, she concludes on a disquieting comparative note. Soviet TV is very earnest, very purposeful, and often very boring. But American TV's obsession with entertainment—pretty low-grade entertainment at that— and its strictly peripheral interest in education raise a question in her mind: "How much can we continue to play while others study? How long can selling through entertainment remain the prime function of the greatest medium of communication in the world?"

A. Doak Barnett provides a panoramic—and sobering—account of the torrential propaganda effort of Red China, which seems to have carried organization, and organized propaganda, to greater lengths than any great power in history. A nation-in-a-hurry, China seeks to extricate itself from the chaos, corruption, and aimlessness of pre-Communist regimes and to instill the vision of a glorious and triumphant future through the union of Marx, Mao, order, discipline, sacrifice, loyalty, and above all, work, work, and yet more work. To achieve the objectives of the state, propaganda must incessantly drive home the Communist message not only through the conventional Communist channels but also through techniques heretofore relatively unexploited.

A revealing account of "group study" appears in Harriet Mills' "Thought Reform: Ideological Re-molding in China." Her portrayal of the anguish of a Western-oriented Chinese girl torn between her convictions and her desire to lose herself, heart and soul, to the Communist movement, and her sense of liberation and exultation when she is finally purged of the Western infection—this is an unforgettable picture for those who regard the coercive subjugation of the mind as the ultimate indignity to be inflicted on a member of the human race.

How far can state-monopolized propaganda go in establishing a monolithic national consciousness, etched at the will of the master manipulators? Given the growing body of scientific knowledge about the human mind, thoughtful people often ask the question and shudder. And the bleak possibilities presented by such as George Orwell in his *1984* and Aldous Huxley in *Brave New World* and *Brave New World Revisited* serve only to heighten our fears.

Yet the human intellect has a toughness, a resilience, and a seemingly inextinguishable desire for at least a measure of freedom which suggests that there are limits to the influence of even the most cunning and ruthless propaganda machine. Russia still produces its Pasternaks, its youthful rebels, and its restless artists and authors after forty-odd years of Communist indoctrination. Red propaganda seems almost ludicrously impotent when imposed upon a subject people—witness the case of Hungary. In China, eight years of the most intensive national brainwashing produced not a hundred but a thousand lusty flowers of dissent when the ill-fated opportunity arrived in 1957. The evidence is far from conclusive, but it is easy to underestimate this marvelously incorrigible instrument—the mind of man.

78. THE SOVIET PRESS:
PROPAGANDIST, AGITATOR, ORGANIZER

by Leo Gruliow *

There is no understanding the Soviet press apart from its role as instrument of the revolution. Ask a Soviet newspaperman to define his work, and very likely he will give you the definition offered in every Soviet journalism textbook, in every lecture and, over and over, in the newspapers themselves. The definition is a phrase from Lenin, describing the press as "not only collective propagandist and collective agitator, but collective organizer."

Lenin coined the phrase in 1901, when he was an editor of *Iskra* (The Spark). *Iskra,* issued by revolutionary exiles, was printed on thin paper so that it might be smuggled into Russia. Small, illegal publications of this kind were virtually the only media which the exiles possessed at that time for reaching an audience inside their country.

In the light of this, Lenin's single-minded concept of the press becomes more understandable. Many of the old Bolsheviks—Lenin himself—listed journalism as their occupation. But their picture of journalism was entirely colored by their obsession with revolution. The press was "propagandist, agitator, organizer" for their cause; any broader view of its functions, including the prime duty of conveying information, as such, was beyond their vision.

Today the revolution has been accomplished, in terms of a shift of power, and the press founded on Lenin's precepts is no longer the isolated voice of a few hundred men smuggling papers over the border. It is the country's monopoly press, responsible for keeping some 200,000,000 people informed. But the revolution continues as an unfinished battle for winning the minds of the people and for changing the face of the land, and the functions of the press remain essentially the same as in the days of *Iskra.* Last year M. Strepukhov, formerly editor of the trade union daily, *Trud* (Labor), and more recently vice-chairman of the Communist Party's propaganda and agitation department, summed up the modern Soviet press as "a powerful instrument for mobilizing the masses to carry out party and government decisions." That anyone might regard the press anywhere as designed primarily to serve the reader with news, rather than merely to influence him for political ends, seems incomprehensible to the Soviet mind.

* Editor of *Current Digest of the Soviet Press.* Lecturer and radio-TV commentator on Soviet affairs. This selection is from Leo Gruliow, "The Soviet Press: Propagandist, Agitator, Organizer," *Journal of International Affairs,* vol. 10, no. 2, 1956, pp. 154-160. By permission of the publisher.

When an American editor told visiting Soviet journalists that he tries to be factual and objective in presenting news, the Russians politely but firmly rejected the notion that such an attitude could be real.

Of course, a good deal of cant and humbug is mouthed in the West about a free and objective press. The very act of selecting and editing news involves some degree of human bias, as the visiting Soviet newspapermen pointed out. But democracy, with its assumption that the reader is entitled to facts upon which to base an independent, private judgment, and the news competition in democracy's comparatively free journalistic market-place, have given rise in many countries to an ideal of factual, speedy and objective news presentation. The ideal is often honored in the breach, yet it is nonetheless real and living. The Soviet press itself prints unwitting evidence of this every day by compiling its daily indictment of the West almost entirely from the news columns of Western papers.

But the Soviet view of the press recognizes no such reality of imperfectly achieved ideals. The Leninist deals in absolutes. Since some measure of human bias is inevitable, runs Soviet reasoning, the question is not "how much bias?" but only "whose bias?" And from this it is one step to Lenin's conclusion that bias, specifically class and party bias (*partiinost'*), is necessary, nay, desirable, and the stronger the better.

At the opposite end of the journalistic spectrum, then, is not necessarily the paper which assails communism with the same vehemence as *Pravda* displays in defending it, but the "newspaper of information," existing even in some countries where the press traditionally has been regarded as a political vehicle.

The One-party Press

When a Soviet editor speaks of the party bias of his press, he has in mind, of course, only one party. The Communist Party is publisher or co-publisher of a majority of the Soviet newspapers.

Other bodies also publish papers—the Soviets, the trade unions, the Young Communist League, the armed forces, the ministries (of various industries, and of transport, agriculture, culture, and so on), the Writers' Union, the Public Society for Cooperation with the Armed Forces. Even if these agencies were not themselves transmission belts for the party, however, power over their press would remain with the party because the appointment, removal or promotion of every editor in the U.S.S.R. requires approval by the local party executive body. Then, to ensure upper-echelon control, it is further subject to confirmation at the next higher territorial-administrative level in the party. Appointments of editors of local papers must be confirmed by province and republic party committees, regardless of whether the papers are published by the party or not. Appointments of editors of newspapers operating on a province or republic scale must be approved by the party central committee itself.

The newspaper staff often includes many persons not enrolled in the party. Even *Pravda*, the party's own central organ, has a number of prominent non-party writers on its staff. But there is no ambiguity about the relationship between journalist and party. The relationship was set forth in an editorial entitled "The Soviet Journalist," in the magazine *Partiinaya zhizn* (Party Life) in May, 1955. The editorial dealt with a familiar topic, the need for close party supervision of the press. "The staff of the newspaper," it said, "is a kind of direct continuation of the party apparatus." Party officials must brief the newspapermen on what to write, advise them and give them constant criticism and guidance, said the editorial.

It is hardly surprising that the party-oriented Soviet press should be dominated by the party's central organ. *Pravda* is set apart in many ways. It is the only Soviet paper published seven days a week. In spite of the country's size, *Pravda* "blankets" the Soviet Union, flying matrices to more than a dozen major cities where local editions, identical with the edition appearing in Moscow, are run off. In circulation it towers over all other papers. Scheduled to reach 5,500,000 this year, the circulation is more than a tenth of the total circulation of all Soviet dailies, thrice-weeklies, twice-weeklies and weeklies combined; it is approximately four times that of the second largest daily, the government organ *Izvestia* (News). Incidentally, *Pravda* and *Izvestia,* alone among Soviet newspapers, maintain foreign correspondents, but *Pravda* has 25, *Izvestia* only eight.

When *Pravda* speaks, it does so with the voice of the top party leadership, and all Soviet and satellite newspapers promptly echo its words. Its editorials and major articles are read over the radio every day. Local papers frequently reprint its editorials in lieu of their own. Whenever policy shifts, it is *Pravda* that gives the signal. A *Pravda* article set off the recent press campaign against the Stalin "cult." It was a *Pravda* article that cut short the talk of consumer goods early in 1955 and turned the emphasis back to heavy industry, foreshadowing the resignations of Prime Minister Malenkov and Trade Minister Mikoyan. When Stalin died in 1953, it was *Pravda* that proclaimed the "collective leadership" slogan.

If other newspapers have taken a stand which differs from that of *Pravda,* they hasten to revise it as soon as *Pravda* appears. . . .

A Journalistic Hierarchy

There have been substantial changes in the tone and manner of the Soviet press since Stalin's death, but there are no signs that the position of *Pravda* is likely to be challenged. In fact, it is *Pravda* that has set the pattern for the changes. Under Stalin it led the pack. . . . Public papers are berated or praised by the "central" press. *Pravda* alone is immune.

A newspaper's criticism of another paper is printed under the standing headline "Review of the Press" or "In the Latest Mail." A characteristic "Review of the Press" in *Pravda* attacked *Udmurtskaya pravda,* organ of a province party committee in the Urals, in these terms:

> The unplanned and not always wise news items and correspondence appearing in the paper's "Party Life" column do not give an idea of the full-blooded activity of the party organizations. . . . How much the paper would gain from lively articles by party officials if it printed them more often; . . . The Udmurt Province Party Committee, of course, reads its paper. Why do they tolerate the paper's aloofness from the life of party organization?

Since Stalin's death there have been occasional instances in which a newspaper has defended itself against this kind of criticism. But only once has a Soviet paper talked back to *Pravda*. On December 9, 1955, a *Pravda* editorial ridiculed a passage from an *Izvestia* article on corn growing. Next day *Izvestia* printed a rejoinder, complaining that *Pravda* had taken the passage out of context.

Uniformity and Diversity

Despite identity of editorial policy, there are marked differences in style and subject matter among Soviet newspapers. At one end of the scale stands *Pravda*, solemn, sober and omnipotent. At the other are the country's four or five evening papers (their present number cannot be determined; they are forbidden for export). One such, the popular *Vechernyaya Moskva* (Evening Moscow), is newsy, sprightly, and regarded as "lightweight." *Komsomolskaya pravda*, aimed at a youthful audience, has the liveliest make-up in the Soviet Union and is written in brighter and simpler style than most papers. *Literaturnaya gazeta*, dealing with many areas besides the literary, caters to intellectuals.

But the outstanding feature of all the papers, despite the diversity of spheres with which they deal and the individual tone which each may seek to create, is the uniformity enforced upon them. In the franker post-Stalin atmosphere, Strepukhov admitted and criticized the uniformity, in an article in a May, 1955, issue of the magazine *Kommunist*, although he carefully avoided touching on the reason:

> Before me lie several issues of province and territory newspapers published on the same day. Above all, one is arrested by the striking similarity of the papers. Like twins, they can hardly be distinguished from one another. If it were not for the masthead and the names of districts, factories and collective farms which are mentioned, any one of the papers could be substituted for another, and neither the reader nor the staff itself would notice.

In any country, news services and syndicates are the channels, if not the reason, for standardization. Tass, the monopoly news service, distributes most of the copy which, appearing simultaneously and identically in papers throughout the U.S.S.R., creates an overwhelming impression of uniformity. In the American press uniformity appears mostly in widely syndicated features. In the Soviet press it is the features which differ from paper to paper, and the news display which is often identical, even to the phrasing, type, size and page position of headlines.

When William Benton, publisher of the *Encyclopedia Britannica*, visited Tass director Nikolai G. Palgunov in Moscow, he called Palgunov's attention to copies of the previous day's papers from all over the country. Each bore the identical headline in the identical type, size and page position, and the same picture of the same event in the same size and position on the page. Palgunov was visibly discomfited, reports Benton, and insisted that the identity of headlines and pictures was only "coincidental."

The following day Benton mentioned the incident to Konstantin Gubin, editor of *Izvestia*. Gubin laughed and said this was "compulsory news"

with "Tass headlines"—categories which, I might add, are well known to
Soviet editors, who receive sealed instructions dictating the treatment of
major stories.

The Confidential News Report

In lectures to journalism students at Moscow University Palgunov presented the Soviet view of news. His lectures were printed last year in a
brochure entitled, "Fundamentals of News in the Newspaper—Tass and
Its Role."

"News must be *organized*," he said, italicizing, "else it is news of *mere
events* and *happenstance*. . . . News must not merely throw light on this or
that fact or event—*it must pursue a definite purpose*. . . . News is agitation
via facts. In selecting the news topic, the writer of the news story must proceed above all from the realization that not all facts and not just any event
should be reported in the press." Tass follows Palgunov's advice that "not
all facts" should be reported.

In his lectures Palgunov noted that the Tass incoming file in 1954
ranged from 670,000 to 700,000 words daily. The outgoing file for Soviet
newspapers is only 60,000 words—40,000 of domestic news and 20,000 of
foreign. What happens to the balance of several hundred thousand words?
A large part is duplication, for the incoming file evidently includes the
reports of foreign news services with which Tass exchanges and which
duplicate one another's coverage. But a part goes into the Tass confidential
news report, each page of it headlined in huge block letters, "Not for Publication." At the end of the day the mimeographed pages are collected by the
messengers who distribute them, so that no copies may be retained by the
editors and high officials who receive it for their own information.

Whenever there has been a major Soviet statement, for example, Tass
rounds up foreign comment. If the comment is unfavorable, Tass releases
for publication such innocuous passages as "All London newspapers print
the Soviet declaration under large headlines on page one," and then rele-
gates to the confidential service the unfavorable editorial comments. Or it
releases an item saying that "many French papers indulge in gross fabrica-
tions, slander and distortion of the Soviet declaration," and saves the substance of the adverse reaction for the confidential service.

This device has been an almost invariable rule in the Tass reporting of
United Nations debates. The Soviet delegate's remarks are reported *in
extenso*, the replies by foreign delegates are disposed of in a phrase such as
"several delegates crudely attacked the Soviet position"—without mentioning what they said. What they said goes into the "not for publication"
service.

A tremendous part of Tass reporting of foreign affairs consists of quotations from foreign newspapers. This enables the official Soviet press to
present views which it might be undiplomatic for it to express in its own
name, and also adds the prestige of the foreign source to the Soviet argument. Anyone interested in the curious consequences of this practice can
study the speeches of the late Andrei Vishinsky, which abound in quotations from the world press, and the columns of *Pravda*, where many of the

quotations had appeared earlier under Tass datelines. The same passages quoted from foreign papers would then appear in *Pravda* a second time in the text of Vishinsky's speeches. Tass is the feeder agency for such quotations. . . .

79. AND NOW A WORD FROM OUR SPONSOR: THE KREMLIN
by Marya Mannes*

The long, bleak drive from Sheremetyevo Airport into Moscow tells the story simply: on every roof, peaked and wooden or square and stone, sprout aerials. Within a ten-mile radius of the capital of the U.S.S.R., five million television sets are registered, with an estimated audience of twenty million people. Television manufacturers make more than two millions sets a year, which they sell immediately, and by 1965 they can assure themselves of thirty million in use. Another five years still may not bring them to our saturation point, but they won't be far. They began only in 1953.

We could comfort ourselves, if we wished, not only with our long head start but by a comparison in programing. It would, in most instances, be highly unflattering to a system entirely dominated by the state. Soviet television is merely another tentacle of the giant octopus of government, and those who run it have no more freedom of direction or choice than the editors of newspapers or the producers of radio.

Dogma throttles the little screen as it blights the printed page and the spoken word. There is, of course, no free discussion, no intrusion of ideas unacceptable to the state, and no importation of foreign material that is not safely historical or wholly escapist. The set is a governess or a professor 90 per cent of the time, and an entertainer or palliative 10 per cent—an almost exact inversion of our programing.

Technically we could feel very smug indeed, for Soviet broadcasting is still astonishingly primitive compared to ours. The television studios, in Moscow and Leningrad, are small, their equipment old, their procedures beguilingly casual. At a rehearsal of a drama in the Moscow studio, a girl not more than 18 held a boom microphone over the actors' heads and an old woman wearing a head scarf and felt slippers held the cable of one of the two cameramen, trailing him as he moved. A scene between a man and a woman was halted again and again with good-humored horseplay because the actress was too short; the camera couldn't get her head in range with her partner's unless she stood on her toes.

On screen and behind screen, poverty of equipment is matched by poverty of imagination. Everything is taken straightforward and head-on, with no manipulation of angles or lights to create fluidity and surprise, no feeling at all of the special idiom of television. When they are not transmitting a film,

* Staff writer for *The Reporter*. This selection is from Marya Mannes, "A Word from Our Sponsor: The Kremlin," *New York Times Magazine*, Mar. 5, 1961, pp. 44, 49-50, and 52. By permission of the author and publisher.

the Russians are photographing a stage play or a radio lecture or a musical concert or a dance performance, as if the function of the medium were merely to make visible what was previously only heard or read.

In short, on the basis of intermittent viewing during two weeks in the U.S.S.R., an American like myself could say, with a yawn of boredom, "Well, here's one field, at least, where we're ahead of the Russians. If any proof were needed of the superiority of free enterprise over state control in mass media, here it is. No medium can develop its full potential within this ideological straitjacket, this bureaucratic dictatorship."

Yet, this kind of dismissal would be a dangerous error. For one thing, our technical lead is being narrowed day by day. New broadcasting centers are rising in both Moscow and Leningrad, equipped with large studios and the latest equipment, including Ampex Videotape. Within four years Moscow will have three channels producing a total of twenty-five hours a day of programing, as against the two channels now providing only nine hours on weekdays and about thirteen hours on Sundays.

Already seventy-five television centers have risen across the U.S.S.R., with each of the fifteen republics broadcasting in its own tongue; and there are now a hundred relay stations carrying the central transmissions from the big cities to remote areas.

The Russians are acutely aware of their present technical shortcomings. Mr. Sakontikov, the chief editor of Moscow programing, and Artist Hero Ezmakov and Mr. Vedensky, both of Leningrad television, all apologized for the primitive conditions.

"We know that you are way ahead of us in this field," they told me, "but we are catching up." When asked if they believed that television could become an art form, they were strongly affirmative. But how, I asked, could television become an art form so long as there were constant limitations on freedom of expression, without which creative impetus cannot exist?

Mr. Sakontikov smiled. "In time," he said, "the machinery of state will wither away and television will become a social function." He hastened to add, and was echoed later by Mr. Ezmakov in Leningrad, that a foreign observer must not think of the state as apart from, and superior to, themselves, the broadcasters. "We are the state," they said, "and what we broadcast is what the people want."

"You think you have free television," they said, "but does not business dictate what people will see?

"We will never use the air for business. We will never interrupt our programs with selling toothpaste, as you do. It is a terrible thing." I forbore to tell them that the difference between our systems was that while we sold many products for many sponsors, they sold one product, dogma, for one sponsor, the state.

I asked each of them then the overriding question: what did they consider to be the prime function of television? Simply, with the utmost conviction, they answered almost in the same words: "To make better people. To develop their tastes."

What is yours in America? they asked. Primarily to entertain, I answered; only secondarily to inform.

Do you think this is right? they asked. No, I said, I do not; but I added
that educational television was making strides and that a sizable body of
people was in a growing state of revolution against the virtual control of
programing by the sponsors. Some day, I felt, the American people would
demand an alternate system. The word "revolution" pleased them and the
climate grew warmer.

We then discussed the relative influence of viewers in the U.S.A. and the
U.S.S.R. on television programing. Did Americans determine what they saw?

I said that we could say what we liked and didn't like by writing letters,
that certain pressure groups could affect broadcasting, that critics could,
and did, write exactly what they felt, however adverse, but that in reality
the program content was determined by the networks and the advertising
agencies on the basis of quantitative viewing as reflected in ratings.

Here my Russian hosts proudly averred that there was a constant contact between broadcasters and viewers in Russia not only by letter but by
direct confrontation. Each major group in Soviet society, whether collective farmers or automobile workers or building constructors or editors or
lawyers, had its television committee which met at regular intervals with
the television authorities. At these meetings, open to the public, complaints
and suggestions were freely offered, they said.

"Sometimes," said Mr. Vedensky, "they are quite insulting. We are told
we bore them too much, they ask for more entertainment, they complain
about our plays and movies, they ask for more treatment of actual problems
in living. As a matter of fact, we started our English lessons a year ago
because so many of them requested them."

Soviet attempts to "make better people" cover a wide range. Besides
their excellent English lessons, I watched a program on ballroom dancing;
a program on how to set a table properly for guests; one on how to perform
acrobatics.

No day passes without a discussion of some phase of science or technology, without a science-fiction cartoon or playlet on space, without a
documentary on farming or building or nature study. Even ostensible entertainment features are larded with party pep talk.

As for news, of course, the Soviet citizen is permitted to see only that
footage which redounds to the virtue or glory of the state and hear only
those dispatches which disparage the Western democracies and exalt the
Communists or neutralist blocs.

Of Khrushchev at the United Nations, the Russian viewer saw no table-
thumping or shoe-waving, only his Chairman speaking, followed by the
applause of the satellites. The camera never included the delegates of
eighty-odd nations who sat on their hands, or, to my knowledge at least,
stayed with a Western speech for more than a moment. Khrushchev, on
Soviet TV and radio, won every round. Only Castro, torch of liberty, savior
of humanity, shared his spotlight.

The only areas free of direct propaganda seem to be the puppet plays
for children, delightfully done, concerts or ballet, costume dramas, or plays
from the repertoire of Russian classics from Ostrovski to Chekhov. As Leo

Paladini, a Russian expert, wrote in the English periodical Soviet Survey last year:

> With a few praiseworthy exceptions, Soviet films and films from the satellite countries fall into two categories, dedicated to two equally misleading myths: historical costume films . . . and films allegedly depicting "modern life" and showing a nonexisting world of the *kolkhoz* [collective farm] with dancing harvest girls and workers who spend their free time enthusiastically discussing how to increase the production of cast iron. Both categories are an escape from reality.

The same can be said of the few foreign films shown: costume escape or "documentary"-type films depicting the worst of slum life in capitalistic countries.

Just how much the drip of doctrine erodes the viewer's judgment is hard to determine. There must be some point at which an unconscious resistance sets in to shield the eye and ear from assault.

Yet some of the propaganda undeniably sticks, if only from cumulative repetition. The Russians really do believe that the West has imperialist designs, that colonialism is the great threat to all mankind, and that only the Soviet Union is the true champion of peace.

My little guide was the only Soviet viewer whose reactions I could observe. She may not have been a typical viewer, but she was a regular one, watching with her husband and family nearly every evening, addicted to romantic films and plays, believing the news implicitly, impressed by the Soviet leaders, delighted with the Chairman's temperament, slightly bored with educational programs but very partial to the English lessons.

I was particularly curious to know if the Russian intellectuals looked at television, and the repeated assurance that they did was confirmed in an interview with Mr. Zakharchenko, the editor-in-chief of a highly popular magazine called Techniques for Youth, a writer himself, and a broadcaster with a wide following.

"We take it very seriously," he said. "In fact, I myself am a member of a television review board that meets regularly with the broadcasters to advise and criticize where we think it necessary."

He admitted freely that their television techniques were lacking in imagination, that there had not yet come into being a group of writers specifically trained for the medium, that some of the programing was static and dull. When I complained particularly about the lack of spontaneity in live discussion programs or even announcements—men and women alike spoke only from notes and there seemed to be a total absence of free give-and-take—Zakharchenko conceded this to be true and blamed it on educational systems of the past.

"We were taught to read and write but not to speak. This results in a certain rigidity, a dependence on what is written down and planned."

New teaching techniques were curing this, he said. He added also that he spoke on television without notes and could say whatever he wanted. Dynamic, breezy, and humorous as he was, I doubt that his freedom of speech was quite that absolute.

He indicated, however, that the size of his mail showed the intensity of public response to an independent, "free-wheeling" personality, that he felt in direct contact with the people and that they expressed themselves without inhibition. Again, one would need access not only to his mail but to the 50,000 letters (a handful by our standards) received yearly by the Moscow station to know just how free this exchange really was.

Speaking of the tendency of television in general—whether government-run or privately owned—to neglect the bond with the public, to lose continuous contact with the audience, Mr. Paladini in Soviet Survey wrote:

> No solution to this problem can be expected in the U. S. S. R. For the public to have an influence on television, it must live within the framework of a society that is very different from the one historically established on Soviet territory, a society, in fact, which allows people to make their own decisions. . . . Any dialogue between television and the public is made impossible if there is an official and sacred truth on one side, and a total lack of autonomous means of expression on the other.

Although the directors of Soviet television periodically announce the receipt of thousands of letters from the public, it seems clear, he went on, that "these are unlikely to have any say in the development of Soviet television."

To take issue with Mr. Paladini's conclusion would demand more contrary evidence than a few weeks in the Soviet Union can provide. The foreign observer must sift through what he is told and by whom. Aside from the various interviews reported above, I can add only one tangible corroboration that some public criticism of television exists.

In a small "comic" book put out by the publishers of the humor magazine Krokodil, several pages are devoted to good-natured ribbing of the small screen. The style is heavy-handed and pun-ridden, but the targets are plain: the silliness of quiz shows, the interminable length of classical symphony concerts, the tendency to leave title and cartoon "frame" on screen for long intervals, the "interviews" with scientists in which the interviewer does all the talking and the scientist none, and, above all, the relentless How-To-Do-It lectures, especially for women.

Hardly corrosive criticisms in our terms, to be sure, but at least a hint of rebellion. It was, indeed, read with chortles of recognitive glee by a Russian sitting next to me on a plane, who later presented me with the booklet in question.

As for the "official and sacred truth on one side, and a total lack of autonomous means of expression on the other," I wonder whether our own "free" television system entirely escapes Mr. Paladini's charge. Since the dawn of our commercial system the broadcasters' "official and sacred truth" has been that the function of television is to sell goods by entertaining the public, and that any other motive or method of transmission is contrary to the principles of free enterprise, impractical, or a plot against the people.

The official and sacred truth is that the value of a program depends on the number of people who look at it and buy the products of its sponsor, that Westerns and crime, variety and quiz shows and old films are What the People Want, and that viewers who do not want them, being a minority of consumers, are unrepresentative and therefore insignificant.

Certainly, the American viewers can squawk and write and sign petitions to their hearts' content, but the effect this has had on programing is slight. Years of strong protests from citizens' groups against the mountainous dosage of crime on our television has not reduced it by one show. Conversely, it is hard to conceive of a body of distinguished Americans demanding Russian lessons in prime time because it is even harder to conceive of the broadcasters acceding to their wishes.

Trendex and Nielsen and Arbitron, to be sure, are supposed to measure public reaction as a guide to programing. But these surveys are purely quantitative. They may show how many sets are turned on at a given time, but they cannot show the degree to which the viewer likes or dislikes what he is seeing.

We can, if we choose, smile at the naïveté of the professed function of Soviet television to "make better people." Against the excellent few in our networks who truly believe that their major function is, indeed, to inform and stimulate and educate the American people, the dominant interests continue to insist that entertainment, first and last, is the medium's major purpose. To keep their franchise, some public-service programs must be included. But, say the broadcasters, let's leave enlightenment to the educational stations: television is a business.

And anyway, we could say, can "better people" truly be made by indoctrinating them hourly with dogma, by withholding the truth, by shutting them out of the world around them, by feeding them superiority, by boring them?

Possibly not. But there are tangible assets in teaching a whole people the language of their greatest rival, in presenting them with the best in their dramatic literature, in music, and in dance, in revealing to them the intricate marvels of nature, in instructing them in a number of skills, in keeping them abreast of their nation's technical advances in many fields, in instilling in them a pride in their labor and destiny.

There is a tangible asset in the use of women in positions of importance in TV, from chief engineer to newscaster, and their presence is one of the industry's most obvious attractions in the U.S.S.R.

There are equally tangible assets in the omissions of Soviet television. Crime and horror, gunplay and brutality are virtually absent from the screen, soap operas are unheard-of, and if much of the fare is unexciting it is also wholly free of the vulgarity, triviality and cheapness that flood our own sets.

When we talk, moreover, of the constant propaganda in Soviet television, we might remember what we are sold on our television, how often, and what this kind of conditioning can do in terms of the life we lead, the thoughts we have, and the aims we aspire to.

Television, no doubt, is making us a better-equipped people, a more comfortable people, possibly even a more relaxed people. Entertainment takes our mind from the grimmer realities, relieves us of the burden of thought and action. And we can always assure ourselves that on Sundays and sometimes—an hour or two a week—at night we can learn things we should know about and listen to our betters.

But does this companion of our days and nights do enough for us in a time of peril and demand? How much can we continue to play while others study? How long can selling-through-entertainment remain the prime function of the greatest medium of communication in the world?

Not, I hazard, very long. In the manipulation of this medium we are still strides ahead of the Russians, and their problem lies less in technical advancement, which is assured, than in keeping their audience baited. They cannot teach if they bore.

We, on the other hand, cannot educate our people to the realities of life and their involvement in it if we bend our major efforts toward their entertainment from dawn to midnight. This might be as good a time as any for the responsible members of our television system to stop polishing up their "image" and start thinking of their country.

What do Americans need to make them better people? What are our lacks? Where are our weaknesses? What must we know to withstand the future? The answers are there. The programing waits.

80. MAO'S AIM:
TO CAPTURE 600 MILLION MINDS
by A. Doak Barnett*

In the beautiful city of Peiping, where golden-tiled roofs of old imperial palaces shine brightly under the September sun, the Chinese Communists are about to hold their first National Party Congress since 1945. The face of the Chinese nation has undergone revolutionary plastic surgery since the last Party Congress, held in the caves and adobe huts of the little town of Yenan in China's remote northwest.

In the eleven years which have passed since the last meeting, the Communists have pushed Chiang Kai-shek and the Kuomintang off the mainland to the island of Taiwan (Formosa), reunified the country and reestablished a Chinese empire, organized the most totalitarian regime in the history of China, suppressed or liquidated virtually all opposition leaders and groups and dispossessed whole classes of society. They have made considerable progress toward collectivizing agriculture and socializing business, and have begun an ambitious program of industrialization. Under party control, a formidable modern army has been trained, and, for the first time in modern history, China has become once again under the Communists what she was in ancient days, the foremost power in Asia.

Impressive as these accomplishments have been, however, they may be of less interest to future social historians than the revolutionary struggle for

* Author of *Communist China and Asia: Challenge to American Policy*. This selection is from A. Doak Barnett, "Mao's Aim: To Capture 600 Million Minds," *New York Times Magazine*, Sept. 9, 1956, pp. 11 and 72-74. By permission of the author and publisher.

control of the minds of men in China which the Communists have waged since they came to power. With relentless energy and the zeal of religious reformers and inquisitors, Mao Tse-tung and his colleagues have attempted to "remold" the thinking of almost a quarter of the human race. They have tried to impose "Marxism-Leninism and the Thought of Mao Tse-tung" as a new ideology on a country which has one of the longest unbroken traditions of culture and philosophy of any nation on earth.

This attempt to reshape the minds of almost six hundred million people has been done partly through negative controls based on repression and fear and partly through a positive attempt to change people's ideas by a tremendous propaganda and indoctrination program. It is the latter which is most fascinating—and disturbing. The ability of a modern totalitarian regime, using police state techniques, to silence opposition and to repress a population into mute submission was fully demonstrated before the Chinese Communists came to power. But the Communists' techniques of mass persuasion and conversion in China are in many respects unique and may well outclass anything the Soviet Union and other modern totalitarian regimes have accomplished ideologically.

On the surface at least, the Chinese Communists achieved spectacular success rapidly. Within a few short years after 1949 the Chinese people appeared to have become regimented yes-men, parroting the Communist party line and speaking in one repetitious, monotonous voice; despite recent indications of some relaxation of control, the uniformity of ideas publicly expressed in China is still startling. A factory worker at the barracks-like dormitories of an industrial plant in Mukden recites the catechism of Marxist philosophy; a professor in distant Lanchow preaches the dogmas of dialectical materialism. Far to the south, the shopkeepers of Canton repeat the clichés of class struggle and world revolution. Shanghai's business men, world-renowned for their aggressive competitiveness, dance in the streets to celebrate socialization of their companies, while peasants in Hunan, wedded for centuries to the idea of owning a small plot of land, speak out in praise of collectivization.

During the past few months, Peiping's leaders have consciously attempted to relax the atmosphere of control. Since May, when Mao Tse-tung proclaimed "let all flowers bloom together and all schools of thought contend," there has been an increase of public "criticism and self-criticism" in China, and the Chinese people have cautiously begun to test a new party line on "free expression" of ideas. But there is no indication to date that this new "freedom," which can be turned on or off at will by the Chinese Communist leaders, permits any opposition to the basic ideology or policies of the regime.

The Communists' Party-Army-Government apparatus has achieved political and ideological control which extends to the grass-roots village level in a way unprecedented in Chinese history. Six and a half to seven million Communist party members, belonging to between three and four hundred thousand party branches scattered all over the country, hold the controlling strands of a complex web of organizations which enmeshes the masses in a system of close totalitarian supervision.

The entire citizenry of China is organized into groups which are easy for the authorities to control. In cities, for example, every fifteen to forty households are grouped into Residents Teams, under the surveillance of local police posts called Security Sub-Stations. The police, although less obvious and oppressive than in Stalinist Russia, are ubiquitous and effective. They keep track of all movements of people and constantly investigate not just the activities but also the attitudes of people in their precincts.

Besides these negative police controls, based on repression and fear, there are numerous mass political organizations through which the regime organizes the population in a more positive sense. Almost everyone belongs to one or more of these associations, established for specific social, economic and occupational groups, including peasants, urban workers, women, youth, students, children, different categories in the arts and professions and even business men. Each of these centrally directed, nation-wide organizations conducts frequent meetings, indoctrinates its members and serves as a channel for propaganda. Through them, active supporters of the regime are put to work, while everyone else is subjected to effective, organized social pressure to submit and conform.

From time to time, specific groups are singled out and subjected to special, frenetic mass campaigns. These have followed one another, with brief lulls between, ever since the Communists took control of China in 1949. Each has been an emotional binge involving large-scale propaganda and indoctrination, mass mobilization of the population to denounce a specific group of people and public confessions by the victims.

In the two most important early campaigns, those against landlords and alleged "counter-revolutionaries," hundreds of thousands, and perhaps several millions, of the victims were executed. But even in these campaigns of physical violence the Communists were vitally concerned with what they called "education of the masses." Instead of disposing of their victims quietly or secretly, they held mass public trials and public executions; mobs mobilized by the Communists often played the role of prosecutor. In the most important subsequent campaigns, the Communists' primary objective has been to obtain public conversion, or at least submission, of the victims rather than to liquidate them.

The "ideological remolding" campaign directed against university professors in 1951-1952 was one of these. For several months classes stopped in China's leading universities, while the professors engaged in orgies of open mutual recrimination and abject self-criticism. At the climax of the campaign, the best-known, long-respected professors in China published lengthy confessions; typical was that of the dean of the Law College of Peiping University who humbly apologized for the "serious mistake of holding on to my views."

All of these campaigns have been an essential part of the Communists' dialectical approach to the revolutionary struggle by the masses, and they have been conducted under the glare of tremendous publicity.

Peiping's enormous propaganda machine has a firm grip on almost every conceivable medium of communication. The propaganda is all-pervasive and insidious. It blares from loudspeakers at captive audiences in the trains and dangles on cloth banners outside prominent buildings. It creeps into songs which schoolgirls learn in class and stares from calendars which gourmets see in restaurants. Propaganda is injected into painting and poster art. Village storytellers have been given outlines for new stories to tell. Diaries are printed with quotations from Lenin, Mao and other Marxist deities on each page. Political slogans have even been knitted into women's garters!

Because illiterates still make up a majority of the population, especially in rural areas, the Chinese Communists emphasize oral propaganda and agitation. If people can be mobilized *en masse* with fly swatters to combat insects proclaimed to be carriers of "American germ warfare," as they once were in Tsingtao, what does it matter if they can't read?

The political missionaries in China's oral propaganda network, which the Communists say will ultimately contain 1 per cent of the population, operate at a village level and "deliver propaganda to the door"; they are even instructed, without a trace of humor, to get ordinary people "to replace family gossip with talk on current events." Public meetings, speeches, slide showings, picture exhibits, simple plays, puppet shows and singing sessions, as well as informal conversation, make up their propaganda repertory.

The daily press, supplemented by the radio, is of primary political importance. The official line emanates from such sources as the Peiping People's Daily and New China News Agency and is then disseminated all over the country. The Communists reject the "bourgeois concept of objectivity"; news is frankly propagandistic. Careful reading of the press, by those who can, is considered to be a political obligation; "neglect of newspaper reading is neglect of politics" which is a "serious manifestation of bourgeois decayed mentality." Collective reading and listening groups increase the reach of both newspapers and radios, as do handwritten village "wall newspapers" and "megaphone broadcasts" in which propaganda agents literally shout the news to villagers from the rooftops.

The screen, too, is conscripted into the cause. Typical of the output of the state-controlled motion picture industry is the film "Women Locomotive Drivers" which chronicles the epic struggle of several young girls to become engineers in order to contribute to "national construction."

The state-controlled publishing industry pours out millions of pamphlets and books; the best sellers have been works on such subjects as the Communists' marriage law and the campaign for suppression of "counterrevolutionaries." To increase the number of people whom the Communists can reach through the written word, a new literature in simple colloquial language has been developed for peasants and workers, and a nation-wide literacy training program is under way, accompanied by a plan to simplify the written language. Novels and plays center on current propaganda themes, defined by writers' organizations.

The all-out assault on the minds of the people is carried on at the level of each individual Chinese with what is perhaps the most effective single technique used by the Communists—indoctrination through small "study-groups." Today, and every single day, millions of ordinary Chinese gather in groups of half a dozen to a dozen people—in factories, shops, schools and offices—to *hsueh hsi* or "study" the ideology and policies of the regime. These groups, meeting regularly under leaders who report the thinking of every member to higher authorities, spend long hours discussing material transmitted to them by the party's propaganda agencies. The party line provides all the final answers in these discussions, but nevertheless the "study groups" examine in great detail all possible opinions on any ideological or political question in order to sweep away every obstacle to complete and unanimous agreement in support of the "correct" party line.

Criticism and self-criticism are the essence of this process. Each group member must participate actively, baring his inner self to the group and confessing past mistakes or lingering doubts. There is, as some Chinese have phrased it, no "freedom of silence" in these groups. No one can be indifferent, passive or neutral. Each member must stand up and be counted.

In this discussion process there is constant emotional and intellectual interaction among all members of a "study group." Each person discovers that when group criticism centers on him, as it does at different times on all members, he is, in a sense, a minority of one whom all the rest try to convert to prove *their* own "progressiveness." As a result, great social pressure is brought to bear on every member of the group. This process, often tense and emotional, takes place under the watchful eye of the leader, who is linked to party authorities and is responsible to them for the successful indoctrination of all group members.

Refugees from Communist China who have come out to Hong Kong assert that prolonged participation in "study groups" does convert many people and often has a subtle influence even on persons who strongly resist indoctrination. One former editor, a man in his forties, says: "You can't think clearly, even if you think you can, when you are taking part in intensive 'study.' You instinctively realize that your real thoughts will some day pop out of your mouth and that therefore to be safe you either have to change your real thoughts or not think at all." A young girl, just graduated from a university in Communist China, reports, "Most students began to change after undergoing 'study.' That doesn't mean, however, that this 'change' was really 'conversion' in many cases. For most students there wasn't much to convert; they had no firm or well-developed ideology; they were an ideological blank. The change, therefore, was an acceptance of new ideas which filled a vacuum."

These comments reveal two important reasons for the success of Communist indoctrination in China: the prevailing fear, or at least healthy respect, for Communist power; and the ideological vacuum which existed during the last years before the Communist take-over. China, after years of political and intellectual confusion, was a fertile field for propagation of a new faith.

The impact of all this propaganda and indoctrination is most carefully investigated by the Communists. Three separate nation-wide systems of organized informers have been established. Public Security Committees are organized in every locality by the police, while two other Government agencies select "correspondents" all over the country. These people check and report on the actions and opinions of everyone within a certain district or organization.

Such widespread investigation, mutual surveillance and organized informing breeds an atmosphere of suspicion which makes most individuals in China feel under continuous scrutiny not only by official personnel but also by other ordinary citizens. Almost anything one does has "ideological implications." One refugee in Hong Kong, a housewife, reports that her neighbors in China watched her return heavy-laden from a shopping expedition and then subjected her to group criticism for indulging in a "bourgeois" diet. A bank clerk says that his residents' group tried to make him cut down on smoking, claiming that he could not be "progressive" if he spent too much money on tobacco.

The Chinese Communists' fanatic, semi-religious drive to get everyone to accept their ideological dogmas leads them to spend an enormous amount of time and effort indoctrinating even those who are jailed or sentenced to forced labor (which is called, significantly, "reform through labor"). The "brainwashing" which Americans imprisoned in China have undergone is not a process reserved for foreigners. It is merely part of the Communists' over-all program of "thought reform"; Chinese prisoners undergo the same thing.

In prison, "thought reform" can be particularly effective because it is carried out in a completely controlled environment and because physical mistreatment, fear and threats play a much greater and more obvious role than in ordinary indoctrination. The unbearable fatigue and psychological pressures of both interrogation and group discussion in jail literally break down a person's mental equilibrium, greatly reducing resistance to complete reindoctrination.

The end product of this totalitarian organization propaganda and indoctrination is efficient thought control. The aim is to create the "new Socialist man"—a man who subordinates his own individual will to the will of the party, who accepts the Communists' code of "truth" and morality defining "good" or "bad" and "friend" or "foe," who is willing to live frugally, accept austerity and struggle for the revolutionary cause, who supports all the policies of the Communist party and fights against anyone or anything identified by his leaders as "feudal, capitalist or bourgeois." Clearly this is a big order, involving head-on conflict with centuries-old Chinese traditions, but it is what the Communists are trying to achieve.

To what extent are they successful? All one can say with assurance is that the Peiping regime *is* reaching the mass of people in China, it *is* teaching them the new ideology, and the people *are* expressing verbal acceptance of it. But this does not answer the crucial question: What is really going on in the minds of those indoctrinated? How many genuinely accept the new ideology? How many people's minds are confused by a combination of partial acceptance and partial doubt? How many people "believe" only because of the unceasing psychological and social pressures upon them? What would happen if the pressures were lifted? How many have built walls around their minds and have tried to stop thinking? How many cling stubbornly to old beliefs despite the necessity of approving the new ideology verbally? These questions cannot really be answered, but it is reasonable to assume that there are many people in China who fit all of these categories.

One thing does seem clear. The Peiping regime is having its greatest success in indoctrinating the youth of the nation. It is the future in which the Communists are interested, and it is the young people who hold the key to the future. Nurtured in a controlled environment, educated in Marxism and subjected to intense and continuous propaganda and indoctrination, the younger generation in China is without question being deeply influenced by the Communists' determined effort to "remold" the minds of an entire nation. Young people are particularly responsive to the Communists' appeals to national pride, as well as their promises of a Utopian future. Millions of children and young men and women in China today do bear the stamp of the "new Socialist man." This is one of the most profoundly disturbing facts about the Chinese revolution.

81. GROUP STUDY IN RED CHINA: BRAINWASHING IN DEPTH
by Harriet Mills*

. . . What are the factors which tend to make group study, tense and painful as it often is, effective? First, there is the essential human need to belong, to achieve and maintain emotional balance. To be unprogressive in China is not simply a political verdict; it is social suicide as well. Second, the constant repetition of correct ideas and particularly the application of them to the public analysis of one's own and others' problems mean that one is forced to give them detailed scrutiny. The Communists are conscious of the value of this. "From habit or pretense," they say, "it may become real." Third—and this is all too often neglected by outside observers—is the crusading idealism, the strong moral note, that runs through all discussion of political, social, and economic steps. Since it is obviously right that China should be made new and strong to assume its long overdue place as a major power, it is right to collectivize so as to mechanize and increase agricultural production. It is right to be Spartan and not demand higher wages so more effort can go into new plants, right to report opposition to the Party that is bringing medicine, schooling, and security to half a billion peasants, right to resist the "aggressive designs" of the United States in Korea, right that women should be emancipated. Fourth, there is the universal knowledge, as the highest spokesmen of the Party have frankly admitted, that in the long run no course but the correct one is open. At-

* Teaches Chinese at Cornell. Spent twenty-five years in China and graduated from the Shanghai American School before returning to the United States to study at Wellesley and Columbia. Arrested in Red China in July, 1951, and imprisoned for alleged counterrevolutionary action until October, 1955. This selection is from Harriet Mills, "Thought Reform: Ideological Re-molding in China," *Atlantic*, vol. 204, no. 6, December, 1959, pp. 73-74. By permission of the author and publisher.

tempts to avoid the tensions of group study by tacit compact to go through the routine or to stick to pleasantries are blocked not only by the fact of the leader's relations with the authorities but by the ever-present possibility that some member, whether motivated by genuine change of heart or by a selfish attempt at winning official favor, might report the group. Thus, there is tremendous pressure both to fall in line and to want to fall in line.

Most important of all, however, is a sense of nationalism, a patriotic pride in China's new posture of confidence and achievement. That China, which in 1948 was economically prostrate under runaway inflation, mal-administered by a weak and corrupt government totally dependent on American aid, incapable of producing motorcycles, much less automobiles, can now fight the United Nations to a draw in Korea, maintain the world's fourth largest air force, produce trucks, jet planes, even establish a nuclear reactor, is an intoxicating spectacle to the Chinese. This pride, in turn, has generated a remarkably effective and spontaneous code of public honesty, courtesy, and civic sense unknown in the old China. To be asked whether an incorrect idea is really worthy of the new China can make one feel guilty. Thousands have asked themselves, "What right have I to disagree with those who can achieve so much?" As a professor of English, remembering China's internal disintegration and international humiliation, explained to me in the spring of 1951, "Now we can again be proud to be Chinese!"

This man, a master of arts from Yale, had taught in an army language program at Harvard during World War II and knew and liked America. No left-wing enthusiast, he was slow in making up his mind about the Communists in the early period of their power, but as they brought the country under control, licked inflation, improved material conditions in the universities, and dared abrogate the unequal treaties, he proudly identified himself with the new China. For him, group study was stimulating. He looked on it as accelerating the weeding out of his undesirable bourgeois liberalism and promoting the growth of new socialist thinking. He had once enjoyed *Animal Farm*, but by mid-1951 he rejected *1984*, though his wife, a graduate of an American university in Shanghai, did not.

The valedictorian of the class of 1948 at the same university—the last class to graduate before the Communist take-over—was a brilliant student of international affairs. His English was good, his French and Japanese serviceable. His burning idealism had led him as a high school student into Christianity. Later, at the university, it led him into the student movement, which, in the last years before the fall of the Kuomintang, was dominated by the left. For months after the Communists came in, he was deeply troubled. His patriotism thrilled to the assurance and vitality of the Communists. Other aspects of his being cringed at their attack on habits and patterns of thinking which he subscribed to, including his Christianity.

One hot summer day he came to see me. "I have studied and studied," he said, using the Chinese term *hsüeh-hsi,* "and thought and thought. I have begun to feel there is more good in the Communist Party than in the Christian church. If I can satisfy myself on this score, I shall join the Party." Shortly afterwards he told me that he had. "Now that you are a Party member," I asked, "do you think group study is still worth your while?" "Oh, yes," he replied, his eyes burning with infectious enthusiasm, "it is indispensable."

Group study can even be exhilarating, particularly for those who, having been heavily criticized or struggled against, admit the error of their ways and are readmitted to the fellowship of the group. My good friend, a young former YWCA secretary, is only one example. Daughter of a Japanese-trained optometrist, she had graduated from the Catholic University in Peking about the end of World War II. A Protestant, she went to work for the YWCA and soon became close to young American students and diplomatic personnel who returned to Peking after the war. Transferred away for a while, she returned to Peking in early 1950 and joined the Central Relief Agency of the People's Government. She was miserable. She welcomed the material advances of the Government but felt that the price, in terms of regimentation, controlled thought, required group study, anti-Americanism, and the like, was too high. "I will go anywhere in the world," she used to remark, "where there is no group study."

Intrinsically honest, my friend's reservations about the regime were all too obvious. She could not fit into, and was therefore cut off from, the mainstream of Chinese life. Her Chinese friends pleaded with her to reconsider her attitude, particularly her relations with me, since by early 1951 I was known to be under suspicion. Her Western friends, knowing there was little possibility for her to leave China, were forced to urge her to compromise. But she remained fiercely loyal to her standards and her friends. For this she eventually landed, on my account, in the same prison cell with me.

In prison, as outside, she soon won the respect of wardens as well as prisoners for her honesty and courage. She did not pretend. Her kindnesses to me, whom the Communists had arrested as an American spy, were unobtrusive, but if discovered she courageously admitted them. For the first time in her life, she met people from many walks of Chinese life, people who, unlike herself, were uneducated, had had no contact with foreigners, people who were wholly and completely Chinese. Some had accomplished amazing things against incredible odds. She began to see a new dimension to her native land, to feel its hope lay within itself. She no longer felt that China was somehow inferior to the West. She began to discover her Chinese identity. But her habits of mind, her desire to look at both sides of a question, to undertake impartial inquiry, her reluctance to be regimented, and particularly her loyalty to her old friends died hard, and she was on one or two occasions briefly struggled against.

The result which I watched was a sort of catharsis. Her point of view changed, and with it her evaluation of past friends and associations. She remained as courageous, fair, and honest as ever, but her frame of reference was new. The joy and good feeling within the cell group that had helped her were enormous and vital. The helpers rejoiced at a black sheep brought home. She rejoiced at the psychological relief of having achieved spiritual integration. Very positive feelings of identification with and gratitude toward the small group and the larger society beyond followed. . . .

CHAPTER XI

Public Relations:
The Engineering of Consent

The evolution of the attitudes of political rulers from "the public be damned" to the public be wooed has been slow, painful, and marked by frequent retrogressions. It might be argued that the American businessman has been no less tardy than the politician in hearkening to the voice of the people. As recently as 1882, railroad magnate Vanderbilt uttered in a moment of provocation his infamous remark and thereby provided a convenient slogan with which to characterize the arrogance of his ilk. But once the business community embarked upon a policy of currying favor with its publics—once, in short, it placed itself in partial bondage to the public relations counselor—there appears to have been no turning back. And it could scarcely be otherwise: The phenomenal development of the media of mass communication, the growth of formal literacy, the increase in leisure time resulting from the shorter work week, the improvement in living standards, the unstinting application of the principle of free association, the legitimation of collective bargaining, and the rapid growth of population have transformed the citizen, the consumer, and the employee into potent forces in the modern world.

What is public relations? Who are its practitioners? What are its origins, its techniques, its applications, and its limitations? What are its present status and future prospects? What is its contribution to the politics and commerce of a free society? These are some of the questions considered in this chapter.

Whether one attempts to define this craft in terms of ends or means, one is struck by its nebulosity. An author of a textbook on public relations reports that "one student of public opinion has collected more than fifty definitions from fifty experts in the field."[1] And certainly the literature abounds in clever capsule characterizations. "Public relations" becomes "PR." The putative father of public relations describes his brainchild, as we shall see, as "the engineering of consent." Heilbroner calls it the Invisible Sell and Dale Carnegie Writ Large. And the "PR"tist is variously referred to as an "image merchant,"[2] a "middleman,"[3] and "a combination

---

[1] Charles S. Steinberg, *The Mass Communicators*, Harper & Brothers, New York, 1958, p. 198.

[2] See Irwin Ross, *The Image Merchants*, Doubleday & Company, Inc., New York, 1959.

[3] "A Special Report on Public Relations Today," *Business Week*, no. 1609, July 2, 1960, p. 42. The reader would profit from this informative report on corporate public relations.

trouble-shooter, adviser, and good-will ambassador."[4] All these labels correctly suggest, however, that the public relations man is both a public opinion analyst and a propagandist. In the former capacity he divines and interprets the moods, desires, and probable reactions of the various publics important to his client. His client (or it could be his employer) may be a corporation, a trade association, a candidate for public office, a government agency, an entertainer seeking to achieve or to retain stardom, a foreign country courting the United States government or American investors, an uplift society interested in reform legislation, a community in search of new industry—any person or group, in fact, with something to sell: a product, a point of view, a talent, an ideology. The publics are equally numerous: customers, stockholders, voters, employees, fans, prospective converts, legislators, bureaucrats, citizens. As propagandist, the PR expert reverses the flow of information and, utilizing his knowledge of communications media and of communications techniques, interprets the client in the most favorable terms to his publics.

Public relations has become big business in America in the past three decades. *Business Week* reports that corporations alone spent an estimated $2 billion on PR in 1960 and that this annual expenditure is expected to triple in less than ten years. The number of PR men has increased a hundredfold since 1930 to an estimated 100,000 at present, and it is predicted that 250,000 will be practicing this profession by 1969.[5] One might be led to conclude, when confronted by these and other statistics which might be cited to document the phenomenal growth of PR, that only those entrenched on the high ground of massive indifference will long avoid being swept before a veritable flood of advocacy.

The first selection in this chapter is drawn from the many writings of Edward L. Bernays, the dean of American public relations counselors. He has served in this capacity with his wife, Doris E. Fleischman, since 1919. His tour de force in securing the participation of President Hoover, Thomas Edison, and Henry Ford in the reenactment of the invention of the electric light on the fiftieth anniversary of that discovery greatly enhanced his own reputation and alerted many to the possibilities of PR. Bernays articulates for us his thesis that, although the people are sovereign in a democracy, they require guidance—the kind of guidance which the specialist in the use of the channels of communication can provide. He concedes that demagogues are as capable of mastering the techniques of consent engineering as the responsible leader and suggests that this is all the more reason for those committed to socially desirable objectives to make use of the communications experts to assure leadership which is in the public interest.

We turn next to Robert Heilbroner for a candid and perceptive report on the current role of public relations in America. He begins with its P. T. Barnum origins and traces its development to its present lofty status. What PR is, how it works, who is using it, and to what ends are reviewed in graphic fashion. The article concludes with some particularly useful remarks on the effectiveness of PR and its contributions as a social force.

The next two selections are specifically concerned with the use of public

[4] Steinberg, *op. cit.*, p. 201.
[5] *Business Week, op. cit.*, p. 42.

relations in politics. First, Stanley Kelley, Jr., discusses the increasingly important role of PR in political campaigns. He observes a fundamental change taking place in campaign techniques: The old-time political boss with his handouts has given way to the expert in molding public opinion. As Kelley notes, "the mass media have now emerged as the most important single road to political power."

Then Irwin Ross supplies a case history of America's most successful specialists in political public relations as he examines the operations of Clem Whitaker and his wife, Leone Baxter, in California politics. One cannot fail to be impressed with the skill and not a little alarmed at many of the tactics of this resourceful pair of propagandists.

Any young, brash, burgeoning profession is likely to be the recipient of considerable criticism, and PR is no exception. In fact, it might be said that the field of public relations is in need of better public relations—and so the PR man joins the ill physician, the disturbed psychologist, and the shaggy barber as one of life's little ironies. Heilbroner, Kelley, and Ross, in their evaluations of public relations, all speak of the resulting debasement of communications. Others feel that too many "consent engineers" are contemptuous of the public which they purport to serve, and that they are inclined to dichotomize the human species into Slobs and Snobs (with dual citizenship perhaps for some) and callously to regard them as objects for manipulation—not, in short, as ends in themselves but as mere means to ends. Still others are fearful that this expensive set of techniques known as PR is available only to those with ample financial resources and that there is no necessary correlation between affluence and devotion to the public weal.

Such criticism understandably disturbs the PR practitioner, but of even greater concern are complaints of unethical conduct. In obvious anger, Patrick Sullivan, public relations director for a large corporation, replies to allegations of dishonesty and deception. "Ethically," he asserts, "the pursuit of public relations is neutral and, as such, can be applied to either good or evil ends." He concedes that PR, like every other trade or profession, is not without its corner-cutters and double-dealers but insists that the vast majority of public relations men are honest. Most of their clients are seeking to have their reputations enhanced and certainly, therefore, would not risk having them besmirched by shabby practices.

82. THE ENGINEERING OF CONSENT
by Edward L. Bernays*

Freedom of speech and its democratic corollary, a free press, have tacitly expanded our Bill of Rights to include the right of persuasion. This development was an inevitable result of the expansion of the media of free speech

* Public relations counselor and lecturer on and sometime professor of public relations. Author of *Crystallizing Public Opinion, Propaganda, Speak up for Democracy, Public Relations,* and other works. Editor of and contributor to *The Engineering of Consent.* This selection is from Edward L. Bernays, "The Engineering of Consent," *The Annals,* vol. 250, March, 1947, pp. 113-120. Reprinted by permission.

and persuasion. .... All these media provide open doors to the public mind. Any one of us through these media may influence the attitudes and actions of our fellow citizens.

The tremendous expansion of communications in the United States has given this Nation the world's most penetrating and effective apparatus for the transmission of ideas. Every resident is constantly exposed to the impact of our vast network of communications which reach every corner of the country, no matter how remote or isolated. Words hammer continually at the eyes and ears of America. The United States has become a small room in which a single whisper is magnified thousands of times.

Knowledge of how to use this enormous amplifying system becomes a matter of primary concern to those who are interested in socially constructive action.

There are two main divisions of this communications system which maintain social cohesion. On the first level there are the commercial media. Almost 1,800 daily newspapers in the United States have a combined circulation of around 44,000,000. There are approximately 10,000 weekly newspapers and almost 6,000 magazines. Approximately 2,000 radio stations of various types broadcast to the Nation's 60,000,000 receiving sets. Approximately 16,500 motion picture houses have a capacity of almost 10,500,000.* A deluge of books and pamphlets is published annually. The country is blanketed with billboards, handbills, throwaways, and direct mail advertising. Round tables, panels and forums, classrooms and legislative assemblies, and public platforms—any and all media, day after day, spread the word, someone's word.

On the second level there are the specialized media owned and operated by the many organized groups in this country. Almost all such groups (and many of their subdivisions) have their own communications systems. They disseminate ideas not only by means of the formal written word in labor papers, house organs, special bulletins, and the like, but also through lectures, meetings, discussions, and rank-and-file conversations.

LEADERSHIP THROUGH COMMUNICATION

This web of communications, sometimes duplicating, crisscrossing, and overlapping, is a condition of fact, not theory. We must recognize the significance of modern communications not only as a highly organized mechanical web but as a potent force for social good or possible evil. We can

---

* *Editors' Note:* In any growing and technologically dynamic society, statistics such as these are likely to be obsolete before they are published. The following changes have taken place since this article was written: (1) The number of daily newspapers has increased to 1,850 (new suburban newspapers have more than offset metropolitan mergers and demises), and total daily circulation is up one-third to 58 million; (2) the number of weekly newspapers has declined to slightly less than 9,000; (3) periodicals now number more than 8,400; (4) the combined total of AM and FM radio stations (approximately 3,300 and 600, respectively) has nearly doubled, and there are now an estimated 150 million radio receivers; (5) the number of conventional motion-picture houses has declined several thousand, but this has been counterbalanced by the increase in drive-in theatres; and (6) in contrast with the less than two dozen television stations transmitting to 300,000 receiving sets in 1947, there are now approximately 550 TV stations and more than 50 million TV sets in use in the United States.

determine whether this network shall be employed to its greatest extent for sound social ends.

For only by mastering the techniques of communication can leadership be exercised fruitfully in the vast complex that is modern democracy in the United States. In an earlier age, in a society that was small geographically and with a more homogeneous population, a leader was usually known to his followers personally; there was a visual relationship between them. Communication was accomplished principally by personal announcement to an audience or through a relatively primitive printing press. Books, pamphlets, and newspapers reached a very small literate segment of the public.

We are tired of hearing repeated the threadbare cliché "The world has grown smaller"; but this so-called truism is not actually true, by any means. The world has grown both smaller and very much larger. Its physical frontiers have been expanded. Today's leaders have become more remote physically from the public; yet, at the same time, the public has much greater familiarity with these leaders through the system of modern communications. Leaders are just as potent today as ever.

In turn, by use of this system, which has constantly expanded as a result of technological improvement, leaders have been able to overcome the problems of geographical distance and social stratification to reach their publics. Underlying much of this expansion, and largely the reason for its existence in its present form, has been widespread and enormously rapid diffusion of literacy.

Leaders may be the spokesmen for many different points of view. They may direct the activities of major organized groups such as industry, labor, or units of government. They may compete with one another in battles for public good will; or they may, representing divisions within the larger units, compete among themselves. Such leaders, with the aid of technicians in the field who have specialized in utilizing the channels of communication, have been able to accomplish purposefully and scientifically what we have termed "the engineering of consent."

THE ENGINEERING APPROACH

This phrase quite simply means the use of an engineering approach—that is, action based only on thorough knowledge of the situation and on the application of scientific principles and tried practices to the task of getting people to support ideas and programs. Any person or organization depends ultimately on public approval, and is therefore faced with the problem of engineering the public's *consent* to a program or goal. We expect our elected government officials to try to engineer our consent—through the network of communications open to them—for the measures they propose. We reject government authoritarianism or regimentation, but we are willing to take action suggested to us by the written or spoken word. The engineering of consent is the very essence of the democratic process, the freedom to persuade and suggest. The freedoms of speech, press, petition, and assembly, the freedoms which make the engineering of consent possible, are among the most cherished guarantees of the Constitution of the United States.

The engineering of consent should be based theoretically and practically on the complete understanding of those whom it attempts to win over. But it is sometimes impossible to reach joint decisions based on an understanding of facts by all the people. The average American adult has only six years of schooling behind him. With pressing crises and decisions to be faced, a leader frequently cannot wait for the people to arrive at even general understanding. In certain cases, democratic leaders must play their part in leading the public through the engineering of consent to socially constructive goals and values. This role naturally imposes upon them the obligation to use the educational processes, as well as other available techniques, to bring about as complete an understanding as possible.

Under no circumstances should the engineering of consent supersede or displace the functions of the educational system, either formal or informal, in bringing about understanding by the people as a basis for their action. The engineering of consent often does supplement the educational process. If higher general educational standards were to prevail in this country and the general level of public knowledge and understanding were raised as a result, this approach would still retain its value.

Even in a society of a perfectionist educational standard, equal progress would not be achieved in every field. There would always be time lags, blind spots, and points of weakness; and the engineering of consent would still be essential. The engineering of consent will always be needed as an adjunct to, or a partner of, the educational process.

IMPORTANCE OF ENGINEERING CONSENT

Today it is impossible to overestimate the importance of engineering consent; it affects almost every aspect of our daily lives. When used for social purposes, it is among our most valuable contributions to the efficient functioning of modern society. The techniques can be subverted; demagogues can utilize the techniques for antidemocratic purposes with as much success as can those who employ them for socially desirable ends. The responsible leader, to accomplish social objectives, must therefore be constantly aware of the possibilities of subversion. He must apply his energies to mastering the operational know-how of consent engineering, and to outmaneuvering his opponents in the public interest.

It is clear that a leader in a democracy need not always possess the personal qualities of a Daniel Webster or a Henry Clay. He need not be visible or even audible to his audiences. He may lead indirectly, simply by effectively using today's means of making contact with the eyes and ears of those audiences. Even the direct, or what might be called the old-fashioned, method of speaking to an audience is for the most part once removed; for usually public speech is transmitted, mechanically, through the mass media of radio, motion pictures, and television.

During World War I, the famous Committee on Public Information, organized by George Creel, dramatized in the public's consciousness the effectiveness of the war of words. The Committee helped to build the morale of our own people to win over the neutrals, and to disrupt the enemy. It helped to win that war. But by comparison with the enormous scope of word warfare in World War II, the Committee on Public Information used primitive tools to do an important job. The Office of War Information alone probably broadcast more words over its short-wave facilities during the war than were written by all of George Creel's staff.

As this approach came to be recognized as the key factor in influencing public thought, thousands of experts in many related fields came to the fore—such specialists as editors, publishers, advertising men, heads of pressure groups and political parties, educators, and publicists. During World War I and the immediate postwar years a new profession developed in response to the demand for trained, skilled specialists to advise others on the technique of engineering public consent, a profession providing counsel on public relations.

THE PROFESSIONAL VIEWPOINT

In 1923 I defined this profession in my book, *Crystallizing Public Opinion*, and in the same year, at New York University, gave the first course on the subject. In the almost quarter-century that has elapsed since then, the profession has become a recognized one in this country and has spread to other democratic countries where free communication and competition of ideas in the market place are permitted. The profession has its literature, its training courses, an increasing number of practitioners, and a growing recognition of social responsibility.

In the United States, the profession deals specifically with the problems of relationship between a group and its public. Its chief function is to analyze objectively and realistically the position of its client vis-à-vis a public and to advise as to the necessary corrections in its client's attitudes toward and approaches to that public. It is thus an instrument for achieving adjustment if any maladjustment in relationships exists. It must be remembered of course that good will, the basis of lasting adjustment, can be preserved in the long run only by those whose actions warrant it. But this does not prevent those who do not deserve good will from winning it and holding onto it long enough to do a lot of damage.

The public relations counsel has a professional responsibility to push only those ideas he can respect, and not to promote causes or accept assignments for clients he considers antisocial.

PLANNING A CAMPAIGN

Just as the civil engineer must analyze every element of the situation before he builds a bridge, so the engineer of consent, in order to achieve a worthwhile social objective, must operate from a foundation of soundly planned action. Let us assume that he is engaged in a specific task. His plans must be based on four prerequisites:

1. Calculation of resources, both human and physical; i.e., the manpower, the money, and the time available for the purpose;

2. As thorough knowledge of the subject as possible;

3. Determination of objectives, subject to possible change after research; specifically, what is to be accomplished, with whom and through whom;

4. Research of the public to learn why and how it acts, both individually and as a group.

Only after this preliminary groundwork has been firmly laid is it possible to know whether the objectives are realistically attainable. Only then can the engineer of consent utilize his resources of manpower, money, and time, and the media available. Strategy, organization, and activities will be geared to the realities of the situation.

The task must first be related to the budget available for manpower and mechanics. In terms of human assets, the consent engineer has certain talents—creative, administrative, executive—and he must know what these are. He should also have a clear knowledge of his limitations. The human assets need to be implemented by work space and office equipment. All material needs must be provided by budget.

Above all else, once the budget has been established, and before a first step is taken, the field of knowledge dealing with the subject should be thoroughly explored. This is primarily a matter of collecting and codifying a store of information so that it will be available for practical, efficient use. This preliminary work may be tedious and exacting, but it cannot be by-passed; for the engineer of consent should be powerfully equipped with facts, with truths, with evidence, before he begins to show himself before a public.

The consent engineer should provide himself with the standard reference books on public relations, publicity, public opinion: *N. W. Ayer & Son's Directory of Newspapers and Periodicals*, the *Editor and Publisher Year Book*, the *Radio Daily Annual*, the *Congressional Directory*, the *Chicago Daily News Almanac*, the *World Almanac*—and, of course, the telephone book. (The *World Almanac*, for example, contains lists of many of the thousands of associations in the United States—a cross section of the country.) These and other volumes provide a basic library necessary to effective planning.

At this point in the preparatory work, the engineer of consent should consider the objectives of his activity. He should have clearly in mind at all times precisely where he is going and what he wishes to accomplish. He may intensify already existing favorable attitudes; he may induce those holding favorable attitudes to take constructive action; he may convert disbelievers; he may disrupt certain antagonistic points of view.

Goals should be defined exactly. In a Red Cross drive, for example, a time limit and the amount of money to be raised are set from the start. Much better results are obtained in a relief drive when the appeal is made for aid to the people of a specific country or locality rather than of a general area such as Europe or Asia.

STUDYING THE PUBLIC

The objective must at all times be related to the public whose consent is to be obtained. That public is people, but what do they know? What are their present attitudes toward the situation with which the consent engineer is concerned? What are the impulses which govern these attitudes? What ideas are the people ready to absorb? What are they ready to do, given an effective stimulant? Do they get their ideas from bartenders, letter carriers, waitresses, Little Orphan Annie, or the editorial page of the *New York Times?* What group leaders or opinion molders effectively influence the thought process of what followers? What is the flow of ideas—from whom to whom? To what extent do authority, factual evidence, precision, reason, tradition, and emotion play a part in the acceptance of these ideas?

The public's attitudes, assumptions, ideas, or prejudices result from definite influences. One must try to find out what they are in any situation in which one is working.

If the engineer of consent is to plan effectively, he must also know the group formations with which he is to deal, for democratic society is actually only a loose aggregate of constituent groups. Certain individuals with common social and/or professional interests form voluntary groups. These include such great professional organizations as those of doctors, lawyers, nurses, and the like; the trade associations; the farm associations and labor unions; the women's clubs; the religious groups; and the thousands of clubs and fraternal associations. Formal groups, such as political units, may range from organized minorities to the large amorphous political bodies that are our two major parties. There is today even another category of the public group which must be kept in mind by the engineer of consent. The readers of the *New Republic* or the listeners to Raymond Swing's program are as much voluntary groups, although unorganized, as are the members of a trade union or a Rotary Club.

To function well, almost all organized groups elect or select leaders who usually remain in a controlling position for stated intervals of time. These leaders reflect their followers' wishes and work to promote their interests. In a democratic society, they can only lead them as far as, and in the direction in which, they want to go. To influence the public, the engineer of consent works with and through group leaders and opinion molders on every level.

VALUE AND TECHNIQUES OF RESEARCH

To achieve accurate working knowledge of the receptivity of the public mind to an idea or ideas, it is necessary to engage in painstaking research. Such research should aim to establish a common denominator between the researcher and the public. It should disclose the realities of the objective situation in which the engineer of consent has to work. Completed, it provides a blueprint of action and clarifies the question of who does what, where, when, and why. It will indicate the over-all strategy to be employed, the themes to be stressed, the organization needed, the use of media, and the day-to-day tactics. It should further indicate how long it will take to win the public and what are the short- and long-term trends of public thinking. It will disclose subconscious and conscious motivations in public thought, and the actions, words, and pictures that effect these motivations. It will reveal public awareness, the low or high visibility of ideas in the public mind.

Research may indicate the necessity to modify original objectives, to enlarge or contract the planned goal, or to change actions and methods. In short, it furnishes the equivalent of the mariner's chart, the architect's blueprint, the traveler's road map.

Public opinion research may be conducted by questionnaires, by personal interviews, or by polls. Contact can be made with business leaders, heads of trade associations, trade union officials, and educational leaders, all of whom may be willing to aid the engineer of consent. The heads of professional groups in the communities—the medical association, the architects, the engineers—all should be queried. So should social service executives, officials of women's clubs, and religious leaders. Editors, publishers, and radio station and motion picture people can be persuaded to discuss with the consent engineer his objectives and the appeals and angles that affect these leaders and their audiences. The local unions or associations of barbers, railwaymen, clothing workers, and taxicab drivers may be willing to co-operate in the undertaking. Grass-roots leaders are important.

Such a survey has a double-barreled effect. The engineer of consent learns what group leaders know and do not know, the extent to which they will co-operate with him, the media that reach them, appeals that may be valid, and the prejudices, the legends, or the facts by which they live. He is able simultaneously to determine whether or not they will conduct informational campaigns in their own right, and thus supplement his activities.

THEMES, STRATEGY, AND ORGANIZATION

Now that the preliminary work has been done, it will be possible to proceed to actual planning. From the survey of opinion will emerge the major themes of strategy. These themes contain the ideas to be conveyed; they channel the lines of approach to the public; and they must be expressed through whatever media are used. The themes are ever present but intangible—comparable to what in fiction is called the "story line."

To be successful, the themes must appeal to the motives of the public. Motives are the activation of both conscious and subconscious pressures created by the force of desires. Psychologists have isolated a number of compelling appeals, the validity of which has been repeatedly proved in practical application.

Once the themes are established, in what kind of a campaign are they to be used? The situation may call for a blitzkrieg or a continuing battle, a combination of both, or some other strategy. It may be necessary to develop a plan of action for an election that will be over in a few weeks or months, or for a campaign that may take years, such as the effort to cut down the tuberculosis death rate. Planning for mass persuasion is governed by many factors that call upon all one's powers of training, experience, skill, and judgment. Planning should be flexible and provide for changed conditions.

When the plans have been perfected, organization of resources follows, and it must be undertaken in advance to provide the necessary manpower, money, and physical equipment. Organization also correlates the activities of any specialists who may be called upon from time to time, such as opinion researchers, fund raisers, publicity men, radio and motion picture experts, specialists for women's clubs and foreign language groups, and the like.

THE TACTICS

At this point it will be possible to plan the tactics of the program, i.e., to decide how the themes are to be disseminated over the idea carriers, the networks of communication.

Do not think of tactics in terms of segmental approaches. The problem is not to get articles into a newspaper or obtain radio time or arrange a motion picture newsreel; it is rather to set in motion a broad activity, the success of which depends on interlocking all phases and elements of the proposed strategy, implemented by tactics that are timed to the moment of maximum effectiveness. An action held over but one day may fall completely flat. Skilled and imaginative timing has determined the success of many mass movements and campaigns, the familiar phenomena so typical of the American people's behavior pattern.

Emphasis of the consent engineer's activities will be on the written and spoken word, geared to the media and designed for the audiences he is addressing. He must be sure that his material fits his public. He must prepare copy written in simple language and sixteen-word sentences for the average school-age public. Some copy will be aimed at the understanding of people who have had seventeen years of schooling. He must familiarize himself with all media and know how to supply them with material suitable in quantity and quality.

Primarily, however, the engineer of consent must create news. News is not an inanimate thing. It is the overt act that makes news, and news in turn shapes the attitudes and actions of people. A good criterion as to whether something is or is not news is whether the event juts out of the pattern of routine. The developing of events and circumstances that are not routine is one of the basic functions of the engineer of consent. Events so planned can be projected over the communication systems to infinitely more people than those actually participating, and such events vividly dramatize ideas for those who do not witness the events.

The imaginatively managed event can compete successfully with other events for attention. Newsworthy events, involving people, usually do not happen by accident. They are planned deliberately to accomplish a purpose, to influence our ideas and actions.

Events may also be set up in chain reaction. By harnessing the energies of group leaders, the engineer of consent can stimulate them to set in motion activities of their own. They will organize additional, specialized, subsidiary events, all of which will further dramatize the basic theme.

CONCLUSION

Communication is the key to engineering consent for social action. But it is not enough to get out leaflets and bulletins on the mimeograph machines, to place releases in the newspapers, or to fill the air waves with radio talks. Words, sounds, and pictures accomplish little unless they are the tools of a soundly thought-out plan and carefully organized methods. If the plans are well formulated and the proper use is made of them, the ideas conveyed by the words will become part and parcel of the people themselves.

When the public is convinced of the soundness of an idea, it will proceed to action. People translate an idea into action suggested by the idea itself, whether it is ideological, political, or social. They may adopt a philosophy that stresses racial and religious tolerance; they may vote a New Deal into office; or they may organize a consumers' buying strike. But such results do not just happen. In a democracy they can be accomplished principally by the engineering of consent.

83. PUBLIC RELATIONS: THE INVISIBLE SELL
by Robert L. Heilbroner *

Mixed up in the affairs of the Atomic Energy Commission, the Institute of Boiler and Radiator Manufacturers, Elvis Presley, and United States Steel; welcomed into the inner sanctum of church, corporation, and cabaret alike; as indispensable to a modern hospital as a surgeon and to a big labor union as an organizer, you will find the representatives of one of the newest, fastest growing, and certainly most significant professions of our times. These are the members of the public relations fraternity—a brotherhood of some 100,000 whose common bond is its profession, and whose common woe is that no two of the practitioners can ever quite agree on what that profession is.

Whatever it is, public relations is the wonder child of our age. Turn back to the Manhattan classified telephone directory for 1935 and look up the listing for public relations: you will find ten names. Go through the catalogues of the universities twenty years back, and you search for a course on public relations in vain. Investigate the public relations staff of General Motors for 1931, and you will discover one man, Paul Garrett, who had just been hired.

Today the listing in the telephone directory runs on for seven columns and over seven hundred names—in Manhattan alone. Last year 653 colleges taught something called "public relations"; eleven (including such pillars of respectability as Columbia and New York University) offered it as an undergraduate major; and one, Boston University, had a School of Public Relations which gave an M.S. degree. And last December when Paul Garrett retired from General Motors as a full vice president (to set up his own public relations firm), his staff numbered some two hundred people, exclusive of clerical help, and cost well over $1,000,000 a year.

* Free-lance writer on economics and public affairs. Author of *The Worldly Philosophers, The Quest for Wealth, The Future as History,* and numerous articles. This selection is from Robert L. Heilbroner, "Public Relations: The Invisible Sell," *Harper's Magazine,* vol. 214, June, 1957, pp. 23-31. Reprinted by permission.

That is, however, only evidence of public relations' meteoric rise. Even more impressive is its present extent. According to *Fortune* magazine, nearly five thousand corporations now support public relations departments or engage public relations counsel. An already outdated report by the Bureau of the Budget lists 5,211 full-time "information officers" for the federal government. Add in the labor unions, the private welfare organizations, the charities, causes, and not least, the celebrities who also buy what public relations men sell, and you arrive at the not unimpressive figure of at least half a billion dollars spent for PR hired help alone. How much is spent not for the hired hands, but on public relations itself, nobody even hazards a guess.

And what is this thing called "public relations" on which all this money is expended? It is not one thing, but many, for the practice in which the brotherhood engages is indeed a motley one. In the name of public relations you will find the boys "institutionalizing" a TV comic, "personalizing" an institution, or just plain peddling a product or an idea. Public relations includes such virtuous aims as making the public "aware" of muscular dystrophy and such dubious ones as putting pressure on a legislature through phony consumer fronts. It runs the gamut from philosophizing on social trends before a board of directors, to advising that same board on how best to pulverize the opposition in a proxy fight. It takes in the planted item in the gossip column and the artfully contrived mention of a client's product in a magazine article ostensibly about something else. It embraces the cozy corporate brochure "About Us Folks," and the hard-breathing advertisement of the "facts" concerning a strike. In a word, public relations covers a lot of acreage—blurring out into advertising, slopping over into selling, dipping down into publicity, and touching—or at least aspiring to—the "making" of public opinion itself.

And what, one may ask, after reading this ill-assorted catalogue, *is* public relations? Perhaps we can sum it up by calling it the business of the Invisible Sell. Public relations is Dale Carnegie writ large: it is the professional winning of friends and influencing of people—only not for oneself, but for one's clients, and not by glad-handing or overtly campaigning for their favor, but by creating "situations of reality" in which their acquiescence and approbation are spontaneously aroused. The public relations man is the stage manager of real-life dramas which contain not a hidden moral, but a hidden commercial. In the arresting, if chilling, phrase of Edward L. Bernays, a pioneer in the field, public relations is "the engineering of public consent."

And this makes the brotherhood somewhat more interesting than just another bunch of guys out to make a buck. For we are all of us to some extent hooked by the Invisible Sell—enthusiastic about people we have never met, persuaded of the virtues of products and institutions with which we have no direct contact, contented captives of ideas we are scarcely aware of having picked up. If the public relations men are capable of *manufacturing* these enthusiasms, persuasions, and ideas, it would not be too much to claim that they practice the most important occupation of our day. Or perhaps one should say the most portentous. Or perhaps merely the most pretentious. Whatever the final verdict, it would certainly seem worth while to meet the fraternity members themselves.

UP FROM BROADWAY

This will not involve us immediately in a series of high-level conferences in paneled board rooms. On the contrary, a Cook's Tour of public relations land begins far from the fluorescent eyries of Madison Avenue, in the hole-in-the-wall offices of another, even dreamier avenue four blocks west: Broadway. For whereas it makes a public relations counselor (and how the trade does love that orotund title) cringe to be told so, he did not spring, full-formed, from the brow of Jove. He crawled up from a lower form of life called the Press Agent. And there on Broadway the evolutionary process can yet be witnessed, as small wriggling things hitch themselves up on the terra firma of respectability, take their first tentative gulp of air, and— if they are still alive—declare themselves to be public relations men.

Back in the primordial ooze itself are the press agents whose "offices" are often only the stuffy phone booths around the corner from Lindy's. At his wilder extremes the press agent is the man who says to his client cuties, "Now when you get turned down for the part, you just walk over to the window and jump. I'll be waiting down below with a net," but in his more prosaic moments he lives off plainer fare called Client Mention. And client mention is still an indispensable part of public relations, even at its most stratospheric. Ben Sonnenberg, for example, who is one of the best-known public relations men in the country, has a special literary knack for leaving his clients' imprints on the sands of *Time*. Even Edward Bernays, who is today about as far from a press agent as one can get, rode to fame on some particularly gorgeous client mentions. One of them involved the fiftieth anniversary of the invention of the electric light, for which Bernays staged a Golden Jubilee at Dearborn, Michigan. Quite by chance, the President of the United States contributed his presence to the shindig and the Postmaster General issued a special stamp in its honor. In the stamp, the Jubilee, the posters, and the news releases, the Mazda bulb quietly glowed, reciprocally lighting up and lit by the luminaries provided by its master PR.

Today the public relations counselor disapprovingly frowns at the mention of the press agent whose motto reads, "Anything goes, so long as you spell the name right." Nonetheless he owes much of his imaginative vitality to his rude forebears. Indeed at the lower echelons of public relations you will find the direct descendants of the press agents, who have learned that a quick and agile mind and some good publicity ideas can be quickly parlayed into cash.

Of the 700-odd public relations firms in New York and the 2,000-odd in the nation, a very considerable number—perhaps as many as two-thirds —represent the ventures of bright young men, who start with a general background in publicity, a client or two, and a few hundred dollars in cash. This is where enterprising youth goes these days, instead of West. A career in point is that of an ex-publicity man named Alan Brandt. Good-looking, voluble, and an absolute garden sprinkler of ideas, Brandt took the plunge sixteen months ago from a well-paid position as publicity director of station WNEW in New York, for which he had gained nation-wide notice with shows such as a disc-less disc-jockey program (calliopes, music boxes, player pianos), a 2:00 A.M. feeding show for parents up bottling their infants, and Esoterica, A Program of Frankly Limited Appeal (Ethiopian music and Gertrude Stein).

"I just got tired of working for someone else," says Brandt, "so I went out and got myself a room with one window, one desk, one phone, one size of stationery, one girl—and one client. I was in business."

The client was the producer of Captain Kangaroo, a TV kiddies' show, and Brandt publicized it as the children's show that *parents* would like. It was a good pitch and made several magazine breaks, and thereupon the phone began to ring. A hair-products firm wanted to know if Brandt could think of some way of publicizing buns and chignons: Brandt got a TV hair styles contest started. A Boston radio station showed up looking for a publicity idea: Brandt printed records which fitted the new Chrysler car-phonograph and which interrupted their music with, "Are you missing the news? Tune in on station WHDH." A TV morning show wanted to be talked about: Brandt put Salvador Dali on to explain that the cauliflower was the basis of all art, and had an art dealer choose between six master-pieces worth over $100,000 and six fake copies worth less than $100, by slashing the fakes—while Brandt quietly perspired behind the camera. A book publisher wondered if something could be done about a novel set in a small New England town. Brandt got an item in the Associated Press about a book that would blow up Gilmanton, New Hampshire, and *Peyton Place* was a best seller before it even reached the bookstores.

It is now sixteen months later, and despite the fact that Alan Brandt is successful enough to need a personal tax lawyer, he sometimes worries about where he goes from here. For if the publicity end of the public relations game is a rich one (at least for those who make the grade), it is also rugged.

"Here I am," said another energetic hustler, "working like a beaver to get my client, call him Bill Blick, into the columns. He's a dog of a client, but finally I get something worth printing. Then I hear it's going to run in a big name column. I call my client's secretary and we all rush out to buy the early edition. And what does the item say?—'What ever happened to Bill Blick?' "

Equally baneful to the publicity man is the fact that his client, a modest soul who just happens to have a few good pictures of himself in case they're needed, is usually blissfully unaware of the writing, the phoning, the glamorizing that have been done to make his pedestrian life fit to print. On the morning when months of patient work finally pays off, he cheerfully calls his PR and says, "Say, did you see what the *Times* wrote about me?" And worst of all is the call that comes on the day when a national break of great importance has finally been landed. The client phones and enthuses.

"Great job! Just what we needed! Thanks a lot! Of course you under-stand that we won't be needing you any more now."

HOW TO CATCH A WHALE

Hence those PRs who cultivate the flowers of publicity raise a lush but quick-wilting crop. It is not surprising therefore that the next step up the evolutionary ladder is to the less spectacular but hardier perennials of Product Promotion. Here is where you will meet nine out of ten PRs who have graduated from the publicity game, tirelessly plugging away for products the majority of which are hardly such as to inspire soaring flights of the imagination. Typewriters, for example. Or wool. Or dog food.

Now since there are very few magazines or newspapers which would be interested in running a story about typewriters, wool, or dog food, and still fewer which would give free advertising to Underwood, the Wool Institute, or the Gaines Dog Food Company, the public relations man must disguise his hook with fancy feathers. The Underwood people therefore prepare "5 Sprightly Stories" on such themes as *How To Keep Your Boss Happy*, or *The Girl With The Halo* (your secretary); the Wool Institute offers *How's Your AQ?* (Appearance Quotient) and *Wool in History and Legend* —"the fascinating story of the thousands-of-years-old romance of the use of wool"; and the dog food people establish the Gaines Dog Research Center—"a research and educational institution created as a public service." These are offered free to editors.

Needless to say, the mortality rate of such PR productions reaches epidemic proportions, but since the birth rate is high, a certain number of brain-children survive. A considerable number as a matter of fact. No PR firm of any stature cannot boast of having "placed" stories in *Life, Look, Saturday Evening Post,* or *Reader's Digest,* not to mention the *New York Times*—although many is the chagrined PR who, having finally inspired a story on his client's industry or interest, reads it with fading smile to realize, at the end, that the goddam magazine never mentioned *his* client once.

One of the most successful product promoters is the firm of Ruder and Finn, which began like Brandt Public Relations, on a shoestring. Not quite ten years ago Bill Ruder, a young publicity man for Sam Goldwyn, and David Finn, a hopeful painter, decided to put their curiously diverse talents together in public relations. They took a room in the Hotel Lombardy— the size of which can be judged by the fact that it is now the hotel linen closet—and landed that essential First Account. It was a promotion job for Perry Como's records, and they performed it so artfully that Como thanked them publicly in an ad in *Billboard.* Then *their* phone began to ring. And they began to think.

"We didn't want to be just publicity boys all our lives," says Finn. "And while we were beating our brains to think of a way not to be, Bill remembered the nation-wide publicity network that Goldwyn used. We decided to try the same deal for product promotion." By writing to independent PRs around the country, Ruder and Finn established a gossamer-thin tie-up with small out-of-town public relations firms, and this they then hawked as the Ruder & Finn Field Network. Into its flimsy meshes promptly swam a whale. A major soap company was about to launch a new soap and it wanted just such point-of-sale promotion. The soap brass descended from its glassy heights to the brownstone basement into which Ruder and Finn had moved their operation (and where they had spent the previous twenty-four hours frantically adding twenty-seven men to their "network"), and—perhaps with suds in its eyes—approved of what it saw.

After that it was easy. Today, with seventy employees, a Field Network of over 190, and a gross take in excess of $1,200,000, Bill Ruder and Dave Finn run one of the six biggest PR firms in the country.

Walking through the pastel-tinted Ruder and Finn offices is not unlike walking through an advertising agency—a resemblance which makes both PRs and advertising men edgy. There is a writing department, a TV and radio department, a magazine department, an art department, and a long string of offices for account executives, supervisors of executives, supervisors of supervisors, and so on. For R & F does a great deal more than publicity for its clients. In fact it does public relations for them.

What is public relations at the R & F level? Of course it includes product promotion via the Invisible Sell, as witness a technique used to push Skotch Koolers, a picnic carrier. R & F sent samples of the Koolers to professional photographers and TV studios, merely suggesting that they might be used as studio props. They were. You may have noticed the Kooler alongside the man with the beard in a Schweppes ad, or next to a bathing beauty extolling skin cream. Without spending a nickel on advertising, R & F dangled its product before the eyes of several million people, a pleasing number of whom swallowed the bait.

But the public relations bait does not consist of products only. Indeed, the publics to which R & F professionally relates its clients tend to include fewer and fewer customers, and more and more groups such as stockholders, employees, or even bankers. For these publics Ruder and Finn will design a client's annual report and compose dignified but warm letters to his shareholders, will edit his employee newspaper, or make his name known among the Wall Street community. Or, in the jargon of the trade, they will create and sell his "image."

For example, in the early months of 1956 Orr & Sembower, a vigorous but relatively unknown firm of boiler manufacturers, came to Ruder and Finn eager to tell the world—that is, the very small world concerned with boilers—that it was "a real forward-thinking company." How do you make a boiler manufacturer look real forward-thinking? The table [on page 432] shows part of the R & F evaluation of their job nine months later.

Comments Ruder and Finn: "We have begun to create in the minds of the various publics the image of Orr & Sembower as a leading manufacturer of packaged heat transfer equipment."

It is not by coincidence that our Cook's Tour of public relations land has taken us from publicity through product pushing to the creation of corporate "images," for the higher up the ladder of public relations you go, the more grandiose becomes its purpose. Indeed, when you arrive at the summit, you can hardly see the customer any more at all. The bait which now dangles from the invisible line is no longer personalities and merchandise, but institutions and ideas.

Thus at the powerhouse of public relations maintained by General Motors, only a fraction of the PR effort is aimed at making people like GM *cars,* and whereas this fraction packs a mighty wallop (the whole idea of Motorama was originally a PR flash of genius), it is hardly central to the company's public relations program. For General Motors—or any large corporation, for that matter—has a more important task for its public relations than the pushing of Chevvies, Buicks, or Cadillacs: Sales Promotion does *that.* What public relations must do is the far more difficult job of selling General Motors itself—as a community asset, a helpful company, a corporation, with solid ideas, a big business with its heart in the right place—in a word, as a great institution, and by implication, one which should not be meddled with.

When Paul Garrett arrived in Detroit twenty-five years ago to begin General Motors' public relations program, the first question fired at him was: "How do you make a billion dollars look small?" Garrett said damned if he knew, and furthermore damned if he thought that was his job. Public relations, he argued, was not an "act," but a continuing effort on the part of management to win the confidence of the people with whom it came into contact. Hence you will find General Motors engaged in a host of activities in which altruism and self-interest come together in a creamy blend. Plant City and Field Relations, for example, stimulates local GM participation in the community affairs of the sixty-eight cities where it has factories, thereby helping both the community and itself. Educational Rela-

Evaluation of a Public Relations Program for a Boiler Manufacturer

WHAT WE PROGRAMMED	WHAT WE ACCOMPLISHED
Minimum of two speaking engagements for Fred Klein, the president	Speeches delivered at two important conventions
Article in *Harvard Business Review*	In the works as the story of a small company in foreign trade
Articles in *Fortune* or *Business Week*	No soap on one; the other now in development
Important newspaper story	Interview in N. Y. *Herald Tribune*
Articles aimed at management, engineers, architects, and heating specialists	Stories in *Factory Management & Maintenance, Power, Progressive Architecture,* and others

tions works with the schools, providing them with such useful educational material as films on safe driving, and providing itself with a flow of applicants for jobs. The Speakers Bureau is glad to send a company-sponsored lecturer to your club or association to edify it with an inspirational talk— or to educate it with a "sound" economic one. Institutional Advertising tells the story of GM's role in supporting some twenty thousand suppliers, and leaves you with the pleasant impression that what's good for General Motors is good for small business, too. The billion dollars may not look any smaller as a result of these efforts. But it looks much, much nicer.

THE IMAGE-MAKERS

This same kind of quiet winning of friends and influencing of people is practiced by the biggest public relations firms. At Hill & Knowlton, for instance, which runs neck and neck with Carl Byoir & Associates as the largest PR outfit in the country (H & K's minimum fee $36,000; Byoir's, $50,000, but H & K has more accounts), only 6 or 7 per cent of the firm's effort is spent on publicity. The rest is largely concentrated on showing corporations how to do Good Works and how to present their side of the story—which is always known as The Facts.

Thus for its biggest account, the American Iron and Steel Institute (which is incidentally the biggest PR account in the country), H & K provides a whole panoply of services, none of which is calculated to sell a single ton of steel, but all of which are calculated to sell the steel industry and its point of view. It publishes *Steelways*, a magazine which is sent to 100,000 key people, such as editors and educators, who pass along interesting bits of information to an audience estimated at 12,000,000. It puts out booklets on "timely topics of importance" such as the industry's lagging profit rate. It runs a field service which counsels individual companies on such matters as how to conduct plant tours, or how to work with the local school board, or who should go on the Institute's mailing list.

And it runs such interesting services as the Community Resources Workshop. This is a project to acquaint teachers with industry and its potential helpfulness in providing educational material. It also aims at giving teachers an insight into the problems of steel—not on a "propagandistic" basis, but just the way steel executives honestly see them. Dr. Albert L. Ayars, the educator who heads the Workshop, has stated that he would resign if his project were ever used for the propagation of distorted facts. "I suppose you could say," he admits, "that as a result of these experiences the teachers will be more receptive to some legislation which would be of benefit to industry and the public. But again, not because they have been coerced into it. All that we would have done from the standpoint of our client, American Iron and Steel Industry, is to have exposed them to the facts."

For those who picture public relations at the summit as the cunning manipulation of minds, or the subtle exercise of devious techniques, the actual practice of Big PR must look tame indeed. That it is often transparently self-serving, under the guise of serving the public, is perfectly true; and that the motives which prompt it are not entirely spiritual, needs hardly to be pointed out. It is the Invisible Sell on a huge scale, but whereas one may not always particularly like what is being sold, it is hard to get much worked up over the salesmanship.

That goes for nine-tenths of Big PR. Of course there is also the tenth tenth. Witness, for example, the public-relations tactics in the Pennsylvania railroad-truckers fight in 1952. The client here was the Eastern Railroads Presidents Conference; the PR firm was that of Carl Byoir & Associates (Hill & Knowlton's big competitor); and the issue at stake was a bill increasing the size and weight limits for trucks on the state roads. It was not by accident that Byoir was chosen for the task of beating the bill. As the company explained in a letter to one of the railroad vice presidents (in charge of public relations), it was good at that sort of thing, modestly mentioning a chain-store bill it had licked in New York State for the A & P, and a tax reduction it had secured in Louisiana for the Freeport Sulphur company. And so, for a fee of $150,000 it got the job.

And brought home the bacon. In due course the bill was vetoed by the Governor.

Not that the Governor acted out of any but the best interests. He had before him, for example, an early report of the Maryland State Roads Commission containing very unfavorable data on road damage. He was faced at every turn by newspaper and magazine articles on the evils of trucking, and across his desk passed a succession of interesting studies by institutions such as the New Jersey Citizens Tax Study Foundation. Certainly not absent from the Governor's mind was the opposition of the State Association of Township Supervisors, which had mailed out thousands of postcards protesting the truck bill, and of the State Grange, a politically powerful organization.

When Governor Fine vetoed the bill, it must have seemed to him that he was only expressing the will of the people: but how much of this will of the people was the result of the activities of the Byoir agency who spent several hundred thousand dollars in their campaign?

There is now pending in the United States District Court for the Eastern District of Pennsylvania an anti-trust action entitled *"Noerr Motor Freight, Inc., v. Eastern Railway Presidents Conference et al."* In support of their position the Plaintiff-Truckers introduced through their briefs and supporting affidavits, and by the testimony of witnesses, evidence to the effect that the Maryland Commission's public relations man constantly visited the Byoir offices and later was given a job by the defendant, the Eastern Railway Presidents Conference; that newspaper and magazine articles were planted by the Byoir agency or based upon material supplied by them; and that the New Jersey Citizens Tax Study Foundation was founded and supported by the Byoir agency. Evidence was also introduced that a Byoir man set up headquarters in the Grange and used the Grange stationery and that the postcards mailed in the name of the Township Supervisors were prepared by Byoir.

It is incidents such as this which give rise to alarm over the power of public relations (although it is worthy of note that not a single client left the Byoir firm, and that the Public Relations Society of America—the "standards-setting" organization of the trade—did not suggest that Carl Byoir & Associates should withdraw). But if within the profession most eyes were delicately averted, outside it voices were raised. In a brilliant exposé by Robert Bendiner in the *Reporter*, the question was posed: "Is this what is meant by the engineering of public consent?"

The indignation was natural, and yet the Byoir episode is not a case by which the power of public relations must be judged. For one thing, as is often the way, the success backfired: Byoir and the railroads are now both entangled in the $250,000,000 suit filed by the truckers. And for another thing, no one has ever denied the power of public relations, in careless or overeager hands, to gain selfish advantage, or to exert legislative influence, on behalf of its clients—whether they are business, labor, farm, or foreign.

All this, however, is aside from the crucial point. It is not the excesses, but the run of the mill of big PR, not its faults but its very virtues which need examination. The basic question is not the power which resides in bad public relations, but that inherent in *good* public relations; not the ability of public relations to subvert, but its capacity to convince. The really important question about the power of public relations is whether it can influence what men *think*.

WHERE THE DOUBT BEGINS

This brings us to an impressive demonstration concerning the making of public opinion that took place in Cincinnati in 1947.

For six months Cincinnati became the focus for an unprecedented crusade—a powerful, well-planned, and well-financed attempt to teach it what to think. Specifically, Cincinnati was the target of an all-out effort to make a typical American city "United Nations conscious."

The crusade was a thorough and intelligent one. It was launched at every level of city life. On blotters, matchbooks, streetcar signs, and billboards, Cincinnatians read "Peace Begins with the United Nations—the United Nations Begins with You." Local radio stations broadcast UN facts and news daily—one of them on 150 spots a week. The newspapers played up the theme. Every schoolchild in the city was given literature about the United Nations to take home; the PTA, the Council of Churches, and the Catholic Church all climbed enthusiastically aboard the bandwagon. Club women rallied round with letters and telegrams pledging their support to the American delegation to the UN. In the last three months as the campaign reached a crescendo, 225 meetings were held; hundreds of documentary films shown, 59,588 pieces of literature distributed.

Then they took a poll of the results.

At the end of six months only *half* as many people considered the United Nations a means of preventing war as thought so at the beginning.

There was almost no change in the number who thought that the United States should take an active part in world affairs.

There was a drop in the number of those who were in favor of having the United States join an international police to keep peace.

Fewer people thought there should be some sort of international control of atom bombs.

There was almost no change in the numbers who knew what the main purpose of the United Nations was, or who had heard of the veto power, or who knew how the UN worked.

In a word, the campaign was a gigantic frost.

Why? The answer may be shocking, but it is simplicity itself: people in Cincinnati just didn't give a damn about the United Nations, one way or another. For all the matchbooks and the meetings, the UN was something far off, vague, abstract, unconnected with daily life. Hence the propaganda went in one ear and out the other, and save for the pleasant friction stimulated in transit, it left no imprint at all.

And the moral, for public relations, seems to be that most people don't give a damn about most things, unless those things are part and parcel of their concrete lives. They just don't listen. For many years, Hill & Knowlton has sought to put across such simple (and true) messages as that the steel industry is not a dangerous place to work, or that steel's profit margins, by comparison with other industries, have been low. The results: slightly *more* people thought steel was dangerous in 1955 than in 1946 or 1943, and there continues to be "considerable belief" (in Hill & Knowlton's own words) that steel's profits are too high.

Or take the case of General Motors. For nearly twenty years, along with seven other large corporations, GM has tested its popularity by means of a continuing opinion poll called the Link Audit. On the face of it, results were excellent: the proportion of people who "liked" General Motors (and all the other companies) rose from less than 60 per cent in the late 'thirties to over 80 per cent today. The only trouble is, no one quite knows what "like" means. Every time there is a strike in any *one* of the eight companies, the popularity of *all* of them goes down. For some unfathomable reason all the corporations are more popular in fall than spring. And every time there is something to get mad about, the Link Audit "liking" doesn't seem to prevent people from boiling up: when Harlow Curtice, GM's president, testily denied to a Senate Committee last year that there was anything wrong with General Motors' dealer relations, something akin to a whirlwind of angry protest materialized out of the blue. Chastened, Mr. Curtice appeared again in a more conciliatory mood. The whirlwind disappeared. And the Link Audit once again showed that everybody "liked" General Motors.

Hence the public-opinion researchers are, to put it mildly, skeptical about the ability of public relations to engineer the public's consent and dubious about the depth of the affections it arouses. "Give the PR something real and specific—a personality, a product, or even a precise enough idea—and he can usually make an impact," says one professional public-opinion measurer. "But ask him to sell a big fuzzy thing like a 'nice' company or a 'sound' doctrine, and the result is usually an absolutely monumental indifference."

Or worse, skepticism. One opinion researcher, Douglas Williams, measuring the effect of a company's efforts to "sell" its employees on Free Private Enterprise, found the net outcome to be an increase in hostility and suspicion. "Those people knew about free enterprise in terms of their own jobs and incomes," he explains. "They didn't like having those realities 'justified' with fancy abstractions. Instead they asked, 'What's really the matter, that they have to sell this thing to me?'"

The wiser public relations men are well aware of these facts. "Make no mistake about it," says Earl Newsom, who counsels, among others, Ford and Standard Oil of New Jersey, "a corporation does not win the confidence of the American people by trying to 'educate' them to its point of view." A case in point is Newsom's client, "Jersey," which has long ago wearily resigned itself to living with the popular opinion that it is still part of the oil trust which broke up some forty years ago. It just doesn't bother to argue any more—because it realizes that it probably wouldn't do any good if it did.

But whereas the public relations men themselves have salutary doubts about the efficacy of their efforts to sell those nice big ideas, their clients share no such hesitations with them. For if there is one part of the public which is really a patsy for the power of public relations, it is that hard-headed pragmatic character, the American big businessman himself. Not content with using public relations to publicize or promote his wares, or to cement his relationships with his employees or stockholders—all of which it can do very well—he is convinced that it can serve to get his "message" across to an eagerly attentive public, and to enshrine his corporation, as well as its products, in their hearts. Nor does he, curiously enough, demand proof of this conviction, for he has swallowed the Invisible Sell hook, line, and sinker.

WHAT IS IT WORTH?

If the public relations brotherhood is not quite so powerful as its enthusiastic clients think, neither can it be shrugged off as just a collection of publicists, pitchmen, and commercial philosophers. Public relations is more than just an occupation or a bunch of occupations: it is a social force—and as such it has left two indelible marks on our world.

The first mark is its part in the general debasement of communications from which we suffer. It is only a banality to point out the need for effective public communication in today's complex society, but communication has become more of a fetish than a function. Science has a technical term which describes the result of forcing more messages along a carrier than it can accommodate: it calls the result *noise*. We live in a noisy society: one in which everyone talks and few say anything; one in which the spurious, the insincere, the meretricious, and most of all the *empty*, crowd out the meaningful, the useful, the important. People who live in such a society learn not to listen—or worse, when they do listen, they learn to disbelieve what they hear.

In this process of the debasement of communication, public relations must bear its share of the blame. No one can quarrel with the essential function that public relations fills as the purveyor of genuine ideas and information. No one denies that many public relations men, working for corporations as well as for colleges or causes, honestly communicate things which are worth communicating. Nor can anyone absolve public relations for loading the communications channels with noise. We read the news and suspect that behind it lies the "news release." We encounter reputation and ascribe it to publicity. Worst of all, we no longer credit good behavior to good motives, but cheapen it to the level of "good public relations."

It is not *that* bad, of course. But if we step back to view that whole big thing called Public Relations and then attempt to weigh what it has meant to our values and beliefs, it is hard to avoid the conclusion that the net effect of the Invisible Sell has been to further a cynical judgment of the motives behind human behavior.

That is one side of the coin, but there is another, and shinier. If public relations has cheapened the face value of good conduct, at the same time it has enormously increased the prevalence of good conduct. For regardless of its motive or its incessant self-advertisement, good conduct *is* more prevalent on the business scene, and public relations can rightly take much of the credit. The reason is a curious one: It is that something called Good Public Relations has come to be regarded as an indispensable attribute of business—as much a sign that a business is "modern and progressive" as a shiny new glass office building (which is also, of course, a good public relations move). Quite simply, business has sold itself the bill of goods it originally intended to sell the public.

"If you ask me," said one shrewd public relations man, "the aim of a big corporation should be invisibility. But no. It insists on being as visible as possible. Its directors get nervous unless people say what wonderful public relations the company has. So it has to *have* wonderful public relations. It has to *act* lovable. It has to *be* progressive. It has to *become* socially responsible—not because the management necessarily thinks that way, but because that's what Good Public Relations is."

Hence by an unexpected twist, public relations has become a weapon whose recoil is greater than its muzzle blast. Good Public Relations has come to be something very much like the corporate conscience—a commercial conscience, no doubt, but a conscience none the less. If the public relations profession can bolster this role, if it can become the corporate conscience openly, fearlessly, and wisely, speaking not only *for* business but *to* business, then it will have more than redeemed its name.

84. P.R. MAN: POLITICAL MASTERMIND
by Stanley Kelley, Jr.*

. . . Despite the fact that mass communication techniques have been undergoing rapid change and development for over half a century, the extent to which they have modified American campaigning is too little recognized. The typical nineteenth-century campaign combined public stumping and private talks with local bosses. Local organizations were the national parties' real point of contact with the voter.

Now, the mass media have given new dimensions to campaigning. They are fast. They allow the campaigner to talk to a truly national audience and to focus its attention on particular events, personalities and issues. They have greatly increased the cost of campaigning, but they have enormously reduced the *unit* cost of reaching voters. They allow political parties to put their cases before a vast group of mass media consumers that local organizations have never been able to interest in politics. By 1952, Presidential candidate Eisenhower's professional advisers were telling him that

* Professor of politics at Princeton University. Author of *Professional Public Relations and Political Power* and *Political Campaigning*. This selection is from Stanley Kelley, Jr., "P.R. Man: Political Mastermind," *New York Times Magazine*, Sept. 2, 1956, pp. 10, 54, and 56. Reprinted by permission of the author and publisher.

in a one-half hour television show he could reach more voters than he could in three years of whistle-stopping at his then current rate.

Just as the big city boss symbolized the political techniques of the nineteenth century, so the public relations man is a characteristic figure in today's campaign. In his brand of politics, propaganda has become the central concern. For the boss, the principal aim was to build a bloc of votes that would stick by him, regardless of the candidates and regardless of the issues. In contrast, the public relations man fights his battles in the mind of the voter; he specializes in building attitudes and standardizing opinions on controversial issues. Says one of them, "We use campaign funds, not to dispense favors, but to mold public sentiment. . . ." This kind of politics has a logic of its own and calls for study of political "markets," alternative ways of framing appeals, and methods of distributing ideas.

It also requires meticulous planning. Neat brochures, one paragraph to a page, for all kinds of projects, are a sort of trademark of public relations men in politics. The 1952 Republican campaign strategy was laid out in advance in a long blueprint that outlined organization, basic appeals, types of speeches, literature, advertising, television and radio programs, the relative weight to be given to the various media, the kinds, places and times of campaign trips and rallies, and the areas in which efforts were to be concentrated.

Advertising and public relations men may sometimes serve as little more than campaign technicians, but it is not unusual for them to have a seat at the strategy table. In California, it is normal practice for major candidates to put the management of their campaigns in the hands of any one of about half a dozen independent political public relations firms. Payment is on a fee basis. In other parts of the country, it is more usual for the public relations man to be the political committee's permanent employee.

What determines the public relations man's political style? Partly it is his judgment of what kind of slogans and candidates the market will bear. The public relations man's conception of his market differs little from that of ordinary political analysis. He, too, is interested in all the groupings of society, whether based on age, sex, income, occupation or some other factor. Though he prides himself on knowing the psychology of the "little man" much more intimately than the client he serves, he checks his feel for the issues with the help of polling and market research organizations. A California public relations man who has worked for both Senator Knowland and Vice President Nixon says flatly that he wouldn't undertake a campaign without an item in the budget for "continuity" polling. In the use of polls the public relations man is less likely to be concerned with his candidate's current popularity than with what he is told about the way the slogans are "taking" or about latent weaknesses in the position of the opposing candidate.

In part, also, the way the public relations expert approaches issues is determined by certain characteristics of mass communication. He is acutely aware that radio and television dials turn easily. He knows that the lead sentences of a newspaper story are those that have the largest readership. He expects to be listened to, but not to be listened to for very long. As a result, he telescopes his arguments into themes and slogans. For the p. r. man, a phrase like "that mess in Washington" may truly cover a multitude of sins. Losing something in balanced discussion, he hopes to gain in emotional impact.

For somewhat similar motives he makes a liberal use of gimmicks. Tricks and novelties—barrage balloons, singing jingles, pretty girls—are essentially a way of attracting the attention of a public that is distracted by thousands of competing appeals. In the modern forum getting attention is the hard first step in selling opinions.

Gimmicks can border on the fantastic. In a Los Angeles mayoralty recall campaign, a prize was offered to the person who most nearly estimated the number of votes by which Mayor Fletcher Bowron would be recalled, thus making the award of the prize contingent on the Mayor's defeat.

The p. r. man is devoted to the strategy of attack. To attack is to choose one's battleground; to defend is to accept the issues as they have been pictured by others. In 1952, constant attack was an essential feature of Republican plans, for Republican strategists hoped to arouse apathetic citizens who had failed to vote in previous elections and win them for Eisenhower. . . .

The p. r. man may help a candidate ride into office on issues, but he has other services to offer as well. In an age of mass media communication, a candidate is in a position much like that of the motion-picture star. Like the star, he must "have something" to begin with, but from then on a great deal depends on his ability to give his name currency and project his personality. Wendell Willkie, a year before the 1940 convention, was a man of stature and ability, but a political unknown. By the time the convention met, he was a candidate. In between were the newspaper and magazine stories, carefully planted by p. r. men, that had fired the public imagination with Willkie's underdog fight against party regulars.

P. r. men may serve candidates as "build-up boys" or, more modestly, simply as coaches. Vice President Nixon's 1952 defense of his political fund has been a subject of great controversy ever since. Friends have emphasized its spontaneity; enemies, its "soap opera" calculation. Both versions have a substantial degree of truth. There is little doubt that Nixon prepared his own speech and that he delivered it only from notes. But there was also a background of careful preparation.

Delivery of the speech was held up to allow public excitement to mount. Wording of the speech was carefully gone over with Nixon's public relations adviser and his television consultant. In his campaign for Senator and all through his campaign for Vice President, Nixon systematically discussed every shortcoming of every television appearance Nixon made.

Nixon and his managers were early in appreciating the subtle changes of style that are required if a new medium is to be used effectively. The newest, television, has been a puzzler for the p. r. man as well as for politicians in general. Early attempts on TV were radio-like speeches, which most professionals now count as dismal failures.

In 1950 Governor Thomas E. Dewey broke new ground with a talkathon, a program format later picked up by other candidates, including a British Conservative M. P. Questions directed at the Governor from citizens on the street gave to Dewey a chance to display an enormous knowledge of New York government and to the whole program a degree of human interest that the traditional speech notably lacks. In Robert Meyner's campaign for Governor of New Jersey, an advertising man experimented with fast-paced documentaries featuring Meyner as a kind of commentator. The latest trend, if it is a trend, seems to be toward making campaign television short, fast and visual.

Once the themes of a campaign are created and the conditions for marketing them carefully studied, they must be worked into the speeches, news stories, television shows and printed literature that will eventually reach the political consumer. With the growth of population and the multiplication of media, distributing a propaganda line has become a problem fully as baffling as creating one. Here again, the lay politician more and more frequently turns to the p. r. man for help.

The method chosen to reach a group of voters will depend in part on the nature of the group. In Maryland's 1950 senatorial campaign, a Chicago p. r. man retained by Republican candidate John M. Butler wanted to get his message before first generation Catholic immigrants. He felt that Butler's pro-McCarthy appeals had a good chance of winning votes in this group of normally Democratic voters—if he could get his story before them. One tactic he tried was to work through a popular bakery supply man who asked local bakers to put in a good word for candidate Butler with their customers. First generation immigrants, he reasoned, had not deserted the bread of the old countries for the cellophane-wrapped product available at the supermarket. He could reach them at the bakery.

Sometimes calculation will proceed in the opposite direction: The p. r. man discovers a ready-made audience and then seeks some way to influence it politically. In an inter-office memorandum, one advertising executive noted that people returning by automobile from Saturday night baseball games form a semi-captive audience. Usually, these people turn on their car radios, tune to a program of popular music, and then sit back and listen. Why not, proposed the memorandum, make the agency's client, the Governor of an Eastern state, a disk jockey? He could play his favorite records, mixing music with a few chatty political remarks.

Discovering the most economical way to distribute propaganda requires an intimate knowledge of listening, viewing and reading habits and of popular behavior patterns in general. Television may be the most powerful communication medium yet invented, but on a sunny Sunday afternoon, radio may be a better bet. To pass on matters of this kind, the p. r. man has to be a kind of practicing sociologist. Even before a number of academic social scientists discovered "opinion leaders"—those people from whom their associates habitually seek authoritative opinions—p. r. men systematically fed them direct mail in campaigns. Probably the opinion leader is flattered by such special attention. In any case, he is in a position to put a general propaganda line before his special public with the force of his own prestige behind it. Other kinds of observation can also be turned to political advantage. One p. r. man put campaign literature into beauty parlors and barbor shops. His theory: Patrons of these establishments read obsessively.

To what extent do all the calculations of the p. r. man end by winning votes? One of the more ironic facts about the deference candidates give to the p. r. man's opinions is that the latter can rarely show the extent to which he caused the voter's decision. The voter's environment is filled with words and images. He casts his ballot. The relation between these two phenomena is rarely clear.

One difficulty in evaluating p. r. practice in politics comes from the fact that the field is new and that there is nothing to prevent anyone from calling himself a "public relations counsel." Probably only a few of the many candidates who seek p. r. help really get competent advice.

That public relations is essentially an art, not a science, offers another difficulty in gauging the effectiveness of p. r. techniques. "An idea that looks good," one p. r. man has said, "may lay an egg. Something you think is barely worth doing may really click."

Still, there is evidence, if not proof, of the value of p. r. skill and knowledge. Good p. r. advice, for instance, may mean the difference between talking to TV sets that are tuned in or turned off. In the 1952 Presidential campaign, the theories that governed Republican and Democratic television time buying were in sharp contrast. The Democrats scheduled regular half-hour spots from 10:30 to 11 P. M. on Tuesdays and Thursdays. The Republicans, acting on professional advice, placed their programs in periods usually taken by the most successful commercial shows, hoping to capture a part of their viewers. Nielsen ratings showed Eisenhower's speeches drew consistently larger audiences than Stevenson's, except in the one case where Stevenson, too, fell heir to a popular feature's time period. Examples like this, bolstered by data from clipping services, public opinion polls and audience rating agencies, help the p. r. man convince his clients that he has a real product to sell.

And however inconclusive such evidence may appear to the skeptical, it is altogether likely that the public relations man will continue to play an increasingly important role in campaigns. With the decline of political clubs and old-fashioned machines in all parts of the country, the mass media have now emerged as the most important single road to political power. The public relations man who took early note of this fact is beginning to reap the rewards.

85. THE SUPERSALESMEN OF CALIFORNIA POLITICS: WHITAKER AND BAXTER

by Irwin Ross*

In the weeks before last November's election, a menacing-looking monkey wrench suddenly became a political weapon in California. The un-

* Free-lance writer and newspaperman. Author of *Strategy for Liberals, The Image Merchants,* and other works. This selection is from Irwin Ross, *The Image Merchants,* Doubleday & Company, Inc., New York, 1959. Copyright © 1959 by Irwin Ross. First appeared as an article in *Harper's Magazine.* Copyright 1959 Harper & Brothers. Reprinted by permission of Doubleday & Company, Inc.

lovely object was flung across billboards, newspaper ads, garish handbills—accompanied by the slogan, "Defeat the Monkey Wrench Tax Bill. Vote No on 17."

Proposition 17 was a complex measure which proposed to rejigger the state's tax system by reducing the sales tax, lowering income tax rates on modest incomes, raising them to 46 per cent on incomes over $50,000. The measure was of doubtful wisdom, to put it mildly, but it was not precisely a monkey wrench either.

The monkey wrench motif, and the "fear campaign" which it dominated, bore the unmistakable touch of Whitaker and Baxter, the remarkable San Francisco husband-and-wife team who have long been the country's outstanding specialists in political public relations. They were the first in the field in the early 'thirties, have since run eighty major campaigns—winning all but six. In the last dozen years, they have paid personal income taxes on over a million dollars. The American Medical Association alone paid them a fee of $350,000 for a strenuous crusade against compulsory medical insurance.

Their performance in the 1958 election measured up to the Whitaker and Baxter legend. Proposition 17 was defeated after a brilliant campaign that threatened Californians with the wreck of the state's entire financial structure and—what was perhaps even worse—the imposing of burdensome new taxes on food, real estate, and gasoline if the Monkey Wrench passed.

While they conducted this crusade in Northern California, Whitaker and Baxter also found time to handle a successful statewide campaign for Proposition 4—a $60 million harbor bond issue—as well as to run Governor Knight for U. S. Senator. They dropped Knight after the primary—because he had refused to follow their advice. He insisted on attacking Knowland, his running mate, rather than turning his full fire on the Democrats. Not many press agents, one can assume, feel sufficiently secure to fire a Governor. Whitaker and Baxter, however, have an exuberant respect for their own political wisdom—and they hate a loser. The November results vindicated their judgment: Knight lost badly.

By this time, Whitaker and Baxter have been fixtures of California politics far longer than anyone in high state office. Clem Whitaker is a tall, spindly man with a deeply-lined, craggy face who looks older than his sixty years. He is something of a non-stop talker in a low, well-modulated voice that is oddly reassuring. Wife Leone Baxter, by contrast, is a surprisingly youthful fifty-two, a pretty redhead with the well-scrubbed, glowing complexion of the ageless American girl. She too is never at a loss for words, though her tone is sprightlier and she often sounds on the edge of breathless discovery.

For a pair of old pros, Whitaker and Baxter are full of surprises. They relish talking about their coups, but betray little of the cynicism of the veteran politico. In their view, professional campaign management is an ennobling effort to raise the level of political awareness in a democracy. "We feel," Whitaker says solemnly, "that people in our state are better informed, more alive to the issues, are better citizens because of our type of activity."

They carry on these educational chores in close unison. At work, the accordion wall is kept open between their carpeted, paneled offices. A visitor who telephones one will often find himself talking to both partners simultaneously. Whenever they have a lecture date, they both perform on the platform. They share profits equally, sign letters together, seldom use the first person singular when the plural will do.

There is some division of effort, however. Whitaker usually plots long-range strategy, while Baxter invents slogans and labors over pamphlet copy. They both write speeches and hate the job. Before an interviewer, each is meticulous in pointing out the specific contributions of the other, but neither likes to be upstaged in conversation. When a question is asked, they both leap forward to answer and will interrupt each other frequently.

Clem Whitaker comes naturally by his tone of moral uplift. His father was a Baptist preacher, an uncle a Socialist Baptist preacher. A precocious youngster, Clem covered the California legislature for the Sacramento *Union* at seventeen, became city editor at nineteen. For a period he was a correspondent for the San Francisco *Examiner,* then in 1921 launched the Capitol News Bureau—a political news service for papers around the state which did not have their own Sacramento correspondents. He had worked up to eighty subscribers and was netting $25,000 a year when he sold out to the United Press late in 1929. He had suffered a difficult siege in the hospital and decided that public relations would be an easier way to make a living.

Whitaker ran some minor campaigns (including a vain effort to abolish capital punishment) before he came upon Leone Baxter in 1933. She was a demure widow of twenty-six who had written a little newspaper copy and now was manager of the Chamber of Commerce of Redding, California.

What brought them together was a referendum over the Central Valley Water Project, an irrigation and flood-control development which had been authorized by the legislature. The Pacific Gas and Electric Company, alarmed because the power generated might be sold to public authorities, then forced a referendum. At a meeting of supporters of CVP, Whitaker and Baxter were urged to take on the campaign.

It was a tough fight. Pacific Gas was well heeled, but the other side could scrape up less than $40,000 for Whitaker and Baxter—a sum they would now regard as laughable. They concentrated their energies on the small towns of central California, which would directly benefit from the project, and did a skillful job of getting their propaganda into small-town newspapers. They also made the first extensive use of radio in a state campaign, handling everything themselves—from the production of scripts to sound effects. When the returns were in, the Central Valley Project had triumphed by 33,603 votes. Impressed by this performance, Pacific Gas and Electric later put Whitaker and Baxter on an annual retainer. They remain a client to this day.

WE WERE SORRY WE HAD TO DO IT THAT WAY

Clem and Leone were now launched as a partnership, though they did not marry until 1938. Their second year, 1934, established them as a formidable team. Not only did they put over George Hatfield as Lieutenant Governor, but they had a large hand in defeating old Socialist Upton Sinclair, who was running for Governor on the Democratic ticket with a bizarre program to End Poverty in California, which thoroughly alarmed conservative citizens. A quarter-century later, W & B are admittedly embarrassed to talk about the Sinclair campaign. "It was one we hated to handle," says Whitaker. "Sinclair was an old friend of the Whitaker family. It's always difficult to fight a campaign against a man you like personally." Half the Whitakers stopped talking to Clem. W & B took the job, they insist, because they regarded Sinclair's program as a great menace.

Hired just two months before election, "we felt we had to do a fast job, we had to make a drastic change in public opinion." Their strategy was the ultimate in what might be called the diversionary technique—shifting attention from Sinclair's program to his personal foibles.

"Upton was beaten," Clem says candidly, "because he had written books." For three days, Clem and Leone secluded themselves with Sinclair's lifetime production, compiling a mass of damaging quotations. Then they hired an artist named Bill LeNoire who did a series of thirty cartoons on "the blot of Sinclairism," in which generally a dismaying quotation would be embedded in a big blob of black ink and flung against some typical scene of American felicity.

Thus, bride and groom, emerging from church, are assailed by a Sinclair comment that in capitalist society the institution of marriage has the qualities of "marriage plus prostitution." Or the picture of a madonna and child is defiled by Sinclair's observation that "of a score of religions in the world . . . *each is a mighty fortress of graft.*" In another cartoon, a huge black ogre labeled "Communism" looms behind Sinclair as he harangues a glowing idealization of Miss California. The Communist charge was frequently thrown at Sinclair, though in that regard he was quite blameless.

Whitaker and Baxter had mats made of the cartoons, shipped them to papers around the state. At least 3,000 appeared in print. "Sure, those quotations were irrelevant," says Baxter. "But we had one objective: to keep him from becoming Governor. But because he was a good man, we were sorry we had to do it that way."

After their imaginative assault on Sinclair, Whitaker and Baxter found themselves in increasing demand. They have handled as many as six campaigns in a single year. They turned back the repeated assaults of the Single Tax, the $30-every-Thursday movement of the late 'thirties, the weird pension proposals of "Gorgeous" George McClain, the Garrison Revenue Bond Act, and an effort to reapportion the legislature. They won an anti-featherbedding drive against the "full-crew" law on the railroads, three times persuaded California's voters to raise teachers' salaries, elected one Mayor of San Francisco, kept another from being recalled, ran three successful campaigns for Goodwin Knight, one for Earl Warren. They have handled but one Democrat, George Reilly, who was defeated for Mayor of San Francisco.

Whitaker and Baxter, incorporated as "Campaigns, Inc.," brought a new approach to political public relations. Long before their advent, politicians and pressure groups had of course hired press agents to write speeches and puff their causes in the papers. W & B, by contrast, provided the entire management of a campaign—overall strategy, organization, financial supervision as well as publicity and advertising.

California provided an excellent market for these services. Its peculiar cross-filing system—allowing Republicans and Democrats to run in each other's primaries—had effectively undercut party identity. A mushrooming population, nonpartisan municipal elections, and a dearth of patronage made it impossible to build stable political machines based on precinct organization. Moreover, incessant use of the initiative and referendum meant that in each election the individual voter had to be continuously harangued about a multitude of complex issues.

Cross-filing and the initiative and referendum, ironically, were reforms of the progressive Republican administration of Hiram Johnson. They were designed, in that distant era before World War I, to break the power of the old-line party machines. They achieved their purpose—eventually at the expense of producing chaos in California politics and making politicians more dependent on the mass media than elsewhere in the country. In California, the great game of politics turned into a branch of public relations.

Year-round the Whitaker and Baxter operation numbers no more than twelve people; at campaign time it is likely to expand to fifty. The firm charges $25,000 to $75,000 to handle a statewide campaign, but this fee is supplemented by the 15 per cent commission charged on advertising placed for clients. (W & B have their own advertising subsidiary.) Annual income is further increased by fees for the public relations "counseling" which occupies the firm between campaigns; its clients include railroads, public utilities, steamship lines. All told, W & B gross about $250,000 a year—exclusive, of course, of the money they expend on behalf of their clients. It is not unusual for a statewide referendum campaign to cost $500,000.

The firm's success can be credited to a variety of factors: shrewd strategy, thorough organization, and an imaginative exploitation of all the media of communications. By the time one of their campaigns is over, the unwary citizenry has nearly drowned in propaganda. Some years back, Whitaker calculated that in a typical campaign they employed ten million pamphlets and leaflets; 50,000 letters to "key individuals and officers of organizations"; 70,000 inches of advertising in 700 newspapers; 3,000 spot announcements on 109 radio stations; theater slides and trailers in 160 theaters; 1,000 large billboards and 18,000 or 20,000 smaller posters.

THE PARTNERS PAUSE TO THINK THINGS OUT

When Whitaker and Baxter take over a campaign, they absent themselves from the office for a few days to work out a detailed Plan of Campaign. This includes the basic strategy, methods of organization, the issues to be stressed, the types and volume of publicity and advertising to be used—and the timing of each thrust of propaganda. As a guide to their own strategy, W & B frequently formulate an Opposition Plan of Campaign.

They also prepare a budget. The client—generally a committee—guarantees the total sum and Whitaker and Baxter handle all disbursements. If the treasury runs low, W & B are in a position to advance as much as $100,000 out of their own funds, thus avoiding any slackening in the pace of the campaign because of financial stringencies. Few public relations firms are in this enviable position.

A basic part of the strategy of any campaign is to undercut as much opposition as possible in advance. Early in 1958, W & B confronted a difficult problem—how to win a referendum in support of a $50 million bond issue to improve the Port of San Francisco. The trouble with this estimable undertaking, they felt, was that only San Francisco would directly benefit, though the voters of the entire state would have to approve. True, the bonds would be repaid out of revenue, and hence would cost the taxpayers nothing—but this was not an easy thought to get across to more than six million voters. "The more you have to explain," Clem Whitaker says sadly, "the more difficult it is to win support."

Their solution was enterprising. One morning at breakfast, Leone read a newspaper story about another bond proposal—a $10-million issue, also self-liquidating, to expand small-boat harbor facilities throughout California. From the look of things, the small-boat bill seemed unlikely to pass the legislature. Whitaker and Baxter had no passion for amateur boating, but they suddenly saw a way of enhancing the attractiveness of their own measure—namely, by amalgamating the two bond proposals.

They mobilized their supporters at Sacramento, got a new bill passed, and were then able to go to the state with a proposal to improve scores of harbors from the Oregon border to Mexico. There followed the usual outpouring of catchy handbills, "mailers," newspaper ads, radio and TV spots —and the voters responded handsomely. "A good example," says Whitaker, "of how you can win a campaign in the board room—long before it starts."

The design of each campaign is different, but all share certain basic similarities. Timing is very important. A cardinal W & B rule is to allocate 75 per cent of their budget to the final three or four weeks of a campaign, when the din of contention has finally aroused the voters. Repetition is equally important. "We assume we have to get a voter's attention seven times to make a sale," says Whitaker. "That's an arbitrary figure, of course, but repetition is the only way to swing someone from no position to an affirmative position."

Every campaign must have a dominant, arresting theme. "The theme," Baxter has explained, "should have simplicity and clarity. Most of all, it must high-point the major issues of the campaign with great brevity—in language that paints a picture understandable to people in all circumstances."

Simplicity, of course, can verge on over-simplification and even fantasy. The Truman Administration's proposal for compulsory medical insurance was, for better or ill, exactly what the term implied. W & B, however, found it more helpful to crusade against "socialized medicine"—a term which they have conversationally abandoned, now that the fight is won.

In 1950, California's voters were presented with a scheme to pay old-age pensions out of the proceeds of legalized gambling. The plan was poorly conceived, but Whitaker and Baxter, who led the opposition, did not confine themselves to attacking its absurdities. Instead they pitched their entire campaign on the theme, "Keep the Crime Syndicates Out!" But nobody had suggested that the crime syndicates be let in.

For each theme, Whitaker and Baxter can of course provide a rationale: compulsory medical insurance would lead to socialized medicine; legalized gambling could lead to corruption. The virtue of a slogan, however, is that it so compresses the sequential relationship that a hypothetical threat becomes an immediate threat.

In its printed propaganda—that is, in the small print—W & B will spell out their rationale. Thus, in 1958, their newspaper ads warned that if the Monkey Wrench Tax Bill passed, the state would have to impose new taxes on real estate, food, and gasoline in order to raise needed revenues. But their highly effective TV spots eliminated the argument and merely demanded, "Do you want to pay a state property tax on your home?" Loud voice in background: "NO!" Announcer: "Then vote NO on Proposition 17—the Monkey Wrench Tax Bill."

Campaigns are dominated by themes and themes are in turn highlighted by "gimmicks," a term which W & B themselves apply. The Monkey Wrench Tax Bill was one such attention-getter. So was the song "I've Been Loafing On The Railroad" when they were campaigning in 1948 against the full-crew law on trains. It was sung at meetings, on innumerable radio spots, and served as caption for a widely distributed cartoon of a railway employee lolling in a bed atop a freight car.

HOW TO LOOK AGGRESSIVE

Torpor is the norm in politics, in the view of Whitaker and Baxter. "The average American," Whitaker once sadly informed a PR audience, "doesn't want to be educated; he doesn't want to improve his mind; he doesn't even want to work, consciously, at being a good citizen. But there are two ways you can interest him in a campaign, and only two that we have ever found successful.

"Most every American loves *contest*. He likes a good hot battle, with no punches pulled. . . . *So you can interest him if you put on a fight!* . . . Then, too, most every American likes to be entertained. He likes the movies; he likes mysteries; he likes fireworks and parades. . . . So if you can't fight, PUT ON A SHOW!"

The show must never lose its aggressive quality—a principle as important as its thematic simplicity. "Even when you're on the defensive, you must appear to be aggressive," says Whitaker. This is not always easy. In 1946, W & B were campaigning to prevent the recall of Mayor Roger Lapham of San Francisco. A recall campaign, unlike an election, does not involve two or more candidates slugging it out. There is no opponent—just the public official defending his record against his detractors. An intolerable situation, W & B felt; their solution was a brilliant improvisation—Mayor Lapham *vs.* the Faceless Man, a sinister type with his tilted derby completely obscuring his face, whom they labeled "The Undercover Candidate for Mayor." The Faceless Man, whose non-face was smeared across billboards and newspaper ads, became a target as vicious as any opponent Lapham might have flailed against. Lapham won.

The success of a campaign, W & B believe, is not only dependent on its aggressive pace and streamlined themes. It also requires grass-roots organization for the most effective distribution of the propaganda packaged at headquarters. In each campaign, the firm spends a good deal of energy rounding up its "natural allies"—local and statewide organizations which have either a direct or peripheral interest in the issue.

Thus, in its 1958 campaign for the harbor bond issue, W & B naturally received endorsements from the Pacific American Steamship Association, the various maritime unions, the California Marine Parks and Harbors Association, and the California Boating Council. But it ventured much further afield—mobilizing such groups as the California Rifle and Pistol Association, the Associated Brick Manufacturers of Southern California, the Fresno Cotton Exchange, the Chambers of Commerce of over forty cities, and the Orange County Farm Bureau. By the end of the campaign, over 150 organizations had affirmed their approval of Proposition 4.

A concerted effort is made to win the editorial support of newspapers. There is nothing subtle about the approach: W & B's missionaries buttonhole editors in their offices. When the firm was fighting a compulsory-health-insurance proposal made by Governor Earl Warren, over 500 newspapers were visited. The results were gratifying: Warren's proposal lost around thirty of its fifty supporters, and the numbers of papers in opposition increased from about one hundred to 432.

W & B do not overlook the helpfulness of advertising in encouraging favorable editorial attention. Reporting in July 1946 to its client, the California Teachers' Association, as one of its pay-raise referendum campaigns got under way, W & B stated:

"Every newspaper in the state has received a check to cover 60 inches of advertising space, reserved for our use during the month of October. The individual papers were advised that the schedule was made possible by the teachers in their own communities—and you can feel very confident, I believe, that no editor is going to develop a distaste for teachers generally or for their publicity stories as a result of it."

Further to increase good will, W & B do not charge small papers the normal 15 per cent advertising commission.

WHAT THEY DID FOR THE AMA

Although most of their work has been in California, Whitaker and Baxter have proved that the techniques developed there can be successfully applied nationally. In 1948, the American Medical Association, alarmed at the Truman Administration's campaign for compulsory health insurance, retained Whitaker and Baxter to turn back the threat. The partners went to Chicago, recruited a staff of around forty people, spent $4,678,000 over a three-and-a-half-year period.

Their approach was strategically sound: organized medicine had to offer a positive program to counter the Administration's plan. Under W & B's prodding, the AMA for the first time enthusiastically backed voluntary group-insurance plans, which provided a persuasive slogan—"The Voluntary Way Is The American Way"—with which to belabor "socialized" medicine.

Whitaker and Baxter then set about to mobilize the nation's doctors to arouse their parents, friends, and every variety of local organization to the Socialist threat. An enormous asset, of course, was the network of county and state medical societies around the country. Chicago headquarters provisioned them with canned speeches, canned resolutions, canned press releases for local use. In 1949, over 54 million pieces of literature were distributed, in 1950 over 43 million. In one two-week period in October 1950, the AMA spent $1,100,000 in newspaper and radio advertising (more than $2 million was also spent by sponsors of tie-in ads).

No angle was overlooked. The personal physicians of Congressmen and Senators were approached to solicit their votes. Doctors who knew newspaper editors were asked to request their support. Over 10,000 endorsements of the AMA position were received from local organizations. These were promptly released to the press and brought to the attention of the President, Congressmen, Senators, and state legislators. In the 1950 Congressional campaign, while the AMA officially remained on the sidelines, "Healing Arts Committees" of doctors and dentists were organized to campaign against advocates of the Murray-Wagner-Dingell bill. The "Socialists" were clobbered. So was their bill. Whitaker and Baxter could boast, with pardonable pride, that they had organized the "greatest grass-roots lobby in history."

Success, of course, breeds imitation. There are now several political PR firms in California, some of whose principals—like Herbert Baus of Los Angeles and Harry Lerner of San Francisco—received their training in Whitaker and Baxter's shop. Alumnus Lerner, in 1956, handed W & B their stiffest defeat on an initiative measure to "unitize" California's oil fields and thereby limit oil extraction.

W & B, retained by the "major" oil companies, argued that it was a salutary conservation measure. Lerner, representing the "independents," attacked it as a restrictive measure designed to favor the huge monopolies. W & B's campaign was temperate (friends said they were restrained by their clients), Lerner's attack was slashing—in a fashion reminiscent of his old mentors. His most effective gimmicks, displayed on billboards and ads, were two symbols for the "oil monopoly"—a hog wallowing in oil and a whale swallowing up the independents. His printed copy and TV spots were equally rough—and he won handsomely: 3,950,532 to 1,208,752 votes.

PATRICK HENRY LAID IT ON

Whitaker and Baxter do not alibi their defeats, but they are of course happier talking about their victories. They have great zest for their work, a quality which they in large part ascribe to conviction. "A campaign is too demanding if your heart isn't in it," says Whitaker. They have never been political neuters, willing to sell their talents to the highest bidder. Republicans from the start, they have regularly worked the conservative side of the street, though certain of their campaigns—like those raising teachers' salaries—had equal appeal for liberal-minded citizens. Dedicated Republicans, they rally spontaneously to any cause which champions Free Enterprise, Personal Initiative, Freedom, or the American Way. Their personal rhetoric at times has a quality of Boy Scout piety, but is so insistent that it inevitably carries the ring of sincerity.

Whitaker is fond of Lincoln's statement, "Public sentiment is everything. With public sentiment, nothing can fail; without it, nothing can succeed."

"If we sometimes go to extremes to create that sentiment," Whitaker has argued, "we can recall that some of the greatest statesmen in American history went to extremes, too. It was Lincoln who said: 'This government cannot endure permanently *half slave and half free.*' That's what we call 'a fear campaign' . . . a picture of dire things to come, unless the issue is resolved.

"And it was Patrick Henry who said, 'Give me liberty or give me death!' That's what we call laying it on with a ladle . . . even in these modern times, that is the kind of dynamic sloganeering that molds public sentiment—and wins campaigns."

These protestations are hardly persuasive. The sad fact is that their mass manufacture of slogans and wielding of ladles has led to a grievous debasement of political debate. It is true that political appeals, long before W & B entered the scene, were hardly distinguished for their intellectual sobriety. Oversimplification of issues, attribution of base motives to the opposition, appeals to prejudice and the most irrelevant ad hominem arguments have long flavored the rhetoric of democratic debate—especially at election time. Whitaker and Baxter's peculiar contribution, however, has been to make a precise art of oversimplification, to systematize emotional appeals, to merchandise the images they create through a relentless exploitation of every means of mass communication. Compared to these virtuosos, the old-time politician seems like an amateur.

WE'VE MELLOWED

In their more reflective moments, the partners occasionally betray some anxiety about the inadvertent effects of their work. Asked whether they have ever been disturbed at the tactics they have had to employ, Whitaker replied solemnly, "We search our souls to be sure we are not using tactics that will do damage to society." Baxter was more troubled: "We've felt that many of our methods have been used by the most dreadful people—like dictators. The only protection is that people in this business are decent." The conversation turned again to the campaign against Upton Sinclair. "We wouldn't operate like that now, would we, Clem?"

Whitaker sighed. "I guess we've mellowed—but on the other hand, we haven't been faced again with the same kind of fight."

Whatever the character of the fights ahead, W & B can look forward to a secure future. The political atmosphere peculiar to California which first nurtured their talents still exists: the lack of strong party organization, the personal character of many political contests, the enormous number of initiative and referendum issues at every election will continue to provide a ready market for their services and those of competing firms. This despite the fact that the cross-filing system, which frequently nullified the value of party affiliation, has recently been on the way out.

For the last few years, a Democrat or Republican cross-filing in the other's primary has had to list his own party label on the ballot, which greatly lessened the chances of capturing both primaries. This past April the legislature finally passed a bill abolishing cross-filing entirely. Thus party labels have begun to mean a good deal again in California. All this, however, has not brought into existence strong party organization on the traditional model (despite the growth of influential Democratic Clubs around the state). Even if they lost political candidates as clients, which seems unlikely, the professional campaign firms could still keep fully occupied with the endless initiative and referendum campaigns.

Outside of California, the Whitaker and Baxter type of operation has not emerged—nor does it seem likely to. The main reason is that party organization is stronger than in California, even in an era of decline for the big-city machine. To hire a PR firm to manage an entire major campaign would involve an unthinkable degree of abdication for a self-respecting political leader. PR people are of course involved in major campaigns in other states. In recent years, they have been put to increasing use and, depending on the prestige of the individual performer, their advice is often taken on issues of policy. But except in isolated instances they are not granted the range of responsibility which W & B take as a matter of course.

On the other hand, the techniques which the California firm pioneered have of course spread throughout the country. The 1952 Presidential campaign—and more particularly the 1956 one—saw a sophisticated effort to merchandise politics with all the gimmickry of advertising and public relations normally applied to the merchandising of soap. We can expect that no future Presidential campaign will be able to dispense with the five-minute TV speech, the thirty-second spot, the canned interview, and the carefully scripted political rally—complete to Hollywood director and three name bands. Whitaker and Baxter can reasonably boast that they have led the way.

86. MADISON AVENUE MAFIA?
by Patrick J. Sullivan*

Several times between now and next November, I freely predict that several articles, and perhaps a few books, will hint darkly that our next President will be selected not by the traditional American system based on ward heelers, county bosses and backroom logrolling at the convention, but by shady public relations men, operating from a mysterious area known as Madison Avenue.

* Public relations director for General Dynamics Corporation. This selection is from Patrick J. Sullivan, "Madison Avenue Mafia?" *America*, vol. 102, issue no. 23, Mar. 12, 1960, pp. 704-705. Reprinted by permission.

From reading the columns of the nation's professionally indignant commentators, one could have gathered the impression that the recently exposed rash of television scandals was the work of the same Madison Avenue mafia.

Now, I am a public relations man and I know most of the influential public relations executives in New York, yet I intend to vote only once next November, and I don't expect to know who our next President will be until the morning of November 9. Right up until he returned from his hegira to the mountains, I thought Charley Van Doren was on the level.

IS MADISON AVENUE HONEST?

Frankly, I'm getting pretty tired of sharing the blame for everything that has gone wrong in this vale of tears since the time of the Flood.

Public relations, as I try to practice it and as it is practiced by the overwhelming majority of my associates, is the business of representing to the public in the best possible light the firms, corporations or associations which employ us. It has been widely implied that public relations is systematic fraud and deceit; I know that it is not.

Ethically, the pursuit of public relations is neutral and, as such, can be applied to either good or evil ends. After all, the relationship of the public relations man to his client is exactly the same as the lawyer's relationship with his employer. The lawyer operates within a formalized system of behavior when he represents widows and orphans, murderers and rapists, soulless corporations and giant philanthropies. In a theatrically arranged courtroom, before a microcosm of public opinion, the lawyer presents his employer in the best available light. In a larger arena, before the whole public, the public relations man performs the same service for his client. Public relations men have to be more selective of clients than lawyers, and yet the law is regarded as one of the learned professions, and as such has the respect of the community.

Selling is also analogous to public relations work. Though not on a par with the lawyer, the salesman is accepted by his neighbors as the follower of an honest trade, and he is accepted as such without reservation.

One group that is sometimes moved to make hostile appraisal of the public relations profession bears, in fact, striking resemblance to the object of its indignation in its own ordinary operations. I refer to the most respected of journalistic professionals, the editorial writers of the nation's newspapers. These holier-than-anybody gentlemen daily compose enough highly opinionated prose to cover profitably most of the nation's arable acres. The opinions they express, however, are paid for by the publisher and may or may not be their own. Yes, the editorial writers are like public relations men.

There are crooks and double-dealers in public relations, just as there are perjurers in the profession of law, uneducated quacks and irresponsible fee-splitters in the medical profession, salesmen who lie about the performance of the products they sell, and Democratic editorial writers who work for Republican newspapers. But even as most lawyers are upright, most doctors compassionate, most salesmen honest in their beliefs about their products, most editorial writers frank about what they think, so most public relations men are also square shooters, and largely for the same reasons. One big reason, of course, is that they have to be square shooters. An organization that is anxious enough about its reputation to hire a public relations man can't afford to be represented by anyone but a man of the highest character. General Motors would not consider for a moment having an ex-ambulance athlete as a member of its legal staff. President Eisenhower selected Jim Hagerty, a man of spotless reputation, to represent his Administration to the press. Men who direct public relations activities of hospitals, colleges, trade associations, leading businesses, philanthropic organizations, dioceses and religious orders usually represent the high moral character of the organizations themselves.

It seems, nevertheless, that only in the field of public relations do people overlook the overwhelming majority of honest men to make a judgment of the profession on the basis of the few mavericks who contaminate every sizable group.

SUSPICIONS WITHOUT BASIS

Why does this attitude persist? There are a couple of reasonable explanations. Public relations is one of the new professions that have become connected with business in the past 50 years as more scientific methods of management have become common. Unlike accounting, insurance management, industrial relations or personnel management—or even advertising—public relations did not grow up in the business framework, but was transplanted almost full-blown from the field of journalism. As aliens from a world romantically misrepresented in the public mind and as agents dealing in the unmeasurable arena of public opinion, public relations people as a group are not too well understood by their associates in business.

On the other hand, some journalists profess to look upon the public relations man as an apostate who has gone over to the enemy camp with the express purpose of using his inside information about newspapers to dupe them into printing false, misleading puffs about his new employers. Yet every reporter knows that in most cases when he talks to a public relations man or reads a news release the facts he gets are correct. I have read statements by newspaper editors and publishers estimating that—in extreme ranges—from thirty to eighty per cent of the stories appearing in American newspapers first come to the attention of the papers in the form of news releases.

Why, then, the persistent denigration of an ethically neutral trade that is generally practiced with some circumspection? Irritatingly enough, I think a good bit of it comes from within the public relations business.

The guilty parties I have in mind are found in all walks of life, but an unfortunately large, stagnant body of them seems to have collected in the public relations business. These are the guys who, when they were in the newspaper business, constantly referred to the paper which employed them as "this rag." During the second week of their tenure they had started griping about the changes from the good old days. If they were on the desk, they complained about inferior reporting; and if they were outside, they complained about the punishment their copy took from the desk. They're the experts on what can't be done.

Naturally, such lackluster personalities don't go far in any business. When they find they are standing still on newspapers, they "take the veil" and give the publicity field a break, since public relations is hungry for any kind of journalistic experience and pays better.

Ten minutes after they are hired, these particular gentlemen start gnawing at the hand of the new master and commence griping about how they've humiliated themselves by taking the additional money they earn in public relations.

They feed this attitude back to their former associates in journalism, and, because most public relations staffs are small and closely knit, they keep the doubts alive in the minds of their more impressionable associates.

Every organization that does business with the public—from the manufacturer of automobile mufflers to governments—can, and in most cases does, utilize public relations counsel. Courses in its techniques are taught at colleges and universities; some of these institutions even offer degrees in the subject. Every branch of the Federal Government and almost every legislator has a public spokesman who would be called a public relations man in any other enterprise.

Yet many of us in the business have not come to grips with the question whether what we are doing is right or wrong, and many persistently refuse to face the question. It must be unsettling to live with an unanswered question like this, but there are even more compelling reasons than this one for public relations men to take a hard look at where they stand with their own consciences.

The only ethics the impersonal large organization knows is the ethics of whether the public approves or disapproves of its policies. As the arbiter of what the public thinks, the public relations man becomes the ethical adviser of the organization which hires him. If he can't decide in his own mind whether what he's doing is supposed to be honest or crooked, he'll have some difficulty giving balanced judgment on the ethical problems on which he is to advise. . . .

CHAPTER XII

Advertising:
The Merchandising of Illusion

If advertising had no more than merchandising significance, its study could be left to the schools of business administration. Because its impact has broad social, ethical, political, and economic importance, however, some consideration of its function and controversial character is called for in a book on public opinion and propaganda.

In the words of Prof. David M. Potter, advertising has become "an instrument of social control comparable to the school and the church in the extent of its influence upon society." Its omnipresence via billboards, newspapers, magazines, trolley cars, radio, TV, and, increasingly, the movies, means not only that its overt message is bound to register but that less conspicuous, sometimes unintended, and possibly even more important collateral messages are profoundly influencing this generation.

One of the questions raised most frequently at advertising conclaves these days is said to be: "Why isn't advertising respected like other professions?" The query reflects the fact that, while criticism of advertising is regarded as virtually un-American in many quarters, some novelists and other prominent public figures have recently subjected the advertising fraternity to a withering series of attacks.

Advertising, they charge, debases the English language, misleads the consumer, perverts his buying habits, adds a tinny veneer to American life, and instills a false sense of values through morally dubious techniques. The defensiveness of many advertising men and their frequently shrill reaction to their detractors speak eloquently, it is said, of their private uneasiness about the intrinsic dignity of their craft.

This is alleged despite advertising's indubitably solid achievements. It brings new products, improved products, and bargain prices to consumer attention. Some of its handiwork is unquestionably entertaining. Part of it has been educational (creating public awareness of the nutritional value of orange juice, for example). On occasions it has cooperated admirably with public service informational campaigns. Above all, mass advertising has created the demand for specific commodities which makes possible mass markets and mass production which make possible the comparatively low prices which make possible the fabled American standard of living.

Even when acknowledging these services, the critics stick to their guns. They ask whether the advertising flood can fail to foster the attitude that the "good life" is the life of ever-increasing consumption. Can exposing the average American, as Vance Packard says in *The Waste Makers*, to over

1,500 sales messages a day reminding him of the delights and indispensability of all these marvelous products do other than accelerate the developing view that Homo sapiens lives fully, richly, and to the hilt only in his capacity as a consumer? What chance has Emerson's warning against "grubby thing-worship" when people are inescapably bombarded by myriad advertising appeals virtually from the time their senses can first absorb messages (and before they are old enough to discount advertising's excesses and recognize its essentially self-serving role)? They are bombarded, too, by men wise in the ways of the subconscious and clinically skillful in exploiting that potentially imperious ally.

Other critics doubt the American consumer has to be goaded so relentlessly into buying the quantity of goods and services needed to keep the economy humming. An informal survey of one's friends, it is said, can demonstrate to anyone's satisfaction that few families would have any trouble finding ways to spend their money even if their incomes were considerably larger—whether increased advertising were present or not. It is conceded that advertising influences the *pattern* of spending, but its influence on the *total volume* of spending is much less certain. Is it just another myth, perhaps, that it takes $12 billion of advertising or more to move the goods of a high-gear economy—a myth, moreover, which nourishes the disquieting claim that artificially created product obsolescence is essential to a dynamic economy? Finally, it is urged that public spending (or public stimulation of private spending) on such projects as adequate housing, highways, hospitals, schools, medical colleges, stream pollution control, reforestation, metropolitan transportation facilities, etc., energizes the economy just as effectively as private spending for less essential purposes.

Vance Packard introduces our readings with a biting attack upon motivational research (which turns out to be a brief summary of *The Hidden Persuaders*). Mr. Packard is concerned about the growing tendency of advertising agencies to exploit people's hidden and often irrational anxieties, fears, and yearnings through advertising appeals based on psychological and psychoanalytical explorations of the customer's subconscious. Granting the usefulness of "depth probing" in certain circumstances, he sees it more often as a cynical attempt to prey upon human frailties for commercial advantage.

Some of Mr. Packard's indictment is now obsolete (subliminal advertising never caught on, and look at the small car market now!), but much of it remains staple ammunition for the advertising critic today.

Mr. Packard is answered by Fairfax M. Cone, who thinks the former is much too careless with his premises, his implications, and his conclusions. Mr. Cone insists that advertisers cannot afford to deceive the public— because the public will not be deceived for long. Motivational research, he contends, is only a logical extension of the timeless salesmanship principle that one should know as much about a prospective client as possible both to enhance the possibility of sales and to acquire the information needed to enable the manufacturer to better meet the consumer's wishes.

Other defenders of advertising point out that advertising often does confer an added value to a product—simply by creating illusions pleasing to the customer. The girl who wears a lipstick which advertising has identified with glamour and romance may actually *feel* more glamorous and romantic when she wears it. The male disturbed by the decline of his physical virility may actually *feel* more vigorous after he hopefully consumes a patent medicine invested with magical powers by advertising. In Martin Mayer's words, "Whenever a benefit is promised from the use of a product, and the promise is believed, then the use of that product carries with it a value not necessarily inherent in the stuff itself."[1]

In "The Propaganda Function in Marketing," Professor McGarry seeks to puncture some of the popular myths he believes have clustered about the field. Among them are the views that there is a real distinction between "artificial" and "natural" wants and that advertising somehow coerces people into buying goods they do not really want. He concludes on the optimistic note that advertising ultimately compels the producer to seek to satisfy an ever wider range of ever more finely differentiated tastes and desires. The results, he believes, will contribute to the diversity which is a "major element" in our standard of living.

87. THE GROWING POWER OF ADMEN

by Vance Packard *

America's advertising industry is moving into a commanding role in our society. Its executives are becoming masters of our economic destiny, the engineers behind some of our most successful political campaigns, major patrons of our social scientists, dictators of the content of most of the radio and television programs we hear, judges with life-and-death power over most of our mass-circulation magazines. Also, they have become our most powerful taste makers. In 1957 they made millions of Americans suddenly feel somehow inadequate because they did not own high-tailed automobiles.

They have, in short, become major wielders of social control in America in this second half of the twentieth century. Their power to do good or non-good is becoming massive, and many are using their power irresponsibly.

The growth of their power is seen in the amount of money entrusted to them to spend. In 1940 they had at their disposal $2 billion to conduct campaigns of persuasion. Today they have $10 billion. If you divide that figure by the total U.S. population, you come up with a fairly startling statistic. Approximately $60 is now being spent each year on *each* man, woman, and child in America solely to coax him or her to use products the admen are promoting.

This growing power of advertising men derives from the dominant role that selling plays in the dynamics of our economy. In the executive suites

[1] "What Is Advertising Good for?" *Harper's Magazine,* vol. 216, February, 1958, p. 28.

* Author of *The Hidden Persuaders, The Status Seekers,* and *The Waste Makers.* This selection is from Vance Packard, "The Growing Power of Admen," *Atlantic,* vol. 200, no. 3, September, 1957, pp. 55-59. Copyright 1961 by Vance Packard. By permission of the author and publisher.

of thousands of corporations the main preoccupation is no longer with production problems but rather with selling problems.

The most obvious explanation for this shift of emphasis is the fabulous productivity of our automated factories. Since 1940 our gross national product has soared more than 400 per cent. In 1954 it was predicted that our GNP would hit the long-dreamed-of mark of $400 billion by 1958. Actually it shot past that figure in 1956 and is expected to reach $600 billion within the coming decade.

To absorb this fantastic outpouring of goods we shall have to step up our personal consumption of goods by almost 50 per cent. As the chairman of America's leading advertising agency proclaimed recently: "We have to expand our levels of consumption in the next ten years by an amount nearly equal to the entire growth of the country in the two hundred years from colonial days up to 1940." The big problem we face, he said, is to cut down the "time lag" in the process by which we ordinarily learn to expand our wants and needs, in order to "absorb this production." Advertising men are the experts who can overcome this lag.

The real needs of most of us were satisfied long ago. About 40 per cent of the things we buy today are unnecessary in terms of any real need. Even our wants are pretty well satisfied. It has become a question of creating in our minds new, unrealized wants and needs.

Happily for the marketers, Americans by nature seem to relish learning to want new things. We are a restless people who like continually to hear of new things to do and buy. (Note the recent popularity of bejeweled fly swatters and mousetraps.) Emerson commented on this trait in Americans when he said that they, unlike Europeans, exhibit "an uncalculated, headlong expenditure." This makes them the world's prize consumers.

Recently the president of the Institute for Motivational Research (which conducts psychological studies for marketers) noted with satisfaction "our increasing willingness to give vent to our whims and desires" and offered the opinion that America is "experiencing a revolution in self-indulgence."

A corollary problem of marketers in moving their goods into our homes is that of making us discontented with what we already have, since most of us already own perfectly serviceable automobiles, washing machines, refrigerators, and clothing. We must be persuaded that the old product has become hopelessly inadequate to meet our needs or desired style of living. Advertising men call this "creating psychological obsolescence."

Another development adding to the power, glory, and prosperity of advertising men is the increased standardization of competing products. Perhaps connoisseurs can still detect significant differences in gasolines, whiskeys, cigarettes, beer, tires, cake mixes, and detergents, but most of us no longer can. Reports on blindfold tests conducted with cigarette smokers and whiskey and beer drinkers consistently reveal an inability of people to spot their favorite brand. A few days ago I heard a gathering of advertising men being advised that in blindfold tests people can't even tell the difference between Coca-Cola and Pepsi-Cola!

It used to startle me to hear advertising men make casual statements that in many fields such as gasoline and cigarettes the products are "all the same." Now it becomes apparent why they can be so complacent. It is the advertising man's genius that makes products seem compellingly different in our minds.

A third reason for the increasing influence of admen is the growth of self-service selling at supermarkets, vending machines, and so on. More and more, machines or systems are replacing people at the selling counter. The product maker can no longer rely on word-of-mouth selling by a clerk, merchant, or attendant. Thus the customer must be pre-sold, through advertising, so that he will have the product's image firmly etched in his mind as he enters the market place.

In the face of all these crying needs for more effective selling, America's 3300 advertising agencies have come to constitute "a great sociological battering ram," to use a phrase current with admen. Individually, advertising men have become "merchants of discontent."

As advertising men by the tens of thousands bring their wiles to bear to stimulate sales of products, we are seeing a massive straining for greater impact. Some months ago a distiller sent a photographic team to the edges of the Sahara Desert in order to obtain a photograph of a martini-filled glass in a setting which would suggest dryness. The photographers faced a crisis when, in searching the fruit markets of Cairo for a sliver of yellow lemon peel to go with the drink, they discovered that lemons sold in Egypt are green. This problem was solved when they arranged for a yellow lemon to be flown over from Italy.

Advertising men now ponder the advisability of making the "entertainment" portion of their TV sponsored programs a little dull so that the commercials will seem more exciting by contrast. In pictorial presentations one trend has been to the absurdly incongruous, to catch our eye as we search for reading matter amid a jungle of ads. Men sell whiskey while seated sideways on white horses, men with beards sell tonic water, shaggy dogs sell rum, kangaroos sell airline tickets. Meanwhile one advertising man complained: "We are suffering from fatigue of believability."

The advertising agencies, in their straining to become more persuasive, have been spending millions of dollars in research designed to learn more about the consumer. Batten Barton Durstine & Osborn has set up a division which it refers to grandiosely as "The National Panel of Consumer Opinion." It consists of several thousand housewives carefully chosen to constitute a "scale model" of the American female populace. These women can earn merchandise premiums by answering questionnaires about products and about their daily habits. Meanwhile Dr. George Gallup, long a researcher for admen, inaugurated a method of probing the consumer which he called "activation research." He set up a "sample bank" of people which he called "Mirror of America," and began probing the people in order to isolate just what triggers the sale of a product.

The most commotion in advertising circles in recent years, however, has centered on a probing technique called "motivation research," which promises to put deeper impact into sales messages. This "depth approach" to consumers involves the use of psychiatry and the social sciences to get inside the consumers' subconscious in order to discover the "psychological hook" which will impel consumers by the millions to buy a certain product.

Most of the leading advertising agencies now have psychologists, psychiatrists, or both on their payrolls. McCann-Erickson recently spent $3 million on a single monumental study of consumer psychology. A Chicago advertising agency rounded up eight leading social scientists in the Midwest (two psychoanalysts, a cultural anthropologist, a social psychologist, two sociologists, and two professors of social science) and had them spend a twelve-hour day in a hotel room watching television programs in order to glean new insights into the appeal of the sponsored programs and the commercials.

Meanwhile several dozens research firms have sprung up, all promising proficiency in depth research. The most famous, the Institute for Motivational Research, commanded by a psychoanalyst from Austria, Dr. Ernest Dichter, occupies a mountaintop castle on the Hudson. The room where local children observe television programs is equipped with hidden tape recorders, one-way viewing screens, and so on, to catch their reactions. Several hundred residents of the area constitute a "psycho-panel." They have been depth-probed and card-indexed as to their hidden anxieties, hostilities, and so forth. If you want to know how much impact a sales message will have on hypochondriacs, for example, Dr. Dichter has a group of bona fide hypochondriacs on call for a trial run.

So far much of the depth-probing of consumers is more hunch than science, but still most of the nation's largest producers of consumer products have been turning to it in an effort to increase their sales penetration. Giant corporations are raiding each other's customers with campaigns mapped by doctors of psychology.

One of the nation's largest advertising agencies now gives every single product it handles a motivational checkup. The merchandising journal *Tide* predicts that within ten years "few national marketers will launch an advertising campaign or introduce a new product without first conducting a thorough study of consumer motivations."

Some of the techniques used to probe consumer motives have been borrowed straight from psychiatric clinics and sociological laboratories: the depth interview (a miniature psychoanalysis without the couch), projective picture and word association tests, galvanometers (lie detectors), hypnosis, and social-layer analysis. When our motives are fathomed the experts then shape and bait psychological hooks which will bring us flopping into their corporate boats.

Among the more common strategies devised to lure us are: building self-images of ourselves into their product (playful gasolines for playful people); reminding us that their product can fill one of our hidden needs (security, self-esteem); playing upon our anxiety feelings; offering us ways, through products, to channel our aggressive feelings; selling us sexual reassurance; encouraging impulse buying; conditioning the young; selling us status symbols; making us style-conscious and then switching styles.

Several of the uses to which the insights are put strike me as constructive, or at least non-objectionable. The technique of gearing appeals to the social class most likely to enjoy your product would seem to be a step toward rationality in marketing. One of the notable cases of ill-considered selling occurred in Chicago when one of the leading brewers developed social pretensions for its brew, which had long been popular with the tavern-type clientele. The brewer's advertising men, in an effort to give the brew more class, began showing it being sipped by fox hunters, concert pianists, and drawing-room socialites. Sales did pick up slightly in the better residential areas but began falling disastrously with old customers. The boys in the taverns found the brew didn't taste right any more, though the formula was unchanged.

Social Research, Inc., looked into this fiasco when it depth-probed several hundred typical beer drinkers for the *Chicago Tribune*. It found that beer drinking in America is accepted as an informal, predominantly middle-class custom. So the brewers' foundation in its ads has recently been stressing the back-fence character of beer drinking.

The recent history of beer marketing reveals another way in which motivational analysts can produce constructive, or at least more rational, results. You may recall that in the mid-fifties many beer producers started to proclaim that their beer was particularly low-caloried and hence relatively non-fattening. The campaign was inspired by the mania for weight reduction which was particularly feverish then. Reportedly there were some impressive gains in sales as a result, but the motivational analysts viewed the low-caloric campaigns for beer with misgivings. Dr. Dichter's depth-probers, in testing the thoughts which sprang into people's minds when they saw the words "low calorie," found people thought of self-deprivation, discomfort. He admonished brewers to play up beer as a pleasure, not a medicine.

Motivational analysts have also performed a constructive service by showing advertising men how to conquer unreasonable prejudice against a product. A classic job in this respect was performed on the prune by Dr. Dichter's institute and advertising men of the prune industry. Prunes simply were not selling, and Dr. Dichter was asked to find why. His depth-probers found the prune, in our society, had become ridden with a host of connotations, all unfortunate. We thought of prunes in terms of dried-up old maids, boardinghouses, constipation, even witches. Under Dr. Dichter's guidance the prune has now been "rediscovered" as the "California wonder fruit," and admen now almost always show it in gay, zestful, youthful, colorful settings. The laxative angle is now mentioned in small type; and the prune industry, at last reports, is showing a hearty revival.

Still another way that the depth approach can perform a valid service is to help people achieve a feeling of self-worth through advertising. A producer of steam shovels found sales lagging. When a motivation study was made of prospective customers, it was discovered that steam-shovel operators play a large role in influencing the decisions of purchasing agents, and shovel operators did not like the shovel in question. A study of the ads that had been used to promote the shovel suggested a clue.

The shovel was always shown at work in all its monumental glory. Its operator was depicted as a barely visible figure inside the distant cab. The operators subconsciously felt their role was belittled. When the advertising men were advised of this source of irritation they began taking their pictures over the shoulder of the operator, with the operator shown as the confident master of the machine. This new approach reportedly brought a marked mellowing in the attitude of operators toward the shovel advertised.

Several of the techniques being used on us by certain of the advertising men (and their scientific allies), however, do give cause for concern. These are the techniques designed to catch us when our conscious guard is down. Here are some of the types of operation I have in mind.

1. Appeals designed to play upon our hidden weaknesses. At one of America's largest advertising agencies, staff psychologists have been exploring the subconscious of sample humans in order to find how to shape messages that will have maximum impact with people of high anxiety, body consciousness, hostility, passiveness, and so on.

In Chicago a smaller agency has conducted a psychiatric study of women's menstrual cycle and the emotional states which go with each stage of the cycle in order to learn how to sell cake mixes to women more effectively. The aim was to learn how to incorporate within one ad a double-barreled message which would appeal to women in the high phase of their cycle (creative, sexually excitable, narcissistic, outgoing, loving) and also at the same time to women who happened to be in their low phase (want attention, affection, things done for them). This could be achieved, the agency concluded, by offering the high-phase woman something new and the low-phase women an easy-does-it meal.

2. Strategies involving the manipulation of children. The agency just mentioned also conducted a study of the psyche of straight-haired small girls to find how best to persuade them and their mothers that the girls might feel doomed to ugliness and unhappiness if they were not somehow provided with curly hair. The agency was trying to promote the use of home permanents on children and used many psychiatric techniques in probing the little girls.

The most inviting opportunity to manipulate children for profit, of course, is via television. Five-year-old children, admen have learned, make mighty fine amplifiers of singing jingles (beer or cigarettes included). They can be taught to sing them endlessly with gusto around the house all day long and, unlike the TV set, they can't be turned off.

3. The use of subthreshold effects to slip messages past our conscious guard. Some advertising men have been investigating, very quietly, the possibility of inserting "flash" sales messages in TV and movie film. The bits of film flash by so fast they are not "seen" by the conscious eye, but are reportedly seen by the subconscious eye. In late 1956 the London *Sunday Times* charged that advertisers had produced a notable rise in ice cream consumption at a cinema in New Jersey during experiments with subthreshold effects. The use of such surreptitious appeals on any substantial basis will raise an ethical question of the most serious nature, particularly if such hidden appeals are used to put across political candidates or points of view.

4. The deliberate sale of products for their status-enhancement value. Automotive advertisers have hammered so long and loud on the theme of bigness that many Americans feel socially insecure in a small or medium-sized car (unless it is their second car or a chic foreign-made car). Although the times cry for more compact cars for our crowded highways and traffic-clogged metropolitan centers, most U.S. car makers stress, in their ads, the luxurious bigness of their cars. A TV commercial for one of the medium-priced cars stressed how Big it was and then, in a bit of theatrics, the announcer exclaimed: "People are getting smart about car buying nowadays!" With that, the screen showed a crowd of "people" chanting, "We're everybody. . . . We want a Big Car and style too."

5. The creation of illogical, irrational loyalties. This occurs most conspicuously in the promotion of gasolines, cigarettes, whiskeys, detergents. The research director of a leading advertising agency which has made a study in depth of cigarette smoking states that 65 per cent of all smokers are absolutely loyal to one brand of cigarettes, even to the extent of walking down five flights of stairs to buy their own brand rather than accept another brand offered by a friend. About 20 percent are relatively loyal. Yet he found in tests where cigarettes were masked that people could identify their brand by only 2 per cent better than chance. He concluded: "They are smoking an image completely."

In the building of images, cylinders of tobacco shreds wrapped in white paper have been invested with a variety of "exciting" personalities, to use one researcher's phrase. One smoke may have an image of elegance, another is daintily feminine, still another has an image of hair-on-your-chest virility. One cigarette company deliberately changed its image to almost a teen-age personality—even though most of the heavy smokers are in the thirty-to-forty age group. The aim reportedly was to recruit more beginner smokers and develop loyalty in them which would pay off on a long-term basis.

6. The exploitation of our deepest sexual sensitivities. According to the Institute for Motivational Research the admen who conceived the cigarette slogan "Like Your Pleasures Big?" were not unaware that the phrase was a *double entendre* with "latent sexual meaning." The same institute counseled motorboat builders that men could be appealed to on the fact that power boats can be used to express a sense of power in "almost a sexual way." A Midwestern advertising agency has discovered that men can be persuaded to buy a new car by the implied promise that the new, more powerful car offers them a renewal of potency.

7. The application of the insights of depth-selling to politics. In 1956 many political candidates, including the heads of the ticket, were counseled by admen to present an attractive image to the public. The most popular models were father images and courageous young Davids. At one quite important level the presidential campaign settled into a battle between advertising agencies: Batten Barton Durstine & Osborn for the Republicans and the smaller agency Norman Craig & Kummel for the Democrats.

The advertising man's approach to politics was perhaps best summed up by ad executive Rosser Reeves, who conceived the ceaseless barrage of half-minute spots on TV and radio in 1952 for the GOP. He said, "I think of a man in a voting booth who hesitates between two levers as if he were pausing between competing tubes of toothpaste in a drugstore. The brand that has made the highest penetration on his brain will win his choice."

The Democratic candidate, Adlai Stevenson (who reportedly became very unhappy about some of the strategies conceived for him by admen late in the campaign), voiced his irritation at the symbol manipulators' approach to politics (at least the GOP variety) by saying: "The idea that you can merchandise candidates for high office like breakfast cereal . . . is the ultimate indignity to the democratic process."

To sum up, I feel that while advertising in general is a constructive— and indispensable—force in our economy, its practitioners are becoming uncomfortably powerful and many of them need to exhibit more responsibility in their use of their new power than they have been doing. This particularly applies to their use of the depth approach to consumers.

The responsible leaders of the industry should, I believe, review the current trends in advertising and admonish practitioners to proceed with greater consideration for the public's welfare in certain areas. As a start they might consider the following broad trends which I believe should be viewed uneasily by thoughtful citizens:

Advertising men are pushing us toward conformity and passivity. Americans by the millions respond to their signals. Perhaps the trend to passivity is more serious than the trend to conformity. Max Lerner, in commenting on the implications he saw in some of the depth persuasion activities I described in my book, made one of the most perceptive and disquieting remarks I have encountered concerning the trend in selling. He wrote: "In motivation research . . . the consumer is always passive. He is analyzed, dissected, acted upon, bought and sold. He is a commodity to be trafficked in. The human being as a commodity, that is the disease of our age."

Many of the efforts of the advertising men provoke lasting anxieties. Economist Robert Lekachman recently speculated that we could only guess at the tensions and anxieties generated by the relentless pursuit of the emblems of success being encouraged in our society today.

The advertising men frequently are encouraging irrationality, as when they persuade us to buy products on the basis of images they have skillfully devised rather than on the merits of the physical product inside the package.

They are tending to demean many scientists who have been lured into serving them. Some of the social scientists collaborating with the advertising men maintain their standards of investigation; others strive to please, and often lay before their employers insights into our vulnerabilities which the advertising men do not hesitate to exploit.

Many of them are encouraging an attitude of wastefulness on the part of the public toward the nation's fast-shrinking resources. One conspicuous way they do this is by deliberately striving to make us dissatisfied with the serviceable products we already own.

Finally they often seek to invade the privacy of the mind. They want to know too much about us, and the inner workings of our emotions, for comfort. We should be able to be a little irrational and neurotic at times without having to fear that we thus become vulnerable to outside manipulation.

If advertising is to represent progress rather than regress for man in his struggle for self-mastery, then these considerations must be honestly faced.

88. ADVERTISING IS NOT A PLOT
by Fairfax M. Cone *

That there are irresponsible people in advertising can no more be disputed than that there are unscrupulous builders, manufacturers, retailers, and even doctors and lawyers. This is unfortunate. However, to assume that the reprehensible are in greater proportion in advertising than in any other field of endeavor is certainly questionable. .

In "The Growing Power of Admen" (*Atlantic*, September, 1957), Vance Packard has collected and collated a number of accusations of base advertising manipulation that add up to a vastly disturbing total picture. To be specific, Mr. Packard states that advertising executives have become the selfish masters of our economic destiny, our most powerful taste makers, major patrons and demeaners of our social scientists, dictators of the content of most of our radio and television programs, and judges with life and death power over most of our mass-circulation magazines.

This power, Mr. Packard believes, comes from $10 billion spent annually by the advertising industry to persuade the American public to buy goods, 40 per cent of which are unnecessary in terms of any real need.

The terms of real need are something I cannot argue. I am certain that few women I know *need* a home permanent wave or five colors of lipstick or an automatic dishwasher or a rotisserie. Few men I know *need* an electric shaver or a power lawn mower or a wardrobe that includes twelve nerve-jarring sports shirts. Few families I know *need* a 21-inch television set to replace an electronically satisfactory 14-inch television set, or need to belong to a book club. Nevertheless they do indulge in just such things. And while it might be interesting and perhaps useful to speculate on what would happen to the American economy if 40 per cent of consumer goods of almost any kind were to be deducted from our gross national income, the subject here is the irresponsibility of advertising people rather than the role that advertising plays in an economy of abundance.

In the first place, of the $10 billion spent on advertising in the United States every year, the total spent through advertising agencies is some $4 billion. Mr. Packard fails to make this distinction clear, and by implication accuses the agencies—which spend little more than a third of the money—of becoming "a great sociological battering ram." This is only one of Mr. Packard's mistakes. A much bigger one, and one that shows a curious lack of understanding of how advertising comes to be, lies in the statement that the expenditure for advertising is entrusted to the agencies.

* Leading advertising figure who organized Foote, Cone and Belding in 1942. This selection is from Fairfax M. Cone, "Advertising Is Not a Plot," *Atlantic,* vol. 201, no. 1, January, 1958, pp. 71-73. By permission of the author and publisher.

This is something, I am sure, that many an agency man and women has wished for, even dreamed of: professional responsibility. But advertising in most businesses is everybody's business and there are no cases on record where any considerable sums of money have been entrusted to anyone for expenditure. Advertising budgets, like advertising plans and advertising messages, are no less subject to management scrutiny than expenditures for plant and equipment and payroll.

The advertising agency in which I am a partner is retained by forty-three advertisers. Their expenditures through this agency in 1957 totaled almost $100 million, and not a single one of these dollars was spent without advertiser authority and without advertiser approval of advertising text as well as schedules. Moreover, the shares of a large number of these companies are listed in the New York Stock Exchange. All are under the constant surveillance of stockholders and security analysts. None entrust advertising expenditures to either inside or outside advertising executives, nor to both together. Chairmen, presidents, and executive committees must pass every advertising budget proposal; and every budget that I know of is presented complete with detailed copy recommendations and layouts for printed advertising and proposed text and storyboards (precise pictorial outlines) for television commercials.

As to the claim that advertising executives dictate the content of most radio and television programs, it need only be said that no half hour of time on any network or independent station is controlled by any advertiser or any advertising agency; nor does any advertiser or any advertising agency dictate the programing. Networks and stations allow only two options: not to buy either a time period or a program that is offered, or not to renew it. Now, to be sure, many an advertiser has dropped a program that someone wanted him to keep on the air. Various reasons are ascribed every time this happens; punishing a performer for failing to hew to some line has often been given as a reason, and I am sure that this has happened. But tune-in is the basis for almost all program decisions. Tune-in guides networks and stations alike in programing; and advertising goes where circulation is, where people in the greatest numbers want to look and listen. Advertising can afford to pay for programs just so long as advertising is effective in selling; it has no other purpose.

Before I come to the role of taste making and the subornation of the social scientists that are ascribed to the advertising industry by Mr. Packard, I think it should be noted that his charge that advertising executives are "judges with life-and-death power over most of our mass-circulation magazines" is made with no shred of evidence, or even an implication, to support the allegation. Our ten largest mass-circulation magazines are the *Reader's Digest*, *Life*, *Ladies Home Journal*, *TV Guide*, *Look*, *Saturday Evening Post*, *McCall's*, *Better Homes & Gardens*, and the weekly newspaper supplements, *This Week* and the *American Weekly*. It would be interesting to have Mr. Packard tell us just which of their editors and publishers are held in advertising bondage; or, better still, tell us *one* who has ever brought up for advertiser or advertising agency discussion an editorial item or feature that he himself questioned, pro or con, on principle.

There have been many disputes by advertisers and their agencies about articles published in magazines to which they took exception, and scheduled advertising has been canceled. But I can see no difference between this and the action of an irate individual who cancels his subscription because of an article or story that he doesn't like. America's periodical publishers, large and small, like the broadcasters and the newspaper publishers, go their own highly individual and independent ways, and advertising follows them; it never leads.

The only "evidence" Mr. Packard submits to sustain his claim that the executives of the advertising industry have become our most powerful taste makers is the assertion that "In 1957 they made millions of Americans suddenly feel somehow inadequate because they did not own high-tailed automobiles." But Mr. Packard charges on. "Advertising men," he says, once again without quoting any source for his statement, "now ponder the advisability of making the 'entertainment' portion of their TV sponsored programs a little dull so that the commercials will seem more exciting by contrast." This is fantastic. What advertising men? Who? Where? And with the connivance of what network or station officials who must suddenly have decided that commercials and not programs attract the audiences by which they live?

The absurdity of most of Mr. Packard's charges should be patent. And nowhere are these more ridiculous than in giving as standards of general advertising agency operation and practice a number of experiments and experiences in so-called motivational research, amateur and professional.

Many, many years ago advertising was defined as salesmanship in print: showing your customer why it is in his best selfish interest to buy the goods you have for sale. This, I submit, is neither dishonest nor demoralizing. American industry has grown great by producing goods that are in many people's selfish interest to buy, and advertising has become the principal means of communication between the maker and the potential customer.

Advertising is not a plot. Nor are most advertising people wily plotters. They are salesmen, in print and over the air. And just as most good salesmen-in-person seek to know all they can about their prospective customers, so do most manufacturers and their salesmen-in-advertising undertake to learn all *they* can about their prospective customers. Motivational research is done primarily for two reasons: first, to find out what people know about products (and services), and second, to find out what people want in products (and services) that may not currently be there.

Frequently, motivational research is done to find out why a certain product isn't selling or why another, competitive, product is selling much better. Sometimes the reason is only that the advertising is stressing a point that the advertiser thinks far more important than the consumer, omitting the real point of difference. In such a case the advertising may be changed to make the important point clear. Or, if there is a lack in the product, the product may be changed.

There is another important use of motivational research. As Mr. Packard points out, in alarm that I cannot share, many competitive products today are very similar in quality and performance, or taste, or appearance. Some critics of our system hold this to result from a concerted effort on the part of many people for standardization in everything we have and think and do; and I think no premise could be more false. Products are more alike today than ever before because few manufacturers can long hold any great advantage of research; competition is knowledgeable and alert and fast on its feet. The result is that more and more products and services are bought as a matter of personal choice than for reasons of large variations in quality or performance or value.

Motivational research is one of the methods used to discover the elements in choice in specific instances and to build products and design services—and advertising—to merit the choosing. To be sure, motivational research has utilized techniques used also in sociological laboratories: the depth interview, projective picture and word association tests, galvanometers, and even, perhaps, hypnosis, as Mr. Packard states. But what Mr. Packard infers is that their use is reprehensible, and this I do not believe. Hypnosis in research is a new idea to me; I can only think that its use (if it has been used) must have been as tentative as the instance cited of a nameless Chicago advertising agency which "rounded up eight leading social scientists in the Midwest (two psychoanalysts, a cultural anthropologist, a social psychologist, two sociologists, and two professors of social science) and had them spend a twelve-hour day in a hotel room watching television programs in order to glean new insights into the appeal of the sponsored programs and the commercials." Not many advertising agencies could afford so fantastic an undertaking, even once; and none that I know of could rebill the cost to its clients.

The use of depth interviews is valuable in many businesses. Projective picture and word association tests are standard in schools and colleges and in the hiring and placing of people throughout industry. And the galvanometer (lie detector) principle is only something that many people have experimented with to measure accurately reactions to parts of radio and television commercials that are lost in recall tests.

I repeat, there is no advertising plotting here. To know more about people and how they think, and what they want and why, is only to make advertising serve better. And now, if I can hear someone say, "serve whom?" I will say, "everybody." The plain fact is that advertising to be affordable must sell the very same products and services to the very same people again and again. If it lies to them or if it builds up false hopes it can only fail, and so must the advertising people who make it, and the advertisers who pay the bill.

No one in business would ever use advertising if he could call on all his prospects in person. In selling many things to many people across the whole United States, the cost of personal selling is obviously prohibitive. The essential thing about advertising is that it is a multiplier of sales messages. It adds very little to the unit cost of most things we buy. As a result, advertising is one of the most important elements in mass production, for it makes mass selling at reasonable cost possible.

No advertising executive that I know wants to debase it. And, fortunately, those who do debase it commit their sins in public. What almost guarantees the honesty of advertising and advertising people is advertising itself. Punishment for sinning is swift and sure. It comes from a public that deeply resents being fooled and that will not buy any product again that has failed to live up to its original advertising promise.

89. THE PROPAGANDA FUNCTION IN MARKETING
by Edmund D. McGarry*

The most controversial aspect of marketing is advertising. Ever since advertising began to appear, moralists and critics have complained that it distorted people's natural desires, misinformed them as to the products they needed, played upon their emotions, and led to waste of resources.

Proponents of advertising, on the other hand, have argued that it is an economical method of distributing goods, that it provides entertainment, and actually adds to the value of the goods advertised. The purpose here is not to discuss these issues directly, but rather to place the advertising process in its proper perspective as a function of marketing.

Advertising as used today is primarily a type of propaganda. The essence of propaganda is that it conditions people to act in a way favorable to or desired by the propagandist. It deliberately attempts to influence, persuade, and convince people to act in a way that they would not otherwise act. Propaganda had its birth in the attempt of the church to propagate the faith. It is used by leaders who seek a following in politics, in religion, and in all affairs which require action by large bodies of people.

In business it is used primary by sellers to obtain a market by conditioning people in the market to accept the particular products offered. The growth of new techniques of communication has greatly extended the range of propaganda penetration, has expanded the number of products advertised, and has increased the total amount of propaganda disseminated; but the aim of the messages carried is essentially unchanged since the beginning of civilization.

In fact, the use of force of argument instead of physical force marked the change from savagery to civilized living. "The creation of the world," said Plato, "is the victory of persuasion over force."

The use of persuasion is part of man's apparatus to adapt his way of life to change. Without some stimulus to action, man tends to be indifferent and apathetic to change, and unwilling to exert the effort which change necessitates. He prefers to follow his preconditioned routines rather than direct his effort in some different way. There must be some extra stimulus

* Professor of marketing and economics at the University of Buffalo. Former associate editor of *National Marketing Journal*. This selection is from Edmund D. McGarry, "The Propaganda Function in Marketing," *The Journal of Marketing*, national quarterly publication of the American Marketing Association, vol. 23, no. 2, October, 1958, pp. 131-139. By permission of the publisher.

to action; and this stimulus is afforded either by compulsion of force or the threat of force, or by persuasion in the form of the written or spoken word.

PROPAGANDA VERSUS EDUCATION

Propaganda differs from education in that education presumably is oriented toward the dissemination of "truth"—dispassionate, objective, and unbiased. Pure education takes an impartial non-partisan point of view. It is not prejudiced; it has no slant. Yet all of us know that education must persuade to get students to study; it must propagandize to get funds.

Propaganda, on the other hand, by definition is biased, partial, and one sided. It has an axe to grind; therefore, it is always controversial. But unlike education, in which there is no sponsor, the sponsor of propaganda, particularly advertising propaganda, is known. And everyone knows what the sponsor is trying to do, what his motives are, and how he would like others to act. The sponsor of commercial propaganda must identify himself and the product he advertises and he must take the responsibility for it; otherwise, his propaganda cannot be directed to his purpose.

Every advertisement is designed to predispose its readers to a favorable consideration of its sponsor and his product. It is deliberately planned to make its readers and listeners take sides—to affiliate and ally themselves under its banner and to ignore all others.

Advertising is the obtrusive display of the conflict of interests in the market place. It represents a parade of the contestants in the battle for market supremacy, each imploring the audience to follow him. By its very nature advertising must be prejudiced in order to be potent.

THE BARRAGE EFFECT OF PROPAGANDA

Commercial propaganda is a social phenomenon, and its analysis must necessarily be in a social framework. It is, in fact, a part of our culture and at the same time exercises a considerable influence on that culture. Professor David M. Potter speaks of it "as an instrument of social control comparable to the school and the church in the extent of its influence upon society."[1]

Like other types of propaganda, advertising has a barrage effect. Although it is designed primarily to induce people who have the money and the need to buy the product, its effect cannot usually be confined to these. It creates a pattern of thought in a much larger population. Its results are diffuse and pervasive rather than selective. Because of this diffusion, many who are not in a position to buy, read, or listen to the advertisement, and many others who do not see or hear the message directly, learn of it from others by word of mouth.

Moreover, the pattern of thought created by advertising is likely to last for an indefinite period. If consecutive appeals are used, the effect tends to be cumulative both because of the widening group which sees it and

[1] David M. Potter, *People of Plenty* (Chicago: University of Chicago Press, 1954), p. 168.

because of the intensification of the impression it makes. This cumulative effect continues to a point of diminishing returns which is reached either through saturation of the market, through the counteracting influence of competing messages, or through the saturation of receptivity.

There is another sense in which there is a spill-over of advertising effectiveness. This is what might be called the cross-product influence. It is said, for instance, that when vacuum cleaners were first advertised the demand for brooms increased; the inference is that the promotion of cleanliness in the home leads to the increased sales of any product that enhances cleanliness.

Still another type of spill-over effect is seen in the case of the firm selling a family of products in which the advertising of any one will increase to some extent the sales of other products in the same group. It seems probable also that the advertising of a particular brand influences the sales of all other products in the same use-class, even if they are marketed by competitors.

It would seem logical to assume that, when two competing advertisers attempt to promote their individual brands for a particular use, the impact will be greater than if only one is advertised; and, if the market can be expanded, the advertising of each will have a complementary effect on that of the other. If this is true, then there is a cumulative effect of advertising generally in the sense that, as more advertising is published, there is developed a greater propensity to purchase advertised goods of all kinds. The increase may be at the expense of nonadvertised goods, it may be at the expense of savings, or it may result in greater effort on the part of consumers to secure more income.

Advertising versus Personal Selling

Advertising today has to take a large part of the responsibility for making sales. To a great extent salesmen, particularly at the retail level, have become anonymous persons—unknown either to the selling firm or to the buyer—who merely facilitate the sale by formally presenting the product and accepting payment. The real job of adjusting the consumer to the product is done by the mass propaganda called advertising.

In taking over the task formerly performed by the salesman, advertising must substitute symbolic language for the personal appeal of man-to-man at a point where the merchandise is itself present and the transaction takes place. The task of persuading the customer is pushed back in time to a point where it can be planned and partly executed months before the product reaches the market. It is removed in space from the point of sale to the business office, where the entire selling technique is planned and developed without benefit of the presence of the buyer. The sale must thus consist of an impersonalized message to thousands of unidentified potential customers, who have no way of communicating their impressions.

Modern advertising has many tasks to perform, which do not arise when selling is done face-to-face at the point of sale:

1. It must create or point out a need by identifying the circumstances under which it arises.

2. It must link the need to the possibility of fulfilling it with a general product, so that when the need arises the respondent will think of the product that will fulfill it.

3. It must differentiate the particular brand and its sponsor from other products which might satisfy the need approximately as well.

4. It must connect the particular branded product with the place and the conditions under which it can be obtained.

5. It must show that the need is urgent and that the task of buying is easy.

6. It must give a rational basis for action, for people do not like to buy goods which they cannot justify to their own consciences.

7. It must stimulate the respondent to make a firm decision on which he will act at a later time.

In accomplishing these tasks, advertising acts under the klieg lights of publicity. Unlike personal selling, where the promotion is carried on in private between two or more people, the messages publicized in advertising are conspicuous and cannot escape observation. This is one of the reasons why advertising comes in for a great deal of criticism that is equally relevant to selling on a personal basis. The so-called abuses which are concealed and disguised in the personal sales transaction are flaunted in the face of the public when they are published on the printed page or appear on the television screen. There is little doubt that there is more misrepresentation, deceit, and fraud in person-to-person sales relationships than in advertising.

The Purpose of Advertising

Commercial propaganda or advertising had its genesis in the need of the mass producer to sell goods in large quantities, and competition of other goods forced him to resort to an anonymous market: an aggregation of people scattered geographically, and unknown and unidentified as individuals. These conditions, and the growing separation of the locus of production in time and space from the locus of consumption, necessitated some means of making an individual manufacturer's product known and thus assuring it a continuous market.

Through the use of propaganda it was possible to create markets that were more stable than their component parts; for, although individual consumers are notoriously whimsical in changing their minds, their reactions in the market as a whole tend to cancel each other out.[2]

In order to accomplish these results the advertiser must use all the tools at his disposal. He must have an intimate understanding of the product advertised and be able to sense these characteristics whether inherent or inferred, which will fulfill the hopes and expectations of the potential owner and user. He must envisage the product in its use-setting. He must comprehend and appreciate the nature of human behavior. And he must be able to use the tricks of his trade—often the same as, and always closely akin to, those used on the rostrum and in the pulpit.

[2] Compare Neil H. Borden, *The Economic Effects of Advertising* (Chicago: Richard D. Irwin, 1942).

If the propaganda which the advertiser writes is to be effective, it must be expressed in terms in which the consumer thinks, with the same overtones and exaggerations of the product that the well-disposed consumer will attribute to it. It must recognize that the consumer to whom it appeals is but imperfectly rational, that he hates the labor of rational thinking, and that he is sometimes more impressed by what seems to others to be superficial than by the real merits of the product.

RATIONAL VERSUS EMOTIONAL APPEALS

In a broad, general sense advertising appeals either to man's reason or to his emotion or to both. It is difficult, of course, to differentiate in any precise way between these; but generally speaking rational appeals seem more effective in deciding alternative means to ends rather than the ends themselves. Emotion, on the other hand, is usually the trigger to action, particularly when the actions mean a change of attitude on the part of the person.

There are many road-blocks to actions based on rational appeals; for rational arguments tend to raise questions rather than to answer them. Emotional appeals, on the other hand, attempt to stimulate the individuals to carry through impulses which he already has. Assuming that this is true, the rational appeal is likely to be more lasting and its secondary effect to be stronger, because people are more likely to repeat rationalizations than they are to communicate their emotional feelings.

Advertising is highly concentrated on marginal products, things that one can do without, things that can be purchased with free income after the more austere basic needs such as necessary food, housing, clothing, etc., are taken care of.[3] It is these marginal products that give the real satisfactions in life. Even in the case of basic products, it is the exotic, the unusual elements—the fringe benefits—that set one off from his fellow creatures and thus claim the attention of consumers.

The Most Common Motives

Some years ago Victor Schwab suggested that there were ten leading motives or desires of the average consumer to which advertising must appeal in order to be effective:[4]

1. *Money and a better job.* "There must always be some kind of short-cut to getting ahead faster."
2. *Security in old age.* "When I get along in years, I want to be able to take it easy."
3. *Popularity.* "It's fun to be asked out all the time, to be wanted by everybody."
4. *Praise from others.* "Praise from others is a nice thing to get and I like to get it when I deserve it, and I often do."
5. *More comfort.* "A lot of people who are not as industrious or as capable as I am seem to have more comforts, so why shouldn't I spread myself once in a while?"

[3] F. P. Bishop, *The Ethics of Advertising* (London: Robert Hale, Ltd., 1949), p. 48.
[4] Victor Schwab, "Ten Copy Appeals," *Printers' Ink* (December 17, 1943), pp. 17ff.

6. *Social advancement.* "Where would a person be if he never tried to better himself and to meet and associate with better people?"

7. *Improved appearance.* "It is awfully nice to have people tell you how attractive and well-dressed you are. If I had the time and money some people spend on themselves, I would show them."

8. *Personal prestige.* "I am going to see to it that my children can prove that they have parents they need never be ashamed of."

9. *Better health.* "I don't feel any older than I did years ago, it's just that I don't seem to have the drive and energy I used to have."

10. *Increased enjoyment.* "I work hard, I do the best I can about things so why shouldn't I get as much enjoyment as I can?"

Advertisers have found by trial and error that these types of appeals are effective. It is evident that each appeal contains a bit of rationality with a large dose of sentimentality. The fact that these appeals are effective simply indicates that "the average human mind is a montage of hasty impressions, fuzzy generalities, bromidic wall-motto sentiments, self-justifications and sentimentalities."[5] It is out of this "jumble of ideas and feelings" that the advertiser must find a background for his appeals.

More and Better Wants

"The chief thing which the common-sense individual actually wants," wrote Professor Frank H. Knight, "is not satisfactions for the wants which he has, but more and better wants. There is always really present and operative, though in the background of consciousness, the idea of, and desire for a new want to be striven for when the present objective is out of the way."[6] Advertising attempts to present goods which are new or additional in the consumers' inventory of wants, and to indicate how they can be realized. In doing this, it both creates a want and the means of satisfying it.

The fact that advertising concentrates its efforts on changing people's customary wants has given rise to the contention that it corrupts people's desires and stimulates so-called "artificial" consuming habits. But this argument is beside the point for, as Professor Knight has indicated, "there is no issue as between natural and artificial wants. All human wants are more artificial than natural, and the expression 'natural wants,' if it has any meaning, can only refer to those of beasts. By the same token, human wants are more sentimental than real."[7]

Most people have always lived rather drab and unimaginative lives. The so-called golden ages of history were golden only to the few. The great masses lived by drudgery, and thought in terms of only the elemental emotions such as hunger and comfort. The so-called "democratic way of life" rests simply on the idea that our present economy is oriented to change the thinking of these masses. Propaganda, if it is to be effective, must appeal to the masses in the terms of their own mental processes.

It is sometimes alleged also that, through advertising, businessmen foist on people goods they do not want. This, of course, is sheer nonsense. There

[5] Same reference, p. 17.

[6] Frank H. Knight, *The Ethics of Competition* (New York: Harpers, 1935), p. 22.

[7] Same reference, p. 103.

are, in fact, few acts necessarily more deliberate than that of the consumer's action in response to advertising.

Picture the consumer in his living room reading a magazine advertisement. He has had to choose the particular magazine, and pay for it; he has had to select from among the hundreds of pages those he wishes to read, and he can either accept or reject the arguments presented. Assuming that he accepts them and resolves to make the purchase, he must still wait hours or even days before an opportune time arises to make the purchase. During the interval between the time he reads the advertisement and the time he undertakes the overt act of buying, he is entirely outside the influence of the message and may deliberate and search his soul to his heart's content either in private or in consultation with his friends. There is not even mass psychology to influence him. He is a free agent and there is no possibility of coercion, duress, or constraint of any kind.

But the impossibility of advertising to force consumers to buy what they do not want should not be confused with the fact that advertisers sometime overstep the bounds of propriety to make claims for their products which cannot be justified. In some product areas effective protection has been provided by law, but in general the chief defense of the consumer lies in his own discrimination of whom he will patronize or refuse to patronize.

THE LARGER SYSTEM OF BELIEFS

In discussing propaganda generally, psychologists Krech and Crutchfield state that suggestions which are accepted as a consequence of propaganda tend to be in harmony with some larger system of beliefs or some already existing predisposition, and therefore presumably with the major needs and interests of the subject.[8]

To put this another way, at any given time the subject of propaganda has many prejudices, beliefs, and attitudes of different intensities. Some are deeply entrenched, while others are at a superficial level. The more deeply entrenched these predispositions are, the more difficult it will be to change them, and some seem to be entrenched so deeply that they cannot be changed by propaganda at all.

Since it is easier and less expensive to modify existing predispositions than to oppose them, propagandists find it expedient to fit their messages into the current pattern of thinking rather than oppose it head on. It is for this reason that most changes in attitudes and wants achieved by advertising are almost imperceptible, and can be objectively observed only over a period of time.

Both in the selection of the characteristics of the product to promote and in the framing of appeals, the advertiser must give attention to consumers' preconceived ideas of what they want. He develops his product and its appeals to fit into these ideas and to project them further. If his advertis-

[8] D. K. Krech and R. S. Crutchfield, *Theory and Problems of Social Psychology* (New York: McGraw-Hill, 1948), p. 347.

ing is successful in selling his product, competitors will find it necessary to discover other new products or new characteristics of old products, likewise in line with consumers' ideas, as a basis for their counter-propaganda. Thus, competition in advertising tends to develop a constantly increasing improvement of the product to fit consumers' wants, while at the same time it raises the standards of wants in the consumers' minds.

Discounting the Message

The very mass of advertising and the great amount that comes to the attention of consumers is often open to criticism. Critics ask, for instance, "Is there no limit to the increasing din of the market place?" "Will it continue until all businesses are wasting their substance and crying their wares?" "Are there no antidotes for this infectious disease?" We suspect there are.

The editor of *Harper's Magazine* puts it this way:

> Perhaps, however, we will in the long run have reason to be grateful to the copywriters and press agents, even the worst of them. It may turn out that thanks to advertising and public relations, the American people will become the first people in history to be impervious to propaganda. Maybe it isn't such a bad thing that the advertisers and other word-manipulators have got us to the point that we never take words quite at their face value. In all events, it is hard to imagine that the people inured to American advertising would wholeheartedly believe the kind of promises and assurances, whereby Hitler and Stalin have enslaved two great nations in our time.[9]

When two advertisers say approximately the same things about their product, the message of one tends to neutralize that of the other, and the public learns to discount what is said by both. In a free world the right to persuade and be persuaded is one of the essential freedoms. We assume that each of us has the mentality and the fortitude to choose—to accept or reject what he hears or what he reads.

Each has the right to act or to refuse to act on the basis of all the propaganda he absorbs, whether it is in the form of advertising or word-of-mouth gossip. That he often rejects propaganda is a matter of record. But we assume that, whether a person acts wisely or foolishly, he will take the responsibility for the act and that he himself will reap the benefits or the penalties of his action. For this reason he will eventually learn to listen more discriminatingly and act more wisely in the light of all the information available.

EFFECT ON MEDIA CONTENT

It is sometimes alleged that advertising, because it pays most of the cost of magazines and newspapers, dominates and controls the information in these media. It is said that, since the advertiser pays the piper, he must call the tune.

[9] Robert Amory, Jr., "Personal and Otherwise," *Harper's Magazine* (September, 1948), p. 6.

Actually this is seldom true because the medium that publishes biased or slanted news tends to lose its circulation when its bias becomes known, and in this way it ceases to be an effective means of communication. Even the most severe critics of advertising admit that this type of direct and overt influence is pretty well eliminated by the intense competition among media themselves.

The effect of advertising on news content and editorial opinion is far more indirect and subtle. Editors themselves are human and they live in the same environment as the rest of us. They, too, are subject to the propaganda which all of us read; and it would be too much to expect that they are not influenced in a general way by what they read. As a part of the total environment it tends to set a point of view which is not unfavorable to advertising.

The Function of Media

From the advertiser's point of view, the function of the newspaper, the magazine, the broadcasting station, or any other medium of publication is to gather a crowd or furnish an audience.[10] Once the crowd has gathered, it must be entertained, amused, or at least interested enough to hold together while the advertiser's message is being delivered. The need for holding the audience arises from the fact that advertising is selective, in the sense that a specific message is likely to have an appeal only to a scattered few among the many in the crowd. As for the many others who have no need or interest in the particular product, they become bored and resentful that their attention has been disrupted.

The fact that advertising is selective in its expectations, though not in its aims, means that its impact on those to whom the message does not apply or who do not care to listen ranges from irritation to exasperation. From the listener's point of view, it is an unwarranted intrusion on their privacy, by some "jerk" who wants to sell something.

Therefore, the advertiser must use every art he can contrive to make his message palatable, even to those who do not want to listen; and at the same time he searches for a vehicle which will capture and hold his audience while he gives them "the works." In rare cases he is able to convert his message into news which is interesting and entertaining in itself; but often there is a trail of resentment left in the listener's mind, and he deliberately tries to develop some means of shutting out the message from his consciousness. The result is that a great deal of advertising never passes the threshold of the reader's or the listener's consciousness.

Although there is danger of exaggerating the importance of advertising in causing certain changes in our culture, it would be erroneous to conclude that its influence is negligible. Advertising is so prevalent, so pervasive, so extensive, and so conspicuous that it would be absurd to argue that it does not affect our attitudes.

On the other hand, the fact that advertising, in order to be successful

[10] See G. B. Hotchkiss, *Milestones of Marketing* (New York: Macmillan, 1938), p. 10.

and economical, "must be in harmony with some larger system of beliefs or some already existing predisposition" indicates that its influence is tangential rather than direct, that it tends to fit in with and supplement other motivational influences rather than act as an independent force.

EFFECT ON CONSUMER STANDARDS

Advertising, both for individual products and in the aggregate, appeals to the anticipatory aspirations of the group.[11] It offers goals of attainment that would not otherwise be thought of. It sets up ideals to be sought after. Its appeals are designed to stimulate action which will result in a more comfortable, congenial, and satisfying life.

Thus, in the aggregate it creates an ever-expanding series of aspirations for the future. In doing this, it shapes the standards of living for the future; and, since man lives largely in a world of anticipation, it lays the basis for much of his enjoyment.

In American business, commercial propaganda is part and parcel of the mass-production process. Our present American business could no more operate without advertising than it could without the automatic machine or the assembly line. By means of this propaganda, the millions of people coming from many nations and races and diverse backgrounds are conditioned to want sufficient amounts of a given standardized product to make it possible to produce that product at a fraction of the cost which would otherwise be necessary.

If left without such propaganda as is found in advertising, people would not choose the same products they do choose. Whether they would choose the same product at a later date is purely a matter of conjecture, but it seems unlikely. If it is assumed that without advertising they would choose something different, then no producer would be able to secure sufficient production to provide these diverse things at prices people could afford to pay. This is another way of saying that standardization of wants through advertising is in part the basis for the economies which come through mass production.

In spite of the necessity that people's wants be so standardized as to secure mass production, the enormous market and the high-level purchasing power available in America have enabled firms to proliferate these standards and to offer a wider variety of goods for sale than would be possible even under a handicraft system where goods are presumably made to fit the consumer's specifications.

Incidentally, the assumption sometimes made, that people would make wiser choices if there were no advertising, ignores the fact that preconceived notions of what they want have themselves been formed by other types of propaganda and other influences no less biased and no more rational than the propaganda used by sellers.

As people get more income, and as competition becomes stronger among sellers for a share of this income, adjustment of goods to the consumer

---

[11] See Wroe Alderson, *Marketing Behavior and Executive Action* (Homewood, Ill.: Richard D. Irwin, 1957), p. 276ff.

becomes finer. More attention is given to the marginal aspects of goods. New quality standards are developed in terms of their psychological rather than their utilitarian values. For instance, people in buying shoes are often more interested in style and how they look to others than in comfort and durability, which are likely to be taken for granted.

These types of desires are often hidden and so subtle that sellers are faced with a continuously changing market, difficult to interpret and almost impossible to predict. They are thus forced to offer their products with infinite variations in characteristics and appeals. To the consumer, the opportunity to choose from this vast variety of products is itself a major element in his standard of living.

CHAPTER XIII

Polling:
The Measurement of Public Opinion

The pollers (or "pollsters," if you prefer a term of derogation) have had their ups and downs: 1936, for example, was a good year. In this, the second year of its operation, Dr. George Gallup's American Institute of Public Opinion capitalized on a golden opportunity to demonstrate the superiority of its polling techniques. Not only did *The Literary Digest* predict a comfortable margin for Alfred M. Landon over FDR, but Gallup, in forecasting a Roosevelt victory, warned of impending fiasco for that magazine because of its reliance on postcard ballots and on samples drawn from lists of automobile owners and telephone subscribers. This, coupled with correct predictions by Roper and Crossley, gave a tremendous boost to the stock of the pollers who were using representative sampling procedures. And 1948 was, of course, a disastrous year for the profession. Success in predicting the outcome of the 1940 and 1944 presidential elections led to overconfidence and carelessness on the part of the commercial pollers. They closed up shop well in advance of the election and spoke of an easy victory for Dewey. Several days before the election, Dr. Gallup announced smugly: "We have never claimed infallibility, but next Tuesday the whole world will be able to see down to the last percentage point how good we are." Pollers have been contrite and considerably more cautious ever since that fateful Tuesday!

Then, early in 1949—to add insult to injury, Lindsay Rogers published his witty, caustic, and devastating attack on "the pollsters." (Examples of tone and style: "If the pollsters sold their product in bottles instead of as news, the Federal Trade Commission would long since have been after them.[1] . . . Instead of feeling the pulse of democracy, Dr. Gallup listens to its baby talk.[2] . . . In politics it is not the accumulation of facts but insight that will find the highroad if and when it is found."[3]) An interesting potpourri of valid and invalid criticism, this book, prepared in large part prior to the 1948 election, did little to advance the cause of polling.

But by 1960 the affairs of pollers were once again at flood tide. After a rather shaky start in which Gallup found only 6 per cent of the voters undecided on August 17, he and his fellow pollers moved on to remarkably accurate final predictions. On Monday, November 7, and on the basis of about 8,000 interviews, Gallup predicted that Kennedy would receive 51 per cent of the two-party vote, which was only 8/10 of 1 per cent above his

---

[1] Lindsay Rogers, *The Pollsters*, Alfred A. Knopf, Inc., New York, 1949, p. 11.
[2] *Ibid.*, p. 17.
[3] *Ibid.*, pp. 238-239.

actual vote. There must have been joy in Princeton as well as Hyannis Port in the wee hours of the morning of November 9—at least over the crucial matter of having picked another winner!

In this chapter we shall examine the techniques of polling and provide a forum for the defenders and detractors of this American institution. We shall attempt, among other things, to dispel some common misconceptions— misconceptions such as (1) polling began with George Gallup, (2) George Gallup is the only poller, and (3) polling consists solely of efforts to predict the outcome of elections by interviewing prospective voters. As noted in one of the selections in this chapter, polling goes back at least as far as the presidential election of 1824, when the *Harrisburg Pennsylvanian* sought to determine how the citizens of Wilmington, Delaware, were going to vote. These so-called "straw polls" were conducted by many newspapers in connection with many elections throughout the nineteenth and early twentieth centuries. And the efforts of the ill-fated *Literary Digest,* which was the best known conductor of polls from 1916 to 1936, were previously mentioned. Thus, Gallup was not even the first person to resort to sampling techniques in polling, but his was the first large-scale organization to utilize systematic sampling procedures with some concern for probability theory. And, as we have also observed in passing, he has had competition from other organizations engaged in public opinion measurement, the measurement not only of voter intentions at election time but also of the sentiment of various publics at different times on myriad issues.

In fact, Dr. Gallup has repeatedly stated that he regards the prediction of elections as the least important of his activities; much more important, he believes, is ascertaining the popular will on significant political, social, and economic issues. Election forecasting is, however, the most dramatic, the most widely publicized, and certainly the most hazardous undertaking of the polling fraternity. The professional poller must surely be ambivalent about making election predictions: On the one hand, there is the undeniable fascination of trying to divine the future (akin, no doubt, to the exhilaration of picking the "daily double"), there is all that wonderful publicity and attention, and there are manifold benefits *if* successful; on the other hand, there is the knowledge that this is one of the few efforts subject to external validation (i.e., the election results), there are the necessary but risky and unscientific adjustments which must be made for voter indecision and for expected voter turnout, and, finally of course, there is the temporary or permanent damage to one's reputation *if* unsuccessful. And all this for an activity really extraneous to the main business of polling!

We begin with a selection from the foreword of *A Guide to Public Opinion Polls* in which Dr. Gallup sets forth briefly ten of the major contributions made by polls to the democratic process. He offers here such incontestable observations as that polls constitute an important check on the power of pressure groups. He makes several statements with which some might argue; for example, in referring to election prediction, "the poll results might be even more accurate as a measure of public sentiment than the official returns." And he affirms his abiding faith in both public opinion and public opinion measurement when he asserts that "public opinion polls have shown that the common people do make good decisions."

In an exceptionally lucid discussion of a difficult subject Maccoby and Holt tell how surveys of public opinion are made. This article was published shortly after the end of World War II. As a result, the examples used refer to that period of our history and sound rather dated.[4] There is, however, no better nontechnical presentation of polling procedures in print. The entire process from defining the objectives of a survey through analyzing the results is described in language the layman can understand.

Dr. Gallup then returns to answer a number of questions the interested layman is likely to ask: "Won't the country suffer when its leaders begin to pay a lot of attention to public opinion polls?" "Just how small can samples be and still be accurate?" "Why haven't I been interviewed?" "What is meant by random sampling?" "What is quota sampling?" "Don't the polls start 'band wagon' movements?" These and other selected queries are handled in straightforward fashion by "Mr. Polling" himself.

The next four articles represent generally critical evaluations of polling. Two free-lance writers on political and social issues, a United States Senator, and a political scientist scrutinize the polls, do not like much of what they see, and tell us why. The least unkind of these appraisals is by Robert Bendiner. He begins by observing that Americans really know very little about themselves despite the endless probing of the pollers and that much of what we appear to know is frequently contradicted by our actions. "What is wrong?" he asks. And he concludes that the trouble with polls is people. Public opinion is basically unmeasurable because each person is infinitely variable. The answers one gets from a respondent depends upon which of his many roles he is playing and which of his many moods he is indulging at the precise moment the questions are asked. But in providing a counterweight to pressure groups, in revealing the willingness of people to discuss presumably hush-hush issues, and in disclosing areas of public ignorance and inconsistency, the polls serve a useful purpose.

Writing in the period of political maneuvering preceding the 1960 national nominating conventions, Samuel Grafton expresses some serious misgivings about the effects of polls on American politics. He views with alarm the increasing use by politicians of private (i.e., confidential and unpublished) polls to discover public sentiment. "Are we heading," he asks, "toward Trendex politics in America"—toward, in short, a political system based like television programming on the lowest common denominator? He also insists that polls tend to influence the very thing which they are designed only to measure, viz., political opinion.

Legislators are understandably hostile toward the polls. They view themselves as the legitimate experts in assessing public opinion, and they are inclined to regard the Gallups as would-be usurpers of their historic pre-

[4] Several of the selections in this chapter (Gallup, Maccoby and Holt, Ranney) are drawn from the immediate postwar period. This in no way detracts from their usefulness. Polling had become big business at this time. Its practitioners were busily lauding their profession, and the growing list of critics was beginning to express reservations.

rogative. This is not to say that legislators make no use of polls both in campaigning and in policy making. In fact, there is evidence of increasing reliance upon polls (both polls that are self-conducted and polls that are administered on contract by commercial pollers) by members of the United States House of Representatives.[5] Senators are notably more skeptical of the value of polls. Typical of senatorial reaction are the remarks of Albert Gore made upon the floor of the Senate immediately after Gallup published his August estimate of the people's choice in the 1960 presidential election. Senator Gore, who is assisted in his scathing indictment of political polls by Senator Russell Long of Louisiana, speaks of them as "almost meaningless" and "in many instances misleading." He has obviously read the Grafton article, since he also speaks of polls becoming a political event, and similarly he refers to election prediction as the "Rose Bowl game" for pollsters, but his homework extended well beyond this single article. He provides a bit of the history of polls, divides their recent history into three distinct periods, details seven problem areas of polling, expresses the typical lay misconception that a major shortcoming of polls is too small samples, legitimately flays the pollers for their tendency to equivocate and straddle in their final election predictions, and offers some perceptive observations about the controversial "bandwagon" effect of polls.

The final critical evaluation of polls is provided in a distinguished and closely reasoned discussion by the late John C. Ranney of the important question: "Do the Polls Serve Democracy?" Professor Ranney does not concern himself primarily, as many do, with the technical competence of the pollers or with the accuracy of poll results. Nor is he interested in the record of Gallup et al. in predicting the outcome of elections. Rather he concentrates on whether the efforts of the polling profession to designate political and socioeconomic issues and to discover the will of the people thereon are in the best interests of a free society. He considers and rejects the frequent objection that the polls are destructive of political leadership. He likewise disposes of the argument that polls publicize the essentially conservative, conventional, and unimaginative views of the mass of the people and thereby impede the forces of progress. He does, however, contend that, although the polls provide a means of testing the claims of potency of special interests and of interpreting public sentiments to political leaders, they misconceive the fundamental nature of democracy. Specifically, they emphasize the *content* and *divergency* of opinion rather than the *process* of opinion formation and adjustment. In short, according to Ranney, the polls have contributed little to the deliberative process which, he asserts, is "the real heart of democracy."

Finally, Dr. Gallup is given an opportunity for rebuttal. He notes that, whereas the editor, the politician, and the academician (as we have just seen) have remained distressingly hostile, the public at large has consistently supported the polls—even after the debacle of 1948. And Gallup appears to regard the 1948 misadventure as something of a blessing in disguise: it provided dramatic proof of the need for improvements, which

[5] See Carl Hawver, "The Congressman and His Public Opinion Poll," *Public Opinion Quarterly*, vol. 18, no. 2, Summer, 1954, pp. 123-129.

were subsequently made. "Some deprecatory voices continue," he laments, and he discusses some of the insinuations of the critics which are particularly galling to him. He concludes, as is his wont, by attesting to his belief in the good sense and wisdom of the common people: "The public," he tells us, "is almost always ahead of its governmental leaders."

90. POLLING'S CONTRIBUTIONS TO THE DEMOCRATIC PROCESS
by George Gallup*

Students of government have noted many contributions to our democratic process made by polls. . . . Suffice it here to review the ten which seem most important:

1. Public opinion polls have provided political leaders with a more accurate gauge of public opinion than they had prior to 1935.

No responsible person in the field of public opinion research would assert that polling methods are perfect. On the other hand, no one who has studied all the methods of gauging public opinion would maintain that other methods are superior to polling methods. Certainly the indices which were relied upon most in the past—letters, newspaper editorials, self-appointed experts, and the like—have been found to be highly inaccurate as guides to public opinion.

2. Public opinion polls have speeded up the processes of democracy by providing not only accurate, but swift, reports of public opinion.

Modern poll procedures make it possible to conduct a nation-wide referendum or plebiscite in a matter of hours, and to report results that would differ by only a few percentage points from the results which would be obtained if the entire voting population of a nation went to the polls. In fact in many situations—particularly those in which a substantial portion of the population fails to take the trouble to vote—the poll results might be even more accurate as a measure of public sentiment than the official returns.

3. Public opinion polls have shown that the common people do make good decisions.

The arguments which have continued from the early days of the country regarding the political wisdom of the common people can now be settled on the basis of a mountain of factual data. The views of the people have been recorded on hundreds of issues and enough time has elapsed to judge the soundness of majority opinion on scores of these problems.

The people have displayed such good sense, and have made such a good record, that the faith of many persons in the basic premises of democracy

* Public opinion analyst and founder of the American Institute of Public Opinion and of other specialized polling organizations. Author of *The Pulse of Democracy, A Guide to Public Opinion Polls,* and other books and articles on public opinion. This selection is from George Gallup, *A Guide to Public Opinion Polls,* 2d ed., Princeton University Press, Princeton, N.J., 1948, pp. ix-xii. Copyright, 1944, 1948, by Princeton University Press. Reprinted by permission of the author and publisher.

has been rekindled. There is little disposition today to refer to the people in slighting terms, as was the case after the first World War, when it was common to think of the people as comprising a "boobocracy."

4. Public opinion polls have helped to focus attention on major issues of the day.

They have provided what Walter Lippmann, in his book *Public Opinion*, asserted was greatly needed by this democracy—a machinery for scoring. By injecting the element of controversy, by showing the division of opinion, in fact by helping to simplify major issues by expressing them in language understandable to the great mass of people, polls have helped to increase public interest in many national issues.

5. Public opinion polls have uncovered many "areas of ignorance."

In performing this service they have brought out certain fundamental weaknesses of our educational system and have pointed to the shortcomings of the whole process of keeping the public well-informed on vital issues of the day.

6. Public opinion polls have helped administrators of government departments make wiser decisions.

The problem of dealing intelligently with the public is one that confronts not only the heads of many government departments, but state and local officials everywhere. Government is learning what business learned years ago—that any program designed to influence the public must be based upon accurate knowledge of public attitudes. Millions of dollars can be wasted by following wrong hunches about the public's information and thinking on important policies.

7. Public opinion polls have made it more difficult for political bosses to pick presidential candidates "in smoke-filled rooms."

The "open" primary was originally intended to give voters a chance to help guide the parties in choosing presidential nominees and candidates for other political office. It was designed to strip political machines of their power to select candidates without respect to the wishes of the people.

Polls can perform this service which the open primary was intended to provide. They can report the popularity of various candidates with the voters. And in doing so they can make it that much more difficult for professional politicians to hand-pick candidates.

8. Public opinion polls have shown that the people are not motivated, in their voting, solely by the factor of self-interest, as many politicians have presumed.

Time after time, poll results reveal the fairness of the people in spreading the tax load to all segments of the population, their resentment at "log rolling" methods, and their concern about the national good, as contrasted with the selfish interests of their own community or state. Too often, officeholders assume that the only road to popularity and to re-election is to grab as much political booty as possible for their own electorate—a fact disproved by poll results.

9. Public opinion polls constitute almost the only present check on the growing power of pressure groups.

Many students of government have been concerned with the great influence exerted upon legislation by lobbyists for the various pressure groups in the country. By exploding the claims of these lobbyists to represent the "unanimous" or "overwhelming" sentiment of the pressure group which employs them, public opinion polls have revealed their real status.

Poll results show that pressure-group spokesmen often represent only a minority of those within their own groups, and prove baseless their threats of political reprisal if legislators do not bow to their wishes.

10. Public opinion polls help define the "mandate" of the people in national elections.

Inevitably many wrong conclusions are drawn from the attempt to read the will of the people on national issues, by examining election returns on individuals. Some of the greatest mistakes of the last thirty years have come about by trying to decide what the public really thought on issues, when it cast its vote for candidates.

Not until elections are changed to permit the public to vote on all the issues which come up in a campaign will it be possible to draw accurate conclusions about the opinion of the majority on specific problems. Meanwhile public opinion polls can perform this service. At the same time that the views of voters are obtained on candidates, the views of these same voters can be recorded on issues. In this way, election results can be interpreted much more accurately than in the past.

91. HOW SURVEYS ARE MADE
by Eleanor E. Maccoby and Robert R. Holt*

The surveying of public attitudes and opinions during recent years has attracted an increasingly large audience. The "public opinion polls" now share newspaper space with the most omniscient columnists and during pre-election weeks they become front-page news.

To most people, who know about polls only what they read in the newspapers, surveying must appear to be a transparently simple procedure. The questions asked seem obvious enough and the percentages always add to a hundred. They seldom suspect the tortuous and detailed labors which lie behind the neat columns of figures. For many such followers of public opinion the final results are doubtless the only part of the process of surveying that has any interest, but there are others who are not so easily satisfied.

This article is meant for those people, not themselves expert in surveying, whose interest in public opinion includes a curiosity as to how the surveys are made, and perhaps an interest in the possibilities of using the polling

* Eleanor E. Maccoby, research associate of the Laboratory of Human Development and lecturer in social psychology at Harvard University, coauthor of *Patterns in Child Rearing* and *Family Savings in Puerto Rico* and author of articles on public opinion, mass media, and child development. Robert R. Holt, professor of psychology and director of Research Center for Mental Health at New York University and author of articles in clinical and social psychology. This selection is from Eleanor E. Maccoby and Robert R. Holt, "How Surveys Are Made," *Journal of Social Issues*, vol. 2, issue no. 2, May, 1946, pp. 45-57. Reprinted by permission.

procedure in their own organizations or communities. It is not intended as a manual of instructions for beginning pollers; no short article could serve such a purpose adequately. It proposes to describe briefly the major steps that are followed in surveying and to answer thereby some of the common questions as to the techniques which lie behind survey findings.

DEFINING THE OBJECTIVES OF THE SURVEY

The first step in any survey, as in any other planned observation, is to define the question which the survey is to answer. The more clearly the objectives of the study are specified, the more likely it is to yield clear-cut results.

Usually the definition of objectives begins with a broad, general statement of the problem and then turns to a listing of all the items of information the survey will gather. The survey director must analyze his problem carefully to make sure that he includes in his study as many of the pertinent aspects of his problem as he can. It is his responsibility to find out as much as he can in this planning stage about the important factors bearing on the subject of the study.

Suppose we consider as an example the problem of conducting a survey on public attitudes toward taxes. It is necessary to define the problem by specifying what varieties of taxes the survey will cover. Attitudes toward federal taxes may be different from attitudes toward state and local taxes, and the survey may deal with all or only some of these. If the survey is to deal with both income taxes and sales taxes, a distinction must be made between them in the detailed plans for the survey. The administration of tax policy would be an important consideration; public reactions to the tax forms, dates and methods of payment should be studied. An effort might be made to find out the extent to which people would be willing to see public services curtailed for the sake of reducing taxes. Full understanding of the attitudes in this area would require data on the level of public information about taxes. Do people know what the tax rates are? Do they know what the money is used for? The survey should also cover the relation, if any, between attitudes toward taxes and other attitudes and personal attributes of the people interviewed. Do attitudes toward taxes differ in different income and education groups? How are they correlated with attitudes toward other governmental activities?

The survey director must consider all these aspects of his problem. It may be that he will not be able to deal with them all, because of limitations of time or money and he will therefore have to limit the scope of the survey. His goal is to specify what aspects of the subject he will cover, and to anticipate exactly what tables he will want in his final report.

CHOOSING THE STUDY DESIGN

While most studies require a single survey of one particular group, this is not always the case. Surveys may be designed in a variety of ways, depending on the objectives of the study. It may be desirable for some purposes to survey two contrasting communities or industrial plants and to compare the two sets of results. In studies where it is important to measure changes or trends in opinions or behavior, a group of people may be selected as respondents and this group may be interviewed several times at specified intervals. When studying cause-and-effect relationships it is sometimes possible to use experimental techniques. To study the effects of a certain motion picture on attitudes, for example, two similar groups might be selected, an "experimental" group who would be shown the film and a "control" group who would not. The influence of the picture on the attitudes of the experimental group could then be studied.

SELECTING THE SAMPLE

As part of the basic planning of the survey, the survey director must define exactly the group to be covered by the survey. If he is studying the opinions of the American people on a certain issue, the group to be studied (the "universe") will probably be the entire adult population. If he is making a morale survey within a certain factory, the universe might be all the employees in the factory. Or perhaps the survey is to cover only the skilled, semi-skilled and unskilled workers, not the clerical and managerial staff.

When the group to be studied has been decided upon, the next question to be answered is: Can the survey include a contact with each member of the group? In a study of employees' morale, it may be possible to interview every employee. In a nation-wide public opinion survey, however, it is obviously impossible to poll each adult person in the country. More often than not, a survey must be based upon a *sample* of the universe. Some individuals must be selected from the universe in such a way that they will represent all the people in the universe.

The most reliable way to choose the individuals to be included in a sample survey is to use some random method of selection. Selecting at random means using some automatic method of choosing which gives each individual in the group to be studied an equal chance (or at least a *known* chance) of being in the sample. To take a random sample of the members of an organization, for example, one might take every tenth card in the membership file. To decide which card to take as the first case, one might open a book at random and take the last digit of the page number. Experience in survey work has demonstrated that if, instead of selecting at random, a surveyer tries to pick a representative sample by choosing certain people or places that he believes are representative, a biased sample will probably result. When surveys are based on random sampling, the probable size of the sampling error can be computed mathematically. The errors in a sample which has not been selected by random methods cannot be estimated in any precise way.

There are many pitfalls in choosing a random sample, many ways in which bias may creep in and prevent the selection from being truly random. Suppose interviewers have been sent to certain blocks in a city and told to visit every fifth dwelling on each block. In counting dwellings, there is danger that the interviewers will miss alley dwellings, basement apartments, servants' quarters over garages, and other inconspicuous households. It is evident that if this happened the sample would be biased in the direction of having too few people in the lower income groups.

Bias may be created when no attempt is made to include in the sample those people who are hard to find at home. If the interviewers take all their interviews in households where they find someone home the first time they call, it is clear that people who are not home much do not have an equal chance of coming into the sample. It is well known to surveyers that people who stay home a good deal differ as a group from people who do not.

When samples are taken from lists of names there is danger that the list will be incomplete. This was apparently partly responsible for the miscarriage of the *Literary Digest* poll of the 1936 presidential election. The sample used by the *Digest*, purporting to represent all voters, was taken from such sources as lists of telephone subscribers. This meant that people without telephones (on the average from a lower socio-economic level than people with telephones) were not represented adequately. An additional bias was probably introduced by the fact that the poll depended on people mailing in the post-cards which they received. The people who mailed in their cards were probably not comparable to the people who did not.

Bias may also be introduced into a sample by allowing the interviewers freedom in the choice of the people to be interviewed. In some polling operations, interviewers are told the number of interviews to take, and they are told that these interviews must be distributed in certain ways. For example, an interviewer might be instructed to take one-half of his interviews with men, the other half with women; one-tenth with Negroes, nine-tenths with whites; and one-fourth of the interviews from each of four income groups. Aside from these restrictions, the interviewer has freedom of choice, and it is evident that he could follow instructions and still interview only "available" people—waitresses, barbers, policemen, people at railway stations, people who sit on their front porches or stroll in the park, and so on. It is clear that with this procedure, certain groups in the population may be under-represented.

Whenever sampling is done by a system of random selection, the more cases the sample has, the more likely it is to represent the universe well. The reasoning behind this is as follows: Suppose a survey is being done of opinions about foreign affairs. This is a subject on which people with different amounts of education differ markedly, so it is important to have college graduates, high school graduates, grade school graduates, people with some grade school, and people with no formal education at all. If only three cases were chosen, they obviously could not adequately represent these five educational groups. A sample of forty cases might easily, by chance, contain four college graduates, or it might contain none—there is not a very good chance that the true proportion of college graduates (perhaps five percent) would be obtained. The larger the number of cases, however, the better the chances that all the levels of education will be represented in their proper proportions. It might be argued that one should deliberately select the right number of people from each educational level and consider this as a representative group. But it would be representative only with respect to education, and there are many other characteristics which are related to opinions on foreign affairs, some of which would not be known in advance. A large sample randomly selected assures a sample which will be reasonably representative of *all* characteristics of the people in the universe.

When random methods of selection are followed, increasing the number of cases will improve the sample by reducing the sampling error, but mere increase in the number of cases will not correct for a bias in the sample. When a sample is "biased" its errors are not chance errors which tend to cancel each other out but are systematic and create deviations in the same direction. For example, in a survey of income and savings the results would be greatly affected by the inclusion or exclusion of a few millionaires. By chance a sample might contain too many millionaires or too few. If this error were purely a matter of random sampling error, an increase in the number of cases would provide a better chance of getting just the right proportion of millionaires. But suppose millionaires could not be interviewed because the interviewers could not get past the butlers and secretaries, or because the millionaires were out hunting in the Maine woods or tarpon fishing off Florida; then all the errors would operate in the direction of including too few millionaires rather than too many and the sample would be biased. Increasing the number of cases in the sample would not reduce the error, since the same cause of error would affect the new cases and in the same direction.

In deciding how many people will be included in his sample, the survey director is usually influenced by considerations of economy. His purpose is not to use the largest possible sample but rather to use the smallest sample which will give results of acceptable accuracy. Sampling experts have worked out formulae for estimating the sampling error which is involved in samples of different sizes. The survey director chooses, then, a sample size which will have a sampling error small enough for his purposes.

Among the factors which determine the number of cases needed for a sample survey, the following are perhaps the most important:

1. The desired accuracy of the survey results. If the survey director wishes to be reasonably sure that his final figures are accurate within one percent, he must have a larger sample than if he is willing to accept a margin of error of five percent.

2. The variability of the characteristic to be measured. It would take more cases to sample for a variable like income, which has a wide range and many different values, than to sample for variables like age or sex.

3. The desired breakdowns of the findings. Fewer cases are needed in a national survey, for example, if the findings are to be used only as national estimates than if they are to be broken down by state or region. In the latter case, it would be necessary to have enough cases in each state or region to represent it separately, while for national figures alone this would not be necessary.

When the objectives of a survey call for a national sample, it is seldom possible to select respondents by taking, say, every ten thousandth person in the country. Travel expenses for the interviewers would be too great; some method must be adopted to reduce the number of communities in which interviews are taken. Usually this is done by first choosing a sample of counties and then selecting a sample of people to be interviewed within these counties. In selecting the counties where interviews will be taken, the survey director can cut down the sampling error by "stratifying" the sample. This means simply that he will arrange all the counties of the country in order according to some characteristic (such as percent of Negro population), divide these ordered counties into strata (high, medium and low), and select sample counties at random within each stratum, thus making sure that a proper proportion of counties with high, medium and low Negro populations will come into the sample.

The "modes of stratification" which are used are always characteristics which are thought to be related to the subject matter of the survey. It would be possible, for example, to stratify counties according to their average annual rainfall, so that a proper proportion of wet and dry counties would be included in the sample. But, to continue a previous example, if the survey were measuring attitudes toward our foreign policy, the sample would not be improved by this stratification since such attitudes are presumably not related to rainfall. A stratification of the counties according to the average educational level might, however, improve the sample, for if education tends to be related to attitudes toward world affairs then by making sure that the sample contains a proper proportion of counties that are high, medium and low in educational status the chances are increased of obtaining a proper representation of people of different points of view toward foreign affairs.

WRITING THE QUESTIONNAIRE

With these phases of study planning completed, the survey director proceeds to write the questionnaire itself. First he must decide whether he will use any "open" questions, or whether they will all be of the "closed" or "polling" variety. Polling questions, the kind most frequently used in the ordinary Gallup and Fortune polls, are questions such as the following:

If the election were held today, who would you vote for—Roosevelt or Dewey?
Roosevelt ....   Dewey ....   Don't know ....

In questions of this sort, the interviewer simply checks the choice which his respondent makes. Polling questions can be more complex than this, of course:

"Which of these comes closest to expressing what you would like to have the U.S. do after the war?" (July, 1945, *Fortune*)
1. Enter into no alliances, and have as little as possible to do with other countries.
2. Depend only on separate alliances with certain countries.
3. Take an active part in an international organization.
4. Don't know.

In using questions like the one above, the interviewer may either read off the alternatives, or he may hand the respondent the list of possible answers and ask him to choose one.

In contrast to these kinds of questions, "open" questions do not present the respondent with fixed alternatives from which he must choose, but ask a general question which the respondent may answer in his own words. The following are examples of open questions: "What do you think will happen to prices of the things you buy in the next year or so?" "Why do you think so?" "As you see it, what is the main thing the U.N. is set up to do?" When questions of this sort are asked, the interviewer must write down each respondent's answer as nearly verbatim as possible, and these answers must be grouped into categories later. When polling questions are used, the interviewer's job is much easier, and the answers are easier to handle in analysis later on.

Polling questions are usually used in surveys to obtain enumerative material, such as age, education, nationality, and the like, or simple statements of fact (Do you own a radio? Are you a registered voter?). They are also frequently used for surveying attitudes if the survey deals with well-understood issues on which people have clear-cut opinions. But in an area where attitudes are complex and confused, there is danger that polling questions will yield misleading results. When open questions are used, people express their views together with any reservations or contingencies which are present in their minds; when they are presented with a polling question and asked to choose one of the alternatives, they may not have an opportunity to express their reservations, unless specific additional questions are asked to bring them out. Polling questions have certain disadvantages, too, when it comes to asking people to make suggestions for improving a situation which they dislike, or to give reasons for their beliefs. If check-lists of alternatives are presented to them, there is the danger of suggesting ideas which were not actually present in their minds. There is also the danger that not all the great variety of possible reasons and suggestions will be included among the poll's alternatives. A common practice in questionnaire construction is to combine polling and open questions. For example, polling questions to which the respondent must answer "Yes" or "No" are often followed by the question "Why do you think so?" and the interviewer then writes down the respondent's reason in the blank provided.

In writing his questionnaire, the survey director must give careful attention to the order in which different topics and particular questions are taken up. The opening questions must be such as to interest the respondent and stimulate his cooperation. The sequence of questions must be orderly, and logical transitions must be made from one topic to another. The context in which a question is asked can have the greatest influence on the answers to it. Likewise the order and number of alternatives can affect the results greatly in a question where the respondent chooses one of a set of alternatives as his answer. To take care of this difficulty, interviewers are sometimes instructed to vary the order in which they present alternatives, or sometimes different forms of the questionnaire are prepared, giving the questions in a different order.

The so-called "funnel" arrangement of questions is often useful. In this procedure, a very general question is followed by one in the same area which is somewhat narrower, and this in turn is followed by a more specific question. This technique permits the respondent to answer the general question spontaneously before any specific aspects of the problem have been suggested to him, but nevertheless pins him down later on specific points. Suppose, for example, that a study is being done on consumers' cooperation with the Government's food conservation program, and the study calls for a table showing how many people are using less bread than they normally would. People may be asked first: "Are you personally doing anything to conserve food?" and if they say they are doing something, they may then be asked "What are you doing?" The answers to these questions will give evidence on what aspects of the food conservation program are upper-most in people's minds, but some people may fail to mention conservation of bread even though they are actually eating less of it. To get specific information, the survey could proceed to a direct question on whether the respondent was conserving bread, and if necessary, could then include questions on the different ways of saving bread.

The task of writing the questions themselves is a difficult one. The writer's first objective must be to make sure that his question is understood. Its wording must be clear and unambiguous, and the words used must be simple enough so that they will be understood by the least educated of the respondents. There are certain regional variations in the use of words which the writer must keep in mind if his question is not to mean different things in different parts of the country. In addition the writer must avoid referring to particular ideas, policies, recent events, or personalities, unless he has some assurance that the respondents will be familiar with them. It is hardly necessary to point out that, in order to be understood, a question must be reasonably brief. If a question contains two or three long sentences, the respondent will often forget what the first part of the question was before he gives his answer, so that he actually responds only to the last few words of the question.

Each question should have a single focus. If it contains several ideas, it is impossible to tell what part of the question the respondent's answer refers to. For example, the question "Do you think a man would be wise to put his money into real estate and securities these days?" is poorly worded, for one man might answer "Yes" when he believes that real estate is a good investment and securities a poor investment, while another man's "Yes" might signify approval of securities but not of real estate.

The writer of questions must keep in mind the fact that the use of prestige words or other emotionally-toned words may materially affect the responses to a question.[1] It is well known, for example, that attaching a prestige name such as Roosevelt's to a policy proposed in a question will increase the proportion of respondents who express approval of the policy. Similarly, it is almost certain that more people would say "Yes" to: "Do you think the United States should send food to the starving people in Europe?" than would agree if the word "starving" were omitted.

[1] Cantril, H., *Gauging Public Opinion*, Princeton, Princeton Univ. Press, 1944, Chapter II.

The survey director must be careful in the use of emotionally-toned words, but there are occasions in which he may find it desirable to employ them. If he is studying opinions about sending food to Europe, he may deliberately use the word "starving" because many people in Europe are, in fact, starving, and because the publicity on the food crisis appeals to people on the grounds that they must help starving people. To omit the word, then, might be to underestimate the number who would be willing to share American food under the conditions actually prevailing. Furthermore, the survey director sometimes finds it desirable to include an emotionally-toned question with the specific purpose of finding out how many people hold their opinions so firmly that they cannot be swayed by devices of this kind.

The question of the effect of emotional "loading" on the answers to a question leads to the more general problem of bias in questions. The point is often raised: Do the answers obtained in a survey represent the "true" attitudes which people have, or have the attitudes been distorted by a "leading" question? In survey research, every attitude must be studied through the answers to questions, and no answer is free from the influence carried by the wording of the question which was used. Every question is "leading," in the sense that it at least specifies the subject-matter about which the respondent is being asked to talk.

For these reasons it is important that each survey finding be interpreted in the light of the particular question which was used. Findings must not be loosely generalized to cover whole areas of opinion. Particularly when a study deals with attitudes which are complex, it is important to ask a battery of questions bearing upon different aspects of the problem, so as to achieve . . . a "well defined context for interpretation."

Although the problems of question-wording need to be emphasized, the survey director in writing his questionnaire can take comfort from the fact that in many cases small differences in question-wording produce relatively little change in public response. Especially when the questions are about facts which are well known to the respondents, it is surprisingly difficult to affect the answers much by context, question order, or the wording of the questions.

PRETESTING THE QUESTIONNAIRE

It is important to give every question a test run before using it. Often questions which appear satisfactory when they are written turn out to be too difficult or ambiguous, or they unexpectedly set off irrelevant trains of thought on the part of the respondents. Questions can be tested for defects of this sort by trying them out on a representative group of people. The answers given on the pretest are taken down in full, and the respondents are asked to explain what they mean by their answers. This procedure enables the survey director to detect questions which are being misunderstood. Often several forms of a question must be tried out before the best wording is found. In the pretest, variations in question order may also be tried out, until a smooth sequence is achieved.

The pretest permits the survey director to check the answers he is getting against the objectives of the survey, to see whether the kind of information being assembled will solve the problems that underlie the survey. Questions must be discarded if it is found that they merely sound interesting but do not contribute anything to the objectives.

ADMINISTERING THE SURVEY

The survey director must make sure that his interviewers are well trained before they begin to work, and arrange for their supervision throughout the interviewing process. Poor interviewing can ruin a survey even though the planning and questionnaire construction have been well done.

The calibre of interviewers needed to do the job depends, of course, on the complexity of the subject, whether polling or open questions are used, and on the amount of freedom which the interviewers will be allowed in the interviewing situation. A certain amount of judgment on the part of the interviewer is *always* required. Respondents frequently make replies which are not answers to the questions at all. In these cases the interviewer must recognize this and repeat the question. Interviewing can never be completely mechanical, if for no other reason than that the interviewer must learn ways to gain the cooperation of the respondent before he can begin the formal interview. For intensive interviewing, in which the interviewer is allowed to adapt his questions to the individual case to some extent, a high degree of skill and training is required. For most surveys interviewers must be personable, intelligent, and tactful.

Perhaps the most important basic principle an interviewing staff must be taught is not to influence the answers of the people being interviewed. This means that they must learn to avoid expressing disapproval or approval of anything the respondent says. When they have some latitude in the rewording of questions they must ask them in a non-directive way. For example, it should become habitual to ask "Are you working now?" instead of "You're not working now, are you?" Similarly, in using open questions in which a respondent gives reasons for his opinion, the interviewer must learn how to stimulate discussion without slanting it. He may try to get the person to express himself more fully by the use of such questions as "Why do you think so?" and "Just how do you mean that?" but must avoid suggestive questions such as: "Is that because of the high cost of living?"

The quality of a survey can always be improved by devoting a good deal of attention to training the interviewers on the specific subject-matter of the survey. There are almost always certain terms which need to be very clearly defined in the interviewers' minds. For example, if an interviewer must check whether or not the respondent is employed, he must learn to know how to classify people who are employed part-time. If he is to include only farmers in the survey, he must have the term "farmer" defined so that he will know whether or not to talk to nurserymen, seasonal farm laborers, small farmers who work part time in the city, and so on.

ANALYZING THE RESULTS

When the interview schedules have been filled out and sent in to a central office, the survey director must tabulate the answers in some way so that the survey results will be summarized and easily understood. The simplest way would be to go through the schedules and tally the answers to each question, so that a count would be obtained. This system is not very convenient for comparisons of groups within the sample, however. To find out how men compare with women on a certain question, it would be necessary to divide the schedules into two groups for men and women, and tally separately. If a count by income groups were desired, a new grouping of the schedules and a new tally would be required.

For large-scale operations where internal comparisons will be needed, it is usually found to be most convenient in the long run to record the answers on punch-cards. Different answers are numbered (or "coded"); each respondent has a separate card, and on this card are punched the numbers which represent his answers to all the questions. After the punching has been done, the process of counting the different answers is greatly simplified, for the sorting and counting machines will sort the cards into any desired groups and count the answers automatically.

Coding is a fairly simple job when the respondent has been presented with a group of alternatives from which he must choose; each of the alternatives can be given a number, and the cards may be punched immediately from the questionnaires which have been filled out. When full narrative answers are given to open questions, however, coding is more difficult. Suppose, for example, that people have been asked to give their reasons for their opinions on a certain issue. A great variety of reasons will be given, and the reasons will be worded in many different ways. These reasons must be grouped into a limited number of categories, and each category must be numbered for purposes of punching on the cards.

It is the responsibility of the survey director to present his findings in such a way as to prevent unsophisticated readers from coming to unjustified conclusions. The problem of misinterpretation of findings very often arises when two percentages are being compared, as in the table below:[2]

Attitude toward continuation of price ceilings:	MARCH, 1945	MARCH, 1946
Favorable	68%	74%
Unfavorable	25%	23%
Don't know	7%	3%
	100%	100%

The question is, has there been a real change in attitudes toward price ceilings? Assume for the moment that the survey reporting these findings had a small sample with a sampling error of five percentage points. Under

---

[2] This table does not represent actual survey findings, but is simply included here for illustrative purposes.

these circumstances, it is quite possible that the true percentage favoring continuation of price ceilings during the two years is, say, 72 percent, that there has been no change in this percentage, but that the two figures which were obtained differed from 72 percent because of random sampling error. A large increase would be needed before one could feel confident that a real change in sentiment has occurred. On the other hand, if the survey were based on a large number of cases, and had a sampling error of only one percentage point, the difference between the percentages shown above could be relied on as showing a real difference, not just a chance one. There are statistical formulae by which the survey director can compute the probable range of error of his percentages, and he must test his differences for reliability before presenting them in his report.

In presenting his findings, it is also the responsibility of the director to caution his readers against generalizing the findings to a different population from the one measured by the survey. If the survey is based upon a sample of midwestern farmers, this fact should be emphasized, so that the reader will not assume that the results apply to all the farmers of the nation.

As has been pointed out earlier, each answer must be interpreted in the light of the particular question asked. Answers to one question cannot be taken to represent attitudes toward other aspects of a broad field of attitudes. For example, if most people say Britain ought to pay for the food which we send to her, it should not be concluded that the majority would recommend withholding food if Britain cannot pay. The survey director must not only avoid drawing unwarranted conclusions himself, but he must caution his readers against doing so. He cannot, of course, prevent misuse of the findings by unscrupulous readers, but he can minimize their misuse by well-intentioned people who will avoid pitfalls if they are only pointed out.

CONCLUSION

The preceding pages outline the steps which are followed in surveying public opinion. The reader may conclude from this description that making a survey is a very complicated business indeed. So it is, and even more so than indicated if one is dealing with a large-scale study of a complex issue on which opinion is confused and contradictory. However, the many precautions and special techniques derive from very simple principles; they are the rules of scientific method which underlie all careful attempts to gather facts reliably and interpret them validly. In its essence, a sample survey is merely a formalized procedure for making observations. It is a device for recording items of information in a systematic way, while eliminating the most common errors of bias, insufficient evidence, and the disregard of negative cases.

For the non-professional student of public opinion, it is not important to learn the detailed methodology which has developed in the surveying field. It is important, however, for him to understand the basic principles of surveying, so that he may evaluate critically the survey findings which he encounters, and seek sound advice if he should desire to utilize the method.

92. QUESTIONS AND ANSWERS
ON SELECTED ASPECTS OF POLLING
by George Gallup*

1

"How can polls aid the processes of democracy?"

Of all writers who have discussed the role of public opinion in American democracy, none foresaw more clearly than James Bryce the importance of a periodic check on the will of the people. Writing some fifty years ago, Bryce said that the next stage in the development of democratic government would be reached "if the will of the majority of citizens were to become ascertainable at all times."

In two respects Bryce saw the need of better methods of ascertaining public opinion. He noted that "the choice of one man against another is an imperfect way of expressing the mind of a constituency." Recent political history provides ample evidence of the difficulty of analyzing election returns on candidates in a way to reveal the will of the people on specific issues.

Bryce also pointed out that with the quickening pace of events, many problems might come up between elections which could not be submitted to the electorate. He wrote that "the action of opinion is continuous, that of voting occasional, and in the intervals between the elections of legislative bodies, changes may take place materially affecting the views of voters." The accuracy of this observation has been borne out innumerable times in the last few years.

By their very nature, modern sampling polls can and do separate the popularity of candidates from the popularity of issues. Polls can report which views of a candidate the public favors, which they reject. The speed with which sampling referenda can be completed for the entire nation is such that public opinion on any given issue can be reported within forty-eight hours if the occasion warrants. Thus the goal has nearly been reached when public opinion can be "ascertainable at all times."

The problem confronting statesmen who have had to rely on guesswork in determining the will of the people was well described three decades ago by President Woodrow Wilson in a talk before the National Press Club. Wilson said to the assembled newspapermen:

> You say, "All the people out my way think so and so." Now, I know perfectly well that you have not talked with all the people out your way. I find that out again and again. . . . The people of the United States . . . are thinking

* Public opinion analyst and founder of the American Institute of Public Opinion and of other specialized polling organizations. This selection is from George Gallup, *A Guide to Public Opinion Polls*, 2d ed., Princeton University Press, Princeton, N.J., 1948, pp. 3-8, 17-22, 25-31, 64-66, 72-73, and 92-95. Copyright, 1944, 1948, by Princeton University Press. Reprinted by permission of the author and publisher.

for themselves, every man for himself; and you do not know, and, the worst of it is, since the responsibility is mine, I do not know what they are thinking about. I have the most imperfect means of finding out, and yet I have got to act as if I knew. . . . I am not put here to do what I please.

2

"Most students of government view with alarm the growing influence
of spokesmen of pressure groups. Can polls do anything to thwart
these lobbyists?"

The chief weapon of the spokesman for a pressure group in seeking special legislative favors is the threat to punish at the next election any legislator who goes contrary to the selfish interests of his group.

To make this threat carry weight, the pressure group spokesman must claim a united front in the organization he represents. He must convince legislators that he voices the unanimous or nearly unanimous views of his membership, that all feel so keenly about the particular legislation in question that they would vote against any candidate for office who opposes it.

Pressure groups have grown to their present powerful position in government because no organization or method existed to deflate their claims. When spokesmen talked about swinging millions of votes for or against a measure, the legislator had no effective way of countering these claims.

Public opinion polls can find out quickly and accurately the views of any group in the population. They can show, and often do, when the rank and file of the membership in a group hold views opposite those of their official spokesmen. Polls can thus limit the claims of pressure groups to the facts, and thus prevent many insupportable demands for special privilege.

During recent years, polls of organized workers have, on many occasions, found them taking exactly the opposite points of view from the spokesmen of labor organizations. Likewise, they have found farmers going contrary to the claims of their leaders, business men taking opposite views from the heads of business associations, war veterans failing to see eye to eye with officers of the American Legion or other veterans' organizations.

3

"Hundreds of minority groups have their spokesmen.
What about the views of the inarticulate majority?"

Public opinion polls can not only deflate the claims of pressure groups and of minorities seeking special privilege, but, more important, they can reveal the will of the inarticulate and unorganized majority of the citizens.

Persons who write or wire their Congressmen and who go to other lengths to put pressure on their legislators usually have a "fish to fry." They have been aptly described as the "articulate minority." Whether their views actually represent minority viewpoints or majority viewpoints can be ascertained only by examination of the views of all citizens. . . .

4

"Public opinion must have its limitations and so must public opinion polls. Are there areas where the views of the people are likely to have little value?"

It should be borne in mind at all times that polling organizations are merely fact-finding agencies. Their responsibility begins and ends with the ascertaining of facts regarding public opinion. They have no rightful concern whatsoever with what is done about these facts. In this sense they perform the same function in the realm of public opinion as the Associated Press, the United Press, or the International News Service in reporting objectively the events of the day.*

Bryce displayed keen insight into democratic government when he wrote: "The people who are by power entitled to say what they want, are less qualified to say *how,* and *in what form,* they are to attain it; or, in other words, public opinion can *determine ends,* but is less fit to examine and select the means to these ends."

The public cannot be expected to render sound judgments on problems or issues about which they are ill informed. Nor, for the same reason, can they be expected to have intelligent views regarding matters of a wholly technical nature.

5

"Won't the country suffer when its leaders begin to pay a lot of attention to public opinion polls?"

A true statesman will never change his ideals or his principles to make them conform to the opinions of any group, be it large or small. Rather, such a leader will try to persuade the public to accept his views and his goals. In fact, his success as a leader will in large part be measured by his success in making converts to his way of thinking.

Throughout history the most effective leaders have been those who have had a keen understanding of the public—leaders who have known the views and prejudices of their followers, their lack of knowledge and misinformation, their hopes and aspirations.

Leaders who do not know what the public thinks, or the state of the public's knowledge on any issue, are likely to be ineffective and unsuccessful leaders, and eventually to lose their opportunity to lead. In the same sense, a military leader who does not take pains to discover the strength and disposition of the enemy troops is likely to lose the battle, and his head.

Great leaders will seek information from every reliable source about the people whom they wish to lead. For this reason they will inevitably pay more attention to facts about the current state of public thinking and of public knowledge. The public opinion poll will be a useful tool in enabling them to reach the highest level of their effectiveness as leaders.

* *Editors' Note:* The United Press and the International News Service were merged into the United Press International (UPI) in 1958.

The answer to the question posed above, then, is not that the country will suffer when its leaders begin to pay a lot of attention to public opinion polls. The country will suffer when its leaders ignore, or make wrong guesses about the public's views on important issues.

10

"Just how small can samples be and still be accurate in predicting the results of elections on candidates or issues?"

Assuming that a sample has been chosen which is truly representative of the voting population, as few as 100 voters might provide a good prediction of an election or a referendum. Obviously, other things being equal, the larger the sample, the greater is the certainty of accuracy. But it does not necessarily follow, as one congressman suggested, that it is as "certain as daylight will follow darkness that a large sample will provide more accurate results than a small sample." A sample of 10,000,000 improperly selected can be less accurate than a sample of 100 properly selected.

Formulae have been developed which give the range of error that may result from the size of the sample used for random sampling. Tables based on these formulae show the range of error at each stage as the size of the sample is increased. For example, if only 100 persons properly selected were interviewed in a national survey, the outside margin of error would be 15 per cent. That is to say, 997 times out of 1,000 on the average, the error would not go beyond 15 per cent. When 900 persons throughout the nation are interviewed, the outside limit of error due solely to the size of the sample is reduced to 5 per cent. When 10,000 people have been interviewed, the range of error has been reduced to 1.5 per cent. From this point on, as the sample is increased, the error continues to be reduced, but at an extremely low rate. Even if 50,000,000 voters were interviewed, a small error would still be present.

The error limitation resulting from the size of the sample varies according to factors inherent in the kinds of stratification used. In general it may be said, however, that the error limits resulting from size of sample fluctuations are not materially different in most public opinion surveys from the figures for random sampling.

When it is taken into account that the expense of reaching 100,000 people is approximately ten times the cost of reaching 10,000, and the cost of reaching 1,000,000 is approximately 100 times the cost of 10,000, it can be seen that there is little sense in paying such a tremendous price for increasing the certainty of accuracy by less than one per cent. To add cases to achieve this additional accuracy would be as profligate for the public opinion researcher as for a farmer to use fifty horses to draw a wagon that could as easily be drawn by two.

Experiments in predicting elections on the basis of extremely small samples are described by Hadley Cantril in *Gauging Public Opinion*. These studies again underscore the importance of the cross section in arriving at accurate results, and the lesser importance of the size of the sample.

The Office of Public Opinion Research at Princeton, headed by Professor Cantril, investigated the voting intentions of a carefully selected sample of just 200 people in New York state, prior to the New York state gubernatorial election in the fall of 1942. The survey was made by a single interviewer who traveled around the state during the week preceding the election.

Interviews were distributed as follows:

	NUMBER OF INTERVIEWS
New York City	
Manhattan	24
Brooklyn	34
Bronx	19
Queens	19
Upstate	
Cities over 500,000	9
100,000 to 500,000	10
10,000 to 100,000	40
2,500 to 10,000	10
Under 2,500	25
Farms	10
Total	200

Persons interviewed were selected in a manner to provide a good cross section of the population with respect to color, economic status, and age. The voting intentions of the 200 persons interviewed were:

Dewey	115
Bennett	72
Alfange	12
Amter	1
	200

The table below shows that the error in predicting Dewey's victory was only 5 per cent, and the average error for the three leading candidates only 3⅓ per cent.

	OPOR SURVEY	ELECTION RESULT
Dewey	58%	53%
Bennett	36%	37%
Alfange	6%	10%

This survey was only 1 per cent less accurate than that of the *New York Daily News*, which based its prediction on 48,000 interviews. The American Institute of Public Opinion, in its prediction, was exactly right on Dewey's percentage and had an average error of only 1⅓ per cent for the top three candidates. The number of cases it based its final prediction upon was 2,500. . . .

11

*"Why haven't I been interviewed? Why have I never heard
of anyone who has been interviewed?"*

These questions come up frequently in connection with modern public opinion surveys, because most persons do not understand how it is possible to get an accurate measurement of public opinion when only a small part of the total population is interviewed.

Old-fashioned "straw polls" relied almost entirely for their accuracy on *numbers*. As shown on previous pages, modern sampling polls rely for their accuracy on an entirely different principle—the careful selection of a *small but representative cross section.*

In this respect, modern surveys merely apply to public opinion research certain well-established procedures which have been used for years in the fields of engineering, medicine, education, and all the social sciences. When an engineer wishes to judge the quality of ore in a mine, he examines a few "samples." From these samples he makes a highly accurate estimate of the amount and quality of ore in the mine. A government wheat tester gauges the quality of a carload of grain by taking a few carefully selected samples.

Samples chosen to represent public opinion provide a faithful replica of the total electorate. It is of little consequence whether this image is life-size or whether it is reduced to a fraction of the original, just as a photograph can be reduced in size and still remain a truthful and accurate portrait.

No case has yet been recorded of a nationwide poll which has gone wrong because too few persons were interviewed. The *Literary Digest* poll of 1936 sent ballots to more than 10,000,000 persons and yet was less accurate than modern polls embracing less than one per cent of this number.

The odds against any one person being interviewed in a modern sampling poll are gigantic. They can be worked out by simple arithmetic. Suppose that a poll in any given week covers a total of 3,000 persons. The chances of being interviewed that week are then 3,000 out of about 94,000,000, the number of adults in the country, or one chance in 31,333.*

With a sample of 3,000 taken weekly, a total of 156,000 persons would be reached in a year, or less than one per cent of the total adult population.

Since the average life expectancy of a person reaching the age of twenty-one is about fifty years, this means that the average person would have less than *one chance in ten* of ever being interviewed in his lifetime, with samples based upon an average of 3,000 per week.

15

*"What is meant by random sampling, and what is meant
by stratified sampling?"*

---

* *Editors' Note:* There were approximately 110 million adults in the United States in 1960, which would reduce one's chances of being interviewed in a sample of 3,000 to 1 in 36,667.

A random sample is one which is selected so that each person in the total population to be covered has an equal chance of being included. If it were possible to line up all the adults in the United States and get them to stand still long enough to permit interviewers to interview every 1,000th or every 1,000,000th person, this would be considered a randomized procedure provided the order in which people were lined up was purely a chance one.

In *stratified sampling* the units to be sampled are first grouped according to certain characteristics, such as geographic location, size of city, type of industry, type of agriculture, etc. Then, if a random procedure is used, units are selected by chance from these subgroups or strata. This tends to increase the likelihood that each of these groups will be properly represented in the sample and at the same time retains all the essential features of a random sample. In terms of the example above, this might mean lining up all the adults in the United States in groups according to the state in which they live and then selecting every 1,000th person. This geographic stratification would increase the probability of getting the proper proportion of residents of each state in the sample. In a similar manner, stratification can be carried out using any other characteristic or characteristics.

16

"What is area sampling? What is quota sampling, and what is the difference between them?"

The two methods of sample design which are now in most general use in public opinion and marketing surveys are most commonly referred to as area sampling and quota sampling.

Area sampling is designed to achieve randomness in sampling. The areas in which the sampling is to be done are selected at random, usually making use of the principle of stratification. The households within these areas are also selected in a random manner. If individuals, rather than households, are to be sampled, the particular individuals within the sample households should also be chosen by chance.

The following statement by Morris H. Hansen, of the Bureau of the Census, and Philip M. Hauser, formerly of the Bureau, provides a description of area sampling:

> To illustrate how and why area sampling works, suppose we are interested in sampling for certain characteristics of the population in a city. For example, we may want to know the total number of persons in certain broad occupational groups, and the number within each of these occupation groups who have a particular opinion, read a specified magazine, or are in a certain income class.

> To estimate the total number of persons having the various characteristics mentioned above, we might proceed by first making an up-to-date list containing the name of every person, or, at considerably less expense, identifying every address or household, in the area to be surveyed, and then selecting a

sample from this listing. Through taking a random sample from such listings of individuals or of households (interviewing all persons within the selected households if households are sampled), we could, with an adequate size of sample, obtain an excellent cross section of the people in the city for any problem. This procedure would lead to highly reliable sample results, but frequently it is not practical for a number of reasons—the principal one being that preparing a listing would cost too much. Moreover, even where a complete pre-listing is already available, it may be too costly to interview the widely scattered sample that would be obtained by sampling individuals (or households) at random from such a listing. One method of getting a reduction in cost over sampling individuals from a pre-listing is to use an area-sampling method in which the individuals interviewed are clustered into a selected set of sample areas.

In area sampling the entire area in which the population to be covered is located is subdivided into smaller areas, and each individual in the population is associated with one and only one such small area—for example, the particular small area in which he resides. Neither the names nor numbers of persons residing in the areas need be known in advance. A sample of these small areas is drawn, and all or a subsample of the population residing in the selected areas is covered in the survey.

A simple illustration will show that if a complete list of areas is available and a random selection of a sample of areas is made, and if the population of these sample areas is completely enumerated, then the chances (or probabilities) of being included are the same for each individual in the population. Moreover, on the average, the population surveyed within such a sample will reveal precisely the characteristics of the entire population from which the sample was drawn. A sample can be made as reliable a cross section as desired, for any characteristics whatever, by merely increasing the size of the sample. Thus, if the population is changing in character, a random cross section of small areas will reveal those shifts.

Quota sampling procedure requires that persons be selected from all major groups in the population in proportion to the numerical size of these groups. The first step in making use of this method of sampling is to divide the total population of the nation or of each state or city into its component parts or strata and to make certain that each part is represented in the sample in proportion to its magnitude.

The individual interviewers are told what assignments they are to obtain in each group. That is, the interviewers are told the number of farmers to be included in completing their assignments, the number of townspeople, the number of men and women, the number in each age group, and the number in any other category used as a "control." While the area in which they are to interview is circumscribed—it may be a block, a neighborhood, a ward, a city, a town, or a county—the selection of the individual respondents to fill out the assigned quotas is left in the hands of the individual interviewers.

A number of sampling operations represent compromises between area sampling and quota sampling. For example, in certain instances the sample will be based upon an area design but the interviewer will have latitude in selecting the individual respondent within each household who is to be interviewed.

17

"What are the advantages of area sampling, and what are the advantages of quota sampling?"

The advantages of area sampling have been stated as follows by Morris H. Hansen and Philip M. Hauser:

> Area sampling eliminates dependence on the assignment of quotas that may be more or less seriously in error, and does not permit the interviewer discretion in the choice of the individuals to be included in the sample. With appropriate methods of designating areas for coverage in the sample, the probabilities of the inclusion of the various elements of the population are known, and consequently the reliability of results from the sample can be measured and controlled. Area sampling, of course, is not the only method that produces such results, but it is frequently an effective method.

The advantages of quota sampling for public opinion surveys are two: greater speed and lower cost. These advantages operate both in the planning of the sample in the first place and in the completion of the interviewing phase of the survey. The setting up of an area sample requires the use of a great many detailed maps and aerial photographs which are expensive and take a great deal of time to assemble. In addition, because of the detailed instructions which must be furnished to the interviewers for selecting each individual respondent, it is a costly and time-consuming process to design the sample. Each survey requires new instructions. On the other hand, quota sampling needs fewer maps; the quotas can be quickly set up using government data, election figures, and other available information; and the same design can be used for a number of surveys without running into the problem of reinterviewing the same respondents.

It is obvious that any system of sampling which requires that certain specified persons be interviewed—with no substitutions permitted—is likely to be far more costly and time-consuming than a system which permits substitutions, or one which gives interviewers some latitude in selection, as in quota sampling. A high proportion of adults are not at home during the normal working day of 9 A.M. to 5 P.M. Therefore any system which requires interviewers to work after these hours or on weekends and to make a number of call-backs can certainly not be expected to be as inexpensive or as fast-operating as a system which permits interviewers to work in those places and areas where respondents are available during these hours. To obtain an accurate cross section of all adults—at least during normal working hours—interviewers must distribute their calls in business, factory, farm, and home areas. However, when the sampling unit is the household rather than the individual, and when any member of the family can report accurately on the subject of the survey, the interviewing part of area sampling is less costly.

While the accuracy of quota sampling cannot be determined from mathematical formulae—principally because of the inability to calculate the interviewer selection factor—there does exist a growing record of performance of public opinion polls which have in the past been operating on quota sampling principles. . . .

49

"To what extent are election returns a guide to polling accuracy?"

The public will probably continue to judge the accuracy of polls chiefly by election returns. For this reason those who conduct polls must be content, rightly or wrongly, to be judged by their election forecasts. But election returns, it should be emphasized, are by no means a perfect measure of the accuracy of public opinion polling techniques.

Election returns are affected by many extraneous factors which have little or nothing to do with the true reflection of the public's views regarding candidates or issues. The weather, corruption on the part of election officials, and the efficiency of political machines in getting their members to the polls, all have an important influence on election returns.

For example, bad weather which keeps farmers from voting would, in elections of recent years, reduce the number of Republican votes cast, because outside the southern states, farmers tend to be more Republican than their city cousins. Corruption has tended to decline with the years, but nevertheless is still present in some cities. Again, it is entirely possible that in a very close race a dramatic last-minute statement or a change of views on the part of one candidate might alter the views of the electorate at a time too late to be measured by any polling organization before election day. Still another extraneous factor which cannot be taken into account by those who conduct polls, and yet which can and does affect election results, is party effort on election day. If one party makes a far greater effort to get its followers to balloting places, poll results obviously are thrown off to this extent. Activity of this sort may be equally effective if operated by some organization other than one of the parties—witness the work of the CIO-PAC in 1944 in educating voters and encouraging them to vote.

Most of these sources of error would be eliminated if a nation required every citizen, on penalty of fine or imprisonment, to cast his ballot. Such a law does exist in Australia. But in the United States in 1940, the last presidential election before the war, the vote was less than 50 million or only five-eighths of the 80 million adult citizens. Elections for Congressmen in off-years attract even fewer voters—34 million in 1946. Elections in some Congressional districts to fill unexpired terms have attracted less than 10 per cent of the eligible voters!

When a considerable number of voters stay away from polling booths on election day, the question inevitably arises as to whether those who do take the trouble to vote represent accurately the views of those who do not.

When the size of the voting group declines to any considerable extent, polling organizations run into a new source of error; for, in addition to the normal error which arises in dividing voters between candidates, or between those who favor and those who oppose a given issue, poll results are subject to a second error which arises from the attempt to determine who will and who will not vote.

If persons who vote were always a perfect sample of the whole—if their views agreed exactly with those who do not vote—this source of error would not exist. The poll prediction would be an accurate forecast since it would be based upon a perfect sample of a perfect sample. But the sample represented by those who vote is rarely a true sample. There is much evidence to prove that those who do go to the polls seldom represent accurately the political views of those who stay away.

Although an error in this kind of election situation certainly has little to do with the accuracy of polls in determining the views of the *entire electorate* on any given issue or on candidates, nevertheless it is a problem which must be solved in order to keep the confidence of the public in polling accuracy.

Much experimental work has been done on the problem of determining who will and who will not vote in a given election, and it can be confidently predicted that ways will be found in the future to reduce the error arising from this factor of turnout.

54

"What chance is there that polls will make wrong forecasts?"

Just as it can be said with certainty that polls will be highly accurate in the vast majority of elections, so with the same certainty it can be said that on occasion they will go wrong. But when they do go wrong, they still should be reasonably close to the mark, if the best practices have been followed.

In thinking of poll accuracy, the terms "right" and "wrong" are wholly inadequate for describing *how* right or *how* wrong a poll is in a given election. Thus, a poll might be "wrong" in naming the winner, yet be within one half of one per cent of the true division of the vote. In short, the accuracy of polls in a scientific sense should be judged solely on *how closely they predict the actual division of votes* on candidates, or the division of opinion on issues. The correct prediction of a winner, but with an error of fifteen per cent, should be regarded as an exceptionally poor forecast; whereas a wrong prediction of one or two per cent should, in a strictly scientific sense, be regarded as a good prediction, even if the winner was not correctly forecast.

The outcome of a national election might be determined by an extremely small number of votes, as in the case of the 1916 election. Polling machinery has not reached, and probably never will reach, the degree of accuracy necessary to forecast an election which is decided by fewer votes than the margin of error under which a poll operates. Since this margin of error averages about two to three per cent, under the best conditions, it is evident that unless a candidate gets 53 per cent or more of the two-party vote, his victory in terms of popular votes cannot be forecast with complete certainty.

One of the things which experience has taught all polling organizations is that accurate predictions of the division of the votes in the electoral college is an almost impossible feat. The reason for this is plain. Theoretically, at least, a mere ten votes out of a total of 30,000,000 cast in the ten largest states could change a total of 249 of the 531 electoral votes of the country.* To measure political sentiment with this degree of accuracy

---

* *Editors' Note:* This was written prior to the admission of Alaska and Hawaii into the Union.

would require methods with the precision of the finest tools used in the physical sciences.

In the 1944 Presidential election, Ohio, with its 25 electoral votes, could not have been placed in the right column unless the polling organization could achieve an accuracy of two-tenths of one per cent! In fact, a total of 165 electoral votes in this election were represented by states where a change of two per cent of the vote would put the 165 electoral votes in a different column.

69

"Don't polls start 'band wagon' movements? Aren't polls harmful in that they not only report but influence election results?"

The band-wagon theory is one of the oldest delusions of politics. It is a time-honored custom for candidates in an election to announce that they are going to win. The misconception under which these politicians labor is that a good many people will vote for a man, regardless of their convictions, just to be able to say that they voted for the winner.

There may have been a time in American political life when people cared so little about political issues or about candidates that the mere pleasure of telling their friends that they supported the winner was enough to make them vote for him. But in recent years no objective evidence has been found to support the contention that poll predictions influence voters. And there is a mountain of evidence to the contrary.

Those who conduct polls are in an excellent position to determine band-wagon influence for the simple reason that the usual polling practice is to measure public opinion at several points in time. Periodic polls record the increase or decrease in any candidate's following. To be specific: suppose that in a given election, candidate "A" is reported as having 60 per cent of the vote as against 40 per cent for candidate "B." The band-wagon theory requires that some of candidate "B's" followers, on learning that he is likely to be the loser, should jump on the band wagon of candidate "A." This means, of course, that candidate "A's" following is increased to the extent of the followers who left "B," and "B's" following is decreased accordingly. The next poll, therefore, would inevitably discover that "A" had not 60 per cent of the major party vote—assuming other factors in this particular election were constant—but that he had more than 60 per cent. In short, the band-wagon theory *absolutely requires* that candidate "A's" following increase to the extent that the band-wagon influence has been present.

Since many factors enter into any single election, it would not be fair to draw conclusions based upon a single election. But if the band-wagon factor were actually important, then certainly in the case of *a great many elections* there must be evidence of this general upward trend in the case of the leading candidate's following.

That this is not the case has been demonstrated in many elections and on many issues. A review of the evidence is enlightening.

In the 1942 governorship race in New York state, Thomas E. Dewey started off with 54 per cent in the first poll. According to the band-wagon theory, he should have improved his position as it became known that he was ahead. But in six succeeding surveys the net change in Governor Dewey's vote was one per cent—and it was a *loss* of one per cent. The campaign ended with his figure at 53 per cent, and he was elected by exactly 53 per cent.

Polls conducted in the Kentucky Senatorial primary in 1938 found voters steadily falling off the band wagon of the leading candidate, Senator Barkley. He started the campaign with 65 per cent in the first poll, and his figure steadily dropped, reaching 59 per cent in the final survey shortly before election day. He was elected with 57 per cent.

In the Maryland Senatorial primary of 1938, polls found a rising trend for the leading candidate, Senator Tydings, but in the South Carolina and Georgia primaries of the same year the opposite tendency was found—a downward trend for the candidates in the lead. The 1936 presidential campaign witnessed an upward trend for Roosevelt, but in 1940 the trend was upward until mid-September and downward thereafter.

On many occasions the Institute has asked voters during election campaigns (1) what candidate they thought would win, and (2) what candidate they themselves were planning to vote for. The result showed that a large proportion of people were supporting the man whom they thought would lose. In 1944, more than seven out of every ten people in the voting population thought Roosevelt would win the election, but only 54 per cent voted for him.

It could, of course, be argued that the band-wagon vote might be present in one election and not in another, or that the losing candidate would have done better if it had not been for a band-wagon psychology. Nevertheless, the weight of evidence is certainly on the side of those who contend that no positive indications exist today to prove the band wagon an important factor.

Indeed, the facts would indicate that party voters generally care far too deeply about who wins an election to vote for a given candidate just to be on the winning side.

The reason politicians hold so tenaciously to the band-wagon theory is that within the narrow limits of professional politics it undoubtedly has great importance to them. Often it is vital for a politician who seeks a job to back the right man at the right time. But the politician is likely to forget that only a negligible number of voters are directly and immediately dependent for a job upon backing the right candidate.

The cases cited above are not isolated cases. They are typical of the election results covered by the Institute during its entire history. The same type of evidence shows that there is no general tendency for winning candidates to increase their lead after poll results have been announced, nor is there any general tendency for the majority opinion on an issue to show a similar trend. A study of issues in which long-time trends have been kept by the Institute reveals no general tendency one way or the other. The majority opinion declines as often as it increases.

93. NATIONAL Q-&-A GAME:
THE POLLS
by Robert Bendiner*

At this moment periodicals all over the country are rushing copy into print to review, interpret, or expand some phase of the most eagerly awaited document since the Declaration of Independence. I refer, of course, to Dr. Kinsey's findings concerning sexual behavior in the human female. The doctor's investigation may establish a new high in interest, but it is just one more expression of what is fast becoming a national faith. This is the belief that the life, thought, and habits of 160,000,000 people can be pinned down, defined, and catalogued if only we ask a "sampling" of ourselves enough questions and arrange the answers statistically.

If the theory is wholly sound, we Americans should already know more about ourselves than any people that ever lived. For years, segments of us have been questioned, polled, or grilled as to our reading habits, our sex habits, our smoking habits. Our opinions have been solicited on national defense, church bingo, flying saucers and free trade; on the Marshall Plan, the Schuman Plan, and the Morris Plan. Our tastes have been explored with respect to music, beer, soap and politicians. All of which—and much more— we have had presented to us in tables of percentages to at least one decimal point.

Yet we are always being surprised at ourselves—that, starting from scratch, for instance, we could emerge victorious from a world war in less than four years and then turn around and win only a draw from North Korea in three. We think we're all set to put Tom Dewey in the White House and we elect Harry Truman. We have to debate with ourselves endlessly as to whether we are really hysterical on the Communist issue or models of prudence and foresight. We think we've gone completely overboard for Douglas MacArthur only to find ourselves dozing as he makes his big pitch at the Republican Convention.

In short, if we know more about ourselves than Australian bushmen, it isn't much more, in spite of constantly taking our national temperature and recording our basal metabolism. Why? What's wrong with all these measuring devices—or do we just expect too much of them?

To begin with, there are polls and polls—and generalization will not do. Ever since a tooth paste concern rolled up sales some years ago by warning that four out of five of us have soft gums, "ad men" have been telling us in mournful numbers just how we are coming apart at the seams. Foundations and "cause" organizations toss off one-shot opinion polls of a somewhat

* Free-lance writer on politics and public affairs, former magazine editor, and American correspondent of *The New Statesman of London.* Author of *The Riddle of the State Department, White House Fever,* and numerous articles. This selection is from Robert Bendiner, "National Q-&-A Game: The Polls," *New York Times Magazine,* Aug. 23, 1953, pp. 13, 36, and 38-39. Reprinted by permission.

more sober variety, though often no more scientific, on subjects ranging from interfaith marriages to anti-vivisection. And many a newspaper in campaign months runs a straw poll that surprisingly confirms its editorial judgment right down to the ground.

All these self-serving, amateur, or counterfeit operations we can dismiss from further consideration here, except to note that they lend a shabby air to the entire business of surveying public opinion, at the expense of legitimate surveyors from Gallup to Kinsey.

Granting the integrity of these responsible pollsters, one is led to wonder why we don't know much more about ourselves than we seem to. Why don't we know whether as a nation we want more defense or lower taxes? A quick end to our involvement in Asia or a smashing triumph over the Communists in that part of the world? More of the McCarthy technique or less? One poll, in 1952, showed that the country expected all-out war within two years, complete with atomic bombing of our cities, while another in the same week indicated that fewer than one-third of us had so much as thought of volunteering for civilian defense work. As a people, then, do we take the threat of war seriously or not? You really can't tell from the polls.

Technicians have brought forth a number of criticisms of the public opinion survey, and they have been endlessly debated in learned journals of sociology. Aside from those that have to do with predicting election results, an especially worrisome procedure since the results are dramatically checked, the big bones of contention are the method of choosing the "sample" to be questioned and the wording of the questions.

As a rule a Gallup poll will involve some 3,000 interviews. That means that each respondent speaks for some 32,000 adult Americans. The most obvious criticism, of course, is that too much ground is presumed to be covered with too few persons, but this is also the least meaningful objection. For if the 3,000 are a fair microcosm of the total population—with exactly the same proportions of rich to poor, male to female, educated to unschooled, rural to urban, young to old, and so forth—then they should perfectly reflect the opinion of the country as a whole. But there's the rub. How is a real microcosm to be picked?

On this there are two schools of thought. For the most part the journalistic poll-takers rely on the "quota" system. Taking the United States Census as their guide, they attempt, rigidly or roughly, to make each sampling group a cross-section of the total population, with just the right representation for each category—income bracket, sex, age, and so on down the line.

But to be really accurate this procedure involves technical difficulties of a formidable sort. The choice of categories to be considered in making up a particular cross-section should ideally be related to the questions to be asked. Then, too, the interviewer is apt to cut corners at times, getting a little careless in satisfying the category requirements in the interest of speed and convenience. And respondents have been thought to knock a few years off their age out of vanity, to add a few thousand dollars to their income, or to pass themselves off as college graduates when they may with difficulty have completed a year of high school. All of which upsets the delicate balance of the cross-section.

Other polls, rejecting the quota system entirely, put their faith in the miraculous law of probability, which is that if you pick a big enough sample completely at random you will get the most representative cross-section possible. Take a box of 1,000 marbles, they suggest, 500 black and 500 white. Blindfolded, pick out 100, and you will come out close to a fifty-fifty division. Two hundred will make it even closer.

The Survey Research Center at the University of Michigan a few years ago made a series of tests on this theory. Taking completely random samplings of 500 to 3,500 persons in various parts of the country, they noted purely factual data, such as age, race and income, and found that their groups conformed remarkably to the national pattern, as shown by census figures. The leading poll-takers were so impressed that they have lately been combining the quota and random technique in a manner too complicated to be described here. All things considered, it is probably fair to say that their samples come close enough to being accurate cross-sections to warrant looking elsewhere for the basic trouble.

Some profess to find it in the questions themselves. Don't they deal with matters too complicated for the average person to have an informed opinion about them, if any? One of the leading poll-takers reports that only 30 to 40 per cent of the adult population is "well informed" on public affairs, to begin with, the rest sloping down from "poorly informed" to a status delicately described as "grossly ignorant."

Human nature being what it is, membership even in this last category does not always inhibit people from the voluble voicing of opinion. A New Jersey bank, eager to improve its services, hired a poll to put questions to passers-by on a street corner, including an inquiry as to whether they knew the function of a trust department. It turned out that 70 per cent did not have the foggiest idea, but such decisive answers were reported as "It's the kitty big capitalists kick into to keep up a monopoly."

If something like one-third of American adults can't tell you what the U.N. is, what illumination can be had from questioning them about reciprocal trade or German unification? The answer of the poll-takers is that they rule out the ignorant. In the jargon of the trade, "questions in depth" are used to discover whether the respondent knows what he is talking about before his opinion is included in the statistics.

Dr. Gallup even has an elaborate "quintamensional plan" for making sure that questioner and respondent are talking about the same thing. Instead of asking a man whether he favors filibusters, for example, he will ask, first, what the respondent thinks a filibuster is; second, what he would like to see done about it. Next comes a question on whether he approves or disapproves a particular move to check filibusters. If he approves, he is asked why and how strongly he feels about it—"very," "fairly," or "not at all." Even so, Rensis Likert, an expert in the field, has been able to cite an instance where two polls asking substantially the same question, but in considerably different language, got answers some fourteen to eighteen percentage points apart.

All of which leads this admittedly unscientific observer to suggest that the comparative weakness of the polls is not of a technological order. They are probably doing as well as they can. The trouble, quite simply, is people.

You can measure their height, their weight and their waistline; but their opinions are too mercurial, often too contradictory, and their frames of reference too varied to make for completely reliable statistics.

Ask the next man you meet whether he thinks we should have more or less in the way of a national defense program. Even if he doesn't know what we have now, he is likely to say more, just on general principle— better be safe than be sorry. After a decent interval of time, ask him whether taxes should go up, stay where they are, or go down. Any doubt about the answer?

If you should then point out that his two answers may be incompatible, he may well suggest as a way out that the Government cut down on non-defense spending. But if he is a farmer, he will oppose the elimination of crop supports; if he is a city worker, he will oppose any slash in social security; and if he ever wore a uniform, he will probably take a sour view of any curtailment in veterans' benefits.

What this gets down to is that the polls come a cropper because people are not all of a piece. Each one is a bundle of conflicting loyalties, responsive to a dozen pressures—his business or union, his church, his friends, his family, his past and, possibly, his conscience. If these are all in harmony, he is lucky—and rare. If they are not, his opinions may be contradictory, depending on whether a particular question hits him at the moment in his role as dairy farmer, New Englander, taxpayer, Democrat, veteran, Jehova's Witness, father or Elk.

If his answer represented a careful weighing of all his interests, if it dovetailed with all his other positions as part of an integrated whole, it would have significance. But how many people go about with a coherent world view, from which flow inevitably their positions on farm prices, Korea, progressive education, Picasso and the Taft-Hartley Law? So few, in all probability, that what the polls record is an aggregation of unsorted prejudices and desires rather than a distillation of the country's wisdom.

What is more, they catch even these prejudices on the fly, as it were, and without conveying their often transitory nature. In spite of formulas for measuring the "intensity" of opinion, I suspect that the respondent's mood at the moment of questioning has a good deal to do with his answer. The man who relates all government activity to his own pocket in March may take a somewhat broader view of national expenditures in June, when the pain in his wallet has abated.

Dr. Gallup recently solicited opinions on the "ideal" number of children per family. Asked on a lonely summer day, with the kids away at camp, a mother may fondly answer three or four, or even more. But put the question to her late on a winter afternoon, with the same blessings tearing up the floorboards, and the answer may be not only different but unprintable.

There are individuals, moreover, who go into a spasm at the mere thought of a world in which foreign policy—any foreign policy—is necessary. Poll-takers are ideal lightning rods for grounding the vague resentments of such as these, but the specific opinions on issues are not likely to have much validity or to be the same two days' running. Given positions of responsibility, these respondents might evolve a coherent policy, of some nature or other; but answering a pollster, they feel no responsibility whatever and are free to indulge their pent-up emotions. Yet they figure in the statistics just the same.

Does this mean that polls, straw votes, and surveys have no real point at all? Far from it. They encourage, even force, people to think concretely about issues that might otherwise remain in a vapory state at the back of their minds. This applies, moreover, not only to the few who are questioned but also to the thousands who read their answers and wonder what they themselves might have said.

The polls have been instrumental, too, in blasting open such traditionally hush-hush issues as birth control and prevention of venereal diseases. People who would not dream of making public pronouncements on such matters have no hesitation in adding their anonymous opinions to a statistical table.

It is no negligible service, moreover, that the pollsters perform simply by spotlighting areas of ignorance and inconsistency, leaving it to the educators and politicians to take over from there.

And, not least, the polls have been known to counteract the work of those pressure groups that swamp Government officials with one-sided mail, sometimes causing them to jump for bandwagons that don't exist.

Viewed in perspective, then, the responsible polls are seen to play a perfectly admirable role in national affairs as long as their limitations are recognized. What those limitations mean, quite simply, is that we unpredictable humans, unlike refrigerators or ball bearings, happily go on resisting the efforts of science to measure us. When it comes to helping us know what we are and what we think, the polls are no substitute for poets, prophets, psychiatrists, novelists, or even good journalists. Neither are they a road map to be followed blindly by politicians in search of votes.

In fairness to the best of our propounders of questions, they claim no such elevated status. "No poll-taker that I know of has ever said that political leaders should suspend their own judgment and follow polls blindly," says Dr. Gallup. "That would be absurd." Yet it is against precisely this exaggerated trust in the question-and-answer game that we must be on guard. Taken along with other revelations of the public temper, as well as an undetermined measure of salt, the polls can be illuminating at best and at worst amusing.

94. THE POLLS GROW: SHOULD THEY?

by Samuel Grafton*

With a Presidential election coming up, the public opinion polls are once more about to have their quadrennial year of conspicuous testing. This is the Rose Bowl game for pollsters. Will their forecasts be on the nose, as in

---

* Free-lance writer and former newspaper editor and columnist. Author of *All Out, A Most Contagious Game,* and other works. This selection is from Samuel Grafton. "The Polls Grow: Should They?" *New York Times Magazine,* Feb. 21, 1960, pp. 15 and 62-63. Reprinted by permission.

1956? Or will they again elect the wrong man, as when all the polls enthusiastically, and, in fact, rather smugly, put Mr. Dewey into the White House in 1948?

The Great Polls Disaster of '48 has been mossed over by time, and so the sporting question of whether the polls are going to be right or wrong in November is not, in the minds of many observers, the chief issue represented by polling today. A greater question stirs, begins to whisper for attention.

The public knows only the Gallup poll, whose predictions are published in a number of newspapers, and the Roper survey, whose findings are broadcast by radio. But there are thirty to forty additional firms which do private (i.e., confidential, and unpublished) surveys of opinion for anybody who cares to hire them. Today almost every prominent American politician has his own public opinion pollster, to whom he goes for counseling and comfort as automatically as a young Broadway actor goes to a psychoanalyst.

These private pollsters (by a technique of divining public opinion, which shall be examined later) presume to tell political figures what issues to discuss, what stands to take, whether to run or not to run, and for what office. The voices of Gallup and Roper constitute less than one-tenth of the total activity in the field. Most polling is private polling, done under contract (at as much as $3,000 per state) for individuals, and the results are not communicated to the general public.

As there are more than thirty firms in this business, there must be thirty degrees of excellence, or lack of it. These firms are having an enormous influence on American politics. Hence the new issue which is arising.

When Gov. Nelson Rockefeller announced his withdrawal from the Presidential race, the question must at once have flared in the mind of almost every political reporter in the country: Did a private poll advise him to quit? That question may be unfair; the Governor has a mind of his own. But he is a great user of private polls and is reputed to have had more than 100 taken during his successful gubernatorial campaign against former Governor Harriman and to have based a good deal of his campaign strategy on them.

One Eastern Senator regularly has the voters in his state quizzed on a list of ten different public issues, to find out which they react to most warmly. The Senator then becomes "hot" about the issues he finds produce a temperature in the voters. Looking at this picture, one is irresistibly reminded of television, which selects the shows it puts on by means of a variety of public opinion polls, such as the Trendex Survey.

Are we heading toward Trendex politics in America, and will the voters be allowed to act only on candidates and issues which manage to get a good enough "rating" to be placed before them? For certain it is, that if the polls, public and private, had shown Governor Rockefeller making a strong enough bid, he would not have left the primary race. He is out of it now, the way the Firestone Hour recently went off television because the ratings showed it to have an audience of only 5,000,000 people, which the network involved considered too few.

Those millions had enjoyed Firestone's music very much, just as millions more had found Rockefeller an interesting candidate. If we are going to have a political system based on the lowest common denominator, may we not in years to come find we must choose, like television viewers, between the political equivalent of the inanities of Westerns and mysteries?

The theory on which polling activity rests is that trained pollsters can determine accurately how the country (or a state, or a city) feels about a personality, or an issue, by questioning a well-selected small sampling of citizens. The sample group must be made up to resemble, in miniature, the entire body politic. It is claimed that if the group be fairly composed it need be no larger than 3,000 people to give accurate results. In theory the size of the group is not as important as that it mirror the whole political body for which it speaks, in terms of income levels, occupation, age, education and racial composition. The polled group is, therefore a foreshortened shadow of the republic.

Both "public polls," those that are published and broadcast, and "private polls," those paid for by individuals for their own information and kept secret, are supposedly conducted by the same methods; there is no difference of technique between them. (For purposes of this essay, "polling" means a sampling of general public opinion, taken in the systematic manner outlined above. It does not mean a telephone roundup of opinions of county political chairmen, or a special private census of insiders, though these, too, are often called polls.)

But even the big public polls, those whose results are published or broadcast, and which try to establish records for themselves under the scrutiny of the people, can go wrong. They have in the past. This raises the cheerless possibility that some candidate may someday decide a question of major importance to the public, such as whether to run, or what issues to raise, on a faulty private questioning of a few thousand persons, by some organization whose name is unknown to most of us.

In the closing weeks of the 1948 Presidential campaign, with every pollster picking Dewey rather than Truman, it began to be observed that Mr. Truman was drawing large crowds at every railroad stop. A news magazine solemnly reported that the people were turning out because Mr. Truman was showing "a growing entertainment value." The crowds increased. Late in October 7,000 people at Auburn, N. Y., stayed through a thunderstorm, wet to their skins, to hear the President. The crowds, growing at every stop, were described by press observers as "merely curious," a "vaudeville audience" which had come out to see the loser.

The President was obviously forging ahead, but the poll-blinded couldn't see it. The polls had been uncannily accurate in 1940 and 1944, coming at times to within 0.2 per cent of being dead right, and confidence in them was high. (A Kansas City milling firm had made up feed sacks, lettered either "Truman" or "Dewey" and had allowed its customers to take their choice. After farmers had taken 20,000 sacks the company dropped the experiment, because the result disagreed with the polls. It showed Truman ahead, and therefore, presumably, it had to be wrong.)

This blinders effect, created by the polls, kept the country from being able to see a reality in front of its nose. One wonders if it isn't a somewhat similar effect which makes television executives continue to show horse operas in spite of the groans of the nation. The 1948 samplings had completely missed the human drama of an under-dog candidate who had traveled 31,500 miles, delivered 350 speeches, spoken 560,000 words and had, by this effort, changed the national political picture when, clearly, if he had been swayed by the polls, he should have stayed at home and accepted defeat as inevitable.

So one-sidedly against Truman were the early poll predictions that the Roper survey gave up issuing regular reports on the 1948 elections early in September, stating that only a "political convulsion" could keep Dewey out of the White House. Mr. Roper added some tart remarks to the effect that "political campaigns are largely ritualistic . . . evidence . . . tends to indicate that the man in the lead at the beginning of the campaign is the man who is the winner at the end of it." He later took it all back, handsomely, and has been a leader in working for poll improvement ever since, but at that moment, the high point of poll self-confidence, he had come close to denying the educational value of political campaigning.

A failure by the polls seems to make everybody happy; there is a kind of national jollification when it occurs. Perhaps this is because there is something galling in the idea that a selected group of 3,000 (or 4,000 or 10,000) citizens can speak for all of us. This assumes, insultingly, that no matter how free a spirit one is, or how preciously unique a soul, he can be represented and spoken for by someone else, in a "well-chosen sampling." Even if he is an odd ball, the thought is there should be enough odd balls in the sample to include his point of view—an infuriating notion.

But the real danger, it would seem, is not that the 3,000 pollees are wrong, or unrepresentative, but that polling of itself has a constipating effect on the political process. It keeps things from happening. If we grant that a different set of poll figures might have kept Governor Rockefeller in the race against Vice President Nixon, who can say what changes in public opinion on our major problems might not have been produced by a vigorous five months of debate between these articulate men? If there had been polling organizations in 1858, Lincoln and Douglas might have been satisfied to take samplings, rather than conduct their debates.

In spite of such doubts, the use of polling by politicians is increasing enormously. Methods tend to catch on among executives as tunes do among teen-agers, and political leaders now imitate each other in paying for private polls on the basis of which they decide where to spend campaign funds (mostly in the areas shown to be about 50-50 in the polls), where to have their candidate make his major speeches (in the towns where he is slipping, of course) and whom to announce for before a convention opens. Private polls are playing a major part in pre-convention in-fighting at this moment, and in the higher levels of American politics the results of private polling circulate constantly, like girly books in a prep school.

The pollsters defend themselves fiercely against criticism. They believe the '48 foul-up was due to the fact that many voters were undecided until late in the campaign; they now consider themselves able, by what Mr. Roper calls "subtle questioning," to detect which way the undecided voter is leaning, and to tell whether he is really undecided, or merely pretending to be.

It is believed by American politicoes that the so-called undecided, silent voter swung the recent British elections, in which the polls did not predict the extent of the Conservative sweep. In this case the silent voter is considered to have been the British working man, feeling prosperous, anxious to keep the Conservatives in power, but unwilling to reveal his intentions to his Labor workmates, or indeed, to anybody.

American pollsters feel that if their latest methods had been used in England, the outcome would have been predicted successfully. The pollsters are convinced that, by careful checks, they have solved the old problems of the "rightward lean"—the fact that poll errors, until a few years ago, seemed always to favor the more conservative candidate, mainly because poll interviewers had a built-in preference for ringing the doorbells of the nicer houses.

A subtler problem is to find out whether the citizen being questioned is going to vote at all. For while a poll theoretically "samples" the opinion of the entire nation, not everybody bothers to vote. This distorts the results. Pollsters actually feel that the accuracy of their findings is not adequately tested by elections. This startling thought is based on the notion that bad weather on election day, local corruption and reluctance to vote may make activity in the polling place a less than accurate picture of national opinion. (A philosopher might say, of course, that a man who does not vote because it is raining is, in his own way, casting a ballot recording the negative intensity of his convictions.)

"Maximum non-voting" takes place in the lowest economic group. If non-voting in this group is overestimated, the poll will lean toward the opinions of the upper economic levels; if it is underestimated, the poll will teeter in the other direction. On these levels, polling is as much art as science. But pollsters feel that new methods of indirect questioning, in which Roper has done much work, now give accurate results.

Gallup believes the polls to be valuable checks against demagogues and lobbyists. "These men always claim they have most of the people behind them," he says. "The polls show it isn't so." Polls revealed a sharp swing away from the late Senator Joseph R. McCarthy at the height of his attack on the Eisenhower Administration for supposedly "coddling Communists."

"Polls often show that the people are more ready for action than their leaders," Gallup says. He cites a long reluctance, at state level, to adopt programs for control of venereal diseases, because of the politicians' fear that the public would be offended by discussions of the problem. Polls showed the public to be not at all squeamish, and control programs were adopted in many states.

But there is a difference between asking a man how he feels about the use of the word "syphilis," and how he feels about the political future. He can readily answer the first question. He may not have the answer to the second question in him; it may be in process of being formed, a long, inchoate thought, without foreseeable end.

Most of the polling organizations are basically market research firms.

They supply undoubtedly valuable information to their business clients about the products consumers would like to have. (Gallup's American Institute of Public Opinion does no private polling for either business or political customers; all the others do.) Roper admits that political polling is more difficult than market research. "We'd have a much easier life if we gave it up," he says, "but we can't resist the challenge."

Gallup, a dedicated worker in his field, says cheerfully that there are only two things in life he feels absolutely certain about—"that at some future date the 'polls will go wrong' again, especially in a close election, and secondly, that no other method will be found—apart from sampling of the kind we do—which is more accurate."

A kind of X-factor enters in when a man is questioned about his political preferences which does not operate when he is asked to describe the kind of automobile upholstery he favors.

The poll itself becomes a political event, interfering with the thing observed. It may set up a bandwagon effect, by giving one candidate an overwhelming early lead; no bandwagon effects are set up for upholstery. Or a negative bandwagon effect may be created, by frightening off other potential candidates, leaving them without the will, perhaps without the funds, to fight. Or a useful debate may be blocked, in the course of which the voter's thoughts might have become clarified, and the shape of his political longing might have become manifest to himself.

For each poll catches the voter at a moment in time, and fixes him there, like a painting; but the political maturation that is going on in him is a process, and he himself may be largely unaware of it. It might even culminate in the way he reacts to a face on the television screen, two nights before election day. Perhaps the X-factor is nothing more than the mind and spirit of man. That is not easy to catch in a net, glory be!

95. A SENATOR LOOKS AT THE POLLS
by Albert Gore*

Mr. Gore: Mr. President, I am concerned with the significance which a considerable number of people attach to political polls. It is because so many people think they are important that they have become an unduly significant factor in our national politics.

This undue influence, as I see it, is the only really important fact about political public opinion polls. But this is important. It is important because our democratic processes are involved, and to some extent prejudiced.

Insofar as accuracy in depiction or prediction of the way the mass of our people will vote in a national election is concerned, I consider most

* United States Senator from Tennessee since 1953, lawyer, and former member of the United States House of Representatives (1939-1953). This selection is from remarks by Senator Albert Gore to the Senate, Aug. 22, 1960, 106 *Congressional Record*, 15775-15780. Deletions *passim*.

of the political polls, including the Gallup poll, as almost meaningless and in many instances misleading. This conclusion is the result of considerable observation and study over a period of 6 months.

Yet I found some Republicans quite gleeful and some Democrats virtually wringing their hands when the Gallup poll published August 17, 1960, showed Senator Kennedy trailing Vice President Nixon 50 percent to 44 percent. I think such an influence is entirely unjustified, and to the extent that it affects or may affect the judgment of the people or the attitudes of our leaders, it is a disservice to our elective process to attach such importance—indeed, any measurable importance—to such a political poll.

The public statements of Senator Kennedy's press secretary, Mr. Pierre Salinger, tend to give the poll some credence. He is quoted as saying:

Polls are not an absolute science; they are an indication.

With respect to Senator Kennedy, Mr. Salinger added, "He's been behind before."

Now, whether Senator Kennedy is behind or out in front cannot be proven by the meager Gallup sample.

I say meager because, in a letter to me on January 3, 1960, which I inserted in the *Congressional Record*, Dr. Gallup wrote:

Our national sampling unit is made up of 1,500 adults.

Now, this amounts to less than two hundredths of 1 percent of the adult citizens of the United States, and, for example, about 1 person, man or woman, well- or ill-informed, in every third county in Tennessee.

It is interesting that Mr. Gallup would find only 6 percent of the people undecided this far from election day. This is particularly interesting in view of the fact that on November 3, 1952—one day before election day—Dr. Gallup showed 13 percent of the people undecided. Now, I have no national poll to prove how many people are now undecided as to how they will ultimately vote in November, but I venture the suggestion that 16 percent or even 26 percent would be more realistic than 6 percent at this date. Indeed, I am reliably informed that another recent poll taken since the two political conventions with a considerably larger sample than Dr. Gallup's meager 1,500, showed 24 percent undecided. . . .

Incidentally, Dr. Gallup has a remarkable record of inaccurate prediction. As an example, I should like to read the first four paragraphs of a column written by George Gallup appearing on the front page of the Washington Post on November 3, 1952. The headline is "Nip-and-Tuck Race Tuesday Indicated in Final Survey":

Princeton, N.J., November 2.—Final poll results, based upon interviewing through Thursday, show Dwight D. Eisenhower and Gov. Adlai E. Stevenson coming down the homestretch in a tight race for the popular vote majority.

That is quite a prediction, is it not, Mr. President? In his letter to me Dr. Gallup claimed he predicted the Eisenhower victory in 1952. Let us see what he said. He said:

> They were . . . coming down the homestretch in a tight race for the popular vote majority.
>
> Latest figures show the race has narrowed since the last report. Continuation or acceleration of the trend to Stevenson, reported in earlier surveys, would give him a majority of the popular vote on election day.

This is his prediction of the Eisenhower victory. I continue to read:

> The electoral vote, which will decide the winner, depends upon four key States—New York, Illinois, Ohio, and California—where latest figures show the candidates running virtually even.

His latest figures, according to the column, indicated the candidates were running virtually even in New York, in Illinois, in Ohio, and in California. When the real poll was taken the next day General Eisenhower received 59½ percent of the total of Eisenhower and Stevenson votes in New York and Governor Stevenson received 40½ percent. In Illinois General Eisenhower received 55 percent and Stevenson 45 percent. In Ohio Eisenhower received 56.8 percent and Stevenson received 43.2 percent. In California Eisenhower received 56.9 percent and Stevenson 43.1 percent. This was the real poll.

I have read from the column and the poll by which Dr. Gallup claims he predicted the Eisenhower victory. If Senators can find such a prediction in it, I shall be pleased for one of them to point it out.

Mr. Long of Louisiana: Mr. President, will the Senator yield?

Mr. Gore: I yield.

Mr. Long of Louisiana: If I correctly understand the Senator's point, he is saying that not only was the Gallup poll incorrect in 1948, but also in 1952, only 4 years later, after the pollsters had undertaken to correct the mistakes which were apparent in 1948. Dr. Gallup predicted a nip-and-tuck race, pinpointing the four major States, and insofar as the general experience in those States was concerned the victory was a landslide victory on that occasion for President Eisenhower.

Mr. Gore: The Senator is correct.

Mr. Long of Louisiana: Four years previous the poll had predicted a landslide for Mr. Dewey, and Mr. Truman was elected?

Mr. Gore: The Senator is correct. Despite this, many people continue to attach great importance to the Gallup poll. I think it is wholly unjustified. It is virtually meaningless.

Mr. Long of Louisiana: Perhaps the significance of what the Senator has said about the Gallup poll in regard to 6 percent of the people being undecided, may be missed. I have known of many polls taken in the State of Louisiana, which had a larger sampling in the State than the Gallup poll has nationwide. In other words, I have seen polls taken in regard to elections with some 1,000 or 1,500 people sampled in the State of

Louisiana alone. The coverage would be 50 times as close as Dr. Gallup was able to arrange.

MR. GORE: It would be 50 times as great.

MR. LONG of Louisiana: I refer to a State which has less than 2 percent of the national population. Almost as many people were polled as Dr. Gallup has polled over the entire Nation. Therefore, the population was covered 50 times as closely, we might say, as the Gallup poll covers the United States, by simply polling 1,500 people nationwide.

About 3 or 4 months previous to an election it is rather typical to find an undecided factor of about 26 percent. That is somewhat normal. My guess is that if Dr. Gallup had been in a position to poll more closely and had placed in doubt those who were really in doubt, he would have come up at this stage with a showing of around 20 to 30 percent of the persons undecided as to how they will vote. It is ridiculous to say that only 6 percent of the people at this time are "undecided." I can assure anyone that such a result would be ridiculous in Louisiana at this time.

MR. GORE: I agree with the Senator that it is ridiculous. In my opinion, if any further evidence were needed to discredit the validity or importance of the poll, this should be it. I thank the Senator. . . .

MR. LONG of Louisiana: Mr. President, will the Senator permit me to engage in a little more colloquy with him?

MR. GORE: I yield.

MR. LONG of Louisiana: My experience in public affairs has been that even in connection with a well-taken poll, in which a relatively high percentage of people are polled, such as the polls to which I have referred that have a coverage of 50 to 100 times as thorough as Dr. Gallup undertakes to achieve, I would nevertheless insist that there must be a margin of error to be expected. A somewhat standard margin would appear to be about 10 percent. With such margin, if the poll predicted that one would get 50 percent of the votes, he might get as high as 55 percent or he might get as low as 45 percent.

MR. GORE: Which would mean the difference between a landslide victory and an ignominious defeat.

MR. LONG of Louisiana: It could very well be.

MR. GORE: Then, there is 1948, when all the polls elected the wrong man. Dr. Gallup predicted that President Truman would receive only 44.5 percent of the popular vote. He missed it by 12 percent—5.4 divided by 44.5. Yet in his booklet entitled "The Story Behind the Gallup Poll," Dr. Gallup claims to have missed it by only 5.4 percent. This is twisted arithmetic. By the same calculation, he claimed that he missed the vote for Henry Wallace by only 1.6 percent. He predicted that Mr. Wallace would receive 4 percent of the popular vote. Actually he received only 2.4 percent. Now, this is a 40 percent error. But by the Gallup computation method of "percentage points" this margin of error is reduced from 40 percent to 1.6 percent.

We recall that in 1956 T. Coleman Andrews, former Commissioner of Internal Revenue, was a candidate for President with a third party nomination. Dr. Gallup predicted that he would receive 1 percent of the vote, or more than 600,000 votes. Actually Mr. Andrews received only 134,000 votes. Yet by the Gallup computation of margin of error he missed the T. Coleman Andrews vote by less than seven-tenths of 1 percent. What a convenient method of calculating one's error. My banker will not let me get by with it.

Mr. Long of Louisiana: Mr. President, will the Senator yield for an observation at that point?

Mr. Gore: I yield.

Mr. Long of Louisiana: If the margin of error were computed in the manner in which I or any layman would compute it, Dr. Gallup missed his prediction by a margin of 4 to 1. He missed it as 1 is to 4. While he predicted that a candidate would receive 600,000 votes, the candidate received only 134,000—one vote for every four that Mr. Gallup predicted. Had Mr. Andrews been paying for this service and the poll taker predicted he would get four times the number of votes which he actually received, he would not hire that group to take any more polls for him, even though the poll taker might think he was within his margin of error.

Mr. Gore: According to Dr. Gallup's computation, if T. Coleman Andrews had received twice the number of votes that Dr. Gallup predicted, Dr. Gallup's percentage of error would have been only 1 percent. If he had received no votes at all he would have been only 1 percent wrong, which is remarkably twisted arithmetic.

This is a publicity guessing game. In addition to its prejudice of our elective process, I am concerned that so many publishers of great newspapers, at a time when world tension and national and international affairs compete for space on the printed pages to inform our people, large areas of printed space on the front pages of our daily newspapers are devoted to this worthlessness.

Mr. Long of Louisiana: Mr. President, will the Senator yield further?

Mr. Gore: I yield.

Mr. Long of Louisiana: I believe one reason why the poll information could not be an accurate reflection of what the people are thinking is depicted in this example. Suppose we should try to find how many persons should be polled in a city the size of New Orleans in order to determine how an election would go. In a city of that size, about 600,000 people, a number of 1,000 would be an appropriate number to sample to see how the election was likely to go.

As the Senator from Tennessee well knows, this is a Nation of 180 million people. As the Senator has so well pointed out, the same principle would be applied if one were to go into his State of Tennessee and ask a single person how that person expected to vote, and then proposed by that person's vote to guess how the people of three counties would vote on the basis of a single expression of opinion. Obviously the sample is much too thin.

Mr. Gore: That person whose opinion was sought might not even vote. He might never have been a voter.

MR. LONG of Louisiana: The number sampled in that case is so very scant, as the Senator said, that it puts one in the position of participating in a guessing game.

In my hometown of Baton Rouge, La., I might very well sample perhaps 300 or 400 people and come up with a fairly accurate guess as to how the city or the parish would go, especially if a scientific sampling principle were used. But if I were to sample only a single person or two or three in that entire city, the chances are very slim that I would come up with an accurate guess.

MR. GORE: The fact that political polls are accurate or inaccurate is not the important element to which I wish to call the attention of the Senate. It is not their accuracy or inaccuracy that urges me to take the time of the Senate to speak upon this subject. They have become political phenomena. The Gallup Poll has become a political event, largely, I believe, because so many newspapers give the poll such wide publicity.

Such polls interfere with our elective processes. Not only do they exercise an influence upon the voters, but we observe events such as occurred recently in connection with Governor Rockefeller of New York. I remember that a story was written after the Governors' conference in Puerto Rico, to the effect that Governor Rockefeller would determine whether he would enter the race for President upon the basis of his standings in the political polls.

When it comes to pass that the Governor of the largest State in our Union can base a major political decision as to whether he will seek the Presidency of the United States upon political polls, then I think it is time for the Senate and the Subcommittee on Privileges and Elections to take a look at political polls.

The danger is that they will be used to influence public opinion, rather than to reflect it. No pollster is held to task for any poll except his last one before election day, and some of them tend, as Dr. Gallup clearly did before the 1952 election, to crowd the middle. What of the interesting polls that are taken 3 months, 2 months, and 1 month before election day? There are many ways that they can be used, to which I will refer later.

MR. LONG of Louisiana: Mr. President, will the Senator yield?

MR. GORE: I yield.

MR. LONG of Louisiana: Of course, the Senator well knows that the important thing in public affairs is not what the people think before they have heard the arguments; the important thing is what they think after they have heard the arguments. It may very well be that when the public has not considered the issue they may think entirely different from the way they may feel after the issue has been discussed. People may have all sorts of misunderstanding about an issue, but when a candidate goes to the people and explains the issue, the people may agree with him, even though they may have been in disagreement with him on the issue before that.

MR. GORE: I would rather risk the opinion of the junior Senator from Louisiana about the political attitude of the people of Louisiana than rely on a poll of 25 or 30 people, well or ill informed, selected at random, in the State of Louisiana. That is only a preface to saying that in all of my talks with my Democratic colleagues—and I have not talked to every one of them, but many of them—only one Democratic Senator has expressed in my hearing the view, either before the national conventions or since, that Vice President Nixon would run as strong a race in his State as Governor Rockefeller would run as the Republican nominee. That opinion is not reflected in the polls. If a real poll were taken, the story might be different.

Mr. LONG of Louisiana: Perhaps those Democratic Senators were speaking in terms of how the people thought they would vote after the issues had been presented, which no poll can show at this point.

Mr. GORE: Dr. Gallup is by no means the only pollster whose polls have been proven almost meaningless. Indeed, there have been many others. Just recently the Chattanooga News–Free Press in my State conducted a statewide poll in the Democratic senatorial primary contest between my colleague, Senator Estes Kefauver, and Judge Andrew Taylor. The final tabulation was 1,913 for Taylor and 1,687 for Kefauver, a 53 percent win by Taylor. But when the real poll was taken, Senator Kefauver won by 65 percent of the vote. I cite, too, the polls in the West Virginia presidential primary. Also the polls on the British election last year.

But despite all this evidence, the political poll and political pollsters are now to have their Rose Bowl game in the presidential election of 1960. Will their forecast be on the nose or will they again elect the wrong man? This is interesting speculation. But if the standing of a candidate in the public opinion polls has a psychological and political effect upon the voters or the candidates, as I regret may be the case, then it is a matter of importance which requires public attention. This is why I speak on the subject today.

Every so often President Eisenhower says something with which I agree wholeheartedly. Such an instance occurred last Wednesday when someone asked the President about the most recent political poll. The President is reported to have said:

> No one should be pessimistic or discouraged by some straw in the wind and certainly he should not be complacent with another straw that seems to point favorably in his direction.

Although the popularity of the political poll has reached a high mark only in relatively recent years, formal political polling is by no means a product of the 20th century. Recognized as the first published American political poll was one conducted in 1824 by the Harrisburg Pennsylvanian at Wilmington, Del. In that poll, Andrew Jackson received almost twice as many votes as the ultimate presidential winner, John Quincy Adams.

The history of election polling can roughly be divided into three distinct periods. The era prior to 1936 has been well described as the "catch-as-catch-can" period and that subsequent to 1936 to about 1950 can be considered as the "quota" period. Since about 1950, we have had the "probability" period. Undoubtedly at any given time during any of these periods it has been thought that the methods employed at that particular time were the ultimate in polling technique. However, the occurrences of mispredictions have convinced the almost unconceivable pollsters that polling perfection was a long way off.

In the "catch-as-catch-can" period, responses were solicited haphazardly by mail, by clip-out ballots appearing in newspapers and magazines, some by personal interview, and by almost any other rapid manner which would add to the total number polled. Emphasis was on quantity. The period ended abruptly with the collapse of the Literary Digest poll. Earlier successes had given the Digest poll tremendous prestige as its predictions in three previous presidential campaigns had been successful. Of all the polls conducted in 1936, the one by the Literary Digest was easily the most widely known; now it is the most widely remembered. The Digest, we may recall, predicted a landslide victory for Alf Landon. Well, there was a landslide all right, only it was in the opposite direction than had been predicted. Franklin D. Roosevelt in that election received all but 8 of the 531 electoral votes. With this demonstration of polling inaccuracy, "finis" was written to the Literary Digest and the "catch-as-catch-can" period and to the political career of Mr. Landon.

The so-called quota sample, which gives the second period its title, was in wide use until a few years ago. A cross section of the adult population was laid out—so many college graduates, so many men under 30, so many women over 50, so many in high income brackets, and so forth. Once the sample was drawn up, the interviewers would have the task of finding the required number of people in each category for interview. This method placed much discretion in the hands of the interviewers and it relied on uncertain predetermined population categories. The biggest reversal in the quota period was the victory of President Truman in 1948, when the Gallup poll and others predicted firmly that the next President of the United States would be Thomas E. Dewey. A letter which I received from Dr. Gallup and which I inserted earlier in the *Congressional Record* stated:

> A whole book was written on the 1948 election, based upon the post mortem conducted by the Social Research Council. Chiefly the error was due to the failure to poll up to the end of the election.

Dr. Gallup says further that his final election survey in 1948 was completed on October 15, only about 3 weeks before the election. He indicates that the lesson he and others learned from the 1948 election was the importance of taking polls right up to the time of the election. Presuming Dr. Gallup's chief reason for the failure of the 1948 polls is fully justified, this leads me to inquire:

Following this line of reasoning, how can Dr. Gallup claim any accurate predictive value in presidential popularity polls taken months before an election, if Dr. Gallup dismisses as unreliable a poll which is completed just 3 weeks before an election?

In recent years, especially since the Truman victory, pollsters have turned from the quota method to the so-called probability sample or a modified version thereof and we are now in the "probability period." The probability sample reportedly is obtained by a technical and complex method whose announced objective is to give every adult in the United States an equal chance to be polled. If for example, one resides in the second house from the corner facing north, there is a slim possibility that one would be included in some sampling unit.

Today, then, political polling is in the "probability period." Twelve years ago, in 1948, a gross misguess by most so-called scientific guessers led to the end of the quota period. Twelve years earlier, in 1936, the "catch-as-catch-can" period ended abruptly with a major polling setback. Whether or not this 12-year progression will continue in 1960 remains to be seen.

I doubt that it would, because some pollsters have learned one lesson. They crowd the center near election day and use fuzzy language to avoid being stuck with gross mispredictions.

From a small beginning in 1824, political polling has expanded, as I have said, until today more than 30 firms are engaged in the public-opinion business. In addition to the type of polling done by Dr. Gallup, Mr. Elmo Roper, and a few others, today much of the polling is private opinion-taking done under contract for individuals. An outstanding feature of the private poll, as opposed to a newspaper survey, is that the candidate who contracts for it is free to make public any favorable finding and, at the same time, suppress any unfavorable findings.

Now I should like to discuss some of the salient points respecting polls and polling technique.

SIZE OF SAMPLE

Dr. Gallup has a sample poll of 1,500. Mr. Elmo Roper has a sample of 3,000. Other pollsters have more, some less. Dr. Gallup and other pollsters contend that the size of the sample is far less important in achieving reliable and valid results than several other factors. I concede there may be some truth in this statement, particularly since I have considerable misgivings about some of the other factors connected with political polling, to which I shall later refer. Still I feel the size of the sample merits close scrutiny. As a layman, I would question that a straw poll of less than 1 percent of the people could under any reasonable circumstances be regarded as a fair and meaningful cross section test. This would be something more than 500 times as large a sample as Dr. Gallup takes.

In 1944 a committee of the House of Representatives, headed by the then Representative and now the junior Senator from New Mexico, Clinton P. Anderson, conducted a study of political polls. The committee appointed a technical committee to examine the data and statements submitted by Dr. Gallup. The committee was composed of representatives from the Bureau of the Budget, the Bureau of the Census, and the Bureau of Agricultural Economics, which, of course, engage in considerable statistical analyses. Upon examination of Dr. Gallup's testimony and statistics, the technical committee stated in its report:

The size of the samples used for many of the States was not large enough, even if properly drawn, to insure reliable individual State estimates based solely on polls of the voting population. The use of a size of sample adequate to insure reliable results for individual States might have involved more expense than the Gallup organization could afford.

Mr. President, this was in 1944. I recognize that, especially because of the historic 1948 miscalculation, polling organizations have made some alterations in their polling methods. I believe, though, that the committee very properly questioned the adequacy of the sample size in 1944. I would still question it today.

SAMPLE SELECTION

Tied in closely with sample size is the selection of the sample itself. I referred to the composition of the sampling unit earlier in tracing the history of political polling. There is widespread agreement that no accuracy whatsoever can be claimed if, from the very beginning, the subjects polled are not truly representative of the entire area polled. Are the middle-aged South Georgia farmer, the young Oklahoma oilman, the New York career woman, and myriad other such groups and classes adequately represented in such a small sampling unit? They should be if the sample selected is to be an accurate mirror of the area polled. Is this usually the case? It deserves looking into.

MAKEUP OF POLLING BALLOT

It is apparent that polling organizations exercise their own judgment in determining who should be considered a political candidate. We are told, in addition to announced candidates, names are suggested by political writers and county political chairmen. Mr. Kenneth Fink, director of the Princeton Research Service, has written me:

I, too, have been disturbed by the fact that the United States has no real national presidential primaries. As a result, the polls, including our own—willy nilly—are in the position of practically determining who the presidential candidates for the two major political parties are to be.

At times the exercise of judgment by the pollster in the selection of names for his polling card may be extremely poor. On occasion the name of a person who in no way expects to be, and cannot logically be, a candidate appears on the polling card. Any votes such a person receives, merely out of familiarity with the name, would detract from the totals of other actual or truly potential candidates, and the results would thus be distorted.

It is generally recognized that the positioning of a key question or a series of questions in itself can make an important difference. Although political polling does not deal primarily with a key question or a series of questions, the positioning of names on the polling ballot is deserving of close study. Is there an advantage given to the name listed first or last? Marketing authorities advise that the first glance in merchandising is of the utmost importance. Does the same hold true for political polling?

FAMILIARITY WITH POPULAR NAME

In response to my question whether political polling is a reflection of familiarity with a name or names, Mr. Roper replied:

> It is certainly much more a reflection of a familiarity with names than anything else—until after the campaign itself has started.

In an experimental poll recently conducted in Washington by members of my staff, we exercised the same privilege which pollsters do. We picked our own candidates and placed them on the ballot card in the order we desired. In addition to the names of more likely candidates, we included two possible but certainly not probable candidates with popular family names. John D. Eisenhower and Franklin D. Roosevelt, Jr. As I reported to the Senate in an earlier address, the attraction of these two well-known names drew either first- or second-place support from 25 percent of the Washingtonians indicating Democratic leanings, on the Democratic ticket.

INTERVIEWERS

Most organized political polling is now done by personal contact. Unrepresentative balloting by mail was held to have been partially responsible for the gross error in the Literary Digest poll in 1936. When a system of interviewers is utilized, there exists the question of objectivity. There is always the possibility that the actions or comments of the interviewers, however slight or unintended they may be, or however intentional they may be, will have an influential effect upon the person being interviewed. Some polling organizations claim to have highly trained and skilled interviewers, and this I do not question.

Referring once more to the investigation of the 1944 political polls, the House technical committee, referring to the 1944 Gallup poll, reported:

> Partly as a result of manpower shortages and to maintain low costs, the 1944 election poll was conducted by relatively untrained enumerators with relatively little supervision in the field. Better training and closer field supervision would undoubtedly improve the reliability of the results obtained and would be important factors in assuring that sampling instructions are scrupulously followed, that a representative cross section of voters is interviewed, and that errors in response are minimized.

Perhaps the Gallup organization has improved. Dr. Gallup, however, recognizes that this is a legitimate criticism.

ESTABLISHMENT OF INTENT OF VOTING

Another pitfall is the fact that the pollster may be able to find out how the voter says he will vote, but cannot determine accurately whether he is really going to vote. A national poll theoretically samples the opinion of the entire qualified adult populace, but not everyone bothers to vote. Many times a series of questions is used in an effort to determine just who is going to vote. But according to Mr. Roper:

Many more people claim they are going to vote than actually do vote. In fact, this is one of the chief problems we face, and we have a rather elaborate battery of questions out of which we hope to gain a fairly accurate impression of who is likely to vote and who is not likely to vote, even though they contend vigorously they will.

In addition to the problem of establishing the intent of voting, the qualification for voting must also be considered. The inclusion of those not qualified or those having no intention of voting would, of course, increase the possibility of error.

HANDLING THE UNDECIDED VOTE

There undoubtedly has never been a time when every person polled had his mind made up as to who his favorite candidate is. We had such an experience in the experimental poll conducted in Washington. It is the undecided vote and how to handle it in the tabulations that poses a major problem for all pollsters. Once more the element of judgment on the part of the pollster enters in deciding how to handle the undecided responses. It is the view of many that the silent vote swung last year's British elections, in which most polls failed to predict the decisiveness of the sweeping Conservative victory. A normal method is to split the undecided vote according to the percentages of the decided vote in the poll. This method, however, has been seriously questioned on the ground that the undecided people are in many ways unique and their mental processes differ from those with strong party or candidate affiliation. There is, therefore, no reason to assume that they will make up their minds and split their votes in the same way as do the "decided" voters. A few percentage points off either way in the tabulation could make a substantial difference in the predicted outcome. . . .

Mr. President, I have referred specifically to seven problem areas confronting the pollster, problems which make precise predictions impracticable and render political polling scarcely more than an informed guessing game. There are other related problems, which I shall not take time now to discuss, which, when coupled with one or several of these seven, or even occurring alone, have the potential to throw an otherwise valid poll off considerably.

Even if the pollsters could come up with a valid poll, we cannot escape the possibility that political polls may be subject to manipulation and misuse. Mr. Roper, in speaking of the political poll, has told me:

> I feel the tool with which we're working is a potentially very valuable one, but like many other thoughtful people, I have misgivings about its possible misuse.

I certainly concur in that statement.

I go back once more to the 1944 investigation. Dr. Gallup has said that—

> From the Gallup Poll started in 1935, we have always regarded ourselves as factfinders—or, in a sense, as score keepers.

In spite of this statement, however, it appears that upon occasion Dr. Gallup, and possibly other pollsters, has exceeded the "factfinders" limit in reporting the poll results. At one point during the 1944 Presidential campaign, Dr. Gallup subtracted 2 percentage points from the Democratic Party total for what he said was an anticipated low turnout. On this point, I refer again to the report of the House Technical Committee:

> The manner of handling the adjustment of anticipated low election turn-out, which resulted in a 2-percentage-point subtraction from the estimated Democratic vote as reported in the actual canvass of the voting population for the three polls published prior to October 27, is subject to criticism. While it is at least debatable whether or not such subtraction was justified in the publication of the early polls, the publication of the estimates, without specific mention of the character and magnitude of the subtraction, may be questioned. This is particularly true, inasmuch as turn-out adjustment had such an important effect in the early Gallup predictions for the 1944 election. Moreover, the adjustments were made on a rough appraisal basis rather than on any basis of precise quantitative measurement, and the same percentage was applied uniformly to the States without regard to local variations. . . .

MR. GORE: Mr. President, it is my hope that some curiosity—and, indeed, some concern—has been aroused about political polling procedure, and especially about some of the pitfalls and some of the dangers to our democratic system that I have mentioned. I submit, however, that concern is of no significance unless the published results of political polls have an influential effect in our election processes or upon our leaders. From my study, I have concluded that polls do, in fact, have an influence which is entirely unjustified.

Most pollsters firmly maintain that there is little evidence that published results of their polls even weeks or months before an election have a "band-wagon" effect, pulling voters to the candidate which polls show is in the lead. They point to the miscalculated 1948 campaign, and state that if the desire to be with the winner had operated, Dewey would have won by the greatest majority of the century. Reasoning, however, does not permit dropping from our consideration the "band wagon" possibility. The operation of the "band-wagon" effect does not necessarily have to lead to an out-and-out victory for the candidate who polls erroneously predict is in the lead.

MR. CARLSON: Mr. President, will the Senator from Tennessee yield?

MR. GORE: I yield.

MR. CARLSON: The Senator from Tennessee has clarified a point I was going to make. He stressed the fact that the polls might influence the voters. But certainly that was not proven to be the case in the 1948 election.

MR. GORE: It was not proven that the polls were decisive in their effect, Mr. President. Nevertheless, I would not want to dismiss as inconsequential the influence of the polls.

It is true that, despite the fact that all the polls showed that Governor

Dewey would be elected, Mr. Truman won. But it does not necessarily follow that the polls had no influence.

Polls may have a very great influence months ahead of a political campaign. They may discourage campaign contributors. They may affect morale of campaign workers. They may influence local political leaders who wish to be with the winner to make an alinement, which they may maintain through the campaign.

The influence of polls in the early stages of the campaign may be more effective than very near the end of the campaign, when some pollsters crowd the middle line in order to protect themselves, as I have said.

There is reason to believe that, especially in the case of early polls, when the minds of many voters have not been made up, published results of polls do exert an influence. Even if such an influence amounts to only 1 percent, the damage to our election processes has been done. That might be the margin between victory and defeat of a good man.

The danger is that polls will be used to influence public opinion rather than reflect it. To the extent that the public considers the polls seriously meaningful, this danger is magnified.

96. DO THE POLLS SERVE DEMOCRACY?

by John C. Ranney *

Most of the current controversy over public opinion polls has centered about the question of their accuracy: the reliability of the sample taken, the impartiality of the sponsorship, the honesty of the interviewer and the person interviewed, the fairness of the questions, the measurement of intensities or gradations of feeling, and the validity of the analysis of interpretation.[1] These are all, admittedly, important questions; but they tend to ignore or to beg one which is both more important and more theoretical: Assuming that the polls were to attain a miraculously perfect and unchallengeable accuracy, would they, even then, contribute significantly to the working of democracy?

One's first inclination is to take it for granted that the answer is "Yes." No principle, in democratic theory, has been more fundamental than the belief that political decisions ought to be made by the people as a whole or in accordance with their desires.[2] Yet no principle, in democratic practice, has proved more difficult of precise application. In theory, even when doubts are entertained as to the rationality, the objectivity, and the

---

* Late professor of government at Smith College. This selection is from John C. Ranney, "Do the Polls Serve Democracy?" *Public Opinion Quarterly*, vol. 10, issue no. 3, Fall, 1946, pp. 349-360. Reprinted by permission.

[1] See, for example, in recent issues of the *Public Opinion Quarterly* (Vol. 9) Edward L. Bernays, "Attitude Polls—Servants or Masters?" pp. 264-268b (Fall, 1945); Gordon M. Connelly, "Now Let's Look at the Real Problem: Validity," pp. 51-60 (Spring, 1945); Leo P. Crespi, "The Cheater Problem in Polling," pp. 431-445 (Winter, 1945-46); and the symposium, "The Discussion Goes On," pp. 403-410 (Winter, 1945-46).

[2] I do not intend to imply, of course, that this is the whole of democratic theory.

capacity of the ordinary citizen, modern democratic writers have continued to find the essence of democracy in popular participation in policy-making.[3] But in practice, it has long been apparent that our electoral system, as a reflection of popular wishes and as a channel for popular activity, leaves a good deal to be desired.

Various improvements have been suggested, ranging from the initiative and the referendum to proportional or functional representation. But none of these devices, except by placing an intolerable strain on the voter, has solved the problem of how to reflect simultaneously the great diversity of his interests and attitudes on different issues.[4] The result, under our present system, is that even if one assumes that the voter does anything more than choose between the personalities of rival candidates, an election approximates what has been called "plebiscitary democracy." It is a way of approving or disapproving in the most general terms the policies of the party or individual in office and of renewing or transferring this exceedingly vague mandate for the coming term of office.[5]

Such a check and consultation is much better than none at all. Notwithstanding its resemblance to some of the dictatorial plebiscites, it permits, in a free society, the expression of at least the major discontents. But consultations which are so sweeping and which occur at such rare intervals are only the thinnest caricature of the democratic belief that the health of the community depends upon the personal, active, and continuous political participation of the body of its citizens.

It is here that the polls are supposed to make their great contribution. By separating the issues from one another, by stating them simply and clearly, and by covering the electorate completely and continuously, they avoid the most obvious obscurities, strains, and distortions of the older procedures. If to these virtues one might add unchallengeable accuracy, the

---

[3] For some recent statements on this subject, see Carl L. Becker, *Modern Democracy* (New Haven, 1941), p. 7; James Bryce, *Modern Democracies* (New York, 1924), Vol. 1, p. 20; Francis Coker, *Recent Political Thought* (New York and London, 1934), p. 293; Carl J. Friedrich, *The New Belief in the Common Man* (Boston, 1942), pp. 31, 221; Harold J. Laski, "Democracy," *Encyclopaedia of the Social Sciences* (New York, 1932), Vol. 3, pp. 80, 84; John D. Lewis, "The Elements of Democracy," *American Political Science Review*, Vol. 34, p. 469 (June, 1940); A. D. Lindsay, *The Modern Democratic State* (London, New York, Toronto, 1943), Vol. 1, pp. 267-268; Charles E. Merriam, *The New Democracy and the New Despotism* (New York, 1939), pp. 11-12; Francis Graham Wilson, *The Elements of Modern Politics* (New York and London, 1936), pp. 189-190, 247.

[4] John Dickinson, "Democratic Realities and the Democratic Dogma," *American Political Science Review*, Vol. 24, p. 300 (May, 1930); Pendleton Herring, *The Politics of Democracy* (New York, 1940), p. 329; E. E. Schattschneider, *Party Government* (New York, 1942), p. 33. For the weaknesses of such devices as the initiative and referendum, see Harold F. Gosnell, "The Polls and Other Mechanisms of Democracy," *Public Opinion Quarterly*, Vol. 4, p. 225 (June, 1940); A. Lawrence Lowell, *Public Opinion and Popular Government* (New York, 1913), pp. 152-235; William B. Munro, "Initiative and Referendum," *Encyclopaedia of the Social Sciences*, Vol. 4, pp. 50-52.

[5] The electoral system is, of course, supplemented by the interpretive work of the pressure groups, and they provide an important instrument for popular political action. But it is obvious that many of them are at least as much concerned with misrepresenting or flouting public opinion on individual issues as with representing it.

well-known dream of Bryce would be realized: the will of the majority of
the citizens could be ascertained at all times; representative assemblies and
elaborate voting machinery would be unnecessary and obsolete.[6]

ATTACKS ON THE POLLS

Not everyone has rejoiced over this possibility. Anyone who agrees with
Hamilton, for example, that the people are turbulent and changing, seldom
judging or determining right, is hardly likely to welcome a device to make
the voice of the people (which decidedly is not the voice of God) more
audible than ever.[7] Nor is this attitude likely to surprise or disturb the
genuine democrat.

What should disturb him, however, is the fact that there are many people
who consider themselves good democrats and who nevertheless consider the
polls a menace to democracy. The objections of this second group deserve
more systematic attention than they have yet received.[8]

THE DESTRUCTION OF LEADERSHIP

The first and most frequent of these objections is that the polls destroy
political courage and leadership. Every adequate government, it is maintained, requires these qualities in its officials. They can exist, however, only
where there is freedom and flexibility and where the statesman is not
bound, either in form or in fact, by rigid instructions from the voters. The
government official, whether Congressman or administrator, has access to
information which is beyond the reach of the ordinary voter, and he has
something more than the ordinary voter's leisure in which to consider it.
To subject his judgment to the ill-informed and hasty judgment of the electorate is to commit the political crime of rendering a decision before considering the evidence on which it ought to be based. It is true that the polls
have no official standing and cannot bind any office-holder. But, the charge
runs, the official who wants to keep his job will abandon his duty of
analyzing and judging proposed policies in favor of the simpler, and safer,
device of deciding as the polls tell him to decide.[9]

So far as the legislator is concerned, there are several weaknesses in this
argument. Simply as a matter of fact, it would be extremely difficult to
show that the polls have had a decisive effect in determining the voting
habits of any substantial number of representatives.[10] It is one of the

[6] *The American Commonwealth* (New York, 1920), Vol. 2, p. 262.

[7] See, for example, Col. O. R. McGuire, "The U.S. Constitution and Ten Shekels of
Silver," *Public Opinion Quarterly*, Vol. 4, pp. 232-235 (June, 1940).

[8] In this discussion I am not taking up the question of the accuracy of the polls,
since the principle at issue is really one of whether even an accurate poll is a desirable
thing in a democracy.

[9] For a concise statement of this position, see Eric F. Goldman, "Poll on the Polls,"
Public Opinion Quarterly, Vol. 8, pp. 461-467 (Winter, 1944-45), and the literature
there cited.

[10] More Congressmen would be influenced by the polls, and the argument strengthened, if there were more general confidence in their accuracy and if the returns were
published by Congressional districts. For evidence of the influence of polls on legislators, see L. E. Gleeck, "96 Congressmen Make Up Their Minds," *Public Opinion Quar-*

dubious advantages of the American system that it is extremely difficult to allocate responsibility; and even in those cases in which responsibility can be fixed, the ordinary voter is only too likely to be ignorant of the voting record of his representative. The average Congressman on the average issue need not worry too much about the opinion of his constituents in the mass. What he does need to worry about is the opinion of specific organizations and individuals inside his constituency, especially the political machines and the organized pressure groups. Any Congressman who is concerned with political realities knows that it is more important to appease a well-disciplined minority, which can deliver the votes on election day, than to gratify an unorganized and casual majority, the intensity of whose convictions and the efficacy of whose action is far less likely to be decisive. If the polls exert any influence at all, therefore, they tend to moderate or deflate rather than to reinforce the special pressures already influencing legislators.[11]

The absence of scientific methods for measuring opinion, moreover, has never prevented politicians from trying to guess what it is. The representative, if such there be, who follows the polls slavishly would have his ear well to the ground under any circumstances. It is hard to see how democracy is undermined or its moral fibre destroyed simply by providing him with more reliable methods of judgment. It can hardly be urged that so long as a representative is going to vote according to public opinion anyway, the more distorted his picture of it, the better. Nor would it be easy to show that, among those restrained by the polls, the idealists seriously outnumber those who would otherwise follow the dictates of selfish and limited interests.

Finally, it should be remembered that public opinion is not so definite and rigid as the argument implies. In some instances, changes have been both rapid and extreme, and political leaders have often been in a strategic position to influence or shape it. In addition, men of intelligence and foresight who understand the probable effects of an unfortunate policy or the misconceptions on which it is based can anticipate the ultimate revulsion of public feeling and act accordingly. Voters, it should be remembered, do not always show great tolerance for the Congressman who excuses his own past mistakes with the plea that most of the electorate, at the time, shared his way of thinking.

Although the argument concerning the destruction of leadership is usually made with the legislator in mind, it actually has somewhat more factual strength in the case of the policy-making administrator. Surveys indicate that he is more likely to pay attention to the results of the polls, and he is also more likely to have expert or specialized personal knowledge as an

---

terly, Vol. 4, pp. 3-24 (March, 1940); George W. Hartman, "Judgments of State Legislators Concerning Public Opinion," Journal of Social Psychology, Vol. 21, pp. 105-114 (February, 1945); Martin Kriesberg, "What Congressmen and Administrators Think of the Polls," Public Opinion Quarterly, Vol. 9, pp. 333-337 (Fall, 1945); George F. Lewis, Jr., "The Congressmen Look at the Polls," Ibid., Vol. 4, pp. 229-231 (June, 1940).

[11] The opposite assumption is the basis for the New York Times' frequently quoted criticism of the polls, November 13, 1936, p. 22.

alternative basis for decision.[12] There is a possibility, at least, that his interest in the polls may indicate a tendency to subordinate his own well-informed judgment to the opinion of the electorate; and there is a further possibility that he may become so dependent upon it that he will take no action at all when that opinion is confused or divided or simply non-existent.

On the other hand, the administrator is, if anything, subject to even greater and more numerous pressures than is the Congressman. For him, therefore, the polls may be even more important as a basis for resisting minority pressures in the public interest. Moreover, like the legislator, he has considerable power to influence public opinion, although his methods are somewhat different; and a precise knowledge of what that opinion is can be an important help in enlightening or changing it.

The factual basis, or lack of basis, for the argument that the polls destroy leadership is less important, however, than two of the argument's theoretical implications.

The first of these is that government officials, whether legislators or administrators, constitute something of an expert body, possessing unusual intelligence, information, and skill, and that to this body the voter, because of his personal inadequacy, should delegate his power.

This argument, however, proves too much. If expertness is to be the criterion for the right to participate in government, the ordinary Congressman would himself have difficulty in qualifying.[13] Even the policy-making administrator, in an age of increasingly voluminous and technical legislation, is likely to be an expert only in the most attenuated sense of the term.[14] To be sure, both he and the legislator must make use of the knowledge and experience of the expert, especially in determining the technical means to achieve broader and predetermined objectives. But when it comes to determining the objectives themselves—and it is with objectives rather than with means that the polls are primarily concerned—the democratic theorist who would free leaders from the restraint of a less well-informed public opinion is, consciously or unconsciously, on the road to what, since the days of Plato, has been the radically undemocratic position of urging rule by some elite.

The second theoretical implication is the even stranger one that ignorance of what the people want and feel is a positive advantage in a democracy. Yet few defenses of democracy have been more persuasive than the one which insists that democracy alone provides the government with adequate information about the desires and attitudes of the people and that, even if these prove to be ignorant or irrational, it is only on the basis of such information that a government can act intelligently. Legislation cannot be

---

[12] Kriesberg, *op. cit.* The polls, it should be noted, are generally concerned with broader matters of policy rather than with the technical matters in regard to which the expert has the greatest competence.

[13] John Dewey, *The Public and Its Problems* (New York, 1927), p. 124; Herman Finer, *The Theory and Practice of Modern Government* (New York, 1934), pp. 100-101.

[14] It is difficult to make a simple generalization on this subject because of the great variety of levels and types of administrative activity. But the quality of mind of the policy-making administrator is fundamentally different from that of the true expert, whose field of competence is necessarily quite restricted.

separated from the practical problem of administration and enforcement; and it is of fundamental importance, in framing and administering laws with intelligence, to understand, as one of the vital factors in the situation, the state of public feeling.[15] This is not to say that opinion is the only factor to be considered. It is saying that it is an essential element in the rational analysis of any political situation. People will not refrain from having opinions and acting upon them simply because they are not asked what they are. Yet statesmen, whether legislators or administrators, are unlikely to have direct personal knowledge of these feelings; and the weaknesses of elections, the press, and other methods of identifying them have been obvious for decades. Here, therefore, if anywhere, the polls, far from being a menace to democracy, give substance and meaning to what has always, in theory, been one of its outstanding advantages.[16]

In short, so far as this first set of criticisms is concerned, the polls are neither, in fact, so destructive of leadership and courage as critics suggest nor, in theory, so incompatible with the traditional meaning of democracy. On the contrary, the unstated assumptions of the critics tend logically to a conclusion which is itself basically undemocratic.

THE POLLS AS A BRAKE ON PROGRESS

A second set of charges is remarkable for the way in which it parallels Hamilton's way of thinking for purposes which are quite un-Hamiltonian. Its authors agree that the intelligence and judgment of the people is to be distrusted—not because of their radicalism, however, but because of their conservatism and complacency. Far from being a source of turbulence and unrest and a menace to private property and traditional ways of doing things, the people are so conventional and so contented with things as they are that they constitute a formidable brake upon progress, slow to see the need for drastic social changes and slow to take the necessary steps, always doing too little and always doing it too late. Public opinion polls, by giving publicity to these attitudes, increase their force. In addition, the attention and deference paid them intensify both the complacency of the people and their confidence in their own mystical rightness. What the people need, however, is to develop some realization of their own shortcomings and some willingness to leave to the expert those matters of which he alone can judge.[17]

Here, as in the case of the first set of criticisms, it would be difficult to prove that the people are actually more conservative than their representatives. Some observers, in fact, contend that the polls have repeatedly shown the people to be far readier than Congress to accept progressive ideas.[18] But even if the people proved, as a regular matter, to be a hindrance to

---

[15] Ernest Barker, *Reflections on Government* (London, 1942), pp. 74-75, 199, 230; John Dewey, *op. cit.*, pp. 206-208; George Gallup and Saul Forbes Rae, *The Pulse of Democracy* (New York, 1940), p. 265; A. D. Lindsay, *op. cit.*, pp. 144, 269-270, 274.

[16] The use already made of the polls by such governmental agencies as the Department of Agriculture indicates their value in making this theoretical advantage of democracy into a real one. See Friedrich, *op. cit.*, pp. 117, 217-221.

[17] Robert S. Lynd, "Democracy in Reverse," *Public Opinion Quarterly*, Vol. 4, pp. 218-220 (June, 1940). See also Lindsay, *op. cit.*, p. 234.

[18] William A. Lydgate, *What America Thinks* (New York, 1944), pp. 2-8.

progress, certain theoretical difficulties would remain. It is undoubtedly true that the process of modern government is too technical and complex to be directed in detail by the ordinary citizen and that the skill and knowledge of the expert must be tapped in a responsible fashion. Yet this argument is too easily confused with the very different argument that the "responsible" expert must be given the power to introduce, according to his own judgment, drastic social changes. There is, to begin with, a certain lack of logic in an argument which speaks of ultimate responsibility to the public while maintaining that "trained intelligence" must none the less be free to introduce the drastic changes which the uninformed public is not prepared to accept. And the more one tries to avoid this dilemma by limiting responsibility to the voter in favor of government by a disinterested, wise, and public-spirited elite, the more the criticism becomes one, not of the polls as a hindrance to the operation of democracy, but of democracy as a hindrance to progress.

The defense of democracy, which is as old as Aristotle, does not need to be elaborated here.[19] But it is essential to point out, as Plato himself came to recognize, that no government, however well intentioned, can force a community to move in directions in which it does not want to move, or to move much more rapidly than it would otherwise move, without resorting to instruments of force and tyranny which are incompatible with both the spirit and the practice of democracy.[20]

THE POLLS AS A MISCONCEPTION OF DEMOCRACY

The third, and by far the most valid, criticism which can be made of the polls is that they represent a fundamental misconception of the nature of democracy. Bryce's picture of a society in which the will of the majority of the citizens would be ascertainable at all times is neither a very profound nor a very realistic picture of democratic society. Democracy is not simply the ascertaining and the applying of a "will of the people"—a somewhat mystical entity existing in and of itself, independent, unified, and complete.[21] It is the whole long process by which the people and their agents inform themselves, discuss, make compromises, and finally arrive at a decision.[22]

The people are not the only element in this process, and they are not necessarily the agent which is best suited to each part of the task. In general, the executive and the administrative services are best fitted to see policy as a whole and to prepare a coherent program as well as to handle the technical details of legislation. The legislature provides a forum in which the different interests within the country can confront one another in a regularized way, as the people cannot, and acquire something of the mutual understanding and comprehensive outlook which is essential for the

---

19 For a further discussion of this subject, see Friedrich, *op. cit.,* pp. 41. 217-218, 220-221; John D. Lewis, *op. cit.;* Lindsay, *op. cit.,* pp. 268-277.

20 Dewey, *op. cit.,* p. 208; Dickinson, *op. cit.,* pp. 301-304; Laski, *op. cit.,* p. 84; John Stuart Mill, *Considerations on Representative Government* (New York, 1862), pp. 55-80.

21 Dickinson, *op. cit.,* pp. 288-289; John D. Lewis, *op. cit.,* p. 471.

22 Barker, *op. cit.,* pp. 36, 67; C. Delisle Burns, *Democracy* (London, 1929), p. 90; Dickinson, *op. cit.,* pp. 291-292; Friedrich, *Constitutional Government and Democracy* (Boston, 1941), p. 255; Lindsay, *The Essentials of Democracy* (Philadelphia, 1929).

satisfactory adjustment of interests. The people themselves, finally, can express better than any other agency what it is they need and want.

None of these functions, it is true, belongs exclusively to any one agency, nor can any be separated rigidly from the others. The process of discussion and adjustment is a continuous one, carried on on all levels. There is a constant interweaving and interpenetration of talk and action subject to no precise demarcation but in which it is none the less essential that each agency refrain from functions which are beyond its competence.[23] In this process the operation of the polls may be positively harmful, not in interfering with "government by experts" as more frequently charged, but in emphasizing the content of the opinion rather than the way in which it is formed and in focussing attention on the divergency of opinion rather than upon the process of adjusting and integrating it.

To say this is not to urge a restriction on popular participation but to emphasize its real nature and function. Popular participation in government is thin and meaningless if it is nothing more than the registering of an opinion. It becomes meaningful to the extent that the opinion is itself the product of information, discussion, and practical political action. There is something not only pathetic but indicative of a basic weakness in the polls' conception of democracy in the stories of those who tell interviewers they could give a "better answer" to the questions if only they had time to read up a bit or think things over. It is precisely this reading up and thinking over which are the essence of political participation and which make politics an educational experience, developing the character and capacity of the citizens.[24]

The polls, however, except as their publication tends to stimulate political interest, play almost no part in this process. They make it possible for the people to express their attitude toward specific proposals and even to indicate the intensity of their feeling on the subject; and they can distinguish the attitudes of different social and economic groups from one another. But they provide no mechanism on the popular level for promoting discussion, for reconciling and adjusting conflicting sectional, class, or group interests, or for working out a coherent and comprehensive legislative program.

In fact, far less perfect instruments for discovering the "will" of the voters are often much more effective in arousing popular participation. The initiative and the referendum, for all their weaknesses, stir opponents and advocates of measures to unusual activity and stimulate a large proportion of the voters, rather than a small selected sample, to consider and discuss the issues.[25] Similarly, the privately-conducted British Peace Ballot proved

[23] Barker, *op. cit.*, pp. 43-44; Dickinson, *op. cit.*, p. 301; Finer, *op. cit.*, pp. 99-101, 369; Friedrich, *Constitutional Government*, pp. 255, 415; John D. Lewis, *op. cit.*, pp. 469-470; Merriam, *op. cit.*, pp. 120-121; Mill, *op. cit.*, pp. 115-116.

[24] To some, this is the greatest justification of democracy. Burns, *op. cit.*, pp. 7, 71-72, 88-89; Coker, *op. cit.*, p. 294; Dewey, *op. cit.*, pp. 206-208; Mill, *op. cit.*, pp. 69-80, 170; Alexis de Tocqueville, *Democracy in America* (New York, 1838), p. 232.

[25] Edwin A. Cottrell, "Twenty-Five Years of Direct Legislation in California," *Public Opinion Quarterly*, Vol. 3, pp. 30-45 (January, 1939). For a different opinion, see Waldo Schumacher, "Thirty Years of People's Rule in Oregon," *Political Science Quarterly*, Vol. 47, pp. 242-258 (June, 1932).

to be an educational experience for the entire British people.[26] Even the much maligned *Literary Digest* Poll performed a greater service in arousing thought and discussion than did its more accurate competitors.

In short, the polls are not concerned with, and provide no remedy for, the gravest weaknesses in the democratic process. If one thinks of democracy in practical terms of discussion and political activity rather than of a disembodied "will," the great need is to get rid of the obstacles to popular education, information, debate, judgment, and enforcement of responsibility. To do this, there must be a multiple effort directed against a multiplicity of evils. To mention only a few of these, the political education in most of our schools, handicapped as they are by conventional school-boards and the fear of controversy, is wretchedly inadequate. In too many cities the sources of information are insufficient, the news itself distorted, and the free competition of ideas seriously restricted.[27] In general, our facilities for discussion—clubs, unions, pressure organizations, forums, round-tables, and the radio—provide no adequate successor to the town meeting in the sense of active and responsible personal participation.[28] More fundamentally, the undemocratic character of much of our economic and social life is a real hindrance to the growth of political democracy.

Moreover, even if our political education were magnificent, the channels of information completely clear, the facilities for discussion abundant, and the spirit of democracy universal, the obscurity and confusion in our political system, resulting from its checks and balances and its lack of party discipline, would make it almost impossible for the ordinary voter to understand what is going on, to pass judgment intelligently, and to place responsibility. Yet any government in which the people are to share must at a minimum be comprehensible. Obscurity and anonymity kill democracy. These defects, however, are present in our government, and about them the polls can do very little.

SUMMARY

The chief advantage of the polls is that, in an age of increasing strain upon traditional democratic procedures, they have made a constructive technical contribution by reflecting sensitively and flexibly the currents of public feeling, by making this information available to political leaders in a way which is neither rigid nor mandatory, and by testing the claims of special interests to represent the desires of the people as a whole. These are services performed by no other agency, and they should not be underestimated.

[26] Dame Adelaide Livingstone, *The Peace Ballot* (London, 1935), pp. 19-29.

[27] The development of the one-newspaper pattern is particularly unfortunate. Oswald Garrison Villard, *The Disappearing Daily* (New York, 1944), pp. 3, 5, 10-12. See also Morris L. Ernst, *The First Freedom* (New York, 1946), xii and *passim* for a survey not only of the newspaper but of book publishing, the radio, and the motion picture.

[28] On the need for new devices for discussion, see Harwood L. Childs, *An Introduction to Public Opinion* (New York, 1940), p. 137; Coker, *op. cit.,* p. 373; Harold D. Lasswell, *Democracy through Public Opinion* (Menasha, Wisconsin, 1941), pp. 80-95; Merriam, *On the Agenda of Democracy* (Cambridge, 1941), pp. 21-22; Joseph R. Starr, "Political Parties and Public Opinion," *Public Opinion Quarterly,* Vol. 3, pp. 436-448 (July, 1939). For a more optimistic picture, see Friedrich, *Constitutional Government,* p. 546.

But if, in a democracy, the health of the community depends upon the personal, active, and continuous political participation of the body of its citizens, this contribution is a limited and even a minor one. Even when used with the greatest accuracy and intelligence, the polls cannot achieve any fundamental improvement until our political system itself is simplified, until the lines of responsibility are clarified, and until devices are discovered for increasing the direct participation of the people, not simply in the registration of their aims, but in the deliberative procedure which is the real heart of democracy.

97. DR. GALLUP ANSWERS HIS CRITICS
by George Gallup *

When the first polls of public opinion appeared in the fall of 1935, politicians viewed them with suspicion. Political scientists and social scientists generally ignored them. And Washington correspondents and columnists openly attacked them. Only a few hardy editors and publishers had faith enough to print poll results.

To many there seemed to be something almost indecent about the very attempt to measure public opinion. Wasn't it an invasion of a field which should be left free and undefiled? Wasn't Montaigne right when he said: "Public opinion is a powerful, bold, and unmeasurable party"?

Those of us who launched this effort to measure public opinion by sampling methods did not regard public opinion as a mysterious force which manifested itself in unknown ways. To us, as to James Bryce, public opinion was the "aggregate of the views men hold regarding matters that affect or interest the community."

EARLY SUCCESS AND OPPOSITION

In the two decades since polls of public opinion were first launched, the frigid climate in which they started has moderated somewhat. But on occasion, icy blasts still sweep down upon us. Since we began this effort to gauge public opinion on a periodic basis, we have had our lucky breaks, as well as our unlucky ones. Against the misfortune of 1948 must be set the good luck of 1936—a time when we required a good break.

When polls were first launched, we had told the world that the new system of sampling was superior to that followed by the *Literary Digest*. In fact, we were emboldened to say in print as early as July of 1936 that the *Literary Digest* would be wrong in November, and we were foolhardy enough to predict just what the *Digest* would find from its post-card poll of many millions.

Our predictions about the *Literary Digest* poll results came true. The

* Public opinion analyst and founder of the American Institute of Public Opinion and of other specialized polling organizations. This selection is from George Gallup, "The Changing Climate for Public Opinion Research," *Public Opinion Quarterly*, vol. 21, issue no. 1, Spring, 1957, pp. 23-27. Reprinted by permission of the author and publisher.

Digest was not only wrong, but its error was almost exactly what we had said it would be. The sampling polls were on the right side, and by this very fact could lay claim to superiority over the straw vote methods which had prevailed up to that time.

The success of the scientific sampling polls in 1936 by no means stilled the critics. Many had paid little or no attention to them up to this point. Now they began to view polls with genuine alarm. Some claimed we were not measuring public opinion; public opinion could not be measured, at least not by the procedures we were using. Others said we were not scientific. Still others thought that we were an evil force which might lead the country straight to Hell—or to direct democracy, which they regarded as equally terrifying. An Oregon congressman introduced a bill to curb polls. The fight was on.

The most bitter critics were those whose political views placed them at the extreme right or left on the political spectrum. I can remember addressing a meeting on a college campus where I advanced the idea that the common people of the country display an extraordinary amount of good sense about the issues of the day. The left-wingers in the group nearly stoned me from the campus. In a naive way I had thought that they would welcome any facts showing that the collective judgment of the little people of the country was surprisingly sound. The extreme right wing was equally bitter in its views. Through the years the *Chicago Tribune* never missed an opportunity to flail us.

THE STORM AND SILVER LINING OF 1948

The battle raged back and forth, with the polls gaining ground through the pre-war and war years. Then came 1948! The avalanche descended. Latent animosities harbored against us were brought to the surface in an explosive manner. To many, the wrong predictions of 1948 proved that we were a snare and a delusion. It mattered little that nearly all the political writers and pundits of the country also were wrong. We were the proper whipping boy. . . .

The reaction of the public to the 1948 debacle—in contrast to that of the critics—was enlightening. The public was quite willing to forgive and forget. We saved many a client newspaper by encouraging editors and publishers to send out their own reporters to poll their readers about polls and whether the newspaper should continue to print them. In every single instance a sizable majority of the public said, in effect: "Everyone makes mistakes. Polls serve a useful purpose. We hope you continue to print them."

In crucial periods support often comes from unexpected quarters. I recall the anguish of the late Dr. Kinsey when his first book had created a furore. He had expected that the ordinary citizens of the land would resent his intrusion into the sacrosanct area of sex, but that his fellow professors and scientists would rush to his defense. He was crushed to find that the opposite was the case. The cruel blows were struck by fellow professors. The public, on the other hand, looked upon his work as a worth-while contribution to a subject which needed ventilation and illumination.

LESSONS FROM ELECTION FORECASTING

All of us in the field of public opinion research regard election forecasting as one of our least important contributions. It has always seemed much more worth while to report public opinion on the political, social and economic issues of the day. At the same time, standing up to the rigorous test of election forecasting has had the effect of improving methods and increasing our knowledge of voting behavior.

Since 1936 we have carried on a broad experimental program to establish a system of predicting voting behavior. As early as 1940 we were experimenting with the use of the voting precinct as a sampling unit. In 1950, for the first time, we based our final prediction of the Congressional elections on a survey of a large sample of precincts. We used a precinct sample again in the 1952 Presidential election to measure late trends but not for our final figures. In 1954 and 1956, however, we depended entirely on the precinct sample.

We do not know whether a better system will be developed or not. The important point to keep in mind is that it took sixteen years of experimental work before we developed the sampling system we now have. Maybe this "lead" time is too long; but it must be kept in mind that congressional elections come only at two-year intervals, and presidential elections at four-year intervals. In most areas of the physical and social sciences, experiments typically can be performed in a short period of time. In polling on national elections, the opportunities to test methods are few and far between.

The 1948 election, bitter experience though it was, proved a blessing in disguise. We learned that political sentiment can shift in the last few days of a campaign, and that we would have to devise machinery which would permit us to measure trends to the very end of a campaign. This we did in the elections of 1950 and 1952.

An interesting fact about the 1956 election is that if polling had stopped as early as it did in 1948, our error, percentage-wise, would have been almost as great as in 1948. When the revolts broke out in Hungary and the invasion of Egypt began, Eisenhower's strength jumped four and one-half percentage points. At election time, Eisenhower received 58 per cent of the national total—or three percentage points more than had been shown by polls made ten days previously.

No system of polling is perfect. And I have stated publicly many times that almost certainly polls will be wrong in some future election, particularly one which breaks near the fifty-fifty line. But we can look forward with greater equanimity to this part of our work. In this department, at least, the labors of the last twenty years have not gone for naught.

SOME DEPRECATORY VOICES CONTINUE

Despite the mountain of evidence that has been built up since 1935 to support the contentions of poll takers regarding the reliability of their findings, acceptance on the part of text-book writers proceeds at glacial speed.

Invariably, any reference to polls must be qualified by some such statement as: "If you can believe the polls . . ." For some strange reason, this
rule seems to apply only to those in our special field of polling. Fellow
workers in other vineyards would regard it as definitely insulting if a survey
of public opinion, undertaken in the Yale or Chicago Graduate School, were
qualified by some such remark as, "If you can believe anything which
comes out of the Yale Graduate School . . ." One can only hope that the
day will arrive when our academic friends and text-book authors will have
enough intellectual courage either to leave out their qualifying remarks, or
else to come right out and say that we are mountebanks!

And while I am on this point, I would like to bring up another long-
standing complaint of those of us who conduct polls. This is the use of
quotation marks around the word "scientific" when applied to polls. If our
work is not scientific, then no one in the field of social science, and few of
those in the natural sciences, have a right to use the word. Even under the
most rigid interpretation of the word I venture to say that our work fully
qualifies.

Another deprecatory word which gets under our skins is the word "commercial." Anything that pays its own way is supposed to be contaminated
in some strange manner. If the same standard is used, then most of the work
which has been carried on in the field of nuclear physics is "commercial."
At least this work is being paid for, and certainly it is not pursued solely
for the sake of science. Most of the work now being done by university
survey centers is paid for by business, charitable, or governmental organizations, but I believe that these university centers would resent the description of their work as "commercial."

WISDOM OF THE PUBLIC

I have often been accused of believing that "the voice of the people is
the voice of God," but the two decades during which I have directed polling
of the American public on nearly all the important issues of the day have
provided me with ample opportunity to judge the collective views of my
fellow citizens.

I am firmly convinced that if, during the last twenty years, public opinion had manifested itself only by letters to congressmen, the lobbying of
pressure groups, and the reports of political henchmen—as it did prior to
the advent of the sampling polls—the country would almost certainly have
been led in the wrong direction at several critical points. The public is almost always ahead of its governmental leaders. This statement has been
made many times, and it can be supported by an overwhelming volume of
evidence amassed during these two decades on nearly every conceivable
issue—political, social and economic.

Perhaps in an ideal state this should not be the case. But the plain, unadorned fact is that it is true, and anyone who wishes to compare the views
of the people, as shown by thousands of cross-section surveys, with official
views expressed in Washington, can easily prove it to his own satisfaction.
It is my earnest hope that future writers on the subject of polls and pollsters
will take time to consult the record before reaching their conclusions.

CHAPTER XIV

The Competence of Public Opinion

Is public opinion equal to the demands of our times? Or is authentic popular government becoming increasingly obsolete as planetary problems of ever-greater scope and complexity crowd upon us, problems which reduce the "average man" to a state of confusion and bewilderment and a sense of helplessness? The symbolic appurtenances of popular rule must of course be cherished, social conventions being what they are, but do not the harsh realities and fateful decisions of the mid-twentieth century demand that experts decide? The power elitists remind us that real power in our technical and specialized society inevitably must and already largely has come to rest in the hands of the experts and the "insiders."

Skeptical of the people's capacity to judge the manifold questions of the 1920s, Norman Angell's skepticism would logically deepen today. The well-informed citizen of the 1960s should presumably know the background, the major current facts, the policy alternatives and their consequences involved in atomic testing and atomic controls, disarmament, American policy toward Red China, the gold outflow, the latest Berlin crisis, the West's worsening position in southeast Asia, our Latin-American relations, the Cuban threat, the Algerian crisis, Arab-Israeli tensions, the problems of the newly emerging African nations, American defense policy, the vital aspects of the cold war, the foreign-aid programs and their pitfalls, the problem of accelerated national growth amidst structural unemployment, inflation, the farm surplus dilemma, Federal aid to education, antitrust policy, tax reform, national emergency strikes, national health insurance, the welfare state, organized crime and its relation to politics, desegregation, and civil rights—to say nothing of the myriad problems of state and metropolitan government and of the local community.

A staggering list, indeed, the mere contemplation of which might tempt the most conscientious citizen to toss in the sponge. And if the conscientious are so tempted, what of the multiplied millions who could not care less or who are simply too busy or too distressed or too harassed to give public affairs the sustained attention responsible citizenship presumably requires? Little wonder, as James Bryce declares in a famous passage, that the common man's ideas "when examined, mostly resolve themselves into two or three prejudices and aversions, two or three phrases or catchwords suggesting or embodying arguments which the man who repeats them has not analyzed."

Yet Lord Bryce reminds us that the relative ignorance of the common man is almost matched by the ignorance of the college educated, whose indubitably superficial acquaintance with political questions provides precious little justification for the smug satisfaction he often feels in comparison with the intellectually unwashed.

If the average man cannot hope to arrive at thoughtful, informed, perceptive opinions on the manifold issues of our day, what is his role? Charles Horton Cooley contends that people may be individually ignorant, but, taken collectively, they are shrewd judges of men. Lord Bryce, too, shares the faith that the common man can distinguish a great man from a demagogue. Yet, vital though this quality may be, the people have not discharged their responsibilities when they mark an X, even a wise X, in a column on a ballot. Democracy is more demanding than that.

A few glimpses into modern democratic political processes may help clarify the issue. Normally, American politics involves a series of struggles between conflicting interest groups representing segments of the people. These groups operate in conjunction with a government which reflects the pressures upon it, but which also expresses the independent judgment of its members to a significant degree. The struggle takes place under the critical surveillance of an attentive minority of journalists, editors, and other influential persons who refine and discipline the interest-group struggle while guiding, warning, stimulating, and restraining the ultimate decision makers. It is no derogation of popular government to recognize that an effective democracy ordinarily depends more on the size, vigor, and quality of its informed minority than upon the knowledge and judgment of its "average" citizen. Certainly this minority is of special concern to public officials, partly because of its directly affirmative contributions, partly because it may rouse the larger public when blunders are made or when matters of great moment are at stake, and partly because it helps create the general climate of opinion which conditions the public at large to think well or ill of an official or candidate or party or administration.[1]

If most people are indifferent to most issues, their deep-lying prejudices, fears, aspirations, and moral sentiments nonetheless set effective limits to the area of choice in which decision makers function (elitists please note). If the various so-called elites ignore or flout these profoundly significant though often unobtrusive attitudes, they will soon enough discover that the somnolent public has become an outraged public which asserts its will and exacts its vengeance in unmistakable fashion. The health of a society, then, depends heavily on the nature of the popular predispositions which determine what a people will not stand for.

Popular opinion is important in another setting, too. When a situation is perceived to vitally affect the "common man's" current or future welfare, a kind of mass awakening will again occur. The public consensus (if one exists) or majority opinion (if it forms) is then reflected either in a popular veto of a proposed course of action or in decisive support for one alternative against others. (If neither a consensus nor a majority opinion becomes apparent, other factors will of course be determinative.) Thus, even if mass opinion rarely expresses itself, its potentiality continuously shapes the

---

[1] It might be added that the defense of civil liberties—except in time of great national tension—depends far more on the courage and democratic commitments of a dedicated minority than upon the sentiments of the people in general. The latter frequently are either unconcerned or disposed to adopt more restrictive attitudes than the traditions of freedom require.

political landscape, and its active expression is always crucial when it bears the stamp of unity.

While all this attests to the crucial character of mass opinion in a democracy, it tells us nothing about its minimum obligations today or about its wisdom. It can be argued that such opinion is qualitatively adequate only if:

1. Political parties feel constrained to present competent candidates, and the public, for the most part, chooses wisely among them.

2. Candidates and elected officials do not jeopardize their careers when it becomes necessary for them to ask the people to accept hardships, make painful choices, and assume burdens commensurate with the urgencies of the times.

How well does mass opinion measure up to these standards? With empirical evidence difficult to come by, it may seem presumptuous to hazard a judgment. Yet most students of politics apparently believe that national party conventions in recent decades seldom reject the clearly superior candidate for the clearly inferior one. Nor has the public been unwilling to follow the great leaders when they have presented themselves—Washington, Jefferson, Lincoln, Theodore Roosevelt, Wilson (in his early presidential years, at least), Franklin D. Roosevelt, Truman (in foreign affairs, at least). But on the other hand, neither did the public become disillusioned with such mediocrities as Grant and Coolidge. In sum, the people will not—usually—reject great leadership, but neither will they demand it. They may be content with, or even enthusiastic about, an undistinguished chief executive, as long as he avoids egregious blunders, isn't too unlucky, and doesn't violate the public's conception of presidential proprieties.

This, surely, is cause enough for alarm. As the twentieth century advances, it is compellingly evident that the people require the stimulus of forceful executive leadership which can limn the problems and imperatives of the times, impress their gravity upon the people, and mobilize popular support for the policies required to deal with them. The nation can afford lackluster legislatures and courts, perhaps, but it can no longer tolerate the proportion of indifferent presidents it has so comfortably endured throughout its history.

Writing seventy-odd years ago, Lord Bryce spoke of the complacency which afflicts a self-governing and prosperous people. They seem "to need a succession of men like the prophets of Israel," he declared. Not discerning these, he found some comfort in the "wholesome irritation" supplied by some leading writers of his day and by "the philanthropic reformers who tell more directly upon the multitude, particularly through the churches." Were he writing today, he might share the common belief that the chief executive and only the chief executive can arouse the people to a recognition of the perils and opportunities of our age.

James Reston, for one, is convinced that "if great and noble ideas cry out above the advertising jingles," the people will respond. They have demonstrated, in his opinion, "a vast capacity for growth and change." Senator Richard Neuberger agreed. He amassed considerable evidence to support his belief that political leaders are too timid and have too low an estimate of public intelligence and public responsibility. He believed that, if politicians on all levels have the courage to spell out the sacrifices and demands that are needed, the political risks are far less than politicians commonly assume.

Concerning himself primarily with foreign policy, Walter Lippmann, on the other hand, asserts that "successful democratic politicians are insecure and intimidated men. They advance politically only as they placate, appease, bribe, seduce, bamboozle, or otherwise manage to manipulate the demanding and threatening elements in their constituencies." It is politically hazardous to be "right too soon. Very often the penalty is political death." Mr. Lippmann goes on to say that "at the critical junctures, when the stakes are high, the prevailing mass opinion will impose what amounts to a veto upon changing the course on which the government is at the time proceeding." Once aroused, however, the public rushes to extremes, expects the impossible, sees the situation in moral terms of black and white, tends to be vindictive, and creates an opinion milieu in which intelligent foreign-policy formulation is well-nigh impossible.

Dexter Perkins dissents, citing chapter and verse to demonstrate that the public, while its insights and behavior have been less than ideal, has responded to challenges in a reasonably mature and intelligent fashion. He is particularly impressed with the people's support of statesmanlike decisions in recent years, including periods when the President was of one party and Congress of another.

Perhaps it should be added at this point that there is sometimes a tendency to blame national shortcomings on mass opinion when other factors are primarily responsible. If leaders are unduly timid, if no one blows the bugle and points the way, whom and where can the people follow? If public opinion is perverted by the anachronisms and delays and minority tyrannies of Congress, by the frustrations of federalism, by the chaos of our party system, and by malrepresentation and gerrymandering, are the people to blame? If the press entertains rather than informs, if TV lulls rather than educates, are the people wholly at fault? If the "experts" and the political leaders offer the people no remedy for their hobbled and hobbling institutions because no consensus on the remedy exists, wherein lies the guilt? We can hope the people will wisely follow, but we can hardly expect them to lead.

And so to the concluding selections of our studies on the competence of public opinion. It has been some time since the notion was held that the voice of the people was the voice of God, although not a few skeptics still incline to the belief that it is the voice of Belial. The editors of *The Nation* remind us it is neither, but rather "the cry of imperfect, struggling, divine-human man."

Carl Sandburg has the last word. Speaking with a historian's perspective, a poet's grace, and a democrat's faith, he says, "The people have the say-so. Let the argument go on. Let the people listen. Tomorrow the people say Yes or No by one question: 'What else can be done?' In the drive of faiths on the wind today the people know: we have come far and we are going farther yet."

98. BABBITT AS MANAGER OF CIVILIZATION—
IN HIS SPARE TIME

by Norman Angell*

. . . At certain intervals—regular under systems like that of the United States, irregular under the parliamentary systems prevalent in Europe—the ordinary busy citizen is asked, on a given day, to sit in judgment upon his rulers. The manufacturer, professional man, artisan, butcher, baker, candle-stick-maker, barber, in addition to being wise about his own personal affairs, has then to be wise about everybody else's as well; to judge the affairs of the world; to become a statesman dealing with extremely difficult and complex subjects. We are on that occasion rulers of one another: the other men's votes may send your children to their death in war; your vote may help to send your neighbor's. An ordinary election, whether in Britain or in America, compels the voter to pass judgment upon public questions which become continuously more complex. Each decade adds new problems.

Consider just a few of those upon which the busy citizen at any ordinary election is now compelled to pass judgment. There is almost always in some form or another the tariff, the whole issue of free trade and protection about which the professors of economics are themselves in disagreement. It involves difficult related subjects like the right treatment of big business on the one hand—involving the complex trust-busting legislation designed to check its power—and the interests of, for instance, the farming population on the other. Which brings in the question of government aid for the farmer, either by attempts to stabilize the price of his product by the government marketing of surpluses or by such relief as better credit might afford; which brings us to the Federal Reserve policy and the complex question of currency and its control; the incidence of tax burdens, the payment by foreign nations of war debts; the World Court; League of Nations; disarmament; prohibition and its vast ramifications; evolution (now, in some states), the crime wave, the relation of public services like the judiciary and the police to politics; immigration; relations with Mexico, with Russia; the Red menace in the Schools; the Catholic menace, the Klan. . . .

The British voter has an even more difficult job because mistakes matter more in his case and he is confronted with vast reconstructions owing to the revolutionary economic changes that have followed the war. When the tariff is presented to him it is allied to questions like imperial preference

* Newspaperman, lecturer, and writer of books and articles on political and economic subjects. Knighted (1931) and awarded Nobel Peace Prize (1933). Author of *The Great Illusion, The Public Mind, The Story of Money, Preface to Peace, Let the People Know, The Steep Places,* and numerous other works. This selection is from Norman Angell, *The Public Mind,* E. P. Dutton & Co., Inc., New York, 1927, pp. 4-10. Copyright, 1927 by E. P. Dutton & Co., Inc. Renewal, 1955, by Miss Barbara Hays. Reprinted by permission of the publishers.

and he is compelled to balance considerations of present advantage for Britain against the desirability of aiding, even artificially, the development of countries which may furnish a future field of emigration for people of our speech and culture. Which brings us, of course, to problems of the political relation of Britain to the Dominions, and of these to the rest of the world; to the future of the Empire, our proper relation to India; to the Orient, and to the government of subject peoples; and that, of course, involving foreign policy, carries us to questions of military strategy, the desirability of creating this or that naval base; the maintenance of the Navy or the Air Force, the future of the battleship; the League of Nations, disarmament, whether they should be opposed or encouraged; foreign trade and its relation to the American debt and the Gold Standard; inflation; deflation; the relation of currency policy to trade depression and unemployment; the coal subsidy; the proper sphere of Trade Unionism; the relations with Russia; Socialism; religious instruction in schools; the liquor problem; Church disestablishment; divorce; vivisection; compulsory vaccination....

These are a mere selection from a much larger number of problems just as difficult, with which the aforesaid business man, dentist, butcher, baker, or barber has to deal—in his spare time.

For that is the essence of the method. These complex matters, often of war and peace (of life and death, that is), must necessarily be settled casually and hurriedly—can only receive a "spare-time" attention. The immense majority of voters are obliged to give most of their attention and energy to the not very easy job of earning a living. Political decisions obviously cannot receive the kind of intensive attention which a man gives to his means of livelihood, his trade or profession, for which he has had a special training. The decisions which, totalled, make public policy, the collective judgments of modern nations, must be made for the most part on the basis of headlines in the newspapers, gulped hurriedly with the morning coffee; or of casual talk in the train; or formed by catchy slogans which seem to hit the case, but probably only so seem because they happen to be alliterative, or carry a certain rhythm which causes them to stick in the memory. Not much more is possible in our busy world. Yet the barber who would not presume to bob the hair of the least flapper, or shave any man's face, without a special preparation for the job, is usually very positive and unqualified in his political opinions, in decisions upon such subjects as free trade, the way to deal with Germany, or Ireland, or India; on unemployment, the school age, the merits of the submarine as against the battleship. Any victim who has suffered much from the talkativeness of the hair-cutting profession might well wish that he could be as sure about any one of those subjects as the politically minded barber seems to be about all of them.

It is hardly necessary to labor the point that the barber's decision becomes every day more difficult: that the mere march of invention has given him problems of which his grandfather never dreamed. If mail-coach drivers struck, it was inconvenient to a few travellers, but there was no such menace of immediate starvation as that which followed the strike of a few hundred locomotive drivers, compelling action by the community (through the Government—that is to say, ultimately, the voters) for its protection. When transport was by wagons and horses no elaborate legislation touching franchises, rates, company acts, limited liability was necessary; but when the railroad came the barber found it necessary to have opinions about those things, to vote on them, to take action deeply concerning his neighbors and their future.

It is noteworthy in this connection that much of the political machinery which we have applied to democratic conditions has come down to us from those simpler times, and that an instrument suitable enough, it may be, for those conditions is being applied to very different conditions.

One realizes this particularly in observing the operation of the American "Long Ballot"—the method of choosing a long list of public officials by the naïve device of popular election. In Washington's day, when great cities were unknown, it was perhaps a feasible and common-sense arrangement for the inhabitants of a village to assemble on the green (or, in the case of the famous New England town meetings, in the Town Hall) and decide that John would make a good magistrate and James a good policeman. The village had known John and James since childhood. The device was feasible enough.[1] But note what happens when the device, serviceable enough in these conditions, is applied to the conditions of a modern city like New York or Chicago. The voter receives a long list—sometimes running to hundreds of names—of men whom, save with rare exceptions, he has never seen, whose qualifications and respective merits he cannot possibly know. They are candidates for such positions as that of judge, city engineer, surveyor, public health officer, keeper of courthouse records, sheriff, chief of the police. The elector is asked to state whether, in his view, the posts of (say) officer of health, public bacteriologist, or county-court judge (his mind being necessarily in most cases a complete blank as to the necessary qualifications for such work) would be better filled by John Smith (whom the voter has never seen) or Henry Brown (whom equally the voter has never seen and does not know). And so on, with a list of names and offices resembling in some "Long Ballots" a public directory. The head of a great business or institution, having given a life-time to learning his particular job, is compelled often to devote laborious days to such decisions as whether A, B, or C (whose records he knows) is best fitted for a position with the functions of which he has been for years familiar. The assumption behind the electoral method presumably is that the voter going into a booth becomes endowed with some magic quality enabling him to perform miracles of selection which would baffle the greatest administrators in the world, without any of the preparatory labor which the humblest administrator in his private affairs knows to be indispensable. Yet this outrageous farce has continued for generations; nor is it a mere oversight or survival like a picturesque bit of ritual come down to us from feudal times. The attempt to change this method has often been bitterly opposed as a movement away

---

[1] "If," as Aristotle said, "the citizens of a State are to judge and distribute offices according to merit, then they must know each other's characters; where they do not possess this knowledge, both the election to offices and the decision of law suits will go wrong" (*Politics*, Bk. VII, ch. iv.).

from democracy, a "distrust of the people," a reflection upon their "great heart and sound sense."

It is true that the fight about the "Long Ballot" is perhaps now settled. The pendulum even in America has swung far indeed the other way, with towns adopting more and more the city manager method or commission government. It is recognized that the barber is not perhaps quite able in his spare time to decide the respective merits of half a dozen candidates for a judgeship, or for a post as engineer or bacteriologist.

But is he any better able to decide such questions as free trade and protection, the merits of the gold standard as opposed to a managed currency or a bi-metallic standard? These are extremely complex questions about which most divergent views are held by specialists and experts who have devoted life-time study to them. Yet he will have to answer them, and we are faced by the problem of enabling him to do that in some form or other; of helping him to judge as between experts, to apply tests in results where he cannot follow details.

But before we can even start on that task we have to take cognizance of certain characteristics of the public mind as we now know it, and the significance of these characteristics.

Looking back upon the decisions of the nations during these last fifteen years, one is brought face to face with the disturbing phenomenon that just when the facts were plainest the decisions have been most erroneous and disastrous. It is a characteristic of the most damaging mistakes that they have been about extremely simple things, about facts of universal knowledge. The errors have not been due to the intellectually baffling nature of the problems, but to the flat refusal on the part of whole nations to face self-evident facts, because to face them would have meant abandoning the indulgence of a temper, or appetite, or emotion.

Now, if that is true . . . it would serve no purpose to make a democracy more "educated" in the sense of possessing a wider range of knowledge. If the people can disregard in their collective decisions the facts of which they are already perfectly well aware, they can just as easily disregard that further knowledge with which a wider education in this sense of "knowing things" might endow them. . . .

99. EDUCATION, WEALTH, AND THE QUALITY OF OPINION

by James Bryce*

. . . Orthodox democratic theory assumes that every citizen has, or ought to have, thought out for himself certain opinions, *i.e.*, ought to have a definite view, defensible by arguments, of what the country needs, of what principles ought to be applied in governing it, of the men to whose hands

* British lawyer, professor of law, member of Parliament, and diplomat. British Ambassador to the United States, 1907-1913. This selection is from James Bryce, *The American Commonwealth*, Macmillan & Co., Ltd., London, 1889, Vol. II, pp. 212-214.

the government ought to be entrusted. There are persons who talk, though certainly very few who act, as if they believed this theory, which may be compared to the theory of some ultra-Protestants that every good Christian has or ought to have, by the strength of his own reason, worked out for himself from the Bible a system of theology. But one need only try the experiment of talking to that representative of public opinion whom the Americans call "the man in the cars," to realize how uniform opinion is among all classes of people, how little there is of that individuality in the ideas of each individual which they would have if he had formed them for himself, how little solidity and substance there is in the political or social ideas of nineteen persons out of every twenty. These ideas, when examined, mostly resolve themselves into two or three prejudices and aversions, two or three prepossessions for a particular leader or section of a party, two or three phrases or catchwords suggesting or embodying arguments which the man who repeats them has not analysed. It is not that these nineteen-twentieths are incapable of appreciating good arguments, or are unwilling to receive them. On the contrary, and this is especially true of the working classes, an audience is usually pleased when solid arguments are addressed to it, and men read with most relish the articles or leaflets, supposing them to be smartly written, which contain the most carefully sifted facts and the most exact thought. But to the great mass of mankind in all places, public questions come in the third or fourth rank among the interests of life, and obtain less than a third or a fourth of the leisure available for thinking. It is therefore rather sentiment than thought that the mass can contribute; and the soundness and elevation of their sentiment will have more to do with their taking their stand on the side of justice, honour, and peace, than any reasoning they can apply to the sifting of the multifarious facts thrown before them, and to the drawing of the legitimate inferences therefrom.

It may be suggested that this analysis, if true of the uneducated, is not true of the educated classes. It is less true of that small class which in Europe specially occupies itself with politics; which, whether it reasons well or ill, does no doubt reason. But it is substantially no less applicable to the commercial and professional classes than to the working classes; for in the former, as well as in the latter, one finds few persons who take the pains, or have the leisure, or indeed possess the knowledge, to enable them to form an independent judgment. The chief difference between the so-called upper (including the wealthy part of the commercial classes) and humbler strata of society is that the former are less influenced by sentiment and possibly more influenced by notions, often erroneous, of their own interest. Having something to lose, they are more apt to imagine dangers to their property or their class ascendency. Moving in a more artificial society, their sympathies are less readily excited, and they more frequently indulge the tendency to cynicism natural to those who lead a life full of unreality and conventionalisms.

The apparent paradox that where the humbler classes have differed in opinion from the higher, they have often been proved by the event to have been right and their so-called betters wrong (a fact sufficiently illustrated by the experience of many European countries during the last half-century) may perhaps be explained by considering that the historical and scientific data on which the solution of a difficult political problem depends are really just as little known to the wealthy as to the poor. Ordinary education, even the sort of education which is represented by a university degree, does not fit a man to handle these questions, and it sometimes fills him with a vain conceit of his own competence which closes his mind to argument and to the accumulating evidence of facts. Education ought, no doubt, to enlighten a man; but the educated classes, speaking generally, are the property-holding classes, and the possession of property does more to make a man timid than education does to make him hopeful. He is apt to underrate the power as well as the worth of sentiment; he overvalues the restraints which existing institutions impose; he has a faint appreciation of the curative power of freedom, and of the tendency which brings things right when men have been left to their own devices, and have learnt from failure how to attain success. In the less-educated man a certain simplicity and openness of mind go some way to compensate for the lack of knowledge. He is more apt to be influenced by the authority of leaders; but as, at least in England and America, he is generally shrewd enough to discern between a great man and a demagogue, this is more a gain than a loss.

While suggesting these as explanations of the paradox, I admit that it remains a paradox. But the paradox is not in the statement, but in the facts. Nearly all great political and social causes have made their way first among the middle or humbler classes. The original impulse which has set the cause in motion, the inspiring ideas that have drawn men to it, have no doubt come from lofty and piercing minds, and minds generally belonging to the cultivated class. But the principles and precepts these minds have delivered have waxed strong because the masses have received them gladly, while the wealthiest or so-called educated classes have frowned on or persecuted them. The most striking instance of all is to be found in the early history of Christianity. . . .

100. WHAT THE MASSES CONTRIBUTE
by Charles H. Cooley*

. . . The sentiment of the people is most readily and successfully exercised in their judgment of persons. Montesquieu, in discussing republican government, advocated on this ground an almost universal manhood suffrage in the choosing of representatives. "For," says he, "though few can tell the exact degree of men's capacities, yet there are none but are capable of knowing in general whether the person they choose is better qualified than

---

* Eminent early twentieth-century (1865-1929) American sociologist and professor of sociology at the University of Michigan. Author of *Human Nature and the Social Order, Social Organization, Social Process,* and other works. This selection is from Charles Horton Cooley, *Social Organization,* Charles Scribner's Sons, New York, 1909, pp. 142-146. Reprinted by permission of Charles Scribner's Sons. Copyright 1909 Charles Scribner's Sons; renewal copyright 1937 Elsie Jones Cooley.

most of his neighbors."[1] The plainest men have an inbred shrewdness in judging human nature which makes them good critics of persons even when impenetrable to ideas. This shrewdness is fostered by a free society, in which every one has to make and hold his own place among his fellows; and it is used with much effect in politics and elsewhere as a guide to sound ideas.

Some years ago, for instance, occurred a national election in which the main issue was whether silver should or should not be coined freely at a rate much above its bullion value. Two facts were impressed upon the observer of this campaign: first, the inability of most men, even of education, to reason clearly on a somewhat abstract question lying outside of their daily experience, and, second, the sound instinct which all sorts of people showed in choosing sides through leadership. The flow of nonsense on both parts was remarkable, but personality was the determining influence. It was common to hear men say that they should vote for or against the proposition because they did or did not trust its conspicuous advocates; and it was evident that many were controlled in this way who did not acknowledge it, even to themselves. The general result was that the more conservative men were united on one side, and the more radical and shifting elements on the other.

The real interest of the voter at our elections is usually in personality. One likes or dislikes A, who is running for alderman, and votes accordingly, without knowing or caring what he is likely to do if elected. Or one opposes B, because he is believed to be in league with the obnoxious C, and so on. It is next to impossible to get a large or intelligent vote on an impersonal matter, such as the constitutional amendments which, in most of our states, have to be submitted to the people. The newspapers, reflecting the public taste, say little about them, and the ordinary voter learns of them for the first time when he comes to the polls. Only a measure which directly affects the interests or passions of the people, like prohibition of the liquor traffic, will call out a large vote.

On this shrewd judgment of persons the advocate of democracy chiefly grounds his faith that the people will be right in the long run. The old argument against him runs as follows: democracy is the rule of the many; the many are incompetent to understand public questions; hence democracy is the rule of incompetence. Thus Macaulay held that institutions purely democratic must sooner or later destroy liberty or civilization or both; and expected a day of spoliation in the United States, "for with you the majority is the government and has the rich absolutely at its mercy."[2] More recent writers of standing have taken the same view, like Lecky, who declares that the rule of the majority is the rule of ignorance, since the poor and the ignorant are the largest proportion of the population.[3]

To this our democrat will answer, "The many, whether rich or poor, are

---

[1] *The Spirit of Laws*, book xi, chap. 6.

[2] From a letter written to an American correspondent in 1857 and printed in the appendix to Trevelyan's *Macaulay*.

[3] *Democracy and Liberty*, vol. i, chap. 1, page 25 and *passim*. Some of Lecky's expressions, however, are more favorable to democracy.

incompetent to grasp the truth in its abstractness, but they reach it through personal symbols, they feel their way by sympathy, and their conclusions are at least as apt to be right as those of any artificially selected class." And he will perhaps turn to American history, which is, on the whole, a fairly convincing demonstration that the masses are not incapable of temperate and wise decision, even on matters of much difficulty. That our antecedents and training have been peculiarly fortunate must be conceded.

The crudely pessimistic view is superficial not only in underestimating the masses and overestimating wealth—which is, in our times at least, almost the only possible basis of a privileged class—but in failing to understand the organic character of a mature public judgment. Is it not a rather obvious fallacy to say that because the ignorant outnumber the educated, therefore the rule of the majority is the rule of ignorance? If fifty men consult together, forty of whom are ignorant regarding the matter in hand and ten informed, will their conclusions necessarily be those of ignorance? Evidently not, unless in some improbable manner the forty separate from the ten and refuse to be guided by them. Savages and gangs of boys on the street choose the most sagacious to lead in counsel, and even pirates will put the best navigators in charge of the ship. The natural thing, as we have seen, is for a group to defer to its most competent members. Lecky would himself have maintained this in the case of Parliament, and why should it not be true of other groups? I see no reason why the rule of the majority should be the rule of ignorance, unless they are not only ignorant but fools; and I do not suppose the common people of any capable race are that.

I was born and have lived nearly all my life in the shadow of an institution of higher learning, a university, supported out of the taxes of a democratic state and governed by a board elected directly by the people. So far back as I can remember there have not been wanting pessimists to say that the institution could not prosper on such a basis. "What," they said, "do the farmers know or care about the university? How can we expect that they should support astronomy and Sanscrit and the higher mathematics?" In fact there have been troublous times, especially in the earlier days, but the higher learning has steadily won its way in open discussion, and the university is now far larger, higher in its standards, better supported and apparently more firmly established in popular approval than ever before. What more exacting test of the power of democracy to pursue and effectuate high and rather abstract ideals could there well be than this? One who lives in the midst of such facts cannot but discover something rather doctrinaire in the views of Macaulay and Lecky.

If it be true that most people judge men rather than ideas, we may say that democratic society is representative not only in politics but in all its thought. Everywhere a few are allowed to think and act for the rest, and the essence of democratic method is not in the direct choice of the people in many matters, but in their retaining a conscious power to change their representatives, or to exercise direct choice, when they wish to do so. All tolerable government is representative, but democracy is voluntarily so, and differs from oligarchy in preserving the definite responsibility of the few to the many. It may even happen, as in England, that a hereditary ruling class retains much of its power by the consent of a democratized electorate, or, as in France, that a conception of the state, generated under absolute monarchy, is cherished under the rule of the people.

As for popular suffrage, it is a crude but practical device for ascertaining the preponderant bent of opinion on a definite issue. It is in a sense superficial, mechanical, almost absurd, when we consider the difference in real significance among the units; but it is simple, educative, and has that palpable sort of justice that allays contention. No doubt spiritual weight is the great thing, but as there is no accepted way to measure this, we count one man one vote, and trust that spiritual differences will be expressed through persuasion. . . .

101. WHEREIN PUBLIC OPINION FAILS AND SUCCEEDS

by James Bryce *

WHEREIN PUBLIC OPINION FAILS

. . . We may wind up the examination of public opinion by considering what are its merits as a governing and overseeing power, and, on the other hand, what defects, due either to inherent weakness or to the want of appropriate machinery, prevent it from attaining the ideal which the Americans have set before themselves. I begin with the defects.

The obvious weakness of government by opinion is the difficulty of ascertaining it. English administrators in India lament the impossibility of learning the sentiments of the natives, because in the East the populations, the true masses, are dumb. The press is written by a handful of persons who, in becoming writers have ceased to belong to the multitude, and the multitude does not read. The difficulties of Western statesmen are due to an opposite cause. The populations are highly articulate. Such is the din of voices that it is hard to say which cry prevails, which is swelled by many, which only by a few throats. The organs of opinion seem almost as numerous as the people themselves, and they are all engaged in representing their own view as that of the "people." Like other valuable articles, genuine opinion is surrounded by many counterfeits. The one positive test applicable is that of an election, and an election can at best do no more than test the division of opinion between two or three great parties, leaving subsidiary issues uncertain, while in many cases the result depends so much on the personal merits of the candidates as to render interpretation difficult. An American statesman is in no danger of consciously running counter to public opinion, but how is he to discover whether any particular opinion

* British lawyer, professor of law, member of Parliament, and diplomat. British Ambassador to the United States, 1907-1913. This selection is from James Bryce, *The American Commonwealth,* Macmillan & Co., Ltd., London, 1889, Vol. II, pp. 315-334, *passim.*

is making or losing way, how is he to gauge the voting strength its advocates can put forth, or the moral authority which its advocates can exert? Elections cannot be further multiplied, for they are too numerous already. The *referendum*, or plan of submitting a specific question to the popular vote, is the logical resource, but it is troublesome and costly to take the votes of millions of people over an area so large as that of one of the greater States; much more then is this method difficult to apply in Federal matters. This is the first drawback to the rule of public opinion. The choice of persons for offices is only an indirect and often unsatisfactory way of declaring views of policy, and as the elections at which such choices are made come at fixed intervals, time is lost in waiting for the opportunity of delivering the popular judgment.

The framers of the American Constitution may not have perceived that in labouring to produce a balance, as well between the National and State Governments as between the Executive and Congress, in weakening each single authority in the Government by dividing powers and functions among each of them, they were throwing upon the nation at large, that is, upon unorganized public opinion, more work than it had ever discharged in England, or could duly discharge in a country so divided by distances and jealousies as the United States then were. Distances and jealousies have been lessened. But under the system of restrictions and balances, the habit of self-distrust and submission to the popular voice has become unexpectedly strong among legislators.

American legislatures are bodies with limited powers, their members less qualified, by shortness of tenure as well as other causes, for the work of constructive legislation, than are those of most European chambers. They are accustomed to consider themselves delegates from their respective States and districts, responsible to those districts, rather than councillors of the whole nation labouring for its general interests, and they have no executive leaders, seeing that no official sits either in Congress or in a State legislature, or possesses any authority in these bodies. Hence if at any time the people desire measures which do not merely repeal a law or direct an appropriation, but establish some administrative scheme, or mark out some positive line of financial policy, or provide some body of rules for dealing with such a topic as bankruptcy, railroad or canal communications, the management of public lands, and so forth, the people must decide for themselves what they want and put their wishes into practical shape. In other words, public opinion must hammer out a project, and present it to Congress or to the State legislature (as the case may be), with such a voice of command as to compel its embodiment in and passage as an Act. But public opinion has no machinery available for the purpose. When members of Congress think the country desires legislation, they begin to prepare bills, but the want of leadership and of constructive skill often prevents such bills from satisfying the needs of the case, and the timidity of Congress, fearing to go beyond what opinion desires, retards the accomplishment of the public wish. The people who are the power entitled to say what they want, are less qualified to say how, and in what form, they are to obtain it, or in other words, public opinion can determine ends, but is less fit to examine and select means to those ends. It is slow and clumsy in grappling with large problems. It looks at them, talks incessantly about them, complains of Congress for not solving them, is distressed that they do not solve themselves. But they remain unsolved. Vital decisions have usually hung fire longer than they would have been likely to do in European countries. The war of 1812 seemed on the point of breaking out over and over again before it came at last. The absorption of Texas was a question of many years. The extension of slavery question came before the nation in 1819; after 1840 it was the chief source of trouble; year by year it grew more menacing; year by year the nation was seen more clearly to be drifting towards the breakers. Everybody felt that something must be done. But it was the function of no one authority in particular to discover a remedy, as it would have been the function of a cabinet in Europe. I do not say the sword might not in any case have been invoked, for the temperature of Southern feeling had been steadily rising to war point. But the history of 1840-60 leaves the impression that the constitutional organs of government did less to grapple with the problem than a people may expect from its organs. . . .

The structure of the government provides the requisite machinery neither for forming nor for guiding a popular opinion, disposed of itself to recognize only broad and patent facts, and to be swayed only by such obvious reasons as it needs little reflection to follow. Admirable practical acuteness, admirable ingenuity in inventing and handling machinery, whether of iron and wood or of human beings, co-exist, in the United States, with an aversion to new abstract propositions, and trains of theoretic reasoning. The liability to be caught by fallacies, the inability to recognize facts which are not seen but must be inferentially found to exist, the incapacity to imagine a future which must result from the unchecked operation of present forces, these are indeed the defects of the ordinary citizen in all countries, and if they are conspicuous in America, it is only because the ordinary citizen, who is more intelligent there than elsewhere, is also more potent. . . .

There is more force in the remark that we must remember how much is gained as well as lost by the slow and hesitating working of public opinion in the United States. So tremendous a force would be dangerous if it moved rashly. Acting over and gathered from an enormous area, in which there exist many local differences, it needs time, often a long time, to become conscious of the preponderance of one set of tendencies over another. The elements both of local difference and of class difference must be (so to speak) well shaken up together, and each part brought into contact with the rest, before the mixed liquid can produce a precipitate in the form of a practical conclusion. And in this is seen the difference between the excellence as a governing power of opinion in the whole Union, and opinion within the limits of a particular State. The systems of constitutional machinery by which public sentiment acts are similar in the greater and in the smaller area; the constitutional maxims practically identical. But public opinion, which moves slowly, temperately, and surely, in the field of national affairs, is sometimes hasty and reckless in State affairs. The population of a State may be of one colour, as that of the North-western States is almost purely agricultural, or may contain few persons of education and political knowledge, or may fall under the influence of a demagogue or a clique, or may be possessed by some local passion. Thus its opinion may want breadth, sobriety, wisdom, and the result be seen in imprudent or unjust measures. The latest constitution of California, the Granger legislation of Illinois, Iowa, and Wisconsin, the repudiation of their public debts by several States, are familiar instances of follies, to use no harder name, which local opinion approved, but which would have been impossible in the Federal Government, where the controlling opinion is that of a large and complex nation, and where the very deficiencies of one section or one class serve to correct qualities which may exist in excess in some other. . . .

The enormous force of public opinion is a danger to the people themselves, as well as their leaders. It no longer makes them tyrannical. But it fills them with an undue confidence in their wisdom, their virtue, and their freedom. It may be thought that a nation which uses freedom well can hardly have too much freedom; yet even such a nation may be too much inclined to think freedom an absolute and all-sufficient good, to seek truth only in the voice of the majority, to mistake prosperity for greatness. Such a nation, seeing nothing but its own triumphs, and hearing nothing but its own praises, seems to need a succession of men like the prophets of Israel to rouse the people out of their self-complacency, to refresh their moral ideals, to remind them that the life is more than meat, and the body more than raiment, and that to whom much is given of them shall much also be required. If America has no prophets of this order, she fortunately possesses two classes of men who maintain a wholesome irritation such as that which Socrates thought it his function to apply to the Athenian people. These are the instructed critics who exert a growing influence on opinion through the higher newspapers, and by literature generally, and the philanthropic reformers who tell more directly upon the multitude, particularly through the churches. Both classes combined may not as yet be doing all that is needed. But the significant point is that their influence represents not an ebbing but a flowing tide. If the evils they combat exist on a larger scale than in past times, they too are more active and more courageous in rousing and reprehending their fellow-countrymen.

WHEREIN PUBLIC OPINION SUCCEEDS

In the examination of the actualities of politics as well as of forms of government, faults are more readily perceived than merits. Everybody is struck by the mistakes which a ruler makes, or by evils which a constitution fails to avert, while less praise than is due may be bestowed in respect of the temptations that have been resisted, or the prudence with which the framers of the government have avoided defects from which other countries suffer. Thus the general prosperity of the United States and the success of their people in all kinds of private enterprises, philanthropic as well as gainful, throws into relief the blemishes of their government, and makes it the more necessary to point out in what respects the power of public opinion overcomes those blemishes, and maintains a high level of good feeling and well-being in the nation. . . .

The conscience and common sense of the nation as a whole keep down the evils which have crept into the working of the Constitution, and may in time extinguish them. Public opinion is a sort of atmosphere, fresh, keen, and full of sunlight, like that of the American cities, and this sunlight kills many of those noxious germs which are hatched where politicians congregate. That which, varying a once famous phrase, we may call the genius of universal publicity, has some disagreeable results, but the wholesome ones are greater and more numerous. Selfishness, injustice, cruelty, tricks, and jobs of all sorts shun the light; to expose them is to defeat them. No serious evils, no rankling sore in the body politic, can remain long concealed, and when disclosed, it is half destroyed. So long as the opinion of a nation is sound, the main lines of its policy cannot go far wrong, whatever waste of time and money may be incurred in carrying them out. It was observed in the last section that opinion is too vague and indeterminate a thing to be capable of considering and selecting the best means for the end on which it has determined. The counterpart of that remark is that the opinion of a whole nation, a united and tolerably homogeneous nation, is, when at last it does express itself, the most competent authority to determine the ends of national policy. In European countries, legislatures and cabinets sometimes take decisions which the nation, which had scarcely thought of the matter till the decision has been taken, is ultimately found to disapprove. In America, men feel that the nation is the only power entitled to say what it wants, and that, till it has manifested its wishes, nothing must be done to commit it. It may sometimes be long in speaking, but when it speaks, it speaks with a weight which the wisest governing class cannot claim. . . .

Under a system of elections one man's vote is as good as another, the vicious and ignorant have as much weight as the wise and good. A system of elections might be imagined which would provide no security for due deliberation or full discussion, a system which, while democratic in name, recognizing no privilege, and referring everything to the vote of the majority, would in practice be hasty, violent, tyrannical. It is with such a possible democracy that one has to contrast the rule of public opinion as it exists in the United States. Opinion declares itself legally through elections. But opinion is at work at other times also, and has other methods of declaring itself. It secures full discussion of issues of policy and of the characters of men. It suffers nothing to be concealed. It listens patiently to all the arguments that are addressed to it. Eloquence, education, wisdom, the authority derived from experience and high character, tell upon it in the long run, and have, perhaps not always their due influence, but yet a great and growing influence. Thus a democracy governing itself through a constantly active public opinion, and not solely by its intermittent mechanism of elections, tends to become patient, tolerant, reasonable, and is more likely to be unembittered and unvexed by class divisions.

It is the existence of such a public opinion as this, the practice of freely and constantly reading, talking, and judging of public affairs with a view to voting thereon, rather than the mere possession of political rights, that gives to popular government that educative and stimulative power which is so frequently claimed as its highest merit. Those who, in the last generation, were forced to argue for democratic government against oligarchies or despots, were perhaps inclined, if not to exaggerate the value of extended suffrage and a powerful legislature, at least to pass too lightly over the concomitant conditions by whose help such institutions train men to use liberty well. History does not support the doctrine that the mere enjoyment of power fits large masses of men, any more than individuals or classes, for its exercise. Along with that enjoyment there must be found some one or more of various auspicious conditions, such as a direct and fairly equal interest in the common welfare, the presence of a class or group of persons respected and competent to guide, an absence of religious or race hatreds, a high level of education, or at least of intelligence, old habits of local self-government, the practice of unlimited free discussion. In America it is not simply the habit of voting but the briskness and breeziness of the whole atmosphere of public life, and the process of obtaining information and discussing it, of hearing and judging each side, that form the citizen's intelligence. True it is that he would not gain much from this process did it not lead up to the exercise of voting power: he would not learn so much on the road did not the polling-booth stand at the end of it. But if it were his lot, as it is that of the masses in some European countries, to exercise his right of suffrage under few of these favouring conditions, the educational value of the vote would become comparatively small. It is the habit of breathing as well as helping to form public opinion that cultivates, develops, trains the average American. It gives him a sense of personal responsibility stronger, because more constant, than exists in those free countries of Europe where he commits his power to a legislature. Sensible that his eye ought to be always fixed on the conduct of affairs, he grows accustomed to read and judge, not indeed profoundly, sometimes erroneously, usually under party influences, but yet with a feeling that the judgment is his own. He has a sense of ownership in the government, and therewith a kind of independence of manner as well as of mind very different from the demissness of the humbler classes of the Old World. And the consciousness of responsibility which goes along with this laudable pride, brings forth the peaceable fruits of moderation. As the Greeks thought that the old families ruled their households more gently than upstarts did, so citizens who have been born to power, born into an atmosphere of legal right and constitutional authority, are sobered by their privileges. Despite their natural quickness and eagerness, the native Americans are politically patient. They are disposed to try soft means first, to expect others to bow to that force of opinion which they themselves recognize. Opposition does not incense them; danger does not, by making them lose their heads, hurry them into precipitate courses. In no country does a beaten minority take a defeat so well....

It is chiefly the faith in publicity that gives to the American public their peculiar buoyancy and what one may call their airy hopefulness in discussing even the weak points of their system. They are always telling you that they have no skeleton closets, nothing to keep back. They know, and are content that all the world should know, the worst as well as the best of themselves. They have a boundless faith in free inquiry and full discussion. They admit the possibility of any number of temporary errors and delusions. But to suppose that a vast nation should, after hearing everything, canvassing everything, and trying all the preliminary experiments it has a mind to, ultimately go wrong by mistaking its own true interests, seems to them a sort of blasphemy against the human intelligence and its Creator. . . .

It has been observed that the all-subduing power of the popular voice may tell against the appearance of great statesmen by dwarfing aspiring individualities, by teaching men to discover and obey the tendencies of their age rather than rise above them and direct them. If this happens in America it is not because the American people fails to appreciate and follow and exalt such eminent men as fortune bestows upon it. It has a great capacity for loyalty, even for hero-worship. "Our people," said an experienced American publicist to me, "are in reality hungering for great men, and the warmth with which even pinchbeck geniuses, men who have anything showy or taking about them, anything that is deemed to betoken a strong individuality, are followed and glorified in spite of intellectual emptiness, and perhaps even moral shortcomings, is the best proof of the fact." Henry Clay was the darling of his party for many years, as Jefferson, with less of personal fascination, had been in the preceding generation. Daniel Webster retained the devotion of New England long after it had become clear that his splendid intellect was mated to a far from noble character. A kind of dictatorship was yielded to Abraham Lincoln, whose memory is cherished almost like that of Washington himself. Whenever a man appears with something taking or forcible about him, he becomes the object of so much popular interest and admiration that those cooler heads who perceive his faults, and perhaps dread his laxity of principle, reproach the proneness of their less-discerning countrymen to make an idol out of wood or clay. The career of Andrew Jackson is a case in point, though it may be hoped that the intelligence of the people would estimate such a character more truly to-day. . . . I doubt if there be any country where a really brilliant man, confident in his own strength, and adding the charm of a striking personality to the gift of popular eloquence, would find an easier path to fame and power, and would exert more influence over the minds and emotions of the multitude. Such a man, speaking to the people with the independence of conscious strength, would find himself appreciated and respected.

Controversy is still bitter, more profuse in personal imputations than one expects to find it where there are no grave issues to excuse excitement. But in this respect also there is an improvement. Partisans are reckless, but the mass of the people lends itself less to acrid partisanship than it did in the time of Jackson, or in those first days of the Republic which were so long looked back to as a sort of heroic age. Public opinion grows more temperate, more mellow, and assuredly more tolerant. Its very strength disposes it to bear with opposition or remonstrance. It respects itself too much to wish to silence any voice.

102. PEOPLE *CAN* RISE TO THE CHALLENGE
by James Reston *

In this week's New Yorker magazine there is a cartoon of an angry bartender saying to a customer on the other side of the bar: "Look, my friend, one more comparison between our civilization and Ancient Rome's and out you go!"

This helps a little, for in recent weeks we have been told by everybody from Adlai Stevenson to former Senator William Jenner of Indiana that we are sick and soft and going merrily to hell.

What Oswald Spengler in Germany, "The Gloomy Dean" Inge in England, Peter Drucker in Austria and Nikolai Berdyaev in Russia said of Europe in the Thirties, an odd, mixed-bag of liberal intellectuals, right-wing politicians and retired generals is beginning to repeat about America.

We are, they say, living in a demented world, and ducking our responsibilities. As Berdyaev put it better than the modern Cassandras: there is something shaken and shattered in the soul of modern man. We are entering the realm of the unknown and unlived, joylessly and without much hope. We are now in a time of spiritual decadence, of loneliness and dereliction.

The criers of havoc have always been interesting in every age, and they have often been right. Moreover, they have something to say to us today about the dangers of easy education, free, endless idiot-box entertainment, cheap booze, high wages for sloppy work and early casual marriage. But is this a fair indictment?

A Noble Record

This nation has not fled from danger. It has not abused its power. It has not been indifferent to the misery of mankind. It has not lost its capacity for daring or pity.

It has broken its tradition of isolation and taken commitments involving the possibility of war to forty-three different nations all over the world. It has accepted peacetime conscription and a high level of taxation.

These are not the actions of a decadent people. On the contrary, no nation in the history of sovereign states has ever responded to such a challenge with more courage or generosity in time of peace. And the surprising thing is that, after all the disappointed hopes of the postwar generation, the main opposition to the Government comes not from the people who want the nation to do less but from the people who want it to do more.

What have the Governments of the nation asked the people to do since the war that they have not consented to do? They cannot be expected to demand higher taxes and a longer military draft when the President is

---

* Chief Washington correspondent for the *New York Times* since 1953. Winner of two Pulitzer prizes, the Overseas Press Club award, and the George Polk Memorial award. This selection is from the *New York Times,* Feb. 8, 1959, p. 8E. By permission of the author and publisher.

telling them that all is well at the Pentagon. Nor are they likely to act like pioneers when Washington tells them that all we have to fear is inflation itself.

Tawdry or Golden Age?

Even if the people get the kind of government they deserve—a disturbing thought these days—somebody has to give a lead. This is especially true when the great issues of government become increasingly involved in the mysteries of science and economics and when the air waves are increasingly full of noise and rubbish.

It is true that there is a rootlessness and spiritual distemper in the land and that the pace of progress in America is not equal to the pace of history, but the people have shown a vast capacity for growth and change in the last generation and will respond if great and noble ideas cry out above the advertising jingles. . . .

103. ARE THE PEOPLE AHEAD OF THEIR "LEADERS"?

by Richard L. Neuberger*

Many members of Congress admit candidly to a belief that practical politics requires them to be extremely wary about acquainting their constituents with the stern realities that face the United States in a troubled world.

In the minds of these Senators and Representatives exists a stereotype of the average voter which adds up to a fellow who, given the choice, will invariably follow the path of least resistance. They fear the people are not prepared for further sacrifices in order to advance America's interests and prestige abroad. They are convinced the public is oblivious to the magnitude of the perils in the present world situation, particularly with respect to the industrial and technological emergence of Russia and, to a lesser degree of Communist China. Nor do they feel that gratitude will accrue to the political leader who endeavors to alert the public to such dangers.

One reason for this rather unflattering concept of the folks back home is the notion, widely held on Capitol Hill, that much of the electorate is more interested in a new hard-surfaced road to the county seat than in what happens to Burma or Iraq. If there is any one maxim which seems to prevail among many members of our national legislature, it is that local matters must come first and global problems a poor second—that is, if the member of Congress is to survive politically. Berlin or Cyprus may be important, but it is at the courthouse and precinct level that votes are won.

* Newspaperman, Oregon state senator, and United States Senator from Oregon from 1955 to 1960 (died, 1960). Coauthor of *Integrity, The Life of George W. Norris, Our Promised Land,* and other works. His wife, Maurine, was elected to the United States Senate in November, 1960. This selection is from Richard L. Neuberger, "Are the People Ahead of Their 'Leaders'?" *New York Times Magazine,* Aug. 23, 1959, pp. 13, 76, and 78. By permission of the publisher and Maurine Neuberger.

And I have heard more than one colleague declare that a lot of his constituents would rather have their taxes reduced than land a space rocket on the far side of the moon.

The results of such beliefs may be discerned in many aspects of governmental policy. Despite the fact that even the President's shaky $77 billion budget is not balanced by existing revenues, in neither the Senate nor the House is strong sentiment apparent to increase taxes so that this generation can take care of its own obligations. The fiscal year just ended saw some $13 billion added to the national debt. The Interstate Highway trust fund is running in the red, but Congress has moved slowly and with great reluctance on the matter, although at last the House Ways and Means Committee has taken partial measures to put the program on a pay-as-you-go basis.

Nor is such political timidity confined to Capitol Hill. Some thirty-four Governors of the sovereign states want the Federal Government to continue providing 90 per cent of the $39.2 billion cost of these interstate roads, but they have petitioned against raising the Federal share of the gasoline tax.

Postal revenues still lag behind expenditures, yet bills to boost postage rates languish in Congressional committees. There is much oratory against special privilege in general, but little is done specifically. Tax loopholes are not closed, despite the obvious discrimination and injustice which they typify. And despite all the fanfare about political reform, bills to control or regulate campaign spending still have gotten nowhere on Congressional calendars.

The glut of agricultural products continues to mount in warehouses and silos, but the sponsors of the Administration's much-heralded program to cut down on wheat price supports did not even seek a Senate roll-call on their own proposal. Key Senators from farm states were reluctant to be forced into taking a stand. The reciprocal-trade structure wobbles when lower bids on electrical equipment from friendly neighboring nations are deliberately set aside by the Government, under heavy political pressure, in favor of paying higher prices to domestic firms.

In the political world there is apprehension over the Presidential elections of 1960. An unwillingness exists to offend blocs of votes. This attitude rests mainly on the thesis that the American public is not ready for sacrifice, that the Presidential hopeful who dared advocate higher taxes or more expensive postage stamps or an end to discriminatory benefits favoring powerful political groups would be out of the running.

In my opinion, such concepts are wrong. I believe that the national leader who promised the public sacrifice rather than subsidies would soon rally a dedicated and informed following in every state. I think he could speak in terms of increased Federal revenues to defend ourselves and the rest of the free nations, and I feel he could challenge many special-interest organizations to relinquish their favored treatment at the expense of the public purse. He would have to be fair, and he would have to voice his advocacies without fear or favor.

Let me make plain what I mean. He could not ask the rural electric farm cooperatives to give up their special 2 per cent interest rate on loans from the Treasury, unless he also challenged the private power companies to abandon their accelerated tax write-offs. But if he did both, I am convinced he would not only get away with it but increase his popularity.

I am aware that my authority for such statements is sharply limited. I am only one of ninety-eight members of the Senate, and I come from a Pacific seaboard state of only 1,800,000 residents. Yet it is not an untypical state, and many national elections have demonstrated that geography rarely influences broad political attitudes in the United States. From the contacts which I have with my constituents—in person and by mail—I think the people are fully prepared for more sacrifices. In fact, it is my view that they are becoming highly suspicious of politicians who imply that the rough trail ahead can be traveled successfully without more sacrifices being undertaken.

A few months ago I decided to put this matter to the test. I introduced four bills to increase Federal revenues by a total of some $3.3 billion. The proposals were (1) a restoration of the excess-profits tax in effect during the Korean war, (2) a reduction in the special depletion allowance for oil companies from 27.5 to 15 per cent, (3) permitting the Post Office Department to set its own rates based on sound cost-accounting methods, and (4) increasing the Federal tax on gasoline and other motor fuels from 3 cents to 4½ cents a gallon.

I suppose it may be said that because the first two of these bills would levy only on corporations they involved no political risks. But the proposals to increase postage rates and gas taxes definitely would affect the public, and can be regarded as some measure of whether or not the people are prepared psychologically for additional sacrifices to bear the necessary burdens of government.

During a ten-day trip across the continent to Oregon, I spoke a dozen times before various organizations. The theme of each speech was the same—that if we expected more benefits and a higher level of services from the United States Government, then we should be prepared to pay for them in the form of increased taxes.

On no occasion did I encounter a reaction which could be regarded as hostile. Indeed, it seemed to me that exactly the opposite was the case. I remember particularly addressing the annual luncheon of the Western Forest Industries Association. This is an organization of prominent lumbermen, who seek additional funds for the Forest Service in order that larger stands of National Forest stumpage may be offered for sale.

In effect, I told these constituents that, while they constantly pressured me to secure more appropriations from the Treasury, I never once had heard from any of them in behalf of augmenting Treasury revenues. Then I offered my belief that this generation should take care of its own needs and obligations, rather than shoving them off onto the Americans of the future, who will have plenty of problems of their own.

I had spoken to the Western Forest Association in the past, but this was the only time I ever received what might be called an ovation. Many members came to the dais and said they were glad to be told the truth rather than being fed "political pap." And my mail still contains letters of approbation from these hardheaded sawmill operators.

This has been the predominant reaction which I have encountered to my tax-increase proposals. For every letter from Oregon criticizing the proposals to boost motor-fuel levies or to authorize higher postage rates, there are at least two letters approving both ideas.

I actually had submitted myself and my political fate to something of this same test last year, when my vote decided the question of higher postage rates on a special five-member Senate subcommittee appointed to consider the issue. The first general rate increase in all categories since 1932 was the result. Political attacks on me in Oregon took place almost immediately. I was accused of putting a tax on the mother writing her GI son in military service, or on the maiden sending a love letter to her boy friend overseas. Among the critics was my senior colleague in the Senate, Wayne Morse, one of the most tireless and effective orators in American public life.

My answer was short and direct. I pointed out that the Post Office Department had been operating at a deficit of $700 million, while paying its clerks and letter-carriers wages as low as $4,000 a year. Should this deficit be narrowed by the people and businesses who were using the mails or should it be heaped on the entire body of taxpayers, now and in the future? I doubt if a dozen citizens came to me all during the autumn with any criticism of my decisive vote to institute higher postal rates.

This is consistent with our whole national past. The American people have never flinched from burdens and sacrifices, despite the frequent effort of demagogues to discourage them from doing so.

During the terrible ordeal of the Civil War, it became necessary for the Federal Government to enact the first general conscription law Americans ever had experienced. The law declared all able-bodied male citizens between the ages of 20 and 45 eligible for military service in the Union Army. Foes of President Lincoln and his Administration spared no effort, fair or foul, to inflame the public against what then seemed an extraordinary demand upon the lives and careers of the nation's young men. Lincoln even had political antagonists in his own Cabinet who administered the law as oppressively as possible, in order to arouse popular indignation, especially among wives and mothers.

Yet, in spite of these appeals to selfishness and cowardice, the people supported the Union war effort and the President who headed it. The so-called "Peace Democrats," who felt the public was unequal to heroic sacrifices, suffered constant repudiation at the polls. President Lincoln won the electoral vote of all except three Union states in 1864.

The lessons of our history point dramatically to a national capacity for sacrifice and great deeds. Yet neither Congress nor the Administration seems disposed to draw on these lessons for guidance in the present crisis of relations between East and West, with the Soviet Union steadily drawing nearer to parity or even supremacy over us in many important realms of technology and production.

The $13 billion added to the national debt in the last fiscal year might have been even greater if some leading Democrats had achieved their wish for across-the-board tax reductions in the spring of 1958.

I would recommend a careful review of an episode which occurred in 1947 when the Republican Eightieth Congress enacted a generous tax reduction, despite the huge national debt left over from World War II and the drastic inflation already setting in after the abrupt removal of price controls. President Truman vetoed the tax-reduction bill and made the veto stick by a narrow margin. "This is the wrong time to provide for tax reduction," he told Congress.

In the elections of 1948 the Republicans seized on this veto as a major issue. Harry Truman not only retained the Presidency, in one of the great political upsets of our era, but the Democrats wrested dominance in the Senate and House from the Republicans, many of whom had assumed that tax reduction would be an issue of overwhelming popularity with the American public.

A new look at public opinion might well be undertaken by the current Eighty-sixth Congress. Predicated on my own mail and on personal contacts with the voters, I would unhesitatingly declare that the public prefers additional sacrifices to either an abandonment of our obvious national needs or to a piling up of further financial deficits. I believe the members of the Senate and the House must be able to separate the clamor of special interests from the legitimate voice of the people.

This sifting is not too difficult. On many issues, the public may be quiescent while a few lobbyists with mimeograph machines and funds for telegrams may seem to take over. Yet this does not mean that the public agrees with the pleadings of the special interests—far from it. And on election day the Jeffersonian axiom of "one man, one vote" generally prevails. Special interests and pressure groups may be able to buy unlimited wires and letterheads, but ballots are not thus readily procured.

Of course, public opinion is never suspended between heaven and earth like Mohammed's coffin. It does not exist in a vacuum. It frequently must be mobilized, cultivated and informed. This is where the executive and the Congress both have an obligation to make every effort to help educate the voters to the realities which confront us all. People rarely can know on their own the specific facts regarding military might of the Soviet Union or the industrial emergence of Red China. These must be disseminated by political leaders who are not afraid to tell their constituents the cold, hard truth, grim and unpleasant though it may be.

This educational process can take many forms—in speeches, direct personal contacts, through the vast torrent of mail which flows out from Capitol Hill and the White House, in press releases and in news letters.

The President possesses the greatest forum in the land, because each word spoken at the White House is magnified countless times. Every member of Congress also has innumerable avenues to his constituents. Thus, public opinion can be created and led, if those in government have the courage to keep the sugar-coating off the prescriptions which they prepare for the American electorate. Indeed, this educational process may be one of the most important duties of those who serve in high national offices. Could Jefferson have acquired the West or Lincoln have held together the Union if they had disregarded the formation of public opinion, even with the relatively crude methods for reaching the people which were available in the periods in which they played their epic roles?

Speaking of a complex and potentially unpopular issue like foreign aid, Senator J. W. Fulbright of Arkansas, chairman of the Senate Foreign Relations Committee, said that only the President could prepare the whole public to accept such a program as this. I agree substantially with the Fulbright thesis, although I would add the one cautionary note that Congress likewise has a duty to spread vital information in support of essential undertakings which may be politically unpopular or unpalatable. And Senator Fulbright recently told his colleagues that he believes the American people "would prefer to pay more taxes, if necessary, than to default to the Soviet Union."

So I hope our colleagues in both chambers of Congress will take a fresh look at the willingness of the average American to face up to realities. I doubt if our people want to be told that they can enjoy increased governmental benefits without paying higher taxes. I doubt if they want to be assured that the Soviet Union can be kept from world domination without many of our young men experiencing rigorous service in their country's uniform. I doubt if they want special privilege, whether it goes to labor unions or to big business.

This same challenge goes, too, to the military hero now serving his final term in the White House. In the last analysis, his is the one national voice in the land—the only voice not anchored to the sectional interests of a single state or region. Harry S. Truman, who has a deep reverence for the high office he occupied for seven years, has written, "It is through the use of these great powers [of the Presidency] that leadership arises, events are molded and administrations take on character."

I think this is sound advice to Dwight D. Eisenhower. If he should seek further sacrifices and national duty of his continent-wide constituency, I have no doubt whatever that the American people will respond with firmness and with courage—as they have to all similar appeals from their leaders since this country was founded under great travail in 1789.

104. THE FAILURE OF PUBLIC OPINION IN FOREIGN AFFAIRS

by Walter Lippmann*

1. Public Opinion in War and Peace

Writing in 1913, just before the outbreak of the war, and having in mind

* Author, newspaper columnist, and former editor. This selection is from Walter Lippmann, *The Public Philosophy*, Little, Brown & Company, Boston, 1955, pp. 16-27. Copyright, 1955, by Walter Lippmann. Reprinted by permission of Little, Brown & Company.

Queen Victoria and King Edward the VII, Sir Harry Johnston thus described how foreign affairs were conducted in the Nineteenth Century:

> In those days, a country's relations with its neighbors or with distant lands were dealt with almost exclusively by the head of the State—Emperor, King, or President—acting with the more-or-less dependent Minister-of-State, who was no representative of the masses, but the employé of the Monarch. Events were prepared and sprung on a submissive, a confident, or a stupid people. The public Press criticized, more often applauded, but had at most to deal with a *fait accompli* and make the best of it. Occasionally, in our own land, a statesman, out of office and discontented, went round the great provincial towns agitating against the trend of British foreign policy—perhaps wisely, perhaps unfairly, we do not yet know—and scored a slight success. But once in office, his Cabinet fell in by degrees with the views of the Sovereign and the permanent officials (after the fifties of the last century these public servants were a factor of ever-growing importance); and, as before, the foreign policy of the Empire was shaped by a small camarilla consisting of the Sovereign, two Cabinet Ministers, the permanent Under-Secretary of State for Foreign Affairs, and perhaps one representative of *la plus haute finance*.[1]

Without taking it too literally, this is a fair description of how foreign affairs were conducted before the First World War. There were exceptions. The Aberdeen government, for example, was overthrown in 1855 because of its inefficient conduct of the Crimean War. But generally speaking, the elected parliaments were little consulted in the deliberations which led up to war, or on the high strategy of the war, on the terms of the armistice, on the conditions of peace. Even their right to be informed was severely limited, and the principle of the system was, one might say, that war and peace were the business of the executive department. The power of decision was not in, was not even shared with, the House of Commons, the Chamber of Deputies, the Reichstag.

The United States was, of course, a special case. The Congress has always had constitutional rights to advise and to be consulted in the declaration of war and in the ratification of treaties. But at the time I am talking about, that is to say before the First World War broke out, it was American policy to abstain from the role of a great power, and to limit its sphere of vital interests to the Western Hemisphere and the North Pacific Ocean. Only in 1917 did the American constitutional system for dealing with foreign affairs become involved with the conduct of world affairs. . . .

This system of executive responsibility broke down during the war, and from 1917 on the conduct of the war and then the conditions of the armistice and the peace were subjected to the dominating impact of mass opinions.

Saying this does not mean that the great mass of the people have had strong opinions about the whole range of complex issues which were before the military staffs and the foreign offices. The action of mass opinion has

---

[1] Sir Harry Johnston, "Common Sense in Foreign Policy," pp. 1-2, cited in Howard Lee McBain & Lindsay Rogers, *The New Constitutions of Europe* (1922), p. 139.

not been, and in the nature of things could not be, continuous through the successive phases in which affairs develop. Action has been discontinuous. Usually it has been a massive negative imposed at critical junctures when a new general course of policy needed to be set. There have, of course, been periods of apathy and of indifference. But democratic politicians have preferred to shun foresight about troublesome changes to come, knowing that the massive veto was latent, and that it would be expensive to them and to their party if they provoked it.

In the winter of 1918-1919, for example, Lloyd George, Clemenceau, Wilson and Orlando were at a critical juncture of modern history. The Germans were defeated, their government was overthrown, their troops disarmed and disbanded. The Allies were called upon to decide whether they would dictate a punitive peace or would negotiate a peace of reconciliation.

In the Thirties the British and the French governments had to decide whether to rearm and to take concerted measures to contain Hitler and Mussolini or whether to remain unarmed and to appease them. The United States had to decide whether to arm in order to contain the Japanese or to negotiate with them at the expense of China.

During the Second World War the British and the American governments had again to make the choice between total victory with unconditional surrender and negotiated settlements whose end was reconciliation.

These were momentous issues, like choosing at the fork of the road a way from which there is no turning back: whether to arm or not to arm—whether, as a conflict blows up, to intervene or to withdraw—whether in war to fight for the unconditional surrender of the adversary or for his reconciliation. The issues are so momentous that public feeling quickly becomes incandescent to them. But they can be answered with the only words that a great mass *qua* mass can speak—with a Yes or a No.

Experience since 1917 indicates that in matters of war and peace the popular answer in the democracies is likely to be No. For everything connected with war has become dangerous, painful, disagreeable and exhausting to very nearly everyone. The rule to which there are few exceptions—the acceptance of the Marshall Plan is one of them—is that at the critical junctures, when the stakes are high, the prevailing mass opinion will impose what amounts to a veto upon changing the course on which the government is at the time proceeding. Prepare for war in time of peace? No. It is bad to raise taxes, to unbalance the budget, to take men away from their schools or their jobs, to provoke the enemy. Intervene in a developing conflict? No. Avoid the risk of war. Withdraw from the area of the conflict? No. The adversary must not be appeased. Reduce your claims on the area? No. Righteousness cannot be compromised. Negotiate a compromise peace as soon as the opportunity presents itself? No. The aggressor must be punished. Remain armed to enforce the dictated settlement? No. The war is over.

The unhappy truth is that the prevailing public opinion has been destructively wrong at the critical junctures. The people have imposed a veto upon the judgments of informed and responsible officials. They have compelled the governments, which usually knew what would have been wiser, or was necessary, or was more expedient, to be too late with too little, or too long with too much, too pacifist in peace and too bellicose in war, too neutralist or appeasing in negotiation or too intransigent. Mass opinion has acquired mounting power in this century. It has shown itself to be a dangerous master of decisions when the stakes are life and death.

2. The Compulsion to Make Mistakes

The errors of public opinion in these matters have a common characteristic. The movement of opinion is slower than the movement of events. Because of that, the cycle of subjective sentiments on war and peace is usually out of gear with the cycle of objective developments. Just because they are mass opinions there is an inertia in them. It takes much longer to change many minds than to change a few. It takes time to inform and to persuade and to arouse large scattered varied multitudes of persons. So before the multitude have caught up with the old events there are likely to be new ones coming up over the horizon with which the government should be preparing to deal. But the majority will be more aware of what they have just caught up with near at hand than with what is still distant and in the future. For these reasons the propensity to say No to a change of course sets up a compulsion to make mistakes. The opinion deals with a situation which no longer exists.

When the world wars came, the people of the liberal democracies could not be aroused to the exertions and the sacrifices of the struggle until they had been frightened by the opening disasters, had been incited to passionate hatred, and had become intoxicated with unlimited hope. To overcome this inertia the enemy had to be portrayed as evil incarnate, as absolute and congenital wickedness. The people wanted to be told that when this particular enemy had been forced to unconditional surrender, they would re-enter the golden age. This unique war would end all wars. This last war would make the world safe for democracy. This crusade would make the whole world a democracy.

As a result of this impassioned nonsense public opinion became so envenomed that the people would not countenance a workable peace; they were against any public man who showed "any tenderness for the Hun," or was inclined to listen to the "Hun food snivel."[2]

3. The Pattern of the Mistakes

In order to see in its true perspective what happened, we must remember that at the end of the First World War the only victorious powers were the liberal democracies of the West. Lenin, who had been a refugee in Switzerland until 1917, was still at the very beginning of his struggle to become the master of the empire of the Romanoffs. Mussolini was an obscure journalist, and nobody had dreamed of Hitler. The men who took part in the Peace Conference were men of the same standards and tradition. They were the heads of duly elected governments in countries where respect for civil liberty was the rule. Europe from the Atlantic to the Pripet Marshes lay within the military orbit of their forces. All the undemocratic empires,

[2] Cf. Harold Nicholson, *Peacemaking*, Chap. III.

enemy and ally, had been destroyed by defeat and revolution. In 1918—unlike 1945—there had been no Yalta, there was no alien foreign minister at the peace conference who held a veto on the settlement.

Yet as soon as the terms of the settlement were known, it was evident that peace had not been made with Germany. It was not for want of power but for want of statesmanship that the liberal democracies failed. They failed to restore order in that great part of the world which—outside of revolutionary Russia—was still within the orbit of their influence, still amenable to their leadership, still subject to their decisions, still working within the same economy, still living in the same international community, still thinking in the same universe of discourse. In this failure to make peace there was generated the cycle of wars in which the West has suffered so sudden and so spectacular a decline.

Public opinion, having vetoed reconciliation, had made the settlement unworkable. And so when a new generation of Germans grew up, they rebelled. But by that time the Western democracies, so recently too warlike to make peace with the unarmed German Republic, had become too pacifist to take the risks which could have prevented the war Hitler was announcing he would wage against Europe. Having refused the risk of trying to prevent war, they would not now prepare for the war. The European democracies chose to rely on the double negative of unarmed appeasement, and the American democracy chose to rely on unarmed isolation.

When the unprevented war came, the fatal cycle was repeated. Western Europe was defeated and occupied before the British people began seriously to wage the war. And after the catastrophe in Western Europe eighteen agonizing months of indecision elapsed before the surprise and shock of Pearl Harbor did for the American people what no amount of argument and evidence and reason had been able to do.

Once again it seemed impossible to wage the war energetically except by inciting the people to paroxysms of hatred and to utopian dreams. So they were told that the Four Freedoms would be established everywhere, once the incurably bad Germans and the incurably bad Japanese had been forced to surrender unconditionally. The war could be popular only if the enemy was altogether evil and the Allies very nearly perfect. This mixture of envenomed hatred and furious righteousness made a public opinion which would not tolerate the calculated compromises that durable settlements demand. Once again the people were drugged by the propaganda which had aroused them to fight the war and to endure its miseries. Once again they would not think, once again they would not allow their leaders to think, about an eventual peace with their enemies, or about the differences that must arise among the Allies in this coalition, as in all earlier ones. How well this popular diplomacy worked is attested by the fact that less than five years after the democracies had disarmed their enemies, they were imploring their former enemies, Germany and Japan, to rearm.

The record shows that the people of the democracies, having become sovereign in this century, have made it increasingly difficult for their governments to prepare properly for war or to make peace. Their responsible officials have been like the ministers of an opinionated and willful despot. Between the critical junctures, when public opinion has been inattentive or not vehemently aroused, responsible officials have often been able to circumvent extremist popular opinions and to wheedle their way towards moderation and good sense. In the crises, however, democratic officials—over and above their own human propensity to err—have been compelled to make the big mistakes that public opinion has insisted upon. Even the greatest men have not been able to turn back the massive tides of opinion and of sentiment.

There is no mystery about why there is such a tendency for popular opinion to be wrong in judging war and peace. Strategic and diplomatic decisions call for a kind of knowledge—not to speak of an experience and a seasoned judgment—which cannot be had by glancing at newspapers, listening to snatches of radio comment, watching politicians perform on television, hearing occasional lectures, and reading a few books. It would not be enough to make a man competent to decide whether to amputate a leg, and it is not enough to qualify him to choose war or peace, to arm or not to arm, to intervene or to withdraw, to fight on or to negotiate.

Usually, moreover, when the decision is critical and urgent, the public will not be told the whole truth. What can be told to the great public it will not hear in the complicated and qualified concreteness that is needed for a practical decision. When distant and unfamiliar and complex things are communicated to great masses of people, the truth suffers a considerable and often a radical distortion. The complex is made over into the simple, the hypothetical into the dogmatic, and the relative into an absolute. Even when there is no deliberate distortion by censorship and propaganda, which is unlikely in time of war, the public opinion of masses cannot be counted upon to apprehend regularly and promptly the reality of things. There is an inherent tendency in opinion to feed upon rumors excited by our own wishes and fears.

4. Democratic Politicians

At the critical moments in this sad history, there have been men, worth listening to, who warned the people against their mistakes. Always, too, there have been men inside the governments who judged correctly, because they were permitted to know in time, the uncensored and unvarnished truth. But the climate of modern democracy does not usually inspire them to speak out. For what Churchill did in the Thirties before Munich was exceptional: the general rule is that a democratic politician had better not be right too soon. Very often the penalty is political death. It is much safer to keep in step with the parade of opinion than to try to keep up with the swifter movement of events.

In government offices which are sensitive to the vehemence and passion of mass sentiment public men have no sure tenure. They are in effect perpetual office seekers, always on trial for their political lives, always required to court their restless constituents. They are deprived of their independence. Democratic politicians rarely feel they can afford the luxury of telling the whole truth to the people.[3] And since not telling it, though prudent, is uncomfortable, they find it easier if they themselves do not have to hear too often too much of the sour truth. The men under them who report and collect the news come to realize in their turn that it is safer to be wrong before it has become fashionable to be right.

With exceptions so rare that they are regarded as miracles and freaks of nature, successful democratic politicians are insecure and intimidated men. They advance politically only as they placate, appease, bribe, seduce, bamboozle, or otherwise manage to manipulate the demanding and threatening elements in their constituencies. The decisive consideration is not whether the proposition is good but whether it is popular—not whether it will work well and prove itself but whether the active talking constituents like it immediately. Politicians rationalize this servitude by saying that in a democracy public men are the servants of the people.

This devitalization of the governing power is the malady of democratic states. As the malady grows the executives become highly susceptible to encroachment and usurpation by elected assemblies; they are pressed and harassed by the higgling of parties, by the agents of organized interests, and by the spokesmen of sectarians and ideologues. The malady can be fatal. It can be deadly to the very survival of the state as a free society if, when the great and hard issues of war and peace, of security and solvency, of revolution and order are up for decision, the executive and judicial departments, with their civil servants and technicians, have lost their power to decide.

105. PUBLIC OPINION AND FOREIGN AFFAIRS: A MORE OPTIMISTIC APPRAISAL

by Dexter Perkins*

. . . Mr. Lippmann seems to think that curbs on the people, and the strengthening of the executive, and a return to the philosophy of Edmund Burke, would accomplish wonders. Of course things will not fall out that way. The popular control of government in the Western World (whether we like it or not) is here to stay. But, aside from this, I for my part distrust

---

[3] "As we look over the list of the early leaders of the republic, Washington, John Adams, Hamilton, and others, we discern that they were all men who insisted upon being themselves and who refused to truckle to the people. With each succeeding generation, the growing demand of the people that its elective officials shall not lead but merely register the popular will has steadily undermined the independence of those who derive their power from popular election. The persistent refusal of the Adamses to sacrifice the integrity of their own intellectual and moral standards and values for the sake of winning public office or popular favor is another of the measuring rods by which we may measure the divergence of American life from its starting point." James Truslow Adams, *The Adams Family* (1930), p. 95.

* Professor emeritus at Cornell. Author of *America and Two Wars, The American Approach to Foreign Policy, The Evolution of American Foreign Policy,* and other works. This selection is from Dexter Perkins, *Popular Government and Foreign Policy,* Fund for Adult Education, Pasadena, Calif., April, 1956, pp. 7, 8, 19-21, 29-30, 33-35, and 62-63. By permission of the Fund for Adult Education.

all elitism, however presented. The best wisdom is to be found in the collectivity, not because any member of the collectivity is himself as wise or as well informed or as disinterested as some notable individuals may be, but because the reconciliation of the wills, the aspirations, and the interests of all, even the prejudices of all, provides a more solid and enduring basis of action than the will, the aspiration, and the interest of any individual or of any class. The free men of the West are not sheep to be driven; they will not be driven. They must find the path to wisdom for themselves, through leadership of course, but through a leadership that understands and represents them. When we deny this, when we denigrate the democratic process, or yield to gloom with regard to popular government, we shake the very foundations on which our polity rests. Let me not fall into melodrama; I do not think that democracy in this country is decaying, or will decay, whatever the criticisms or the doubts expressed. But I think the prescription for strengthening it and for overcoming its manifest limitations must be a positive prescription, and that even that will not avail without faith....

No one pretends, certainly no one ought to pretend, that the American record is perfect. To make a reasonable judgment about foreign affairs, or about any large problem, it is necessary to begin by recognizing the large margin of uncertainty that exists in human affairs, and especially in human affairs of any complexity. The immense scope of the problems of diplomacy makes miscalculation easy. It is hard to get all the facts; it is almost impossible to see far ahead; and in large areas we simply do not control the situations with which we have to deal. Nor is this all. The answer to the important question that diplomacy has to face is by no means entirely a matter of intellect. It is a matter of profound emotion. The critics of our foreign policy often speak as if the emotional element were something particularly connected with popular government. But it is really quite unhistorical to assume that only the "masses," to use the favorite term, are governed by feeling. Diplomats also feel; dictators feel; oligarchs feel. To assume that there is any form of governmental organization that will exorcise sentiment and install pure and abstract reason on the throne would be to take a view of human nature that has little warrant in experience. We shall never understand human affairs aright if we treat a social problem on the basis of an intellectual syllogism....

But let us look at the Treaty of Versailles more narrowly. Walter Lippmann has some bitter criticism of it. ". . . as soon as the terms of the settlement were known," he writes in his recent book, "it was evident that peace had not been made with Germany. . . . the liberal democracies failed. They failed to restore order in that great part of the world which—outside of revolutionary Russia—was still within the orbit of their influence. . . . In this failure to make peace there was generated the cycle of wars in which the West has suffered so sudden and spectacular a decline. Public opinion, having vetoed reconciliation, made the settlement unworkable." Is this a just judgment on the statesmen who gathered in Paris in 1919? Is it a just judgment on the people they represented? I do not so regard it.

The principal folly connected with the Treaty of Versailles was undeniably the handling of the reparations question. It is quite true that French and British public opinion was absurdly preoccupied with making Germany pay immense sums to compensate for the sacrifices of the West. It is quite true that French and British insistence on these payments was sharpened by the insistence of American opinion on getting back the sums that had been lent to the Allies during the war. It is quite true, too, that, as matters fell out, French opinion led to an utterly foolish effort to exact reparations from Germany by the occupation of the Ruhr valley and that, in the struggle that ensued, the German middle classes were brayed in a mortar. But let us look at the other side of the case. The perversion of public feeling on the reparation and war debt questions was not long-lasting. By 1924 the reparations question had been placed on what at the time looked like a reasonable basis. Soon after, the question of the war debts received a temporary solution. True enough, these arrangements broke down with the advent of the Great Depression. But what happened then? The whole problem disappeared, and no one seems to have bothered about it since. This is not a noble record, but it does show some capacity on the part of the democratic peoples to learn from harsh experience and to accept the inevitable gracefully when it arrives.

Moreover, the democracies went further. Mr. Lippmann says they vetoed reconciliation. Precisely the contrary is true. In the Treaties of Locarno, and in the admission of Germany to the League of Nations, the democracies *approved* reconciliation. They worked out an elaborate series of agreements looking to the security of all of Western Europe and to the peaceful settlements of disputes arising between the signatories of the Treaty of Versailles. In the middle twenties an optimist might have been pardoned for believing that a new age had dawned. Mr. Lippmann says that the peoples "failed to restore order." On the contrary, they made a great effort to restore order.

Was this an unjust order? Justice means different things to different people. But as I view the territorial terms of the Treaty of Versailles, I cannot find them brutal, certainly not brutal by the standard fixed by a Hitler or by the Russia of Stalin in dealing with the defeated enemy. Let us examine them. They did indeed involve the separation of considerable territory from Germany. But the territories taken away were not taken away vindictively, or on the basis of popular passion. Most people would agree that the retrocession of Alsace-Lorraine to France was in line with the desires of its inhabitants in 1919. The detachment of the Saar valley was temporary, and provision was made (and honored) for its return to Germany. The northern and eastern frontiers of Germany were largely settled by plebiscites and several of these plebiscites came out in favor of the Germans. Virtually no one at the time foresaw the problem of the Sudetenland, the German-speaking part of Czechoslovakia which Hitler was to claim in 1938. The limitation imposed on the union of Germany and Austria was an error, but not an irrevocable one, under the terms of the treaty. Taken altogether, these terms, I submit, were not such as represent an unreasoning desire for vengeance. They seemed at the time to have a moral basis. One does not need to reproach the democracies with folly and vindictiveness on this basis.

It is true there was a flaw in them, and a serious one. They depended upon collective power for their maintenance. They were terms that Germans could not accept as lasting if their old urge to power and domination reasserted itself. But here we come back to the old problem, the problem of preserving a given settlement if the balance of physical power shifts dramatically. It was not in the peace-making that the democracies went astray. It was in allowing themselves to be divided and distraught in the years that followed. There is much truth in the admittedly self-justificatory comment of Lloyd George that it was not the statesmen at Versailles who erred but the statesmen who permitted the position of the democracies to be shaken in the period of the thirties. It was not popular government in the twenties that made the major errors but popular government in the thirties. . . .

In a passage from Walter Lippmann's *The Public Philosophy* one finds him declaring that "the prevailing mass opinion will impose what amounts to a veto upon changing the course on which the government is at the time proceeding. Prepare for war in time of peace? No. . . . Intervene in a developing conflict? No." There are other generalizations, but let us look for a moment at these two. Is not Mr. Lippmann wrong? Mass opinion in 1940 *did* favor preparing for war when we were at peace, not so early as might have been wished but as soon as the peril became a lively one. Mass opinion was *not* averse to intervening in a developing conflict in 1940 and 1941. On the contrary, it moved more and more in the direction of intervention. Of course it was not united. I know of no way in which uniformity of opinion can be produced in a democracy in advance of actual involvement in the struggle. There will, I repeat, always be a lag in action as distinguished from the action of a totalitarian state. This is one of the risks of democracy. But we came through, after all.

When we come to the war itself, we find a magnificent achievement. We have no occasion to analyze that achievement in detail. But surely it may be said that no nation has made a national effort in any way commensurate with that of 1941 to 1945. Popular government vindicated itself in the actual waging of the war, as it vindicated itself in 1917 and 1918. Some people would say that it vindicated itself more fully for, on the whole, with the exception of the tragic position of the Nisei, a genuine blot on the record, the war was fought with full respect for civil liberty and in the finest tradition of free government. Moreover, it illustrated a point which it is desirable to emphasize. Mr. Lippmann, in his book *The Public Philosophy* sees the necessity of strengthening the Executive if our form of polity is to function successfully. I shall not argue the matter in detail here, but I do wish to suggest that in times of emergency our government almost automatically tends to concentrate power in the administration. This was true in the Civil War and in the First World War. And there would be many who would contend that the reaction that comes with peace towards a more equal relationship between the legislature and the Executive has much to be said for it. If one puts the matter another way, we do not seem to suffer from a deficiency of governmental power when there is a profound need for such power; and the libertarian spirit which fears undue concentration of authority in time of peace is something of which many of us, both in theory and from the practical point of view, would be disposed to approve. . . .

Now it is quite true that we reacted foolishly at the end of the war. We did blithely assume that matters were settled; we not only dismantled our military machine with inconsequent haste, but we rushed towards the removal of governmental controls. We were wrong, no doubt about it, in our assessment of the kind of world we live in. But the amazing thing to me is the rapidity with which the American people learned. Of course there is no doubt of the context in which they learned. The men in the Kremlin not only saw us demobilize, but they thought they saw us headed towards an economic depression. And they proceeded to take advantage of what they estimated the situation to be. They stalled on the making of peace; they stirred up trouble wherever they could; and they appear to have preferred a disorganized Germany to any other kind. Now how long did we stand for this kind of thing? We stood for it for less than two years, not a very long time as the historian measures time. We were beginning to react in 1946, and the speech which Winston Churchill made at Fulton, Missouri, in the winter of that year had a considerable impact on the public mind.

But we get the clear signs of the public mood in 1947. Let us review the circumstances. The Russians had been stirring up guerrilla warfare in northern Greece. They had egged on their satellites to do so. And the British, who had entered Greece in the course of the war in 1944 and who had garrisons there in 1947, felt compelled for fiscal reasons (so they said) to bring their troops home. At the same time the Russians were bringing pressure to bear on Turkey, looking to the cession of two border provinces and to eventual Russian control of the Dardanelles. It was in these circumstances that President Truman came before the Congress on the 12th of March, 1947 with a request for an appropriation of $400,000,000 for assistance to these two countries, threatened by Soviet intrigue and possible aggression. Now the Congress was a Republican Congress; in other words, from the purely partisan angle it might have taken a dim view of the President's recommendations. And behind the Congress were the American people who, we are told, are not really competent to oversee their own public affairs and who can be depended upon to make a botch of things where diplomacy is concerned. Well, what happened? By a very large bipartisan vote, the President got what he asked for. And the policy adopted in 1947 has resulted in a tranquil and prosperous Greece and in a Turkey infinitely stronger than the Turkey of eight years ago.

But more was soon to come. The state of Europe in the Winter of 1947 was indeed precarious. It was one of the bitterest winters in the recent history of the continent. The social disorganization created by the war still left its mark. The possibility of an economic collapse was real. Such a collapse involved enormous dangers for the interests of the United States. And what happened? Speaking at Harvard University on the 5th of June, Secretary of State Marshall brought prominently to public attention a plan already projected for economic assistance to Europe. He did not dot the "I" and cross the "T," but he propounded a policy. And this same Republican Congress, which had voted aid to Greece and Turkey, initiated the Marshall

Plan. It did so by overwhelming votes; it did so in such a way as to leave no doubt of the good sense and of the good will of the American people. . . .

The criticism of our foreign policy in the last decade, at any rate the criticism on the higher levels, has been useful and suggestive; it is often the product of high intelligence and of sincere desire to promote the welfare of the Republic. But at times the critics seem to be denigrating the democratic process itself; they seem to betray a deep distrust of popular government. Such distrust is dangerous and, as I see it, is not supported by the facts.

In the last forty years, and especially in the last fifteen years, the American people have emerged from their continental isolationism and have, by the ineluctable logic of events, come to play a central part on the stage of the world. On the whole, they have played a worthy role; they have twice rolled back the forces of German militarism in victorious wars; they have met the new challenge of Russian Communist imperialism more promptly and more intelligently than their long tradition of non-entanglement would have suggested. They have reinvigorated Europe and strengthened its defenses; they have met and stalemated aggression in the Orient; they have accepted reluctantly, but with clear minds, the necessity for the building up of their physical power; they have improved the mechanisms through which they act in the field of foreign affairs. They have erred and will err; for the very complexity of the problems makes infallibility impossible. But the more we contrast their record with the record of the totalitarians, the better it seems; and, wholly apart from the fact that, in any case, we have a popular government and mean to keep it, there seems no reason to believe that the people are more prone to make mistakes than any particular group or element in society. Folly is not confined to a democratic electorate; it extends to those numerous classes out of which an elite might be formed. The business classes are not always right in judging large issues, neither are the technical experts, neither are the academics, neither are the newspaper columnists. If there is wisdom to be found in the world, it will be a collective wisdom; it will be the distillation of the thought of the many, and of the aspirations of the many, rarefied and purified by special knowledge, chastened by a love of moderation, evolved from practical experience, and modified with the passage of time. Such wisdom is not easy to come at; but it may well be that it is more easily attained under popular government than in any other way.

106. THE VOICE OF THE PEOPLE: NEITHER GOD NOR BELIAL*

Editors of *The Nation*

. . . To-day we are ready to subscribe to the motto of Vox Populi Vox Dei. To-morrow, in our wrath, we shall write it Diaboli. While complete analysis and understanding of popular opinion are impossible, they are also

* This selection is from "Vox Populi," *The Nation*, vol. 91, Sept. 29, 1910, p. 283. By permission of the publisher.

unnecessary. The trouble is not so much our inability to comprehend the phenomenon, puzzling as its operations often are, as it is our half-views of it when we are laboring under blinding disappointment and despair over its faulty working.

In the first place, we all recognize that there are matters for the masses and matters for the experts. We know, when we stop to think, that there is a large field of human interest open to us all which only a few really enter into and possess. Art and science are realms which we penetrate in varying degree, and certainly there is no obligation resting upon us to explore completely or not at all. Yet, partly because of the easy humor of it, partly because of the serious need, critics more or less competent make it one of their regular tasks to point anew to popular shortcomings of taste, of knowledge, and of judgment in these matters. They do it, moreover, with an air of half-amused, half-bored hopelessness that suggests and is meant to suggest the worthlessness of popular notions about anything. Now, it is well to insist that art and science must be approached seriously, and that one cannot precipitate himself into the midst of their oceanic vastness. It may also be true that the general opinion, if there is any, in these matters will always be negligible, except as an item in the history of culture. But all this proves absolutely nothing regarding the worth of the public judgment in other fields.

But, however it may be in things intellectual, it is not lack of ability that disheartens one in the public's handling of affairs more suited to it. Its critics do not weep over its native political incapacity; they scold it for its indifference, its tardiness, its careless and criminal stupidity. One day the great beast is afire with a well-directed energy that removes mountains. The next it is sunk in lifeless torpor. It is necessary for the impatient observer to hold fast to two considerations if he would rightly understand the prodigy. One is that the public consciousness is not simply a weighing-machine. It is, on the contrary, a huge personality, an immense bundle of nerves, responsive in varying degree to a multitude of influences, and, in our present state of psychological knowledge, to be prophesied about only with the greatest presumption. It is suspicious of professions of disinterestedness in its behalf, and an enthusiastic worshipper of a long succession of heroes. It is subject to moods, has its political fads and fashions, and is, altogether, anything but a sober, steady, mechanical shopkeeper. Nevertheless, its heart is in the right place, a balance-wheel that controls, with whatever imperfections of adjustment, its shortsightedness, its impulsiveness, and its inertia.

A consideration equally important is that the fallibility of the popular judgment is not utterly condemnatory of it. In our endless seeking for a sign we have, naturally enough, elevated the voice of the people into the place of an oracle. Some one must speak the final word, and how can it be final unless it is correct? Such a test applied generally would destroy confidence in the value of all authority. Our longing for the absolute, essential as it is to progress, must not be allowed to tempt us to depreciate the worth of the relative and the finite that is within our grasp. The voice of the people is neither the voice of God nor the utterance of Belial—it is simply the cry of man. Sometimes it is muffled by weakness, sometimes rendered inarticulate by artificial barriers, raised sometimes in misapprehension and sometimes clearly for wrong. But always it is the cry of imperfect, struggling, divine-human man, and, like him, the most puzzling, the most irritating, and the most hopeful phenomenon on the planet.

107. THE PEOPLE, YES
by Carl Sandburg*

Always the storm of propaganda blows.
Buy a paper. Read a book. Start the radio.
Listen in the railroad car, in the bus,
Go to church, to a movie, to a saloon.
And always the breezes of personal opinion
are blowing mixed with the doctrines
of propaganda or the chatter of selling spiels.
Believe this, believe that. Buy these, buy them.
Love one-two-three, hate four-five-six.
Remember 7-8-9, forget 10-11-12.
Go now, don't wait, go now at once and buy
Dada Salts Incorporated, Crazy Horse Crystals,
for whatever ails you and if nothing ails you
it is good for that and we are telling you
for your own good. Whatever you are told,
you are told it is for your own good and not
for the special interest of those telling you.
Planned economy is forethought and care.
Planned economy is regimentation and tyranny.
What do you know about planned economy
and how did this argument get started and why?
Let the argument go on.

The storm of propaganda blows always.
In every air of today the germs float and hover.
The shock and contact of ideas goes on.
Planned economy will arrive, stand up,
and stay a long time—or planned economy will
take a beating and be smothered.
        The people have the say-so.
        Let the argument go on.
        Let the people listen.
Tomorrow the people say Yes or No by one question:
        "What else can be done?"
In the drive of faiths on the wind today the people know:
"We have come far and we are going farther yet. . . ."

* Poet, biographer, novelist, lecturer, and American folk song recitalist. Author of *Chicago Poems, Rootabaga Stories, Abraham Lincoln: The War Years, Remembrance Rock, Always the Young Strangers,* and numerous other works. This selection is from Carl Sandburg, *The People, Yes,* Harcourt, Brace & World, Inc., New York, 1936, pp. 280-281. Copyright 1936 by Harcourt, Brace & World, Inc.